Goldman: *Globalisation and the Western Legal Tradition: Recurring Patterns of Law and Authority*

Gobert & Punch: *Rethinking Corporate Crime*

Harlow & Rawlings: *Law and Administration*

Harris: *An Introduction to Law*

Harris, Campbell & Halson: *Remedies in Contract and Tort*

Harvey: *Seeking Asylum in the UK: Problems and Prospects*

Hervey & McHale: *Health Law and the European Union*

Holder & Lee: *Environmental Protection, Law and Policy*

Kostakopoulou: *The Future Governance of Citizenship*

Lewis: *Choice and the Legal Order: Rising above Politics*

Likosky: *Law, Infrastructure and Human Rights*

Likosky: *Transnational Legal Processes*

Maughan & Webb: *Lawyering Skills and the Legal Process*

McGlynn: *Families and the European Union: Law, Politics and Pluralism*

Moffat: *Trusts Law: Text and Materials*

Monti: *EC Competition Law*

Morgan & Yeung: *An Introduction to Law and Regulation: Text and Materials*

Norrie: *Crime, Reason and History*

O'Dair: *Legal Ethics*

Oliver: *Common Values and the Public–Private Divide*

Oliver & Drewry: *The Law and Parliament*

Picciotto: *International Business Taxation*

Reed: *Internet Law: Text and Materials*

Richardson: *Law, Process and Custody*

Roberts & Palmer: *Dispute Processes: ADR and the Primary Forms of Decision-Making*

Rowbottom: *Democracy Distorted: Wealth, Influence and Democratic Politics*

Scott & Black: *Cranston's Consumers and the Law*

Seneviratne: *Ombudsmen: Public Services and Administrative Justice*

Stapleton: *Product Liability*

Stewart: *Gender, Law and Justice in a Global Market*

Tamanaha: *Law as a Means to an End: Threat to the Rule of Law*

Turpin & Tomkins: *British Government and the Constitution: Text and Materials*

Twining: *General Jurisprudence: Understanding Law from a Global Perspective*

Twining: *Globalisation and Legal Theory*

Twining: *Human Rights, Southern Voices: Francis Deng, Abdullahi An-Na'im, Yash Ghai and Upendra Baxi*

Twining: *Rethinking Evidence*

Twining & Miers: *How to Do Things with Rules*

Ward: *A Critical Introduction to European Law*

Ward: *Law, Text, Terror*

Ward: *Shakespeare and Legal Imagination*

Wells & Quick: *Lacey, Wells and Quick: Reconstructing Criminal Law*

Zander: *Cases and Materials on the English Legal System*

Zander: *The Law-Making Process*

Housing Law and Policy

DAVID COWAN

CAMBRIDGE UNIVERSITY PRESS
Cambridge, New York, Melbourne, Madrid, Cape Town,
Singapore, São Paulo, Delhi, Tokyo, Mexico City

Cambridge University Press
The Edinburgh Building, Cambridge CB2 8RU, UK

Published in the United States of America by Cambridge University Press, New York

www.cambridge.org
Information on this title: www.cambridge.org/9780521199971

© David Cowan 2011

First published 2011

Printed in the United Kingdom at the University Press, Cambridge

A catalogue record for this publication is available from the British Library

ISBN 978-0-521-19997-1 Hardback
ISBN 978-0-521-13719-5 Paperback

To my brother, Andrew,
and
Zeddles
xxx

Contents

Preface

As always, the real energy and enthusiasm for a book project comes in the opening stages. This book was originally devised as a joint project with my colleague, friend and collaborator, Morag McDermont. When Morag went on to better and higher things, I chose to take on writing this book alone. Morag's influence, however, appears on almost every page that I and she have read (and re-read), and it is to her, first and foremost, that I owe a debt of gratitude. Had Morag joined me in writing this book, I strongly suspect that it would have taken a different form (especially Chapter 5, which Morag, whose special subject that chapter concerns, felt was too reductionist, but I felt it could not take the sort of lengthy excursus which she encouraged).

As it is, there is only one style of writing that I use and that is, to confound authorial convention, non-neutral. My previous attempt at a text such as this did rather make me blush at its overly heart-on-sleeve attitude, so this text has been toned down considerably. But, I keep hold of the view that housing law is not a neutral subject and to present it as such is a mistake. Housing law is political; I have a view and expect others to have a view. We can (and should) argue and I know that I am not always right (indeed, often wrong); but to present this subject, about which I am passionate, in a neutral way does violence to both of us (the subject and me). The style is also conversational, without, I hope, being too personal. I also hope that, if you engage with the text, you will correspond with me and, if so, I look forward to hearing from you (my email address appears at the end of this preface).

This book presents an account of English housing law and policy which is structured on the basis of three organising parts: regulation; access; rights and responsibilities. The structure is by no means perfect and there are oddities because of the tenure-basis of the subject (where do modern interventions such as shared ownership 'fit'?). It is recognised that this approach differs from that commonly pursued in law books dealing with the subject, but the structure used here offers a world view of the subject that lends coherence to the book's core aim, the integration of housing law and policy within a conceptual schema. The ambition of this project is to provide the basis for a cross-disciplinary conversation on equal terms.

Its limitation is that it deals only with English law and policy, on the basis that to include devolved approaches would require the book to be two or three times as long. There are many similarities, but there are also considerable differences in approach and it seems clear that Scotland is leading the way with tenure reform, but that Wales may not be far behind. There are other limitations – for example, I decided to write out certain elements of the subject which others might have included (particular issues with long leaseholds, such as service charges and enfranchisement etc.); not because they did not fit (they do), but because I could only scratch the surface and others have provided an excellent narrative of the issues.

This book is avowedly *socio-legal*, a descriptor discussed in Chapter 1. That chapter also provides an overview of the terms 'law' and 'policy', and their relation with 'housing', as used in this text. In particular, I take a broad approach to the meaning of law, which other scholars regard, I think, as broad notions of legality (which may not represent 'the law'). Although this book appears in the *Law in Context* series, I see no contradiction – indeed, socio-legal studies is about the study of law in society. Having said that, though, one must also anticipate the observation that those contexts can be independent of law – this appears in some studies of law in society – but the central point is that law may be just one of those contexts. It is important to note when it is and is not one of those contexts. This can hardly be a striking, or novel, interpretation of those contexts – everyday decision-making is conducted in hard-pressed, underfunded, local housing offices by mostly committed officers who often have little, if any, legal education, or by a landlord (characterised in this text as mostly amateur) making a decision to evict a tenant. In one sense, socio-legal studies sets out to identify and appreciate those contexts, and I have made ample use of this literature wherever it is available (and, generally, it is plentiful, thanks to interdisciplinary advances).

Having said that, though, I have willingly conceded to the desire of others that more 'hard' law should be included in this text. That is because you only know it is being used/manipulated/translated/avoided when you know it. If socio-legal studies seeks to get a handle on law in society, that law provides one of the contexts, but that is not to say that I place 'law first' in my analysis. The best example of this is with the law regarding eligibility for assistance, dealt with in its own chapter (in itself, something which sets this text out from others). The law here is complex, hard-nosed and just plain hard. It is designed to exclude (in a 'Fortress UK' kind of way), but to retain a commitment to international treaties to which the UK is signatory. It is based on some unproven empirical observations as to human nature (in particular, the belief that the greater the denial of rights, the less likely the UK will be regarded as a beacon – which perhaps says more about those who conceived the rules who assumed the knavish attitude of incomers). An alternative observation is that it is designed to offer comfort to UK citizens (or, at least, those UK citizens who are habitually resident in the UK) who should know that they are entitled over a considerable number of others who are ineligible. The problem is that they don't. There has been an ineffective translation of this complex law in society; indeed, various myths are perpetrated about this law, but government does little to assuage those concerns; indeed, some appear to try to exacerbate those myths. The law, then, is an important battleground – certainly for lawyers, but also for its translation in society.

Readers will find plenty of other examples in this book, from the everyday to the extraordinary. One of the particular interests of socio-legal studies lies in the mundane, and uncovering the truths that these mundane practices shade. I have previously argued that the identification of the mundane involves a value-judgment and that issues which appear mundane, or are treated as mundane, usually have significant repercussions; an 'ordinary' three-minute possession hearing is, on one level, mundane (as a judge said to me, 'pretty boring stuff') but may lead to the loss of the occupier's home. Underpinning that hearing is a raft of what Emilie Cloatre has termed 'socio-legal objects' including the construction of tenure and 'the' social (2008).

I have tried my utmost to make that law palatable to non-lawyer readers, but, if that has been unsuccessful, I feel that the point will have been proved as well. Housing law is a ridiculously complex, unsatisfactory amalgam of diverse historical leftovers topped with sprinklings at different times of bits and bobs, without attention being given to its ultimate 'consumers', i.e. ordinary people. Although I have never wholly bought into the simplification agenda, the law lacks conceptual coherence. Because the subject is political, one just gets more sprinklings from generally non-specialist housing ministers who are in the job for a few minutes before they move on (upwards or out); their feel for the subject is hampered by their lack of knowledge and appreciation of the sector and its own politics. These games are also played out in this book – much of the innovation flows from the entrepreneurial juices beyond the state, which create their own local (or, indeed, national) laws.

As I was putting the final draft of this book to bed, the Conservative-led Coalition government decided it would be an appropriate moment to add its own sprinklings to others' leftovers and sprinklings. At the time of writing they have issued two consultation papers on which the Localism Bill is based – it is to be noted that the deadline for responses to the second, crucial consultation paper was the date of the second reading of the Bill, which may tell you something about this government's approach to consultation. But that is really beside the point for this book. Where relevant, chapters in this book have a final section entitled 'the future', which refers to the consultation papers (and not the Bill on the assumption that clause numbers are likely to change in the Act and, therefore, it would only confuse) and discusses the changes. Those changes can only really be appreciated by reference to the inherited social and political settlement of housing. The rest of each chapter provides the basis for that appreciation. Readers are likely (already) to be able to tell where I stand on these reforms, but I repeat that I am often wrong.

The final substantive point to make is that I have tried to wear my theory lightly in this book. Readers versed in the work of Foucault and Latour, and their followers, may be seen smiling at certain points because they have unlocked the code; but those unversed in that literature should not be bothered to find that code for, hopefully, it won't be necessary.

Ultimately, though, I want you, the reader, to be engaged in this subject and, if this book assists in that process, I feel that I will have succeeded; even if you disagree with me (I hope you do).

There are five groups of people who have contributed to this text.

First, there are a number of academic colleagues to whom I owe considerable debts. Specifically, and in no particular order, Caroline Hunter, Helen Carr, Hal Pawson, Alex Marsh, Sarah Blandy, Martin Partington CBE QC, Sally Wheeler, Sue Bright, Judy Nixon and Simon Halliday have not only been collaborators over many years, they have also read chapters of this book for me, corrected errors, introduced other ideas, and been generally engaged in this project (or just listened to me moan on). Put simply, this book would not have been possible without them and their work. This book may be seen as a successor to Martin's classic book in this series, *Landlord and Tenant*; if that is the case and if it is regarded as half as good as that book, I will be delighted. I was granted a period of study leave to enable me to finish this book and I am grateful to my colleagues at Bristol who took up the slack during that year.

Many of the ideas in this book have been developed alongside them, and I have tried to credit them fully – this is particularly apparent in the most current issue, proportionality, where the discussion in Chapter 16 draws heavily on theoretical and empirical work in which I have been fortunate enough to have been involved with Caroline and Hal; parts of Chapter 3 are derived from work which Alex and I began, but never completed (we were always too busy) on a monograph, *Regulating Renting: Governing the Private Rented Sector*. Other parts of this book come from papers delivered at various locations, but I would particularly like to thank the Housing Law Practitioners Association for giving me the opportunity to bring my thoughts about IHO together for a conference session, and the product of that can be seen largely in Chapters 10 and 16. Hayder Al-Hassan, Simon Marciniak and Rajea Sultana have also provided me with the opportunity to flesh out and test some of the ideas in this book.

Second, when the idea for this book was originally presented to Cambridge University Press as a possible project for the *Law in Context* series, I was in the middle of my pupillage at Arden Chambers. That Chambers showed enough confidence in my abilities to accept my application as a non-full-time member of their Chambers. As a group of people, their engagement with housing also fills these pages, mostly anonymously, although the Chambers' mission to drive on and extend housing law has been responsible for a substantial part of the major developments in the law discussed here. Although perhaps invidious, I should extend particular thanks to David Carter and Jonathan Manning, my pupil supervisors; David has guided me through issues in my incipient practice as well as being gracious enough to lead me in a case; Terry Gallivan has also assisted me and led me in *Poplar HARCA* v. *Howe*; Christopher Baker, my mentor; Clare Roberts and Toby Vanhegan provided considerable assistance with the chapter on eligibility, and Toby corrected a number of errors in my draft; Sally Blackmore, who has assisted with my appreciation of various subjects covered in this book; Robert Brown, whose encyclopaedic knowledge of disability law, in particular, has been helpful; Iain Colville for his appreciation of shared ownership (and to whom I am indebted for an important point in the penultimate section of this book); last, but certainly not least, Andrew Arden QC himself – I doubt that he will agree with much in this book, but it is his drive and passion which largely created it.

There is no doubt that the following pages have been enlivened by my occasional forays into practice. I pay tribute to all the housing practitioners who work under increasingly strained conditions for the good of their clients.

Third, these pages are also enlivened by copious references to the Nearly Legal blog (www.nearlylegal.co.uk/blog), a specialist housing law and policy blog. The original Nearly Legal and subsequent contributors, most of whom are anonymous, have kept me updated and sustained my interest in this subject. They deserve considerable credit and gratitude for the decidedly free (and witty) service they provide to the community – they are housing 'nuts'. I think that the statistics of my visits to the site will demonstrate my addiction. It is thoroughly recommended.

Fourth, I always said that I would die happy if I got a book into the *Law in Context* series. I am grateful to Cambridge University Press, and especially Sionadh, for making it possible for my cadaver to have a smile, as well as being so generous when the final, final, final, final deadlines were not met. Marie Selwood has been a wonderful copy-editor to work with.

Fifth and finally, my partner and children have suffered the insufferable while I wrote this book, but did so with good grace. It was my pleasure to pay homage to my father in my inaugural lecture in 2005 and I repeat that here – he has never quite understood why I became an academic but has been hugely supportive over the years. This book is dedicated, however, to two people. First, my brother, Andrew, chief executive at Devonshires, who has done more for the cause of social housing over the years, and, indeed, for our family, than could be measured. We are usually on opposite sides of the ideological divide which housing creates, but we also bore for England (and, in his case, the UK) about our subject. It is also dedicated to my youngest son, Zachary (aka Zeddles).

The usual caveats apply. And remember, do feel free to get in touch with me.

Dave Cowan
Bristol/London
d.s.cowan@bris.ac.uk

List of abbreviations

ABC	acceptable behaviour contract
ALMO	arms length management organisation
ASB	anti-social behaviour
ASBI	anti-social behaviour injunction
ASBO	anti-social behaviour order
AST	assured shorthold tenancy
AT	assured tenancy
BRE	Building Research Establishment
BRMA	broad rental market area
BSA	Building Societies Association
CBL	choice-based lettings
CCHPR	Cambridge Centre for Housing and Planning Research
CCT	compulsory competitive tendering
CHAC	Central Housing Advisory Committee
CHR	Centre for Housing Research
CICC	Commission on Integration and Community Cohesion
CIH	Chartered Institute of Housing
CJC	Civil Justice Council
CLG	(Department for) Communities and Local Government
CML	Council for Mortgage Lenders
CPA	comprehensive performance assessment
CPR	Civil Procedure Rules
CURS	Centre for Urban and Regional Studies
DCA	Department for Constitutional Affairs
DCSF	Department for Children, Schools and Families
DDA	Disability Discrimination Act 1995
DETR	Department of the Environment, Transport and the Regions
DHSS	Department of Health and Social Security
DoE	Department of the Environment
DRC	Disability Rights Commission
DSS	Department of Social Security
DTLR	Department for Transport, Local Government and the Regions
DWP	Department for Work and Pensions

ECtHR	European Court of Human Rights
EEA	European Economic Area
EHRC	Equality and Human Rights Commission
FIT	family intervention tenancy
FOS	Financial Ombudsman Service
FSA	Financial Services Authority
FSMA	Financial Services and Markets Act 2000
HAG	Housing Association Grant
HAT	Housing Action Trust
HB	housing benefit
HCA	Homes and Communities Agency
HHSRS	Housing Health and Safety Rating System
HMO	house in multiple occupation
HOS	Housing Ombudsman Service
HPU	Homeless Persons Unit
HRA	Human Rights Act 1998
IEA	Institute of Economic Affairs
IHO	intermediate home ownership
JCHR	Joint Committee on Human Rights
KLOE	key lines of enquiry
LAG	Legal Action Group
LCD	Lord Chancellor's Department
LHA	local housing allowance
LSVT	large-scale voluntary transfer
MCOB	Mortgage Code of Business
MoJ	Ministry of Justice
MPPI	mortgage payment protection insurance
NACAB	National Association of Citizens Advice Bureaux
NASS	National Asylum Support Service
NCSR	National Centre for Social Research
NFALMO	National Federation of Arms Length Management Organisations
NFHA	National Federation of Housing Associations
NHF	National Housing Federation
ODPM	Office of the Deputy Prime Minister
OFT	Office of Fair Trading
PAP	pre-action protocol
PPO	postponed possession order
PRP	private registered provider of social housing
PRS	private rented sector
RPTS	Residential Property Tribunal Service
RTB	right to buy
SEU	Social Exclusion Unit
SPO	suspended possession order

TMO	tenant management organisation
TRO	tenancy relations officers
TSA	Tenants Services Authority
UKBA	United Kingdom Border Agency
UKBIA	United Kingdom Border and Immigration Agency
VOA	Valuation Office Agency

Table of legislation

Primary Legislation

Secondary Legislation (Rules, Regulations etc.)

Codes, Guidelines etc.

Draft legislation and Governmental/advisory documents

Table of international instruments

European Legislation

European Treaties and Conventions

Table of cases

1

Locating housing law and policy

It probably seems strange to begin a book about housing law and policy with a chapter which seeks to 'locate' the subject. In one sense, the location of the book is determined by its subject-matter – housing – and its descriptors – law and policy. However, the purpose of this chapter is somewhat deeper than that narrow sense. The purpose of this chapter is to locate the ways in which we think about housing law and policy by uncovering the assumptions and (to a certain extent, hidden) truths of the dual disciplines of law and policy in relation to housing. This is an ambitious way to start a text, but it is important in appreciating both the limits of thought about housing law and policy as well as their current constitution. If you like, the attempt here is to provide a partial genealogy of the subject because the subject was not preordained and, indeed, remains an ongoing project. It is an ongoing project for at least three reasons – first, the history of housing law and policy is a history to a large extent of cycles of failure and re-invention; second, it is a history in which state sovereignty and individual responsibility have vied for primacy; and, third, housing's uncertain relationship with the welfare state is reflected in the identity of the subject to the extent that we might ask, 'what is social about social housing?' (discussed in Cowan and McDermont 2006). In large part, it is these three ideas that are the underlying themes of this book.

Thus, this chapter concerns what is meant by the study of housing law and policy, locating the law–policy interaction, and how this identity of the subject-matter maps on to the structure adopted in this book. The opening sections identify the disciplines of housing law and policy separately through certain analytical themes which are brought together in these subjects. What this discussion is designed to demonstrate is that both housing law and housing policy are 'destination subjects'. They bring together within their rubric a variety of ideas, theories and perspectives drawn from other sources. To put it another way, they are parasitic on those other sources. In demonstrating this, the task of explaining the evolution of today's housing relations is also begun.

There is a final point to this chapter and this book. Housing law and policy have developed to reflect, perhaps inadequately, what might be termed an evolution in our ways of 'holding' housing. At the turn of the twentieth century, it is said that around 90% of the population lived in privately rented accommodation; most other households were owner-occupiers (see Malpass and Murie 1999: 11). In 2007, in contrast, just under 69.5% of the population were owner-occupiers, around 17.5% rented from social landlords, and just 13% were living in private rented accommodation (www.communities.gov.uk/housing/ housingresearch/housingstatistics/housingstatisticsby/stockincludingvacants/ livetables/: table 104). Understandings of housing law and housing policy have developed alongside this evolution, driving, supporting and responding to that change as well as raising problems; to an extent, also, the law has facilitated this change without necessary alteration, particularly regarding one aspect of ownership, namely mortgage lending (Whitehouse 2010).

The structure of this chapter is as follows. In the first part, I set out my stall about the interrelationship between housing law and policy and describe the structure of this book. Subsequently, I take the subjects of housing law and housing policy separately, describing the influences on their modern apparel, both historic and current. Separating them out in this way is a convenient, analytical device, which also draws attention to their separate influences. However, the point of this book, as is emphasised in the opening section, is to demonstrate their complex interaction.

Housing law and policy

The separation of housing law and housing policy is a convenient device that reflects both the separate development of the disciplines as well as the way in which they are often currently presented. But it is a false division. One simply cannot understand, let alone appreciate, the one without the other. Housing policy texts make some reference to housing law, and vice versa. However – and this is no criticism of these works because it is not their purpose – they rarely bring the two together. They offer a partial picture of their subject as a result.

Even the most commonplace application of housing law is infused not just with that law but with housing policy. This is often done silently, with the stamp of a judge and possibly little recognition that they are performing an interdisciplinary act. Most private sector tenancies can generally be terminated by giving the occupier 2 months' written notice that the landlord requires possession of the property. Once that has occurred, the court must grant the possession order. Stripped of its technicality for present purposes (discussed in Chapter 11 below), this is understandable law. However, when a district judge makes such an order, usually without an oral hearing, they are performing a housing policy which has prioritised and produced a private rented sector (PRS) which offers temporary security to tenants. They are the implementers of the law, for sure, but they are also participating in the policy behind it (and there may be little a district judge can do about that). It may also be that the occupier does not go through with the court proceedings, as they are but a mere formality (although, see Chapter 16). In doing so, the occupier is acting out housing policy. Historically, that temporary security represents a major shift in policy.

But this book is not just about housing law, it is about housing policy and its uses of housing law. Housing policy interventions may be by way of formal law – by which I mean statute or secondary legislation, and its interpretation by judges – or by informal law – such as guidance which is enforceable by another means (and may be more readily applied by its targets because it is more digestible and is written for them). Housing policy does not necessarily need to use either method of law. There are a variety of other more indirect methods – such as targets and financial penalties or rewards/incentives, bidding criteria (such as a requirement for partnerships before being awarded a grant), performance standards and inspection regimes – which are equally, if not more, important and may also take on the character of 'law' at least between the people involved. These softer regulatory tools are employed by policy-makers and others in sometimes vain attempts to achieve implementation of policy goals. They have become increasingly frequently used in housing policy, as elsewhere.

One important clarification, then, that can be taken from this conjunction between housing law and policy is of the subject-matter of housing law itself. That clarification is one which will be familiar to most, if not all, lawyers, but particularly those with a socio-legal bent. The paradigm of socio-legal studies has opened our eyes to the diverse places and understandings of housing law, whether it be in the courts or in everyday life. The interaction and interrelation between housing law and policy offers the opportunity for a socio-legal analysis of what used to be called the housing system, the agglomeration of tenures, policy and law (but is perhaps more accurately referred to as the housing sys-tem*s*). The socio-legal question can be framed like this: how does housing law operate in society?

In thinking about this question, we need to be alive to the diverse regulatory techniques of housing policy, as well as the self-governing capacities of individ-uals. In the course of a study about harassment and unlawful eviction in the PRS in 1999, a private landlord said to us – and I paraphrase – that he considered that placing a bunch of flowers in a property for a new occupier was a much more effective regulatory technique than a contract which nobody read. Albeit slightly extreme, this understanding opens our eyes to the different regulatory techniques which can be used by the different actors in housing relationships. In another guise, Daintith (1994) categorised regulatory techniques by reference to the concepts of imperium – commands backed by force, like the contract – and dominium – incentives to comply, at a stretch the bunch of flowers. Throughout this book, we are just as interested in the contract as the bunch-of-flowers approaches to regulation. When we think about homelessness law, for example, we need to be alive not just to the law itself but also the findings of research pro-ject after research project, that, as Loveland (1991a: 22) expressed it,

> Legalism is an intruder into the administrative arena. It does not prescribe deci-sion-making, rather it gets in the way. It is not respected, but ignored. And if it cannot be ignored it is grudgingly accepted as an unrealistic impediment to rational decision-making.

This may be an overly pessimistic assessment and recent research has stressed, more positively, certain criteria through which law might have more sig-nificant impact on decision-making practices (for example, Halliday 2004). Nevertheless, we need to be sensitive to the different influences on decision-making beyond the law and what the objects of study – housing officers, ten-ants, landlords, applicants, lenders, even judges – regard as 'law'. This is what I think Rose and Valverde (1998: 545) had in mind when they argued that there is no such thing as 'the law'. They argue that:

> Law, as a unified phenomenon governed by certain principles, is a fiction. This fiction is the creation of the legal discipline, of legal textbooks, of jurisprudence itself, which is forever seeking for the differentia specifica that will unify and rationalize the empirical diversity of legal sites, legal concepts, legal criteria of judgement, legal personnel, legal discourses, legal objects and objectives.

The task of writing this book, then, is ultimately both ambitious and contra-dictory. It sets out relevant parts of the law, while simultaneously seeking to pull back from the fiction that this is 'the' law, as opposed to one set of formal rules which may well be ignored, supplemented, interpreted or translated, and only very occasionally invoked. In summary, what people think of, and act out, as law is far more important than my (or your) versions of truth (for *the* clas-sic text on law in society, see Ewick and Silbey, 1999). As a legal practitioner, I recognise the power of law; as a socio-legal academic, I recognise that is but one version of law competing against other versions which have their own internal logics and power.

Structure of this book

Having outlined the approach taken in this book, I take the opportunity to set out its overall structure. This book has three parts following this introductory chapter.

The three parts of the book discuss the following issues: the *regulation* of the housing systems; *access* to housing; and individual *rights and responsibilities* in housing.

Taking each in turn, the regulation of housing systems is concerned with the ways in which different types of regulation have been used to stifle or stimulate the development of each tenure (a concept discussed in the next sections of this chapter). Although this may be unfamiliar terrain for some lawyers and law students, it provides essential background information which, often, becomes foregrounded in subsequent chapters. It offers some explanation as to why legal values may be less important in decision-making because it offers an appreciation of the regulatory matrix of the housing systems which goes beyond the formal law. Finally, it explains what is possible – that is to say, it explains the constraints within which each tenure operates as well as the constraints (self-imposed and otherwise) within which regulation operates.

Our thinking about access to housing has been dominated by two concepts, need and affordability. There is a rough and ready distinction which one might operate here: access to social sector accommodation is based upon a household's housing need, whereas access to private sector accommodation is based upon affordability. In this part, we interrogate these concepts in relation to access to the different housing tenures, although it is most convenient here, for reasons which will become apparent, to link social housing together.

In the third part, we are concerned with rights in housing, including security in housing. The general observation one might make is the shift in concern away from rights towards responsibilities, particularly to one's community. This is, perhaps, paradoxical in light of the incorporation of the European Convention on Human Rights and Freedoms into domestic law in the Human Rights Act 1998 (referred to throughout this book as the HRA). However, the predominant concerns of policy-makers are to ensure that these rights do not trump the interests of neighbours and the local community, bodies which equally have rights of their own, as well as the interests of the housing providers themselves. Sometimes, it must be said, the rights do appear to trump the interests of the providers, but these occasions are infrequent.

In each part, we can observe an appreciation of, and response to, discrete policy issues and approaches. It is also important to appreciate that these parts have intersections and overlaps – it is by no means a perfect structure. Nevertheless, the structure itself does work because, at the end, you should appreciate that there is a complex interplay between each part. Each chapter can, of course, be read separately, and hopefully there will be valuable material there. But the bigger point, indeed the purpose of this structure, is that the foundational context of each chapter can be found within that structure.

Of the examples of this interplay, the one most uppermost in my mind at present (for reasons with which I won't bore you) is security of tenure, the opening chapter of Part III. It is noted at the outset of that chapter that tenure is the oddest thing and, I might have added, security of tenure is even odder. It just makes no sense – indeed, it is nonsense – on its own. The different ways in which the law provides security of tenure are fundamentally justified by the different modes of funding and regulating each tenure, discussed in Part I. But, when one considers that tenure itself is often an accident and, indeed, unclear at the point of access, that justification is just nonsense.

These introductory points now complete, I move on to discuss the subjects of housing law and housing policy separately.

Housing law

I begin with a story to introduce the identity of housing law. It is a story of the history of the subject in part, and its current identity. The story begins in 2005–06. The Law Commission had been set the task of developing a model of proportionate dispute resolution in the context of housing disputes. Where should it start? It began its work by seeking to classify different types of housing problem to which the law offers some remedy (Law Commission 2006a: paras. 1.18–24). From here, it identified certain core housing disputes, where the occupation of a 'home' is under threat. Next, the Commission identified certain other peripheral areas outside that core concerning issues relating to the peaceful occupation or enjoyment of that home, purely financial matters, and long-term security-related issues. A second set of issues were identified as being concerned with legal relationships. The core here was said to concern 'pure' landlord and tenant matters, because this followed on from their previous work about landlord and tenant. Other legal relationships were at the periphery. The Law Commission was able to present these levels of analysis in the form of an onion so that one could peel back the layers of housing law (Law Commission 2006b: Part 3).

Ultimately, though, it gave up with these approaches (to mix metaphors, the onion hit a brick wall). It did so for a revealing reason. The classification of housing problems approach, it was said, 'risks glossing over the differences in individual perspectives, whether between the two parties to a particular housing dispute, or between different individuals engaged in superficially similar disputes' (Law Commission 2006b: para. 3.18(2)). The legal relationships analysis did 'not bring out the underlying personal relationships, wider social, physical, economic or other problems or the role of, and effects of the dispute on, third parties' (para. 3.18(1)). Instead, the Law Commission developed what it termed an 'accountability space' analysis which focused on the construction of disputes by reference to dispute resolution processes (paras. 3.13–7).

This story is designed to illustrate a simple point – there is no single, uniform understanding of housing law. The parameters of the subject are shaped not so much by the subject-matter – housing – but by legal processes as well as the authors and practitioners who develop and test their ideas. Of course, this is probably likely to be true of all classifications within the law curriculum; but, underlying the debate about the parameters of housing law lies a rather more complex history.

It should be remembered, first and foremost, that housing law is a relatively new subject within the law curriculum. In their preface to the first major text on the subject, Andrew Arden and Martin Partington (1983: v) noted the diverse locations of their subject and that, conventionally, housing law had meant 'public housing law'. It was the achievement of those authors that they brought together the diverse, apparently unconnected sources of law concerned with housing. Over the subsequent twenty-five or so years, we have developed a better understanding of the terrain of housing law but, as the Law Commission so vividly demonstrated, it remains incomplete and obscure. The analytical approach pioneered by Arden and Partington in that and subsequent work has been to begin with an outline of the different types of legal relationships, or statuses, which occur in housing, followed by a 'function'- or 'problem'-based approach. They were able to develop that structure because, by that time, the sources of housing law were converging, most particularly around the theme of consumerism which had been a particular issue in this area from the 1970s (Loveland 1992).

Strands of housing law were apparent before that time, although they had not been interwoven. A number of themes arose at different times and for different reasons, and (perhaps counter-intuitively) despite prevailing political orthodoxies (cf. Englander 1983; Wohl 1977: 19). In the remaining part of this section, these strands of housing law are introduced.

Poor Laws

One strand of housing law can be derived from the Poor Laws. This should neither be over- nor underestimated. It should not be overestimated because the Poor Laws were abolished by the National Assistance Act 1948, s. 1. Therefore, they have no formal existence; although certain concepts are reminiscent of those laws (such as the equation of settlement under the Poor Law with local connection under the homelessness legislation – discussed in Chapter 6 below) and the local administration of public sector housing. Equally, their influence should not be underestimated because, as Cranston noted (in the broader context of the welfare state, but which is equally applicable to housing):

> When modern social rights are examined … many of the themes identified in the discussion of the poor law … recur – notably the character of social rights, the

incorporation of morality in social welfare law and administration, and the centrality of work in social welfare policy. (Cranston 1985: 44; see also Harris 1999)

Relevant themes of the Poor Laws include the principle of less eligibility, the importance of locality, and the distinctions between those deserving of assistance and those undeserving of it. This is not the place for a full examination of the Poor Laws (as to which see, for example, Cranston 1985).

The principle of less eligibility was most clearly framed in what is known as the New Poor Law, which came into being in 1834, and was a product in part of the Royal Commission report of 1832. It incorporated a particular understanding of a broad division between those deserving of assistance and those undeserving of assistance. The principle was that relief should not be given so as to produce a better situation for the recipient than the lowest-paid worker:

> The first and most essential of all conditions, a principle which we find universally admitted, even by those whose practice is at variance with it, is that [the recipient of Poor Law relief's] situation on the whole shall not be made really or apparently so eligible as the situation of the independent labourer of the lowest class ... Every penny bestowed that tends to render the condition of the pauper more eligible than that of the independent labourer, is a bounty on indolence and vice. (Poor Law Report, in Checkland and Checkland 1974: 335)

The principle was produced from concerns that 'outdoor relief' – commonly, some form of payment in money or in lieu – actually caused both the breakdown of family ties as well as claims for relief: 'In abolishing punishment, we equally abolish reward ... idleness, improvidence, or extravagance occasion no loss, and consequently diligence and economy can afford no gain' (Checkland and Checkland 1974: 156). The concern was to identify the pauper from the pauperised. The pauperised was a category of poor person who was made idle by the system – those who won't labour – as opposed to those who, despite the system, tried to find work or remained in work – the industrious poor (see Dean 1992: 220; Procacci 1991: 158, who refers to pauperism as 'poverty intensified to the level of *social danger*' (original emphasis)). The construction of workhouses in this period was specifically designed to demonstrate this principle both to the inmates as well as those on the outside. They became a powerful means of disciplining populations both inside and outside their walls (Foucault 1991).

At the risk of accusations of historicity – an overly linear understanding of history – one can say that these debates remain prevalent in housing law and its administration today. Law reformers at the heart of government, for example, had a rallying cry in the early 1990s that rehousing assistance should be targeted on married couples, or those who are holding off marriage until they find suitable accommodation. In 2008, a new housing minister, Caroline Flint, fresh from the Department for Work and Pensions (DWP), argued that housing allocation should be linked by a 'commitment contract' to job-seeking (Wintour 2008), a point reinforced by the Coalition government in its programme for welfare reform (DWP 2010c, with the sub-title 'welfare that works').

Sanitation

For some, housing law itself was born during the nineteenth century. It was during this time that the first legislative interventions in the relationship between landlord and tenant – fragments of which remain extant today – occurred (and are touched on again in Chapter 13 as they remain relevant). These interventions concerned the state and condition of rented properties. They resulted, in part, from problematic limitations on the responsibility of landlords through the usual principles of contract law. However, to see such judicial limitations as the cause would in itself be insufficient.

During the nineteenth century, it has been said that there was an 'avalanche of statistics', the science of the state (Hacking 1991; Foucault 1991). Many of these interventions were to focus on the housing conditions of the poor and, most particularly, stamping out the production of disease, such as cholera, which affected all classes. Hence, the poor are often written out of the accounts of investigators in the early to mid-nineteenth century (Poovey 1995: 82; Hamlin 1998: 211). Perhaps the classic text of this early period is Edwin Chadwick's *Report on the Sanitary Condition of the Labouring Population of Great Britain*, published in 1842. In this publication, Chadwick summarised the local reports of his investigators. As Hamlin (1998) explains, Chadwick's reading of the local reports and his summary were designed in part to bolster the New Poor Law, which Chadwick himself had devised, and to create a limited public health in which certain explanations of disease, such as destitution and poverty, were written out. This necessitated buying into certain theories of disease, notably the miasmatic version (through which disease was airborne), and discrediting others. Sanitation fulfilled a number of ends, and was used to explain and solve all; principally though, it bolstered the New Poor Law project (Hamlin 1998; Dean 1991).

In this report and subsequently, the primary target of intervention became the poor themselves and, more specifically, the moral condition of the poor (Gauldie 1974). Principal concerns were overcrowding and certain types of housing – 'common lodging houses' – which were regarded as unhygienic and ethically problematic. Overcrowding produced incest and sexual promiscuity, referred to by Chadwick euphemistically as 'promiscuous sleeping' (see Flinn 1965: 194). Lodging houses were regarded in the 1842 report as inherently contagionist, but this was not necessarily the focus of the accounts: they stressed the 'moral depravation' encountered in these transient locations. By their transient nature, the occupiers lent themselves to such depravation (see, further, Gauldie 1974: 245). There was a 'long succession of works whose literary merit and statistical accuracy may have varied, but whose cumulative influence was considerable' (Gauldie 1974: 147). One particularly influential work was Reverend Andrew Mearns' one penny pamphlet, *The Bitter Cry of Outcast London* (1883). This pamphlet provided shocking examples of apparent degradation and vice, from which the poor were said to be in need of evangelical rescue.

The Royal Commission on the Housing of the Working Classes (1885a: 14) was particularly engaged with the question: 'Is it the pig that makes the stye or the stye that makes the pig?' To put this slightly differently, the question which animated the inquiry was whether, if the quality of the housing were improved, would that also impact on the moral delinquency of the inhabitants? In one form or another, it was this question which dominated Victorian inquiry and became understood as public health.

Public health was a legitimate organising metaphor for intervention in the free market but it was combined with a sense of concern for the morals of the occupiers. The legislation during this period (according to Wohl (1977: 73), there were forty major Acts dealing with public health) has been categorised as follows:

i)   the Public Health Act powers over new building, and (less comprehensive and more difficult to exercise) to prevent the unhealthy use of existing houses and to remedy conditions that were dangerous to health;

ii) powers to close or demolish individual houses that were unfit for human habitation;

iii) powers to demolish and clear areas of insanitary housing. (Holmans 1985: 27)

Such neutral presentation of the laws, however, does little justice to the role they had in making visible not only the conditions of such housing but also the types of occupier. In particular, attention was focused on not just the criminal classes but what Octavia Hill (a pioneer housing manager and member of the 'five per cent' philanthropists) referred to in her evidence to the 1885 Royal Commission as the 'destructive classes' for whom a 'paternal supervision' was necessary (1885a: paras. 9122–4). The principal reason for slum clearance and housing improvement powers was understood to be dealing with deviance:

> The first and most sweeping improvement schemes were deliberately driven through the most criminal areas, with the dispersal of criminals from their haunts, and the suppression of crime as the first motive. The fact that these haunts were in most cases also the most insanitary parts of the cities was a secondary consideration. The frequency with which the emotive phrase 'dens of vice' crops up is some indication of attitude. (Gauldie 1974: 267)

It was not until the Housing of the Working Classes Act 1885 that Parliament introduced an implied condition of fitness for human habitation into the contract between landlord and tenant (against the furious protests of the judiciary – see Reynolds 1974: 381). The provision was, perhaps unsurprisingly, narrowly interpreted and (as demonstrated in Chapter 13) practically useless, but it remains an important provision in that it interfered, for practically the first time, in an important matter: the landlord–tenant contractual relation. It brought into effect, in slightly different form, a recommendation of the 1885 Royal Commission (1885a: p. 56) that 'there should be a simple power by civil procedure for the recovery of damages against owners or holders of property by those who have suffered injury or loss by their neglect or default in sanitary matters'.

Security

Concerns over sanitation subsequently gave way to more pressing concerns about security and housing costs during the First World War. The development of rent control (under which rent increases were set centrally) and security of tenure (under which tenants could not be evicted without a court order available on a number of narrow grounds) were made more likely due to wartime conditions. As Holmans (1987: 387–8) has put it, rent control fitted into the complex of direct controls over prices, materials and manpower: 'the capacity of the building industry was for the time being greatly reduced and new house building at a virtual halt'. Thus, the increasing demand could not be met with an increase in supply. That rent control came earlier than other controls may well be due to the impact of rent strikes by munition-workers, particularly in Glasgow.

The clamour for reform began in, and was centred around, Glasgow where, before the war, accommodation shortages had existed. These were only exacerbated by the arrival of around 16,000 workers into the city's munitions factories at the start of the war. Shortages meant that rents were continually increased and non-payers evicted. Such were the inexorable rises in rent that, even at the outbreak of war, there were 13,000 empty houses in the city (Damar 1980: 90). Rent strikes occurred throughout 1915, together with ambushing of officials conducting the evictions. The government was inactive on the rents issue, and was more concerned with munitions output (legislating to outlaw strikes and regulate working conditions: see Watchman 1980: 27–30). In mid-1915, about 20,000 tenants were withholding their rent and, when the sheriff stayed an eviction after a demonstration of between 10–15,000 workers, a telegram was sent to the Prime Minister:

> That this meeting of Clyde munitions workers requests the government to state, not later than Saturday first, that it forbids any increase of rent during the period of the war; and that, this failing, a general strike will be declared on 22 November.

The government then indicated that it would legislate and the Bill became law within 4 weeks of being presented to Parliament. The legislation – the Increase in Rent and Mortgage (War Restrictions) Act 1915 – was due to expire within 6 months of the end of the war, but, in fact, set the tone for the structure of rent legislation for the next 40 years. Whereas other controls ended shortly after the war, this legislation was a permanent feature of the terrain, in some form or other, until it became a politically contested issue during the late 1950s.

The shadow of that first statutory intervention into security of tenure and rent control is lengthy. A set of understandings about its failure or success dominated debate and remain the backdrop to our current understandings of the 'problem' of security. The failure of rent control is a classic economic study, apparently taught in first-year undergraduate economics; there are more than 500 academic papers on the subject and, it has been said, there is more work to be done on it (Turner and Malpezzi 2003). To preface Chapter 3, the deregulation of private renting in the 1980s and subsequently has been premised on the failure of long-term security and rent control/regulation; and that premise is also inflected in the Coalition approach to the social sector (discussed in Chapter 11).

Tenure

Security was the foundation stone for the Arden and Partington approach because it attached to types of tenure (specifically, the landlord and tenant relation). Tenure is used rather imprecisely here. For property lawyers, tenure has no real relevance for our current understanding of the ways in which people hold property (see Chapter 11). In fact, property law divides the holding of land into two predominant types of estates – freehold and leasehold. The notion of the estate identifies the time period for which the land is held.

For housing lawyers, by contrast, tenure means something rather different. It is also a bit messy. Tenure is related to the identity of the owner, or the holder, of the property. It also reflects the different types and range of rights and obligations held by the occupier. As a result, we split housing tenure into four important categories, or housing sectors: owner occupation, private renting, local authority and private registered providers (PRP).

One needs to acknowledge at the outset that these categories are hardly watertight. They interact with each other in different ways. Long leaseholds are usually placed in the owner-occupation category, but it is unclear precisely why that should be. There are rather complex rules about extending leaseholds, for example, which are specific to this segment. It is unclear where licences – personal occupation rights, which may or may not be long term – fall, although the identification of the individual who grants the licence will usually be determinative. The categories are not closed either. The government keeps statistics on housing tenure using this four-tenured system but, for a considerable part of the twentieth century, PRPs[1] (then termed housing associations) were lumped in with the PRS. It is only since the early 1980s that they were separated out

---

[1] Throughout this book, I have decided to use the term 'private registered providers' and abbreviated it to PRPs. This is primarily for convenience, consistency and to assist the reader. The term derives from the boringly titled (but significant) Housing and Regeneration Act 2008 (Consequential Provisions) Order 2010, SI 2010/866, which defines such providers as private registered providers of social housing. The use of the term is, it must be accepted, unfortunate and historically inaccurate. These organisations are what were once known as housing associations, then registered social landlords (under the Housing Act 1996, Part I), and now PRPs (as a result of the implementation of the Housing and Regeneration Act 2008) (McDermont 2010 provides excellent discussion of the history of this sector and the significance of labels).

from each other. We are gradually becoming more accustomed to referring to the 'social rented sector', linking together local authority and PRP-provided housing (there is lengthy examination of this identification in Cowan and McDermont 2006; 2009). The production of the social rented sector has been an ongoing project (see, in particular, the Cave review of the regulation of social housing: Cave 2007). Apparent policy and practice innovations, such as shared ownership, take their shape within already existing legal structures and cause particular issues for law and policy as a result (discussed in Chapter 16 below).

The reason for those changes, as will become apparent particularly in the first part of this book, was political. Tenure does political work. It may be criticised as imprecise, or quasi-scientific (Barlow and Duncan 1989: 220), but it is critical to an appreciation of the way housing law works. Government interventions are usually targeted on one particular tenure or other, although it is sometimes the case that understandings developed in one tenure are translated or seep into the practices of another tenure. As is suggested in subsequent chapters, the different ways in which the tenures are regulated and financed form the basis for most of the different ways in which we use tenure in housing law; but, and here's one oddity about tenure, as discussed in much of Part II of this book, access to particular tenures does not necessarily depend on choice. Nevertheless, first and foremost, security is often different between the tenures. This makes the identification of housing tenure the crucial first analytical step.

The identification of tenures in this way enables government to separate out housing problems and identify separate regulatory arenas. If governments favour owner-occupation, for whatever reason, it can be increased from within the sector (for example, by facilitating the first-time buyer through mechanisms such as the production of cheaper properties for sale or encouraging lenders to lend more), or by encouraging cross-fertilisation between the sectors (for example, through the right to buy (RTB) a council home, combined with a financial incentive).

Furthermore, and linked in with that point, research on the meaning of home demonstrates that this identification of tenure has resonances in society. Gurney, for example, demonstrates in a coherent body of work how owner-occupation – or, home ownership – is identified as being coupled with a 'moral responsibility to look after one's property', whereas tenants are 'negatively associated … with profligacy and waste' (1999b: 1711), particularly council tenants (p. 1716). These identifications of tenure do not reflect variations in quality or experience, nor do they offer a coherent explanation of tenure choices. Tenure divisions are categories of consumption. Consumption is affected most particularly by the production and financing of housing. Owner-occupation is now the dominant tenure largely because private renting became unprofitable and speculative housebuilders began building for ownership at key moments when finance was in high supply (Craig 1986); its promotion in housing policy is consequential on that development, but it also fulfils certain ideological aims of government.

Modern sources

The previous parts have drawn attention to historical antecedents of housing law and policy. There are other rather more modern strands which both limit and expand the parameters of housing law.

The first modern source concerns devolution. This limits the ambit of this book because it is jurisdictionally confined to a study of English housing law and policy. Devolution has produced separate understandings of housing law and policy within the United Kingdom. Scotland has taken a series of progressive steps – for example, a single social housing tenancy – which mean that the law together with underlying policy are rather different both in substance and operation (Robson and Halliday 1998). Wales has also made some alterations, for example, around homelessness law (see Arden et al. 2010; Luba and Davies 2010), and has subsequently been granted more generous powers in relation to social housing tenure, for instance (National Assembly for Wales (Legislative Competence) (Housing and Local Government) Order 2010, SI 2010/1838, Article 2). There are rumours of more radical changes around tenancy law. Northern Ireland landlord and tenant law has different emphases (see, for example, Paris 2002). Devolution has created a laboratory for the study of comparative housing law and policy. One cannot enter that laboratory without a clear appreciation of the separate development of housing law and policy in those jurisdictions. This book provides one element in that overall make-up, being about England only.

Second, the HRA and the jurisdiction of the European Court of Human Rights (ECtHR), under the European Convention on Human Rights, has resulted in the questioning (at least) of a number of principles and interventions in housing law. These sources can be overestimated – most human rights challenges are unsuccessful – but have made a significant difference in some areas. So, for example, in Chapter 16, we ask, as a direct result of human rights jurisprudence, are mandatory possession proceedings really 'mandatory'? In some areas, though, this 'new' jurisprudence has left housing law in a state of uncertainty and anxiety. Much printer ink has been spilt in seeking to determine whether a PRP is a 'public authority' or 'exercising public functions' under the 1998 Act, s. 3, which would cast the net of substantive and procedural protections wider (see *Poplar HARCA* v. *Donoghue* [2002] QB 48; cf. *YL* v. *Birmingham CC* [2008] 1 AC 95; *R (Weaver)* v. *London & Quadrant HT* [2010] 1 WLR 363). From a theoretical and practical perspective, the questions raised in HRA-related litigation involve questions of jurisdiction and scale (Valverde, 2009).

Third, any student of housing law and policy needs to be aware of both the potential for housing litigation as well as the problems of funding such litigation (as regards public funding, see MoJ 2010). There is plenty of housing law out there. That public litigation is likely to be the tip of the iceberg. Most housing law takes place outside the courts or is settled at the threshold of the court; sometimes, the 'shadow of the law' may affect the outcome but most often it does not because people often 'lump' (that is, do nothing about) their housing problems (see Genn 1999; Bridges et al. 1995; Mnookin and Kornhauser 1979). Satisfaction surveys of housing tenure often mask housing law problems (see the insights of Mulcahy and Tritter 1998 in the context of the medical profession, many of which are equally applicable to the housing context). Assumptions (usually of lawyers) that court decisions will have an impact both within the organisation in question and a ripple effect are unlikely to correlate with reality or, indeed, have unforeseen side effects (Halliday 2000a; 2000b; 2004).

Equally, the housing law which *is* reported is unlikely to be representative of the housing law which actually takes place in a crowded courthouse in everyday life (see, generally, Galanter 2004). This is because, most usually, the reported housing law cases are at the higher levels. Housing law at lower levels of the court system (by which I mean the daily routine of county courts and district judges) is unseen. Furthermore, a housing problem may not be thought of as a 'legal' problem by the parties involved. A housing problem may not have a court-based solution. Housing law has largely gone underground – it can be witnessed not just in the county courts but also through the different avenues which now exist for redress. These avenues are both administrative – for example, the right to have a decision reviewed or just simply to complain about a particular service – and adjudicative – the Residential Property Tribunal Service (RPTS) now has substantial jurisdiction in housing matters, as do the various ombudsman services (the local government ombudsman, the housing ombudsman, the removals ombudsman and the estate agency ombudsman, to name four such services).

Finally, one must be aware of funding limitations for housing law. Funding housing law is currently in a state of flux (MoJ 2010). If you can afford it, there are plenty of practitioners who can help. If you cannot afford it, legal aid funding is limited. Controls on suppliers of housing law advice through the legal aid scheme have, for some suppliers, made it uneconomic. Some suppliers have left the market place. The ability to seek legal advice can be compromised by the existence of 'advice deserts' in certain parts of the country. The Legal Services Commission, which administers legal aid, is in the process of developing Community Legal Advice Centres and Community Legal Advice Networks but concerns over quality and the effect on Citizens Advice Bureaux have been raised (see Griffith 2008).

Conclusions

Housing law tries to make sense of the evolution of housing tenure with which this chapter began. It does so by providing a structure through which diverse strands can be analysed (and often found wanting: Law Commission 2003). One particular result of these different strands is complexity. Complexity is, in some respects, what divides off housing law from the crowd. The Arden and Partington approach offers one method of simplifying that complexity. Housing law is like a maze, but, worse, without a vantage point at its centre because there is no centre point (or, its centre point depends fundamentally on one's starting point). One thing which can be drawn from the above (and which is unlikely to provide much comfort to the reader) is that to appreciate housing law, one must go beyond its mere description. There are some clear themes which can be identified – such as morality and techniques of governance – but they are apparently without much coherence within the subject as a whole. There is a politics of housing law (and, it should be remembered, neutrality is in any event a political statement). That politics may have dimmed somewhat since the 1970s, but it remains evident, sometimes silenced, but always structuring our truths about the subject. One particular example is the formation of two professional organisations of housing lawyers – the Housing Law Practitioners Association, which predominantly has a tenant focus, and the Social Housing Landlords Association, which (unsurprisingly) predominantly has a landlord focus.

Housing policy

Housing policy is a slippery term, just like housing law. The destination subject of 'housing studies', which is concerned largely with the study of housing policy, has diverse roots, partly in the way housing has been consumed, and the classes of such consumption (classically, see Rex and Moore 1967); partly in the economics of housing; and partly in a critique of consumption which focused on the production of housing (Ball 1983).

Housing as public policy

From one perspective, housing policy refers to centrally planned interventions in housing designed to achieve economic or other goals (Mullins et al. 2006). This suggests a level of coherence which is unlikely to be justified by an examination of the production of housing policy. This sense of housing policy refers to public policy. One of the key elements of housing policy during the twentieth century became the promotion of owner-occupation as a tenure, while welcoming the demise of renting. In large measure, this predilection for ownership and consumption is what governs housing policy today and, indeed, has done so for much of the post-war period (Murie 1998). This direction was a result of both ideological and economic choices (while not always being entirely consistently pursued).

There are a number of key questions here which form the concern of housing policy. They can be summarised in the fairly consistent, broad formulation of the goal of housing policy since the end of the Second World War: a decent home for all at a price within one's means (for discussion, see Hills and Mullings 1990; cf. Cowan and Marsh 2001a). This formulation of housing policy is one with which few could disagree. However, its breadth of ambition has enabled a significant number of contradictory state interventions in housing, for example, from financing the production of public sector housing to plotting its decline (implicitly within its ambit, if not explicitly). For much of the twentieth century, the concern was with quantity – that is to say, the numbers of properties being built – and controlling, or regulating, the cost of housing consumption. Housing need was, at this time, a question of housing shortages. To an extent, this understanding of housing need remains current (thus, the development of a system of affordable rent in the social sector has been tied in with the production of more units of social housing to meet need/demand). Concurrently, housing need became equally concerned with the bureaucratic distribution of accommodation to households in need of accommodation. Both versions of housing need subsist side by side, with complex interactions and balances between them which change depending on the political complexion of the government in Westminster (see, for example, CLG 2010e).

One particular concern of those who follow this public policy perspective is the relationship between housing and the creation of the welfare state. It is sometimes assumed that one of the reasons for the production of public housing by local authorities is that link with the development of the welfare state. However, there can be little doubt that the better explanation lies in the impact of the two World Wars. As Cole and Furbey (1994: 60) memorably put it, 'Adolf Hitler proved a more decisive influence than William Beveridge in shaping the housing requirements of post-war Britain.' In the immediate aftermath of both World Wars substantial programmes of reconstruction were undertaken, and predominantly by local authorities. But it is also clear that this programme was contingent in the sense that it was always anticipated that the private sector would take over (and, comparatively, most other countries in Europe developed housing through housing associations or companies rather than local government). So, after the First World War, the call for 'homes fit for heroes' was met with housing commissioned and managed by the public sector but constructed by the private sector and it was assumed that this would be for a limited period only (as is evidenced by the reports on the PRS at that time, discussed in Cowan and McDermont 2006: ch. 2).

Malpass (2003) has demonstrated how the incoming Labour government at the end of the Second World War inherited and largely accepted the plans laid down by the Coalition government that preceded it and which were based on the ideas inherited from the inter-war period: 'As a result policy was dominated by urgent quantitative imperatives rather than systemic reform objectives' (ibid. p. 591). Housing has been referred to as the 'wobbly pillar' of the welfare state (Torgerson 1987) because, unlike health and education, it was dominated by the private market. Perhaps ironically, as the welfare state is being dissolved through the influx of private sector values, the demands for responsibility and lash-ups with crime control policy – broadly the shifts to prudentialism, individualisation and responsibilisation (Rose 1999; O'Malley 2004) – housing can now be regarded as having a closer relationship with the welfare state than before. Housing policy has, however, led the way, and it can plausibly be argued that developments in housing policy have been pushed out to the welfare state (Malpass 2008).

If one adopts the perspective of housing as public policy, the key question from the latter part of the twentieth century is the extent to which housing policy has declined or collapsed as a central concern of the state. At the end of the twentieth century, key housing policy analysts were arguing over whether housing policy had a future. Many of the housing problems of the twentieth century had either disappeared or changed shape – gross housing shortages were no longer at their post-war levels, the quality of existing housing stock had been raised, and the conditions which gave rise to public involvement in housing had evaporated (Malpass 1999). The focus had shifted to the identity of the provider and facilitating growth in ownership to sustainable levels, so that policy interventions in housing appeared to have a different end.

Whatever the rights and wrongs of that debate, it now has a kind of *fin de siècle* feel to it. Housing as public policy appears in rude health. It has of course changed as new problems have begun to be recognised and understood (for a brilliant essay on the discovery of housing problems, see Jacobs et al. 2003; and for a similarly brilliant essay on the partial understandings developed in reviews of mixed estates, see Bond et al. 2011); and the interdisciplinary nature of housing as public policy has shifted in line with the new emphasis on 'responsibility' within the welfare state as well as within crime control policy. Indeed, from around 2000, there has been what can only be described as an avalanche of housing policy activity across the housing tenures.

One critique of this housing as public policy position is that it has failed to identify key drivers in the housing system. Housing as public policy has often failed to deliver on its intentions. This is the problem sometimes referred to as the 'implementation gap' (Pressman and Wildavsky 1973). For example, despite a range of initiatives to revive the PRS in the late 1980s and 1990s, the tenure remained stubbornly resistant. It is true that it did not decline further and may have slightly increased, but the attempts to engage new model landlords were by and large seen as failures. By contrast, the development by mortgage lenders (as opposed to the state) of the 'buy-to-let' mortgage was, for some time at least, considerably successful in bringing new money and (more) amateur landlords into the sector (Rhodes 2007).

Key policy interventions have not emerged from Whitehall but from other sources (referred to sometimes as bottom-up implementation – for a 'state of the art' discussion, see the papers in the symposium edited by Schofield and Sausman 2002). Perhaps the most significant such intervention occurred in the otherwise apparently sleepy backwaters of Chiltern, where a local authority sold its entire housing stock to a housing association in the early 1980s. This transaction was developed by the local authority's housing officers and was innovative in the sense that this was the first time a local authority had engaged in such a transaction in relation to housing in the modern era. Such a transaction has become known as a 'large-scale voluntary transfer' (LSVT) and, from today's vantage point, has changed the face of social housing. It became accepted as, and limited by, public policy.

A second level of critique lies in the problematisation of housing; or, rather, why are certain housing problems produced? As Rose and Miller (1992: 181) note, 'the articulation of government has been bound to the constant identification of the difficulties and failures of government'. Researchers, the media, statisticians, housing practitioners and, indeed, all of us are bound into this production of housing problems. However, just because something becomes a housing problem does not necessarily mean that it is a problem, or, indeed, that it is *the* problem (see, further, Jacobs et al. 2003). Policy reviews may also provide a partial picture of the terrain when they speak to a government with a clear policy desire:

> within the reviews there are indications of the deficiencies of the evidence base, but it is interesting that rather than focus on the implications of the quite considerable weaknesses, except for the two journal articles, the reviews mostly sought to emphasise (indeed, over-emphasise) what they could say about the positive effects of tenure mix. It is suspected that this is a function often of their raison d'être, namely to provide evidence for policy, and yet such a purpose could equally justify a more critical stance. (Bond et al. 2011: 87)

What/who is housing policy for?

I have argued (Cowan 2008) that there now seems to be a sense of existential angst at the heart of housing policy about the big question: what is housing policy for (or, rather, what can housing policy do)? We know that the mortgage market is influenced by factors outside our control, which was emphasised by the Northern Rock problem (that is, the 'run' on the Northern Rock Bank leading to its actual nationalisation under the Banking (Special Provisions) Act 2008) and the collapse of Lehmann Brothers. We know that the poorest households are concentrated in social housing. We know that homelessness and housing need will not disappear, unless one defines them out of existence altogether (but the problems of homelessness and housing need would remain). We know that, however much we try to alter behaviour, there is low and high-level deviance in the form of what is termed 'anti-social behaviour' (ASB) (although its definition is contested terrain). We know that the PRS is unlikely to offer more than an intermediate, short-term tenure (as successive incentive schemes have demonstrated). We know that whatever happens to the PRP sector, our governmental strategies are cornered by the enormous influence of private lenders. We also know that there is a deficit in the implementation of housing policy – what happens in Whitehall is not easily translated into on-the-ground practice.

That sense of angst is compounded by the relatively low status of the office of housing minister; its changing location within government (DoE, DTLR, DETR, ODPM, CLG); the lack of specialist knowledge offered by its various incumbents (with one or two exceptions); and the high mobility of those incumbents. Few housing ministers remain in the job for more than a few years and each new minister brings their own distinctive flavour (witness the comments of the minister, Caroline Flint, appointed in 2008 fresh from the DWP, about the possibility of a link between housing allocation and security, on the one hand, and job-seeking on the other). Responsibility for housing also cross-cuts government departments, so that coherent policy across the domain appears practically difficult. There is often a disconnect between what is desirable from a housing policy perspective and an economic management perspective. Increasing rents in the social sector, for example, has a knock-on effect on housing benefit (HB), employment, mobility and treasury management, all of which have to be negotiated.

A clearer answer to this question was emerging from the avalanche of activity under the New Labour governments to which reference was made above. Housing policy was for occupiers as consumers. One question embedded in this statement is 'consumers of what?', and recent policy documents have suggested that the experience of housing cannot be divorced from the 'place-shaping' role of housing providers, although this may be contested. Place-shaping means 'the creative use of powers and influence to promote the general well-being of a community and its citizens' (Lyons 2007: para. 14). Despite that contestation over role, the notion that housing policy is for consumers is not uncontroversial. Housing policy has been dominated by concerns about providers, whether it be obsessing about contracting out, enabling a mixed economy of provision, creating the conditions within which private lending and private providers can flourish, and one could go on. Tenant participation has been a theme of social housing policy at least since the early 1980s, but this has always been as a check only on housing management.

Second, the focus on the occupier as consumer is also controversial. Labels are important and identifying occupiers as consumers implies a host of rights and obligations that suggest activity and choice on the part of the occupier (which might not be possible or appropriate). It also implies an identity of the occupier as, to use the terms adopted by Le Grand (1997; 2003), 'knaves' and 'knights'. In this work, Le Grand sought to identify the assumptions about human behaviour that underpin welfare policy. He used these terms, together with the identity of 'pawns' to denote those understandings. The 'knave' term denotes a construction of policy which reflects an understanding of its subject as self-interested; the 'knight' has a predominantly public-spirited or altruistic attitude; the 'pawn' is passive and unresponsive to change. As Le Grand (1997: 154) puts it, 'Conscious or not, the assumptions [about human behaviour] will determine the way that welfare institutions are constructed.' The assumption of welfare policy (and, indeed, housing policy) has been that welfare recipients are 'passive recipients of landlord bounty' (Gilroy 1998), and are pawns whose behaviour requires reshaping. The direction of social housing (including HB) policy appears almost entirely based on this understanding; hence, the demand for, and focus on, 'responsibility'. Their construction as consumers also implies a role as 'knights' and 'queens' (the most powerful of all), for the consumer is sovereign (for example, blowing the whistle on an underperforming PRP – see TSA 2010a; CLG 2010k). Equally however, the focus on choice in housing policy (particularly apparent in its allocation/letting or the RTB – see Chapter 7 and Chapter 10) has an understanding of the consumer as 'knave', for those choices assume that consumption motivations can be affected by certain incentives to act in a self-interested way. That is not to say that there was a clear direction, consistency and coherence for housing policy and its influences; far from it, in fact, for, as is developed in subsequent parts of this book, housing policy often seems incoherent and inconsistent, sometimes made 'on the hoof' and lacking direction.

These identities are not only about the consumer but also changing incentives regarding housing management. The LSVT process, for example, can be understood as a way of seeking to alter the motivations of housing managers to act more as knaves, with one eye on the margin of surplus, than might otherwise have been the case. More mundanely, performance measures operate in similar vein, individualising and comparing each officer's performance against a norm (if properly constructed, cf. Jacobs and Manzi 2000).

Social justice

A further dominant theme of housing policy has been its pursuit of social justice. This is, in fact, a rather unhelpful statement because the notion of social justice is contested – its identity depends on political and theoretical perspective. Social justice may be about equality, but this does not take us much further because different political ideologies have different ways of working through equality. So, liberalism and its relative neoliberalism assume that markets provide equality and, as such, prescribe limited state intervention. Although not entirely coherent in this respect, it can be said that the Thatcher government exemplified that neoliberal tradition, particularly as regards its deregulatory impetus. Deregulation of housing markets, particularly in relation to private renting and mortgage lending, was in this vein. The creation of markets, and market-like technologies, in public services may also be included here.

Social democratic ideologies tend the other way: towards state intervention to produce equalities, based on the identity of citizens as rights-bearing. The production of council housing, the creation of legislation designed to assist the homeless in obtaining council and other housing, and the creation of benefits to enable people to pay for their housing (such as HB) are all examples of interventions in the market which assist in the production of equality (and may also have stigmatising effects: Titmuss 1974). Communitarianism emphasises the role of community and, most particularly, the interdependent nature of citizens' responsibilities. The Conservative and New Labour governments' emphasis on and production of ASB are prominent examples of this position. Equally, the focus on tackling social exclusion in the early Blair governments may be considered within this frame (although see the assessment of Levitas 2005).

Another way of approaching the social justice question is by searching for inequalities, or disadvantages, in the housing system. Housing studies have, therefore, spent considerable efforts on isolating specific inequalities – gender, ethnicity, disability (see, for example, Morris and Winn 1990) – whereas the tendency today is towards the analysis of intersectional disadvantage. Intersectionality focuses not on isolating specifics but in obtaining a broader picture of disadvantages as they impact on individuals. The move towards a single equality position under the Equality Act 2010 is likely to highlight this further. An approach which focuses on inequalities in this way will highlight rather different social justice problems.

The problem of tenure

Just as with housing law, the usual starting point for analyses of housing policy is with tenure, identified in much the same way as housing law does (cf. Blandy and Goodchild 1999). However, for those writing from the housing studies perspective, housing tenure is problematic because these are categories of consumption. These categories of consumption are misleading because experiences are likely to differ depending on the nature and location of the dwelling (Kemeny 1992: ch. 1) and on the production of housing (Ball 1983). Early studies in this tradition focused on housing classes – the classic study, Rex and Moore's study of Sparkbrook analysed housing classes in this way. They argued (1967: 274) that 'too much political debate about housing is based upon the assumption that all problems can be discussed simply in terms of the rights of landlords and tenants'. The housing classes thesis has received less prominence as it relates less to public policy and more to empirical questions of aspiration and status values. Yet, it remains important in identifying differential experiences within tenures as well as the inequalities produced by housing class.

Less obviously, perhaps, in focusing on categories of consumption, we miss one of the fundamental points of housing studies – the structures of housing provision. The housing system has been defined by the way in which housing has been produced, predominantly by speculative housebuilders in the private sector, and funded, in the early part of the twentieth century by building societies (see Ball, 1983; 1986). In the inter-war period, owner-occupation began to gain prominence because of the structure of housing provision, which made mortgages more attractive to potential owner-occupiers and less attractive to landlords, and the structure of finance: one result was a controversial set of collaborative arrangements between housebuilders and building societies (Craig 1986). As a policy idea, the structure of housing provision is translated into questions of housing supply, which, in turn, are translated into a quantitative position (identifying how much more housing is required to meet population needs – see for example, Barker 2004). The housing supply issue periodically appears on the policy agenda.

Tenure itself has also been problematised. It presents apparently tightly framed categories but there is also a sense within the literature and, indeed, housing policy itself of moving 'beyond tenure'. This is discussed in particular in Chapters 9 and 10 below, but refers to apparently new hybrid statuses such as shared ownership, under which households buy a share in the property with the option of buying further shares (a process known as 'staircasing'), or other products such as equity release, including sale-and-rentback. Furthermore, the 'hierarchy' of tenures that might exist in national policy discourse is not always mirrored exactly locally – there is spatial differentiation and fragmentation within each tenure so that generic discussion of tenure (and individual characteristics) is, in itself, inaccurate (see, for example, Karn et al. 1985).

The professionalisation of housing

Another theme that has developed (and to which, perhaps, less emphasis has been given than it merits) is the professionalisation of housing (see Laffin 1986; Mullins et al. 2006: 213–17). The development of a profession of housing management, in particular, has been influential both in terms of the development of shared norms and purposes, but also as a vehicle for policy (McDermont 2007). In particular, the housing profession has developed norms around the identification and management of housing need (Cowan and Marsh 2005). Equally, identifying the proper terrain of housing management enabled judgments to be made about its effectiveness, which, in turn, influenced the policy drift about its potential for privatisation.

Most attention has focused on the professionalisation of social housing management, but this would be inadequate if it failed to give attention to the developing phenomenon of professionalisation of private sector housing. Organisations of private landlords, for some time dogged with the stigma of 'amateurism', are developing professional ethics which in turn make private landlords governable (Cowan and Carr, 2008). This is significant because, for some time, they were regarded as 'ungovernable'. Equally, the professionalisation of social housing management is an ongoing process (see Laffin, 1986). It has highly contested and unstable identities (discussed in Chapter 4 and Chapter 5 below) which are defined for different purposes at different times. For example, in the late 1980s, some definition was required because there was an attempt to work out the nature and effectiveness of local authority housing management as opposed to PRPs; the current need is to provide a definition to enable the costs of local authority housing management to be calculated (see Chapter 4).

Modern themes

Over the past thirty years, housing policy has been the site of consistent, varied and diverse innovation. This is the first modern theme – keeping up with the pace of change. In contrast to the housing as public policy analysis, one of the keys to current housing policy is its dislocation from the centre. Housing policy is developed both by the state and in diverse locations beyond the state (which may subsequently get adopted and/or adapted by the state). We might refer to this as a recognition of the significant government of housing that takes place beyond the state (Cowan and McDermont 2006; McKee 2009). It is unlikely that this is a product of the present, but it has become more apparent as housing searches for innovation. This point is not to suggest that state governance has become irrelevant – far from it, as has been highlighted above – but that the watchword of the government of housing is *partnership*.

Partnership may be expressed in any number of ways. For example, partnership may be encapsulated by contracts, which may or may not be enforceable, but which anticipate an ongoing relation between the contracting parties (and, possibly, others). This type of relation most clearly occurs where a local authority decides to sell off part or all of its housing stock to another housing provider. At the other end of the spectrum, partnership may be expressed loosely, such as in the partnership between local authorities and private landlords. Here, at its loosest, local authorities, who are the primary regulators of the PRS, take on the role of promoting it through advice and the provision of information in local fora. Another version of partnership are the contracts which individuals might enter into with their landlords regarding their future behaviour. Partnership, then, is a way of governing the future, managing the risks and seeking to engender trust.

Another way of expressing partnership is through the term 'mixed economy'. This term refers to the policy that different housing providers should be working in the same areas. Generally, the term refers to the social sector, but the notion of a mixed economy also pulls in private sector tenures. There is no necessity for these different providers to work in partnership with each other but the everyday reality is that they do because it is both in their interests and they are often bound together by regulatory or contractual requirements. This multi-tenured or 'mixed communities' approach is the preferred method of producing the ultimate goal of housing policy: *sustainable communities*.

Much housing policy (at whatever spatial scale) is directed to the production of sustainable communities, whether it be at the production or consumption end of the housing cycle. This suggests (again) a level of coherence that has not necessarily been met by clarity in the concept. The notion of sustainable communities is, indeed, very unclear (see ODPM 2003b). It goes beyond the pure production of housing, for sure, but housing policy has always been directed beyond that anyway. We might sum it up through the jargon of place-shaping although this does not take us much further. The Sustainable Communities Act 2007 provides us with the following definition: 'encouraging the improvement of the economic, social or environmental well-being of the authority's area, or part of its area' (s. 1(2)). Social well-being is further defined to include 'participation in civic and political activity' (s. 1(3)). The concept remains, at best, extremely broad. With notable understatement, the Cave review (2007: para. 5.122) pointed out that '[w]ith the increasing interest in sustainable communities, this complexity [of housing provision] is likely to increase rather than diminish'.

Although the focus here has been on policy labels, and their indeterminacy, there has been much policy activity around them and in their name. A raft of activity falls within their brief, from dealing with ASB, homelessness, housing construction and supply, housing quality, environmental considerations, housing finance – indeed, the whole gamut of housing policy itself. They raise serious questions about the nature of housing consumption, particularly over security.

Security is being used here in two senses. The first sense is over the security which we have in our accommodation – the inability of our provider or lender to evict us without some form of court order, perhaps available on limited grounds only.

The second sense is more theoretical and relates to risk. We are now accustomed to the ubiquity of risk. Risk assessment and risk management have a significant role to play across housing policy. Most obviously, perhaps, risk assessment and management appear in private sector policies and practices, such as the decision to make a loan to a household to buy a property. That individual decision is mediated by local practices – the lender's policies and practices – as well as the national – for example, the regulation of lenders and ownership policies – and the global – the regulation of financial markets. As the ongoing effects of the credit crisis (sometimes called the 'credit crunch') demonstrate, the global has a considerable effect on local decision-making both for the future and the past. Lending policies and practices which seemed reasonable once – for example, lending a high proportion of the value of the property or multiples of the household's income – subsequently become, or seem, risky. Risk assessment and management also form a significant part of the governance of social housing – this can be at the level of the risky individual but also the risky organisation (such as a social housing provider which is financially over-stretched).

Conclusion

In this chapter, the structure of the rest of this book was laid out, followed by locating housing law and policy. What may have seemed self-evident at the outset has been shown to have diverse influences, which have been (and continue to be) contested. These themes return throughout this book. Readers will find links – and tensions – between, for example, ideas of need, choice, sustainability, and risk, fleshed out. Many of these links and tensions are ongoing, but equally the legacy of the past has enabled certain truths about housing to have become accepted. The structure of this book is designed partly to enable all of this to emerge. It should not be regarded as fixed – certainly not – for there is considerable seepage between the three parts; but separating out these three broad parts of regulation, access, and rights and responsibilities enables a considerable number of analytical points to be made, which draw on and develop the above discussion further.

Part I
Regulation of housing tenure

Introduction to Part I

This part of the book considers the ways in which each of the housing providers in the identified tenures – owner-occupation, private renting, local authority and PRP – has been and are regulated. 'Housing providers' in this context means not only those who are actually responsible for the provision of housing but also those who facilitate it. For example, public and private finance plays a crucial role in the regulation of all housing providers and this is reflected in the succeeding chapters. Public finance has been gradually drying up since the 1970s and the housing system has begun to draw upon private finance in increasingly innovative ways. As that market has been deregulated, the provision of finance has become more complex and financiers have (for example) sought to impose private sector disciplines on the provision of social housing. The marketisation of social housing is reflected both in the regulation of its development and consumption. To take one example, the importation of 'direct line' methods into social housing ('one call does it all') is a by-product of these changing structures and identities. The marketisation of private housing has been reflected in changing regulatory and institutional structures. This complexity is important for it shows the critical role that central government has had in influencing the development and/or regression of each tenure. However, this part is also concerned with regulation from diverse sources, not just central government. The most significant changes in regulation have occurred from unexpected sources beyond the state, and this part takes account of these sources, particularly as they have affected the development of tenure. Indeed, what this part begins to unpick is how, despite regulatory differences between tenures in the social sector, these differences are becoming regarded as unsustainable because of the significant cross-over between those tenures.

Each chapter in this part develops a broader appreciation of the notion of regulation, beyond that which many texts adopt (although see Prosser forthcoming). This broader appreciation provides the basis for a partial understanding of the different trajectories of each tenure, on which Part II particularly expands, as well as Chapter 11. The chapter on owner-occupation, for example, begins with a section, 'regulating desire', to demonstrate the interaction between that tenure's promotion and individual desire. Equally, all chapters in this part take a perhaps narrower view of regulation, 'regulating law', to demonstrate the crucial mechanisms through which law regulates tenure and their supposed impacts (which have particularly affected the ways in which we now view regulation of the PRS).

The approach in each chapter is partly historical and partly current (indeed, taking account of the Coalition government's reforms) because the history underpins the diagnosis of current regulatory crisis and/or concerns. It might be said that this notion of regulatory crisis is double-edged. On the one hand, there are concerns that the regulation of housing is overdone. This is what has underpinned the Coalition government's reforms of PRP regulation, in particular. This concern is also relevant to the forms of regulation used in the PRS. There has been a sharp shift away from intrusive regulation of that sector, in some respects, because of concerns that over-regulation will lead to its stultification. However, that is not all one way and, as is observed in that chapter, the regulation of the PRS discloses no internal coherence or consistency. On the other hand, there are concerns that, if regulation is underdone, the lack of oversight will lead to crisis. This is what appears to animate the Financial Services Authority's (FSA) approach to mortgage regulation, and what led to concerns in the PRP sector after the high-profile failure of one PRP. The optimum forms of regulation, which much of the broader regulatory literature seeks out (see for discussion Morgan and Yeung 2007), has not necessarily infiltrated into the regulation of all housing tenures.

2

Regulating ownership

Contents

In this chapter, the different ways in which ownership is regulated are considered. Three different types of regulation are examined. The first, regulating desire, is broader than formal regulation, but concerns the ways in which desire for ownership is produced within the housing system. This section deals with the policy through which home ownership (and the use of the word 'home' in conjunction with 'ownership' is important here) has been promoted at the level of the state and beyond. The second, regulating law, concerns the rather different effects that the law of property has on that regulation. It is sometimes suggested, or believed, that the law should mirror the promotion of home ownership and, as a result, protect those owners. The law, however, has not reached this state of recognising a home interest. The focus here is on the conflict which arises between individual home owners and their lenders. The third section concerns the regulation of the banking and building society industry. At the time of writing, this has become *the* hot topic.

Regulating desire

In this section, we are particularly concerned with the general housing policies which have promoted home ownership, influencing the desire so to speak. The importance of this discussion to housing studies as a discipline is significant: there is considerable work about the (social) constructions of ownership, but it is also important that this discussion links in with the next section about the regulating effects of law. The two are intimately related (see the discussion in FSA 2010a about 'responsible borrowing').

Surveys consistently show that demand for home ownership remains fairly constant at around 90 per cent (DETR/DSS 2000: para. 4.1). Yet, as Forrest and Murie (1991: 123) suggest, 'tenure preferences are not formed in a vacuum but are heavily influenced by the pattern of subsidy, general housing policies and the individual judgements regarding financial expectations and changes in family circumstances'. One particular aspect of the tenure which made it more desirable was the incentives given to local authority and some PRP tenants to buy the properties in which they were living or an alternative (for example, the RTB or acquire, discussed in Chapter 10 below). The growth of ownership was contingent on other factors, not just the promotion of ownership by the state, but, and this is the crux of the debate, 'certain attributes of the tenure were increasingly identified as if they were inherent to it and were the underlying reason for its promotion' (Murie 1998: 82).

General housing policies emphasise the label '*home* ownership', whereas others live in dwellings (Murie et al. 1976: 171). The use of the word 'home' is indicative of something rather more than a dwelling. As Gurney (1999a: 172) put it, 'of all the lexical expressions in the English language "home" is perhaps the most evocative. In short, it is more than a word in the normal sense; it is an idea.' Others have sought to demonstrate that desires for home ownership satisfy an ontological craving for security (Saunders, 1990). The principal benefits of ownership in one study were said to be financial as well as providing independence and autonomy (ibid. p. 84). King (2010: 5–6) makes similar strong claims in respect of the RTB:

> It let many working-class households use their dwelling as they saw fit for the first time. Instead of being constrained by the landlords, they could now paint their dwelling how they liked, change it, improve it or even leave it be, and it was their problem and not an issue for others to interfere in. The RTB allowed households to be independent and act in the responsible manner that they were always capable of if only they had been allowed to.

In a study of housing policy documents in the post-war period, Gurney refers to the normalising discourses of home ownership in these documents. Home ownership was said to be a 'basic and natural desire' (DoE 1977: 50), or a 'deep and natural desire ... to have independent control of the home that shelters him

and his family' (DoE 1971). In its 1995 White Paper, the DoE argued the case
for home ownership in these terms:

> A high level of home ownership, alongside a healthy rented market, is good
> for the country and good for the individual. 80% of people favour home own-
> ership over other forms of tenure. They value independence and control over
> their own home. Buying a home is often cheaper than renting. Home owners
> know that in later life, when the mortgage has been paid off, they will have
> the security of an asset which will help maintain their living standards. (DoE
> 1995a: 12)

As Gurney (1999a: 173) puts it, that White Paper expresses the notion of
home through 'ideas of love, warmth, comfort, pride, independence and self-
respect'.

Much of this discourse of home ownership can similarly be found in the self-
help literature of the nineteenth century, especially that which associated itself
with the values of building societies. Here, one finds a link between thrift, on
the one hand, and ownership (specifically of land), on the other. For example,
Samuel Smiles' book, *Self-Help* (1859), extols the virtues of economy:

> Economy may be styled the daughter of Prudence, the sister of Temperance, and
> the mother of Liberty. It is evidently conservative – conservative of character, of
> domestic happiness, and social well-being. It is, in short, the exhibition of self-
> help in one of its best forms.

And Price (1958: 139–40) quotes a lecture given by Smiles in 1864 in which the
virtues of thrift are explicitly linked with those of ownership:

> The accumulation of property has the effect which it always has upon thrifty
> men; it makes them steady, sober and diligent. It weans them from revolution-
> ary notions, and makes them conservative. When workmen, by their industry
> and frugality, have secured their own independence, they will cease to regard
> the sight of others' well-being as a wrong inflicted on themselves; and it will no
> longer be possible to make political capital out of their imaginary woes.

These links between economy, property and conservatism (as opposed to the
pauperised revolutionary) became part and parcel of the social identity of
home ownership during the twentieth century. Harold Bellman, manager of the
Abbey Road Building Society and chair of the Building Societies Association
(BSA), for example, noted that (1927: 54):

> Home ownership is a civic and national asset. The sense of citizenship is more
> keenly felt and appreciated, and personal independence opens up many an
> avenue of wider responsibility and usefulness … The benefits of home ownership
> are not only material, but ethical and moral as well. The man who has something
> to protect and improve – a stake of some sort in the country – naturally turns his
> thoughts in the direction of sane, ordered and perforce economical, government.
> The thrifty man is seldom or never an extremist agitator.

Bellman went on to note the comment that ownership provided a 'bulwark against Bolshevism and all that Bolshevism stands for'.

The discursive nature of home ownership is at its most profound when it is compared with the alternatives. The principal point of comparison is usually between ownership and renting, which some have broadly equated to power and powerlessness or normal and abnormal (see also Saunders 1990; King 2010). Gurney (1999b) is able to illustrate this apparent dichotomy further through the use of well-known aphorisms and metaphors about home ownership, for example: 'an Englishman's home is his castle'; 'it's yours at the end of the day'; 'renting's just money down the drain'. These aphorisms and metaphors form part of the everyday understandings of persons, are value-laden and expressions of 'common-sense', but they also construct a morality about housing tenure. In a separate, but related (and equally engaging), study of the private garden, Blomley (2005) reflects that the act of gardening enacts property, it symbolises the values of property.

Yet there is other powerful research which reflects on the variations in the experience of ownership. Home ownership as a tenure reflects diverse, fragmented experiences (Forrest et al. 1990: 2). Gender, ethnicity and disability, for example, all impact on the experience of ownership (see Watson 1999; Bowes and Sim 2002). In this literature, the focus is less on the promotion of home ownership as a choice, than on the balance between that exercise of choice and the constraints on its exercise. Constrained choice might arise from an inability to access other tenures because of one's exclusion, and, more broadly, what has been described as 'ethnic penalties' (a phrase which can be adapted to each and all such groups) (Karn 1997). For example, evidence from a study conducted in the late 1970s of areas of low-income home ownership in Birmingham and Liverpool suggested that home ownership was 'a squalid trap':

> Unlike many owners who might expect capital gains on their property and the possibility of movement to a different strata of the market, these owners may suffer real capital losses and far from being able to move they will be forced to stay in a deteriorating asset which will be in a deteriorating condition. (Karn et al. 1985: 106)

Indeed, the policy focus has, more recently, been on producing *sustainable* ownership. This refers to the policy need for ownership to be affordable and for the state to intervene only where it becomes unaffordable. Rather than praising the values of home ownership, the 2000 Green Paper, for example, emphasised the need for householders to make realistic appraisals of its affordability and, in doing so, set limits for the proper role of government:

> Everyone who buys a home has an obligation, before entering such a major financial commitment, to make a realistic appraisal of their capacity to maintain payments over the life of a mortgage and to keep the property in good repair. Of course, in some situations, people's circumstances can change unexpectedly, perhaps as a result of long-term sickness, injury or loss of employment. Government

support is available in such cases through benefit help, which covers interest payments on mortgages. (DETR/DSS 2000: para. 4.6)

The Green Paper emphasised a rather different assessment of home ownership
that is required of putative homeowners concerning its risks. Ford et al. (2001:
7–8) point out that these risks require an assessment of the impact of the global
on the local. They are both direct and indirect. Direct risks concern the market
and its associated uncertainties – what has become known as the boom and bust
phenomenon – which are linked with the global financial marketplace; indirect risks concern other areas of social and economic life, such as employment
insecurities. Risk provides a useful practical and theoretical prism for analysing home ownership, as Ford et al. demonstrate in their study of the possessions process (2001) (see Chapter 14 below). Risk individualises – the choices
are made by individuals within the context of a market in which the state has
delimited its role. Malpass (2008: 9) refers to the coming together of understandings of welfare and state support for owner-occupation, both of which
emphasise the responsibilities of individuals, to form a 'homeowners' welfare
state'. In this context, ownership is being used by the state as a method to reduce
the wealth gap, on the (then) assumption that house price values increase over
time, but also as a method of reducing public expenditure through rhetorical
devices of requiring owners to use their capital for the payment of their residential care as they get older or for home improvement (ibid. p. 13).

Regulating law

In this section, the structuring understandings of land law are discussed. They
are structuring understandings because they structure the ways in which we
conceive of land and, more particularly, its uses. The housing studies literature on ownership is immense, as suggested by the previous section, but it
rarely touches on the significance of the regulatory structures of land law. This
clearly is not the place for a detailed summary of property law (for which you
are referred to Clarke and Kohler 2005; Gray and Gray 2008); the more limited
purpose of this part is to demonstrate how the structures and purposes of land
law have facilitated the growth of ownership. While policy discourses are significant, they must be co-located with legal discourses which support and feed
them. It is something of an irony that, while land law facilitates the promotion
of home ownership, it rarely recognises the home interest (Fox 2007).

What it does recognise are certain incidents, or effects, of ownership in land.
Classically, as Honore (1987: 167) put it, these encompass: the right to possess;
the right to use; the right to manage; the right to the income of the thing; the
right to the capital; the right to security; the rights or incidents of transmissi-
bility and absence of term; the duty to prevent harm; liability to execution; and
the incident of residuarity. Of these, the most significant is the right to possess,
which 'is the foundation on which the superstructure of ownership rests' (ibid.).

It is this right on which we will focus here, but before doing so, it is necessary to have a whistle-stop tour of the underlying purposes of the law of property. From there, we will reach out to this notion of possession.

At a fundamental, conceptual level, the purpose of the law of property has become the facilitation of the alienation of land. It may not seem that way when you are, if lucky enough, battling with the conveyancing process (the process of buying and selling land), but that is its underlying rationale. It does so through various mechanisms which are designed to produce certainty in transactions affecting land. These mechanisms were the subject of important reforms in the late nineteenth century – particularly in the Conveyancing and Law of Property Act 1881 and Land Transfer Act 1875 – and in the series of Acts between 1922 and 1925 – especially the Law of Property Act 1925, Land Registration Act 1925 and Land Charges Act 1925. These radically reconfigured the law of property into its current state. These Acts simplified the law of property by reducing the number of rights which are capable of existing at law, while at the same time increasing the security in transactions around land (at least for the careful and/or advised).

Part of this radical reconfiguration was a liberalisation of the laws on the creation of mortgages. Prior to this period, a legal mortgage of land could only be created by a process of conveying the whole land to the lender with a provision for re-conveyance when the loan had been paid off; or by handing over the title documents to the lender. The innovation of these Acts was to enable a legal mortgage or charge to be created by a simple deed and, as necessary, registration (see now, Land Registration Act 2002, s. 27). Although this may not be immediately obvious, this was quite a revolutionary procedural step because it enabled multiple legal mortgages or charges to be created (hence the second mortgage industry today). There were other revolutionary changes, such as the promotion of the leasehold relation to an estate in land (rather than the awkwardly framed chattel real). However, the change in mortgage practice has had increasingly significant effects.

One element of the law of property which was not affected particularly by this raft of legislation was the notion of possession. This notion has an ancient common law basis as requiring both factual possession and the intention to possess. Possession, however, is being used negatively in this context to mean exclusion. Possession, which is the foundation of estates in land, means the right to exclude all others. The intention to possess means the intention to exclude all others. English land law was founded on this understanding (the term *seisin* was used) and it is reflected in our understandings of private property today. It is jealously guarded – a trespass arises by the mere fact of entry onto land without permission. While English land law has moved away from proof of ownership by long possession, as a result of the formalisation of title through land registration, nevertheless the concept of exclusion remains significant and, indeed, increasingly enacted in everyday life.

In this vein, Atkinson and Blandy (2007: 444) develop the concept of 'defensive home ownership', arguing (from Bauman, 2005) that the insecurity of everyday life 'has generated an imperative for the control and handling of domestic territory that seeks autonomy and refuge from dangers, as well as connecting to prevailing ideologies that celebrate personal autonomy and control'. This notion of defensive home ownership offers, then, a different operationalisation of risk. It territorialises risk and has, as its foundations, the link between property and crime control strategies. We are here confronted with 'the two major social facts of the last third of the twentieth century: *the normality of high crime rates* and *the acknowledged limitations of the criminal justice state*' (Garland 2001: 106; original emphasis).

Defensive home ownership is a response to these social facts, one consequence of which has been the architectural and urban planning demand to enhance security. Manifestations of this security are all around us (such as CCTV, lighting etc.) but these techniques also implore us to act responsibly and, in effect, to self-police our space. The 'gated community' is a particularly valuable example of the link between the understandings at the root of property law and our everyday lives. Although the term gated community is a contested concept in itself (see, for example, Bottomley 2007), one common thread is of interlocking legal rights and obligations, often through the use of covenants, to enforce community norms: 'a legal framework which allows the extraction of monies to help pay for maintenance of common-buildings, common services, such as rubbish collection, and other revenue costs such as paying staff to clean or secure the neighbourhood' (Atkinson and Blandy 2005: 177; see also Blandy and Lister 2005). As such, they represent the apotheosis of the logic of property law – a community divided off from the outside by its own local law.

But there are limits to property's focus on exclusion. These limits might come in the form of statutory controls, such as the right of utility companies to access land. Atkinson and Blandy (2007: 448–50) draw attention to the debate over the conviction of Tony Martin, a farmer who took it upon himself to shoot two burglars, one of whom died as a result. Martin was convicted of murder (which was subsequently reduced to manslaughter on the grounds of diminished responsibility). The case became something of a cause célèbre for those who sought to apply the logic of property law (implicitly) by arguing, unsuccessfully, for the right to defend one's home.

Similarly, Fox (2007), in an extended study of the concept of home in law, draws attention to the apparent disparity between home in policy and culture, on the one hand, and as conceived in law. Fox's specific target is the relation which exists between the owner's 'home interest' and their lender. The problem here lies in what Merret (1982 : 72) referred to as the 'magnificent contradiction' that, while adequate housing is a basic necessity both for the self and for the labour market, it cannot be afforded by those in work. We need a mortgage and our lender is not particularly bothered by unquantifiable ideals of home, but by the commercial imperative.

Fox (p. 14) notes that it is a 'truism that, in disputes between creditors and occupiers, the creditor almost invariably wins'. If property law is most concerned with the facilitation of alienation, and alienation is generally practically impossible without the aid of a mortgage, then it follows that the law will generally seek to protect the creditor's interest. However, there are exceptions to this truism and it is not always the case that, in the battleground of a local county court (as opposed to the higher echelons of the court system, where cases are reported), the creditor's interest prevails (see Chapter 14).

One example of a situation where the interests of the creditor and the occupier of the property come into conflict is where the occupier wants to stay in the property and the creditor wants a sale. Where the basis for the occupier's occupation is more than one person's financial contribution to the purchase of the property, they will occupy under a trust of land and will be, in the legal vernacular, a beneficiary. A creditor can request that the court make an order. The Trusts of Land Act 1996 prescribes the criteria by which the court considers whether to accede to that request. The criteria are as follows:

(1) The matters to which the court is to have regard in determining an application for an order ... include –
   (a) the intentions of the person or persons (if any) who created the trust,
   (b) the purposes for which the property subject to the trust is held,
   (c) the welfare of any minor who occupies or might reasonably be expected to occupy any land subject to the trust as his home, and
   (d) the interests of any secured creditor of any beneficiary. (s. 15(1))

The court is also to have regard to include the circumstances and wishes of any beneficiaries of full age and entitled to an interest in possession in property subject to the trust or (in case of dispute) of the majority (according to the value of their combined interests) (s. 15(3)).

Although these factors appear neutral between the occupier and the creditor, the way they are played out and prioritised in court proceedings involving a creditor is anything but neutral. So, in *First National Bank* v. *Achampong* [2003] EWCA Civ 487, Ms Achampong was seeking to resist the claimant's application for an order for sale. The bank had, in fact, begun proceedings in 1993 (twice), but, as Blackburne J put it, the matter 'went to sleep' twice further for extended periods. It was restarted in 2001. The Court of Appeal first held that the bank's charge did not affect Ms Achampong's interest because it had been created by the fraud of her husband and his cousin. The final question was whether sale should be ordered. Ms Achampong resisted this on the grounds that this property was meant as a family home which included not just her children but also her grandchildren. One of her children suffered from a mental disability. The bank could have sought recovery of their money from Ms Achampong's husband and cousin, who were living in Ghana, although this was not a consideration of any weight (at [63]). The court, however, observed that the principles which had been developed laid particular concern to the debt to the bank. There was a significant effect of refusing a sale on the bank which would 'condemn the bank to wait – possibly for many years – until Ms Achampong should choose to sell' (at [62]; applying *Bank of Ireland Home Mortgages Ltd* v. *Bell* [2001] 2 All ER (Comm) 920), while in the meantime the contractual debt would only increase. It was not for Ms Achampong to say that there had been considerable delay in the bank bringing the proceedings because, after all, she had the benefit of the property during the hiatus (at [62]).

As for her family home claim, Blackburne J. made the following observation:

> Insofar as the purpose of the trust – and the intention of the Achampongs in creating it – was to provide a family home and insofar as that is a purpose which goes wider than simply the provision of a matrimonial home, I am unpersuaded that it is a consideration to which much if any weight should be attached. The children of the marriage have long since reached adulthood, one of them is no longer in occupation. It is true that the elder daughter … is a person under mental disability and remains in occupation but to what extent that fact is material to her continued occupation of the property and therefore to the exercise of any discretion under section 14 is not apparent. (at [65])

The court made an order for sale.

So, by way of summary, what we can say is that English property law is based on rights to exclude and, taken to its logical extent, this allows for defensive home ownership. There are limits to this, though. One by-product of this right of exclusion is that it is productive of a positive understanding of home and the security which that provides. There is a considerable degree of assonance between the state policy of promoting home ownership and property law. Yet, this assonance also runs into conflict with other rights in the home – those of creditors – which tend to be prioritised over the occupiers. There is a logical property law explanation – the facilitation of the alienation of land; the assumption that legal constraints on lenders may result in negative changes to lenders' policy, which, in turn, will affect the sale market. Property law is in thrall to lenders, without which it will be unable to produce the desired marketplace.

Regulating lending

This section focuses on the regulation of lending but, underpinning that discussion is also an understanding of the causes of, and regulatory responses to, the credit crunch. There is a degree of historical analysis required. The starting point is a discussion about building societies and the values they espoused, the reasons for their decline and the growth of the mainstream banking industry. We then go on to consider the current and future regulation of the mortgage industry.

Building societies: background and association

The first building societies grew out of the processes of urbanisation during the early industrial revolution. The first records relate to a society set up at the

Golden Cross Inn in 1775 (Boddy 1980: 5). That they should have been related to inns reflects the fact that they tended to be working-class organisations based on a particular locality. Basically, a number of people agreed to pay a fixed sum of money every month to a member of the organisation. The money which accrued was then used to buy a plot of land and build a house on it (and so on until all the members were housed). The organisation terminated when the last member was housed. Such associations soon became anachronistic and only the very first of them actually involved the members in *building*. Associations subsequently took in funds from those simply requiring interest rather than accommodation and this money was used to fund the property side. Depositors were paid their interest out of the sums paid by borrowers. A cycle of deposit and lending was built up, with each supporting the other. Between 1845 and 1873, these associations gradually came to be permanent, as opposed to terminating, societies.

Although originally associated with voluntarism and amateurism, by the mid-nineteenth century, they had taken on a professional ethic, their practice was underpinned by 'a sound mathematical reasoning' and expertise, and they had formed themselves into a strong pressure group which clearly had irked successive governments (see below). A key figure, almost totally neglected in housing studies, was Arthur Scratchley who was largely responsible in the 1840s for developing actuarial practices and tables to govern building societies, and who was probably responsible for developing permanent building societies (see Price 1958: 118). Permanent building societies, rather than meeting in the pub, were associated with the temperance movement. The Leeds Permanent Building Society, for example, began as a society for working men but, by the 1870s, was dominated by lending to the middle classes and the wealthy; indeed, the evidence suggested that by this stage, most of its lending was to petty landlords (Royal Commission 1885b: paras. 10,865–9). Despite the public face of building societies' support for ownership, in the latter part of the nineteenth century they tended to concentrate their loans on landlords: 'owner-occupation played a larger part in building society ideology than in most societies' mortgage portfolios until well into the 20th century' (Craig 1986: 89). Nevertheless, as Craig points out, the ideals and purposes of the movement chimed with the political settlement after the second Reform Act. They encouraged self-help, deservingness, respectability, thrift and order (Gauldie 1974: 206–7).

Under the Building Societies Act 1874, societies became subject to the same regulatory structure as friendly societies because their shares were based upon membership as opposed to capital (they thus avoided regulation through company status: Boddy 1980: 9). That Act permitted societies to loan money only by way of mortgage. They were able to take short-term deposits, to invest a specified proportion in mortgages (up to two-thirds) and the remainder was to be placed in safe securities. The Act remained in place subject to minor amendments until 1986 and provided the foundations for the twentieth-century expansion of the permanent building societies.

Over the past couple of centuries, building societies have been looked on with some favour as organisations because they have encouraged thrift, forward planning and activity on the part of a certain class. Although it is probably true that the middle classes obtained most benefit from them during the nineteenth century and they had little impact on property ownership beyond landlordism, they proved adept at self-publicity, self-formation and producing a set of truths about their role. Property ownership made citizens, but it was the building society which facilitated that transition. The formation of an association of building societies in the nineteenth century was also significant in developing a relatively clear regulatory space for their operations (see, generally, Cleary, 1965).

Property ownership gained during the inter-war period, probably at a greater rate than state-provided housing, as a result of the widespread investment by building societies in the ownership market combined with investment through state subsidy and cosy relationships with builders. Building societies were able to do so as a result of what was termed the 'sheltered circuit', a title which reflected the protection given to both income and capital streams.

As regards income, societies were able to offer better rates to depositors than competitors because they were able to tax interest payments at source at a lower rate (the composite rate) than other organisations; and, in this crucial period, mortgage interest rates payable by borrowers reduced at a slower rate than the base rate. As a result, building societies became cash rich and, for the purposes of their business, needed to lend that money for house purchase. For example, they liberalised the terms they offered to borrowers, increasing the length of mortgage terms (and therefore lowered interest payments widening the affordability bracket) and they reduced the initial deposit which the potential home owner had to provide. The latter was achieved partly through alliances with housebuilders, through a system known as 'pooling' under which the building societies would essentially be guaranteed against loss over a certain loan to value ratio (the disastrous consequences of this scheme for the buyers are considered in Craig 1986; Piratin 1978: 41–2). Building societies also had an effective monopoly over mortgage lending because of a 'corset' around banks' involvement in that market. The Bank of England effectively penalised banks' involvement in the mortgage market through credit control (Holmans 1987: 234–51). Holmans (1987: 235) notes that 'the amount the [banks] lent was subject to quantitative restriction as a result of official "requests" at various times between the mid-1950s and the later 1960s'.

Between 1939 and 1983, the BSA set the interest rates for both deposits in societies and mortgages paid out by them. From 1973, societies protected their market monopoly by operating a cartel under which the largest societies accepted those rates (although smaller societies oscillated within and around them: Boddy and Lambert 1988). The basis for setting the rates appears to have reflected 'the requirements of the housing market, the general level of interest rates, the conflicting interests of investors and borrowers and the societies' need to maintain adequate operating margins and liquid assets' (Boddy 1980: 87; although it was often inaccurate: Boddy and Lambert 1988). A significant factor was the involvement of central government, particularly when market interest rates rose rapidly in the 1970s. During the early 1970s, governments paid bridging loans to societies in order to keep mortgage interest rates at acceptable levels (which contrasts with the exhortatory tactics used in the 1950s and 1960s) (Holmans 1987: 278–82).

High interest rates in the 1970s effectively ended the cosy monopoly enjoyed by the building societies, as the beneficial advantages of the taxation environment were gradually eroded (and withdrawn in 1982); and the banks began to compete more effectively for mortgage and savings business as restrictions on their doing so were gradually whittled away. Higher interest yielding accounts became a major new source of deposit but this led to 'a squeeze on margins and evidence of a reduced rate of growth' (Boddy 1989: 94). At the same time, the increased competition between societies ended the cartel, particularly given that the broader financial marketplace was rapidly being deregulated. The knock-on effect of the competition for investors, through increasing interest paid on deposits, was higher mortgage rates to offset those increased costs (Ball 1983: 36) which therefore provided an incentive to other organisations to join the mortgage market. Finally, when interest rates began to fall, the money markets became more competitive and provided an alternative, higher yielding outlet for personal savings.

Mutuality

One of the governing principles of building societies is mutuality – when there is talk of demutualisation (for example, takeovers by banks, or simply taking corporate status), mutuality is talked of as a hallowed principle and one of the hallmark benefits of the organisation. Mutuality means that depositors and borrowers are members, who are entitled to a say in the direction of the society, and the societies themselves are non-profit-making organisations (although they are entitled to make a surplus). As mutual societies, they were supposed to have 'an equitable balance' between the interests of their members – borrowers and depositors – even though that balance was difficult to maintain (Holmans 1987: 219; for a critique, see Barnes 1984). Mutuality was recognised as the guiding principle in the earliest legislation. Mutuality may well have been a principle which guided their initial development but, subsequently, societies' practices have shown that this ideology has long been shaken off. For some, the credit crunch has been caused by the effects of demutualisation: 'The wheezes, laxer standards and greed would appal the Victorian grandees who set up these institutions to help people move from slums into comfortable properties, which were built so well that millions of us are still living in them.' ('Home truths', *The Times*, 16 June 2008: 2, perhaps playing fast and loose with the history of societies – see, for example, Piratin 1978; Craig 1986.)

The search for 'surplus' also effectively contradicted their mutuality. In seeking new markets in the 1980s, after their monopoly had ended, it was natural that societies called mutuality into question. The BSA sought to resolve this issue by focusing on expanding the role of building societies in the housing market, emphasising their distinctiveness (Boddy, 1989: 97). Talbot (2008) has helpfully identified five factors which caused the retreat from mutuality: the increasing dominance and control of the sector by the largest societies; the limiting structures of the legislation (limiting in the sense of business opportunities); the monopoly and cartel practices of the BSA; the liberalising ethos of the Thatcher governments and the production of liberalising laws affecting societies, in the Building Societies Act 1986; and the ambition of building society managers. One should add the demise of the corset in the early 1980s to this list, because, for the first time, banks were competing in the mortgage market, as well as the fact that building society members' commitment to mutuality was no more than skin deep (Stephens 2007: 210).

Deregulation, competition and the Building Societies Act 1986

The Building Societies Act 1986 provided a new regulatory regime, enabling societies to expand and diversify their enterprises, as well as compete with other mortgage lenders more effectively. The competition of the early 1980s left societies at a disadvantage because of their reliance on personal savings in a market in which better returns could now be gained elsewhere on alternative investments. Additionally, the technological revolution affecting the major clearing banks enabled those institutions to become more efficient and cost-effective. Increasing competition from other financial enterprises in the mortgage market also revolutionised the previously cautious lending practices of societies. This was manifested by higher loans-to-income and loans-to-value ratios than had previously been available (Doling and Ford 1991: 112–13), which brought greater risk of individual borrower's default to the mortgage lending market (although not completely, as societies relied on mortgage indemnity guarantees to limit their losses).

Building societies' agitation for reform in the early 1980s raised the issue over their separate regulatory status. As mutual societies, they were supposed to act in the interests of their members – borrowers and depositors – but they tended to 'be closed oligarchies subject to little control by the membership … so [their] objectives became closely linked to the importance for senior management of high salaries, status, perks and power: all of which are associated with increasing size in terms of turnover, branches, etc.' (Ball 1983: 296). The 1986 Act was a result of a close working relationship between the government, the BSA and the societies individually, which determined the shape of the Act throughout (Boddy and Lambert 1988; Boddy 1989). The strength of the BSA lay in its ability to represent and negotiate within its membership (as different societies had different interests, depending, for example, on their size). They had a neat fit with government housing policies which sought to develop 'new model landlords' (see Chapter 3). They were given much wider purposes under the 1986 Act, enabling them to diversify their portfolios within limits (see Gibb and Munro 1993) but became subject to a new regulator – the Building Societies Commission. The commission had various powers, for example, to set levels of capital adequacy before societies were allowed to diversify into other investments, together with certain obligations to investigate. Societies were willing to accept this slight intrusion as a quid pro quo of their broader powers, partly because they recognised that there was a gap between their management and members (Mabey and Tillet 1980; Hawes 1986) and partly because of high-profile scandals in the late 1970s. The building societies ombudsman also became foisted upon the societies in Part IX of the 1986 Act (see James 1997).

After the 1986 Act, societies diversified their assets, buying into the life insurance market, for example, and essentially joining the consumer market for financial services. They have been considerably assisted by a regulatory environment which has shifted its boundaries when required. The benefits for members of mutual societies have had to be put on hold in order for the societies to keep faith within the 'market' (Kearns and Stephens 1997: 26). Instead of expanding their branch networks, mergers occurred for efficiency gain (ibid.).

The most significant effect of the 1986 Act has been the movement to demutualisation either through takeover (by banks) or through members' vote. The Abbey National was the first to vote in favour of taking corporate status in 1989 and in 1997 the Halifax joined the Abbey together with the Alliance & Leicester, Woolwich and Northern Rock. Conversion reflected the decline in the mortgage market (particularly during the recession at the end of the 1980s and into the 1990s) and, consequently, the desire to expand into other markets beyond the limits allowed by the 1986 Act. Additionally,

> The most compelling reason for conversion is that it will allow the larger societies to gain access to equity finance to allow them to take over other financial institutions. In this case, conversion can be seen as part of a wider consolidation in the financial services industry, combined with the move towards generic financial institutions offering the complete range of personal finance products. (Stephens 1997: 199)

Ironically, demutualisation took place at the same time as the deregulation initiatives had begun to roll back the legislative barriers created in the 1986 Act (Stephens 2007: 208). The Building Societies Act 1997 considerably broadened the ability of societies to engage in the marketplace. A new principal purpose provision included the ability to own residential property to let and borrowers now do not need to be members (s. 1). Loans secured on land must account for at least 75% of the societies' assets but there are few controls over the destination of the other 25%. Just 50% of the societies' funds must come from deposits, the rest may come from the wholesale markets. Under the Building Societies (Funding) and Mutual Societies (Transfers) Act 2007, the Treasury obtained powers to increase the amount societies can obtain from the wholesale markets to 75% (although the need for such an increase was not immediately obvious: Treasury 2008).

In terms of the mortgage market, the outcome of this fairly rapid transition, largely caused by the deregulation of the 1980s and what was known as the 'big bang' on the London Stock Exchange, was the creation of a space in which there was open competition for lending to borrowers. This competition was not just between institutions which depended on depositors but also on a new model type of lending institution, which relied on being able to sell off their loan books on the open market to finance their lending. These institutions had no branches and, critically, did not need to pay heed to the capital reserves of retail banks (Wainwright 2009: 378–80). Initially, these interventions were unsuccessful as they were caught in the downturn in the early 1990s and withdrew from the market (ibid.). The pressures of a competitive market have had effects in different directions. Simultaneously, there was considerable product innovation, including the increased use of interest-only mortgages; increased term lengths; self-certification (by which the lender does not verify the borrower's stated income); the opening up of the mortgage markets to households previously regarded as 'high risk', for example as a result of a form of previous insolvency, county court debt judgment/s, and previous mortgage default; and increases in loan-to-value (for example, up to 125 per cent of the value of the property), loan-to-income (for example, six times a household's income), and debt-to-income ratios (Stephens 1997; Scanlon et al. 2008; FSA 2010a; see also Chapter 10 and Chapter 14 below).

The mortgage industry in crisis

The state has a stake in a significant proportion of the major lending organisations. The roots of this crisis lie in the local and global processes through which lending institutions both changed form and developed the marketplace in respect of the more risky households. Behind both was the development, and increasing sophistication, of securitisation techniques. Securitisation is complex but based on a relatively simple set of transactions. Essentially, a mortgage lender creates a separate entity – sometimes known as a 'special purpose vehicle' (SPV) – which is designed to handle the entire loan book. That vehicle then sells on bonds under which it promises to pay to the bondholder a certain percentage annually during the mortgage term. These bonds can then be sold on, traded and have other transactions performed on them (such as credit default swaps).

A bondholder could assess the risk of these investments by reference to their credit rating, which was provided by a ratings agency. If this works well, then the SPV obtains a capital investment from selling the bonds and the bondholder obtains a valuable income-producing asset. This investment structure facilitated the creation of mortgage lenders which did not rely on depositors at all, because their capital could accrue through the bond process. This process also encouraged a trade in what was known as the 'sub-prime' market – those households which were more risky because of their past credit histories. Techniques were developed to rate a household's riskiness through credit rating it, and products were designed to make ownership affordable to such households (such as low-rate payments for a short period) but which always required the household to pay a premium during the mortgage term. In other words, they were more expensive for those households but, even so, they did enable those households to access home ownership. So successful were these processes in the US that, in its 2000 Green Paper, the DETR wondered why more use had not been made of them in the UK:

> In the United States of America, most home loans are securitised. That is to say, lenders sell on mortgages by issuing bonds. The bonds are a low risk investment and therefore generate funds at low rates of interest. The securitisation process also increases competition because it breaks up the mortgage process into its component parts (attracting customers, processing applications, raising finance and servicing mortgages) and allows mortgage providers to out-source the components that can be provided more cheaply by others. If the process is successful in increasing competition and reducing finance costs, it should lead to lower mortgage interest rates.
>
> The key question in relation to securitisation in this country is why it is not happening already. We will be reviewing this issue with lenders to examine whether there is scope for encouraging a more active secondary market in mortgages. (DETR/DSS 2000: paras. 4.12–3)

As Wainwright (2009) demonstrates, the US securitisation process was moderated as a result of UK laws and innovations were required to appeal to the broadest market; as a result, securitisation proceeded apace, particularly to avoid the rules regarding capital reserves. All of this was fine in a marketplace which was predicated on increasing house prices (thus facilitating remortgaging the property), the availability of credit, stable interest rates, and trust in credit-rating agencies. When interest rates started to rise, credit became less available, interest rates rose further, and the credibility of the credit ratings assessments were questioned: the basis for the risk assessments became falsified. Those assessments and calculations were based on data and projections which were no longer accurate so that 'systemic uncertainty' prevailed (Langley 2008: 485). The securitisation process, then, melted down. At the bottom of the pile lay those owners who were sold 'affordability products', which turned out to be anything but affordable, and concerns over the potential possessions crisis (see, generally, Bone and O'Reilly 2010; also Chapter 14).

Current regulatory structures

The current regulatory structures for the first mortgage market hinge around the FSA, set up under the Financial Services and Markets Act 2000 (FSMA), which promulgates the Mortgage Code of Business (MCOB) (FSA 2008a) and which reflects the outcome of the convergence between banks and building societies, both of which now fall within this regime. Other lenders fall within the regulatory embrace of the Office of Fair Trading (OFT) under the Consumer Credit Act 1994, as amended. This awkward regulatory split was to be remedied by the New Labour government but, as yet, remains in place (see Treasury 2009a).

The Financial Services Authority

The FSMA lays down certain regulatory objectives of the FSA: market confidence, public awareness, the protection of consumers and the reduction of financial crime (ss. 3–6). The FSA must also have regard to certain other factors in running its affairs including facilitating innovation and competition, as well as 'the principle that a burden or restriction which is imposed on a person, or on the carrying on of an activity, should be proportionate to the benefits, considered in general terms, which are expected to result from the imposition of that burden or restriction' (s. 2(3)(c)).

The FSA was an agglomeration of a number of regulators (including some of the Bank of England's responsibilities) into one body. At an early stage, the FSA developed an innovative approach to regulation which focused on risk assessment and management – Advanced, Risk-Responsive Operating Framework, known as ARROW (or more precisely ARROW II – FSA 2006). Risk here is used to refer to the 'potential to cause harm to one or more of [the] statutory objectives' (para. 2.10). Different risk assessment approaches were used depending on the size of the regulated firm (para. 4.5). In a risk-based approach, there is no such thing as 'no risk', everything is a risk. However, the FSA adopted a policy of erring 'on the side of assuming that a firm poses no risk when in fact it does subject to considerations of impact' (Black 2005: 520). This then fed in to the determination of where resources should be focused. But the risks concerned were not just about the regulated firm but also defending the FSA itself – ARROW was developed as a defence mechanism (or sold to its staff as such) and defines 'what, to [the FSA's] mind, are the acceptable limits of its responsibility and hence accountability' (Black 2005: 541).

In a prescient comment, Black (2005: 535) noted that 'one of the dangers of focusing only on firm-specific risks is that regulators may miss trends … of events external to the firm which might affect its risk assessment'. The failure of Northern Rock in 2007 provides one such example, which did in fact lead to criticism of the FSA for failing to build the external environment into its regulation of a mortgage lender operating in a risky climate (Treasury Select Committee 2008). Northern Rock, designated a high-impact firm but a low-probability risk by the FSA, was nevertheless allowed to operate a risky revenue practice, increasing its exposure within the mortgage lending marketplace exponentially at a time when its share price was falling (paras. 37–40). These warning signs were not picked up by the FSA. Northern Rock relied on four sources for its revenue: securitisation; the wholesale market; covered bonds;

and individual deposits, which fell as a proportionate share of its revenue from around 63% in 1997 (when it demutualised) to 22% in 2006 (para. 17). When these different markets closed to Northern Rock, it went under. The risk that these markets would all close to Northern Rock was unforeseen because it was unprecedented (reflecting the important point that risks can only be predicted based on past occurrences): 'It was a low probability, high impact risk.' (FSA 2008b: para. 3) The FSA was 'roundly criticised' during the Select Committee's inquiry (2008: para. 64) and the conclusion was that it did not supervise Northern Rock properly because: 'It did not allocate sufficient resources or time to monitoring a bank whose business model was so clearly an outlier; its procedures were inadequate to supervise a bank whose business grew so rapidly.' (ibid. para. 66) However, the conflicting objectives of the FSA as a regulator also played a key role because running against the FSA's supervisory role was the need to 'create incentives for firms to do the right thing in return for a regulatory dividend – that is less regulatory intervention' (FSA, 2008b: para. 16, citing a speech by the FSA's then chief executive to the Securities and Investment Institute Annual Conference, 9 May 2006).

Basis of Financial Services Authority regulation

As regards the more general basis for regulation, the FSA lays down certain principles as high-level standards for the operation of a mortgage (or, indeed, other regulated) business (MCOB: 2.1) (see Table 1)

It will be readily apparent that these principles operate at a very high level of generality. Principles-based regulation is in vogue. As Black (2008: 3) has noted, principles 'can provide flexibility, facilitate innovation and so enhance competitiveness' for firms; and, for the regulator, they have similar benefits but particularly in terms of flexibility and durability 'in a rapidly changing market environment'. Firms can be policed on the basis of the spirit of the principles as well as their letter, 'avoiding "creative compliance" and the need for the rules to anticipate every possible situation' (Black et al. 2007: 192). Their effectiveness is dependent, to a considerable extent, on the senior management within the regulated firm itself and requires a constant iterative process between the regulated firm and the regulator. Black (2008: 20–1) draws attention to the development of Principle 6, through the FSA's 'treating customers' fairly' initiative, the requirements for which are 'elaborated in a series of "statements", "cluster reports", self-assessment questionnaires, fact sheets and worked examples' (Black et al. 2007: 197). Black (2008: 24–36) identifies certain paradoxes inherent in the principle-based regulatory approach, most notably that this type of regulation can lead to a more ethical approach in the regulated firms but, because non-compliance can be an option, could also erode that ethical approach (although this is likely to be true of other regulatory models).

These high-level principles are supplemented by further guidelines. So, for example, MCOB 11 deals with responsible lending, which requires lenders to have a 'written policy setting out the factors it will take into account in assessing

Table 1. FSA principles

1	Integrity	A firm must conduct its business with integrity.
2	Skill, care and diligence	A firm must conduct its business with due skill, care and diligence.
3	Management and control	A firm must take reasonable care to organise and control its affairs responsibly and effectively, with adequate risk management systems.
4	Financial prudence	A firm *must maintain adequate financial resources.*
5	Market conduct	A firm must observe proper standards of market conduct.
6	Customers' interests	A firm must pay due regard to the interests of its customers and treat them fairly.
7	Communications with clients	A firm must pay due regard to the information needs of its clients, and communicate information to them in a way which is clear, fair and not misleading.
8	Conflicts of interest	A firm must manage conflicts of interest fairly, both between itself and its customers and between a customer and another client.
9	Customers: relationships of trust	A firm must take reasonable care to ensure the suitability of its advice and discretionary decisions for any customer who is entitled to rely upon its judgment.
10	Clients' assets	A firm must arrange adequate protection for clients' assets when it is responsible for them.
11	Relations with regulators	A firm must deal with its regulators in an open and cooperative way, and must disclose to the FSA appropriately anything relating to the firm of which the FSA would reasonably expect notice.

a customer's ability to repay' (MCOB 11.3.4(1)). MCOB 11.1 also makes clear that 'A firm must be able to show that before deciding to enter into, or making a further advance on, a regulated mortgage contract, or home purchase plan, account was taken of the customer's ability to repay.' There are also standards regarding promotion, disclosure and the information to be provided to borrowers (for example, MCOB 3, 4–7).

The Financial Ombudsman Service (FOS) maintains a high-profile role in the field dealing with maladministration by a regulated body (for example over the mis-selling of endowment policies linked to mortgage products). In 2008, it received over 150,000 complaints regarding home finance (FOS 2009: table 2.1); and from 2007 and 2010 between 37–40 per cent of such complaints were upheld (FOS 2010). Its jurisdiction is currently derived from Part XVI, FSMA and, like the FSA, it was an amalgamation, of previously existing ombudsman services. The FOS has compulsory jurisdiction in certain matters where the complainant wishes it to deal with a complaint concerning an activity regulated by the FSMA (s. 226). The FOS determines a complaint 'by reference to what is, in the opinion of the Ombudsman, fair and reasonable in all the circumstances of the case' (s. 228(2)). The determination is binding on all parties, provided that the complainant accepts the determination (s. 228(5)). A determination may specify a monetary award against the firm and a direction for the firm to take such steps as the FOS considers 'just and appropriate' (s. 229(2)). Such determinations are enforceable (s. 229(8)–(9)).

Gilad (2008a; 2008b; 2009) has shown how diverse influences have impacted on the FOS' jurisdiction, how it approaches its task with complainants, and how it manages its extensive powers. For example, rather than creating precedents, the usual practice of the FOS is to deal with cases on a case-by-case basis as a result of interventions because of industry concerns about adverse precedents (Gilad 2008a: 8–11). While the formal academic literature on ombudsmen is generally concerned with the just resolution of complaints and more general quality assurance, Gilad (2008b) demonstrates that the everyday work of the FOS adjudicators is as much concerned with managing the expectations of its complainants, including empathising with complainants and bypassing questions of responsibility. External influences on the FOS include its relationship with, and management of, the media (so that, for example, the FOS avoids naming and shaming non-compliant firms). Gilad (2010: 307) has also suggested that the FOS' dispute resolution process 'is explicitly designed to offset some of the advantages enjoyed by [repeat players] in court litigations' and, thus, neutralise complainant's disadvantages (referring to the classic study of Galanter 1974). Also of considerable interest is its relationship with the FSA combined with the potential sanction of informing the FSA about non-compliant firms albeit with uncertain outcomes. Gilad (2009: 15) tentatively suggests that the variation in firms' response to FOS decisions related to the firms' own 'relative tolerance to the risk of regulatory enforcement and the costs of applying the ombudsman's decisions across the board, given the number of similar complaints and the average redress per complaint'.

The Office of Fair Trading

The OFT's role concerns second-charge lenders (with some exceptions: ss. 16A–C, Consumer Credit Act 1974), which it has said it regards as generally 'high risk' and, consequently, attracts a high degree of regulatory scrutiny (OFT 2009: para. 1.6). All firms must have a licence from the OFT, which has considerable powers in relation to their grant and subsequent variation and revocation (ss. 25–6). Courts are also given considerable powers, for example to determine that an agreement is unenforceable or to vary the loan terms under certain conditions (ss. 127, 135–6), as well as intervening in unfair credit relationships (s. 140A–D, discussed in Chapter 10 below). Given the statement that such lending is high risk, it is surprising that the OFT developed its regulatory guidance rather later than might have been anticipated (discussed in Nield 2010: 614). It published guidance in 2009, which provides general principles of fair business practice (OFT 2009: para. 2.1). In particular, it says that there is to be no **irresponsible lending** with all underwriting decisions being subject to a proper assessment of the borrower's ability to repay the loan without undue hardship and without resort to the security (with the exception of those very limited circumstances where it is agreed expressly that the loan will be paid off by the security), taking full account of all relevant circumstances and any reasonably foreseeable future circumstances. (ibid. original emphasis)

There is to be full disclosure and information, no 'high-pressure selling', and lender incentives must not be undue, any recommendation given is to be in the best interests of the borrower (ch. 3, as required by the Act, in particular ss. 55 and 55A). Further guidance on irresponsible lending was issued in 2010, after a lengthy gestation period. In general terms, the OFT outlined that creditors should:

- not use misleading or oppressive behaviour when advertising, selling, or seeking to enforce a credit agreement
- make a reasonable assessment of whether a borrower can afford to meet repayments in a sustainable manner
- explain the key features of the credit agreement to enable the borrower to make an informed choice
- monitor the borrower's repayment record during the course of the agreement, offering assistance where borrowers appear to be experiencing difficulty and
- treat borrowers fairly and with forbearance if they experience difficulties. (OFT 2010: 13)

The response to the mortgage crisis

The most immediate response to the mortgage crisis has been the intervention of the state in the banking industry – in essence, as Black (2010: 39) puts it:

The crisis has … led to the creation of novel and challenging roles for the state, and the creation of a bespoke administrative apparatus to manage them. The Treasury has become the owner and manager of two banks, the dominant owner of another, and the significant owner of a further. It is also an asset manager, and a guarantor of banks' wholesale liabilities.

It does so through a number of arms-length bodies (including the Asset Protection Agency and UK Financial Investments Ltd) which have to walk something of a tightrope between responding to the market, concerns about their potential dominance within the market, and protecting the financial investment of the state. The FSA and OFT have both recognised that increased controls need to be in place over lending practices (FSA 2009a; 2010a; OFT 2010). The FSA has made clear its view that income verification should apply to all sales (FSA 2010a: paras. 2.22–4; 2.34) and that 'a robust and effective assessment of individual affordability has to underpin any sustainable lending model' (para. 1.6); affordability is to be calculated on a presumed 25-year mortgage term; a 'buffer' is to be built into mortgage applications where the applicant has a credit-impaired history; greater regulatory intervention on product development and governance, stopping short of a ban on certain products (para. 3.3) to avoid 'toxic lending' (i.e. where the risks are too high); measures to facilitate 'responsible borrowing' on the basis that many borrowers seemingly fail to engage with the risks or comparative, cheaper products (ch. 5); and possible measures to impose enhanced capital requirements on non-banks (para. 6.19).

Finally, and more fundamentally, the Coalition government is engaging in a process of fundamental reform of the regulation of the banking industry, including consulting about the transfer of part of the FSA's responsibilities concerned with client-facing services to a consumer protection and markets authority (Treasury/DBIS 2010a) and transferring the OFT's responsibilities to that body as well (Treasury/DBIS 2010b).

Conclusion

Diverse regulatory and other influences have impacted on the growth of owner-occupation in England. In this chapter, we have considered three such influences – the promotion of home ownership; the assumptions in land law about ownership as exclusion and its consonance with the values of defensive home ownership; and the growth of mortgage lending during the twentieth century. However, as regards the last, that growth in the latter part of the twentieth century and the early twenty-first century has been facilitated by innovations that were, or became, unsustainable in the market conditions which prevailed from 2007 and which have lead to major regulatory innovations. At its core, what underlies all these forms of regulation is a set of assumptions about risk, which has become the predominant feature of the regulatory terrain.

3

Regulating private renting

Contents

In the previous chapter, we looked at the ways in which the ownership market is regulated. In this chapter, our focus turns to the regulation of the PRS. We have already observed that private renting was in decline throughout the twentieth century, and it may well be that decline began in the late nineteenth century as a result of unaffordable rent rises (Ball 1983: 26, 205–6). Renting went into decline to the extent that, by the 1970s, as one author put it, renting was no longer considered 'an appropriate activity for private enterprise' (Berry 1974: 123). In this chapter, one central purpose is to explain the relation between the decline of the sector, its subsequent revival, and the relationship of both with changing regulatory structures and strategies.

In the first section, the focus is on what is known about the sector in terms both of the types of persons who become landlords and tenants, as well as the type (or, rather, quality) of property which becomes the subject of a private rental agreement. This is essential background material because it should define whether, how and why the sector is regulated. In the second section, we look to the regulating effect of law, drawing attention to the particular importance of the tenancy agreement on which statutory regulation bites. The interest here lies not just in the way in which the law constructs a tenancy agreement, as opposed to some other form, but also its regulating effects. We then go on to analyse briefly the history of general regulation, explaining the concept of security of tenure and the different ways in which the state has sought to deal with the amount landlords can charge for their tenants' occupation of the property. In the third section, the focus turns to the Housing Act 2004. Beyond explanation of this complex Act, the panoply of regulatory techniques employed in that Act is interesting because it discloses no coherent regulatory strategy. In the final section, consideration is given to the different reform strategies for the sector. Few now believe that the sector operates as a perfect market, but there are different views about the way in which that market should be regulated in the future. This process of holistic review has stalled, however, under the Coalition government.

Private renting: current knowledge

In theory, at least, regulation should be sensitive to context. The relevant contexts discussed in this section concern what is known about the cadre of tenants, landlords and property quality in the sector. It will readily become apparent that talk of a single PRS is a misnomer, because of the diversity within it. That is why academics routinely now refer to the 'private rented sectors', while paying lip-service, to an extent, to the official categorisation.

Tenants

In its 1995 housing White Paper, the DoE stated that a healthy PRS can:

- Provide an essential first stage for young people leaving home, including students and those saving a deposit to buy their own home;
- Contribute to a healthy economy by assisting labour mobility;
- Provide a home for people facing a change in their personal or domestic circumstances;
- Accommodate anyone who prefers to rent rather than own. (DoE 1995: 20)

It could also assist in providing accommodation to those on low incomes (who, subject to income and capital thresholds, might be entitled to a personal subsidy to assist with their rent, known as housing benefit (HB) – discussed in Chapter 9 below).

This statement of policy also reflects the current position. In particular, private renting has become a tenure for the young – 36% of households between 25 and 29 years old live in private renting, and 22% between 30 and 34 years old (NCSR 2008: table 5.3). Over half of new households entering the sector in the 12 months prior to 2006–2007 were in the 16–24 age range (ibid. p. 126). This is partly due to the expansion of tertiary education in England (the term 'studentification' is often given to the effects of this particular market – see CLG Select Committee 2008: para. 179 – which trebled between 1988 and 2000 – Kemp and Keoghan, 2001: 31) as well as other broader housing market factors, such as increasing prices of owner-occupation and early career labour mobility (see, for example, Rugg and Rhodes 2008: 16–17). A rather different market is made up of low- and no-income renters, who are reliant on HB, some of whom are using the sector as a stepping stone to or from social housing, but the proportion of claimants of HB in this sector has declined over the past ten years (NCSR, 2008: 136). There remain a small number of usually older households who retain accommodation that was let to them some time ago (often quite lengthy periods, reflecting different regulatory structures prior to 1989). In general, the PRS offers a transitional tenure for many households as they move through it and either into a further rented property, or ownership, or social housing (Kemp and Keoghan 2001: 33).

Other high-profile groups of users of the sector include those who do so by virtue of statutory routes. Under this category fall those homeless persons who are provided accommodation by local authorities under Part VII, Housing Act 1996, either by way of temporary accommodation or permanent accommodation (see Chapter 6 below and also, CLG, 2010e). Equally, destitute asylum seekers may qualify for housing provided through the UK Border Agency (UKBA), which took over responsibility for this provision from the National Asylum Support Service (NASS) (see Chapter 8 below). Some of this accommodation is in the PRS.

Landlords

From the landlord perspective, renting is predominantly a cottage industry which is best characterised generically by the word amateurist. Most landlords are individuals or couples, and this proportion has risen recently (from 61% in 1993/94 to 73% in 2006 – Rugg and Rhodes 2008: table 2.4). Of these landlord types, 71% own fewer than four properties and 44% owned just one property (ibid.). These types of landlords often enter the PRS by default – they inherit a property, they have been affected by the slump in the housing market and are thus unable to sell their property, or they have a spare property after coupling up so to speak (ibid.). These landlords are sometimes referred to either as business landlords (who obtain most of their income from lettings) or sideline landlords (who obtain a minority of their income from it and may view the property as an investment) (Thomas and Snape 1995).

Successive governments since the early 1980s have sought to rectify this imbalance by giving sweeteners to commercial organisations to enjoin them to enter the sector. These organisations were predominantly involved in the sector before the mid-twentieth century. It seems to have been felt that these organisations would offer the sector 'a significant difference to the scale, professionalism and reputation of private landlordism' (Crook and Kemp 2002: 742). There was a 'bewildering display of projects and acronyms' (Carter and Ginsburg 1994: 106) from the early 1980s designed to re-introduce them to the sector: BES (Business Expansion Scheme); HIT (Housing Investment Trust); HAMA (Housing Associations as Managing Agents); REIT (Real Estate Investment Trust) (see Jones 2007, on prospects of REITs). In general, these initiatives have not been successful over the longer term at least. There are a number of key reasons for their lack of success: the complexity of some of these schemes; insufficient profit from private renting, despite tax incentives; the risk of what would be a new investment (which would therefore require higher returns); the lack of a ready market to buy into (Crook and Kemp 1996; 2002; Crook et al. 1995).

In fact, the most successful scheme in terms of potential growth has come from beyond the state, so to speak, and been provided by the mortgage-lending industry. From the mid-1990s, that industry began offering 'buy-to-let' mortgages, which offered good interest rates to buyers who wished to let property. In 2006, there were about 850,000 such mortgages, which was sufficient for this vehicle to be regarded as a 'phenomenon' (CLG Select Committee 2008: para. 160). The principal effect of this vehicle over time has been that it 'has increased the role of individual investors while the share of rented housing owned by institutional investors has continued to decline' (ibid. para. 161). Such landlords generally fall into the typology in roughly similar proportions to other landlords more generally – most regard renting as a sideline activity and have fewer than five properties (Scanlon and Whitehead 2005). Post-credit crunch, however, this market appears to have suffered badly by the decline in the availability of credit.

A rather different way of typologising landlords has emerged in policy documents. These have drawn a division between 'good' and 'bad' landlords, most particularly in the 2000 Housing Green Paper (DETR/DSS 2000). While the government took a broadly non-interventionist stance in that document, it was unable to ignore apparent problems afflicting the sector, concerning property quality and management standards, to which some form of regulatory response would seem appropriate. In order to manage this tension, the document divided landlords between the 'many good and well-intentioned landlords' and 'a small minority of private landlords [who] set out to exploit their tenants and the community at large in flagrant disregard of the law' (para. 5.4). The dividing strategy had both moral and ethical overtones, and the regulatory strategies proposed for each group diverged sharply. For the former, responsible self-government, community regulation and self-policing (voluntary licensing, accreditation, kitemarks) were deemed appropriate. For the latter, an array of more intrusive, disciplinary regulation was prescribed – licensing, HB restrictions, risk-based regulation of property quality.

As Blandy (2001: 79) argued, this good–bad division was a discursive 'technique … used to justify intervention in a sector which in general the government is concerned not to over-regulate'. It involved an identification of, and link between, dangerous persons – the 'anti-social', the 'bad', and the 'exploitative' – and dangerous places – 'low demand'. The broad-brush distinction offered by the Green Paper suggested stability in that categorisation. Yet, such categories are unlikely to be stable over time and landlords may be both 'good' and 'bad' at the same time. The government was able to exploit the established *image* of the PRS as Rachmanite (see below), while at the same time maintaining both that problems are not widespread – 'a small minority of landlords' – and are overstated: 'All of this earns for the sector as a whole a far worse image than it deserves.' (para. 5.5)

The Green Paper did not see the categories 'good and well-intentioned' and 'bad' as separating the law-abiding from those acting unlawfully. It argued that many good and well-intentioned landlords face a 'great mass of legislation' and 'fall foul of the law … more often than not … through inadvertence' (para. 5.10). Hence, the identification of these categories became decidedly problematic and turned on the identification of those who are 'well-intentioned'. The lack of empirical evidence as to the categories was implicit in the Green Paper: 'We *believe* that most private landlords are basically well-intentioned and anxious to do a good and responsible job.' (para. 5.8, emphasis added) In contrast, what we know is that:

> Areas of low housing demand face severe and complex problems … This often attracts unscrupulous, even criminal, landlords and anti-social tenants, who may have been evicted from social housing. Together they may force out law-abiding tenants and owner-occupiers …
>
> In such areas unscrupulous landlords can operate on a large scale and to the detriment of the community as a whole (not least responsible landlords and tenants). (DTLR 2001: paras. 3 and 13)

In the consultation document from which these quotes are drawn (on selective licensing of landlords), it subsequently became clear what 'unscrupulous' landlords do – they 'take no interest in their tenants or the neighbourhood. Some may even encourage anti-social behaviour in order to intimidate owner-occupiers into accepting low offers for their properties' (para. 15). This knowledge was not supplemented with information about the scale of the problem; rather the concern was to establish that landlords should take responsibility not only for their own behaviour but that of their tenants.

These discursive divisions at the policy level, while significant, are paralleled at the local level by a rather different set of understandings. This set of understandings gained prominence during the 1990s, at a time when social housing provision was at a low ebb, and changed the focus of the relationship of local authorities with the PRS (Cowan and Marsh 2001a). Local authorities are the sector's formal regulator but it was recognised that the PRS could be used to work with local authorities in meeting their statutory obligations to the homeless and to other households in housing need. Rather than Rachmanites, landlords began to be constructed as partners in meeting housing need. Most local authorities now have a type of (voluntary) accreditation scheme for local landlords, involving both carrots (such as fast-track HB, provision of information and advice, grant aid) and re-thinking the sticks (from prosecution to compliance – see Chapter 12 below), with some preconditions for entry (such as relating to property quality) (see, generally, Leather et al. 2001; CIH 2006: 16–23).

The final point about landlords is, perhaps, the most significant for the purposes of this chapter, as it concerns their governance and regulation. A number of representative bodies have developed – the National Landlords Association (formerly the Small Landlords Association), the Federation of Residential Landlords, and the Residential Landlords Association – which are largely in competition with each other for members (Cowan and Carr 2008). Only a minority of landlords are, in fact, members of any of these bodies. However, they 'punch above their weight' precisely because of the conception of landlords as amateurs and individuals (which makes them ungovernable) and the sector as necessary. They lobby government, often successfully on behalf of landlords generally and fund certain legal action on behalf of their members to develop the law in the direction they wish it to go. They have self-regulatory structures for their members, although there may be issues over the enforcement of their standards. They are, in other words, crucial parts of the regulatory and governing structures of the PRS.

Property quality

By most measures, the quality of property offered in the PRS is poor and that has been the case for some time. The Survey of English Housing found that the PRS was most likely to have Category 1 hazards for the Housing Health and Safety Rating System (HHSRS) (discussed below and Chapter 13). Further:

> 2.25 In 2008, 3.1 million 'vulnerable' households were living in the private sector of which 1.2 million (39%) were living in non-decent homes, the remaining 1.9 million (61%) were living in decent accommodation … There has been no significant change since 2006.
> 2.26 Vulnerable households who privately rent their accommodation were more likely to live in non-decent homes compared to social tenants (51% and 26% respectively) … (CLG 2010c; vulnerability being defined by reference to receipt of certain benefits)

Although more properties now meet the decent homes standard, this is likely to be the result of the influx of new properties through the buy-to-let scheme and, in any event, the number of properties failing the decent homes standard has not significantly dropped (CLG Select Committee 2008: para. 29). Some research has referred to a new, or rather a revamped, category of PRS – slum renting, the characteristics of which relate to poor quality property in the least desirable neighbourhoods, in which occupier and landlord crime is endemic (Rugg 2008: 21–3; Rugg and Rhodes 2008: 101–2). More general concerns link property quality with the (nebulous) concept of ASB as we have seen above.

More specific concerns have been expressed about certain types of properties. Principal amongst these concerns are properties termed 'houses in multiple occupation' (HMOs). One starting point here is that statistical knowledge about the numbers of HMOs is unclear because different data sources base their estimates on different definitions. Another starting point, though, is that these properties are inherently risky because they house vulnerable people in poor conditions with poor quality management of the property itself. Furthermore, there are specific concerns about general health and safety and fire hazards (see, generally, BRE 2007: chs. 4–5).

Regulating law

The starting point for any analysis of the law is the agreement between landlord and tenant because the law gives, and has always given, primacy to the contract between the parties. Statutory interventions tend to write certain terms into certain agreements by implication. Many of these terms cannot be excluded by the parties, because it is assumed that there is a basic and general inequality of bargaining power between landlord and tenant. These terms, again generally, are only written into tenancy agreements and not other agreements which are nevertheless included within the category of private renting. The reasons for this primacy being accorded to tenancy agreements are primarily historical on the basis that such agreements were most prevalent at the time and also because, instinctively, tenancy agreements create property rights, as opposed to personal rights. It is the colonising success of property law which has largely been responsible for this baleful binary divide. The status of landlord and tenant as well as the agreement which creates that relation are, therefore, crucial starting points. From this perspective, the identity of the PRS as a 'tenure', which includes a diverse set of legal arrangements, is not one which has any purchase in law.

Defining a tenancy

The tenancy status was contested terrain in law as landlords sought to avoid the regulatory embrace of these statutory protections. This area is less contested today because the levels of protection given to tenants are less significant. However, the result of that contestation is that there is a developed body of case law which, while not entirely consistent, does indicate the basic elements of a tenancy. The contrast in the law is between, on the one hand, a tenancy, which creates enforceable property rights and into which the law implies terms; and, on the other hand, a licence which, at least in theory, creates only personal rights between licensor and occupier.

In order to create a tenancy, the essential elements are that there must be an intention to grant to the occupier exclusive possession for a term (*Street* v. *Mountford* [1985] 1 AC 809). Intention is key but we do not look to the form of the agreement, or indeed, to what the parties themselves believed they were creating. Labels used by the parties are irrelevant – so, if the parties call a document a licence, that in itself is meaningless. Lord Templeman in *Street* made the following much-loved analogy:

> If the agreement satisfied all the requirements of a tenancy, then the agreement produced a tenancy and the parties cannot alter the effect of the agreement by insisting that they only created a licence. The manufacture of a five pronged implement for manual digging results in a fork even if the manufacturer, unfamiliar with the English language, insists that he intended to make and has made a spade. (p. 819)

Intention, is considered objectively, by which is meant for these purposes the effect *in law* of the agreement. One perhaps absurd effect of this objectivity is that an occupier may have a tenancy where the landlord has no title to grant such an agreement, terms the agreement a licence, but nevertheless grants the occupier exclusive possession for a term. This is known as a tenancy by 'estoppel' because the landlord cannot deny that they have title to grant a tenancy if they have represented in the grant that they do (*Bruton* v. *London & Quadrant HT* [2000] 1 AC 406).

Exclusive possession (a term that is wider than 'occupation' in that one is not necessarily required to occupy to possess a property) means that the tenant must possess the property exclusively. Exclusively here means that the occupier has the right to exclude all-comers from the property, including the landlord. Landlords often write into tenancy agreements that the occupier must allow the landlord entry to the property on reasonable notice for limited purposes such as to make repairs to the property or check its state and condition. Rather than deny exclusive possession, such limited reservation of rights by the landlord 'only serves to emphasise the fact that the [occupier] is entitled to exclusive possession' (p. 818). The basis for this observation is the double negative that, if exclusive possession had not been granted, there would be no need to reserve that right. Landlords might retain keys to the property but, in itself, this does not deny the grant of exclusive possession – the reason why the landlord retained the keys must be interrogated (*Aslan* v. *Murphy* [1990] 1 WLR 766). Exclusive possession is not granted where the landlord provides serviced accommodation, which requires unrestricted access to and use of the premises by the landlord, including their employees (*Street*, at p. 818).

Even if exclusive possession is granted, there are exceptional cases where the agreement is referable to some other type of relationship. These include the following: where there is no intention to create legal relations (such as where the parties are friends or relations) (*Booker* v. *Palmer* [1942] 2 All ER 674); where the occupier is living in tied accommodation that is necessary to enable them to perform their employment better (*Norris* v. *Checksfield* [1991] 1 WLR 1241); where the occupation is referable to some other relationship such as between a charitable trustee and a beneficiary (*Gray* v. *Taylor* [1998] 1 WLR 1093). As regards the first category, intention is being used differently, by looking to the background circumstances to the agreement, the relationship between the parties and their conduct.

As regards the term, this means that the length of the agreement must be certain at the outset (*Say* v. *Smith* (1530) 1 Plowd 269). An agreement for the duration of the Second World War was, on this basis, held not to be valid (although an agreement to last for 99 years or the duration of the war, whichever was the earlier, would have been valid because the agreement could not last for more than 99 years: *Lace* v. *Chantler* [1944] KB 368). Difficult questions have arisen in relation to periodic tenancies. These types of agreement occur where the tenancy is for a period, such as a month, but rolls on to further periods. At the outset, it is unclear how long the agreement will last. This was resolved by saying that one period was the term and that is certain in itself (*Prudential Assurance* v. *London Residuary Body* [1992] 2 AC 386). A contractual term is void where one of the parties is only entitled to determine the agreement in a specified circumstance, as occurred in *Prudential Assurance* (where the landlord could only determine the lease if the land was required for road widening and the landlord at the time of the action had no road-widening powers). Although that remains good law, the Supreme Court is shortly to hear an argument as to whether such a tenancy may in fact still exist, but is recognised only in equity (*Berrisford* v. *Mexfield Housing Co-Operative Ltd* [2010] EWCA Civ 811).

In *Street* v. *Mountford*, it was also said that rent was an essential indicator of a tenancy. This was an incorrect statement of principle because the definition of a tenancy in the Law of Property Act 1925 explicitly says that a tenancy may or may not require payment of a rent (s. 205(1)(xxvii); *Ashburn Anstalt* v. *Arnold* [1989] Ch 1). If a rent is paid, then that will certainly be an indicator that the parties intend to enter into legal relations and, conversely, if no rent is paid an indicator that they have no such intention (*Vesely* v. *Levy* [2007] EWCA Civ 367).

Where there are two or more occupiers of a property, there is a further requirement where the occupiers claim possession of the whole of the property. The requirement is that they must be found to hold the property jointly (or, confusingly, the correct analysis in law is that they hold the property as joint tenants). The particular problem for the law arises where the occupiers take the property under separate agreements which often also have separate rent obligations. Here, in principle, no joint tenancy can arise because the law requires there to be joint rent obligations contained in the same document signed by all the occupiers (the unity of interest and unity of title). In such circumstances, the solution developed by the House of Lords was to ask whether the agreements were 'interdependent' – one would not have been signed without the others – or 'independent' of the others (*AG Securities* v. *Vaughan; Antoniades* v. *Villiers* [1990] 1 AC 417). If interdependent, as in *Antoniades*, the House of Lords felt able to read the documents together as one. If independent, as in *AG Securities*, there was no cause to do so. However, in *Mikeover* v. *Brady* [1989] 3 All ER 618, on similar facts to *Antoniades*, the Court of Appeal felt it impossible to regard the agreements as interdependent because 'One cannot add up two several obligations to pay £X so as to construct a joint obligation to pay £2X.' This seems inconsistent with the House of Lords' decision in *Antoniades* but, in any event, it has never been entirely clear why alternative solutions are not canvassed (see, for discussion, Bright 2007: 99).

There is one final consideration. Although statutory intervention is not relevant to determining whether an agreement creates a lease or a licence, Lord Templeman made clear in *Street* v. *Mountford* that 'the court should be astute to detect and frustrate sham devices and artificial transactions whose only object is to disguise the grant of a tenancy and evade' those statutory protections (pp. 819 and 825). Subsequently, and possibly because the courts adopted a rather narrow definition of the word 'sham', Lord Templeman said that he preferred the word 'pretence' (*AG Securities* v. *Vaughan; Antoniades* v. *Villiers* [1990] 1 AC 417, 462). Where agreements have terms which, on their face, would deny the occupier exclusive possession, but neither party intends them to be enforced, such terms are likely to be considered pretences. For example, in *Antoniades*, a clause enabling the landlord to introduce further persons to the property was held to be a pretence because the parties did not intend that to be enforced by the landlord (the property was suitable only for a couple and the occupiers were living in what Lord Templeman referred to as 'quasi-connubial bliss').

Rather more difficult is the problem raised in *Bankway Properties Ltd* v. *Pensfold-Dunsford* [2001] 1 WLR 1369. Here, the landlord imposed a term which, while unfair, the landlord did intend to enforce and which did not avoid the protection of the Housing Acts, at least initially. Pensfold-Dunsford took a tenancy of a bedsit with a friend at a rent of £4,680 per annum, the rent being paid through HB. The agreement provided for a rent increase 2 years after the agreement to £25,000 per annum, which was designed to take the tenancy out of the protection of the Housing Act 1988 (which prescribed an upper limit of £25,000 at that time). There was no way that the tenant could pay that figure as the landlord knew, and Pensfold-Dunsford ran into arrears of rent. The landlord sought a court order evicting the tenant for non-payment of rent. Although its reasoning was not entirely consistent, the Court of Appeal held that the rent increase was inconsistent with and repugnant to the purpose of the protection given by the Housing Act – long-term security of tenure. It was an impermissible device because the rent increase, once levied, meant that in practice the landlord would be able to evict the tenant whenever they wanted because the tenant would always be in arrears of rent (for further discussion of this case, see Bright 2002).

Ownership v. tenancy

This is a slight detour, but an important one, because the legal relation of land-lord and tenant masks an overlap between the PRS and ownership. Although there has been legislative intervention in this arena, generally the outright own-ership of flats is not possible because it would give rise to the problem of enfor-cing the relationship between the flat owners. The solution consistent with the law of property is that flat owners usually take under long tenancy agreements of say 99 or 999 years. For property lawyers, they are part of the PRS; but for the householders themselves, they more usually perceive themselves to be owners (see Blandy and Robinson 2001; Cole and Robinson 2000; Robertson 2006). This complexity is manifested often in a lack of control exercised by the tenant-owner in what they are able to do to their property, the sometimes inadequate management of common parts, and the payment of often considerable sums for repairs to those parts. Additionally, there are particular problems when the length of the agreement runs down. Statute has provided complex solutions to these difficulties, as well as mechanisms of resolving problems through tribu-nals as opposed to courts. These are not discussed further in this book because, to do them justice, would require a rather fuller examination than is available here (see Bright 2007: chs. 20 and 25 for discussion).

Security of tenure

Since 1915, the landlord and tenant relationship of residential property has been the subject of statutory intervention, with varying degrees of control over that relationship. The focus here is on two interrelated interventions: rent control/regulation and security of tenure. These have commonly been cited as the reasons for the historic decline in the PRS (Kemp 1992a; Crook 1992). Introductory economics texts draw on rent control as an example of regula-tory failure causing the sector to decline (see, for example, IEA 1972; Albon and Stafford 1987). The extent to which this version is justified depends on the extent to which one subscribes to a decontextual reality.

Rent control was the original blunt method adopted in the Increase in Rent and Mortgage (War Restrictions) Act 1915. Rent control meant that rents were frozen at certain levels, and rent rises were set centrally. Rent regulation allowed rents to be set between the parties, but at a level designed to be fair to both parties 'in which the over-all pattern of prices responds to changes in supply and demand, while the local impact of severe and abnormal scarcities is kept within bounds' (Donnison 1967: 266). Regulated rents were set on the basis of all the circumstances including the age, character, locality and state of repair of the property (disrepair was to be disregarded), and scarcity (Rent

Act 1977, s. 70). Such rents could be registered with the local rent officer and subject to appeal to a rent assessment committee (as to which, see, generally, Partington 1980). For those tenancies which remain subject to rent regulation (broadly those created between 1965–89), rent rises are now set by reference to the retail price index (Rent Acts (Maximum Fair Rent) Order 1999, SI 1999/6). The current position under the Housing Act 1988 is to enable the rent to be agreed between landlord and tenant on market principles (see Chapter 11 below for fuller discussion).

It has been generally acknowledged that rent regulation or control on its own is insufficient because 'fear of dispossession would in practice nullify any legal rights' (Holmans 1987: 386). Thus, security of tenure is attached to rent regulation or control. Security of tenure affects the landlord's right to possession of the property by reducing it to certain grounds and requiring the landlord to obtain a court order which can only be made on one or more of those grounds. The current rules concerning security of tenure are discussed in Chapter 11 below but, in summary, two types of tenancy are now protected: an assured tenancy (AT), and an assured shorthold tenancy (AST). The latter is a species of the former, is most commonly found today, and grants limited security for a minimum period of 6 months (s. 21(5), Housing Act 1988).

Protecting tenants: a socio-political history

It is not possible to appreciate the issues around security of tenure and rent control/regulation without an appreciation of their historical foundations. The arguments for and against both are steeped in that social and political history. Their emergence in statutory form in the Increase in Rent and Mortgage (War Restrictions) Act 1915 was the product of wartime conditions (see Chapter 1 for the historical background to the passing of this Act).

The controversy produced by the rent control legislation in the post-war period, however, was not just related to the economic impact of this range of controls, but went to the heart of the shift from liberalism to welfarism that was ongoing during this period. What then occurred at the close of the war were a series of official reports, chaired by the 'great men', ostensibly concerned with an enquiry and report on the workings of the law. However, these reports were designed to determine whether and when the state could withdraw rent controls and security of tenure from the PRS. In the inter-war period, there were five such reports (Ministry of Reconstruction, 1918 (the Hunter Report); Ministry of Health, 1920 (the Salisbury Report), 1923 (the Onslow Report), 1931 (the Marley Report), 1937 (the Ridley Report)).

At stake in these reports was the cause of the housing problem – was it a temporary result of the war or were there fundamental concerns over the capacity of the private sector to provide appropriate quality housing (Bowley, 1945: 15)? However, at a deeper level, what was at stake was the political rationality of liberalism – to what extent should the market be left to its own devices? What is apparent in these reports is the clear view that the private sector should be made free as soon as possible and, only at that point, it was thought that it would be able to cater for the population. As Malpass (2005: 40) puts it: 'Despite the salience of housing as a political issue and the intense pressure on the state to respond, the market was left in place and the plan was to return to a free market once the supply bottleneck had been sorted out.' The evident belief was that the free market would provide decent quality housing at an affordable rent, if it was only given the chance. It was a belief in the value of enterprise, here conceived as providing a 'social service'.

With dramatic consequences, including the part responsibility for the fall of the Conservative government in 1964, the Rent Act 1957 on its face decontrolled the sector when the tenant moved from the property (known as 'creeping decontrol'). Peter (or Perec) Rachman is intimately associated with these dramatic consequences. Indeed, such was the intensity of the debate caused by 'Rachmanism' that all subsequent political debates have been shrouded by his persona, even though little is known about him (see Kemp 1997b). His career is discussed in greater detail in Chapter 12 below (concerned with unlawful eviction and harassment). For now, what is important is that Rachman represents the unacceptable face of PRS management (see further, Nelken 1983; Milner Holland 1965).

Rachmanism – the charging of exorbitant rents for poor quality housing – represents political risk. Although political divisions over the future of renting are to a considerable extent also ideological, it is the 'ghost of Rachman' which is commonly summoned to frame debates. It symbolises the image problems of the sector and is sometimes said to operate as a disincentive against institutions being involved in private renting. It was this image problem which the Conservatives party sought to address in the 1980s. John Patten, the Housing Minister in the mid-1980s, said that he was trying to create a legion of 'new model' landlords, 'it's like motherhood and apple pie' (cited in Kemp 1992a: 66). Although the sector was deregulated to an extent in the Housing Act 1988, the then Conservative government sought to defuse the potential of such deregulation to produce new model Rachmans by increasing protections to occupiers against unlawful eviction and harassment (discussed in Chapter 12).

Until recently, when a period of Butskellite equanimity towards the PRS has become apparent, its history was pockmarked by intense and emotional political debate. As Kemp put it:

> For the Conservatives … the private provision of rented housing has often been portrayed as self-evidently beneficial; the problem is merely that the governments have imposed rent controls on the sector which have made it unprofitable and which only need to be removed for the sector to revive. In contrast, for Labour, the private provision of rented housing is just as obviously pernicious; and rent regulation is needed to curb the worst excesses of the market and in particular to prevent unscrupulous private landlords from exploiting their tenants. (Kemp 1997a: 82–3)

New Labour set out its stall early on regarding the PRS, saying effectively that it would not seek to alter existing arrangements regarding the landlord–tenant relation (DETR/DSS 2000). Nevertheless, these extreme positions do come to the fore in parliamentary debate albeit from the backbenches.

Regulating law?

As perhaps can be recognised, there are clear battlelines over rights which have been tightly contested. But the remaining question is the extent to which these rights are actually recognised by landlords and tenants in the sector. The available evidence is thin but – rather depressingly – suggests that landlords and tenants are often not aware of their rights and responsibilities. Cowan (2001), drawing on research evidence of focus groups with tenants and interviews with landlords, suggests that tenants did not appreciate what sort of agreement they held. Furthermore, 'few tenants appreciated the basis for termination of any types of tenancy – many believed that they remained in their properties as a result of the good faith of their landlords and not as a result of legal frameworks of security of tenure' (p. 254). The landlord sample had been introduced to the researchers by the local authority, which implied that they were at the 'good' end of the sector, but 'considerable ignorance of the law' (p. 258) was found.

Rather than drawing on the formal law, then, the sector may well work to informal sets of understandings about appropriate behaviour (on both sides), a sense which may well be exacerbated by the influx of amateurism as a result of the buy-to-let sector. Lister's study with young tenants (2007: 78) demonstrated how, rather than finding the bargain in tenancy agreements, 'the nature of the bargain is unspecified in advance, and its fulfilment is at the parties' discretion. The complex nature of tenancy relationships becomes evident here as misunderstandings and a mismatch of expectations arise early on in the relationship.'

Using language more associated with the study of crime, Lister (2005) refers to the overt and covert surveillance techniques used by landlords both inside the property and outside. That being said, though, national landlord associations often draw distinctions between what they see as the landlord's proper role – controlling behaviour inside the property's boundaries – and that outside the property, which is the proper province of the public police (Carr et al. 2007: 119–21). Cowan and Carr (2008: 163) note that the two largest national landlord associations:

> shared similar positions about this thing called anti-social behaviour. It is not their fault. Such behaviour is endemic in society. Others – teachers, police, mental health and other authorities – have responsibility. Landlords are not an instrument of government policy (although they accept that they are, in terms of the supply of tenants). Their relation of control is through the tenancy agreement which is property-specific. They are not behaviour managers.

The important consideration here concerns the human rights of landlords in the technical (i.e. legal) sense. In *Boyle* v. *Northern Ireland Housing Executive* (Northern Ireland High Court, 14 March 2005), it was surprisingly held that a compulsory registration scheme for HMOs breached Article 1 of the First Protocol to the HRA because it required landlords to be responsible for the behaviour of their occupiers outside the property. Article 1 of the First Protocol says:

> Every natural or legal person is entitled to the peaceful enjoyment of his possessions. No one shall be deprived of his possessions except in the public interest and subject to the conditions provided for by law and by the general principles of international law.
>
> The preceding provisions shall not, however, in any way impair the right of a State to enforce such laws as it deems necessary to control the use of property in accordance with the general interest or to secure the payment of taxes or other contributions or penalties.

Girvan J was clearly influenced by a more general concern that overbearing regulation would have an impact on the availability of HMO accommodation, but he did make clear (in tune with the landlords' views) that control of behaviour in property is the proper subject of regulation through the terms of the tenancy agreement (para. 54).

Housing Act 2004

The Housing Act 2004 contained regulatory controls, drawing on a wide, potent mixture of governance techniques – licensing, regulation, codes of practice and the creation of standards. No coherent approach to the sector's regulation appeared. As Jones (2009: 8.6) put it, in a government review of regulation in the UK housing market:

> The complexities of regulation of private landlords mean that they can be subject to registration, licensing or accreditation schemes that can vary by location and status, depending for example whether it is a HMO or not and the policy of the local authority. The result is that the meaning of these terms has become rather stretched and difficult for a housing professional, never mind a lay person, to comprehend the layer differences.

It offered partly a targeted form of control (HMOs and selective licensing), and partly general (tenancy deposits and housing conditions). It marked a shift away from concerns about individual rights of occupiers to the construction of a 'healthy' sector (Blandy 2001), one in which abuses might be minimised or controlled; the techniques can best be seen as the use of diverse forms of governing, or managing, risk and upskilling our knowledge of various sub-sectors stigmatised as ungovernable. The focus in what follows is on an understanding of techniques of governing and knowing, followed by a detailed appreciation of HMOs and selective licensing, and then a brief consideration of tenancy deposits and the shift to health and safety. The latter are brief because they are considered in depth in Chapters 9 and 13 below; they are relevant here because they contribute to the present discussion about the techniques of governing in the 2004 Act.

Techniques of governing

Carr (2005b) has memorably encapsulated the question facing New Labour as how to govern the ungovernable. The ungovernability of the sector 'is stressed in explanations … which highlight its fragmentation, its incoherence, its polar-isation, its very unknowability'. It formed a policy arena in which common sense knowledge about landlords and the sector became combined with certain statistical knowledge about risk and dangerousness – for example, we were told that there was uncertainty in the definition of an HMO but, nevertheless, these are the most dangerous, unhealthy parts of the sector (see DETR 1999a). We were told that unscrupulous landlords were attracted to areas of low demand and worked in tandem with anti-social tenants (DTLR 2001), but there was no statistical evidence demonstrating that attraction nor any attempt to identify the meaning of 'unscrupulous' or 'problem' landlords (see Valverde 2003a: 239, for discussion of the link between licensing and area, something perhaps less apparent as regards the HMO sector). As has been suggested:

> The central paradox is that the pace of change in some private rented areas makes the need for evidence-based policies and practices paramount – yet it is precisely the housing sector where robust evidence is most difficult to obtain. (CLG 2006a: 8)

Licensing was the prescribed solution for both – compulsory licensing for HMOs and (area) selective licensing for the unscrupulous. The approach to licensing envisaged was not just one way:

> The Government would like to see as a starting point a local compact between local authorities, [PRPs], landlords, police and other agencies. This would be based on an understanding that local authorities and others would provide guid-ance and practical support, with police back up where necessary, while landlords would meet their side of the bargain by abiding by licence conditions. (DTLR 2001: para. 25)

Licensing as a governance technique is, then, a multi-faceted enterprise involv-ing different ranges of expertise. It fills a knowledge void and enables constant surveillance (see Valverde 2003b: 238). The body responsible for the licens-ing schemes is the local authority (s. 232(1)(a)). It is also clear that the local authority's role is not primarily a prosecution one, but is designed as enabling and facilitative – compliance is best achieved through 'collaboration and co-operation' as the Law Commission (2007: 3.3) put it – although this role is not one which appears on the face of the Act.

The other aspect to be considered here might be described as governing the governors – that is, directions of appeal – and we find this is in something of a mess. As Carr et al. (2010: 6) note:

> There are a range of potential dispute resolution mechanisms, from courts, tribunals, ombudsmen, internal reviews, external reviews; and styles, from adversarial, inquisitorial, investigatory, administrative checking. It is perfectly possible for a dispute to be open to more than one and, further, it is not always apparent which forum/style would be most appropriate for the particular dispute.

Although this is a general comment, it is particularly apt when thinking about the PRS, and even more so in relation to the 2004 Act. One of the less frequently observed characteristics of the 2004 Act was that it expanded the jurisdiction of the RPTS to cover significant parts of the jurisdiction over HMOs, selective licensing, and the HHSRS, but not the tenancy deposit regime. There was little public discussion about the expansion of the RPTS jurisdiction but it does reinforce the observation about a lack of coherence in the governance of the sector. As Jones (2009: 8.13) put it, 'The landscape of redress in the housing market is rapidly changing … The system may not be a maze if you are in it but to the outsider looking in it seems unnecessarily complex with consequent fears of a lack of consumer confidence and opportunities for unscrupulous practice.'

Houses in multiple occupation

HMO licensing was a New Labour manifesto commitment in 1997 and 2001. Its final statutory form, however, in Part II of the 2004 Act left much to be desired and it has been supplemented with other frankly impenetrable secondary legislation. An HMO is defined through five tests: the standard test; self-contained flat test; converted building test; where an HMO declaration has been made by the local authority; and a badly converted block of flats. The first three tests relate generally to property type, the relationship between the people living there, and the sharing of basic amenities. Under s. 254(2), the standard test is satisfied if (a) there are one or more units of living accommodation which are not self-contained flats; (b) the living accommodation is occupied by persons who do not form a single household; (c) it is those persons' only or main residence; (d) their occupation is the only use of that accommodation; (e) rent is paid by at least one of the occupants; and (f) two or more households share one or more basic amenities (toilet, personal washing facilities or cooking facilities, or the accommodation is lacking one or more of these: s. 254(8); at one stage it was the rule that each room had to have its own basin, but this was ameliorated by the Licensing and Management of Houses in Multiple Occupation (Additional Provisions) (England) Regulations 2007, SI 2007/1903). However, there are also a number of exclusions contained in Sch. 14 to the Act (for example, where the building is managed or controlled by the public sector) and in the Licensing and Management of HMOs and Other Houses (Miscellaneous Provisions) (England) Regulations 2006, SI 2006/373.

Even if the property is an HMO, it only needs to be licensed if it complies with certain conditions or the property is in an area designated by the local authority as subject to additional licensing (s. 56). In the first category, the conditions are that:

(a) the HMO or any part of it comprises three storeys or more;
(b) it is occupied by five or more persons; and
(c) it is occupied by persons living in two or more single households.
(reg. 3(2), Licensing of Houses in Multiple Occupation (Prescribed Descriptions) (England) Order 2006, SI 2006/371)

The local authority is entitled to make its own requirements for the application, subject to any regulations made by the Secretary of State (s. 63). The application is also governed by the Licensing and Management of Houses in Multiple Occupation and Other Houses (Miscellaneous Provisions) (England) Regulations 2006, SI 2006/373 and Sch. 3, 2004 Act (as amended by reg. 12, Licensing and Management of Houses in Multiple Occupation (Additional Provisions) (England) Regulations 2007, SI 2007/1903).

In essence, a licence application must be refused where the property does not come up to scratch in terms of sanitary equipment, space heating, fire precaution and basic amenities. A licence may be granted where the property is not to be occupied by more than the maximum number of persons or households (see also Sch. 3, Miscellaneous Provisions regulations), provided that the proposed licence holder is a fit and proper person; that the proposed property manager or their agent/employee has control of the property; that the proposed manager is a fit and proper person; and the proposed management arrangements for the property are satisfactory (s. 64(3)). The fit and proper person test must concern at least whether the applicant or the proposed manager (or persons associated or formerly associated with them, or other relevant information) has committed certain criminal offences, practised unlawful discrimination in relation to any business or contravened landlord and tenant law (s. 66(2) and (3)). A licence must be granted subject to certain conditions, for example relating to the provision of a gas safety certificate, and may include other conditions (s. 67). Managers have duties in relation to certain matters, such as fire safety (ensuring that exits are not blocked), maintaining water supply and drainage, gas and electricity (regs. 3–9, Management of Houses in Multiple Occupation (England) Regulations 2006, SI 2006/372); and there are correlative obligations on occupiers (reg. 10).

Failure to obtain a licence when one is required is a criminal offence, as is allowing more households to occupy the property than is authorised by the licence (s. 72). Where an HMO is unlicensed, the occupiers still have to pay rent but may apply to the RPTS for a rent repayment order in certain circumstances. Where a local authority has paid HB in respect of the rent, the authority itself may apply for such an order (see, generally, ss. 73 and 74; see *Newham LBC* v. *Ring*, 7 November 2007, RPTS, www.rpts.gov.uk/Files/2007/November/0010366F.htm).

Research into the impact of the scheme has suggested that there may be significant problems. First, although the definition of an HMO appears fixed, it is clear that a property may go into and out of the formal requirements in successive tenancies, and landlords have also sought to avoid the scheme by reducing the number of occupiers (and, indeed, storeys) in the property (BRE 2010: 5.1 and 7.1). Further, by 2008, a substantial proportion of the sector probably remained unlicensed because the landlords had not applied for a licence. The research estimated that there were about 56,000 licensable HMOs in England, around 23,000 of which were not licensed (p. 37). There is, then, at least a suggestion of creative and actual non-compliance, caused in part by the nature of the obligations and the cost of licensing (which depends on the local authority area).

Second, although this may be to put it a little too high, there is something of a postcode lottery at different phases. This not only applies to the different costs and processes across local authorities, but also some of the authorities' discretionary conditions imposed on licensees, which the researchers described as 'onerous, unreasonable or unnecessary' (ibid. p. 47). One non-postcode issue related to delays in processing applications, in part because the relevant secondary legislation was not in place (pp. 102–4). Many local authorities had focused on the bureaucratic process of licensing at the expense of enforcement and prosecution of non-compliers. This may reflect the trend identified in Chapter 12 below about the shift from prosecution to collaboration with landlords; in the context of HMOs, this may well have further impetus because it should be assumed that these properties are where low- and no-income households live and there is likely to be a conjunction between these households and the operation of duties towards the homeless (that is, homeless households may well be placed in HMO properties and this results in a particular incentive for local authorities to work with the landlords, as opposed to developing an adversarial relationship with them, which may have repercussions in fulfilling obligations to the homeless: Chapter 6). However, although more is now known about the sub-sector, it is clear that the consequence of this more generally is that there is less trust between landlords and local authorities:

> Licensing has had quite an impact on relations between the LA and landlords. The amount of communication between local authorities and landlords has increased greatly because of licensing; unfortunately not all of this has been positive. The teething problems that most local authorities encountered as a result of delays to the issuing of Statutory Instruments related to mandatory licensing and the lack of national standards, fees and application forms has led to some disquiet among landlords. (BRE 2010: 101)

Third, although licensing was designed to be stock-neutral, recognising the significance of this sector for marginal populations, its impact appears to have driven a number of landlords out of the sector. Thus, converting property to studio flats to avoid the licensing regime and other methods of exit, including from the sector entirely, appear to have occurred at least in some areas (para. 7.1.2–3), and it is said that certain lenders were reluctant to lend on HMOs as a result of the regime (para. 7.1.4). This may have been desirable, as it might be assumed that those landlords exiting from the sub-sector were of the type that the regime was aimed at (the unscrupulous, etc.). However, this cannot be assumed and, after all, weak enforcement/prosecution is counter-productive as it might be assumed that non-compliance will not affect the landlord's operation. Where there have been prosecutions, fines have been low (although see http://nearlylegal.co.uk/blog/2010/12/theres-no-place-like-hmo/).

Fourth, the research found that the benefits of the regime were unclear in some respects and in some areas. For example, tenants had not noticed an improvement in management standards:

> Tenants complained that landlords and managing agents were hard to contact and act when needed in the case of disrepair and that they continued to enter the property without giving notice. The majority of local authorities rely on complaints from tenants to identify poor landlords, however, generally tenants will not complain because they do not want to jeopardise their tenancy, or do not know who to complain to. Unscrupulous landlords are taking advantage of this and even with licensing in place little improvement to the management standards in HMO properties has taken place. (BRE 2010: 95)

Similar findings were made in relation to the state and condition of such properties. The concern about unscrupulous landlords unlawfully evicting tenants to avoid licensing was unclear because the data was simply not available to the researchers (ibid. p. 99) – local authorities tend to be reactive and rely on tenant complaints.

Selective licensing

The selective licensing regime draws on the same statutory principles and develops them in this specific context. Selective licensing can only operate in certain areas and only with the approval of the Secretary of State (s. 79(2); the latter requirement was dropped by ministerial approval, dated 30 March 2010). The local authority must consult with affected persons and can only designate an area in respect of two circumstances on the face of the Act: where the area has low demand and designating the area in combination with other strategies will contribute to the improvement of the social or economic conditions in the area (s. 80(3)); where there is significant and persistent problems of ASB, some or all landlords are '… failing to take action to combat the problem that it would be appropriate for them to take', and designation will reduce or eliminate the problem (s. 80(6)). A local authority which seeks to designate an area for selective licensing must also 'adopt a co-ordinated approach in connection with dealing with homelessness, empty properties and anti-social behaviour' (s. 81(3)) and may only designate an area after considering, for example, alternative options (s. 81(4)(a)). Designation will apply to all properties let on a tenancy or licence unless they are excluded (such as HMOs (s. 85(1)(a)), local authority and certain tied accommodation, holiday homes, or where accommodation is shared with the landlord or member of their family – see Selective Licensing of Housing (Specified Exemptions) (England) Order 2006, SI 2006/370). Failure to obtain a licence for rented premises in a designated area is a criminal offence and the landlord is disentitled from using the notice-based procedure for evicting assured shorthold tenants.

The BRE research (2010) found 11 local authorities which operated 15 selective licensing schemes, and 28 local authorities considering making an application for designation. The process itself is daunting, which partly explains the low number of applications (p. 119), and dependent on political will. As the researchers put the latter issue:

> [The] decision on whether to apply for selective licensing is a political one that will depend critically on the views and knowledge of elected members and the perceived priority of private sector housing within the council's remit. Too often it is seen as a 'Cinderella' service and inadequate consideration given to its huge impact on people's lives. (2010: 130–1)

The BRE found evaluation of the impact of these schemes difficult, because they are usually one of a number of renewal initiatives being undertaken. The researchers suggest that the clearest impact was on the management practices of landlords (para. 10.5), but equally it appears from their data analysis that certain households found it more difficult to access properties in such areas because of increased vetting, which 'raises the question of where these tenants are finding housing and whether they are congregating to create problems elsewhere' (ibid. p. 176).

Housing Health and Safety Rating System

A rather different regime applies to property quality, an area in which there has been significant statutory intervention since the mid-nineteenth century. Part I of the 2004 Act implemented an innovative, risk-based regime known as the 'Housing Health and Safety Rating System'. Influenced by the relation between poor quality housing and health, together with a range of expertise, this Part of the Act reframed the previous responsibilities (which were framed around fitness standards) and brought it into line with other statutory regimes (see Burridge and Ormandy 2007). Local authority environmental health officers are to assess the risks, or hazards, of properties against certain broad requirements: physiological, psychological, protection against infection and against accidents (ODPM 2004a).

There is a mass of guidance produced to amplify these requirements (see in particular ODPM 2004a – discussed in Carr et al. 2005 – and CLG 2006a), but the emphasis is on their reflexive use and their adaptation to the particular household concerned. Indeed, it is this use that creates the area of uncertainty which calls for professional judgment. The HHSRS in other words is a clas-sic example of the 'variable array of assemblages of risk and uncertain elem-ents' (O'Malley 2004). This assemblage was made possible by the development of sophisticated computer programmes, transferable onto PDAs, which 'standard[ise] the risks of all hazards on the basis of equivalent annual risk of death creat[ing] an objective measure of risk and allow[ing] comparisons across hazards' (DETR 2001: para. 3.3).

Tenancy deposits

What does not necessarily fit within this regulatory schema, at least super-ficially, is the new system designed to deal with tenancy deposits (ss. 212–15 and Sch. 10). This system requires landlords of certain ASTs to pay the deposit received from tenants into one of two types of compulsory scheme (custodial or insurance) before a certain time or be at risk of a significant penalty (three times the amount of the deposit) and/or be unable to use the notice-based pos-session process for such tenancies (discussed in Chapter 11 below). Certain prescribed information must also be given to the tenant at the same time (s. 213(5)). Schemes can be maintained by professional organisations. They are, in this sense, an example of enforced or co-regulation. One might well ask whether this was a necessary response to the much publicised issue of landlords withholding some or all of the deposit at the end of the occupation (see NACAB 1998; and www.citizensadvice.org.uk/winnn6/index/campaigns/social_policy/ parliamentary_briefings/pb_housing/cr_tenancy_deposit_scheme). The ODPM's own research suggested that the problem was probably not significant enough to require a legislative scheme (Rugg and Bevan 2002) and any intervention was decried by the landlord lobby.

On one level, these provisions might be perceived as a success of the 'anti-landlord culture' (Rugg and Rhodes 2003: 943–4), but Carr's sensitive analysis suggests a rather different, more complex story in which the anti-landlord mes-sage was wrapped up in a campaign to regenerate the image of the sector. It 'is focused on addressing expressed concerns and the creation of trust' but at the same time 'allows space for the reassertion of neo-liberal rationalities simultan-eously with the protection of tenancy deposits'. Thus, private landlord agency organisations might apply to run such a scheme – indeed, some did so on a vol-untary basis (see Carr et al. 2005: para. 10.22).

Regulatory reform[1]

There is no question but that the law and broader regulation of the PRS is in a mess. It is complex, confused and lacks clarity of purpose. We are dealing

---

[1] I should note here that I was involved with a small part of the Law Commission project discussed in this section (Law Commission 2006a; 2006b).

with groups of people (landlords and tenants) who are generally not experts but amateurs, and with properties many of which are outside the appropriate quality norm. One problem is that there is little agreement about what to do – as Rugg and Rhodes (2003) suggested, we are between a rock and a hard place. In a substantial body of work, the Law Commission (2001; 2002a; 2002b; 2003; 2006a; 2006b, 2006c; 2008) sought to deal with these issues by producing a coherent strategy and structure for both the law and broader regulation designed to provide a simpler, more understandable framework as well as to ratchet up standards.

The range of proposals was largely based on two relatively simple ideas: the first is that status and its effects should not be related to the type of landlord (local authority, PRP, or private); and the second that the foundation for the system should be a consumer protection approach (set out in depth in Law Commission 2002a: Part 6; the approach was foreshadowed by the earlier work of the lead Law Commissioner, Martin Partington 1990; 1993). The consumer protection approach implied both that there should be a written contract with standard terms, other terms being subject to unfair contract terms regulations, as well as minimum standards concerned with transparency and fairness. Related to this new underpinning of security of tenure, consideration was given over to the appropriate forum for dispute resolution, framed in terms of 'proportionate' dispute resolution. The Law Commission suggested that the jurisdiction of the RPTS could and should be increased at the expense of the county court.

The Law Commission also approached the question of how best to improve standards in the PRS outside the formal law. Taking account of regulatory theory, it argued in favour of a 'smart regulation' approach and broadly for the provision of more information to landlords combined with a 'housing standards monitor' together with a single code of good housing management practice. One proposal (with which most would agree) was that there is a strong case for the regulation of letting agents, which are (remarkably) currently unregulated.

The New Labour government was reticent in its response to the Law Commission's work to the extent that the CLG Select Committee (2008: 155) pronounced itself 'disappointed' by the non-response. CLG instead saw fit to announce a further review of the PRS which was completed in 2008 (Rugg and Rhodes 2008). By any standards, this was a report of indifferent quality and apparently unaffected by advances in regulatory theory; although it is fair to say that it demonstrates that, whatever regulation there is, that regulation needs to be sensitive to the context of the various sub-sectors which the report is able to identify.

In a quite remarkable page, the review managed to write off the Law Commission's proposals on the basis that they 'offer little advantage in terms of added security to PRS tenants' and 'it could be argued that the principles underlying [two of the Law Commission's recommendations concerning simplification and tenancy length] could be met within the existing frameworks' (ibid. p. 82). In a final section concerning 'directions of travel', the authors recommend that there should be a licensing scheme for all landlords, run by an independent body. The licence would be given on the payment of a cash sum but the landlord could be removed from the scheme at the local authority say-so (e.g. where the landlord is guilty of retaliatory eviction) but the authors did not spell out the criteria for removal – the suggestion was that local authorities should start with the worst landlords but this rather begs the question discussed above about problems of identification.

All in all, this was an extremely disappointing, poorly thought-out set of conclusions – however, it (rather than the Law Commission work) formed the basis for discussion in policy circles (see CLG 2009g). The New Labour government dismissed the Law Commission work on the basis that it was

> firmly of the view that the time is not right for the type of upheaval for tenants and landlords which this would entail. We are particularly concerned that changing tenure arrangements would mean imposing an additional burden on landlords and introducing uncertainty for both tenants and landlords at what is a difficult time for housing markets. This would lead to a very real risk of the rented sector – both private and public – contracting at a time when it is most needed. (CLG 2009g: para. 17)

Rather than take on the suggested reforms from the Rugg and Rhodes review, however, CLG developed its own set of proposals as part of what it described as a 'conversation', including a national register of landlords; written tenancy agreements; full mandatory regulation of letting and managing agents by an independent body; increasing the rent limit for the exclusion of tenancies from the security regime under the 1988 Act; and various measures to support the development of the PRS. On receiving responses to this document, CLG (2010a) then, in essence, reaffirmed its commitment to the broad ideas, while accepting that some of it required further thought.

However, after all this hot air, the Coalition government announced that these reforms would introduce too much additional red tape (other than the rise in AST limits – see Chapter 11). Despite the production of a considerable degree of consensus across the range of stakeholders in the field – no mean feat – nothing is to be done. What has, however, crept through the net has been the potential requirement for all rented properties to have energy assessments (contained in the Energy Bill). Such regulations can only be imposed after an energy efficiency survey of the PRS and

> if, having regard to the report, the Secretary of State considers that the regulations –
> (i)   will improve the energy efficiency of the domestic PR properties to which the regulations relate, and
> (ii) will not decrease the number of properties available for rent. (cl. 37(1)(b))

The sub-clause (ii) encapsulates the problem of thought about regulation in the PRS – the concern that any regulation will result in its decrease and harm its revival.

Conclusion

What we are left with is a regulatory space which is not fit for purpose but in stasis. It is not fit for purpose because it is based on outmoded ideas of law; is insufficiently nuanced; catering for landlords and tenants who are often amateurs as well as vulnerable; contains the highest proportion of the lowest quality stock of any tenure; and lacks (at a fundamental level) any regulatory coherence. However, reform is impossible because, although we all know it is necessary, the government is concerned about its impact on the sector. This overly simplistic proposition, which harks back to the type of concerns expressed about regulation of the PRS in much of the twentieth century, is surprising because of the depth of knowledge which now exists about the sector together with the degree of consensus about the need for reform. We have travelled a long way from the public-health-based reforms, rent control and security, but the legacy remains problematic.

4

Regulating local authority housing

Contents

current stats?

In the previous two chapters, we looked at the regulation of private sector housing – owner-occupation and private renting. In this chapter and the next (concerning PRPs), our focus shifts to what has become known as the 'social sector' or, more simply, 'social housing'. This phrase is controversial, but broadly is taken to mean the provision of low-cost housing by non-profit-making providers to households in need (see Cowan and McDermont 2006; 2009). Just under 17.5% of properties in England are rented from social housing providers; and just under 9% are rented from local authorities. At its peak, though, around 30% of properties were rented from local authorities. The decline in local authority housing stock has taken place largely in the last thirty years. Nevertheless, council housing remains responsible, in numerical terms, for 1.8 million properties – a decline from the 3 million for which it was responsible in 2000 (CLG 2010d).

In years to come, it may well be that both the social housing chapters will be able to be combined because the regulatory structures and strategies will be the same. It may also be that direct provision of housing by local authorities will have been phased out. However, we have not reached that point yet. Housing law and policy currently remains stubbornly different in relation to each of the social housing tenures. While PRPs are given more freedom, local authorities are relatively constrained in what they are able to do.

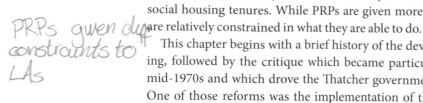

PRPs given diff constraints to LAs

This chapter begins with a brief history of the development of council housing, followed by the critique which became particularly prominent from the mid-1970s and which drove the Thatcher government's reforms of the tenure. One of those reforms was the implementation of the Tenant's Charter in the Housing Act 1980, which also formed the springboard for various other rights (such as the right of certain tenants to buy the property they occupied). Since that time, council housing has been the subject of particular interventions by way of privatisation and managerialism. This forms the centrepiece of the discussion in the following section, which also demonstrates how the power of audit now dominates the regulation of council housing.

The development of council housing

The origins of direct provision of housing by local authorities can be traced back to the mid-nineteenth century and the particular contestation over whether this was a suitable object for public bodies. The development of council housing now seems like a practical inevitability, given the apparent failure of charitable organisations, the failure of private renting in the ten years before the First World War, and the political imperative to build 'homes fit for heroes' in its immediate aftermath (Englander 1983; Daunton 1983; Holmans 1987). However, that original contestation underlies the development of council housing, which should properly be considered contingent on a variety of external factors (Malpass 2005). As Malpass (2005: 31) observes, 'the story ... is one that shows how the role of the state in housing is essentially to support the market rather than challenge or replace it'. The development of council housing was, on one view, a merely temporary phenomenon until the private sector could, once again, take up its historic role.

Although local authorities were given the power to build housing in the Housing of the Working Classes Act 1890, much of this was required to be sold within a ten-year period and, in any event, only around 20,000 properties were built under this Act. Part of the reason for this lack of development lay in some authorities' unwillingness to be involved in such an expansive policy, but part also lay in the lack of subsidy for such development. By contrast, in the inter-war period, local authorities built around a million new properties. The local authorities were chosen for the post-war housebuilding campaign, not because they had a good record, but because there were no viable alternatives at that time. In any event, the state had controlled the market for building materials during the First World War and in its immediate aftermath. Local authorities did so under different subsidy regimes and programmes which balanced the

council and private sectors differently. Subsidy was generally calculated per
property and, naturally, the higher the subsidy, the higher the quality of the
property. The focus of the policy and subsidy gradually shifted from building
new properties in the immediate post-war period to rehabilitation and slum
clearance during the financial crisis of the 1930s.

The construction of council housing was undertaken mainly by the private
sector using private finance. Central government partly financed the servicing
of these debts by providing fixed sums for certain periods (a system in practice until 1972). So, for example, central government provided subsidy under
the Housing (Financial Provisions) Act 1924 at £9 per annum per house for
40 years (see Buck 1991: 77). The figure varied, however, and it was this variable which was reflected in the quality of housing design and construction. The
quality of housing partly reflected the subsidy regime under which it was built.
The remainder, including for example management and maintenance costs, was
paid from other sources. One such source was council rents. The standard form
of private lending involves heavy interest charges at the beginning of the loan
when the amount of capital is highest. It follows that newer properties required
higher rents than the older ones. After attempts at requiring council housing
to adopt private-sector rent levels were abandoned (because the market itself
was so varied – Malpass 1990: 67), the Housing Act 1935 instigated the process of rent-pooling, although this was not explicitly central government policy
until 1955 (see Malpass 1990: ch. 5). Rent-pooling enabled rents to be set across
a council area, so offsetting the higher costs of new building against the lower
costs of older developments on which the loans were running (or had run) their
course.

Drawing on state records, Malpass (2003; 2005) has argued that housing
policy in the aftermath of the Second World War was strongly influenced by
what occurred in the inter-war period. In the short term, there were 'urgent
problems calling for special measures' (Malpass 2005: 58) but it was assumed
that the private sector would gradually return to its prominent role. Until that
could happen, local authorities were, in the words of Aneurin Bevan, 'plannable
instruments' (see Donnison 1967: 164), capable of meeting the planned, ambitious production targets. It follows, then, that the development of council housing should not necessarily be depicted as forming part of the welfare state, but
rather as a temporary exigency.

In this post-war period, both Labour and Conservative governments set
ambitious targets for council housebuilding. The Labour government of
1945–1951 oversaw the construction of just over a million properties (including prefabricated structures), and the subsequent Conservative government
was responsible for 871,000 new public-sector properties. As regards the latter, this may appear surprising but, as Holmans (1987: 113) put it: 'The government wanted houses built by anybody that could get them built, local
authorities included.' It was only subsequently that the much-maligned development of flats and tower blocks took prominence, but only for a short period

(ibid. p. 115). Even so, housing became subservient to economic and political demands – more housing for less subsidy was the requirement – as council housing returned to its immediate pre-war role of rehousing slum-dwellers.

Development of council housing management

It has been suggested that, amidst all this welter of activity, 'councils became landlords without commitment, plan or forethought' (Power 1987: 66). It seems to have been assumed that the 'heroes' themselves would not require management. It was only subsequently that housing management came to the fore, and was championed by government agencies as a result of the changing needs of the occupiers (in particular, the Central Housing Advisory Committee (CHAC) – see CHAC 1938; see Cowan and McDermont 2006: 39; Cowan and Marsh 2005: 30–1). The focus, then, was on the management of occupiers and not properties. As Ravetz (2001: 114) puts it, '[housing management] dealt with two low-status things – housekeeping and working-class affairs – it is not surprising that its importance and complexity were unrecognized'. There were different approaches to housing management at this time and it was only gradually that a professional body – the Institute of Housing (now Chartered, CIH) – was formed. The formation of this body and the development of advice by central government, together with other factors, such as the discovery that certain parts of the sector were unpopular, meant that housing management appeared to have become a relatively defined matter; but that has not been the case (see also the discussion in Chapter 5 below). Its range today, as Franklin (2000: 914–5) expresses it, is enormous:

> The message conveyed [by the social, political and institutional context] seems to be that those working in housing are expected to be all things to all people: policy implementers, performance monitors, rational bureaucrats, caring professionals, job providers, anti-poverty strategists, community developers, agents of social control, promoters of well-being, immigration controllers, custodians of public health and morality, and proponents of better education.

This range foreshadows much of the subsequent analysis in this chapter and, indeed, the rest of this book. Many of these roles are modern phenomena, although some have their roots in earlier generations. In the late 1970s, by contrast, housing management was described as free from these external constraints and expectations – it had 'the greatest degree of discretion and autonomy from external forces, particularly central government' (Merrett 1979: 205). This discretion and autonomy was emphasised by statutory provisions:

> The general management, regulation, and control of houses provided by a local authority under this Part of this Act shall be vested in and exercised by the authority, and the authority may make such reasonable charges for the tenancy or occupation of the houses as they may determine. (s. 83(1), Housing Act 1936)

The assumption at that time was that control should be exercised not by law, but through the ballot box (ibid.). One particular outcome of this was local variation (see, for example, Spicker 1987) and what has been characterised as paternalistic approaches to 'doing the job' (Cole and Furbey 1994: 126). Conventionally, discussions of housing management in the literature generally relate to housing allocation and do not make reference to the law.

But how did the law respond to this discretion and autonomy? Two brief case studies are worthy of mention because they demonstrate both the role of the courts in different jurisdictions (public and contract law) as well as general approaches. In *Shelley* v. *London CC* [1949] AC 56, the House of Lords had to adjudicate on the scope of s. 83, Housing Act 1936, in relation to claims for possession brought by the London County Council. The tenants themselves had committed no, or no serious, breach of the tenancy agreement. The House of Lords held that the management of the properties was a matter for the local authority itself under the Act. As Lord Porter expressed it (at p. 66):

> It is to my mind one of the important duties of management that the local body should be able to pick and choose their tenants at their will. It is true that an ordinary private landlord cannot do so, but local authorities who have wider duties laid on them may well be expected to exercise their powers with discretion and in any case the wording of the Act seems to me to necessitate such a construction.

The courts at this time gave over jurisdiction in these matters of selection and eviction to the council itself. As we see below and in Chapters 6–7, matters are rather different today.

Liverpool CC v. *Irwin* [1977] AC 239 is of a rather different order. Most first-year law students are set this case to read as an example of the courts implying terms into contracts – in this case, a tenancy agreement. It is used rather differently here: as an example of a housing management style which paid little heed to the rights of occupiers of council housing. The case concerned a tower block, Haigh Heights in Everton. The council sought possession against a number of residents. The residents had withheld their rent because of the alleged failure of the council to repair and maintain the common parts of the block (such as rubbish chutes and lifts). The question for the House of Lords concerned the nature and extent of the council's duty to repair and maintain those common parts. Lord Wilberforce began the substantive part of his judgment (pp. 252–3) as follows:

> The first step must be to ascertain what the contract is … We look first at documentary material. As is common with council lettings there is no formal demise, or lease or tenancy agreement. There is a document headed 'Liverpool Corporation, Liverpool City Housing Dept.' and described as 'Conditions of Tenancy.' This contains a list of obligations upon the tenant – he shall do this, he shall not do that, or he shall not do that without the corporation's consent. This is an amalgam of obligations added to from time to time, no doubt, to meet

complaints, emerging situations, or problems as they appear to the council's officers ... At the end there is a form for signature by the tenant stating that he accepts the tenancy. On the landlords' side there is nothing, no signature, no demise, no covenant: the contract takes effect as soon as the tenants sign the form and are let into possession.

The point of this lengthy quotation is this – tenancy agreements, which are today regarded as a *sine qua non*, were non-existent. Occupiers of the property were told what they could not do; council housing management's role was not restricted in any way and, indeed, contained no positive obligations on the council (beyond implied statutory covenants, to which we return in Chapter 13 below). The outcome of the case is less important here (the House of Lords implied certain obligations on Liverpool and terms to 'complete' the agreement and make it workable).

The critique

What emerges from the above is that the development of council housing was contingent on the perceived and actual failure of the other tenures to perform the required task, which was framed in quantitative terms. The qualitative experience of occupiers was not necessarily at the top of the agenda. Rather than change, policy was framed by reference to the apparent successes of previous 'experiments' (Bowley 1945). By the 1970s, though, it is clear that the policy direction had altered. This was not just a result of changing directions in the Conservative party – which were clearly significant – but also concerns were expressed by the Labour party. Other broader structural and external shifts, such as towards consumerism and greater judicial activism in the public law of housing, played a significant role in the development of housing management as well as occupiers' rights (see Loveland 1992).

The first Thatcher government picked and chose those parts of New Right ideology in which political advantage was foreseen. There was clearly such advantage in the policies developed out of the critique of state housing. The large-scale bureaucracy required to manage council housing was a key target. Council housing itself was portrayed as being poorly designed and charged out at rents which defied market principles. In essence, the critique was that the state had proved itself as a landlord to be 'insensitive, incompetent and corrupt' (Thatcher 1993: 599). For the Conservatives, the collective consumption of council housing represented a fundamentally flawed denial of the market (see Stewart and Burridge 1989: 66); individual home owners were praised, council tenants attracted sympathy. One of the key successes of the first Thatcher government was, then, its ability 'to consolidate the move from a crisis *of* council housing to a crisis *in* council housing' (Cole and Furbey 1994: 212, original emphasis).

These critiques struck a chord because, in part, they were true. It was difficult to justify certain stultifying management practices (a sample of which can be found in Saunders 1990: 88 *et seq.*), particularly as council tenants themselves had begun to use home ownership as a comparator (Cairncross et al. 1997: 104–7).

Allocation practices tended to favour the better-off working class who were regarded as the deserving, while the undeserving remained within the PRS. However, this part of the critique was based upon a lack of empirical appreciation, for management practices were, at worst, uneven in application. Some areas with strong commitments to the tenure often produced enlightened policies although the impact of Fabian mores ('the delivery of efficient public services through rational bureaucratic organisation': Cole and Furbey 1994: 126) might have tended to undermine them. But, it was no surprise that the rights agenda of the 1970s partly concentrated on housing.

Complaints about the design of the stock reflected the time at which it had been built. At different periods throughout the century, political pressure, the necessity for the housebuilding programme, central specifications, the need for economy, all made the design of council housebuilding uneven. Some of it was very good and some very poor (see, for example, Cole and Furbey 1994: ch. 4; Forrest and Murie 1991: 36).

A further concern was that the rent-pooling system paid heed neither to national policy, nor to local preferences, nor the efficiency of local housing management and housebuilding. Rather, and this was the central argument levelled by the Conservatives against the system for some time, rent-setting depended upon when properties were built: the older the properties, the lower the rent; the newer the properties, the higher the rent. This factor was exacerbated by the accounting method adopted by local government, known as historic cost accounting, which valued properties on the basis of how much they cost to build as opposed to their current market value. The consequence of this was that authorities with similar stock would commonly have radically different rent structures and costs which neither reflected the market nor the efficiency of their management.

Reforming council housing

Given the strength and broad base of the critique of council-housing management and provision by the mid-1970s, some form of reform was almost inevitable. Although that reform can be periodised in the sense that different emphases have been predominant at different moments (see Cowan 1999), there are two broad and interrelated themes which have underpinned the various reform programmes: privatisation and managerialisation. As regards the first, various schemes under the broad heading of 'low-cost home ownership' have been significant (see Forrest et al. 1984) followed by the development of a programme under which local authorities have sold part or the whole of their housing stock to other social landlords. It may be unlikely that many local authorities will hold a stock of housing at all in the near future. Managerialisation has different strands, from the broad inculcation of a private sector management ethos into local authority housing to a 'shared' understanding of the role of local authorities as place-shapers.

In this section, these themes are developed through an analysis of the following factors: occupiers' rights; the RTB; the enabling role; the Housing Action Trust (HAT) programme; LSVT; performance management and audit; the arms length management organisation (ALMO) programme; and the housing revenue account. Each of the themes of privatisation and managerialisation are interweaved with each of these interventions. We have strayed some distance from a simple accountability link between council housing and the ballot box towards a broader sense in which accountability is linked with the legitimacy of public provision – both our themes are infused with different understandings of accountability and public choice as befit a late-modern world in which complexity and the drive for progress has become inexorable (see Cochrane 2004; Pawson and Jacobs 2010).

Under New Labour, that drive for progress was underpinned by the promulgation of the Decent Homes Strategy (DETR/DSS 2000: para. 7.7; ODPM 2003b: 16; 2004e CLG 2006d; Davidson and Piddington 2007; discussed further in Chapter 13 below). A target was set under which all social landlords were expected to ensure that all homes were decent by 2010 (CLG 2006b: para. 2.7), and the government expected 95 per cent of all social housing to be decent by that date (ibid. para. 2.8). Decades of underinvestment in the housing stock have left much of it in a poor state of repair. A major policy conundrum was how this could be resolved. The first step was to set a standard for decency (ODPM 2004e; CLG 2006b), and the second was for local authorities to determine how they could meet that standard through a 'housing options' appraisal. As regards the second, there were three possible options: housing stock transfer; ALMO for 'high performing' local authorities; or use of the private finance initiative. For some time, there was no 'fourth option' of enabling local authorities to tackle the problem themselves. As the House of Commons ODPM Select Committee (2004b) put it, the decent homes target was used as a 'Trojan horse by the Government in a dogmatic quest to minimise the proportion of stock managed by local authorities'. PFI has proved to be rather more complex and less used in practice (see, generally, PA Consulting 2008; although its discursive formation is perhaps more significant).

Occupiers' rights

As we have seen above, the broad thrust of housing management and housing law was to construct the occupier as a passive recipient with few express rights. Today, that construction of the occupier seems like another world – the occupier is now constructed as an active customer, or consumer, of the housing service, and that activity is both individual – in the sense that the customer has rights and can expect a decent service – and collective – in the sense that the customer can (and is expected to) engage in their own housing management. This shift is not necessarily specific to housing but can be located across the welfare and crime control sector (see Garland 1996; Levitas 2005; Rose 1999;

Walters 2000). It represents a significant part of the challenge to the autonomy and independence of the housing management profession (Clarke and Newman 1997).

The initial development of rights for council housing occupiers was to provide them with security of tenure. This was a cross-party initiative, developed by the Labour administration in the late 1970s under the banner of the Tenant's Charter and subsequently implemented, in amended form, by the Conservative administration in the Housing Act 1980. Its implementation was, however, for a rather different purpose. Although it accorded certain occupiers security of tenure, it was the springboard for a welter of other rights and obligations both on the occupier and the council (Loveland 1992: 350–1).

The rights contained in the 1980 Act were subsequently amended in the Housing Act 1985, Part IV, which remains in force and are discussed in detail in Chapter 11 below.

Perhaps the most significant of these rights, at least today and at the macro level, are the statutory and non-statutory rights which broadly fall within the umbrella term 'tenant participation', but which are now termed 'resident empowerment' and the 'tenant empowerment programme' (CLG 2008a; 2008b). This programme is partly concerned with providing information and some financial support (for example, for those tenants considering the options discussed below) (CLG 2008b: 11).

The tenant participation agenda has derived mostly from council practice and housing policy interventions (see Cole and Furbey 1994: ch. 8 for discussion). In addition, New Labour's broader ideal was to give the local council the role of place-shaper and consulter while also empowering tenants (see CLG 2006d; Lyons, 2007). So, for example, one of New Labour's first interventions in housing was the development of tenant participation compacts which could be negotiated between tenants and the landlord council (DETR 1999b). Enforcement took place in extra-statutory and modern fashion, not through the courts but through performance ratings. However, this tenant participation agenda has lengthy roots and diverse models – there is, at least, a certain tension in the literature that suggests that landlords view tenants as engaging in tenant participation initiatives out of self-interest, whereas tenants view landlords' engagement as a cynical exercise (see Cairncross et al. 1997).

One specific, significant element of the tenant participation agenda was the development in the 1990s of tenant management organisations (TMOs) statutorily expressed as the right to manage (ss. 129–34, Leasehold Reform and Urban Development Act 1993). A TMO takes over part or all of the management of certain properties, the ownership of which remains with the local authority. TMOs have become particularly significant as the current guidance makes clear that it wishes to promote TMOs and that local authorities 'are expected to promote positive information for tenants and residents about the possibilities for taking control of some or more of their local services' (CLG 2008a: 12). As a result, there is a new voluntary method for transferring management responsibilities to residents through a 'local management agreement'. In 2008, there were over 230 TMOs (CLG 2008a: para. 2.3), although this is a constantly changing figure as new ones are created and existing ones wound up (Cairncross et al. 2002: 2.03). Their promotion is partly on the basis of research which suggested that, in terms of effectiveness, TMOs generally 'compared favourably with the top 25% of local authorities in England' (Cairncross et al. 2002: 5.03); but, it is also to be noted that, in terms of efficiency, such measures 'remain elusive' (para. 4.10) because the data was not available.

Under s. 27, Housing Act 1985, as amended, local authorities have the power to contract out their housing management to an external body, subject to the Secretary of State's approval of the management agreement (and there has been a general consent specifically for the modular management agreement for TMOs, which is also applicable when used by local management agreements). Section 27AB, Housing Act 1985, gives wide-ranging powers to the Secretary of State to make regulations 'imposing requirements' on local authorities – after tenants have served a notice proposing that the council should enter into a management agreement with them – and issue guidance. Relevant regulations are now contained in the Housing (Right to Manage) (England) Regulations 2008 (SI 2008/2361) and guidance has been issued (CLG 2008b). Regulation 11(1) of the 2008 regulations requires that the council should accept a notice served by the tenants (subject to certain provisos) and, furthermore, once such a notice has been accepted, the council must provide support and co-operation for the proposed TMO (reg. 12). Support can include 'premises, training, some equipment and money to pay for advice in negotiating an agreement' (CLG 2008b: 18). After the notice, the council and the tenants are required to produce a 'feasibility report' jointly, and an approved assessor is required to have found the TMO competent against a set of criteria which relate to governance, financial controls, community involvement and effective plans (reg. 14; CLG 2008b: 19–23); following which the council makes an 'offer' to tenants on which tenants are balloted secretly. If successful, the council and the TMO then enter into an agreement.

The right to buy

The RTB also flows from the security of tenure provisions and gives certain secure tenants the right to buy the property they occupy. The right is contained in Part V, Housing Act 1985, as amended most recently by the Housing Act 2004. Although the details have changed over time, there are some constant criteria over and above the occupier fulfilling the secure tenancy criteria. First, certain properties are excluded from the right, although these exclusions are limited by area and type; second, the tenant must have occupied the property for a certain period; third, the tenant is entitled to a discount on the purchase price which is partly related to their length of occupation of the property and its type (broadly flat or house); and fourth, the tenant is entitled to require the council to complete the transaction by obtaining an injunction. An additional criterion gives a council the power to require repayment of some or all the discount where the property is sold on within a set period after exercise of the RTB. There is a certain set process through which the tenant and the local authority serve formal notices on each other. These processes and rules are discussed in Chapter 10 below – the focus here is on the broader regulatory effects of the right.

When implemented in the Housing Act 1980, the RTB dominated debate. It seemed to represent a radical break in the relationship between central and local government. As suggested above, this relationship had been cosy although it had altered during the 1970s as financial restrictions impacted. What the 1980 Act did, however, was coerce local authorities into compliance either at the instance of their tenants or at the instance of the Secretary of State. Section 23 empowered the Secretary of State to intervene and take the powers of the local authority, including the powers to complete individual sales, where 'it appears to the Secretary of State that tenants … have or may have difficulty in exercising the right to buy effectively and expeditiously'. Lord Denning remarked that this section was 'a most coercive power' (*Norwich CC* v. *Secretary of State for the Environment* [1982] 1 All ER 737; Forrest and Murie 1991: ch. 9). Unlike practically all other statutory duties on local authorities (Kay et al. undated), the DoE put authorities' response to the new duties under rigorous surveillance: 'Impressions of progress or delay were also obtained from letters of complaint from or on behalf of tenants, from press reports and from informal discussion between the Department and local authorities' (Forrest and Murie 1991: 208). Any sign of delays would be met with formal approaches. The Norwich saga is instructive for the council's refusal to sell was neither absolute nor based on inefficiency. Rather the council was concerned at being able to balance its obligations to those in housing need against those who wished to purchase their accommodation (ibid. p. 212).

Just over 1.75 million council properties have been sold under the RTB in England (www.communities.gov.uk/documents/housing/xls/671.xls, last visited 18 January 2011). From the outset, it became clear that the better quality properties have been sold to the more affluent council tenants, who themselves were generally middle-aged two-parent families with children of (or older than) school age (see Forrest and Murie 1991; Dunn et al. 1987; Williams et al. 1986). This suggested spatial, class and life-cycle dimensions in answering the question of which tenants were buying which properties, but, more generally, the impact of the RTB has been uneven across the council sector. Jones and Murie (2006: 50–1) describe the process as a lottery depending on the tenant being 'in the right place at the right time' but the key point is that those occupying the better quality housing were more likely to accept the incentive to buy (which also impacted on certain black and minority ethnic groups: Peach and Byron 1994). The characteristics of the tenant purchasers' housing histories also suggest that 'many purchasers would have been characterised at earlier stages as "problem" tenants with little prospect of purchasing' (Forrest and Murie 1984: 37). The RTB affected different council's differently (Forrest and Murie 1991). Even so:

> In the strict sense every locality is unique. There are nevertheless a number of general processes at work which can be abstracted from the detailed case studies. Moreover ... local housing market factors such as the relative sizes of the tenures, the level of differentiation within the council stock, and the buying/renting cost gap can interact with broader socio-economic processes to produce quite different outcomes. Equally, apparently similar outcomes can be the product of a different combination of factors. (Forrest and Murie 1991: 195)

The generic impacts of the RTB have been described as exacerbating the residualisation of the sector and increasing the marginalisation of its occupiers (Forrest and Murie 1991: 65–85). Broadly, these terms mean that the poorest, most marginal populations are accommodated in a sector which is numerically declining and in which the best quality properties have generally been sold off. These processes were already 'in place and their impact was clear' prior to 1980 (Murie 1997). These issues remain key policy questions.

The enabling role

Enabling has been a fairly consistent theme within the local authority housing regime, again with subtle shifts in meaning and emphasis (see Goodlad 1993). So, for example, post-First World War local authority housebuilding might accurately be described as having been 'enabled'. Local authorities borrowed money from private sector lenders, they employed a private sector workforce, and the land developed was owned privately (see, for example, Merrett 1979: ch. 2; Short 1982).

However, when the housing White Paper in 1987 prescribed 'enabling' as the future role for local government, it was widely believed to foreshadow a rather different approach for council housing management:

> Local authorities should increasingly see themselves as enablers who ensure that everyone in the area is adequately housed; *but not necessarily by them*. (DoE 1987b: para. 1.16, emphasis added) ...

> The future role of local authorities will essentially be a strategic one identifying housing needs and demands, encouraging innovative methods of provision by other bodies to meet such needs, maximising the use of private finance, and encouraging the new interest in the revival of the independent rented sector. (ibid. para. 5.1)

This shift in emphasis confirmed a radical reappraisal of the role of local authorities not just in the provision of accommodation but also how it was to be managed. It reflected broader changes in the welfare state to split the role of purchaser and provider (see Stewart 1996). Although not expressed as such in legislation, the enabling role was prominent as a criterion for the distribution of capital finance – there were clear steers in DoE guidance that new council housing would not be supported but that relations with developing PRPs and the broader private sector were determining factors (Malpass 1994; 1997: 8; Cole and Goodchild 1995).

New Labour's indication was that the enabling role was not just to be continued but also enhanced – in relation to tenant participation initiatives and the shift to more diversified provision of social (as opposed to council) housing, a position which is also apparent in the Coalition government's approach to housing provision. In the 2000 Green Paper, the enabling role was said to involve local authorities in 'identifying, co-ordinating and facilitating all the resources and agencies that can contribute to the delivery of the strategy' (DETR/DSS 2000: 3.6; also Cowan and Marsh 2001a: 266–9). The policy development of the council as a 'place-shaper' was an advance on this role, subtly altering its focus (CLG 2006c; 2006d; Lyons 2007) in tandem with other initiatives (most notably the statutory duty to devise and deliver a community strategy 'promoting or improving the economic, social and environmental well-being of their area and contributing to the achievement of sustainable development in the United Kingdom': ss. 1 and 4, Local Government Act 2000). Whereas enabling seemed to require local authorities to take a back-seat role, or at least a partnership role, their place-shaping role appears to be one of leadership and delivery. Place-shaping involves local authorities giving 'strategic leadership to help bring together various local agencies and groups in order to build a vision of how to respond to and address a locality's problems and challenges in a co-ordinated way' (CLG 2006c: 5.5). Community strategies are linked with various non-formal local strategic partnerships and local area agreements.

Housing Action Trusts

Although HATs have become a mere footnote in housing policy and law (because they have ceased to exist), they are significant because they symbolised both the second Thatcher administration's focus on, and disenchantment with, local authority housing management, as well as the negotiated implementation of housing policy. They were promoted in the DoE's housing White Paper in 1987 along with a programme known as 'tenant's choice' (DoE 1987b: chs. 5 and 6), and given statutory purpose in the Housing Act 1988. Although the focus is on HATs here (because they were partially successfully implemented), both policies were significant in creating a climate of 'exit' from council housing. To put it another way, if the intention was to create incentives for exercising the RTB or LSVT (see below), it was entirely successful (Ginsburg 1989).

HATs and the legislation underpinning them were developed in a climate of conflict. In 1987–1988, 'Department of Environment officials and their private consultants were to be seen looking round estates for likely candidates' for the HAT programme (Ginsburg 1989: 71). That programme concerned the proposed transfer of parts of a local authority's stock to this new vehicle, the HAT. The first six estates were announced on 11 July 1988, before the 1988 Act had completed its course through Parliament. However, none of these were eventually chosen and the high profile policy begun to disintegrate. The 1988 Act went through a number of different manifestations as far as HATs were concerned (Tiesdell 2001). Gregory and Hainsworth (1993: 114) noted

> [that the final result was] framed in a way which sees little need to meet the anxieties of tenants, much less those of local authorities. Once the HAT is approved in principle there is no control over ministerial appointments to the board, no control over how the Trust exercises its functions and no right of return to local authorities with a guaranteed ability to repurchase properties.

Parliamentary debate took place against a backdrop of political animosity, uncertainty about 'secret discussions', as well as the structure of the proposed legislation (see Karn 1993). One critical point was over whether tenants themselves were to have a vote over the transfer to a HAT and, eventually, the government conceded the point. A variety of non-statutory concessions were given, such as that the estates could be transferred back to the local authority when the HAT had run its course; and tenants and councillors could be represented on the board of the HAT. These shifts did not assuage tenant concerns (Woodward 1991) and all the initial HATs failed to get off the ground. As has been suggested, government will on its own would hardly have been enough for successful implementation without local authority and tenant support (Karn 1993).

Eventually, six different HATs were created, emerging through a process of negotiation between local authorities and the DoE. They represented different communities and different issues, which were not entirely congruent with the original idea, but local authorities opted in 'as a means of improving poor quality housing, albeit with certain strings attached' (Tiesdell 2001: 369). They were extremely well-resourced, with one estimate suggesting that, comparing staff costs, HATs were between 25 and 150 per cent more expensive than PRPs (Evans and Long 2000: 308–9). Nor have they been responsible for large or small-scale exit from the sector. As Tiesdell (2001: 376) put it: 'Initially perceived to be exit mechanisms for local authority housing and as a means for developers to asset strip that housing, they were subsequently commended for their holistic and comprehensive approaches to regeneration.'

Performance management and audit

Performance management is a 'soft' extra-legal mechanism of controlling service delivery, particularly when combined with the technique of audit, which controls quality. It closely links with the development of the customerisation thesis of housing management, and, drawing on private sector principles, seeks a closer relation between the customer and the service delivery itself (see, generally, Bramley et al. 2004: ch. 8). Whereas the Conservative government employed a relatively blunt instrument – called compulsory competitive tendering (CCT), which did what it said – New Labour employed rather softer tools although with a harder edge to them. Although both sets of governments were concerned with efficiency and the 'business-like' nature of public service, the emphasis under the Conservatives was firmly focused on contracting out and, while that remained a priority under New Labour, that administration was less doctrinal and more concerned with modernisation, which encapsulates much of what appears above and below. There has also been a transitional phase in which the performance management tools were simplified and assessment tools altered.

Much here also depends on the production of academic knowledge about housing management. Once we can get a handle on what it means, its extent and scope, we can set about reforming and comparing it. The academic literature has meandered to an uncertain conclusion, but earlier studies demonstrated that it was possible to compare council housing management with that of PRPs (CHR 1989; Bines et al. 1992). Although not necessarily based on such evaluations, the *Citizen's Charter*, the centrepiece of the Major administration, argued that housing management had 'seemed too remote, impersonal and out of touch with the day-to-day concerns of tenants' (Cabinet Office 1991: 15). Consequently, it was proposed, amongst other interventions, that: performance standards would be provided directly to tenants who could then 'identify the standards of service they [could] properly expect, and create pressure for improvement and action where performance is unacceptable' (ibid.); and CCT would be applied to housing management because 'Some councils still patronise their tenants, apparently believing that only the council itself can provide the required service.' (p. 16)

Now, in fact, CCT had little impact, most contracts being delivered by in-house providers. The enduring influence has been the development of performance standards through the production of performance indicators. These have fed into a number of techniques of control, most particularly the benchmarking of service delivery quality and the comprehensive performance assessment (CPA) through which quality was graded and matched with prospects for improvement. Poor performing authorities faced greater prospects of intervention; high performing authorities were given more freedoms, including the ability to set up an ALMO. Various schemes were in place to assist poor performing authorities to improve (see Rashman et al. 2005, on the beacon scheme; and Turner and Whiteman 2005, generally). However, according to Andrews et al. (2005: 654), the CPA process was 'flawed by the failure to take account of circumstances beyond the control of local policy-makers' which distorted the league tables.

The focus of CCT was on the 'three Es' – economy, efficiency and effectiveness – but mostly on the former two. New Labour shifted attention in the 'Best Value' programme, which focused also on effectiveness. The Best Value approach was based upon the pragmatic principle of 'What matters is what works' (DETR 1997: para. 1.6). And: 'Achieving Best Value is not just about economy and efficiency, but also about effectiveness and the quality of local services – the setting of targets and performance against these should therefore underpin the new regime'. Local authorities, furthermore, were required to deliver the 'four Cs': 'challenge' why and how services are being provided; 'compare' with others in both public and private sectors; 'consult' with tenants, residents and the 'wider community'; embrace fair 'competition' (DETR 1999c: para. 4.5). Competition remained a key to the process together with central government and auditors' control.

Financial control was to be increased by the development of a Housing Inspectorate within the Audit Commission's best value team (DETR 1999c: part 6), which had a duty to inspect all local services not already inspected under some other regime (what Boyne et al. 2002: 1197 dubbed the 'Heineken inspectorate'). Ultimately, government retained the right to intervene in service delivery on certain conditions being fulfilled but the prize for the best performers was 'earned autonomy' (Downe and Martin 2006: 468). The Audit Commission's star ratings, based on its inspections (which were scaled down) and its output data, became important signifiers not just of the assessed quality of service but also the possibilities of authorities for greater freedoms. The commission developed key lines of enquiry (KLOEs), which are discussed in greater detail in the next chapter.

Best Value and the CPA was the inspiration for much of New Labour's incentivisation and privatisation instinct. Wrapped up with its various ambitious policy commitments to 'decent homes' and others which are detailed in other parts of this book, the main instruments through which such commitments were implemented were 'reviews', 'strategies' and 'options' (a situation which was in crisis in 2002: Downe and Martin 2006: 467). For hard-pressed council managers, it would not be too far-fetched to say that we now have government by strategy (which also implies a degree of self-management: Cochrane 2004: 491). Important elements of such strategies lie in the general, broad power to promote social and economic well-being and the requirement to produce a strategy for the same.

As Cochrane (2004: 484) puts it, 'modernisation is about cultural change'. Millward (2005: 598) suggests that what was different about New Labour was 'the ability of organisations to demonstrate their support for the government's current projects – before those projects have really been defined'. The point (put slightly more positively) is that New Labour's policy development occurred through conversations over strategies, not over a nice cup of tea (or beer), but in written strategies bidding for money. Playing the game was not just about seeking to deliver, but about using the right language in these documents (Millward 2005). Local authorities became good at playing the game to the extent that, despite a decline in public satisfaction with services and overall performance of local authorities, 75 per cent were judged to be good or excellent in the CPA (Downe and Martin 2006: 469–70). Indeed, Pawson (2009: 12) suggested that, between 2003 and 2009, council housing management performance had improved significantly across three core areas (rent collection, void management and response repairs), which was not entirely driven by the over-performance by the better (or differently) funded ALMO sector.

Recognition of this over-performance against satisfaction has heralded a shift from CPA to Comprehensive Area Assessments. The latter focus more clearly on partnership arrangements (Local Government and Public Involvement in Health Act 2007) and seek to create targets for 'improvement in the economic, social or environmental well-being' in the area (s. 105, 2007 Act). There was also a deregulatory emphasis underpinning these shifts. It was recognised that local authorities were reporting against between 600–1,200 performance indicators, and these were reduced to 198, 35 of which are the targets in the Local Area Assessment (CLG 2006c: para. 6.33–4) which is itself assessed as part of the Comprehensive Area Assessments (CLG 2007b).

This is a mere whistle-stop tour of some of the various initiatives, strategies, targets, plans etc. which have been introduced to direct local authorities in the provision of housing and service delivery around it. One might reasonably speculate whether the 'impact' on service delivery of softer performance management and measurement, together with audit, has been greater than the more strained, specified CCT programme (Vincent-Jones, 2001). However, whichever system is in place, there is always scope for resistance to its techniques for perfectly rational reasons. For example, as Jacobs and Manzi (2000: 97) suggest, 'the fear of the consequences of failure acted as an incentive for staff to disguise mistakes'. Concerns are regularly expressed that a focus on numbers and outputs fails to take account of the inputs, the real people in their everyday lives who are the subjects of service delivery (Cowan and Morgan 2009; McKee 2009). McKee (2009: 168), like others, has noted the 'subversive strategies', such as "putting on a show" for the purposes of the Inspectors – a show that was not necessarily in concurrence with the actual daily practices of the organisations or the professionals within it'.

Large-scale voluntary transfer

An LSVT involves the transfer of all or part of the local authority's housing stock to a PRP, which is often a specially created vehicle for this purpose (Pawson and Mullins 2010: table 2.4 identify that 150 of 170 transfers have been to new, independent PRPs). LSVT PRPs have overtaken most other standard PRPs in terms of scale and importance (Malpass and Mullins 2002). The process began in the mid-1980s, pioneered by Chiltern District Council and the disposal of its entire housing stock to Chiltern Hundreds Housing Association under general powers (contained in s. 32, Housing Act 1985). Unlike most other privatisation initiatives, LSVT took shape through the activities of council officers, but was increasingly and enthusiastically adopted by the Conservative governments and then propelled further by the New Labour governments. LSVT cannot be seen in isolation from the series of policies being promoted and implemented at that time (such as the ill-fated tenant's choice programme and the HAT process), which created a climate in which local authority housing could justifiably be said to be in crisis (see Ginsburg 1989; Malpass 1990).

One might say that, of all innovations in housing, LSVT has proved to be the most enduring in the transformation of the social housing sector (Murie and Nevin 2001). By 2008, over 1.1 million properties had been transferred to PRPs in England under LSVT (Pawson and Mullins 2010: table 2.2). It has become an increasingly popular vehicle for local authorities (of whatever political hue), which can be seen both as benefiting the housing stock, the local authority and central government (which would benefit by securing repairs to existing housing stock and meeting future housing needs with a much reduced impact on public spending, and the levy paid by local authorities to the Treasury was designed to meet increases in HB expenditure in part). LSVT was given a significant nudge, as we have seen, through the decent homes strategy.

For both government and the PRP sector, the principal reason for promoting the programme of LSVT, in addition to the sense of coerced choice over the decent homes strategy (referred to by Pawson et al. 2009, as 'second generation' LSVTs because of the different policy background) and the policy choice in favour of PRPs more generally, has been financial (see Chapter 5 below). When a local authority transfers its housing stock to a PRP, the local authority usually receives a capital receipt for the stock (depending on value, stock condition and other factors). Stock transfer levers private funding into social housing, mixing with public grants, which can then be used to improve current housing stock as well as develop new stock. In addition, this change in status from public to private, which could be seen as simply an accounting sleight of hand, enables the PRP to implement a programme of repairs and improvements without affecting public expenditure as PRPs are non-state bodies for these purposes (for discussion, see Pawson and Mullins 2010: 70–3). Both the purchase and the repair programme would be funded by loan, to be repaid out of rents received.

The effect of the LSVT was to place the housing stock outside the direct control of both central and local government. The PRP created for the purpose, in theory, was an organisation which was self-governing within the regulatory confines of the Housing Corporation/Tenants Services Authority (TSA). Within this new structure, it was the board of the PRP that was ultimately responsible and accountable for the actions of the organisation (McDermont et al. 2009) and, in particular, the development of the business plan for the organisation (Pawson et al. 2009: ch. 3).

The innovation of LSVT was that, in theory, it offered benefits to staff managing the housing, occupiers of the housing, the local authority and central government. For housing officers, it offered the opportunity to escape a depressed sector and engage in the same job, but in a more optimistic climate (Kleinman 1993: 169). They had a vested interest in transfer, although it is also the case that job security is affected (negatively) by transfer (see Pawson and Mullins 2010: 84–6). Advocates of transfer have argued that it can lead to a 'substantive change in culture' in housing management (DETR/DSS 2000: 63), with a more consumerist approach emerging (Pawson et al. 2009: ch. 5). Pawson and Mullins (2010: 82) draw attention to two particular Whitehall assumptions: (a) social housing is a 'capital asset and that its husbandry should be run as a business with decision-making motivated by hard-headed commercial considerations' (thus falling within the New Labour modernisation project); and (b) PRPs are more effective managers of housing stock than local authorities, possibly because of their assumed political neutrality.

For the occupiers, the principal benefits were said to be, first, that a transfer to a PRP was, perhaps paradoxically, the least change option. With central government controls over local housing stock becoming more significant over time, combined with the uncertain prospects for the sector as a whole, transfer offered the opportunity of stability albeit with a new landlord. Even though the landlord was new, current housing officers would transfer to the new PRP. Governance arrangements, although different, would not directly impact on most occupiers. Indeed, the direct impact of transfer on occupiers was the prospect that the backlog of repairs and improvements to the housing stock would be speeded up, with a programme put in place for their delivery.

Occupiers also had the opportunity for direct democracy – part of the transfer process requires a positive vote in favour of a transfer by a majority of tenants. Only then will a transfer be approved by central government. As part of the 'offer' made to current occupiers, in addition to repair and modernisation commitments, they are usually given a guarantee that their rent will not increase above a certain percentage point every year for five years, a commitment to improve housing management, enhanced tenant involvement, certain commitments regarding security of tenure over and above that usually available to PRP occupiers, and possibly a regeneration element (Pawson et al. 2009: 19–20). Such guarantees may not apply to persons who take occupation of property after the transfer. This guarantee may be sacrosanct in that all parties expect it to be honoured, but, more recently, some private lenders have taken the view that it can be broken if the PRP develops revenue problems (see Cowan, McDermont and Prendergrast 2006: 10). The sale process, however, can be conflictual and difficult to manage, with the outcomes uncertain and contingent despite the guarantee (see, in particular, McCormack 2009; Pawson and Mullins 2010).

The benefit to the local authority is that, where the stock receives a positive valuation, the local authority receives a capital receipt which can be used to pay off historic debts and for other purposes (subject to the payment of any financial levy imposed by the Treasury). Where the stock receives a negative valuation, there are still benefits in pursuing stock transfer because the local authority divests itself of its obligations, particularly financial obligations to improve the stock to the decent homes standard, and it can negotiate a reduction of the financial levy to the Treasury.

This is not to say that all LSVTs successfully get off the ground, although it is the case that a higher proportion do so now. One of the highest profile failures occurred in Birmingham, where the stock was subject to a negative valuation, a substantial future repairs bill and a capital debt of £600 million. The LSVT failed because the tenants were unpersuaded by the council's plans. Daly et al. (2005: 334) provide the following explanation: there was a lack of political coherence locally in that there were divisions amongst local and national politicians about support for the transfer; the trade unions did not support the transfer; there was an effective no campaign led by Defend Council Housing, a national group with local roots; a lack of tenant confidence in the council and its housing department which meant that the case for transfer was not effectively presented and tenants were unconvinced by the financial argument for transfer as well as the guarantees offered by the council regarding rents and security of tenure.

It should also be recognised that there is an important, ongoing relationship between the PRP and local authority, which requires continuing management and oversight (Cowan and Morgan 2009). A breakdown in this relationship can affect the day-to-day viability of the LSVT PRP as the local authority is primarily responsible for introducing new occupiers – from the housing register or homelessness system – and the local authority can also affect the development opportunities available to the PRP.

Arms Length Management Organisations

ALMOs are the children of the decent homes standard. They are independent vehicles set up by a local authority to manage its housing stock with a specific mandate to manage and improve that stock. They are generally companies that are entirely owned by the local authority. The provisions of ss. 27 and 105, Housing Act 1985 apply, together with the general powers of well-being in s. 2, Local Government Act 2000, all of which provide the requisite authority for local authorities to agree to let another body exercise all or some of its management functions in relation to all or part of its stock. A key condition for a successful bid for resources is that the ALMO must be rated as either excellent or good with prospects of improvement by the Housing Inspectorate (ODPM 2004c: para. 2.20; Reid et al. 2007: para. 7.2).

The council remains the landlord with strategic housing responsibility (although some of those functions may also be contracted out – see, for example, Local Authorities (Contracting out of Allocation of Housing and Homelessness Functions) Order 1996, SI 1996/3205), tenants remain tenants of the council with the same rights, but the ALMO itself is given a degree of independence in its management of the housing stock. The board of an ALMO is made up of tenants, councillors and independent persons (but, unlike an LSVT, there is no requirement for each constituency to act 'neutrally': see ODPM 2004c: 12; Cowan, McDermont and Prendergast 2006: 31).

ALMOs are, or can be seen as, a compromise option, where, for example, an LSVT has been rejected and the 'ALMO option is tantamount to "staying with the council" and the sense that it offers a continuance of local accountability'

(Reid et al. 2007: 16; Pawson and Mullins 2010: 247–8). Tenants must vote in favour of the ALMO option in order to obtain the approval of the Secretary of State for the transfer, but the documents supporting the ballot do not have to be 'balanced'. In *R (Beale)* v. *Camden LBC* [2004] EWHC 6 (Admin), Camden's documents sent to tenants were 'uniformly positive about the merits of an ALMO ... and contain[ed] only praise for the ALMO. ... in part at least, they have also been, and intentionally so, persuasive rather than merely informative' (at [39]) and partly inaccurate (at [40]). Nevertheless, Munby J found that there was no requirement for neutrality; the question was whether Camden could reasonably have regarded the process as having been sufficient, and it was, not least because of the publicity generated by the 'no' campaign (at [45]). Ultimately, it is for the Secretary of State to make a decision as to the benefits of the ALMO and tenant support for it (ODPM 2004c: para. 9.10(j) requires local authorities to evidence tenants' support for the proposals).

The first round of bidding to the (then) ODPM to create an ALMO was in 2001 and there were five subsequent rounds. In just six years, ALMOs grew to manage over one million local authority properties (Pawson and Mullins 2010: 241). The degree of independence to a certain extent depends on the contract between local authority and ALMO, which is standardised but can be the subject of a 'pick and mix' (in the sense that they can opt in and out of certain clauses). It is also influenced by the external environment, including government guidance. That external environment may be one of considerable complexity in which ALMOs will be working alongside PRPs, TMOs and, possibly, also a partial LSVT, so that the contractual environment is crowded and day-to-day administration potentially problematic (see NFALMO 2009a; 2009b: 10). That having been said, the evidence is that ALMOs have ratcheted up the quality threshold in local authority housing management and incorporated increased tenant involvement (Cole and Powell 2010: 54–5). There may be other explanations for this service improvement, but it may well be that the linking of finance with performance may have been significant. Pawson and Jacobs (2010: 88–9) question 'how effectively such incentives embed a framework for performance maximization'.

Finally, the primary purpose and function of ALMOs will no longer be relevant after the decent homes programme has run its course – so, the new policy question is 'what next for ALMOs'? (NFALMO 2009a). One option has been to transfer the stock to a PRP, but other options are available (such as a TMO or bringing the service back 'in-house'), and the final decision may be dependent on the outcome of the demise of the housing revenue account (discussed below; see Pawson and Mullins 2010: 266–72; Cole and Powell 2010).

Finance

Finance was the mechanism used by the Conservative governments to rein in local authority housing, both stopping its development and hemming in rent-setting ability so as to raise those rents significantly. This occurred in two tranches in 1980 and 1989. New Labour gradually unravelled some of those policies, while also enhancing others.

Since 1935, housing authorities have been required to hold 'housing revenue accounts'. Since 1919, central government has paid subsidy to local government on the basis of what was required in order to balance revenue and expenditure (Malpass 1991: 66). Other than in the 1972 Act, local authority rents have been charged on the basis of what is 'reasonable', with central subsidy making up the deficit. It was the flexible, non-justiciability of this reasonableness criterion which enabled the first Thatcher government to achieve its objective of reducing central government subsidy at the same time as manipulating significant rent increases. Between 1980 and 1983 rents rose by 82 per cent (Malpass 1990: 140) as a result of subtle alterations to the housing revenue account in the Housing Act 1980 which, in themselves, were the product of cross-party consensus (Malpass 1991: 70). The most important changes effected by the 1980 Act were, first, to remove the no-profit rule from the housing revenue account, so enabling authorities to make a surplus; second, to base government subsidy on *notional deficits*. Subsidy was based on central government's assumptions about the appropriate levels of income and expenditure in individual local authorities, although they were at liberty to depart from these levels (leaving their autonomy in place, however constrained) (for the issues over rent-setting, see Malpass et al. 1993: 15; Malpass 1990: 142–4).

This system broke down because, by the mid-1980s, most local authorities had gone 'out of subsidy' (i.e. the housing revenue account had balanced or was in surplus) and were outside central government controls as a result (Malpass 1990: 150–1). The increase in rents was counterbalanced by an increase in targeted rent rebates (which became included in the HB system in 1982) paid out of the DHSS budget. Surpluses made on the housing revenue account could be transferred to the Rate Fund and vice versa (Ginsburg 1989: 64). As the system was based on notional deficits, local authorities could also be in surplus but have a notional deficit. The actual surplus could be transferred to the Rate Fund but the government would continue to pay subsidy.

The Local Government and Housing Act 1989, Part VI, provided the principal mechanisms for the implementation of changes to this policy. Local authorities were required to ring fence their housing revenue account so that it was no longer possible to make contributions to or from it. Schedule 4 set out what items might be regarded as credits and debits to the account and did not include interest on capital receipts. Central government's subsidy and the amount paid in respect of rent rebate became combined into one subsidy. Immediately, this simple adjustment put all local authorities' housing revenue accounts into deficit because rent rebate was now counted as expenditure (whereas before it had been an item of income, combined with rents). Local authorities therefore became reliant on central subsidy again, which returned the lever over rent levels to central government (Malpass 1991: 72). Central government believed that eventually rents would increase to levels which would reduce government subsidy, reducing government's exposure to rent rebate, so that (crudely) richer tenants would support poorer tenants.

Central government would set a guideline rent increase as well as an allowance for management and maintenance. There was 'a desire to produce a pattern of rents which is more closely related to local and regional variations in the value of property in the private sector, and to encourage a pattern of [management and maintenance] spending which is related to differences in stock characteristics' (Malpass et al. 1993: 21). However, local authorities could raise rents outside that guideline to the level they wished as well as increase the amount spent on management and maintenance. Problems arose with the system from the beginning because it was implemented before 'certain key aspects … had been finalised' (Malpass and Warburton 1993: 97) and issues arose about the basis for assessing management and maintenance costs (Malpass et al. 1993: 47). This occurred because the level of management and maintenance required on the stock in urban areas was generally above that which tenants were able to pay outside the subsidy arrangements.

Rent levels were also problematic because increases in London and the South-East had to be dampened (Malpass 1991: 73), which effectively required north to subsidise south. Rent levels actually set by local authorities generally overshot the guideline increases set centrally, mainly to offset management and maintenance expenses greater than notionally allowed by central government. Of the two elements of subsidy – the government element and the HB element – by 1995/96, rent increases had eliminated government subsidy and were eating away at the HB element (Wilcox 1997; Malpass 1990: 176–7).

Rent rises, however, affect HB and affect inflation as well (Warburton 1996: 118). Affordability became the crucial issue reflecting the tense battle being fought between the DoE/DETR and the DSS over HB levels in the 1990s (the latter being responsible for the rebate element of subsidy). As the DoE put it in the 1995 White Paper: 'We are now approaching the limits of what can be achieved through higher rents. … To increase rents much further could increase the cost to the taxpayer, because of the increased benefits bill and damage to work incentives.' (DoE 1995a: 27)

The 1995 White Paper promised to encourage local authorities to make greater use of an ignored provision of the 1989 Act requiring them to have regard, when setting reasonable rents, to the principle that that the rent levels in classes or descriptions of properties should be proportional to those in the private sector (s. 24(3); Walker and Marsh 1997; DoE 1995a: 27). But the problem of implementing this principle was that tenants were insulated from rent rises by HB entitlements 'and in any event the ability of tenants to move in response to [the new signals] is severely limited by the lack of stock into which they can move' (Walker and Marsh 1997: 44; 1998).

New Labour left the housing revenue account in place but within a new financial framework. The government shifted the accounting basis from historic cost to resource-based to reflect the lifetime use of its assets. As part of this frame-work, the New Labour government introduced the major repairs allowance to deal with capitalised repairs. Most radically, perhaps, it introduced a rent restructuring programme which developed the work of the Conservative gov-ernment as well as aims towards convergence of rents in the social sector within ten years (by 2012). This ambitious programme sought to make rent-setting 'fair, more affordable and less confusing for tenants' as well as making a 'closer link between rents and the qualities which tenants value in properties' (ODPM 2002: paras. 1.1 and 1.2.1). The formula for rent-setting matched county average earnings (at 70 per cent), with an allowance for the number of bedrooms in the properties and relative property values (30 per cent) (although this was initially limited to an RPI+½% formula because of concerns over undue rent increases, and there was a cap on rent increases). As Walker and Marsh (2006: 203) note, the important point was that, by way of contrast to previous rent-setting policy initiatives, the formula 'completely removes social landlords' discretion' other than in relation to its implementation time-scale, but without amending pri-mary legislation. There were no provisions for enforcement beyond the Best Value indicator specifically designed for this purpose.

The story about council housebuilding is fortunately simpler. The system of distributing capital credit approvals essentially was weighted against the provi-sion of housing by local authorities. However, New Labour's agnosticism about tenure, its promotion of the idea of 'what matters is what works', together with a recognition that PRPs would be unable to provide the estimated numbers of new social housing units without assistance from local authorities, as well as shifts towards a prudent approach to capital funding and deregulation of con-trols on local authorities, persuaded it that local authorities should be able to deliver new social homes but 'only where [the council] offers better value for money than other options' (CLG 2007a: 78; enabled by s. 313, Housing and Regeneration Act 2008, which amended s. 80B, Local Government and Housing Act 1989). The focus would be on value for money and deliverability, as well as controls on public spending and borrowing (ibid.). Financial disincentives to local authorities were removed so that the new stock would operate outside the housing revenue account subsidy system and to recover 100 per cent of the receipts from RTB sales on such properties, under what are termed 'section 80B agreements' (CLG 2009a; at present 75 per cent of such receipts are pooled for redistribution amongst local authorities: ODPM 2004d).

The future

In addition to what might be termed 'tidying up', there are two major issues that are currently in the Localism Bill. As regards tidying up, for example, the broad well-being power in the Local Government Act 2000 requires fur-ther widening after a restrictive Court of Appeal decision (*Brent LBC* v. *Risk Management Partners Ltd* [2009] EWCA Civ 490). As regards the larger issues, first, there is reform of local authority housing finance; second, reform of regulation.

As regards, the first, New Labour governments had done a considerable amount of preparatory work to clear the way for an innovative proposal for reform of the housing revenue account, with the aim that local authorities were to become self-financing with 30-year business plans (CLG 2007b; 2008c; 2009h; 2010i). New Labour left office prior to implementation of this radical scheme, the basis of which was for local authorities to service their debt out of their rents, with an initially generous allowance for management and mainten-ance, as well as repairs to the stock to enable local authorities to meet the decent homes standard. This was an ambitious programme which set out the notional basis on which the current debts would be allocated between government and individual local authorities; and there would be sufficient 'headroom' to enable local authorities to 'deliver a substantial new build programme without increas-ing borrowing above the opening level under self-financing' (CLG 2010i: para. 1.6). It was recognised, however, that the programme would need to wait for the spending review and was dependent on at least some local authorities upskill-ing in certain respects (ibid. para. 1.12).

The Coalition government, however, has brought ahead this process for essentially the same reasons as New Labour:

> For far too long, councils have been frustrated in their efforts to meet the housing needs of their residents by a discredited system for financing council housing. Under the current system, Whitehall makes a series of complex annual decisions about what councils should raise in rents and what they should spend on their homes. On the back of this, government redistributes income between councils. The result is that councils have no certainty about future income, no ability to plan long term, and few incentives to drive up efficiency. (CLG 2010e: para. 9.1)

The outcomes appear to be the same as New Labour was planning, but the inputs (the resourcing of the scheme) may well be different. It is unclear whether the Coalition will be as generous in terms of the 'headroom' it gives to local authorities for management and maintenance, repair and new-build costs.

Part of this process required a definition of 'housing management' for these purposes. If the housing revenue account is to be abolished in favour of a new mechanism for funding housing management, one needs a definition of hous-ing management. The definition structuring the current approach identifies core services, core-plus services and non-core services (CLG 2010i: 58–60). This definition is likely to become significant because, although designed for this specific purpose, it might conceivably be used to structure the answer to a different question concerning the amenability of PRPs' housing management services to judicial review and within the HRA (this is discussed extensively in the final section of Chapter 5).

As regards the second, under New Labour, there was a shift in regulatory ideal to harmonise regulation across the social housing sector. This was one of the key suggestions of the Cave review of social housing regulation on the basis that the distinctions between provider were irrelevant to the objects of the provision, i.e. tenants (Cave 2007). A subsequent review established a workable programme to be implemented to avoid 'artificial distinctions between providers and equivalent protections, regardless of … landlord' (Cole 2008: para. 2.8), so that certain aspects of the regulation of local authority housing were also transferred to the TSA (see Chapter 5 below). The subsequent demise of that body under the Coalition government (CLG 2010e: ch. 8, in the Localism Bill) means that this programme is in a state of flux with an uncertain future.

Two further reforms are also significant. First, the Audit Commission is to be abolished in the Localism Bill, to be replaced by locally appointed auditors from the private sector on the basis that 'the work of the Commission has increasingly become less focused on accountability to citizens and more on reporting upwards to Government, judging services largely against top down imposed Government targets' (CLG 2010j; also in the Localism Bill). Second, the housing element of the local government ombudsman is to be transferred to the Housing Ombudsman Service (HOS), which is discussed in the next chapter. The vision for the new housing ombudsman is as firefighter in an enhanced regulatory role, and this is also discussed in the next chapter.

Conclusions

The picture presented in this chapter is one of complexity, diversity and fragmentation. Although the various items in the previous section were separated out, together they produce both complexity and diversity. That complexity and diversity is manifested not just in the different forms in which housing is provided and serviced locally, but also in the regulatory and accountability 'space' (Hancher and Moran 1989; Law Commission 2006b) which is bottom-up (from occupiers), horizontal (from other local authorities through benchmarking, beacon schemes etc.) and top-down (inspections and central government policy implementation). Different schemes have different focal points and impacts, with the production of various strategies etc. as the precursor to most policy implementation. However, this has also become a fast-moving target. It is clear that the direction of travel is towards an increasing role for tenants in the management of their housing, incorporating a proactive role of holding the authority to account. The future for local authority housing is also uncertain because the basis on which local authorities are to become self-financing has not yet been made clear.

5

Regulating private registered providers

Contents

In the previous chapter, we considered the reasons for the relative decline of local authority housing. PRPs now occupy centre ground in the development of the social housing sector, despite having had a relatively marginal position in housing policy for the first three-quarters of the twentieth century. Their statistical significance in terms of numbers of properties owned is clear. In 1981, the PRP sector accounted for 498,000 properties against a local authority stock of 6,305,000 (about 7% of the social housing stock). By 31 March 2010, PRPs owned just shy of 2.5 million properties (TSA 2010b), accounting for about 58% of the social housing stock.

This growth is due to a number of policy and fiscal choices concerning the identity of appropriate bodies to develop the social sector. In the previous chapter, it was noted that local authorities were largely regarded as a stop gap, before the private sector took over. The demise of private renting and growth of ownership to levels which were regarded as having reached sustainable limits required an alternative source to be developed in the 1980s. PRPs filled that role, and the reasons why they were chosen are part of the focus of this chapter. Such growth also creates tensions, which are also discussed in this chapter. For PRPs, these tensions include concerns about the independence of the sector, its status as a coherent movement and shifts in the internal understanding of such organisations to enable them to meet the policy challenge. For policy-makers, the tensions concern the regulatory structures of the sector, its affordability both in capital and revenue terms, and the tightrope of controlling the sector while seeking to maintain its independence. This latter point is significant in terms of the shifting identity of the sector on the public–private continuum, which has become a crucial issue not just for regulation, but also for a range of consequential duties and responsibilities (under the HRA and Equality Act 2010).

The first section of this chapter analyses the types of bodies which have become PRPs and the processes through which they have adopted this status. This section also identifies the reasons and processes for their growth. The second section considers the regulatory strategies and structures supporting this growth. The third section draws on recent case law to identify their status within the public–private law continuum.

Private registered providers: definition and types

In this part, an explanation is offered for the phenomenal growth of PRPs together with an analysis of the tensions which this expansion has created. The understanding which has now become standard in housing studies is that the history of PRPs is one of continuity and discontinuity (Malpass 2000a). PRPs have developed at different times for different reasons. The development has come about either in reaction to the state of the tenure or, more commonly, to take advantage of the uneven playing field created by government. As Malpass (2000b: 210) puts it, 'This has been an important source of strength and innovation: change has been achieved by bypassing existing organisations and setting up new ones.' One consequence of this change is that there is little merit now, if there ever was, in thinking about the tenure as being a coherent 'movement'. Different types of PRP have different motivations, although it is also fair to say that for developing PRPs the key motivation and regulator is money (McDermont 2010: ch. 5).

Definition of private registered provider

This lack of coherence is, indeed, furthered by the Housing and Regeneration Act 2008. Prior to this Act, the definition of a PRP was that the body was required to comply with the following conditions: it was either a registered charity, registered Industrial and Provident Society, or a company; in addition, 'the body is non-profit-making, and is established for the purpose of, or has among its objects or powers, the provision, construction, improvement or management' of accommodation (s. 2, Housing Act 1996). Registration with the then Housing Corporation, the regulatory and funding body, was then possible (s. 3). The non-profit-making element had been a core value of the PRP sector and had emerged in the immediate post-war period to distance the tenure from commercial organisations so that it became eligible for subsidy (Malpass 2000a: 121).

This element has, however, gradually been whittled away. The 1995 White Paper first threatened to consign this notion to a bygone, supposedly golden era by arguing that profit-making companies should be able to register on the basis that:

> This will bring the benefits of increased competition, improved value for money in the building programme, wider choice and improved efficiency in housing management. (DoE 1995a: 30)

Almost the entire consultation process at that time was conducted on the basis that profit-making companies would be allowed to register with the Housing Corporation. For example, a linked consultation document placed consumerism in the forefront by attempting to define the 'social housing *product*' (DoE 1995b: emphasis added). The profit-making proposal was dropped after careful lobbying. Nevertheless, the proposal retained its salience for the Blair governments and profit-making private companies became eligible to obtain grants as a result of a controversial amendment introduced into the Housing Act 2004 at a late stage (s. 220). This reform was promoted on the basis that 'it would add an extra dimension to the bidding process, challenging PRPs to compete with private developers on price, and developers to compete with PRPs on meeting the Corporation's scheme development standards' (ODPM 2003a: para. 50).

As a result, the position taken in the Housing and Regeneration Act 2008 can be portrayed as incremental change. Rather than defining registrable organisations by reference to their product, registrable bodies must intend to provide or be providers of social housing in England, and must satisfy the registration authority about their financial situation, constitution and arrangements for their management (s. 112). Section 115 requires that the registration denotes whether the body is or is not profit-making because different rules apply (for example, regarding payments to members – s. 122). Thus, the non-profit-making element has effectively been withdrawn. Indeed, the 2008 Act provides a definition of 'social housing' for the first time as either low-cost rental accommodation or low-cost home ownership accommodation (s. 68(1)). Section 69 defines the former type in the following terms:

Accommodation is low-cost rental accommodation if –

(a) it is made available for rent,

(b) the rent is below the market rate, and

(c) the accommodation is made available in accordance with rules designed to ensure that it is made available to people whose needs are not adequately served by the commercial housing market.

Low-cost home ownership is dealt with further in Chapter 10 below but, for present purposes, is defined as one of three types (shared equity, shared ownership, or shared ownership trust) and 'the accommodation is made available in accordance with rules designed to ensure that it is made available to people whose needs are not adequately served by the commercial housing market' (s. 70(3)). The latter qualification, applicable to both types of social housing, provides the fundamental, perhaps only, coherence in the PRP sector; as such, its significance cannot be overestimated but nor can the deviations from this principle, for the sector is sufficiently differentiated and fragmented for at least some PRPs to offer properties on a commercial basis. Further, the notion of rent below the market rate must be treated with some caution because, certainly in some areas (predominantly in the North of England), it is the case that PRPs' rents are higher than local authorities' and there have been concerns that they have reached market levels (Malpass 2000a: 212–18).

Types of private registered provider

As has already been noted, PRPs are diverse organisations. Approximately 2,000 PRPs were registered with the Housing Corporation before it was dissolved. They range from ancient almshouses to philanthropic organisations founded by Rowntree and Cadbury, from organisations designed to alleviate the crisis in private renting in the 1960s to organisations set up to take over local authority stock. Their purposes range from providing accommodation for general needs to specific types of accommodation, such as sheltered accommodation for elderly households. The types of accommodation developed range from improvement and repair of older property to new build. Most PRPs are small organisations with a few properties only; increasingly, the larger PRPs are dominating the sector.

This diversity was and is clearly influenced by the external policy environment as it developed particularly during the twentieth century. Malpass (2000a: 95–104) has noted how, despite a relatively favourable committee report chaired by Lord Moyne in 1935, PRPs were sidelined by the government, leaving them in a subordinate position to local authorities. And, in the 1939–1961 period, the 'government's position was quite clearly that [PRPs] should supplement rather than substitute the work of local authorities … [and PRPs] were encouraged to focus on other types of need, especially housing for elderly people' (Malpass 2000a: 123).

From this position of relative marginalisation, PRPs moved quite abruptly to the centre stage in the provision of social housing (Langstaff 1992). The funding environment from 1974 encouraged this shift and the consequence is that they have, as a result, become instruments of housing policy (Malpass 2000a: ch. 8).

One particular type of PRP has overtaken the others in terms of scale and importance: the LSVT PRP (Malpass and Mullins 2002; see Chapter 4 above). This type of PRP is formed expressly to take over the whole or a proportion of housing stock transferred from a local authority. For both government and the PRP sector, the principal reason for promoting the programme of LSVT, in addition to the sense of coerced choice over the decent homes strategy, as well as the development of PRPs more generally, has been financial (as we saw in Chapter 4).

The development of private registered providers

How and why did PRPs become such predominant vehicles for the development of social housing in England? In this section, the history of the development of PRPs is traced back to certain key moments in time (1974 and 1988 – although it is accepted that these moments were influenced by prior events: McDermont 2010) to provide at least a partial explanation both of the present and the form of the present.

Housing Act 1974

The Housing Act 1974 was a Labour government measure, although it had initially been promoted by the previous Conservative administration to provide for the rehabilitation of property (Back and Hamnett 1985: 402). That the Act survived at all was significant; that it survived in similar form, with public funding aplenty, led to considerable development within the sector until 1980. This cross-party support was significant, although based upon different rationales. The Conservative administration preferred PRPs 'as semi-private supplements to, covert competitors with, or even potential replacements for local authority housing'; on the other hand, the Labour administration saw the opportunity to create a 'centrally controlled housing service' in contrast to 'the relative autonomy of local authorities' (Noble 1981: 173). Indeed, the rehabilitation of private property would mean that PRPs would take control of some of the privately rented stock, and as such was 'an astute method of achieving social ownership' (Back and Hamnett 1985). It has also been noted that many prominent members of the Labour party were also supporters of the PRP movement (for example, through one of its arms, the housing co-operative) (Best 1991: 154).

The 1974 Act contained two major innovations of which the most prominent was the new funding mechanism. A treasury-based capital grant, called Housing Association Grant (HAG), was made available to PRPs to cover the difference between the costs of a scheme and the available revenue stream (mostly through rents charged). Additionally, a treasury-based income grant, known as Revenue Deficit Grant, shored up any subsequent revenue gap. PRPs were, in other words, totally protected within the public sector. A prerequisite of this financial protection was that PRPs were required to register with the Housing Corporation which had been set up in 1964 to promote an ill-fated intervention into cost-rental schemes and to promote the sector.

The second major innovation of the 1974 Act was that the Housing Corporation gained the power to act as mediator between the PRP and the DoE in the provision of finance (although it had been empowered to provide loans in the Finance Act 1972) as well as gaining powers of monitoring and supervision of PRPs. The subsequent registration process appears to have been chaotic, both in the application and interpretation of registration criteria, as well as a certain bifocalism between promotion and registration models ('the existence of dual functions ensures administrative failure': Noble 1981: 179; see also Lewis and Harden 1982). McDermont (2007a), however, tells a slightly different story, one in which the chaos was managed by the PRPs themselves through their Federation, which extracted the maximum benefit for its membership.

It was the strong level of *public* funding through HAG which ensured that the first Thatcher government lumped PRPs together with local authorities. This was clearly signalled by that government's evident desire to include all PRP properties in the RTB part of the Housing Act 1980 (which was defeated at least in relation to charitable PRPs) The favourable funding regime was also reined in under the incoming Thatcher government, leading to fewer completions (Malpass 2000a: 176).

Mixed funding

By the mid-1980s, PRPs had become regarded as key players in the provision of social housing. One problem with the provision of housing by local authorities – for a cost-conscious government – was that any spending by them would count as 'public sector' spending within Treasury conventions. On the other hand, it was possible for PRPs to raise private finance and spend it without that money being regarded as public expenditure under the same conventions; only the level of HAG paid out would be regarded as public sector expenditure. That private sector nature, in terms of Treasury conventions, enabled the

Conservative government to break its self-imposed shackles and begin a significant social housing development programme, reversing reliance on state funding and increasing risk through reliance on private lending (McDermont 2010). The experiment began in the mid-1980s with support from the then Housing Minister, John Patten (Malpass 2000a: 178).

The move towards 'mixed funding' arrangements (that is, a mix of both public and private funding) was justified in a consultation paper as creating 'new incentives to associations to deliver their service in the most cost-effective manner, bringing to bear the disciplines of the private sector and strengthening the machinery of public support' (DoE, 1987a: para. 2).

The housing White Paper in 1987 praised pre-existing mixed funding arrangements as facilitating 'improved efficiency and allow[ing] public resources to be used more effectively' (DoE 1987b: para. 4.5). Obtaining private finance was to be made easier by bringing PRPs within the definition of bodies able to grant *private sector* tenancies in the Housing Act 1988, as a result of which rents could potentially be charged up to market levels thus ensuring a rate of return on investment. So, tenants would bear the burden of the new market involvement and, realistically, in the new regime of providing housing at increased rental costs to low-income tenants, it followed that reliance would be placed upon the individual subsidy of HB.

A number of ends were served by these reforms, much of which took place without the need for further legislation but within the regulatory powers of the Housing Corporation and its funding arrangements with central government. Huge benefits could be foreseen by those able and willing to enter into development of new stock. It has been this development which has been responsible for the phenomenal growth of PRPs.

Tensions

The changed environment can be considered by looking at four tensions created or exacerbated by the post-1988 regime: risk; affordability; central control; and governance.

These major tensions appear throughout the rest of the discussion in this chapter and beyond. They form the essential backdrop to the difficult changes currently still under way within the sector. Their global manifestation in practice relates to the loss of *autonomy* – who runs the PRP? That loss of autonomy was apparent already from the development of PRPs in the latter half of the twentieth century, and exacerbated by the implications of the 1974 Act, discussed above.

Risk

HAG had previously been paid at the end of the project and thus, if development costs increased, the public purse bore the brunt. After the 1988 Act, HAG became 'frontloaded' – that is, paid at the outset on the basis of assumed costs and calculated against figures set by the DoE through the Housing Corporation. Any unforeseen increases in development costs would be the responsibility of the PRP (see, generally, Randolph 1993; Langstaff 1992).

Private finance brings its own risks. For example, the 1987 White Paper assumed that finance would be gained on the basis of low-start payments (i.e. low payments at the beginning, increasing over time). However, developing PRPs found that low-start finance made any subsequent development more difficult. A conventional interest-rate-based package enabled PRPs to use properties developed earlier to be used subsequently as security against further loans (see Chaplin et al. 1995: 13). Added to these developmental risks, the most significant risk was the threat of insolvency and repossession (although increased competition has also led to mergers and takeovers, see below), although this was only a threat at that time. However, in 2007, the high profile insolvency of Ujima Housing Association occurred. Ujima collapsed because it became financially unviable.

The level of risk will differ depending on the exposure of the PRP to the market. What is perhaps less obvious is that the level of risk will also differ depending upon the size of the association prior to the move to mixed funding. PRPs with larger portfolios were able to use their asset wealth as security to gain greater (and cheaper) loans, increasing their own portfolios at a rate unavailable to smaller PRPs. Thus, larger PRPs, often operating on a national basis, were able to capture most of the available funding and increased their proportion of total PRP stock. In 1983, PRPs with more than 2,500 dwellings owned 47% of the total stock in the sector. In 1995/96, 105 PRPs (or 5% of the total number of PRPs) with more than 2,500 dwellings owned 70% of the total stock (Housing Corporation 1997: table 2.2). In 2010, 90% of the stock was owned by 18% of PRPs (TSA 2010b; see further below).

Affordability

McDermont (2010: ch. 6) has argued that 'one reading of the history of the [PRP] sector would be as a series of attempts to resolve the problem of affordability'. At the outset of the new regime, in the crucial early period after the introduction of mixed funding, the Housing Corporation stressed the need for PRPs to charge 'affordable' rents without defining the term (leading to frustration which brims over in some publications – see, for example, Randolph 1993: 44 – 'Rents were at the same time to be both deregulated but restrained!'). The sector's welcome of the new system was tempered with concerns that rents would become unaffordable to the poorest households (Randolph 1993). Central government would not accept responsibility for defining what affordable meant (Malpass 2000a: 213). It was the sector's national representative body, the National Federation of Housing Associations, which took on the role of attempting to define affordability and monitoring rent levels. The federation's affordability campaign linked the *freedom* to set rent levels with the responsibility to set affordable rents. It attempted to define affordability through *affordability ratios*. The federation's initial assumption was that rents would be affordable if they took up no more than 20% of net household income, which was subsequently revised to 22%. An extensive system for recording and monitoring housing association rents, called CORE (Continuous Recording) was established.

However, the upward spiralling of PRP association rents – between 1988 and 1994 they had increased by 80%, while the Retail Price Index increased by only 30% (Malpass 2000a: 214) – dramatically affected the proportion of public spending going into the social security budget and threatened to 'crowd out' other priorities (Kemp 2000: 268). At first, it was argued that HB could 'take the strain' of the higher rents. As an increasing number of their tenants have become reliant on HB, so too have PRPs and their funders. This was a dangerous policy option embraced by PRPs, which is continually under threat (see Chapter 9 below). Rent levels began to be challenged by local authorities (which are responsible for administering HB) in the late 1990s, although the prevailing experience was that they were not challenged (Bramley 1995: 29; Rugg and Wilcox 1997; Chaplin et al. 1995: 36). Limits on HB therefore mean that a PRP's rental stream is at risk, which is not necessarily in anybody's interest.

Many PRPs found it difficult to dampen their rent levels: 'By the mid-1990s, rents for new homes were likely to require those working as a bus driver, postman, clerical officer or bricklayer all to become reliant on housing benefit' (Best 1997: 115). Equally, the importance given to affordability impacted on the output of PRPs in terms of build and design quality. Karn and Sheridan have noted 'a continuing decline in the standards of homes built by housing associations' (1994: 93); in 1991/92 68 per cent of newly built general needs accommodation was built 5 per cent or more below the space standards (see, further, Goodchild and Karn 1997).

The solution to the affordability problem developed by the Conservative administration in documents linked to its 1995 White Paper was to restrict the ability of PRPs to raise rents to a formula linked to the retail price index '+/– X%'. This formula was incorporated into Housing Corporation regulatory standards where the 'x factor' was limited to 1 per cent and any PRP with increases beyond that would be required to justify the increase (Housing Corporation 1997).

The Blair government's approach to rent-setting was based on a rather different rationale. The housing Green Paper proposed a uniform system of setting rents across PRP and local authority housing (DETR/DSS 2000: ch. 10). The restructuring proposals had a number of aims: keeping rents below market levels; providing a closer link between the qualities tenants value in a home, and how much they pay; reducing what were perceived as unfair inequalities between rents set by different social landlords; and making landlords more efficient by reducing possibilities for using rent increases to cover up deficits arising from organisational inefficiencies (Marsh 2004: 290–1). It was unclear whether the restructuring proposals settled on by central government met those aims or, indeed, offered a robust methodology for the purpose (Marsh 2004: 190–1 and 197; Walker and Marsh 2003: 2028).

The proposals for restructuring that the then DETR settled on aimed to create even closer links between market mechanisms and rents, by setting out a rent-setting system based on property values (seen as an indicator of the relative attractiveness of properties to tenants), and local earnings indices (as the indicator of affordability – Marsh 2001: 190; DETR 2000). The formula required that rents were determined in the following proportions: 70% of the national average rent weighted by average local earnings relative to national earnings, and adjusted for bedsize of the property; and 30% of the national average rent weighted by the value of the individual property relative to the national average property value of the sector in which the dwelling is located (Walker and Marsh 2003: 2028). The system was implemented in 2003 through Housing Corporation regulation and guidance. Concerns have been expressed that it would have particular effects on bedsit-type properties, was likely to reflect property price differentials between north and south, and placed greater reliance on HB where rents increase to market levels (Tang 2008).

Central control

The philosophy of the 1980s was increasing central control over local institutions (McAuslan 1989: 403). The Thatcher administration's interest in PRPs mirrored, to a certain extent, the motivations of the previous Labour administration. We have already noted Malpass' point that PRPs have become instruments of housing policy – he went on to note (2000a: 224) how 'the detailed pattern of [PRP] development activity strongly reflects Ministers' definitions of needs and their relative priority at any given time'. Central government could control PRPs' local provision and development of housing at the same time as withdrawing funding for local authorities. This control could be exercised through the purse strings – the amount of money given to the Housing Corporation for development. Central government was (and remains) able to set the priorities for the development programme and, in this way, to influence who is allocated capital grants from the relevant body. Furthermore, the government is able to set the average total cost that it is prepared to fund through Social Housing Grant (SHG – the successor to HAG), as well as fixing the development costs.

Central government is, therefore, able to influence who gets funding, the level of that funding, and the priorities. So, for example, PRPs have become key players in the development of low-cost home ownership initiatives because this has been a priority area for successive governments (Malpass 2000a: 224; these are discussed in detail in Chapter 10 below). Initially, the level of state capital funding was fixed at 75% but this has gradually declined (e.g. to 54% in 1998–1999) and the current watchword is efficiency; some PRPs are now able to develop new properties with nil grant, recycling grant from previous developments (see Housing Corporation 2008c: paras. 195–7). The remainder is required to be raised through private finance or other sources (sometimes involving local authority assistance). Sometimes, the level of government involvement has unforeseen consequences which affect wider policy. A classic example of this has been the move away from improvement of existing properties, rehabilitation (a key foundation of the post-1974 expansion). Rehabilitation work is, quite simply, too risky in the 'frontloaded' funding environment. At the beginning of a rehabilitation project, estimations of capital costs are not always clear and easy to budget, because it is not always possible to predict how much work is required on a building. On the other hand, the development of new sites is much easier to budget and, consequently, less risky (see Best 1997: 115–16; Randolph 1993: 50–1; Harrison 1992: 22–3).

As we see below, the extent of central government control over PRPs and the Housing Corporation was questioned for some time, but particularly as a result of parallel initiatives in 'better regulation'. A rather different aspect of central control is the way in which public bodies, such as local authorities, can influence the development programmes of PRPs. Local authorities' move towards an 'enabling' role meant that they stopped developing new housing. They have, however, been able to control the level of PRP development through, for example, having partner PRPs (which the Housing Corporation took into account in considering whether to fund development) and/or the provision of cheap land with planning permission in return for allocation rights (which therefore reduced the PRP's development costs). Thus, local authorities were able to influence not only the level of new building in their area, but also *who did it*. This influence has run through development plans, so that, for example, bids for the 2008–2011 development programme required 'the full engagement of local authorities as potential developers, as local planning authorities and as strategic housing enablers and as potential developers' (Housing Corporation, 2008c: para. 31).

Governance

The level of control exerted by central government, the sector regulator and private finance finds its ultimate impact in the PRPs' level and type of service provision. PRPs are voluntary organisations. People became involved in their governance primarily because of a desire 'to contribute to society and/or help the needy' (82.2 per cent in one survey said this was their motivation – Kearns 1990: 44). Such idealism has been gradually eroded in favour of a more professionalised, expert, new public management ethos (Walker 1997; Walker and Smith 1999; Walker 2000; McDermont 2010). PRP governing bodies have been encouraged primarily through their relations of dependency with private lenders to engage in business models of corporate governance (McDermont

2010: ch. 8). Board members, who for some time were not paid (in line with the voluntarist spirit), may now be paid. The National Housing Federation, the current name for the PRP representative body, has sought to re-model PRPs through a campaign headlined 'iN Business for Neighbourhoods', which as Mullins (2006: 245) puts it 'effectively stitched together the tendencies towards a business orientation and those toward neighbourhood accountability'.

A 'competitive ethos' dominates the sector and prefigured the significant shift towards entrepreneurialism and innovation (Manzi 2007 : 259). Certain elements of the Housing Corporation development programme in the early 2000s encouraged a tendency towards growth and organisational mergers or partnerships between PRPs through an efficiency agenda and an explicit 'investment partnering' scheme as part of its development programme in 2004–2006. Cowan (1999: 116) made the point that, at that time, 'we may not have reached the stage of the predatory PRP, looking to monopolise its position through takeovers, mergers and the like ... however we cannot be far off it'. It is now clear that the era of the predatory PRP is in full swing on the basis that the bigger an organisation the more it can insulate itself from external risks (see, for example, Mullins and Craig 2005). Mullins and Craig (2005: 5) identify different types of organisational structure on a range from single independent organisation to enforced transfer of engagements, but across that lie a variety of arrangements including partnerships, contracts, alliances, group structures, amalgamations and voluntary transfers.

At the same time, this new ethos has led to expanding competition between PRPs. In what has been described as the era of 'comfort' – 1974–1981 – PRPs often worked together and respected each other's 'territory', a process known as pepperpotting (see Bramley 1993: 164). Locally based PRPs remained firmly local. The new environment is one of competition for reduced funds but with larger expected returns on investment. Larger PRPs are best placed because they are able to pool the capital costs of development across their whole stock and are therefore able to build more for less – they can often reduce their development costs below the prescribed level. If the major criterion for the receipt of public funds is cost-effectiveness – or building as many properties as possible for less public money – then such PRPs are in the best position to 'win' public funding by 'selling the family silver' (Best 1997: 116). Locally based PRPs lose out in this competitive process because their limitation is that they are local. In this context, it is perhaps no surprise that many of the former local PRPs have changed their names to reflect broader spatial interests (for example, North Housing Association became Home Housing Association).

The extent and impact of these shifts can be seen from research conducted by Pawson and Sosenko (2007) for the Housing Corporation into the restructuring of the sector. They demonstrate that 60 per cent of PRP stock has been subject to some form of constitutional change in governance between 2002–2007, the majority of which was agglomeration of landlords and the development of group structures. They suggest that this is a continuation of processes which were already in place during the 1990s. Some groups which existed in 2002 have formed what the authors refer to as 'supergroups' through agglomerations (p. 15). General justifications for constitutional change were analysed as financial efficiency; business/administrative efficiency; positioning for the future; and improved service delivery (p. 22). The effect of this change has meant that there is now a greater concentration of stock amongst the largest PRPs. LSVT PRPs have significantly altered their governance pattern, more than half of which operated as group subsidiary bodies by 2007, suggesting that a process of integration of these organisations into the PRP sector more generally is under way (p. 29).

It might be noted here that this activity, when compared to the rationale for the preference for PRPs in the 1980s over local authorities, offers a paradox: if the original rationale was based on the identity of PRPs as controllable, small, local organisations, subsequent government/Housing Corporation policies and practices have created a national sector of large organisations, which has considerable power itself over the development of housing policy. In particular, the largest PRPs have organised themselves into what has been referred to as a 'dining club' called the G15, and it is this organisation more than any other which now has the potential to emerge as a leading policy-maker for the sector should it so wish.

Internally, PRPs' management is increasingly dictated not by housing issues per se but by finance (Chaplin et al. 1995; Pryke 1994: 249). As McDermont (2007b: 81) notes, 'given the expectation of many [PRPs] that they should be expanding to become more competent social *businesses*, it is unsurprising that the sector's perspective on governance has been coloured by events and developments in the business sector' (original emphasis). Various committees of inquiry have firmly established the corporate model and financial aspects of governance on PRP practice. Private sector practices, such as call centres and 'gold standard' rewards for tenants, are now almost de rigueur (Walker 2000; Lupton et al. 2003; Flint 2004).

Regulating private registered providers

The funding and regulation of PRPs after the Housing and Regeneration Act 2008 was implemented, from 1 December 2008, is now conducted by two bodies: the Homes and Communities Agency (HCA) is concerned with funding; and the TSA is concerned with regulation (although see below for changes to this duopoly in the Localism Bill). These two bodies have taken on the functions previously exercised solely by the Housing Corporation.

What has altered is the purpose of regulation. Much navel-gazing was done by government here, which commissioned a report from Professor Cave (2007), the outcome of which has been that the purpose of regulation should be refocused to benefit occupiers; a shift conveyed by the title of the Cave report: *Every Tenant Matters*. In the first part of this section, we look at the problems which were said to be caused by the Housing Corporation role and the diagnosis offered by Cave. In the second part, we look at the primary method of regulation of PRPs, entitled *Performance Standards*, developed by the Housing Corporation, which was continued for a period by the TSA, as well as other methods such as the use of Circulars. We assess the problems of this strategy, which were highlighted in the case of *Ujima HA*. We also detail the relevant provisions of the 2008 Act. In the third part, the role played by the Audit Commission's Housing Inspectorate is discussed. In the fourth part, we widen our focus away from state regulation and ask about alternative forms of regulation beyond those narrow institutions. Five such groups are identified here: residents, private lenders, the National Housing Federation, local authorities and the housing ombudsman. This prefaces the final part of this section, 'The future'.

The Housing Corporation

In any study of regulatory bodies, the Housing Corporation would have stood out as almost anomalous because of its triple role – registration, regulation and funding. Whether it should have retained those roles, particularly regulation and funding, was a consistent debate in the sector. Numerous reviews considered the question and, until 2007, found that it was appropriate for a single body to have these roles (see, for example, DETR 2000; ODPM 2004b). This answer was generated, partly, because regulation and funding are intimately linked – receipt of public funding should imply some degree of central regulatory oversight to ensure that the money is being used appropriately. As Malpass (2000a: 246) put it, there was 'the simple ground that it is easier to ensure compliance with the requirements of the regulator if that body is also responsible for the distribution of grant aid'. Partly, that response was influenced by the extent to which central government should control the sector. If central government was going to provide substantial funds for the development of the sector, it had a genuine interest in the sector contributing to central government housing policies (DoE 1995a: 30). The concern that arose as a result was that the Housing Corporation had 'lost its vision as it has become increasingly confined to delivering increasing numbers of Government programmes rather than helping to develop overall policies and strategies' (ODPM Select Committee 2004a: para. 15).

A further criticism of the Housing Corporation was that, historically, it had not necessarily responded appropriately, and with sufficient foresight, to the developments in the sector in the late 1980s and beyond. It was, for example, caught out by the funding shift in the late 1980s, which meant that it 'literally ran out of money' and had to draw down funds from subsequent financial years (Randolph 1993: 43–4). It was also caught out by the collapse of Ujima in 2007. Since its foundation, seismic shifts had taken place in the sector; but there had also been significant developments in regulatory practice and theory at a generic level. In particular, the Better Regulation Commission promulgated a series of regulatory good practices.

In terms of its regulatory role, continual concerns had been expressed about the overburdening of PRPs to a diverse set of regulators (Elton 2006: para. 2). Depending on the PRP's status, it might be regulated by the Charity Commission or the FSA, the Audit Commission, other specialist regulators, such as the Care Standards Authority, as well as the housing regulator. The Housing Corporation did seek to address some of these concerns through moving to a more light-touch regulatory oversight and a new regulatory approach – *Performance Standards* – with desk-based regulation and self-certification.

CLG commissioned the Elton review to inquire into the regulatory burden on PRPs. The review framed a fundamental question concerning the Housing Corporation's approach to risk-based regulation as follows: 'how can the Corporation give effect to the aim of standing back from well run associations while retaining the degree of regular assurance that it and other stakeholders need?' (2006c: para. 34). It welcomed the shift to less intrusive regulation heralded by the deregulatory emphasis of the Housing Corporation's approach but noted that this 'itself carries some risks'.

These risks were amply illustrated by the failure of Ujima. In June 2007, the Housing Corporation found that Ujima was viable, properly managed and properly governed. It did find that Ujima had failed to meet its development target (despite having been given the largest grant allocated to a PRP of £47 million). The Housing Corporation's assessment was based on Ujima's own self-assessment. By December 2007, Ujima was insolvent with over £40 million of losses, and swallowed by London and Quadrant HA (a merger arranged by the Housing Corporation). It is clear from the review of the Housing Corporation's engagement with Ujima (Housing Corporation 2008a) that: serious failures occurred in the internal governance of Ujima, which were not shared with the Housing Corporation; Ujima's 10-year development plan (Project Jerusalem) was viewed by the Housing Corporation as lacking substance; and Ujima was uncooperative with the Housing Corporation's regulation. A finding of the review was that:

> The Corporation, therefore, faced an increasingly uncooperative PRP. In such circumstances the Corporation's approach to regulation, which depended on the provision of information from the association, was not fit for that purpose, with an insufficiently strong process for dealing with non-compliance. The practice of amending traffic lights only as a last resort effectively tolerated non-cooperation and the Corporation's Assessments, which are public documents, provided misplaced comfort to Ujima's various stakeholders. (para. 13)

The announcement of a further review in 2007 – the Cave review – could hardly have been a surprise to any interested party, although that it was conducted at breakneck speed was surprising. The Cave review began with an interesting and important description of the sector, not as a sector, but as a 'domain'. The domain was said to include PRPs, ALMOs, local authority and the private-for-profit sector (para. 2.7). This was an important sleight of hand because, as subsequently became clear, one of the aims of the review was 'to lower barriers to entry and encourage wider private sector participation. The review therefore expects that all parts of the domain will, in future, have relationships with lenders.' (para. 5.30) So, regulation was being used to move the sector away from its non-profit-making basis.

In terms of problems with the current regulatory system, Cave identified the following: the system focused on providers of housing and not the consumers (identified as tenants and communities: 2007: para. 2.45); the regulatory burden was too detailed and onerous (para. 2.54); and there had been unrestricted policy-passporting: 'the practice of securing the implementation of a range of government policies through the regulatory system is an endemic feature of the present arrangements' (para. 2.59). Regulatory purposes, it argued, should include policy objectives but this needed to occur with greater certainty about their extent and cost (para. 2.60). Other problems were unused financial capacity of PRPs (para. 2.62) and weak accountability to, and involvement of, tenants and stakeholders as well as consumer disempowerment (paras. 2.64–72).

This latter point was also significant because the Cave prognosis was to refocus the purpose of regulation as the empowerment of consumers across the regulatory domain arguing that the experience of being a tenant should not be different but should be 'comparable and improving' (2007: para. 2.71). That basis was 'grounded in the view that increasing consumer power and choice is what tenants want and that it will, over time, improve the performance of providers and reduce the need for more intrusive regulation' (para. 2.76). Partly for this reason, Cave proposed a regulatory body for the whole domain (para. 4.9), something which was not initially accepted by the CLG (2007d: para. 7.29).

The problem for Cave, though, might best be expressed by reference to the potential 'regulatory space' of the sector because this space is so densely populated (McDermont 2007b). This problem meant that the range of regulatory strategies and structures was effectively confined. So, for example, the impact of private finance was expressed thus:

> The existing £35 billion private investment in the sector is now larger than the government's input over the same period. Action that undermines the confidence of lenders will produce a significant increase in costs, undermine development of capacity and increase the cost of new supply for the public purse. (2007: para. 4.44)

On the other hand, local authority impact on the range of regulation was effectively discarded on the bases that a national regulator was required, and there is a difference between constructive engagement and co-operation, on the one hand, and regulation, on the other (ibid. para. 4.33).

The review plumped for a co-regulatory approach, a mix of contract, direct regulation and self-regulation and regulatory specification (para. 4.42). Some of the advantages of this approach were stated to be:

> The greater freedom to operate and self regulate – but within a domain wide framework of standards and agreement – should stimulate innovation and responsiveness to local circumstances.

It would provide more safeguards for tenants than the preceding options and be more challenging than pure self regulation.

The continuation of regulation of the financial viability and governance of housing associations (albeit on the basis of risk) together with a wider spectrum of intervention options would maintain the current terms of lending and encourage lender confidence. (2007: ibid.)

Central government's policy-passporting was to be limited to rent-setting and housing standards (paras. 5.12–4). The core responsibility of the regulator was to be the delivery of good quality housing services, which required the definition of such a service (para. 5.41). The government accepted most of the recommendations of the review (see CLG 2007a).

Regulating private registered providers after 2008

The Housing and Regeneration Act 2008 implemented most of the Cave review's recommendations. It provided the statutory basis for the roles and functions of the TSA and HCA. The Act set out ten 'fundamental objectives' in no particular order, with a direction that the TSA 'shall perform its functions with a view to achieving them' (s. 86(1)). These objectives are: to encourage and support a supply of well-managed social housing, of appropriate quality, sufficient to meet reasonable demands; to ensure that actual or potential tenants of social housing have an appropriate degree of choice and protection; to ensure that tenants of social housing have the opportunity to be involved in its management; to ensure that registered providers of social housing perform their functions efficiently, effectively and economically; to ensure that registered providers of social housing are financially viable and properly managed; to encourage registered providers of social housing to contribute to the environmental, social and economic well-being of the areas in which the housing is situated; to encourage investment in social housing (including by promoting the availability of financial services to registered providers of social housing); to avoid the imposition of an unreasonable burden (directly or indirectly) on public funds; to guard against the misuse of public funds; to regulate in a manner which minimises interference, and is proportionate, consistent, transparent and accountable (s. 86). The TSA can balance those objectives as it sees fit.

Beyond that, the TSA essentially had a blank sheet, except as regards rent-setting which remained an area where policy-passporting is possible (s. 199) and appropriate (given the state's investment and concern about rents). For its first period of operation, it worked under the Housing Corporations' regulatory material (Housing Corporation 2005), circulars and other documents. These circulars governed a number of key government policies, including rent-setting (04/08), tenant involvement in housing management (05/07), and tenancy management (eligibility and eviction: 02/07). The TSA developed a Concordat with the Audit Commission Housing Inspectorate (established under the Local Government Act 1999,

s. 10, and extended to the PRP sector in 2001), which remains in place at present (see below).

The TSA engaged in one of the largest-scale consultation exercises conducted by a government agency, engaging with over 27,000 tenants, and produced an early attempt to map out the regulatory terrain and approach (TSA 2009a). This set out the regulatory ideal of 'co-regulation', so that PRPs self-regulate against national standards, but that they also set local priorities as well. The justification for this approach was, in particular: 'The balance between direct regulation and self-regulation enables the standards framework to be more tailored to local priorities than may be possible with uniform national standards prescribed by the regulator. It also generates a degree of ownership in the framework from landlords and tenants' (para. 3.7). The vision of co-regulation was to encourage 'landlords and tenants to engage together with a shared aspiration of improving the standard of service delivery', which then delimited the TSA's regulatory activity (para. 3.5). This co-regulation was also risk-based – following a similar model to that of, for example, the FSA, with 'Senior Risk and Assurance Managers' leading – and the assessment of risk will 'determine proportionate, targeted and consistent use of our limited resources' (para. 3.15). The focus of the TSA regulation was to be finance and governance but will also be 'outcome-based', so input processes were less important. Thus, the role of the TSA was envisioned, effectively, as a back-stop to self-regulation. Thus, information to be collated by the TSA would be such as 'enables it to establish an acceptable minimum level of confidence about landlords and the social housing sector as a whole' (para. 5.12).

The document also foreshadowed the development of broad regulatory principles and standards for the sector, which is what followed in 2010 (TSA 2010a). In this document, *The Regulatory Framework for Social Housing in England from April 2010*, the TSA (re)asserted the essential role of co-regulation as requiring 'robust self-regulation … subject to a "backbone" of regulation by the TSA' (para. 1.1). The TSA set six standards relating to tenant involvement and empowerment; home; tenancy; neighbourhood and community; value for money; governance; and financial viability. These applied across the domain, including local authorities (which were excepted from the last of these). Each standard has 'required outcomes' and 'specific expectations'.

Policy-passporting was to be permitted in respect of quality of accommodation, rents and tenant involvement and empowerment. It was also anticipated, even by Cave, that rents would form part of central government's legitimate role. The framework, therefore, repeats the CLG direction that PRPs rent increases each are to be no more than RPI+½%+£2 to a certain limit (Tenancy Standard: 2.2), but this is subject to an exception:

> Where the application of the Rents Standard would cause registered providers to be unable to meet other standards, particularly in respect of financial viability including the risk that a reduction in overall rental income causes them to risk failing to meet existing commitments such as banking or other lending

covenants, the TSA may allow extensions to the period over which the requirements of the Rents Standard are met. (TSA 2010a: 2.3)

The rent-setting standard is designed, then, to fulfil the ultimate objective
(identified in Chapter 4) of rent-convergence across the social housing domain
(see now TSA 2010c).

The significance of provider–tenant negotiated outcomes in relation to the
standards (and beyond) was a crucial element of this new approach. Thus,

> The TSA standards place a strong emphasis on providers involving their ten-
> ants to shape local delivery to local priorities and scrutinise performance. The
> primary focus for discussions on service delivery and improvement should be
> between providers and their tenants rather than between the regulator and the
> provider (TSA 2010a: para. 1.2)

The central role of the tenant as 'knight' and 'queen' (to use Le Grand's terms
discussed in Chapter 1) was emphasised throughout in terms of the 'service
offer' of the PRP to the tenant: reporting to tenants on performance; tenant
involvement in development and scrutiny of the PRP annual report; having a
clear and accessible complaints policy; and the general expectation that providers will 'engage meaningfully with tenants and offer them opportunities to agree
how service delivery against the TSA standards can be tailored to reflect local
priorities' (para. 1.11). Further, 'Every tenant matters. We expect providers to
understand and respond to the particular needs of their tenants and to demonstrate how they have taken into account the needs of tenants across the [equality
duty]' (para. 1.12). These standards offer a broad set of principles which might
be said to operate as 'tin-openers rather than dials' (Day and Klein 1995: para.
3.13) and require regulatory communications between the TSA, the PRP, and
its tenants; but it is also clear that the primary regulatory conversations need to
be between the PRP and its residents. Compliance with these standards was to
be through annual reports, performance outcomes promised to tenants, existing information sources, analysis of complaints, external validation, the absence
of non-compliance, inspection, and further information (para. 3.6).

On its face, this regulatory framework was a significant volte-face from the
previous regime, which had seemed to prioritise governance, business planning, and financial viability (see McDermont 2007b; McDermont et al. 2009).
However, it is also clear that these elements are central to the TSA approach for,
as the regulatory framework makes clear: 'Good governance is a universal principle and is essential to the quality of service delivery, financial robustness and
value for money' (para. 1.14). Further, PRPs with more than 1,000 properties

> will remain subject to a level of direct scrutiny of financial and governance per-
> formance to enable the TSA to maintain an independent review. We intend to
> continue publishing judgements for these providers, as this is supported and val-
> ued by lenders and providers themselves. The supply of financial information,
> both annual accounts and forecast information, will remain a key part of our
> regulation of all non-local authority landlords' governance and viability. From 1

April 2010 we will expect the same type of financial information as previously from these providers. We will, also as previously, keep the specification of these returns under review, working with providers and stakeholders to keep them fit for purpose, and ensure this information complies with the general principle of 'used and useful'. (2010a: para. 3.8).

Regulatory judgments form a considerable part of the TSA role. They publicly grade the viability and governance of the PRP against the regulatory framework requirements and provide a qualitative assessment. These areas are the focus because 'these are key areas where lenders, boards and others value our assessments' (para. 3.21). Like the Housing Corporation, however, the TSA's approach to regulation is risk-based – PRPs where there are no indications of risk of standards of failure and no other contra-indications of compliance can expect light-touch regulation; those where the information suggests cause for concern can expect increased engagement (para. 3.15).

The Housing and Regeneration Act 2008 may assist the TSA in similar circumstances in the future because of the general powers and functions which it gives to the TSA (chs. 4, 6 and 7) as well as powers to require the provision of certain information and disclosure from other public authorities (ss. 107–9).

Housing Inspectorate

The Audit Commission's Housing Inspectorate took over from the Housing Corporation in 2002. The Inspectorate carried out inspections of various aspects of individual PRP management and governance, although a request must first come from the TSA (and are predominantly of the short-notice type: TSA/Audit Commission 2010a: para. 9). It measured PRP performance against published 'key lines of enquiry', referred to as KLOEs (Audit Commission 2007), adapted to the new environment (TSA/Audit Commission 2010a: 4), and arrived at a score of excellent, good, fair, or poor (and a star system – three stars for excellent, no stars for poor) as well as considering prospects for improvement. The KLOEs were supported by a system of self-assessment and disclosure of documents by the PRP, followed by an inspection of specific elements of the service. The Audit Commission instituted a process of 'short notice' inspection, sampling PRPs on the basis of risk assessment priorities such as results of performance indicators over a three-year period (Audit Commission 2008: para. 3.2). It provided a scoring system based on strengths against weaknesses (para. 9.1). This section is written in the past tense because the Commission is scheduled for abolition (see below).

Other regulatory groups

So far, the analysis has been top-down, but it is an important feature of the regulation of PRPs that much regulation takes place in different spaces and by different groups. All of these regulatory groups do not operate in isolation but, most usually, in concert. They also change shape over time and depend on the PRP's governance as well as development. Five groups are identified here (although there are undoubtedly more which could be considered): tenants; private lenders; the National Housing Federation; local authorities; the housing ombudsman. Each of these are now discussed in turn.

Tenants

Tenants, as we have seen, have become a principal regulatory purpose, in the sense that regulation is being designed for their benefit, as well as co-regulators in their own right. There are other methods by which they can take on the governing role. For example, it has been a regulatory requirement that PRPs with more than 1,000 properties should have at least one tenant member of the board. It has also become accepted practice that LSVT PRPs' governing bodies should be made up of one-third of tenants. McDermont et al. (2009) have identified two issues with this process of direct governance – the neutrality and expertise required of board members. Board members are expected to be neutral and not represent the interests of, for example, the tenants. Board members represent the PRP. These issues are thrown into sharp focus when, as was suggested default practice (under the Housing Corporation's Circular 05/07), the tenant is elected to the board (presumably by other residents). Expertise can be developed and, indeed, may well already be attained through experience, knowledge, or training, but it is usual for the other governing body members to have relevant qualifications (legal, accountancy, estate management etc.). These two issues operate as potential constraints on the policy and potentially counteract the positive impacts which tenants can make to boards.

Indirect governance is through tenant participation, such as associations, which also feed into the decisions taken by the board. Such is the significance of this within the new regulatory regime that it is the *first* standard under which:

Registered providers shall support co-regulation with their tenants by:

- offering all tenants a wide range of opportunities to be involved in the management of their housing, including the ability to influence strategic priorities, the formulation of housing-related policies and the delivery of housing-related services
- consulting with their tenants and acting reasonably in providing them with opportunities to agree local offers for service delivery
- providing tenants with a range of opportunities to influence how providers meet all the TSA's standards, and to scrutinise their performance against all standards and in the development of the annual report
- providing support to tenants to build their capacity to be more effectively involved. (Tenant Involvement and Empowerment Standard: para. 2)

Its significance was re-emphasised in the first joint research project between the TSA and Audit Commission (2010b), which set out the rationale for tenant involvement and its significance for the tenant experience (see especially para. 26: there is a strong relationship between tenants' satisfaction with overall services and satisfaction with opportunities to participate), as well as a 'menu of involvement' (at p. 16). It recognised also that the unintended consequence of the underspecification of the standard 'is that co-regulation is not well understood by tenants or landlords' and landlords were unsure as to the requirements on them (para. 57). The report sought partly to assuage these concerns and partly to upskill PRPs through providing models of practice (ch. 4).

Lenders

The second regulatory body is the private lenders and, one might add, their representative association, the CML. The former have a significant direct regulatory role when lending money because they will inspect the PRP's books and raise any issues with the board, which they are also likely to scrutinise in terms of their expertise. At a relatively early stage of their involvement in the sector, they also influenced the Housing Corporation's regulation in two specific ways. First, there was a shift in the presentation of accounts to merge the requirements of private lenders with Housing Corporation practice. Lenders, typically, are used to dealing with accounts provided in the format of plcs and it was natural for them to require PRPs to provide their accounts in that format. Housing Corporation practice changed as a result to synchronise with lenders' understandings. Second, Housing Corporation performance review reports in the 1990s were simplified to make them palatable to private lenders (Day et al. 1993: 22). The system involved a grading (with three grades), with 'sanitising performance reports so that [PRPs] can make them available to their funders' (Mullins 1997: 309); the regulatory judgments described above perform a similar role. There are just four mentions of the word 'lenders' in the regulatory framework and lender reassurance appears as one of nine specific objectives (para. 6.26). The suspicion may be that as PRP lending has become more mainstream for lenders over time there is less of a requirement for regulation to be conducted to give them comfort; to put this another way, the maturity of the market enables the PRP-lender relationship to be negotiated and governed internally with rather less reliance on external regulatory assessments (although these may be significant if less than positive).

The representative association has an impact on the development of housing policy at the macro level, essentially representing the interests of private lenders in negotiations around policy and legislative changes. They have been extremely active and influential in that process.

National Housing Federation

The third body, the National Housing Federation, has been the subject of an important recent study (McDermont 2010), which demonstrates its influence in terms of developing policy for the sector, representing the sector, as well as setting out influential strategic approaches which are adopted by its members (such as the 'iN Business for Neighbourhoods' strategy, noted above).

Local authorities

The fourth body, local authorities, also have a significant regulatory role. For at least part of the twentieth century, some local authorities offered loans to PRPs to develop certain types of accommodation. As we have seen, authorities became 'enablers' of housing provision from the mid-1980s, now recast as convenors (ch. 4). As McDermont (2010: ch. 4) points out, that role facilitated the development of PRP accommodation by transferring local authority land at low (or no) cost to the favoured PRP, which lowered the cost of that development. In return, the local authority usually extracted rights to nominate households to that accommodation. Regulation here is intimately linked to promotion and accountability (see Cave 2007), because the PRP then became accountable to the local authority in relation to those nomination rights, and effectively lost its independence (nominations are discussed in detail in Chapter 7 below).

Housing Ombudsman Service

Fifth, the HOS has been involved in dealing with individual complaints from PRP residents for some time (and under different labels). Section 51, Housing Act 1996, and Sch. 2 created a system of redress for aggrieved tenants of PRPs. PRPs were required to belong to an approved scheme (i.e. the HOS). The Housing and Regeneration Act 2008 retained the HOS for the sector (s. 124), but this was more than mere 'retention', for the role envisaged for the HOS, in effect, was more visible and much enhanced. If tenants were to be the co-regulators, one of the means through which they exercise that regulatory ability is through complaints. As the HOS noted in its evidence to the Cave review: 'complaints about repair have slipped from first to second place in the scale of the most common causes of reference to my service. Instead, the principal issue complained about was how landlords handled their original complaint.' (Cave 2007: para. 2.52; cf. HOS 2010: 66) Indeed,

> The evidence of failure in too many internal complaint handling procedures underscores the continuing importance of ensuring consistent access to Ombudsman services for all tenants across the domain. The HOS devotes considerable resources to dispute resolution which goes beyond the core role of investigation and adjudication. The review considers this wider role to be valuable and believe that these benefits should extend to all parts of the domain. (2010: para. 5.109)

Under the TSA regulatory framework, the HOS' role becomes highly significant. First, where complaints to the HOS indicate systemic failure, these can be referred to the TSA (2010: para. 1.2). Second, under a memorandum of understanding between the HOS and TSA, which recognised their 'mutual dependence for information' (TSA/HOS 2010: para. 2.1), the HOS shared information with the TSA on a quarterly basis (para. 4). Third, there have been year-on-year rises in the number of complaints to the HOS, which might be expected to continue, given its profile in the TSA regulatory framework (HOS 2010 reports a

21 per cent increase in 2009). Fourth, the Cave review recommended that the HOS and local government ombudsman roles be joined to create a cross-domain ombudsman. This was initially rejected by CLG (2007d) but, as we shall see below, is one of the Coalition projects.

Since 2008, the HOS has adopted a more active interventionist approach to dispute management, as opposed to a more passive 'adjudicatory' approach, because of a shift to encourage early and proportionate dispute resolution. The core purpose of the HOS was redefined as 'enabling early and fair dispute resolution in housing' and uses a variety of different alternative dispute resolution methods (conciliation, mediation, arbitration, adjudication with a hearing, adjudication on the papers, and early neutral assessment: HOS 2010). It offers early advice to potential complainants about advice agencies and appropriate alternative dispute resolution fora. It also offers advice to disputants during PRPs' internal complaints handling processes, and promotes early dispute resolution rather than steering disputants through an internal complaints service. This is a markedly different approach to some other traditional ombudsmen who, in relation to individual complaints, tend to adopt a more adjudicatory, less proactive stance in relation to whether maladministration or service failure has taken place.

The future

The review of social housing regulation

The Coalition government came into power with a 'quango-burning' agenda, in part. One of its targets was the TSA. In October 2010, the government reviewed social housing regulation, and the outcomes of that review represent significant changes to the regulatory terrain (CLG 2010k). This will affect not only the identity of the regulator but also the style of regulation. The review proposed the abolition of the TSA, with its functions to be moved to a specially constituted committee within the HCA (a statutory regulation committee), but separated off from the HCA's funding functions, although serviced by HCA staff (paras. 8.10–3) (thus, responding to the Cave review's concerns regarding functional integration); the Audit Commission is also to be abolished with the new regulation committee having power to commission audit from a full range of providers. As regards economic regulation, the review proposed largely to keep the TSA's current oversight role (albeit within the HCA). The reasoning placed the financial environment at its forefront:

> There is a clear rationale for the continuation of the regulator's proactive stance in relation to these activities to prevent organisational failure and defaults on loans. These activities also help support the confidence of private lenders to provide funds at competitive rates. (para. 5.2)

However, there are two riders to this apparent continuity. First, there will be an overriding duty on this new committee to minimise interference with PRPs, and second the new committee will be expected to be more proactive in achieving value for money in an increasingly constrained financial environment (paras. 5.3–4). Whereas the statutory objectives set for the TSA in the 2008 Act entitled the TSA to balance them as it saw fit, the new regulatory environment is designed to ensure that the tenth objective becomes an overriding duty to 'reflect the Government's intention that proportionality and minimal interference should shape the exercise of all regulatory functions' (para. 3.9).

Reflecting that shift, the significant changes are in the area of 'consumer protection'. Here, the prescription for the new committee is that it should adopt a *reactive* role. It is the regulator of last resort, which should only engage where there are reasonable grounds for believing that there has been 'serious failure':

> We recommend the regulator should only be able to exercise its monitoring and enforcement powers with respect to its consumer protection standards if, in its opinion, there are reasonable grounds to suspect there has been – or that there is a risk of – a breach of a standard(s) resulting in a serious detriment to tenants. In reaching this opinion, we envisage the regulator would have regard to the severity and the extent of the impact. Thus failures resulting in a severe impact on a large number of tenants would represent strong grounds for intervention. (CLG 2010k: para. 4.27)

Information from which this 'serious failure' might be deduced include: nature and volume of complaints; performance information; local intelligence; evidence from other expert bodies; and whistle-blowing (para. 4.29).

The Coalition's approach, then, radically re-envisions co-regulation, as having a far more limited role for the regulator beyond standard-setting. Who is to take up the slack? The Coalition's answer is tenants and their representatives (here conceptualised as elected representatives, MPs and councillors, and tenant panels), with an enhanced role for the HOS (which will take on the housing functions of the LGO) but with the important introduction of a filter for complaints:

> We therefore propose that **tenants should contact MPs, Councillors, or a tenant panel** once the landlord's complaint procedure has been exhausted, and that **MPs/Councillors/tenant panels should intervene in order to attempt to resolve the problem and only then refer the complaint on to the Ombudsmen if the matter cannot be resolved**. We anticipate that the majority of tenant complaints will be resolved at the local level. (CLG 2010k: para. 4.5, original emphasis)

The development of tenant panels, and their significance for the regulation process, is a major innovation; alongside this, the linear process of complaints as the consumer protection regulator, together with the filter and subject to a backstop of the regulatory committee involvement, is equally significant. These roles are to be facilitated by the production of '… **timely, useful performance information to tenants in order to support effective scrutiny**' (para. 4.17, original emphasis); however, the requirement for the PRP to produce an annual report is to be repealed, in essence leaving it to the PRP to decide how to present the information to its tenants (para. 4.19). While recognising that PRPs have different processes, the 'linear process' of complaining is to allow the escalation of complaints from a first-stage review to second stage followed by a complaint to the ombudsman (subject to the filter). At the second stage, 'A tenant panel could play an important role in forming part of the review or indeed conducting the review without officer involvement (as currently happens in some landlords)' (para. 4.23). The panel might also assist the PRP with learning from complaints or act as advocates for tenants (para. 4.24). The tenant involvement and empowerment standard is to be enhanced to account for these roles without being prescriptive as to how PRPs arrange these roles – it is to be exhortatory (para. 4.25).

Issues

The CLG review is a powerful document, with a clear prospectus for increased tenant involvement, which is clearly underpinned by a cost-cutting agenda. These rationales, while convincing on their face, raise empirical issues concerning the spaces in which PRP accountability takes place; the understanding of complaints; tenant capacity and conflicts; the HOS 'filter'; and the power of audit. Each point is taken in turn.

As regards the spaces in which PRP accountability takes place, the CLG model was characterised above as 'linear', making assumptions about the progress of complaints. However, research into complaints suggests a far messier environment with overlapping accountability spaces (Law Commission 2006a; 2006b). Different fora exist for 'complaints' depending on their construction by the process – and there are a variety of processes in which tenants might engage other than by making a complaint. This may depend on their interactions through which the subject is mediated. Further, as the Law Commission (2006b: para. 2.2) put it:

> Processes of adjudication mould disputes. They identify disputes, generally expanding or narrowing them to certain issues. In this sense, they act as an audience for the dispute, transforming and rephrasing it: 'where there are written legal codes and an official language of disputing, language may become an even more critical variable shaping the disputing process.' The adjudicatory process overwrites the language of the participants with its own language, operating through a set of behaviours and codes which can be unwritten or secret. Even where the adjudication processes, principles and practices are formally open, it is often unrealistic to expect the lay participants to access the set of knowledges and expertise in them. (References in the original text have been removed, but see, in particular, Cain and Kulcsar 1981–1982.)

The point is that complaints are socially constructed, and dependent on a variety of external filtering factors. Repairs are said to be the main issue with which the HOS deals. In its work, the Law Commission identified sixteen possible responses to a fairly 'standard' disrepair issue, but none of those responses help the occupier 'unless she is sufficiently confident to decide that she has the ability to do something about her unhappiness. She must also be aware of the existence of one or more of the agencies to whom she might turn for further advice and assistance.' (Law Commission 2006a: para. 2.4)

As regards the understanding of complaints, the first point here is that it requires a service failure to be identified as a 'complaint' (Felsteiner et al. 1980–81); and, even if it is, it requires the occupier to take action in a defined way. The occupier may not even identify something as a complaint, but seek to hold the PRP to account more generally for dissatisfaction or some other form of self-identified harm (see, in particular, Lloyd-Bostock and Mulcahy 1994). Socio-legal research into complaining, however, demonstrates that many people 'lump' their problems – they do nothing about them for a variety of reasons – and that general finding is equally relevant to housing (Genn 1999). There are various barriers to complaining, such as the resources (in the widest sense) available to tenants, including their perception of the seriousness of the issue, and the practices of the landlord (see Karn et al. 1997: ch. 7). As regards occupiers, Cowan and Halliday et al. (2003: ch 5.) postulate the following barriers (in that research, to homelessness internal reviews, but they argue that their findings may be generalisable): ignorance of the process; scepticism; rule-bound image of the process; complaint fatigue; 'satisfaction'. However, the point of that study was to demonstrate that the pursuit and non-pursuit of a grievance substantially depended on the interaction between the applicant and the bureaucracy. Thus, the practices of the PRP are central, for they have to identify something as a complaint.

The point about tenant capacity and conflicts follows on from these points, but is more specific to the relatively undefined identity of tenant panels. There are two points to make here, the first about educating tenants to take on this role, and the second about the role of tenant members of the PRP board (from which tenant panels might be drawn). The first point is that education offers contested terrain in itself. Tenants are required to become 'experts' in housing management beyond their expertise as occupiers and the construction of that training package may emphasise the limits of management as the context for the role (McDermont 2007b). As Furbey et al. noted (1996: 262), in relation to TMO training programmes, these '… embodie[d] a diagnosis for the problems of council housing informed by "dependence" and "enterprise" and financed the entry of consumer–citizens into a limited marketplace of options'. The second is about the identity of tenant panels – for example, if they are constructed from the PRP management board itself, this risks role-conflict, for board members are required to be neutral (even if elected). In their study of 'Wandland', a newly formed LSVT PRP, McDermont et al. (2009: especially 682–90) found that neutrality model punctuated at certain times. For example, the question over policy on rent arrears

produced three poles – the knowledge of tenants as tenants as to why rent arrears arise in the first place; the nature of the tenant as board member; and the strategic role of the board … The issue divided tenant board members and, at heart, concerned the extent to which they were willing to ally themselves with occupiers generally or accept a 'business' approach; it concerned the representative nature of board members at the sharp end. (p. 689)

This construction and expertise of tenant panels is significant for the following issue, concerning the HOS filter, for they are one of the mechanisms through which the HOS will be entitled to adjudicate on complaints in the future. Other filter mechanisms include MPs and local councillors. This filter process is similar (albeit more extensive) than that which applies to the Parliamentary Commissioner for Administration. Complaints under that system are filtered by MPs. Harlow and Rawlings (2009: 445) offer the following perspective on that filter:

A 'top-down' perspective focuses on the notorious 'MP filter' at which many incumbents of the office chafe … This filtering function we might see as either a way of maintaining the workload of the [commissioner] (the real dispute-resolution machinery) within manageable proportions, or as an obstacle to justice. A 'bottom-up' perspective would evaluate the MP's service as a complaints handling system in its own right. It might then appear as an effective, cheap and accessible complaints system, providing quick, cost-free solutions for very ordinary people and taking the load from more formal dispute-resolution machinery. This, however, calls for empirical research.

Thus, it is unclear what purpose/s the filter system actually serves. Subsequently, however, they note (pp. 532–3) that commissioners themselves together with a Cabinet Office Review (2000) had called for the filter to be abolished to enable the commissioner to act effectively. Thus, there are concerns that the inquiry into maladministration causing injustice is not well-served by the filter. One might raise a similar concern here, perhaps more so because there may be pressures to resolve complaints internally. This is a particular concern as the regulation of consumer protection requires the efficient management of complaints.

Finally, it should be noted that, despite the demise of the Audit Commission, audit practices remain a principal form of regulatory control over PRPs and principally seem to operate (certainly within the confines of the review) as a form of comfort for private lenders. However, these practices are to be more diffuse, shared between private providers. The regulator retains the ability to conduct inspections but the anticipation is that there will be a small number of more-targeted inspections. Joint research projects are a thing of the past. With the backstop role of the regulatory committee, audit is likely to become a principal form of control and the body of expertise will grow accordingly. Although audit has a claim to neutrality, it seems perverse to rely so extensively on it when it is, in essence, a congenitally failing enterprise (as one might see from its role in the global credit crisis) (see, generally, Power 1997). Individually negotiated contracts between PRPs and auditors, like companies, may be regarded as something of a Trojan horse in future.

Regulating law

So far, we have considered soft law only. PRPs have largely operated in the shadow of the law without actually creating that shadow. They grant private sector tenancies (from 1989) and their primary relationship with law has been through private law. That makes sense, on one view, if they are regarded as private organisations by the Treasury for accounting purposes. However, the introduction of the HRA raises this issue squarely, albeit in a different context.

Section 6 of that Act provides that it is unlawful for a public authority to act in a way which is incompatible with a Convention right (included in Sch. 1 to that Act). If PRPs fall within the definition of public authority, then they must comply with those rights; furthermore, they will come under a duty to comply with the 'general equalities duty' (s. 149, Equality Act 2010), which came into force in April 2011. The key definition of 'public authority' is broader than might be thought. It *includes*: 'any person certain of whose functions are functions of a public nature' (s. 6(3)(b)); but *excludes*: 'In relation to a particular act, a person is not a public authority by virtue only of subsection (3)(b) if the nature of the act is private' (s. 6(5)). Bodies which fall within s. 6(3)(b) are commonly referred to as 'hybrid public authorities' in the sense that only some of their functions, which are tinged with the requisite degree of publicness, fall within the scope of the HRA. Other bodies, such as local authorities and courts, are 'core public authorities' because all of their functions are automatically public (s. 6(3)(a)).

The hard-edged questions, then, are whether (in this context) PRPs are exercising functions of a public nature and, if so, which acts are private. To preface the following discussion with the outcome (to date): they generally exercise functions of a public nature, although certain stock is excluded, but only in relation to acts of management. In this section, the background to the issue is discussed briefly through the development of the law here; there then follows a discussion of *R (Weaver)* v. *London & Quadrant HT* [2010] 1 WLR 363 – this is extensive because of the significance of this issue to the functioning of PRPs and its implications; finally, a critique of the decision is offered. The Supreme Court refused permission to appeal in *Weaver* because of the unsatisfactory way in which the appeal came about; but it did indicate that the issue is 'live' and would consider 'leapfrog' appeals (by-passing the usual appeal structure).

Background

Even before this period, the courts had regarded PRPs as outside the realm of public law. In *Peabody HT* v. *Green* (1979) 38 P&CR 644, the Peabody Trust sought to evict occupiers of a building which had been shortlife housing at one stage. The occupiers challenged Peabody's attempt at summary eviction by arguing that Peabody had taken account of irrelevant considerations in the exercise of a statutory power (a straightforward public law *Wednesbury* claim

(*Associated Provincial Picture Houses Ltd* v. *Wednesbury Corporation* [1948] 1 KB 223)). The Court of Appeal rejected this challenge on the basis that the mere receipt of public funds did not turn the exercise of a private power – through the rules of the trust – into a public act. As Browne LJ put it (p. 653), 'In my judgment, the powers of a housing association to manage its affairs are not derived from any statute but are derived from its own constitution – in this case, the rules of the plaintiff association.'

Although this case is an historical artefact, pre-dating as it does the tremendous developments in judicial review as well as the outward growth of the bodies which are susceptible to such proceedings (see *R* v. *Panel of Takeover and Mergers ex p Datafin* [1987] QB 815 and *R* v. *Disciplinary Committee of the Jockey Club ex p Aga Khan* [1993] 1 WLR 909), the arguments deployed there have become both familiar and well-rehearsed in subsequent cases, albeit with more sophistication, concerning the amenability of certain bodies to challenge under the HRA. That sophistication can be found in a series of cases concerning the question whether a particular body, such as a PRP, a parish church council, or a care home, is exercising functions of a public nature under the HRA (respectively, *Poplar HARCA* v. *Donoghue* [2001] EWCA 595, *Aston Cantlow PCC* v. *Wallbank* [2003] 3 WLR 283, *R (Heather)* v. *Leonard Cheshire Foundation* [2002] 2 All ER 936 and *YL* v. *Birmingham CC* [2008] 1 AC 95).

As a general rule, the courts in these cases have resisted the formation of general guidelines. But, Lord Nicholls in *Aston Cantlow* made the following observation:

> What, then, is the touchstone to be used in deciding whether a function is public for this purpose? Clearly there is no single test of universal application. There cannot be, given the diverse nature of governmental functions and the variety of means by which these functions are discharged today. Factors to be taken into account include the extent to which in carrying out the relevant function the body is publicly funded, or is exercising statutory powers, or is taking the place of central government or local authorities, or is providing a public service. ([12])

Others have found assistance in the neologism 'governmental' (for example, *Aston Cantlow*, at [10], Lord Nicholls ('a useful guide'); Lord Mance in *YL*, at [91]), by which is meant 'of government', although one might remark that this is merely an unhelpful tautology.

After *Aston Cantlow*, in which it was held that a parochial church council exercising its rights to levy for chancel repairs was not exercising functions of a public nature, it was asserted that the earlier decision in *Poplar HARCA* was incorrectly decided. In *Poplar HARCA*, the Court of Appeal held that Poplar HARCA, an LSVT PRP, was exercising functions of a public nature in terminating Ms Donoghue's AST by means of the mandatory notice procedure (s. 21(4), Housing Act 1988, discussed in Chapter 11 and Chapter 16 below). The Court of Appeal held that 'in providing accommodation for the defendant and then seeking possession, the association's role was so closely assimilated to that of the authority that it was acting as a public authority'. This was a decision clearly on the facts of the case – Ms Donoghue had been provided temporary accommodation in satisfaction of the authority's duties under Part VII, Housing Act 1996, pending their enquiries (discussed in Chapter 6 below). It was only after that point that Poplar HARCA took over the management of the property.

A number of factors were cited as pushing the particular claim into the public function bracket, although this was regarded as a 'borderline case' in which questions of fact and degree played a significant role (at [56]). Lord Woolf LCJ argued that what can make an act, which would otherwise be private, public, is a feature or a combination of features which impose a public character or stamp on the act. This includes statutory authority, the extent of control over the activity by a public authority, and the extent in which private acts are enmeshed in the activities of a public body. At the time of transfer, Ms Donoghue was a sitting tenant of Poplar HARCA and it was intended that she would be treated no better and no worse than if she remained a tenant of Tower Hamlets. While she remained a tenant, Poplar HARCA therefore effectively occupied the position previously occupied by the transferring local authority.

In *YL*, Baroness Hale, who was in the minority, and Lord Mance, who was in the majority, suggested that Lord Woolf had paid too much attention to the historical links between Poplar HARCA and the council, rather than on the nature of the act there in question (at [61] and [105] respectively). Although Lord Woolf had suggested that there was considerable overlap between the scope of judicial review and the concept of functions of a public nature, Lord Mance noted that 'while authorities on judicial review can be helpful, section 6 has a different rationale, linked to the scope of State responsibility in Strasbourg' ([87]). It seemed that *YL* was not only an important decision in its own right in relation to care homes, but, more generally, re-opened the question about whether PRPs were caught by s. 6(3)(b).

The *Weaver* litigation

In *R (Weaver)* v. *London & Quadrant HT* (Div Ct); [2010] 1 WLR 363 (CA), Ms Weaver sought to challenge the use by London and Quadrant (L&Q) of the mandatory ground for possession for rent arrears (Ground 8, Housing Act 1988) in the alleged absence of pursuing other reasonable alternatives. The claim was that this was a breach of her legitimate expectation that L&Q would follow the relevant regulatory guidance issued by the Housing Corporation. Further, it was argued that such legitimate expectation also led to a breach of Article 8 and Article 1 of the First Protocol to the HRA. Put this way, the claim raised the question of whether L&Q was subject to the jurisdiction of the court by way of judicial review and, in exercising functions of a public nature, subject to the HRA.

The Divisional Court [2009] 1 All ER 17 held that L&Q was indeed exercising 'functions of a public nature' under s. 6, HRA in the management and allocation of their housing stock and was subject to judicial review of the same. However, in deciding to seek possession on Ground 8, Housing Act 1988, the court held that L&Q was not acting in breach of a legitimate expectation derived from Housing Corporation regulatory circulars and guidance, and nor was that decision against Ms Weaver's rights under Article 8. As Richards LJ put it, this was a finding 'which in my view takes the claimant nowhere on the facts of this case, and I think it unlikely to be of great practical significance in many other cases' (at [63]). The latter observation considerably underplayed the significance of the discussion.

When the matter came to the Court of Appeal, it proceeded 'in somewhat unusual and not altogether satisfactory circumstances' (Elias LJ, at [2]) because L&Q decided to appeal against the finding as to its public law status. The Divisional Court, as a result, made a formal declaration that L&Q's management and allocation of its housing stock was a function of a public nature for the purposes of s. 6(3)(b), HRA, and was accordingly amenable to judicial review in respect of its performance of those functions. The general nature of that declaration, however, was criticised by the Court of Appeal because it did not actually deal with the real question in the case and lacked 'context' (at [6], Elias LJ; [87], Lord Collins; [115], Rix LJ), that is: whether the termination of a tenancy was a private act within s. 6(5). Nevertheless, the Court of Appeal, by a majority (Rix LJ dissenting), found that L&Q's act of terminating Ms Weaver's tenancy was the exercise of a public function, not a private act, and amenable to judicial review.

Elias LJ, with whom Lord Collins agreed (giving a substantive judgment), first discussed the role of PRPs in relation to the provision of social housing, noting, amongst other matters, their regulation by the then Housing Corporation which also provided grants (matched with private funding); their role in assisting local authorities to carry out their statutory housing policies (drawing attention to the duty to cooperate with local authorities to such extent as is reasonable in the circumstances: s. 170, Housing Act 1996) as well as the practical reality of the importance of nomination agreements (through which local authorities nominate applicants for housing to PRPs); the role of LSVT; and their statutory powers in relation to the conduct of their tenants (e.g. applying for ASBOs or parenting orders). The appeal was concerned with matters before the implementation of the 2008 Act. Elias LJ noted, though, that, if L&Q was unsuccessful in arguing that termination of a tenancy was a private act in this case, 'then inevitably it will not be under the tighter regulatory regime of the 2008 Act' (at [18]).

He then proceeded to discuss L&Q, specifically noting that it was founded in 1973 and operates with a group structure that includes a diverse portfolio of operations and housing stock (from outright ownership through to social renting). It is funded through rents, private borrowing and grants (between 2004 and 2006, the group borrowed £268.7 million, although this was less than half of its capital finance: at [23]). L&Q has control of its stock, subject to nominations agreements from which 64 per cent of its new lettings came (at [24]).

He then discussed the distinction between 'public *functions*' and 'private *acts*' (emphasis added) noting that the distinction between functions and acts was 'not altogether straightforward' (at [29]). He made the important point that once it is decided that a body is a hybrid public authority within s. 6(3)(b), then the only question is whether the particular act in question is a private act (at [28]). In relation to 'private acts', Elias LJ drew three 'tentative propositions' from the authorities:

> First, the source of the power will be a relevant factor in determining whether the act in question is in the nature of a private act or not. Second, that will not be decisive, however, since the nature of the activities in issue in the proceedings is also important. This leads on to the third and related proposition, which is that the character of an act is likely to take its colour from the character of the function of which it forms part. (at [41])

Lord Collins went further on the first point: 'It is not easy to envisage circumstances where an act could be of a public nature where it is not done in pursuance, or purportedly in pursuance, of public functions'. (at [100])

These points were significant because it had already been conceded by L&Q that it was a hybrid public authority in respect of some of its functions.[1] The only question for the court, then, was whether the act of termination was a 'private act'. That is not to say that the general discussion of whether L&Q is a hybrid public authority was irrelevant; indeed, the reverse is the case because 'the wider context of the housing function' remains important to the s. 6(5) question (at [57] and [66]; also Lord Collins at [95]). The relevant factors, which operated cumulatively and in light of the 'broad and generous construction of the concept of a hybrid authority' (at [72]), were: L&Q places significant reliance on substantial public *capital* subsidy; L&Q operates 'in very close harmony' with local government in respect of its allocations functions, reinforced by voluntary transfers of stock; the provision of subsidised housing is a governmental function making 'a valuable contribution' to the government's objectives; together with supplementary factors (L&Q acts in the public interest and has charitable objectives); 'intrusive' regulations are designed to ensure government policies are achieved, particularly on aspects of allocation and management (at [68]–[71]). Lord Collins, in agreement with Elias LJ, added that the statutory protection afforded to social housing tenants, and the various other activities which were conceded to be, or suggested by the interveners as being, public functions was a further factor (at [101]).

Elias LJ accepted that *Aston Cantlow* and *YL* could be read so that the focus should be on the source of the power being exercised – here, of course, directly on the contract of tenancy. However, he pointed out that the outcome in those

---

[1] Note Elias LJ's comment in parenthesis: 'It could, perhaps, have been suggested that the powers to obtain parenting orders or anti-social behaviour orders were simply powers and not functions, but that argument was never advanced.' [52]; Lord Collins referred to the interveners observations that the powers to demote tenants and for family intervention tenancies were functions of a public nature.

cases would have been different 'if they had found that the nature of the functions in issue in those cases were public functions.' In any event, if the source were the focus of enquiry, it would 'significantly undermine the protection' afforded to victims of hybrid authorities (at [77]). He said:

> In my judgment, the act of termination is so bound up with the provision of social housing that once the latter is seen, in the context of this particular body, as the exercise of a public function, then acts which are necessarily involved in the regulation of the function must also be public acts. The grant of a tenancy and its subsequent termination are part and parcel of determining who should be allowed to take advantage of this public benefit. This is not an act which is purely incidental or supplementary to the principal function, such as contracting out the cleaning of the windows of the Trust's properties. That could readily be seen as a private function of a kind carried on by both public and private bodies. No doubt the termination of such a contract would be a private act (unless the body were a core public authority.) (at [76]; see also Lord Collins at [102])

He went on to consider – and this must, strictly, be *obiter* (and so non-binding) because it was not necessary to the decision – whether the protection should shroud *all* tenants of L&Q. He agreed with the Divisional Court that it should:

> The effect of the grant is not merely to assist the Trust (and other RSLs similarly placed) in being able to provide low cost housing to the tenants in the properties acquired by the grant; it necessarily has a wider impact, and bears upon its ability to provide social housing generally. Furthermore, it would be highly unsatisfactory if the protection of human rights' law depended upon the fortuitous fact whether a tenant happened to be allocated to housing acquired with a grant or not. (at [80])

However, it was accepted that the protection would not extend to tenants 'not housed in social housing at all' (at [81]; it is not clear what he meant by the term 'social housing', but it may be by reference to the definition in the 2008 Act).

Much attention has already been given over in the commentaries to the robust dissenting judgment of Rix LJ (and rightly so). He first analysed the Strasbourg and domestic jurisprudence, indulging in a lengthy but narrow reading of the cases. So, for instance, he noted that there was no example of a non-governmental provider of social housing coming before the Strasbourg court (at [118] although now one might look to *Zehentner* v. *Austria* and the discussion in *Manchester City Council* v. *Pinnock* [2010] 3 WLR 1441, at [50]); his reading of *Poplar HARCA* was that: 'It is clear that this court felt that it was highly relevant on the particular facts that provision (which had started with Tower Hamlets pending an investigation of intentional homelessness) and termination (which only occurred in the light of Tower Hamlets' decision that the defendant was intentionally homeless) were all part of the same function.' (at [125]) He was doubtful even that the minority judgments in *YL* would have supported the Divisional Court's conclusions (at [149]). He then offered ten reasons why, in his view, L&Q's act of terminating the tenancy was a private act for the purposes of the HRA. The focus here is on just some of those reasons, which are of particular significance. In an important passage, which offers a critique of the use of the word 'management' in the context of the way the case came before the court, he said:

> 'Management' is a vast and undifferentiated area which, as it seems to me, inevitably includes functions and acts which are most unlikely to be of a public nature: such as the commercial acquisition or even development of property, or the financing of it (even on the basis that public subsidy plays an important role, as to which see below), or the maintenance and repair of it, or the daily grind of administering a very substantial portfolio of property of all kinds. In my judgment, the acceptance that management of social housing is essentially a single integrated function of a public nature is most unlikely to be correct. Moreover, the Trust operates and manages substantial amounts of property outside the sphere of social housing, or where local authority allocation plays no role: see the figure of 36% implicit in the figure quoted at para 24 above. However, there has been hardly any examination of this issue of what 'management' comprises in practice, and the divisional court has proceeded on the basis that management is essentially a function of either a public or a private nature and chosen between these extremes in favour of the former. It has seemed to me that both sides of this dispute have had an interest in advancing an argument which would dispose, once and for all, of the issue whether an RSL is for all purposes a hybrid public authority or not. (at [151])

He then went on to distinguish between allocation and termination. If allocation was a public function, that did not mean that termination was also a public function because, after an allocation, the tenant takes under a contract regulated through private law. And it was 'counter-intuitive' to suggest that such agreements, which are so well used in private/commercial agreements on a daily basis, would depend on Convention rights, more particularly so because such a contract is for the specific purpose of determining the rights of the parties. (at [153])

Weaver: a critique

There are two issues on which comment is made here: first, the question of the ambit of 'management'; second, the generalisability of the judgment to all of a PRP's social housing stock.

Management

Until twenty or so years ago, the practice of housing management had not been defined in any systematic way. This was partly because of the rich diversity in, and gendered nature of, the history of social housing management (see Kemp and Williams 1991). CHAC considered that the term '*must be used in a sense wide enough to cover the care and well-being of an estate as a whole*' (CHAC 1959: para. 15). However, in the 1980s, defining housing management became a pressing problem in a context in which it was sought to prove – or perhaps identify – the efficiencies of the PRP sector particularly by way of comparison with the inefficiencies of the local authority sector (see, for example, CHR 1989). Lists began to be circulated of the tasks of housing management, which ranged in one list from debt counselling and benefit advice through to community development (newsletters, residents meetings) (see, for example, Clapham and Franklin 1994). Even after this, though, the ambit of housing management remained unclear. In one study, it was noted that housing officers, when questioned about the range and rationale of their tasks, reacted with

> contradiction, insecurity and even puzzlement. While there was general agreement about the core of tasks centred around property management – allocations, lettings, rent collection, management of voids, repairs, maintenance – there was far less agreement about the scope of those tasks which centred on tenancy management – the people end of the service. The role of housing officers was seen to be problematic in terms of definition, and guidance from managers was lacking. (Franklin and Clapham 1997: 15)

The TSA's consultation paper (2009a: para. 4.59) on its approach to regulation, in a section on neighbourhood and estate management, suggested that management is a wide-ranging activity:

> Neighbourhood and estate management covers all aspects of how landlords manage communal areas of housing estates and/or social housing – that is those parts of the property that they own and manage which extend beyond the immediate front door of their tenants' homes. This standard would also deal with grounds maintenance and cleaning of communal areas.

These extracts illustrate the lack of fixity in the notion of housing management (see also the discussion in Chapter 4 above, both generally and concerning its definition for the purposes of the new financial regime); its ambit develops over time in response to different considerations (including government and regulatory policy); it is context-specific; its core may just about be clear, but it is less clear whether other non-core activities are part of housing management; and, finally, some specific activities within the range that are regarded as management in some contexts may not be regarded as functions of a public nature. Indeed, there is no precision in the term and there is some danger in overextending its reach (in the form of defensive practices or just ignorance of the developing law).

There has been little assistance from Parliament either. The Housing Act 1985 defined housing management, albeit it in a different context, as matters related to 'the management, maintenance, improvement, or demolition of dwellinghouses' or 'the provision of services or amenities in connection with such dwelling-houses' (s. 105; cf. Housing (Scotland) Act 2001, ss. 54(2)(a)–(b)). Leaving aside the circularity of the first part of the definition, this still does not delineate the ambit of housing management with sufficient certainty.

This brief survey supports Rix LJ's analysis of the notion of management as a 'vast and undifferentiated area which, as it seems to me, includes functions or acts which are unlikely to be of a public nature … [T]he acceptance that management of social housing is essentially a single integrated function of a public nature is most unlikely to be correct.' And it is to be noted that rarely in this literature has management extended to tenancy termination (indeed, the emphasis now is on management to avoid termination through the provision of welfare benefits advice, for example).

Generalisability

The majority in *Weaver* held that the protection of the HRA (and, it followed, judicial review) extended to all of L&Q's tenants who occupy social housing, not just those occupying properties acquired from state grants, but probably not as far as those tenants who are market renting. The reference to 'social housing' must be taken, one might reasonably assume, to refer to the definition in the Housing and Regeneration Act 2008 (as to which, see above).

One can, of course, see the logic of Elias LJ's position on this. State subsidy cannot be viewed in monochrome but as part of a mechanism through which a PRP pools its entire resources to acquire new properties. But the point of opposition to this logic is that it treats PRPs as homogenous organisations, whereas the reality is messier and becoming more so as these organisations agglomerate, merge and develop their entrepreneurial spirit. Mullins and Craig (2005), discussed above, identified different types of PRP organisational structure on a range from single independent organisation to enforced transfer of engagements – but, across that range, there could be found a variety of different arrangements. From this heterogeneity, questions must arise for PRPs like L&Q (and, one might suspect, all G15 PRPs and similar entities) about the extent of the judgment. Would their 'care and repair' arms fall within the scope? Is it realistic to suppose that shared owners and equity owners are both within the scope? Would this be desirable? Clearly, there is much left unanswered that the courts can now expect to be faced with over the coming years.

Conclusion

The shift in the provision of social housing from local authorities to PRPs has been one of the most significant elements in housing policy engineered in the latter part of the twentieth century. PRPs themselves have also engaged in a process of altering their own internal structures in line with a more private sector ethos. Now these practices have become ingrained, the debates have moved on to consideration of the mission of social housing, and some now raise the following, rather tricky, question as the terrain of social housing becomes further dominated by the influence of private finance: what is social about social housing (see Cowan and McDermont 2009)?

The more pressing questions for the PRP sector, however, relate to the future of its regulation and the extent to which the current and future regulation is fit for purpose. Perhaps it is perfectly proper for the regulator to be a last resort and to rely on complaints. However, the available literature does not necessarily support that confident assertion of the Coalition and there must be concerns about the capacity of tenants to take on that enhanced role. One must also speculate whether the new regime will be sufficiently robust to 'pick up' organisational failure early enough to stave off insolvency and failure (will Ujima happen again?).

If PRPs are public organisations for the purposes of law, the subsequent question concerns whether, and to what extent, that will have an impact on PRP practices at a local level and, more generally, their development programmes. My suggestion is that, if there is any effect, it is likely to be limited because PRPs may well feel that they are protected from challenge if they operate in compliance with Housing Corporation/TSA regulation; likely to influence different PRPs differently, as one might anticipate given their different orientations; and, in any event, will permeate housing management only over a period of time which might, in some cases, be lengthy. As Halliday (2004) notes, the extent of impact of public law depends in part on the legal conscientiousness of the organisation – an observation to which we return throughout Parts II and III of this book.

Part II

Access to housing

Introduction to Part II

It is a common mantra that social housing is allocated according to need while private sector housing is allocated according to affordability. Such assumptions underline much government thinking on allocation of social housing – even though, as we shall see, the government has shifted its thinking, relying to a greater extent on 'choice' in the process; nevertheless choice is balanced against need. However, one of the themes of this part of the book is that these concepts are far too blunt as evaluative tools to explain and justify actual practice(s) as well as the legislation involved in many cases. Indeed, we do not need to draw up sophisticated analytical, jurisprudential, or any other theoretical interpretation of these concepts. Rather, although it might surprise the reader, we find that the law and policy combine often to deny allocation according to need whereas the market (as well as government's influence in it) distorts the notion of allocation according to affordability. In fact, when we talk about need and affordability, we are employing a set of values which themselves flesh out the principles involved. These values are *political, historical, economic, class and 'race'-based*, as well as *spatial*, and provide the basis upon which tenure choice is made.

So, for example, it was not inevitable that home ownership should become the majority tenure. Indeed, as we have seen, this only became true in the twentieth century and for quite specific reasons. Far more important have been the political signals of favouritism (tax breaks and 'talking up'), the decline of other tenures for one reason or another, the incline of mortgage finance, together with the (at times) apparent economic benefits of home ownership compared to other tenures (capital gains). However, it is certainly the case that these benefits have changed over time and at any one time will be spatially differentiated. Furthermore, it is clear that these factors, broad as they are, contain only part of the matrix. All of this makes the task of providing a general account of allocations a daunting prospect.

It is in this context that the notion of 'affordability' must be interpreted. Accommodation becomes more affordable when government involves itself in providing individuals (effectively) with a subsidy to pay for it, and less affordable when government changes the rules so as to withdraw the benefit. Becoming a 'citizen' has seemed to mean engaging in the marketplace as a 'legitimate' consumer (see, for example, Rose 1999). Intervention in the PRS made that market affordable for some. However, it may well be that government involvement creates a sub-market for those who need individual subsidy to access such accommodation. The trap attached to needing such individual subsidy is that it effectively operates in an exclusionary way. The fact that benefits can be lost disproportionately to other income coming in means that receipt of benefits operates as a disincentive. Thus, access to housing for such people can often involve exclusion from other consumptive and labour rights. In other words, the market and its affordability are manipulated by government, as well as other forces, in ways that are not always obvious. Just as government may become committed to support, it can withdraw that support (see the discussion of HB).

'Social' housing allocation takes place in an imperfect quasi-market. This quasi-market actually threatens our use of the terminology, for there is nothing particularly or inherently 'social' about social housing. It was, as we have seen, essentially non-profit-making. However, it becomes apparent that power is involved and exercised either individually or bureaucratically. An individual applicant's power is based upon that individual's *knowledge* of the available options and ability to negotiate a system replete with gatekeeping mechanisms. Administrative processes place an interpretative layer upon the notion of need. This point is elegantly made in the following quotation:

> Housing consumption … is the arena in which systematic inequalities in the social structure are mapped on to systematic differences in the housing stock; and it is a medium through which qualitative variations in the housing stock themselves accentuate and sustain different forms of social differentiation. This occurs in a number of ways, relating to the rules and procedures routinely administered by public bureaucracies, to the market-related criteria invoked in the apportionment of housing finance, and to the broad shifts of power, resources and influence between different tenure sectors that are determined by central government, either directly through housing policy or indirectly through broader strategies for managing the economy. (Clapham et al. 1990: 65)

Often, what it comes down to is that social housing is allocated according to a set of centrally determined priorities that also enables morality – and, specifically, a person's deservingness – to pierce and influence the general principle of needs-based allocations. Certain priorities are set.

The second theme running through this part of the book is of *tenure neutrality* or at the very least *tenure reciprocity*. These terms require explanation. The latter, being the more obvious argument, can be dealt with first. The succeeding chapters in this part deal with issues of access in a broadly tenure-based way, beginning with issues of access to council housing and ending with issues of access to home ownership. Our analysis begins with homelessness but this does not mean that homelessness issues do not infiltrate into other areas. For example, there is an intimate connection between housing solutions for homelessness and home ownership, as one of the housing options available to the homeless is home ownership. So, Forrest and Murie (1991: 132) found that 'many [RTB] purchasers would have been categorised at earlier stages as "problem" tenants with little prospect of purchasing'.

There are links in other ways too. Some social housing is prized because, while it leads to a council tenancy, it carries the further benefit of enabling tenants to purchase their accommodation at discounts which increase(d) depending on length of residence. So, the process of bureaucratic, allocation feeds into, and influences, who purchases their council homes. This raises important questions about who is allocated which property, for there will always be those who are more inclined to buy as well as those properties which would fare well in the home ownership market.

Tenure is fluid, not fixed. This is what I mean when using the term 'tenure neutrality'. I am not saying that there are no distinctions between the tenures – although I am placing a bookmark for the discussion in the next part of this book – but that accessing the different tenures is not in itself tenure-based. So, being accepted as homeless or at the top of the housing register does not automatically lead to being allocated local authority property. It can also lead to allocation in PRP property, in the PRS, or even home ownership (as we have seen). The underlying message, then, is that certain important parts of the consumption of housing are not tenure-based. However, and this is the point, how can we then justify having different methods, bureaucracies, procedures, legislation (or anything else for that matter) of allocating housing which are tenure-based? If we are to have coherence in housing allocations, as seems entirely reasonable, we must accept this facet of post-Thatcherism and re-orient the (broad) law of housing allocations. What we find, though, in Part III of this book, by contrast, is that tenure really does matter, and that rights of occupiers are cast differently depending on tenure. If access operates on a tenure-neutral basis, or leads to tenure shifts, then that tenure difference makes little sense – but that is a point to which we return in the next part.

In this part, two further elements of the new housing system are introduced and discussed: sale-and-rentback and shared ownership. These are similarly examples of tenure shifting. In the former case, this is literal as the seller becomes a renter; in the latter, this may be metaphorical because, in law, the shared owner is, in effect, a renter under a long lease, but the shared owner is also likely to believe that they are the 'owner'. These types of relationship create policy and legal puzzles, as we see, and partly because they do not necessarily 'fit'. That having been said, shared ownership, at least, has and will become an increasingly important part of the policy and legal terrain; and sale-and-rentback is likely to become as much a complex part of the legal terrain as a subject of regulation.

6

Homelessness

Contents

Homelessness is one of the most researched areas of interdisciplinary study. A huge body of knowledge has been accumulated, and some questionable assumptions generated (for example, about its causes – see Fitzpatrick 2005 for discussion). In this chapter, rather than engaging with that broad literature, we undercut it. One of the issues might be framed as 'what is homelessness?'. One can theorise about this question (see Neale 1997 for an excellent account), of course, but here an account is developed which places the legislation (Housing Act 1996, Part VII) and, more, its construction both by the courts and everyday decision-making, at the forefront. All too often accounts of 'homelessness' fail to appreciate that the legislation provides an important context to the discussion, or that legislation is misinterpreted. This is the case in media accounts, particularly, but it is also true of accounts given by those who should know better, particularly politicians.

This focus on homelessness law does not diminish either the politics of homelessness or exaggerate the importance of that law. Homelessness law is intensely political and politics drips both from the wording of the legislation as well as the words uttered by judges. Indeed, that law has been cited as a particular cause in itself of homelessness: people make themselves homeless, it is said, in order to take advantage of the legislative protection. It creates a 'perverse incentive' (DoE 1994: 2.7–8).

Homelessness is, of course, a sharp form of housing need; but homelessness law is not designed, or at least not entirely designed, to assess housing need: 'Legislation has always required us to oppress the homeless by making *moral judgments*, not about their housing need, but about *why* the homeless become homeless in the first place.' (Cowan 1997: 21, original emphasis) That is a view to which I remain wedded and seek to demonstrate in this chapter. It remains the case that those who are characterised as the most deserving or less blameworthy (depending on your view) are those who are likely to complete what has been described as the 'obstacle race' (Watchman and Robson 1981).

One critical question in this chapter concerns not just the implementation of homelessness law but also its 'impact'. Homelessness law is just one of the contexts in everyday decision-making of housing officers charged with its implementation; and that law may be of secondary importance. It is interpreted by local authorities which employ officers to make these decisions, often in self-contained homeless persons units, and it is the local authority which has the decision-making obligation as well as the duty to provide assistance to applicants. However, it needs to be recognised that homelessness law is 'living law', by which is meant that it is an everyday act (or, as we shall see in some cases, omission).

Homelessness law: a brief history

Although the current law is contained in Part VII, 1996 Act, that formulation borrows and only slightly develops its key concepts from the Housing

(Homeless Persons) Act 1977. Previous generations did not entirely absolve themselves from obligations towards the homeless, but the fulfilment of those social obligations was usually combined with stigma on its recipients. Cranston (1985: 35), for example, refers to 'the Act of 1697 (8 and 9 Will III c30), which obliged all those receiving poor relief to wear the letter 'P' on the right shoulder of their uppermost garment (s. 2)'. The 'new' Poor Law, designed by Bentham's disciple, Edwin Chadwick, stigmatised the poor through the workhouse which operated as a disciplining device for those both inside as well as outside its walls (see Longmate 2003). The ideology underlying the stigma applied to recipients has never been entirely removed and the metaphorical effect can be similar.

We should not be surprised by this. The inheritance embraced by the homelessness legislation, from the various Poor Laws to the National Assistance Act 1948 (which supposedly abolished the Poor Laws) to the various interdepartmental circulars about the implementation of the 1948 Act and the way in which that Act was administered, was difficult to shake off as hard as some people tried. For example, the BBC television play *Cathy Come Home* was, for some, the pivotal moment in the modern development of the homelessness legislation (see Loveland 1991b; cf. Jacobs et al. 1999). The play provided a vivid portrayal of a blameless two-parent family which became homeless, were separated, had their children taken into care, and then received dormitory-type accommodation from administrators more concerned as to Cathy's spiritual and moral well-being than her housing need. When efforts were made to redress the outrages perpetuated by that scheme in the Housing (Homeless Persons) Act 1977, the emphasis of the new scheme retained much of the old despite the initial beliefs of Stephen Ross MP, who brought forward the original Bill.

Breaking tradition? The National Assistance Act 1948

The 1948 Act was part of the new social welfare legislation produced by the Labour government which came to power at the end of the Second World War. It was designed to alter the structures of social welfare provision at a fundamental level and mark a break with the past. Thus, s. 1 pronounced that the existing Poor Law was to be repealed. Part III provided the criteria governing the provision of residential accommodation as well as temporary accommodation. Interpretation of those criteria and the duties to provide the appropriate type of accommodation were placed on the National Assistance Board and local authorities (which were taken over by local authority social services departments after the Local Authority Social Services Act 1970). Section 21(1)(b) 1948 Act made it a duty on those bodies to provide

(b)   temporary accommodation for persons who are in urgent need thereof, being need arising in circumstances which could not reasonably have been foreseen or in such other circumstances as the authority may in any particular case determine

The criteria in para. (b) reflect both moral blameworthiness and supply. Thus, the section was supposed to provide for the 'unforeseen and unforeseeable misfortune' (for example, fire razing a home to the ground) and not for 'negligent' or 'foolish' action (the foreseeable eviction): HC Debs, vol. 448, col. 690–2 (5 March 1948). Robson and Poustie (1996: 39) draw attention to those

> Members of Parliament [who] forcibly argued that the effect of the foreseeability test would be to call upon local authorities to exercise an unacceptable degree of moral censorship in determining applications for assistance under the Act and, therefore, should be omitted. The Ministry of Health, however, [successfully argued] that the foreseeability test would cause little practical difficulty. That view was not borne out.

Even though subsequent ministerial circulars suggested that the duty did extend to households who had been evicted, judicial opinion did not go this far (see Hoath 1983: 3; *Southwark LBC* v. *Williams* [1971] 2 All ER 175). The supply element is reflected by the fact that only temporary accommodation was to be provided as well as the apparently limited number of people who would fit within the criteria. Such a 'permissive duty' could be defined by those charged with its interpretation so narrowly as to avoid any obligation.

These two elements were also the central reason for the failure of the Act when implemented. As *Cathy Come Home* visibly showed, both elements represented part of the misery of homelessness. The 1948 Act was really just an extension of the old Poor Law even to the extent of using the same accommodation for its recipients (see, for example, Greve et al. 1971; Bailey and Ruddock 1972; Bailey 1973). Families were separated; people were afraid to apply in case their children were taken into care; the accommodation provided was sometimes in the form of a dormitory.

Ambivalence: 1968–1977

In 1968, the Seebohm Committee on Social Services questioned whether homelessness was a subject which should fall within the proper remit of social work, as opposed to being a housing function. The justification for this view seems to have been that it would remove the 'degrading stigmas and social distinctions' (Seebohm 1968: para. 401). That report was followed by the CHAC report (1969), which suggested that indicators of housing need should also include 'social need' (paras. 56–62), and thus also homelessness. As well as these pivotal reports, there were others written by academics all making similar points (see Greve et al. 1971; Glastonbury 1971).

The point to which these reports were generally moving was simple. Homelessness was not a symptom of personal inadequacy. Nor was homelessness something for which (at that time) traditional methods of social work could or should largely assist. Rather, homelessness could also be seen as a symptom of the failure of the housing market (CHAC 1969: para. 332 where this point was mooted). Both Seebohm and Cullingworth also pointed to the fact that welfare was a function of county councils, county borough councils and, in London, the London borough councils, whereas housing was a responsibility of them all except county councils so that: 'Any successful policy for the homeless therefore depends entirely upon good co-operation being established between a county and perhaps as many as twenty or thirty district housing authorities in its area.' (Seebohm 1968: para. 388)

The confusion between social need, on the one hand, and housing need, on the other, tends to characterise this period and was exacerbated by a subsequent government circular issued by the DoE and the DHSS (DoE Circular 18/74). This circular probably represents the only government action under which the morality of the applicant's actions played no part in local authority decisions. For example, it said:

> The Government believes that all those who have no roof, or who appear likely to lose their shelter within a month, should be helped to secure accommodation by advice, preventive action or, if these are not enough, the provision permanently or temporarily, of local authority accommodation. (para. 8)

The circular accepted that some areas suffered from more acute housing stress than others and thus directed housing authorities, who became the responsible agency, in these areas to give 'first claim ... to the most vulnerable' defined as:

> families with dependent children living with them or in care; and adult families or people living alone who either became homeless in an emergency such as fire or flooding or are vulnerable as a result of old age, disability, pregnancy or other special reasons. (para. 10)

Implementation of the circular, however, was patchy at best. A DoE review suggested that only 60 per cent of housing authorities had accepted responsibility and furthermore that the principles enunciated by the circular were not being followed (DoE Press Notice 15 December 1975, no. 1232; see Carnwath 1978: 21). The legal problem was that the 1948 Act duties remained with social services departments, whereas Circular 18/74 located the responsibility on housing departments. Acts are enforceable; circulars, without the authority of Acts of Parliament, are only exhortatory. The practical problem was that neither agency wished to accept responsibility. Homeless people were often therefore treated as 'shuttlecocks' between the different agencies, neither of which wished to accept responsibility (see Bailey 1976).

Housing (Homeless Persons) Bill 1977

The Housing (Homeless Persons) Bill was introduced by Stephen Ross MP as a private member's Bill, although it had the support of the DoE, and was closely modelled on Circular 18/74. Homelessness was defined as having no accommodation; the priority groups were retained under the term 'priority need'; the principle of not separating families remained an important part of the ideology of the Bill and was expressed as such in its terms; and responsibility for homelessness was 'clearly in the sphere of housing' (HC Debs, vol. 926, col. 899 (18 February 1977)) and thus was to be the responsibility of the housing department.

Nevertheless, the Bill was substantially amended before being enacted, partly because of 'a peculiar juxtaposition of political forces' (Loveland 1995: 69). Some less well-meaning concepts were required to be translated into statutory form. The two initial enquiries required of local authorities – whether a particular applicant was homeless as well as being in priority need – were overlaid with a third and fourth enquiry – whether an applicant was 'intentionally' homeless and whether the applicant had a local connection with the authority to which the application was made.

The drafting of these additional enquiries reflected some of the more concerned remarks of parliamentarians. It seems to have become clear from an early stage of the parliamentary procedure that two central issues would dominate the debates.

The first was the belief that some people would make themselves homeless in order to take advantage of the beneficial effects of the Act. This was variously expressed as 'self-induced' homelessness, 'self-inflicted' homelessness, or 'intentional' homelessness.

Second, it was believed that such people would make themselves homeless to 'jump the housing queue' (see, for example, HC Debs, vol. 926, col. 914 (18 February 1977) *per* Paul Channon; cols. 929–30, *per* Toby Jessel; cols. 957–8, *per* Hugh Rossi). The leading parliamentary opponent of the Bill, William Rees-Davies, exemplified its beneficiaries as scroungers, scrimshankers and queue jumpers (see, generally, HC Debs, vol. 926, cols. 972–5). The Act was not allowing for more accommodation to be built – it was supposed to be cost neutral – rather it was concerned with re-ordering priorities and the administration. Thus, the concern of Rees-Davies and others was that this re-ordering would mean that homeless people would infiltrate their constituencies and take housing away from locals. Rees-Davies argued in this way so that his authority would be able to say to the applicant:

> No – a pox on you. Go back to where you come from. We will not be the local authority responsible for looking after you. (HC Debs, vol. 934, col. 1659 (8 July 1977))

Summary of criteria

The criteria inherited by the 1996 Act from these shenanigans were that applicants – which include both the applicant and any person who normally resides with that person or who might reasonably be expected to reside with that person – have to be found (a) homeless; (b) in priority need; (c) not intentionally

---

[Handwritten marginal note:] The Housing (Homeless Persons) Act 1977 came about as a result of the move to classify homelessness as a housing issue as opposed to a social issue. The initial private members bill was based on circular 18/74. Circular 18/74 was unique amongst governmental policies on homelessness in that it did not seek to make moral judgements on why a person was homeless, but to help those that were roofless (street homeless) to find accommodation. This approach was adopted by the Private Members Bill which defined

homeless. These were by no means 'fixed' concepts, but framed to give local authorities considerable discretion in their interpretation. The definition of homelessness, which appeared the most fixed, was that a person was homeless if they had no accommodation in which they had a licence or some other interest; this clearly extended beyond rooflessness and street homelessness. If the applicant jumped these obstacles, the local authority would be under certain obligations to provide accommodation although, if the applicant did not have a local connection with that authority, the authority had a discretion to refer the applicant back to a local authority with which a local connection existed. These key concepts remain in place although they have been the subject of amendments over time which have increased the scope of the discretion available to local authorities and the complexity of the law.

This history is important for a further reason. Through the apparent dichotomy of whether homelessness should be a responsibility of social services or housing, it highlights the almost inevitable requirement that there should be close interaction between them. As a number of studies (and indeed court cases) have demonstrated, however, this interaction was and remains a key problem (Cowan 1997). Furthermore, the dichotomous nature of the obligations was not removed by the 1977 Act; indeed, subsequent legislation concerning community care and children in need impose separate accommodation obligations on local authorities. One key battleground discussed below involves the relationship between these organisations and pieces of legislation.

Housing Act 1996, Part VII

In this section, we deal with the legislative criteria in more detail (although it should also be recognised that we are skimming the surface of the case law, on which more detail can be found in Arden et al. 2010; Luba and Davies 2010). The essential points to note here are the quantity and depth of the case law; local authority homelessness officers are not always best placed to interpret it as they are unlikely to have the necessary training and updated knowledge; finally, the higher courts have gone out of their way to narrow down the scope of potential challenges to individual decisions, a point to which we come in the next section concerning challenging decisions. Local authorities are required to have regard to the Code of Guidance (CLG 2006e) in the exercise of their functions under Part VII (s. 182). Such guidance is just that, i.e. guidance, and not to be regarded as superior to the legislative provisions – it can be found to be incorrect – but it is often interpreted as if it were 'the law'.

Generic issues

Gatekeeping applications

The threshold for making a homelessness application is low. Providing that 'the authority have reason to believe that he is or may be homeless or threatened with homelessness' (s. 183(1)), the authority has a duty to make relevant enquiries (s. 184(1)); and, if it has reason to believe that the applicant is also eligible and in priority need, it has a duty to provide temporary accommodation, pending its decision (s. 188).

The process of implementing the homelessness legislation is often a complex method of rationing access to a limited supply of accommodation, which operates in a number of ways (see, generally, Lidstone 1994). Carlen (1994) identifies bureaucratic or professional procedures which have the effect of deterring applicants (from calling themselves homeless), denying applicants (the legal status of homelessness), and disciplining applicants into withdrawing their status. 'Front of house' staff can misdirect a person away from the Homeless Persons Unit (HPU) to a different part of the authority (Lidstone 1994: 469; Anderson and Morgan 1997). The HPU officers' interviewing techniques can be aggressive or make the applicant feel that they have no hope of accessing accommodation in this way (see Malos and Hague 1993: 42). Decision letters might not be sent to applicants who are then expected to find out about decisions by osmosis or telephoning the authority (a daunting process in itself) (Cowan and Halliday et al. 2003).

The notion of gatekeeping must also be related to the direction of housing policy, which is (naturally) to reduce the numbers of homeless households. There has been some remarkable success in the prevention of homelessness revealed by the CLG's experimental statistics on the subject (CLG 2010h). These estimate that 165,200 cases of homelessness prevention or relief took place in 2009/2010; of these, 61 per cent were assisted to obtain alternative accommodation and the rest were assisted to remain in their own homes. On any view, it must be better to prevent homelessness both for the potential applicant and the state. However, these statistics are also worrying from the perspective of social justice; that is, at least some of these applicants may have been entitled to make homelessness applications and obtain accommodation through the Part VII process. This may be an overtechnical concern (it may be better for all to override due process in this way), but the issue is how to balance the Part VII threshold and that natural desire to prevent homelessness. Put another way, and to mix metaphors a little, some potentially vulnerable applicants may slip through the net.

How was this 'success' achieved? One significant policy intervention has been the requirement contained in the Homelessness Act 2002 for local authorities to conduct homelessness reviews, one purpose of which is 'prevention of homelessness' (ss. 1–2; ODPM 2005a: 13–17), which 'should be a key strategic aim' (CLG 2006e: para. 2.3). CLG set a target of halving the number of households living in temporary accommodation by 2010. It is well on the way to doing so.

A key mechanism now used by most local authorities is the provision of 'housing options' advice alongside other techniques, such as mediation between family members (to avoid evictions from the family home) and the provision of rent deposits to facilitate access to private renting (which causes some difficult decisions about gatekeeping, see *R (Raw)* v. *Lambeth* [2010] EWHC 507 (Admin); *Hanton-Rhouila* v. *Westminster CC* [2010] EWCA Civ 1334). Some mediation schemes report high levels of success (Pawson, Netto, Jones et al. 2007). However, there has been concern that these targets and processes encourage, indeed 'incentivise', gatekeeping and result in unlawful practices given the low threshold for making an application (Pawson, Netto, Jones et al. 2007: 872). For example, failing to participate in mediation and reports from mediators can result in a 'not homeless' finding, which effectively compels participation (the antithesis of mediation, a voluntary process). The tightrope on which local authorities walk between empowering individual choice and denial/deterrence is illustrated by the Code of Guidance:

> In many cases early, effective intervention can prevent homelessness occurring. Housing authorities are reminded that they must not avoid their obligations under Part 7 of the 1996 Act ... but it is open to them to suggest alternative solutions in cases of potential homelessness where these would be appropriate and acceptable to the applicant. (CLG 2006e: para. 2.3)

In *Robinson* v. *Hammersmith & Fulham LBC* [2007] HLR 7, the Court of Appeal was faced with the problem of a local authority which, while Robinson was 17 years old (and therefore in priority need on the facts of the case), sought mediation between Robinson and her mother. That effectively enabled the authority to delay its decision until she was 18 years old (and not in priority need). The court clearly encouraged the use of mediation but not as an alternative to homelessness decision-making; as Jonathan Parker LJ put it 'the process of mediation is wholly independent of the s. 184 inquiry process ... a local authority has, in my judgment, no power to defer making inquiries pursuant to s. 184 on the ground that there is a pending mediation' ([42]).

In *R (Kelly & Mehari)* v. *Birmingham CC* [2009] EWHC 3240 (Admin), Birmingham was found to have been unlawfully gatekeeping its temporary housing stock by refusing to provide applicants with temporary accommodation pending the investigation of the application, unless there was a risk of harm to the applicant. Although the council argued that this was the fault of individual officers, it was also likely to have been a policy of the council – at least, none of the information and internal guidance notes actually referred to the duty to provide temporary accommodation pending enquiries. As Hickinbottom J said (at [39]):

> I cannot accept the submission put on behalf of the Council that the errors in those two cases were the individual errors of Council Officers who, contrary to the Council's proper practice and procedures, erred in deciding whether to offer interim accommodation to Mr Kelly and Mr Mehari pending a completion of the enquiries being made under Section 184. With respect to the Council, that appears unfair to those officers ... None of the officers purported to apply the Section 188 criteria. None of the Council's documents explained that they should

do so, nor did their external documents explain or suggest to applicants that those criteria would be applied. The Section 188 duty to afford interim accommodation pending the conclusion of enquiries under Section 184 is part of a comprehensive and coherent statutory scheme: but the Council treated what they called the application for 'emergency accommodation' as a discrete and separate exercise, divorced from the substantive housing application. There is certainly some evidence that housing applications are not registered until after the initial approach, and even as late as the housing interview: but I do not have to make findings in that specific regard. I am satisfied that, far from the errors in these cases being of individuals who went outside the Council's practice and procedures, the relevant officers were following the practice and procedure they were encouraged to follow by the Council themselves.

Matters got worse for Birmingham, however, in *R (Khazai)* v. *Birmingham CC* [2010] EWHC 2576 (Admin). On 24 February 2010, a direction was sent to senior officers to cascade down to other officers, in the following terms: 'Please note with immediate effect all single homeless who are presenting as homeless/roofless and Domestic Violence victims requiring refuge must be referred to the appropriate funded support service. We should not be completing a homeless application.' This was clearly unlawful, bearing in mind the threshold for completing a homelessness application. Although it was claimed that this direction had been retracted, the evidence was less clear and the judge was unable to conclude that it had been retracted effectively (partly because an internal email said that non-compliance with the direction was being monitored). It was also argued that the council had a 'same day' policy for its decision-making to avoid the requirement to provide temporary accommodation pending the decision – that argument was not accepted by the judge, although it does appear to have been marginal. It had also been argued that the manager responsible for the direction was guilty of misfeasance in public office, which, again, was unsuccessful. In the event, the judge granted a declaration against the council on the basis of its unlawful gatekeeping practices around applications, because:

> [what is] unique to the present proceedings, is that there has been a significant history of criticisms of the Council in operating Part 7 in the past and a decision of this court only a couple of months or so prior to the material decisions in the present cases which roundly condemned the systemic failure then perceived to be affecting the decision-making processes. A declaration from the court can reinforce the message that the house needs to be put in order and is justified on the basis that it fosters good administration. (at [78])

Meaning of 'accommodation'

Although an apparently neutral word used throughout Part VII, a considerable body of law has formed around the meaning of the word 'accommodation'. Initially, the definition of homelessness was simply having 'no accommodation' and there was similarly no qualification to the nature of the accommodation to be provided to successful applicants. In *R* v. *Hillingdon LBC ex p*

Puhlhofer [1986] 1 AC 484, the House of Lords held that a family with two children living in one room in short-term accommodation was not homeless. Lord Brightman (at p. 517) argued that:

> In this situation, Parliament plainly, and wisely, placed no qualifying adjective before the word 'accommodation' in section 1 or section 4 [of the 1977 Act], and none is to be implied … Nor is accommodation not accommodation because it might in certain circumstances be unfit for human habitation … or might involve overcrowding.

Puhlhofer did not disturb the earlier High Court decision that accommodation in a refuge for victims of domestic violence would not be 'accommodation' for the purposes of the Act (*R* v. *Ealing LBC ex p Sidhu* (1982) 80 LGR 534).

The Housing and Planning Act 1986, subsequently introduced two amendments to the legislation in order to combat this judicial approach. First, the definition of homelessness was amended so that the accommodation previously occupied had to have been 'reasonable for [the applicant] to continue to occupy'; reasonableness was also related to the local authority's housing circumstances (following the definition of accommodation in the intentional homelessness provision). Second, the accommodation to be offered to the applicant would have to be 'suitable'. The first amendment left the relationship between homelessness and intentionality open to question.

In *R* v. *Brent LBC ex p Awua* [1996] AC 55, the House of Lords again returned to this issue, the question being in part: 'when is accommodation unreasonable to continue to occupy?' Lord Hoffmann said (at 68A–C):

> [T]here is nothing in the Act to say that a local authority cannot take the view that a person can reasonably be expected to continue to occupy accommodation which is temporary … [T]he extent to which the accommodation is physically suitable, so that it would be reasonable for a person to continue to occupy it, must be related to the time for which he has been there and is expected to stay. A local authority could take the view that a family like the Puhlhofers, put into a single cramped and squalid bedroom, can be expected to make do for a limited period. On the other hand, there will come a time at which it is no longer reasonable to expect them to continue to occupy such accommodation.

All of this raised the question whether *Sidhu* had been correctly decided and, indeed, how long a household living in overcrowded accommodation could be expected to remain in it. These formed the questions for another House of Lords decision, in the joined cases of *Birmingham CC* v. *Ali* and *Manchester CC* v. *Moran* [2010] 2 AC 39. *Ali* concerned in part whether the duty to households, which occupied overcrowded accommodation such as to render them statutorily homeless, could be met by simply leaving them in their current accommodation until accommodation became available. Was that accommodation 'suitable' even though it was unreasonable to continue to occupy? Birmingham, being a particularly large, hard-pressed authority, was unable to provide such accommodation in some cases for considerable periods of time. The alternative for the households was to spend lengthy periods in temporary accommodation. *Moran* essentially raised the *Sidhu* issue, so that the question was whether accommodation provided in a refuge for victims of domestic violence could nevertheless be accommodation which it would be reasonable to continue to occupy for a period.

Baroness Hale gave the only speech (acknowledging assistance from Lord Neuberger in its preparation). Her position was to attempt to assimilate *Sidhu*, *Awua* and, to an extent the *dicta* in *Puhlhofer* by emphasising the words '*continue to* occupy', arguing that this expression looks to the future as well as the past. This sleight of hand was significant because it then enabled her to say that, in the *Ali* cases,

> this interpretation has the advantage that the council can accept that a family is homeless even though they can actually get by where they are for a little while longer. The council can begin the hunt for more suitable accommodation for them. Otherwise the council would have to reject the application until the family could not stay there any longer. (at [38])

So, suitable accommodation could be accommodation which it would not be reasonable to continue to occupy, but that did not mean that Birmingham could leave the households there indefinitely: 'There are degrees of suitability. What is suitable for occupation in the short term may not be suitable for occupation in the medium term, and what is suitable for occupation in the medium term may not be suitable for occupation in the longer term.' (at [47]) Whether accommodation became unsuitable was a question for the authority on the particular facts of any case (at [49]).

As regards *Moran*, Baroness Hale was able to come to the same outcome on essentially the same analysis as the Birmingham cases. Ms Moran's eviction from the refuge could not result in a finding that she was intentionally homeless because it was not accommodation which she could reasonably be expected to continue to occupy: 'The important principle established here is that in most cases a woman who has left her home because of domestic (or other) violence within it remains homeless even if she has found a temporary haven in a women's refuge.'

On a separate point, secondary legislation also prescribes an affordability criterion in relation to accommodation, both as regards reasonableness and suitability (Homelessness (Suitability of Accommodation) Order 1996, SI 1996/3204).

The household 'package'

We have already seen that one of the principal purposes of the homelessness legislation was to keep families together. One thing which the founding parents of the legislation could not have foreseen was changes in approaches to co-parenting after separation or divorce. Where the parties agree informally, or a court orders, that the parties' children are to reside with both parents in their separate households (a 'shared residence' order) under the Children Act

1989 (s. 8), do the children '[normally] reside' or 'might [they] be reasonably expected to reside' with one or other or both parents? This question is relevant to whether accommodation is 'available for [the applicant's] occupation' and thus whether the applicant is homeless, intentionally homeless (if they give up their current accommodation) and in priority need.

This question, which had caused considerable practical difficulties for local authorities, arose most forcefully in *Holmes-Moorhouse* v. *Richmond LBC* [2009] 1 WLR 413. There, the family court had made a shared residence order by consent (as a means of effectively mediating between parents, the male partner having been accused of domestic violence which he disputed) and subsequently requested that the local authority provide the male partner with accommodation to fulfil that order. Although Richmond found Mr Holmes-Moorhouse was homeless, it said that his children did not normally reside with him and he did not have a priority need as a result (he did not have a priority need on any other ground).

The House of Lords held that this decision was one for a local authority, not the family court, to make. The essential questions were fundamentally different between homelessness and Children Act proceedings. The welfare of the children is a relevant consideration for the latter, whereas the former is concerned with broader issues concerned with housing the homeless. In twenty-first-century Britain, a child of seven is usually expected to live with the mother, that is the 'objective social norm' to which the Act appeals: 'But the social norm must be applied in the context of a scheme for allocating scarce resources.' (Lord Hoffmann, at [12]) The question for the authority was 'whether it was reasonably to be expected, in the context of a scheme for housing the homeless, that children who already had a home with their mother should be able also to reside with the father'. The council should have regard to the family court's opinion, especially where it gave a reasoned judgment, as well as the wishes of the parents and the children. Ultimately, though, the decision was one for the local authority. The Family Court had been wrong to make the aspirational order that it had made and had no power to 'conjure up resources' where none existed (Baroness Hale, at [37]–[38]).

Disability

This is a slight detour, but an important one, as it has become apparent that certain obligations under the Disability Discrimination Act 1995 (DDA), s. 49A, must also underpin Part VII decision-making. If that was the case, the same is likely also to be true of s. 149, Equality Act 2010, which came into force on 6 April 2011. These obligations should also underpin decisions of public bodies more generally, but they have arisen in the course of Part VII decision-making and are, therefore, considered here for the sake of convenience (but the discussion here should be read across to other chapters). This section begins with a discussion of the meaning of disability before discussing s. 49A and its effect, and then moving on to s. 149.

Definition of 'disability'

A person has a disability for the purposes of the DDA if, subject to the provisions of Sch. 1, 'he has a physical or mental impairment which has a substantial and long-term adverse effect on his ability to carry out normal day-to-day activities' (s. 1, DDA). Schedule 1, para. 2(1), prescribes that an impairment has a long-term adverse effect if: it has lasted at least 12 months, the period for which it lasts is likely to be at least 12 months, or it is likely to last for the rest of the life of the person affected. If the impairment ceases to have a substantial adverse effect, it is treated as if it is continuing if the effect is likely to recur. Where 'An impairment which would be likely to have a substantial adverse effect on the ability of the person concerned to carry out normal day-to-day activities, but for the fact that measures are being taken to treat or correct it, is to be treated as having that effect' (Sch. 1, para. 6). The relevant 'normal day-to-day activities' are restricted to the following: (a) mobility; (b) manual dexterity; (c) physical co-ordination; (d) continence; (e) ability to lift, carry or otherwise move everyday objects; (f) speech, hearing or eyesight; (g) memory or ability to concentrate, learn or understand; or (h) perception of the risk of physical danger (Sch. 1, para. 4).

The guidance indicates the broad range of conditions which fall within the definition of disability including those conditions which have fluctuating or recurring effects (such as, for example, depression) (*Disability Discrimination Act: Guidance on matters to be taken into account in determining questions relating to the definition of disability*, 2006: para. A6). The cause of the impairment is not generally relevant. The use of the word 'substantial' in the DDA 'reflects the general understanding of disability as a limitation going beyond the normal differences in ability which may exist among people. A substantial effect is one that is greater than the effect which would be produced by the sort of physical or mental conditions experienced by many people which have only "minor" or "trivial" effects' (para. B1).

A number of factors are relevant in considering whether the relevant disability is substantial, such as: the time taken to carry out an activity; the way in which the activity is carried out; the cumulative effects of the impairment; the effects on behaviour; effects of environment; effects of treatment (where the effect is to create a permanent improvement (Sch. 1, para. 6(2)) (paras. B2–B16). Treatment, which delays or prevents a recurrence, and the impairment would be likely to recur without that treatment, is to be ignored and the effect is to be regarded as likely to recur (para. C9). The guidance refers to the list of activities contained in Sch. 1, para. 4, as a list of capacities. As long as one of the capacities is substantially affected, directly or indirectly (para. D11), that is sufficient – for example, the guidance specifically highlights the example of an inability to go shopping because of restricted mobility (para. D3). Inter alia, the guidance gives indications of certain activities which would be regarded as substantial impairments, such as leaving home with or without assistance (mobility, para. D20). Further, the guidance lists certain normal day-to-day activities, including the following: 'shopping, reading and writing, having a conversation or using the telephone, watching television, getting washed and dressed, preparing and eating food, carrying out household tasks, walking and travelling by various forms of transport, and taking part in social activities' (para. D4).

Section 49A, Disability Discrimination Act

Section 49A said:

(1) Every public authority shall in carrying out its functions have due regard to –
    (a) the need to eliminate discrimination that is unlawful under this Act;
    (b) the need to eliminate harassment of disabled persons that is related to their disabilities;
    (c) the need to promote equality of opportunity between disabled persons and other persons;
    (d) the need to take steps to take account of disabled persons' disabilities, even where that involves treating disabled persons more favourably than other persons;
    (e) the need to promote positive attitudes towards disabled persons; and
    (f) the need to encourage participation by disabled persons in public life.

A public authority included the local authority as its 'functions are functions of a public nature' (s. 49B(1)(a)), unless the nature of the act is private (s. 49B(2)). The discussion about *Weaver* v. *London & Quadrant HT* [2010] 1 WLR 363 in Chapter 5 above was, therefore, of particular significance here. It will be remembered that the Court of Appeal held that the act of terminating a tenancy was an act of management which, in the context of a PRP, was a function of a public nature. It follows that the same was also true here.

The then Disability Rights Commission (DRC) (now the Equality and Human Rights Commission (EHRC)) issued a Code of Practice concerning the obligations under s. 49A (as it was entitled to do, by s. 53A, DDA) (DRC 2005; the EHRC has adopted that Code). The Code said that 'the underpinning principle is the requirement to take steps to take account of disabled persons' disabilities, even where that involves treating disabled persons more favourably than other persons' (para. 2.4). Section 49A(1)(d) has been described as a 'most important component of the general public duty': *R (Brown)* v. *SSWP* [2008] EWHC 3158, at [37].

In *Pieretti* v. *LB Enfield* [2010] EWCA Civ 1104, the Court of Appeal considered the operation of s. 49A(1)(d) in the context of the authority's exercise of its functions under the homelessness provisions of the Housing Act 1996 and a specific determination by Enfield on review of its own decision. The Court of Appeal gave general guidance as to the meaning and interpretation of that provision. First, and significantly, it found that s. 49A(1)(d) applies both in drawing up general policies as well as in their application in individual cases (at [26]). Further:

For disability to play its rightful part in determinations made by public authorities (including under those areas of Part VII to which Mr Rutledge refers) there must (so Parliament clearly considered when enacting s. 49A(1)) be a culture of greater awareness of the existence and legal consequences of disability, including of the fact that a disabled person may not be adept at proclaiming his disability. (at [28])

The duty to 'have due regard to … the need to take steps to take account' is, for practical purposes little different from a duty to 'take due steps to take account': 'If steps are not taken in circumstances in which it would have been appropriate for them to be taken, i.e. in which they would have been due, I cannot see how the decision-maker can successfully claim to have had due regard to the need to take them' ([34]).

In *R(Brown)* v. *SSWP* [2008] EWHC 3158, the Court of Appeal stressed the limits of the general duty under s. 49A:

There must, therefore, be a proper regard for all the goals that are set out in section 49A(1) paragraphs (a) to (f), in the context of the function that is being exercised at the time by the public authority. At the same time, the public authority must also pay regard to any countervailing factors which, in the context of the function being exercised, it is proper and reasonable for the public authority to consider. What the relevant countervailing factors are will depend on the function being exercised and all the circumstances that impinge upon it. Clearly, economic and practical factors will often be important. Moreover, the weight to be given to the countervailing factors is a matter for the public authority concerned, rather than the court, unless the assessment by the public authority is unreasonable or irrational. (at [82])

As regards s. 49A(1)(d), the court said that this involved a duty to take steps to 'gather relevant information in order that it can properly take steps to take into account disabled persons' disabilities in the context of the particular function under consideration' (at [85]). There was no duty to 'achieve results' ([81]), and the court will only interfere if the public authority has 'acted outwith the scope of any reasonable public authority in the circumstances' ([84]). At [90]–[96], the court put forward six tentative propositions concerning the duty under s. 49A(1)(d):

a. Those in relevant public authorities making decisions which affect disabled people must be made aware of their duty to have due regard to the identified goals: 'an incomplete or erroneous appreciation of the duties will mean that "due regard" has not been given to them' ([90]);
b. The duty involves a 'conscious approach and state of mind' before and at the time that a particular policy is being considered: 'Attempts to justify a decision as being consistent with the exercise of the duty when it was not, in fact, considered before the decision, are not enough to discharge the duty.';
c. The duty is a substantive one and not simply a box-ticking exercise to be integrated within the discharge of the public functions of the authority. A failure to mention the specific duty is not determinative of non-performance

but it is good practice to make reference to the relevant provisions of the statute and codes;

d. The duty is non-delegable;

e. The duty is a continuing one; and

f. A record of decisions taken is both good practice and, if not kept, 'it may make it more difficult, evidentially, for a public authority to persuade a court that it has fulfilled the duty imposed by section 49A(1)'.

The application of these principles, and the finding that they were relevant on individual applications in *Pieretti*, meant that the obligation under s. 49A(1) (d) infused *all* aspects of the Part VII decision-making process. It was immaterial, therefore, that the disability issue had not been raised at the review stage, because the duty was on the authority to take steps (cf. *Cramp* v. *Hastings BC* [2005] HLR 48). The authority was under a duty to make further inquiries into whether the disability existed and its relevance to the decision (in that case, that the applicant was intentionally homeless) (at [36]). *Pieretti* demonstrates just how wide-ranging this provision can be and, equally, how it reverses the burden onto the authority to make relevant enquiries.

Section 149, Equality Act 2010

By s. 149, Equality Act 2010, the s. 49A duty has been altered, indeed expanded, to take account of the reframing of the various types of equalities laws, together with new equalities laws, as 'protected characteristics'. There are eight protected characteristics: age; disability; gender reassignment; pregnancy and maternity; race; religion or belief; sex; and sexual orientation. Section 149 came into force on 6 April 2011. It reads:

(1) A public authority must, in the exercise of its functions, have due regard to the need to –

   (a) eliminate discrimination, harassment, victimisation and any other conduct that is prohibited by or under this Act;

   (b) advance equality of opportunity between persons who share a relevant protected characteristic and persons who do not share it;

   (c) foster good relations between persons who share a relevant protected characteristic and persons who do not share it.

(2) A person who is not a public authority but who exercises public functions must, in the exercise of those functions, have due regard to the matters mentioned in subsection (1).

(3) Having due regard to the need to advance equality of opportunity between persons who share a relevant protected characteristic and persons who do not share it involves having due regard, in particular, to the need to –

   (a) remove or minimise disadvantages suffered by persons who share a relevant protected characteristic that are connected to that characteristic;

   (b) take steps to meet the needs of persons who share a relevant protected characteristic that are different from the needs of persons who do not share it;

(c) encourage persons who share a relevant protected characteristic to participate in public life or in any other activity in which participation by such persons is disproportionately low.

(4) The steps involved in meeting the needs of disabled persons that are different from the needs of persons who are not disabled include, in particular, steps to take account of disabled persons' disabilities.

(5) Having due regard to the need to foster good relations between persons who share a relevant protected characteristic and persons who do not share it involves having due regard, in particular, to the need to –

(a) tackle prejudice, and

(b) promote understanding.

(6) Compliance with the duties in this section may involve treating some persons more favourably than others; but that is not to be taken as permitting conduct that would otherwise be prohibited by or under this Act.

In *Pieretti*, it was suggested that this is a wider provision than s. 49A, which it replaced. The expression public functions in s. 149(2) is a function of a public nature for the purposes of the HRA – thus, *Weaver* is as relevant here as under s. 49A. Local authorities also have specific duties under the 2010 Act, for example, to prepare and publish equality objectives and other information (see, in particular, Equality Act 2010 (Statutory Duties) Regulations 2011). It is clear that the duties under this section apply to all their work, 'including services, policymaking, employment, planning, procurement and statutory decision-making' (EHRC 2011: 41).

Key Criterion 1: homelessness – specific considerations

We have already dealt with the definition of homelessness above. The Act does, however, indicate certain other considerations for local authorities. First, Part VII ironed out an ugly distinction which arose on the terms of the previous legislation between violence which occurred inside the home (i.e. domestic violence) and violence which occurred outside the home. The former would result in homelessness, the latter only if it was unreasonable to continue to occupy the home. Part VII was placed in line with domestic violence legislation and now concerns 'domestic violence or other violence', where violence also includes threats of violence which are likely to be carried out and domestic violence from an associated person (s. 177; as Baroness Hale suggested, there is little reason for the retention of the phrase 'domestic violence', beyond the history of the provisions – *Yemshaw* v. *Hounslow LBC* [2011] UKSC 3, at [9]–[10]). Thus, this new provision is capable of extending, for example, to racial harassment. Second, there has always been provision made for those 'threatened with homelessness', that is to say the applicant is likely to become homeless within 28 days.

On the first point, a difficult question has arisen in relation to the meaning of the word 'violence' – is it limited to physical violence or threats of physical violence, or does it have a broader meaning (to include threats of violence, acts or gestures)? In *Danesh* v. *Kensington & Chelsea RLBC* [2007] 1 WLR 69, the Court of Appeal adopted the restrictive meaning, i.e. physical violence only, partly because the then Code of Guidance seemed to suggest that conclusion (cf. *Bond* v. *Leicester CC* [2002] HLR 6, Hale LJ). The Code was, however, subsequently redrafted and included the following:

> 8.21 The Secretary of State considers that the term 'violence' should not be given a restrictive meaning, and that 'domestic violence' should be understood to include threatening behaviour, violence or abuse (psychological, physical, sexual, financial or emotional) between persons who are, or have been, intimate partners, family members or members of the same household, regardless of gender or sexuality.
>
> 8.22 An assessment of the likelihood of a threat of violence being carried out should not be based on whether there has been actual violence in the past. An assessment must be based on the facts of the case and devoid of any value judgements about what an applicant should or should not do, or should or should not have done, to mitigate the risk of any violence (e.g. seek police help or apply for an injunction against the perpetrator). Inquiries into cases where violence is alleged will need careful handling. See Chapter 6 for further guidance.

Despite that redraft, *Danesh* was accepted as good law by the Court of Appeal in *Yemshaw* v. *Hounslow LBC* [2010] HLR 23; where the Code conflicts with the statute, it is the statute which must prevail (at [29]). The Code, in this case, was wrong. Further, the court agreed with part of the reasoning in *Danesh* that the broader interpretation

> would inevitably give rise to greater practical difficulties on the part of the housing authority than a definition limited to physical violence. An assessment would have to be made of the subjective views and objective vulnerability and sensitivity of those claiming to be the subject of domestic violence, making the allocation of the scarce resource between competing applicants even more difficult. Those are precisely the type of considerations for which the Secretary of State might feel compelled to make provision in an Order under section 177(3). (at [32])

On appeal, however, these decisions were overturned by the Supreme Court ([2011] UKSC 3), unanimously (but not without some hesitation – see Lord Brown). Baroness Hale began by acknowledging that there was a 'passporting' effect of the violence provision because, once accepted, then it is no longer reasonable for the applicant to continue to occupy accommodation, which also means that the applicant could not be found intentionally homeless and nor could they be referred back to another local authority where the perpetrator lived ([7]–[8]).

The court held that violence extended beyond actual physical violence, and adopted the definition used in family court proceedings: "'Domestic violence" includes physical violence, *threatening or intimidating behaviour and any other form of abuse which, directly or indirectly, may give rise to the risk of harm'* (*Practice Direction (Residence and Contact Orders: Domestic Violence) (No. 2)* [2009] 1 WLR 251, at [2], emphasis added; *Yemshaw*, at [28]). The court did so partly through historical analysis of the ambit of the provisions and partly by reference to a principle of statutory interpretation which regards a statute as 'living law'. In other words, in this particular context, the meaning of the statutory provision could not be regarded as fixed in time but developing alongside our broader understandings alongside a purposive approach to the provisions (see *Fitzpatrick* v. *Sterling HA* [2001] 1 AC 27). The purposes of this provision were regarded as follows:

> In this case the purpose is to ensure that a person is not obliged to remain living in a home where she, her children or other members of her household are at risk of harm. A further purpose is that the victim of domestic violence has a real choice between remaining in her home and seeking protection from the criminal or civil law and leaving to begin a new life elsewhere. (at [27])

It was recognised that this interpretation gives rise to difficult questions of fact for the local authority, but that the key question is not about the past acts but the probability of them happening in the future (as to which, see *Birmingham CC* v. *Ali* and *Manchester CC* v. *Moran* [2010] 2 AC 39; in this sense, one might see this question as a risk assessment). In what is likely to become a widely cited comment, Baroness Hale said by way of conclusion:

> I accept that these are not easy decisions and will involve officers in some difficult judgments. But these are no more intrinsically difficult than many of the other judgments that they have to make ... Was this, in reality, simply a case of marriage breakdown in which the appellant was not genuinely in fear of her husband; or was it a classic case of domestic abuse, in which one spouse puts the other in fear through the constant denial of freedom and of money for essentials, through the denigration of her personality, such that she genuinely fears that he may take her children away from her however unrealistic this may appear to an objective outsider? This is not to apply a subjective test ... The test is always the view of the objective outsider but applied to the particular facts, circumstances and personalities of the people involved. (at [36])

Baroness Hale left open the ambit of the words 'other violence', as she could see both sides of the argument (at [35]). Baroness Hale's judgment in *Yemshaw* may, in future, be regarded as a state-of-the-art reflection on the interpretation of the 1996 Act.

Key Criterion 2: eligibility

This is dealt with in Chapter 8 below.

Key Criterion 3: priority need

The Act identifies four generic groups of applicants with priority need. One we have already dealt with above – where the applicant has dependent children who reside with, or might be reasonably expected to reside with, the applicant (s. 189(1)(b)). A second is a pregnant woman or a person with whom she resides or might reasonably be expected to reside. The third group is of particular interest because it is the main way in which single homeless persons can be found to be in priority need. It also demonstrates the difficult nature of the discretion open to local authorities as well as the judicialisation of key phrases in the Act:

> (c) a person who is vulnerable as a result of old age, mental illness or handicap or physical disability or other special reason, or with whom such a person resides or might reasonably be expected to reside;

The main question concerns the meaning of the word 'vulnerable'. The first point to make is that the notion of vulnerability should be related to the particular criterion being considered. The formulation of vulnerability approved by the courts is that an applicant is vulnerable if they would be 'less able to fend for [themselves] than an ordinary homeless person so that injury or detriment to [them] will result when a less vulnerable [person] would be able to cope without harmful effects' (*R* v. *Camden LBC ex p Pereira* (1999) 31 HLR 317, 330 (Hobhouse LJ), approving a line of cases in this regard). This formulation – one that I have always found quite astonishing – should not be read as a statutory provision. In *Osmani* v. *Camden LBC* [2005] HLR 22, Auld LJ clarified that it requires a local authority officer to ask themselves a hypothetical question about the likely future effects of street homelessness on the applicant, as set against the ordinary homeless person (at [38] 5)). As the Court of Appeal noted in *Shala* v. *Birmingham* CC [2008] HLR 8 at [24], it is 'a legal test which itself makes the dubious assumption that homelessness is something fit people can always cope with'. Being less able to fend for oneself is not just related to finding and keeping accommodation but is more general than that (for example, having regard to the debilitating effects of depressive disorders when facing or coping with street homelessness: *R* v. *Newham LBC ex p Lumley* (2003) 33 HLR 111, [63], Brooke LJ).

Difficult questions arise over medical evidence concerning vulnerability. Local authority officers clearly need assistance from their own medical experts. They can be expensive to employ and operate at different levels within recognised hierarchies (e.g. from nurse to consultant). Entrepreneurialism operates here so that some local authorities outsource their medical advice; one such company, NowMedical, advises 'over 100 housing organisations throughout the UK', charging £35 for 'general' cases and £50 for 'cases assessed by our psychiatrists' (www.nowmedical.co.uk/ – accessed 21 September 2009). It was set up by a GP, Dr Keen, whose reports are well-known by any reader of multiple homelessness assessments. In *Shala* v. *Birmingham CC* [2008] HLR 8, Birmingham's use of Dr Keen's medical assessment was called into question. Here, the applicant was a Kosovan refugee, three of whose children were missing. The medical evidence on her behalf was that she was vulnerable, suffered from severe post-traumatic stress disorder, and was 'quite' depressed for which she was taking 'high dose' anti-depressants. As the internal review process went on, the medical reports became more severe and the local authority's decision that she was not vulnerable was flawed because it had failed to give consideration to those reports which were of real, and possibly decisive, relevance (at [15]).

The Court of Appeal went on, however, to consider Dr Keen's role. He had originally said that the applicant was not vulnerable (he had not seen the subsequent medical reports) as there was 'no particular assertion of severity' by Ms Shala's medical advisors. His opinion was not matched against the opinion of Ms Shala's medical advisors. The court made general comments about Dr Keen's role. He was a GP and not a qualified psychiatrist; he had not examined Ms Shala (which should have been taken into account by the local authority); and did not contact her medical advisors to discuss their opinions. The court said at [22]:

> Advice has the function of enabling the authority to understand the medical issues and to evaluate for itself the expert evidence placed before it. Absent an examination of the patient, his advice cannot itself ordinarily constitute expert evidence of the applicant's condition.

The decision is one for the local authority and it must balance between the opinions of medical advisors.

Secondary legislation has broadened the scope of priority need to include certain other groups as having a priority need, such as: 16- and 17-year-olds who are not owed accommodation obligations under the Children Act 1989; applicants under 21 who were formerly looked after, accommodated or fostered (s. 24, Children Act 1989) between the ages of 16 and 18; a person who is vulnerable as a result of membership of the armed forces, certain custodial offences, and 'as a result of ceasing to occupy accommodation by reason of violence from another person or threats of violence from another person which are likely to be carried out' (Homelessness (Priority Need for Accommodation) (England) Order 2002, SI 2002/2051). It should, however, be noted and remembered that under-eighteens are not entitled to hold a legal estate in land and, therefore, arrangements need to be made in this regard (see Cowan and Dearden 2001; and for the inconvenient outcome, see *Alexander-David* v. *Hammersmith & Fulham LBC* [2010] Ch 272).

Key Criterion 4: intentional homelessness

Section 191 provides the following definition of intentional homelessness:

(1) A person becomes homeless intentionally if he deliberately does or fails to do anything in consequence of which he ceases to occupy accommodation which is available for his occupation and which it would have been reasonable for him to continue to occupy.

(2) For the purposes of subsection (1) an act or omission in good faith on the part of a person who was unaware of any relevant fact shall not be treated as deliberate.

A local authority must show five things: there was a deliberate act or omission; which caused the loss of accommodation; there must be a cessation of occupation (and not failure to take up other accommodation); that accommodation was available for the applicant's occupation; and it would have been reasonable for the applicant to continue to occupy it (see Arden et al. 2010: para. 6.6). Originally (and not unreasonably) described as 'gobbledegook', the provision has been the subject of considerable judicial examination. In one of the earliest cases, Brightman LJ was forced to change the tenses of the section to achieve the desired result (*Dyson* v. *Kerrier DC* [1980] 1 WLR 1205). It is, perhaps, best approached through examples:

Example 1: The applicant left secure accommodation for a winter let which automatically terminated. It was held that the applicant's deliberate act of leaving the secure accommodation for insecure accommodation caused the homelessness (*Dyson* v. *Kerrier DC* [1980] 1 WLR 1205).

Example 2: The applicants were incurring substantial arrears of rent on their accommodation. They were advised to await the result of possession proceedings by the local authority but they left before those proceedings had begun. The House of Lords upheld the local authority's finding of intentional homelessness because the voluntary decision to leave the accommodation was the cause of the homelessness (not the substantial arrears of rent) (*Din* v. *Wandsworth LBC* [1983] 1 AC 657).

Example 3: Deliberate failure to pay rent or mortgage payments which results in eviction is also likely to lead to a justifiable finding of intentional homelessness (*Robinson* v. *Torbay BC* [1982] 1 All ER 726).

Example 4: Deliberately committing an offence (in this case, paedophilia), the result of which, if caught, would lead an ordinary reasonable person to expect that the applicant would be given a long prison sentence which would lead to the loss of the applicant's accommodation (*R* v. *Hounslow LBC ex p R* (1997) 29 HLR 939). This would be the case even if the applicant arranged to have the rent paid during incarceration but that arrangement was never carried out (*Stewart* v. *Lambeth LBC* [2002] HLR 40).

Example 5: Deliberately taking on a mortgage which, taking account of the applicants' previous financial history, and which was about £124 more than the applicants' previous rent per month, caused the loss of accommodation when the mortgagee took possession of the property (even though one such immediate cause was the applicant's loss of employment) (*Watchman* v. *Ipswich BC* [2007] HLR 33).

One key question discussed in the authorities is how an applicant can remove the tarnish of a potential intentionality finding. One answer is through accessing 'settled accommodation', which then acts so as to break the chain of causation; what is settled accommodation is a question of fact and degree. The chain of causation can be broken by other accommodation, but it is unclear what such accommodation might be (and accommodation in a prison is not sufficient: *Stewart* v. *Lambeth LBC* [2002] HLR 40). Accommodation which is unaffordable and occupied only so that the applicant can make a second application (after a previous finding of intentional homelessness) was not sufficient (*Mohammed* v. *Westminster CC* [2005] HLR 47).

An addendum to the Code of Guidance provides advice on intentional homelessness in the context of mortgage possessions, making clear that local authorities 'will need to look at the substantive causes of that homelessness prior to surrender or sale of the property or refusal of an offer of assistance under the MRS [Mortgage Rescue Scheme] or HMS [Homeowners Mortgage Support]' (CLG 2009c: para. 12 – for a discussion of these schemes for assisting borrowers in default, see Chapter 14 below).

The final point concerns acts or omissions in good faith. In *Ugiagbe* v. *Southwark LBC* [2009] HLR 35, the council had made a finding of intentional homelessness where the applicant had refrained from making a homelessness application (as advised by a law centre) because she did not want to be considered homeless. Her landlord allowed her to remain in her accommodation while she bid for accommodation through the waiting list. Eventually, he asked her to leave and she did (without a court order). The council said that, had she sought advice or made a homelessness application, it would have advised her to wait for a court order. Her claim was that she had acted in good faith. Lloyd LJ said that bad faith 'carries a connotation of some kind of impropriety, or some element of misuse or abuse of the legislation' (at [27]). This would catch dishonesty and 'wilful blindness in the Nelsonian sense comes close to that.' But Ms Ugiagbe was not turning a blind eye: 'On the contrary, she had been led to think that she would be treated as within the scope of the homeless duty, and wanted to avoid that if she possibly could. Foolish or not, her subjective motivation seems to me to be the opposite of bad faith' (at [28]).

Duties to the homeless

Where it appears to an authority that the applicant is eligible, homeless and in priority need, the authority comes under a duty to provide temporary suitable accommodation pending its inquiries (s. 188(1)). Bed and breakfast accommodation, which was used considerably by local authorities, is now not to be regarded as suitable for families unless there is no other accommodation available and, even then, only for a maximum period of 6 weeks (Homelessness (Suitability of Accommodation) Order 2003, SI 2003/3326). Accommodation can, however, be outside the local authority's boundaries (although it should be within its boundaries 'so far as reasonably practicable': s. 208(1)) but the local authority must have regard to the particular circumstances of the applicant and their household (*R* v. *Newham LBC ex p Sacupima* (2001) 33 HLR 1). If they place an applicant outside their area, they must give notice to the other authority (s. 208(2)–(4)).

If an applicant is subsequently found to be eligible, homeless, in priority need and not intentionally homeless, the local authority comes under a duty to secure suitable accommodation that is available for the applicant's occupation until the duty ceases (s. 193). Such accommodation will not be secure unless the authority says so. The duty ceases in three broad types of situation – where the applicant no longer meets the above criteria; where the applicant refuses or voluntarily ceases to occupy suitable temporary or permanent accommodation; and where the applicant accepts a qualifying offer of accommodation (s. 193(5)–(7); as synthesised in *Griffiths* v. *St Helens MBC* [2006] 1 WLR 2238, at [34]). The suitable accommodation to be provided may be temporary or permanent. Section 193(5) has been construed as temporary accommodation:

> The local housing authority shall cease to be subject to the duty under this section if the applicant, having been informed by the authority of the possible consequence of refusal [and of his right to request a review of the suitability of the accommodation], refuses an offer of accommodation which the authority are satisfied is suitable for him and the authority notify him that they regard themselves as having discharged their duty under this section.

Permanent accommodation may be provided by the local authority under s. 193(7):

> (7) The local housing authority shall also cease to be subject to the duty under this section if the applicant, having been informed of the possible consequences of refusal and of his right to request a review of the suitability of the accommodation, refuses a final offer of accommodation under Part 6.
>
> (7A) An offer of accommodation under Part 6 is a final offer for the purposes of subsection (7) if it is made in writing and states that it is a final offer for the purposes of subsection (7).
>
> ...
>
> (7F) The local housing authority shall not–
> (a) make a final offer of accommodation under Part 6 for the purposes of subsection (7);
> (ab) approve a private accommodation offer; or
> (b) approve an offer of an assured shorthold tenancy for the purposes of subsection (7B),
> unless they are satisfied that the accommodation is suitable for the applicant and that it is reasonable for him to accept the offer.

(8) For the purposes of subsection (7F) an applicant may reasonably be expected to accept an offer even though he is under contractual or other obligations in respect of his existing accommodation, provided he is able to bring those obligations to an end before he is required to take up the offer.

A local authority may also offer the applicant a 'qualifying offer' of an AST in the PRS but the duty only comes to an end if the applicant, having been provided with specified information, accepts the offer. It does not come to an end if the applicant rejects the offer (s. 193(7B)–(7D)).

The difficult issue which has arisen is over the division of offers between s. 193(5) and (7). The route is significant because the questions to be addressed on any review are different – s. 193(5) only requires the accommodation to be suitable; s. 193(7) requires the accommodation to be suitable *and* that it is reasonable for the applicant to accept the offer (*Slater* v. *Lewisham LBC* [2004] HLR 37). In *Griffiths*, the Court of Appeal held that an offer of an AST in the PRS could be an offer of temporary accommodation under s. 193(5) (the provisions in s. 193(7B)–(7D) are for a permanent offer discharging the authority's duty). In *Ravichandran* v. *Lewisham LBC* [2010] HLR 42, the Court of Appeal held that, where an offer under s. 193(7) is made, the applicant is entitled to three potentially separate reviews: suitability, whether it was reasonable for them to accept the offer, and the authority's decision to discharge duty. Those reviews could sensibly be rolled up together:

> If, however, the decision of the authority as to the discharge of its duty does not take place at the same time as either the review of the suitability requirement or the reasonableness requirement, matters relevant to those requirements which were not taken into account on the earlier review must be taken into account by the authority on the decision review if the matters existed prior to the refusal of the offer, even though they were not raised by the applicant at the earlier review. (at [35](8))

It is always the case that an authority should make it clear which type of offer is being made (that is, under which provision) (*Ravichandran*) but it is not determinative if it does not do so (and applies the s. 193(7F) test: *Vilvarasa* v. *Harrow LBC* [2010] EWCA Civ 1278).

It has always been difficult to challenge successfully an assertion by a local authority that accommodation is suitable, given the wide margin of appreciation and the room for the exercise of discretion enjoyed by local authorities in this regard (see, for example, *R* v. *Camden LBC ex p Jibril* (1997) 29 HLR 785). In *Birmingham* v. *Ali*, discussed above, a further question was whether the applicants, having been found homeless, could be left in their current (over-crowded) accommodation – i.e. that, even though they were homeless in that accommodation, it was nevertheless suitable in terms of the performance of that duty. The House of Lords drew a distinction between accommodation which it would not be reasonable to occupy in the long term (and thus result in a finding of homelessness) and accommodation which, although not reasonable to occupy in the long term, could nevertheless be reasonable to occupy in the short term. Thus, the households could be left where they were for the short term: 'it must be a question, which turns on the particular facts, whether, in any particular case, the period [they continued in occupation of the property] was simply too long' (at [49]). As Baroness Hale put it (at [48]):

> Birmingham were entitled to decide that these families were homeless even though they could stay where they were for a little while. But they were not entitled to leave them there indefinitely. There was bound to come a time when their accommodation could no longer be described as 'suitable' in the discharge of the duty under section 193(2).

However, if the applicant has no local connection with the local authority to which application was made ('the first authority'), and has a local connection with another authority ('the second authority'), the first authority can refer the applicant to the second authority (ss. 198–201; see also the guidelines for local authorities and referees in relation to the procedure for local connection referrals contained in Annex 18 of the Code of Guidance, although this is not part of the statutory Code).

Where an applicant is found eligible and homeless but not to have a priority need and to be intentionally homeless (or not, as the case may be), the authority has a duty to provide 'advice and assistance in any attempts he may make to secure that accommodation becomes available for his occupation' (ss. 190(3), 192(2)); and, in the same circumstances, if the applicant is not intentionally homeless, the authority has a power to provide accommodation (s. 192(3)). Where the applicant is found eligible, homeless, in priority need but intentionally homeless, the duties are to provide advice and assistance as well as to secure accommodation for such period as will give the applicant a 'reasonable opportunity' to secure accommodation. It is also to be noted that applicants who are found to be homeless are afforded a 'reasonable preference' in the allocations scheme (s. 167(2)(a)).

A pause for thought ...

Let us now take a pause from this heavy duty, complex law and approach decision-making from an alternative angle: what do we know about decision-making itself? Socio-legal researchers have been particularly active in assessing decision-making, not just its quality but also the types of practices involved. From the outset, this research suggested that decision-making practices were often characterised by unlawfulness (Loveland 1993; 1995, ch. 7; Widdowson 1981; Birkinshaw 1982). Loveland's research (1995: 190–2) had raised the question about differential awareness of, and conformity to, lawful decision-making procedures and outcomes. His research found *ultra vires* decision-making to the extent that, in withering terms, he characterised (1991a: 22) legalism as

> an intruder into the administrative arena. It does not prescribe administrative behaviour, but challenges it. It does not facilitate the decision-making

process, rather it gets in the way. It is not respected, but ignored. And if it cannot be ignored it is grudgingly accepted as an unrealistic impediment to rational decision-making.

Perhaps the most significant recent research is that reported by Halliday (1998; 2000a; 2004). Halliday asks a slightly different question to Loveland about the *impact* of law, or, more precisely, what are the barriers to the influence of case law on bureaucratic decision-making? And, because of this question, his research took place in three HPUs which had been the subject of intensive judicial scrutiny. Like Loveland, Halliday notes the importance of the contexts in which decision-making takes place. Homelessness assessment departments are complex, heterogeneous organisations with different pressures forcing different types of approaches. In relation to the decision-making environment, he notes (ch. 5) the influence of a number of (non-inclusive) factors: the importance of local resources, especially as regards the provision of temporary accommodation; performance audit and the impetus of Best Value in setting targets for decision-making together with performance-related pay; political pressure from councillors (which might also lead to 'subversive' decision-making); and what he refers to as 'more remote features of the political, social and economic landscape' (2004: 99), such as around the construction of bogus welfare claims.

Subsequent qualitative research in two assessment departments characterised them as 'the audit authority' and 'the risk authority' because of the importance of these influences (Cowan and Halliday et al. 2003). The former refers to the governing practices implied when an organisation makes the value(s) of audit uppermost in its organisational culture; the latter where the department prioritises the applicant's tenantability and uses the legislation as a risk assessment tool (asking the question: on the basis of our knowledge of this applicant, will they make a good tenant?). In the latter case, there was a multiplicity of interlocking and overlapping databases used by the authority through which risk was defined and assessed (albeit crudely and in a limited fashion).

Halliday also notes two characteristics of the decision-making he observed which were resistant to the influence of the wealth of law discussed in the previous section. These were 'professional intuition' and a 'culture of suspicion'. As regards the former, this was an on-the-job, learned skill which was part of the routinisation of decision-making and concerns whether an applicant is telling the truth or not. It is 'gut feeling' and particularly applied to intentional homelessness. The 'culture of suspicion' was 'organisationally produced and reflects organisational culture' (p. 55) and concerned the openness and truthfulness of applicant's accounts. He talked of a 'siege mentality' among the officers he observed – that is, officers perceived themselves to be besieged by bogus applicants and applications: 'The belief was that applicants learned how to "play the game" when making a homelessness application – that they became aware of how to fill in applications and answer interview questions in order to secure an offer of housing' (p. 56). This culture 'rested in part on ethnic stereotyping ... or in relation to immigrants' (ibid.). These are powerful findings, sufficiently so for

Halliday (2000b) to refer to them as producing institutional racism in decision-making.

The outcomes of this research are important in assessing the value(s) of all this law. It must be remembered that law is but one influence in decision-making and it may not be the most important such influence. Other factors can predominate. Lawyers may seek to (and may have to) make sense of these factors within their frame. As an HPU manager said to Halliday (2004: 66):

> it is so stacked against the applicant that when the barrister draws up an affidavit and puts down what you were actually thinking when you made that decision, it just can get you out of so many things that maybe you didn't think of, that you always thought that you could justify almost any decision that you made ... [W]e won most of the cases, not because we're brilliant, but because, one, it's stacked against them, and, two, we've got a good barrister.

This comment nicely prefaces the next section concerning challenges to decision-making.

Challenging decision-making

Once a local authority has made a decision, it must communicate that decision to applicants including its reasons for a negative decision (s. 184(3) – sometimes referred to as a 'section 184 decision letter'). Applicants have the right to request that the local authority conduct a review of most negative decisions (s. 202), and must do so within 21 days from the date of notification of the decision (s. 202(3)). Such a review, if conducted by an officer, must be conducted by an officer who was not involved in the original decision and is senior to the original decision-maker (Allocation of Housing and Homelessness (Review Procedures) Regulations 1999, SI 1999/71, reg. 2). Generally, such reviews must be conducted within 8 weeks of the request for the review (reg. 9(1)(a), although different time limits apply in relation to certain cases such as local connection referrals) but a longer period can be agreed between the parties in writing (reg. 9(2)). If the applicant remains dissatisfied, they have a right of appeal to a county court on a point of law (that is, the usual grounds for judicial review) within 21 days of being notified of the review decision: s. 204 (time will run from the date of notification of the applicant's agent, if prior to the applicant being informed: *Dharmaraj* v. *Hounslow LBC* [2011] EWCA Civ, 24 January 2011). If the applicant remains dissatisfied, there is the further opportunity for a 'second appeal' to the Court of Appeal, but again on a point of law.

A brief history

Originally, applicants who were dissatisfied with the decisions on their application had to apply to the High Court for a judicial review of the decision. Considerable disquiet had been expressed by the judiciary about the volume of judicial review cases in homelessness. In a much-cited part of his judgment in *R v. Brent LBC ex p Puhlhofer*, Lord Brightman expressed concern at the

> prolific use of judicial review for the purpose of challenging the performance of local authorities of their [homelessness] functions … I think that great judicial restraint should be exercised in giving leave to proceed by judicial review … [I]t is not, in my opinion, appropriate that the remedy of judicial review, which is a discretionary remedy, should be made use of to monitor the actions of local authorities under the Act save in the exceptional case. ([1986] 1 All ER 447, 474)

Subsequent research demonstrated, in fact, that concern about the use of judicial review in homelessness cases was misplaced. Sunkin (1987) reported that there had been just 66 applications for leave in 1985. By 1992, the level of applications for leave to apply for judicial review had risen to around 400 (Bridges et al. 1995: 28–9). This represented less than a fifth of all leave applications for judicial review, and was less than the number of applications in immigration cases (although this figure was subject to considerable fluctuation) (Bridges et al. 1995: ch. 2).

Expressed as a percentage, the proportion of unsuccessful homeless applicants who used judicial review was less than 3 per cent (although this did not include potential cases challenging decisions about local connection or the suitability of accommodation). Further, there was evidence to suggest that some local authorities were using the leave stage to filter out applications, caving in just before the leave hearing (ibid. p. 120). Nevertheless, despite this empirical data, the government's 1994 consultation paper repeated concerns about the 'substantial number of cases in which there is an application for judicial review' and consulted on whether local authorities should be required to have their own 'appeals mechanisms for handling disputes' (DoE 1994: para. 16). The introduction of internal review which followed in the 1996 Act was part of a dual strategy to relieve the pressure on the High Court. The local county court was granted jurisdiction to hear appeals on points of law from aggrieved homeless applicants, with the aim of substantially reducing the judicial review workload. Significantly, homeless applicants must go through the internal review process before an appeal to the county court is possible.

Experiences of internal review

Cowan, Halliday and Hunter (2006) demonstrated that numbers of requests for internal reviews had increased over time since its introduction in the 1996 Act, perhaps because of an increase in volume of homelessness decisions. In terms of overall volume, the numbers of applicants making use of the internal review process was 'much greater' than the use made of judicial review (perhaps not surprisingly given the costs of judicial review). What was particularly interesting, though, was the differences in volume of requests and outcomes between apparently similar authorities. In their qualitative work, part of which involved interviews with unsuccessful applicants who did not use the internal review process, Cowan and Halliday et al. (2003: ch. 5) developed an 'interaction perspective' to demonstrate the barriers to seeking internal review. These barriers were said to include: ignorance of the right to review; scepticism about internal review; a rule-bound image of decision-making; applicant fatigue; satisfaction with a negative decision (i.e. non-aggrieved); does not want/need long-term housing. The point of the interaction perspective was that messages gleaned by applicants from the application process, including interactions with officers, produced these barriers.

Challenging reviews

At a general level of administrative justice, the right of review is the bargain basement. It is cheap and efficient; done well, it can increase the quality of decision-making and may well have an impact in ratcheting up the quality of initial decisions (Cowan et al. 2006). The whole process has been held to be compliant with Article 6, Sch. 1, HRA (*Runa Begum* v. *Tower Hamlets LBC* [2003] 2 AC 430); and is a function capable of being contracted out (Local Authorities (Contracting out of Allocation of Housing and Homelessness Functions) Order 1996, SI 1996/3205; *Heald and Others* v. *LB Brent* [2010] 1 WLR 990, contracting out 'as if it were the town hall catering contract' at [65] Sedley LJ. The process of authorising the contracting out must comply with the governing provisions of the contracting out legislation (Deregulation and Contracting Out Act 1994, ss. 69–70; failure to do so may render the contractor's decision-making void: *Shacklady* v. *Flintshire CC* (2010) November *Legal Action* 20; Carter and Cowan 2010).

Challenging reviews – whether they have been done well or badly – on a point of law is, however, extremely difficult in terms of grounds. The spirit of *Puhlhofer* lives on in this regard. In *Holmes-Moorhouse* v. *Richmond-upon-Thames LBC* [2009] 1 WLR 413, Lord Neuberger said (at [47]–[49]) that decision-letters are not to be closely scrutinised and it should be recognised that review officers themselves are unlikely to have legal experience or training. If decision-letters were over-scrutinised, they would provide less full reasoning, which would not be in the interests of justice. He went on (at [50]):

> Accordingly, a benevolent approach should be adopted to the interpretation of review decisions. The court should not take too technical view of the language used, or search for inconsistencies, or adopt a nit-picking approach, when confronted with an appeal against a review decision. That is not to say that the court should approve incomprehensible or misguided reasoning, but it should be realistic and practical in its approach to the interpretation of review decisions.

This is but one of many such comments which demonstrate how the law is stacked against the claimant. There is something to be said for such sentiments – decision-letters have become of inordinate length (especially in potentially contentious cases) precisely because local authorities are seeking to make their decisions 'bullet-proof' (Halliday 2004). However, at the same time, given that the burden of proof on a claimant to succeed on a point of law is high, such sentiments act to increase the likelihood of failure – they stack the decks even further in favour of the decision-makers.

Other statutory obligations

Although Part VII is the main route for homeless applicants, alternative avenues do exist depending on the applicant's circumstances. The two further housing obligations considered here are owed to certain minors (Children Act 1989) and those in receipt of community care services (National Assistance Act 1948). These obligations belong to social services departments. There are interlocking obligations so that social services departments and housing authorities are entitled to ask each other for assistance (s. 27, Children Act 1989; ss. 170 and 213, Housing Act 1996; and through policy interventions such as the Supporting People programme, as to which see Carr 2005a) but such interlocking obligations are generally weak and ineffectual (see, for example, R v. *Northavon DC ex p Smith* [1994] 2 AC 402). These areas have, unfortunately, generated quite a body of case law for one simple reason: financial restrictions. The applicant becomes a shuttlecock between the departments, which are often at war with each other in seeking to protect (or gatekeep) their budgets (see, for example, *ex p Smith*).

There is plenty of attention given over in guidance to the need for joint assessments and joint working (CLG 2006e: chs. 5 and 12; DoH 2000: para. 5.72; CLG/DCSF 2010) as well as in the case law, but the problem has always been more than financial, branching into the 'discursive'. The discursive problem is caused not just by the different language used by the different departments, but also by different professional approaches (Cowan 1997).

Schemes such as the Supporting People programme do potentially offer a way around these problems, but, as Carr (2005a: 404) suggests, this has been done through 'attempts to weld together an ambitious alliance of welfarist, therapeutic, consumerist, commercial and administrative government practices [which] are inevitably fragile and failure may not be avoided'. Allen (2003) casts a warning note to those who seek to 'join-up' thinking. Drawing on a study of foyers, which offered joined-up working, he suggested that there was a tendency to shift blame onto '"recalcitrant individuals" who were now culpable for their own situation' (p. 299), resulting in a tendency to exclude. As Allen (2003: 304) puts it, 'Strong versions of joined-up thinking make use of holistic practices, which are infallible because they can "see everything, know everything, and do anything"'.

Children Act 1989

The Children Act 1989 contains specific duties to accommodate children in need in certain circumstances, although not necessarily with their parents (s. 20; *R (G)*

v. *Barnet LBC* [2003] UKHL 57). A child in need is defined in relatively broad terms (s. 17(10)). The s. 20 obligation arises in relation to any child in need:

> within their area who appears to them to require accommodation as a result of
> (a) there being no person who has parental responsibility for him;
> (b) his being lost or having been abandoned;
> (c) the person who has been caring for him being prevented (whether or not permanently, and for whatever reason) from providing him with suitable accommodation or care.

The notion of being prevented from providing accommodation has been given a wide construction so that 'children are not to suffer for the shortcomings of their parents or carers' (*R (G)* v. *Barnet LBC* [2004] 2 AC 208; *R (G)* v. *Southwark LBC* [2009] 1 WLR 1299).

The 1989 Act was amended by the Children (Leaving Care) Act 2000 which imposed continuing obligations on local authorities after certain children in need, including those accommodated under s. 20 for a total of 13 weeks or more, had reached 18 years of age and extending at least until the child reached the age of 21. One can see, therefore, that the potential financial consequences of providing accommodation under s. 20 (or, indeed, any of the other general powers in the 1989 Act) could be significant; and, more to the point, it could be avoided by the housing department meeting the accommodation need through Part VII obligations. In *R (M)* v. *Hammersmith & Fulham LBC* [2008] 1 WLR 535, the social services department had effectively passed the 'child in need' on to the housing department which assumed it had an obligation to house her and did so. The House of Lords was distinctly unimpressed by the approach taken by the council (regarding the social services authority as effectively having avoided its responsibilities – see Baroness Hale at [4]), but, nevertheless, found that M was not entitled to these additional services because she had not been provided accommodation under s. 20.

It was not long, however, before the House had to consider the matter again, the other way around: *R (G)* v. *Southwark LBC* [2009] 1 WLR 1299. This time, it was the social worker who had made the Children Act 1989 assessment and referred the matter to the HPU as the child was in need of accommodation and other referrals. Of course, the 2002 priority need SI would automatically mean that a child in need of 16 or 17 years old would be in priority need. However, the House of Lords also drew attention to the exceptions to that, which include where the social services authority was providing accommodation under s. 20. The point, according to their Lordships, was that primacy should be given to the 1989 obligations; the 2002 order was designed to pick up applicants who, for one reason or another, had no such entitlement, 'not to enable a children's authority to divert its duty under section 20 to the housing authority, thereby emasculating the assistance to be afforded to children of 16 or 17 who "require accommodation"' (at [40], Lord Neuberger; also Baroness Hale at [4] and [7]). CLG and the Department for Children, Schools and Families (DCSF) issued guidance on the interaction between the 1989 and 1996 Acts in light of these decisions (CLG/DCSF 2010). The guidance emphasises that it is best for families to stay together, the need for co-ordinated services, as well as noting that some authorities now have integrated services for this client group, and the importance of a joint working protocol.

Community care

Housing obligations are to be found in the National Assistance Act 1948, Part III, and are accessed after an assessment by the social services department (s. 47, National Health Service and Community Care Act 1990). The main accommodation obligation is contained in s. 21(1):

(1) Subject to and in accordance with the provisions of this Part of this Act, a local authority may with the approval of the Secretary of State, and to such extent as he may direct shall, make arrangements for providing

   (a) residential accommodation for persons who by reason of age, illness, disability or any other circumstances are in need of care and attention which is not otherwise available to them; and

   (aa) residential accommodation for expectant and nursing mothers who are in need of care and attention which is not otherwise available to them.

Although expressed as a power, para. (a) becomes a duty (circuitously) 'in relation to persons who are ordinarily resident in their area and other persons who are in urgent need thereof' for persons over 18 years old as well as certain other persons suffering from mental disorder (Department of Health, Local Authority Circular 93(10), Appendix 1, para. 2). The phrase 'residential accommodation' is construed widely to include a range of accommodation, from general needs stock to institutional or sheltered accommodation (*R* v. *Bristol CC ex p Penfold* [1998] 1 CCLR 315; *R* v. *Islington LBC ex p Batantu* (2000) 33 HLR 871). The means of fulfilling that obligation, once it arises, can be through the housing department's lettings policy or through other means, but it is a positive obligation to meet that need once it has been assessed as arising (*R* v. *Kensington and Chelsea RLBC ex p Kujtim* (1999) 32 HLR 579). Challenging a negative assessment is extremely difficult, unless it can be said to be perverse, because, as Hale LJ put it: 'need is a relative concept which trained and experienced social workers are much better equipped to assess than are lawyers and courts provided that they act rationally' (*R (Wahid)* v. *Tower Hamlets LBC* [2003] HLR 2 at [33]; also *R (Ireneschild)* v. *Lambeth LBC* [2007] HLR 34 at [71]). It has also been suggested that the words 'which is not otherwise available to them' are significant in limiting local authority social services' obligations (*R (Wahid)* v. *Tower Hamlets LBC* [2003] HLR 2, at [28]). Be that as it may, it remains a method of circumventing a negative homelessness finding in certain cases (see *R (Bernard)* v. *Islington LBC* [2002] EWHC 2282 (Admin)).

The future

The principal policy issue in relation to homelessness, which has particularly influenced past Conservative governments (e.g. DoE 1994), has been the concern that there is a perverse incentive to use this 'route' into social housing, rather than seek a private sector 'solution' to housing problems. This concern has resurfaced under the Coalition government. In its consultation paper, the government argued that the existence of the homelessness 'route', together with the main homelessness duty under s. 193(7)

> encourages some households to apply as homeless in order to secure reasonable preference and an effective guarantee of being offered social housing. Around 21 per cent of social lets to new tenants are allocated to people owed the main homelessness duty, many of whom will have been provided with expensive temporary accommodation while waiting in the housing queue. (CLG 2010e: para. 6.8)

Households may have a priority need for housing, it continues, but that does not necessitate the provision of *social* housing. Therefore, the proposal, incorporated in the Localism Bill, is to alter the way in which the duty can be brought to an end to include consideration of the provision of an AST in the PRS for a minimum term of 12 months; and the duty would recur if the applicant becomes homeless again within 2 years of that offer (paras. 6.10–17). This amendment effectively returns to the original position under the 1996 Act (the main homelessness duty was amended by New Labour thereafter) but the recurrence of the duty is new (and, perhaps, suggests that the Coalition government has learnt a political lesson from the perceptions about the 1996 Act as originally drafted).

Conclusions

What we can (amply) demonstrate from this chapter is the juridification of homelessness. Homelessness itself has been abstracted and relocated within the court system, leading to complex decision-making and haphazard outcomes. Judges have been extremely wary of getting into the minutiae of decisions, deferring their role to the busy reviewing officer who provides that link between the authority and the courts. Yet, one question concerns the extent to which any of this law really matters. Here, as the research suggests, one needs to be alive to the contexts in which decision-making takes place; it is these contexts which shape the outputs, decisions and reviews, as much as, if not more than, the law. And it is those contexts which are obscured by the welter of law.

7

Allocating social housing

Contents

In the previous chapter, we saw that there has been a process of juridification around the concept of homelessness, which simultaneously obscures the social processes underlying homelessness law. It thus fits neatly into the governing themes of this part of the book, of top-down law and bottom-up implementation, the former making assumptions about the latter, while the latter being seemingly often blissfully ignorant of the former.

This chapter discusses the broader process of social housing allocation – that is, the allocation of social housing units to households in need (which might include homeless households). The same themes re-emerge here but in different patterns. There is law – not as much as in homelessness, but enough to produce retrenchment; and government policy has moved in tune with local entrepreneurial initiative, thus marginalising the law. There have been policy shifts away from bureaucratic allocation of social housing to a market-based system of letting households choose their housing (choice-based lettings (CBL)).

Underlying the chapter is the basic assumption that has, in the past, often been made that the allocation of social housing must be made according to some criteria of need. This is based on an assertion of demand for a limited resource. In a general way, this may or may not be right but, like all general assertions in housing at any rate, it needs to be modified. In high-density housing areas, like London or some other urban centres, demand for social housing may well outstrip its supply. However, that is not always the case and, increasingly, social housing providers have to change their orientation – rather than waiting for households to register with them, they have to compete for occupiers along with other sectors of the housing market. Indeed, and this takes the argument one stage further, it has been suggested that a reliance on just housing those in need not only marginalises those offered housing but it also produces socially excluded problem estates. The goal, then, for practitioners, is for mixed communities which, so the argument goes, are more sustainable (Page 1993). One consequence of this is that need has become a highly contested concept; indeed, some question if it is fit for purpose (see, generally, Dwelly and Cowans 2006). A further consequence is that the Coalition government's reforms take the increase in social housing waiting lists as their starting point.

In the first section, the history of this area is set out and a specification of failure is drawn up, answering the question, what went wrong? Two themes are identified in the following section – CBL and sustainable communities – which together have been seen as part of the solution. We then go on to analyse the extent to which law intrudes onto these policy solutions. In the next section, we look at the vital role played by PRPs in social housing allocation. It will be remembered from Part I of the book that, for the past twenty or so years, the domain of social housing providers has expanded considerably. PRPs are now central figures and local authorities must rely on them to fulfil their duties. On the other hand, PRPs have their own pressures and are independent organisations. Our essential question in this chapter is about the ways in which law can insert itself into these bureaucratic processes. We cannot hope to provide a comprehensive analysis (for which, see Arden et al. 2010; Luba and Davies 2010) but an overview, and one which demonstrates the inherent tension in the concept of 'housing need'. Finally, attention is given to the Coalition's proposals for reform.

What went wrong?

History

It is reasonably clear that, when social housing was first developed on a mass scale in the post-First World War era, little thought was given to who was going to use it. Anne Power (1987: 66) memorably has noted that 'councils became landlords without commitment, plan or forethought'. The idea that the state was going to produce 'homes fit for heroes' (as discussed in Chapters 1 and 4 above) makes certain assumptions, not just about the failure of other housing tenures. This new housing was to be fit for *heroes*, a tall order by any stretch, and consequently expensive; indeed possibly too expensive for many of the heroes themselves to rent (Bowley 1945: 129). But that was not quite the point. The assumption was that this new housing would produce a 'filtering-down' process. Those who could afford the new housing would move into it, and thus free up their housing for other households. In time, the poorer quality housing would fall into disuse and be replaced by better quality housing. That assumption proved false (see Burnett 1986: 242; Cowan and McDermont 2006).

The Ministry of Health provided guidance in 1920 which suggested 'the careful selection of tenants' and 'the elimination of unsatisfactory tenants', but did not offer any criteria under which such assessments could be made. Housing need was invented, it was fair to say, to answer this question subsequently, when it was realised that the filtering-down assumption was false and, perhaps more fundamentally, when the 'big question' of social housing was asked: who was this new building for? This problem became more and more significant during the 1920s as properties were being mass constructed and at a time of impending financial crisis. It was now that the welfare role of council housing was given prominence. In a succession of Ministry of Health annual reports, beginning in 1929–1930, the problem of administration of council housing came to be constructed as a problem of need, requiring the development of new techniques of management. It was said that the purpose of local authority housing was to provide for those 'who are least eligible in the eyes of the private owner' and made reference to the statutory 'reasonable preference' to be given to those with larger families. Although this was said to produce difficulties in rent collection, the ministry advised on the use of differential rents (requiring better off households to pay more, to offset the rents of those who were less well off: Ministry of Health 1930).

In the subsequent report, the question of rent was linked with need – there were those tenants who could afford private sector rents 'and whose continued occupation of the houses at subsidised rents means the exclusion of those whose need is unquestionably greater' (Ministry of Health 1931: 97). Thus, in identifying need as an organising concept, the Ministry of Health was also identifying the role of council housing: it was the provision of property at a subsidised rent for the short term until the household could afford to exit the tenure for private renting. The limited, residual role envisaged for municipal landlordism mirrored the prevalent belief that the private sector would soon be able to provide for all.

The Committee on Local Expenditure (1932), set up in the wake of recession, gave just two paragraphs to the 'management and allocation of accommodation' and echoed the ministry's view on targeted assistance: 'subsidies should not be wasted by being given to those who do not need them'. The committee thought that tenants who could afford to should pay higher rents 'to increase the revenue obtainable to reduce the loss arising from housing estates'; or vacate their properties which could then be sold on the open market or let to poorer households (para. 95). Thus, in this period the notion of need mutated into an organising principle not only of who should get council housing, but also how long they should get it for. Indeed, the London County Council wrote to 300 tenants in 1933 suggesting that they vacate their properties in the interests of those persons whose need was greater.

By this time, the emphasis on need as the selection criterion was also required because the focus of council housing had shifted away from new building for the better-off working class to slum clearance and the rehousing of slum dwellers. This was accompanied by a shift in focus towards more intensive 'management' of occupiers.

Slum clearance devalued the tenure in the popular consciousness: slum clearance estates were 'stigmatized as "rough" and their occupiers sometimes shunned' (Holmans 1987: 178). Some local authorities were also concerned at the slum dwellers' 'bad influence on other council tenants' (Schifferes 1976: 66). Thus, councils experimented with methods of dealing with this pauperised population, of discipline and normalisation by cutting them off 'in special blocks under close supervision until they proved themselves capable' (Kemp and Williams 1991: 130). Before households were accepted or offered housing, they were subjected to the 'housing visitor'. Damer (1976: 73) draws on the forms used by these personnel in Glasgow which required the visitor to differentiate the type of person, cleanliness, and furniture from 'very good' to 'unsuitable'. Such judgments were largely based on the 'detective work' of these employees who were specifically employed because of their experience as middle-aged married women (Damer and Madigan 1974: 226).

Although housing need appears neutral, this brief foray into its emergence and development suggests that it is anything but neutral. It was used to legitimate decisions about entitlement based on who was most deserving, and to legitimate most intensive 'management' of those who were not in that category. This history is important because 'housing need' subsequently becomes an object – a mantra – which is repeated again and again as the positive reason for not only having, but also needing, social housing itself. Indeed, in the post-Second World War period, housing need became the subject of technical expertise. So, for example, in its 1949 report, a CHAC sub-committee considered that properties should be let to those 'in the greatest housing need', which implied a hierarchy of housing needs and which were subsequently specified (overcrowding, ill-health, lack of a separate home, condition of dwelling, exceptional cases, and other factors) (CHAC 1949: paras. 7 and 15–24).

Objectivity was the key to housing need, and this objectivity was emphasised in this and subsequent reports of the CHAC. Thus, schemes which took no account of housing need – such as allocation on the basis of date of registration (a strict queuing scheme) or on the basis of 'pure' discretion (or, more brutally, political whim) – were deprecated. Schemes based on the awarding of points to households for need, or banding schemes (under which households would be placed into broad bands of housing need), were generally regarded as proper.

A specification of failure

It is now generally acknowledged that the principles of housing allocation developed during the twentieth century were flawed at a pretty fundamental level. In short, they became overly bureaucratic, often opaque (and thus lacked transparency), discriminatory, and often resulted in the wrong households being allocated the wrong housing. Four broad reasons form the epicentre of this critique: discretion; complexity; risk; and the production of problem estates.

The first part of the critique concerned the use of discretion. The open-ended obligation that 'reasonable preference' should be accorded to certain types of households provided a discretion which was too broad:

> discretion was depicted as the bug in the system – a source of deviance which allowed short-term management goals to compromise the principle of social justice. It was the smokescreen behind which housing departments infused an agreed hierarchy of needs with a range of other, more dubious, allocative principles. (Smith and Mallinson 1996: 341)

The solution, on this view, was to provide closer attention to rules, the supposed binary opposite of discretion (cf. Sainsbury 1992). A further problem with discretion was opened up by a more discrete research enquiry into the role of selection and allocation systems in the systematic direct and indirect processes of discrimination against black and ethnic minority households (see, for example, the classic study by Henderson and Karn 1987). Yet, more formally bounded rules did not alter these effects because of the impact of broader socio-economic disadvantage. Indeed, Jeffers and Hoggett (1995) found, in a study of Haringey and Lambeth, that even when systems were designed explicitly to avoid discrimination, black and minority ethnic households still ended up with worse quality housing.

What emerged from the abundant research into council house allocation was the way in which the operationalisation of need depended on a system of 'political influence, by possessing a bargaining counter, or by articulacy and social acceptability' (Jones 1988: 98). Political influence was not just a question of individual households being assisted, but also of the more systematic way priority was given to households wishing to transfer within the sector (Clapham and Kintrea 1986; see also above). This could be justified in a number of ways – as rewarding long-standing tenants, as opening out the accommodation they were leaving for new tenants, as being a rational use of available accommodation. Broadly, however, its effect was that those who could 'afford' to wait longest were rewarded with the best properties. One might say, then, that despite the discourse of social housing management emphasising the role of need, it relied for its efficacy upon bargaining instincts similar to those in the private sector, and that leads inevitably to inequity.

Second, schemes had become incredibly complex, running to pages and pages in some high-demand areas. This was a direct result of the solutions emerging from the rule–discretion debate. Indeed, a casual reading of the CHAC reports of 1949 and 1969 make clear that a shift to rules required greater complexity. However, it was also made possible by the development of technology:

> Allocations systems seemingly have become ever more complex, designed to reflect the range of nuance of housing need, a trend made possible by the development of the first computerised allocation administration in the late 1970s and early 1980s. Computerisation is now universal, except amongst the smallest housing associations. (Pawson and Kintrea 2002: 648)

Third, a by-product of this sophistication was an increasing reliance on risk as a housing management tool (Cullingworth 1973: 51; Gray 1979: 207). To some degree this represents a return to themes prominent in the 1920s. It is possible to think of housing management in terms of risk management and minimisation, with one option being to screen high-risk households out of the sector through the selection and allocation process. As this type of risk management became more prominent – or at least more widely recognised – it has become plausible to portray need not as the organising criterion but largely as window-dressing: the overriding factor was that new tenants should not be a burden on housing management – what Cowan (1997) has referred to as 'tenantability'. In housing management speak, some risky households are referred to as the 'unhouseables' – households which require such high levels of intervention, or are so problematic in some way (for example, a known paedophile), that they would have a seriously detrimental effect on a neighbourhood. The selection process provided one method of insuring against that potential burden. Schemes divide populations into good risks and bad risks, filtering out some of the bad risks and subsequent management practices 'engage in "close watching and masterful inactivity" to weed out the bad who slipped through and the good who succumbed to the insurance temptation' (Baker 2000: 570).

Fourth, an increasingly important critique of needs-based allocation concerned the 'discovery' of unpopular estates and their links with allocation schemes. The creation of such 'problem estates' (as they were labelled in policy terms) was related to the stigma slum dwellers carried with them to their new properties and to complex, localised sets of circumstances (Damer 1974). In the PRP sector, this result has been particularly harshly felt and debated following the publication of *Building for Communities* (Page 1993), in which it was asserted that there was a 'spiral of decline' on PRP estates. This report created what has been described as a 'paradigm shift' in the thinking of the PRP sector (McDermont 2010). An over-reliance on providing accommodation for those in the greatest need has, perhaps paradoxically, resulted in ghettos of unpopular housing.

Certainly, labelling an estate in this way could create a self-fulfilling prophecy in that properties on such estates were often matched with the more desperate (Bottoms and Wiles 1986). These areas then became the focus of a series of criminological studies, and were constructed as criminological problems – Bottoms and Wiles (1986), for example, referred to 'residential community crime careers'. Some academics and policy-makers tended to see one-dimensional causes and solutions – the architecture, the management – to these multi-dimensional issues (see, for example, the much criticised work of Coleman 1986). Thus, for example, during the 1980s, the Priority Estates Project employed a decentralisation approach to housing management to cure the ills of the worst estates, to less than emphatic evaluations (Cole and Furbey 1994: 213–15). More recently, policy pre-occupations have linked the turning around of such estates to a notion of a more active citizen/tenant of housing, who would participate in their housing management (see Chapter 4 and Chapter 5 above).

Similarly, it has been asserted that, as social housing has become a tenure of last resort, more must be done to encourage diverse households to apply. The question has been framed in terms of the mission of social housing – is it, as Cole et al. (1996) put it, about 'creating communities or welfare housing'? This is a tough question to answer, but broadly the opposition suggested in the question is not necessarily accurate. Housing organisations are going out of their way to produce communities within social housing. Thus, the pressure to make social housing more desirable, particularly in areas where the housing stock (or some of it) is hard to let, has made these organisations expand their understandings of 'housing need'. They have actively sought to debureaucratise themselves, creating more welcoming spaces, estate agency-like offices with shop fronts, and better marketing.

Towards stable communities

Choice-based lettings

CBL is a heavily touted, high-profile government policy under which, rather than being allocated property, households on waiting lists bid for properties advertised by local authorities and sometimes also by PRPs and private sector landlords. It has certainly captured the hearts and minds of many in the social sector, as a better way of managing allocations (or 'lettings' in the terminology of the CBL process). The rather mundane definition of such schemes – as those which 'incorporate an advertising scheme' (CLG 2008d: para. 2.7) – belies their significance both as a matter of policy and culture change, and has had considerable impact in some areas where outcomes are 'demonstrably different' (Pawson et al. 2006: para. 9.13).

CBL came rather out of the blue as a policy pronouncement in the 2000 housing Green Paper (DETR/DSS 2000a: ch. 9). It had been pioneered in Delft (and is sometimes known as the 'Delft scheme') and initially piloted in England in Market Harborough. The Green Paper trumpeted the benefits of CBL in perhaps typically New Labour terms as leading to households having 'a longer term commitment to the locality', promoting 'more sustainable communities', and will 'increase personal well-being, and help to reduce anti-social behaviour, crime, stress and educational under-achievement' (para. 9.7). It is important that choice and need are somehow balanced. The Green Paper restated the government's commitment to housing need – 'We want to promote a more customer-centred approach, *but without changing the fundamental role of social housing in meeting housing need*' (para. 9.2, emphasis added). This commitment was, however, more wavering than before as 'there may be occasions when it is necessary and desirable, for some wider community benefit, to allow exceptions to this' (para. 9.12).

The ideological shift embraced by CBL will be well appreciated by those conversant with shifts in understandings of welfare, as it requires an 'active homeseeker' to whom a property is let, rather than a passive household who is allocated a property (see Cowan and Marsh 2005). Effectively, households conduct a 'self-assessment' of the likelihood of success in the bidding process for individual properties. That self-assessment is deliberately modelled on private sector approaches, as the Green Paper suggested:

> Even in the private sector, people cannot always live exactly where they would like. They must make choices. Choice implies a trade-off between people's needs and aspirations on the one hand, and the availability of housing they can afford on the other. Those who cannot afford housing in one area may have to look elsewhere, and are free to do so. But the more opportunity people have to decide these things for themselves, the more likely they are to feel ownership of the decision and to be satisfied with the outcome. And the more information they have on which to base their decisions, the better those decisions are likely to be. (DETR/DSS 2000: para. 9.6)

CBL, then, is a market-based model of social housing selection and allocation. Its basis is an analogy with assumptions about the ways in which the private sector works; as well as the benefits of the private sector approach. Thus, for example, under CBL, households are entitled to refuse accommodation they bid for, on the basis that they would be able to do so in the private sector (see Marsh et al. 2004: para. 10.17). This marketised model of the process, so the claim runs, will allow people more ontological security as they have chosen their property: they will feel ownership of *their* decision and get satisfaction with that.

Choice itself has always been part of the system – generally, applicants have always chosen the areas for which they wanted to be considered and, at some level, usually were entitled to refuse a property. CBL simply changes that particular timing. However, CBL is a global expression under which fundamental changes are taking place in allocations schemes. Most significantly, in order to run an effective CBL scheme, households need to know what properties they are likely to 'win'. In order to do this, they need to know where they stand in the queue. Thus, going hand-in-hand with the choice element of CBL is wholesale reform of allocation schemes (as well as housing options schemes, discussed in the previous chapter, which emphasise the realistic).

CBL harnesses technology – for example, in many schemes, households bid for properties on-line – and, in the process, it is recognised that it produces different vulnerabilities (such as, for example, lacking access to sources of information on vacant properties and bidding mechanisms – see Marsh et al. 2004: ch. 6; Pawson et al. 2009: paras. 2.16–20). The CBL Code of Guidance discusses how schemes should assist potentially disadvantaged households (CLG 2008d: paras. 5.7–9 and 5.22–8), and recognises that the required level of assistance will depend on the type of disadvantage. A good practice guide has been produced to assist local authorities in identifying such households and developing processes to assist them, including recognition of the importance of joint working (Pawson et al. 2009: especially ch. 6). However, the overriding feeling is that matters have not particularly improved since Pawson et al. (2006: para. 9.15) found that 'very few [providers] systematically monitor the participation of "potentially disadvantaged" households or the letting of properties to members of such groups'.

Most particularly, the Green Paper suggested that, instead of giving households points to reflect their housing need, allocation schemes should employ broad bands of housing need, into which households would be placed, with waiting time as the currency in each band (also ODPM 2002: paras. 5.10–11). Points schemes encouraged the use of discretion and lacked transparency. It was often impossible in such schemes to give an indication of waiting time before a household would be offered a property. A simpler banding scheme, in which queue jumping is minimised and allocation is on the basis of waiting time within bands, encourages transparency. Applicants can see where they are on the housing register and how long they need to wait before they will be able to bid successfully for a particular property. This can also affect area choice because it is usually possible to say statistically how long a household would need to wait before they would be likely to make a successful bid for that area.

There are divergent schemes in operation now across the country, although many take banding households as their starting point (Pawson et al. 2006: chs. 2–3). Some schemes have priority cards for certain groups (although these are not entirely in accordance with the underlying thrust of CBL in terms of transparency and are not recommended by the Code of Guidance: CLG 2008d: paras. 4.29–33). Most would laud the shift to scheme transparency in banding households.

One particular, and slightly different, thrust of CBL has been a rethinking of scale. If choice is the key, why restrict that choice to a geographic area based on the vagaries of the political boundary process (i.e. constituting each local authority area), rather than on where households might want to live? This was a question which presented itself at an early stage, particularly to those local authorities with an entrepreneurial bent as an opportunity to develop their policies on a regional basis. A number of such schemes are currently in operation across the country. They have been given a particular boost by the CBL guidance (CLG 2008d) which describes sub-regional and/or regional schemes as being the government's 'policy objective' as 'the best way to achieve the greatest choice and flexibility in meeting tenants' housing needs' (para. 7.1). In particular, the encouragement to labour mobility, cost-sharing between different providers, and the benefits of a larger pool of housing are all important (para. 7.2).

There are, though, potential issues which CBL may throw up. The principle that the longer a household waits, the more priority it will have might seem defensible but it creates a market, together with the bargaining inequalities engendered by markets. The bargaining chip is waiting time, and some people can afford to wait longer than others. Here, it is worth thinking about the findings of Jeffers and Hoggett into the Haringey and Lambeth allocation schemes in the mid-1990s:

> It also became clear to us that many applicants, particularly those living in temporary accommodation, when asked the question 'where would you like to live?', reinterpreted this question in terms of 'how long do you wish to wait for an offer?'. This in turn related to the position of the player in the allocations game ... Given that black applicants were disproportionately represented in the homeless families channel, this put them at an initial disadvantage in the game, compared with existing tenants who were seeking a transfer. (Jeffers and Hoggett 1995: 336)

The evidence, however, is that CBL may have led to deconcentrations of minority ethnic settlements in social housing, which is an important effect and runs counter to alternative perspectives that minority ethnic households choose to concentrate together (Pawson et al 2006: 6.14–37; cf. Van Ham and Manley, 2009). It is also likely that young people who have no history of independent living will have to wait longer than under previous schemes. Others, such as those households that are new arrivals in a particular local authority area, will have to build up 'credit' through waiting time.

Towards sustainable communities

CBL fits into a broader, less defined general policy idea that social housing should provide 'sustainable communities' and that allocations policies have not facilitated that process. There is some evidence that CBL has facilitated the sustainment of tenancies (Pawson et al. 2006: para. 9.23). The notion of sustainable communities, sometimes the word stable is used, is not one which is really capable of definition. It seems to depend on a variety of different factors, from architectural design (especially 'designing out' crime and low-level deviance through use of streetlights, cctv and the like) and estate-profiling to more micro-objectives summarised as 'local' or 'community' lettings policies. The sustainable communities goal had come to the forefront after the Page report in 1993, but one of the reasons why that report had such purchase was because it tapped into the concerns and consciousness of housing officers who were expressing these concerns. Housing Corporation priorities for funding new housing association developments shifted in the 1990s in an attempt to ensure new housing schemes met the sustainability criteria (see Chapter 5).

Allocation solely according to housing need was already being challenged during the 1990s. So the 2000 Green Paper, in which the government opened up a discussion of whether it was appropriate to provide social housing solely on the basis of need, continued that train of thought:

> We do not believe that social housing should only be allocated to the poorest and most vulnerable members of the community … [W]e recognise that there may be occasions when it is necessary and desirable, for some wider community benefit, to allow exceptions to this. (DETR/DSS 2000a: para. 9.12)

One way in which sustainable communities can be created is through 'local lettings schemes', which (again had been in existence prior to the Green Paper and which were suggested as an option in the Green Paper: paras. 9.29–32). These schemes use the lettings systems to achieve ends such as a reduction in child density on particular estates or the encouragement of particular social groupings (key workers, the employed, etc.) to live in them (and were welcomed in, for example, the Page report). However, there is also a tension here between two 'social mix' and 'safety net' objectives. As Fitzpatrick and Pawson (2007: 177) have put it: 'The most obvious tension between these objectives is the requirement "to make more space" for better-off groups in a sector continuing to contract.'

The Housing Corporation's regulatory code and performance standards regarded these policies as acceptable for PRPs, with certain safeguards, since the mid-1990s making allowance for such policies in the regulatory guidance itself. Their 1997 regulatory guidance, *Performance Standards*, had already accepted that housing need could be overridden 'where this would lead to unsustainable tenancies or unstable communities', although only exceptionally (Housing Corporation 1997: 38).

Although these paragraphs of the Green Paper were less than explicit on this point, certain vulnerable households must be divided off because they are not community-minded or community builders. Some community lettings policies make the questionable assumption that 'the problem of anti-social behaviour is best dealt with by excluding or removing anti-social elements' (Griffiths et al. 1996: 21). The schemes come in a variety of formats but all are involved in one way or another in discriminating between applicants. Cole et al. (2001: 50–1) refer to five different strands of local lettings schemes which work in a variety of combinations: economic; family and friends; local links; community contribution; household characteristics. Flint (2002: 632) describes the practices of a 'lettings committee' in Glasgow:

> This process involved social housing staff and tenants in classifying individual applicants in relation to locally defined norms and values. On occasion, where individuals were seen to be incompatible with, or deviant from, this constructed community identity (eg because of prior convictions for drug dealing) they were

refused a tenancy. Tenants were involved in both seeking to direct the conduct of future tenants, and in the making of populations and the construction of community identities.

The 2000 Green Paper promised powers to suspend the anti-social from the housing list or have their priority reduced – a disciplining mechanism with the possibility of redemption held out for such households who were to 'be given a clear indication of what they needed to do to get the restriction lifted' (DETR/DSS 2000: para. 9.13). This suggestion was made law in the Homelessness Act 2002, which introduced s. 160A(7)–(8). These provisions gave local authorities power either to exclude or reduce the reasonable preference owed to members of those households who have been guilty of certain unacceptable behaviour and, when the application is made, are 'unsuitable to be a tenant of the authority by reason of that behaviour'. The definition of 'unacceptable behaviour' is that it must be serious enough to make the applicant unsuitable to be a tenant of the authority; and that is further defined as behaviour which would have entitled the authority to an order for possession which would have been sufficient to obtain an outright possession order against such a household. Now, on any view, this convoluted provision is extremely difficult to put into practice because the local authority must decide what a judge would make of that behaviour and, in particular, whether such a judge would make an *outright*, as opposed to a suspended or postponed, possession order (PPO). However, it is also clear that any such decision by a local authority would be difficult to challenge unless it reached the threshold of being *Wednesbury* unreasonable. That threshold is difficult to reach because the decision is essentially one for the local authority (see *Dixon* v. *Wandsworth LBC* [2007] EWHC 3075 (Admin)).

The 'BNP' effect

The British National Party (BNP) achieved some limited success in the 2009 local elections. One reason for this success, it was thought, was due to the perpetration of the myth that social housing was being allocated to those who have, it is said, no legitimate right to it. Economic migrants were one such group pinpointed, in fact by a government minister, Margaret Hodge, in an unfortunately misinformed intervention (http://news.bbc.co.uk/1/hi/uk_politics/6673911.stm; see Chapter 8 below). If the point of CBL was to provide a clearer, more transparent system of social housing allocation, it was not affecting popular misconceptions of the process (CLG 2009b: 29). The question then became the extent to which 'local connection' could and should be prioritised in local (or regional) schemes, and how publicising the fairness of schemes could dispel the myths and misperceptions of local communities. The answer given by the CLG (2009b: 32) was that local communities should be actively engaged through 'effective, transparent communication'. Local authorities are under a duty to consult on changes to their scheme or where they create a new scheme (s. 167(7), Housing Act 1996) and the advice is that they should do so at an early stage (CLG 2009b: 42) as well as have monitoring and evaluation of the outcomes published (ibid. p. 51). The guidance also makes clear that 'there is nothing to prevent [local authorities] from framing their allocation scheme to include local connection as a policy priority, provided that overall the scheme continues to meet the reasonable preference requirements in s. 167' (ibid. p. 63).

The intrusion of law

For most of the twentieth century, law rarely intruded on this administrative arena. Until the Housing Act 1996, which substantially reworked the law, there was not even a requirement on local authorities to maintain a housing waiting list of applicants (and, in fact, that requirement no longer exists). The House of Lords, in *Shelley* v. *London CC* [1948] 2 All ER 898 made clear that the selection and allocation of local authority housing was for the local authority itself and not for the courts. The broad framework had been set in the Housing (Financial Provisions) Act 1924, s. 3(1)(f), which required local authorities, as a condition of receiving grants for development, to give 'reasonable preference' to households with large families. After that, the notion of 'reasonable preference' became detached from receipt of grant and became the basis for determining housing need. The categories were expanded in the consolidating and amending Housing Act 1935, to include those living in insanitary, overcrowded or unsatisfactory housing conditions. These categories remained unchanged until 1996, although, as we have seen, certain categories of homeless persons were added in 1977.

One of the principal questions addressed here is the extent to which prioritisation should reflect differences in housing need. Until recently, the jurisprudence proceeded on this basis, perhaps too single-mindedly, but not unreasonably given that this was considered the purpose of Part 6, Housing Act 1996. It has, however, been unravelled by a more flexible jurisdiction opened up by the House of Lords which, at best, discourages legal challenges to allocations schemes.

The Housing Act 1996, Part VI

Part VI governs the allocation of accommodation by local authorities; a Code of Guidance and supplements (ODPM 2002; CLG 2009a; 2009b) have been produced to which local authorities must have regard (s. 169). Under s. 159(1), an allocation occurs when a local authority either offers its own accommodation, nominates the household to another body capable of granting a secure or introductory tenancy, or nominates an applicant to a PRP for an AT (which would also include an AST). Local authorities can, however, contract out part of their allocations/lettings process, including the assessment and review functions, to another organisation (Local Authorities (Contracting out of Allocation of

Housing and Homelessness Functions) Order 1996, SI 1996/3205); many do so, particularly after an LSVT, depending in part on the numbers of officers remaining with the authority after transfer and whether the authority is rural or urban (Pawson et al. 2009; Pawson and Mullins 2010: 291–4). Nominations are dealt with below. Originally, existing tenants who wished to transfer to alternative accommodation were excluded from the register, but the Homelessness Act 2002 required these households to be included on the register with all the other households (s. 159(5)).

Provided an applicant complies with the local authority's procedure, they shall be considered for an allocation (s. 166(3)). The threshold for such an application is, therefore, low. After a brief hiatus, there is no longer a requirement on a local housing authority to maintain a waiting list or housing register, although it is the case that most do. Any such list or register should not, however, be taken to represent a statement of the housing needs of households in the local authority area. Certain households are regarded as ineligible (s. 160A, Housing Act 1996; dealt with in Chapter 8 below), subject to a right to review (s. 167(2)(4A)). It is the case, though, that local authorities must have a published allocation scheme which includes 'all aspects of the allocation process, including the persons or descriptions of persons by whom decisions are to be taken' (s. 167(1)). Schemes have been held to be unlawful in part as a result of not giving sufficient information about a policy (see, for example, *R (Lin)* v. *Barnet LBC* [2007] HLR 30, at [48]; *R (Faarah)* v. *Southwark LBC* [2009] HLR 12; cf. *R (Van Boolen)* v. *LB Barking & Dagenham* [2009] EWHC 2196 (Admin)).

Allocations schemes are, however, the province of local authorities as is emphasised by s. 167(6). There is, though, a constraint on them in that they are required to give 'reasonable preference' to certain categories of household. These are politically contested.[1] The Housing Act 1996 also included a category to which 'additional preference' should be accorded, but this was watered down in the 2002 Act so that additional preference can be given to certain categories of persons with urgent need. These categories are defined as follows:

[margin note:] Homelessness Act 2002

(2) As regards priorities, the scheme shall be framed so as to secure that reasonable preference is given to –
  (a) people who are homeless (within the meaning of Part 7);
  (b) people who are owed a duty by any local housing authority under section 190(2), 193(2) or 195(2) (or under section 65(2) or 68(2) of the Housing Act 1985) or who are occupying accommodation secured by any such authority under section 192(3);

---

[1] For example, a Code of Guidance issued in 1996, offered the following extra-legal advice: 'Recognising the importance of a stable home environment to children's development, the Government believes that local authorities should give priority to ensuring that families, particularly married couples, with dependent children or who are expecting a child have access to settled accommodation. Consideration should also be given to those who have delayed starting a family because of the inadequacies of their accommodation.' (DoE 1996: para. 29) The paragraph was removed from the subsequent edition of the guidance.

(c) people occupying insanitary or overcrowded housing or otherwise living in unsatisfactory housing conditions;

(d) people who need to move on medical or welfare grounds (including
grounds relating to a disability); and

(e) people who need to move to a particular locality in the district of the
authority, where failure to meet that need would cause hardship (to
themselves or to others).

The scheme may also be framed so as to give additional preference to particular
descriptions of people within this subsection (being descriptions of people with
urgent housing needs).

Local authorities can 'determine priorities' by reference to the household's financial resources, the behaviour of any household member, and local connection with
the authority (s. 167(2A), Housing Act 1996); but the authority is entitled to use
other criteria. As we shall see shortly, this proviso in s. 167(2A), introduced by the
Homelessness Act 2002 and initially thought simply to give further leeway to local
authorities, partly produced the downfall of 20 years' worth of jurisprudence.

One of the interesting, initially rather odd, aspects of the revamped Part VI
was that it did not seem on its face to say much at all about CBL. It gave local
authorities power to make provision to allow households to make an application for specific accommodation (for example, through bidding for it) and for
an allocation to be made to persons of a particular description (for example, in
a particular band or with particular needs) (s. 167(2E)). And the scheme itself
must have a statement about choice as well as applicants' ability to express preferences (s. 167(1A)). Nothing more, though – the question raised, then, was
whether the new, high-profile, high-cost schemes were lawful? After an awkward hiatus, it now appears that they are.

(De-)judicialising allocations

Commensurate with the development of judicial review and the more contested approach to housing rights, the courts have sought to clarify what is
meant by the notion of reasonable preference. In the face of challenges to allocations schemes, the courts have been cautious, making clear that allocation
schemes are the province of the local authority and not the courts. Provided
the local authority does not stray from the Act and is not *Wednesbury* unreasonable, the courts are likely to refuse to intervene. Furthermore, the courts'
jurisdiction is limited by the quite open-ended discretion given to local authorities. Nevertheless, a certain number of principles did emerge from a developing body of case law, which may be summarised as follows:

- Reasonable preference was taken to mean a 'reasonable head start' (*R* v.
Wolverhampton MBC ex p Watters (1997) 29 HLR 931, 938);
- Applicants whose households appeared in one or more of the reason-
able preference categories were entitled to greater preference, referred to as

'cumulative preference' or 'composite assessment' of need (*R* v. *Lambeth LBC ex p Ashley* (1996) 29 HLR 385; *R* v. *Islington LBC ex p Reilly and Mannix* (1999) 31 HLR 651; *R* v. *Westminster CC ex p Al-Khorsan* (2001) 33 HLR 77);

- Applicants with a reasonable preference should not be considered alongside applicants who have no such preference, even where the latter constitute no more than a small proportion of applicants on the waiting list (*R (A/Lindsay)* v. *Lambeth LBC* [2002] HLR 57; *R (Cali/Abdi/Hassan)* v. *Waltham Forest LBC* [2007] HLR 1);
- If a scheme is unlawful on any of the above points, it is not 'saved' by giving applicants a choice of accommodation;
- Having a reasonable or cumulative preference does not guarantee an allocation.

All of these points were brushed aside, however, by the House of Lords which considered Part VI for the first time in *R (Ahmad)* v. *Newham LBC* [2009] HLR 31. Newham's scheme was the sort of scheme which failed to satisfy most, if not all, of the above principles in the previous case law. In summary, the council had two separate categories – those to whom offers were made directly, and those who were given a choice. The former category accounted for 25 per cent of all the properties let; the people in this group accounted for extremely narrow categories of applicants with the most pressing need for housing. An additional preference category (giving the household priority over those in other bands), for example, required not just a medical condition but one which made it impossible for the sufferer to continue to occupy their accommodation. In the choice group, the remaining applicants were placed in one of three categories: priority homeseekers who fell into one or more of the reasonable preference categories; transfer applicants who were not priority homeseekers; and other homeseekers (who were rarely made offers and were regarded as irrelevant for these purposes). No more than 5 per cent of allocations could go to tenants seeking a transfer. Priority between members of the same category was decided on the basis of waiting time only (calculated by the date on which they registered).

Not surprisingly, the scheme was regarded as *ultra vires* in both the High Court and Court of Appeal. The priority homeseekers group did not distinguish between relative needs in that it made no allowance for cumulative preference; and the allocation of 5 per cent of stock to households without any reasonable preference was also unlawful. The House of Lords disagreed. It upheld both the lawfulness of the scheme and its rationality. The policy considerations are relatively clear. The House of Lords was concerned that, as the law was developing, most schemes were capable of being challenged successfully leading, as Lord Scott put it, to 'endless challenges, based on comparisons between the points awarded to the complainant and the points awarded to others in the same priority band'. The Lords were united in their approach that the circumstances of the Ahmads – which were written out of their judgment – were irrelevant;

however much empathy they inspired, that should not affect the outcome (Lord Neuberger, at [60]). In parenthesis, it might be noted that, while the earlier courts may have been swayed by the Ahmads' situation, the House of Lords was evidently swayed by the council's predicament (see e.g. [7], Lord Scott, [25] and [61]–[62], Lord Neuberger). What is the court to do in such cases because, after all, it only has the complainant before it and not others – as Baroness Hale said: 'The court is in no position to re-write the whole policy and to weigh the claims of the multitude who are not before the court against the claims of the few who are.' (at [15]) Furthermore, rewriting such policies would, in itself, over-extend the role of the courts and take them into the realms of policy which is the province of the local authority.

On the first point, Lord Neuberger offered five reasons why the notion of a composite assessment was an incorrect interpretation of s. 167(2). First, the opening words of s. 167(2) do not suggest that such an assessment is required. To read it as requiring such an assessment 'involves those opening words performing, as it were, a double duty, and therefore places more weight on those words than, in my view, they naturally bear' (at [39]). Second, the power to accord additional preference 'appears to me to permit, and therefore impliedly not to require, an authority to carry out the very exercise which, on the respondent's case, it is their duty to do' (at [40]). Third, the use of the word 'may' in s. 167(2A) again 'makes it clear that authorities can have priority rules as between reasonable preference applicants, which strongly suggests that they are not required to do so' (at [42]). Fourth, reference was made to the Green Paper and the suggestion there that banding would be appropriate (at [44]). Fifth:

> as a general proposition, it is undesirable for the courts to get involved in questions of how priorities are accorded in housing allocation policies. Of course, there will be cases where the court has a duty to interfere, for instance if a policy does not comply with statutory requirements, or if it is plainly irrational. However, it seems unlikely that the legislature can have intended that Judges should embark on the exercise of telling authorities how to decide on priorities as between applicants in need of rehousing, save in relatively rare and extreme circumstances. Housing allocation policy is a difficult exercise which requires not only social and political sensitivity and judgment, but also local expertise and knowledge. ([47])

Having made these general observations, the next question was whether Newham's scheme was, in fact, irrational. Given the high bar set, it was hardly surprising that it was found not to be so. On their interpretation of Part VI, the scheme 'plainly' (at [50]) satisfied the statutory requirements and accorded with the Green Paper policy. Waiting time, it was said, is an important factor which a housing authority could regard as 'very significant' (at [52]). Although 'rough and ready', such a simple scheme had advantages over a more nuanced scheme because 'it is very clear, relatively simple to administer, and highly transparent' (at [51]). Any alternative would be more expensive, time-consuming, based on value judgment, open to argument and more opaque (at [51]; also Lord Scott, at

[5]). Furthermore, the scheme did allow for additional preference and multiple needs to be taken into account, albeit the criteria are 'very stringent' (at [54]). Given Newham's housing difficulties in terms of supply and demand for social housing, there was nothing inherently absurd or arbitrary about that.

The second issue concerned the mixing of non-preference tenants seeking a transfer and preference households. The argument on this point, as Baroness Hale put it (and she dealt with this point), 'the people in [the reasonable preference] groups must be given preference in relation to every property which is let under the scheme' (at [17]). She had already noted, though, that Part VI involves something less than a target duty because 'there is not even a duty to provide [social housing], although there is a duty to have and to operate a lawful allocation policy' (at [13]). So, her position on this issue was robust. As she put it, the requirement is only 'reasonable preference' (and she like the others did not define this criterion and did not approve the *Watters* definition):

> It does not require that they should be given absolute priority over everyone else. Still less does it require that an individual household in one of those groups should be given absolute priority over an individual household which wishes to transfer. The decision in *R (A)* v. *Lambeth London Borough Council* [2002] HLR 998, 16–17, 37, appears, in part at least, to have been based on this mistaken premise. The scheme is about the overall policy for allocating the available housing stock between groups. (at [17])

Having said that transfers due to under-occupation and like-for-like transfers are 'good housing management … Happy tenants are more likely to be good tenants' ([20]), she went on to make the points that only 5 per cent of properties were allocated to transfer households and transfers are effectively neutral in terms of allocation (because they free up a unit of housing which can be allocated).

If schemes themselves cannot be challenged, the direction of travel is to challenge either the local authority's interpretation of its scheme (for example, *R (Alam)* v. *Tower Hamlets LBC* [2009] EWHC 44 (Admin)) and/or its application in any particular case (*R (Van Boolen)* v. *Barking & Dagenham LBC* [2009] EWHC 2196 (Admin)) (see Baker 2009; Cowan and Marsh 2009). Certainly, such challenges are harder to mount but it is also notable that the House of Lords itself, in the first related case it heard after *Ahmad*, struck down part of an allocation scheme on the basis that it was irrational (*R (Ali)* v. *Birmingham CC* [2010] 2 AC 39 (discussed in Chapter 6) – distinction between priority awarded to 'homeless at home' and homeless in temporary accommodation without rational justification).

Private registered providers and housing need

To focus solely on local authority allocation to local authority accommodation would undoubtedly be an anachronistic analysis. The mixed economy of provision of social housing means that, in any area, there are diverse providers of social housing. In some areas, the local authority itself retains the housing obligation but has no housing stock at all to fulfil that obligation after an LSVT (see Chapter 4 and Chapter 5 above). From the 1940s, PRPs entered into agreements with local authorities under which the latter could nominate households to PRPs (McDermont 2010). These 'nomination agreements' are now common not just in LSVT areas – Pawson and Mullins' survey of the 'top 250' PRPs found that, of the 176 respondents, 88 per cent had documented nomination agreements with the local authority (2003: 54).

Nomination agreements have become particularly prominent since the development of the PRP sector in the 1980s, as the power over development was one of the key bargaining tools which local authorities had (and for which they were able to extract nomination agreements) (McDermont 2007b). In some areas, nomination agreements have been developed further into common housing registers between the local authority and other PRPs operating in the area. The degree to which PRPs had been captured by government housing policy was reflected in the Housing Corporation's *Regulatory Code and Guidance* (2005). The TSA standard for allocations is as follows:

> Registered providers shall let their homes in a fair, transparent and efficient way. They shall take into account the housing needs and aspirations of tenants and potential tenants. They shall demonstrate how they:
> - make the best use of available housing
> - are compatible with the purpose of the housing
> - contribute to local authorities' strategic housing function and sustainable communities
>
> There should be clear application, decision-making and appeals processes. (TSA 2010a: 25)

The specific expectations of PRPs are

> 1.1 Registered providers shall co-operate with local authorities' strategic housing function, and their duties to meet identified local housing needs. This includes assistance with local authorities' homelessness duties, and through meeting obligations in nominations agreements. Where, in exceptional circumstances, registered providers choose not to participate in choice-based lettings schemes in areas where they own homes, they shall publish their reasons for doing so.
>
> ...
>
> 1.4 Registered providers' published policies shall include how they have made use of common housing registers, common allocations policies and local letting policies. Registered providers shall clearly set out, and be able to give reasons for, the criteria they use for excluding actual and potential tenants from consideration for allocations, mobility or mutual exchange schemes. (TSA 2010a: 26)

This goes further than the statutory obligation to 'co-operate to such extent as is reasonable in the circumstances in offering accommodation to people with priority on the authority's register' (s. 170, 1996 Act). Regulation clearly seeks to align PRPs' allocations policies with local authority assessments of need (which was effectively the position adopted in the late 1980s – Levison and Robertson 1989: 25).

There is a tricky balance between, on the one hand, the retention by the PRP of the power of choice over who should get its stock, and thus independence from the state, to becoming an arm of the state in meeting housing need, and thus losing control. Thus, amongst non-LSVT PRPs, the norm is that nomination agreements allow local authorities to nominate to 50 per cent of all vacancies (Pawson and Mullins 2003: 56). In practice, the issue may become contested when the local authority nominates a household which is then rejected by the PRP. PRPs can (and often do) implicitly assert their independence by re-assessing nominated households. A significant proportion of PRPs at least 'occasionally' reject nominee households after such an assessment on the grounds that they are 'unsuitable' or 'ineligible' or, less often, not a rehousing priority (Pawson and Mullins 2003: 61 and 62–4). This leads to allegations from local authorities that PRPs cherry-pick their nominees; that is, they only pick the 'better' households for their accommodation and, in the process, ignore housing need. For a PRP, this can make sense because the management problems caused by certain occupiers can have a significant impact on the business interests of the PRP (Cowan et al. 2009: 295).

The Housing Corporation's regulatory code entitled PRPs to exclude households from allocations '[w]hen the [household's] unacceptable behaviour is serious enough to make them unsuitable to be a tenants and only in circumstances that [PRPs] are not unlawfully discriminating' (para. 3.6c). A Housing Corporation circular expanded on this in relation to exclusions for rent arrears and ASB (Housing Corporation 2007). The circular suggested that there should be no blanket bans: 'rent arrears should not be an automatic barrier to access'; and that exclusions relating to ASB should be based on evidence of the behaviour within the previous 2 years. It is important to note, though, that these are broad threshold criteria and that there is considerable variation in practice between PRPs. One particular issue, which prompted the circular, was the prevalence of PRP exclusion policies and practices to avoid potential management problems (Parker et al. 1994; Pleace et al. 2007).

In a report on their study of three areas, a research team discussed what they termed problematic nominations (Cowan and Morgan 2009; Cowan et al. 2008; 2009). They demonstrated how nominations agreements themselves were often largely ignored at the outset but were then dusted off to resolve acrimonious disputes, or just to maintain relations between the organisations. It is, though, important to see the nominations process taking place over time and the developing relations between organisations, as well as the impact of internal organisational developments, as being crucial contexts. In one of their study areas, an LSVT area (which they call Trumpton), the LSVT PRP had developed an exclusions policy and practice which was unpublished but which had a significant impact on the local authority, which found itself unable to fulfil its statutory obligations to households. They reported a Trumpton housing manager saying:

> This is the issue of obligations. We have a statutory obligation around homelessness, around trying to meet housing needs. The associations, whoever they may be, stock transfer or whatever, have a moral obligation not a statutory obligation and they play fast and loose with that. (Cowan and Morgan 2009: 169)

The frustration felt by this manager was clearly exacerbated by the powerlessness of the local authority in the face of the apparent intransigence of the predominant housing provider. There was a loss of confidence in the PRP, but, equally, a reliance on it.

Despite these concerns, there have been no legal challenges to a particular nomination failure by any of the parties (local authority, PRP or applicant). One reason for this may be that, although they may produce animosity between local authority and PRP, there is an ongoing relation between them based not only on contract (or something like that) but also on an ongoing relationship. PRPs need local authorities for a steady supply of households; local authorities rely on PRPs to provide accommodation for households. Policy structures further demand this mutual reliance placing regulatory and financial constraints on the parties. Law, therefore, is an interesting absence, and that absence tells us a lot about the structuring factors of the social housing 'market'. A rather more important reason uncovered by Cowan et al. (2008) was that such challenges rely on a disappointed applicant to make a claim. However, such applicants may not be aware that they are the subjects of a nomination:

> In the final analysis, we can reflect on how the nominee households are written out of many of the stories told by our interviewees and the nominations process. Problematic nominations were not people but institutional problems. Of course, some households are or become known as problems, but these are then refocused on the interactions between LA and [PRP]. The nominee is, thus, mostly invisible in our data …

Cowan (2008b) subsequently speculated that if one impact of CBL is transparency, then applicants will come to know of their failed nomination and may well challenge it (a prediction which has yet to be fulfilled).

Reform

Allocations/lettings is politically contested terrain. The questions discussed above remain pertinent. It can be seen that, over time, the drift has been towards centralisation of the specification of the criteria for allocations/lettings, exemplified by the 1996 Act (as amended by the Homelessness Act 2002). The Coalition government's localism agenda operates against this tide, and it was no surprise, therefore, that the earliest announcements of that government were incorporated in its consultation paper (CLG 2010e).

In essence, the aim of this document and the Localism Bill is to turn the clock back to the unamended 1996 Act. So, local authorities are to be given the opportunity to specify who is entitled to appear on the waiting list as qualifying persons (instead of the current open list); and existing PRP and local authority tenants who are seeking a transfer are to be taken off the list. These changes were heavily trailed, including by the Prime Minister, but are controversial in part because they give some rein to local authorities to exclude households and possibly, subject to interpretation, appear to change the balance between existing and aspirant tenants in favour of the former.

As regards the former – the exclusions – the concern is that waiting lists are too long and many households stand little chance of obtaining a letting. They encourage the (mistaken) perception that anyone waiting long enough will obtain an allocation/letting (para. 4.6). Apparently with support, despite their questionable legality, the document refers to local authorities which actively seek to deter applicants who stand no chance in the process (para. 4.7). The governing rationale for this change is as follows:

> We take the view that it should be for local authorities to put in place arrangements which suit the particular needs of their local area. Some local authorities might restrict social housing to those in housing need (e.g. homeless households and overcrowded families). Other local authorities might impose residency criteria or exclude applicants with a poor tenancy record or those with sufficient financial resources to rent or buy privately. Others may decide to continue with open waiting lists. If, having taken into account the views of their local community, local authorities decide that there are benefits in maintaining open waiting lists (for example, to stimulate demand for social housing), we believe they should be able to do so. (CLG 2010e: para. 4.9)

The government will reserve a power, however, to list qualifying and non-qualifying households. This return to the 1996 Act raises concerns that the problems experienced in the implementation of that Act will re-occur. Most local authorities excluded applications from those who did not have a local connection with the area; under eighteens; those with a history of ASB; and, in particular, those with previous rent arrears (see Butler 1998; Cowan 1998: 231–6). Indeed, the pre-consultation paper trailing of the proposals suggested that local connection was the prime motivation for these reforms (see Woolf 2010).

As regards the second change – excluding transfer applicants from the list – the purpose here is rather different for the assumption is that such applicants will at some stage be offered a different property. The problem set up in the consultation paper is that such applicants will often have less apparent need than other applicants and, therefore, suffer by comparison in the allocations/lettings process:

> As a result many social tenants have been trapped for years in housing which they don't want to live in, unable to change their housing circumstances because they do not have sufficient priority under the local authority's allocation scheme. In 2008/9, out of 139,000 local authority lets (excluding mutual

exchanges), only 32,000 (23 per cent) went to existing tenants. (CLG 2010e: para. 4.19)

The prescription is to increase lettings to such persons, partly to facilitate their mobility. Various non-statutory schemes have been trailed to develop this process, including national home swap programme and other web-based services (see ch. 5 of the consultation paper). In theory, and as accepted by all parties in *Ahmad*, transfers are stock neutral because, at the end of the process, there will usually be an allocation/letting to a new applicant. However, this returns us to the situation where a transfer applicant will usually have a greater bargaining chip than others because they can wait longer for the better property to become available. New applicants are unlikely to have that luxury. What one might expect, therefore, is that the allocations process involves a gradual ratcheting up in the quality of accommodation, with new entrants receiving the worst quality stock but then transferring to better stock. Households will work their way up the quality ladder (Cowan and Marsh 2009). There must be concerns, therefore, that this scheme will formalise certain dimensions of inequality (see, for example, Ginsburg 1988; see also the critique of CHAC 1969).

Conclusion

In the previous chapter, we asked whether homelessness law is capable of being fully implemented in practice. We noted its obscurity, its reliance on homeless persons challenging local decision-making, and the problem of 'impact' of law (not least, that it is unclear what impact means in this context). This chapter has approached the question of law rather differently. The law on social housing allocations has more than likely been one of the factors which produced complexity, but other factors were involved as well and, in any event, fulfilling the law now looks rather simpler than it did. Housing management, as we noted in Chapter 1, has developed into a profession, and allocations is one aspect of that profession. Together with reliance on advisory committees and guidance, professionalisation may well have produced complexity. And, as a result, a different professional expertise and a reversion to simplicity has been required to get us out of the mess. The question of law in this chapter has been whether the resulting initiatives and the drive for choice, simplicity and transparency could be supported without further changes to the law, a question largely resolved in the affirmative after *Ahmad*. The question of policy is the extent to which housing need can continue to be supported within a policy framework that promotes both a choice agenda and sustainability. This question remains open.

8

Eligibility

Contents

This chapter concerns eligibility for the range of benefits and resources considered in this part (i.e. HB, homelessness and an allocation of housing, Chapter 9, Chapter 6, and Chapter 7 respectively). Eligibility is in some respects the gateway into the assessment obligations of local housing authorities, but extends beyond this to other services, such as those provided through the support available to asylum seekers. It is a relatively new arena, which is generally aimed at asylum seekers and other persons from abroad, and one which has been highly contested. The 'time when the welfare state did not look at your passport or ask why you were here' has passed (*R (Westminster CC)* v. *National Asylum Support Service* [2002] 1 WLR 2956, at [19] *per* Lord Hoffmann).

As Morris (2009: 32) has put it, in the context of citizenship (or rather non-citizens), the law works through a process of 'civic stratification … which operates through a series of differentiated legal statuses with different rights attached'. The law – by which is meant not just the legislative settlement, but also the complex of secondary legislation, tertiary guidance and circulars, and judicial authority – is particularly complex and sometimes difficult to find.

One has to have in mind that the law is being interpreted on a day-to-day basis by housing officers who may be skilled in the interpretation of housing law but for whom eligibility is, to adapt LP Hartley's famous metaphor from *The Go-Between*, 'another country' in which things are done differently. There is some qualitative research evidence, from a study of three local authority HPUs' decision-making processes, that 'institutional racism may operate in the social construction of "bureaucratic knowledge"' (Halliday 2000b: 451) as a result of ethnic stereotyping or 'produced from a more subtle combination of various characteristics of its decision-making culture focusing on a certain "type" of situation which gave rise to homelessness' (p. 452). Whatever conclusions are drawn from the evidence, one thing is clear – housing decision-makers have been drawn into ('responsibilised' by) the broad immigration decision-making process ('a scrutiny which often goes beyond legal requirements': Sales 2002: 461).

After a context-setting section, this chapter considers the regulations affecting asylum seekers, and those who unsuccessfully seek asylum; it then moves on to regulations which translate the freedom of movement granted to European Economic Area (EEA) residents into UK law; the habitual residence test, which affects certain households who are otherwise presumptively eligible; and, finally, considers the problems where the household contains an ineligible family member of an otherwise eligible main applicant.

Background

The development of policy towards the entitlement of asylum seekers and persons from abroad has proceeded on certain empirically unproven assumptions about economic migration, which is sometimes translated as 'welfare scrounging', and (rough) binary distinctions between the 'bogus' and the 'genuine' (Sales 2002; on the lack of empirical evidence, see, for example, Joint Committee on Human Rights (JCHR), 2007: para. 5). So, for example, the 1998 White Paper argued that: 'There is no doubt that the asylum system is being abused by those seeking to migrate for purely economic reasons. Many claims are simply a tissue of lies', while at the same time noting that 'the very nature of illegal immigration makes it difficult to assess the total number of people in the country without authority and so liable to removal' (Home Office Border and Immigration Agency 1998: paras. 1.14 and 1.15 respectively).

The bogus are 'inappropriate' applicants for welfare, justifying penalising legislation which affects the broader category of persons (Cowan 1997) and which links in with what Rutherford (1997) termed the 'eliminative ideal'. As Michael Howard, the then Home Secretary, put it in 1995, 'Britain should be a haven, not a honeypot'. Peter Lilley, the then Secretary of State for Social Security, played to the audience at the 1993 Conservative Party Conference by offering the following pastiche:

We have all too many home grown scroungers, but it is beyond the pale when foreigners come here expecting handouts …

It's not so much a Cook's tour but a crooks' tour … Just imagine the advice you might find in a European phrasebook for Benefit Tourists. 'Wo is das Hotel?' – where is the housing department? 'Ou est le bureau de change?' – where do I cash my benefit cheque? 'Mio bambina e in Italia' – send child benefits to my family in Italy. 'Je suis un citoyen de l'Europe' – give me benefits or I'll take you to the European Court.

The Conservatives were not alone in such parodies. More recently, Margaret Hodge, the MP for Barking, wrote an open letter to her fellow immigrants in *The Observer* saying:

We should … look at drawing up different rules based on, for instance, length of residence, citizenship or national insurance contributions which carry more weight in a transparent points system used to decide who is entitled to access social housing. There are a small number of confirmed refugees who, of course, would receive the same entitlements as British citizens. However, most new migrant families are economic migrants who choose to come to live and work here. If you choose to come to Britain, should you presume the right to access social housing?

Hodge was giving voice to what is an undoubtedly widely held and reported belief that asylum seekers and other persons from abroad do rather better in the allocation of scarce welfare resources than the 'indigenous' population (to use a vague and undefined word in common currency – see, for example, Woolf 2010), views which were found in studies (see, for example, Cowan and Halliday et al. 2003: 129; CICC 2007; IPSOS MORI 2009; Rutter and Latore 2009) and formed the core rationale for the redrafted Code of Guidance on allocations on the proper way to address this (mis-)perception (CLG 2009b: paras. 34–53).

The story as presented of preferential treatment 'sounds right'; it has been treated somehow as an established truth in the popular media, so that 'the imaginary figure of the asylum seeker as a threat to well-being and national belonging became ingrained with the national psyche and "we" learnt to desire and demand "their" exclusion' (Robinson 2010: 62). It also latches on to the historical antecedents (Cowan 1997: 154–60). As is demonstrated below, the law is tipped against such persons because most will fail the eligibility gateway. Furthermore, the evidence suggests that, on arrival and after a successful application for asylum, such households have a limited understanding of their housing rights (Rutter and Lahore 2009: ch. 5; Robinson et al. 2007). Although they are not 'powerless pawns', they have limited room to exercise choice which is also combined with a lack of information, so that any decision-making they do have is often a 'take it or leave it' type of decision around which their construction of place and neighbourhood is managed (Robinson *et* al 2007; Spicer 2008; Hynes 2009).

Asylum seekers

In general, until they are granted refugee status, asylum seekers are ineligible for HB, assistance as a homeless household, and for an allocation of social housing (respectively: Immigration and Asylum Act 1999, s. 115(1)(k), subject to certain exceptions in the Social Security (Immigration and Asylum) (Consequential Amendments) Regulations 2000, SI 2000/636; Immigration and Asylum Act 1999, s. 118 and Housing Act 1996, s. 185, subject to exceptions contained in the Allocation of Housing and Homelessness (Eligibility) (England) Regulations 2006, SI 2006/1294; and Housing Act 1996, s. 160A, subject to exceptions contained in the Allocation of Housing and Homelessness (Eligibility) (England) Regulations 2006, SI 2006/1294). Instead, their rights to assistance are dealt with by a combination of the Immigration and Asylum Act 1999 (the 1999 Act; as amended, in particular by the Nationality, Immigration and Asylum Act 2002 (the 2002 Act), s. 55) and the National Assistance Act 1948 (the 1948 Act, as amended, in particular by the 1999 Act, s. 96). In summary, the support provisions under the asylum Acts are provided by the United Kingdom Border Agency (UKBA) and offer certain asylum seekers accommodation and/or support on the fulfilment of certain conditions. Provision under the 1948 Act is by social services authorities and includes accommodation and other support. Asylum seekers whose application for asylum is unsuccessful are offered limited support given the fulfilment of certain criteria.

The 1999 Act support provisions now draw a distinction between applications for asylum 'made as soon as reasonably practicable after the person's arrival in the United Kingdom' (discussed below as section 95 cases) and others (2002 Act, s. 55(1)(b)). In the case of the former, entitlement to a range of specified support (1999 Act, s. 96) is provided by the UKBA subject to certain criteria being fulfilled, or under the 1948 Act. In the case of the latter, the specified support may not be provided by the Secretary of State other than 'to the extent necessary for the purpose of avoiding a breach of a person's Convention rights (within the meaning of the HRA)' (s. 55(5)(a)) and certain other protected categories (including those under eighteen). The UKBA apparently takes 3 days as a 'reasonable period' provided that the asylum seeker had no opportunity to claim asylum within that time (JCHR 2007: para. 88). The rationale for this distinction lies in the belief, first articulated by Michael Howard as Home Secretary in 1995, that those who apply for asylum at the port of entry or as soon thereafter as reasonable are more likely to be genuine. However, as Lord Brown put it in *R* v. *Secretary of State for the Home Department ex p Limbuela* [2006] 1 AC 396, at [101], to be considered below:

> I do not wish to minimise the advantages which the government seek to gain from their policy towards late claimants. But nor should these be overstated. It is in reality unlikely that many claims will be made earlier as a result of it. Nor do the statistics suggest that late claimants make a disproportionate number of

the unmeritorious claims. But more important to my mind is that ... the policy's necessary consequence is that some asylum seekers *will* be reduced to street penury.

Section 95 cases

Section 95, 1999 Act, gives the Secretary of State the power to provide accommodation and other support to those asylum seekers and their dependants 'who appear to the Secretary of State to be destitute or to be likely to become destitute within such period as may be prescribed' (the latter is fulfilled by a 14-day rule: Asylum Support Regulations 2000, SI 2000/704, reg. 7). That power is residual, in the sense that it operates only when there is no other obligation on other bodies, such as a duty on local authorities under the 1948 Act (see below for further discussion; *R (Westminster CC)* v. *NASS* [2002] 1 WLR 2956), or accepted by others, such as a charitable organisation (see Asylum Support Regulations 2000, SI 2000/704, reg. 6(4)). The destitution test is satisfied if

(a) he does not have adequate accommodation or any means of obtaining it (whether or not his other essential living needs are met); or
(b) he has adequate accommodation or the means of obtaining it, but cannot meet his other essential living needs. (s. 95(3))

In essence, the Secretary of State, acting through the UKBA's 'New Asylum Model' (through which a UKBA official has complete 'ownership' of an application for asylum and assistance, in succession to the agency set up to administer the 1999 Act support provisions, the NASS), operates a compulsory dispersal scheme for those seeking the provision of accommodation. That is, to remove the burden which fell disproportionately on local authorities in certain parts of London and the South East, asylum seekers are dispersed to other parts of the country under arrangements devised between NASS/UKBA through contracts made with providers (local authorities, PRPs, voluntary agencies and private landlords usually operating through consortia) on a regional basis. Asylum seekers are moved on from emergency accommodation to other areas on a no-choice basis, irrespective of their preference (s. 97(2)(a)) after completion of a lengthy form (Hynes 2009: 106). Refusal of accommodation terminates the support offered, subject to an appeal to Asylum Support Adjudicators. At the end of the first quarter of 2010, there were 27,455 asylum seekers in receipt of this support (Home Office 2010: 14). Where the UKBA decides that the applicant is not qualified for support under s. 95 or the UKBA decides to stop providing support, the applicant has a right of appeal to the First-tier Tribunal (Asylum Support) (s. 103, 1999 Act).

The 1999 Act requires the UKBA to take into account 'the desirability, in general, of providing accommodation in areas in which there is a ready supply of accommodation' (s. 97(1)(b)) and there is no right of appeal against the adequacy, nature and quality of the accommodation offered (leaving the only prospect of judicial review). This is generally taken as meaning areas where there is low demand for housing, whether social or otherwise. Those areas are by their nature the least desirable, with poor housing quality and other neighbourhood issues, such as racial harassment and attacks (see Robinson et al. 2007; Hynes 2009; Dwyer and Brown 2008; Phillips 2006: 544–6, referring to a picture of 'housing insecurity, deprivation and disadvantage'); it is, perhaps, not surprising that a significant number of asylum seekers forego s. 95 accommodation (see Phillips, 2006: 542). Asylum seekers were '"parachuted" into [these] deprived areas, with little preparation beforehand' (Phillips 2006: 546; also Anie et al. 2005; cf. Darling 2010, on Sheffield's development of 'City of Sanctuary' status). Hynes (2009) found that her sample of asylum seekers tended to wrap up voluntary agencies with the UKBA 'extending the cycle of mistrust' (p. 109; to similar effect, see Griffiths et al. 2006); that relocation to other areas during dispersal was common and built into the NASS system (p. 110); and that 'unmonitored use of accommodation providers opens up channels of potential exploitation' (p. 111).

On determination of the asylum application, the provision of accommodation is also terminated, subject to 28 days' notice being given if asylum is granted. A successful claim for asylum means that the household is entitled to the full range of benefits. Importantly, such a household is 'provided with' a local connection with the local authority into which it has finally been dispersed (s. 196(6) and (7) – see Chapter 6 above for local connection). An unsuccessful claim means that the household must rely on s. 4, 1999 Act, for support (see below). The research suggests that the 28-day notice period is often insufficient and households, lacking knowledge and information together with sometimes inadequate access to advice, are vulnerable to homelessness as a result (see, for example, Dwyer and Brown 2008; Phillips 2006; Hynes 2009).

Other cases

The question in relation to those asylum seekers to whom s. 55(1), the 1999 Act, applies (i.e. those who do not make an application for asylum within a reasonable period after entering the UK) is at what point it becomes necessary for the Secretary of State to intervene to avoid breach of the HRA. Articles 3 and 8 are particularly in issue here, although the focus in these cases has been on Article 3. That Article is expressed in the most forceful way as far as a Convention right goes: 'No one shall be subjected to torture or to inhuman or degrading treatment or punishment.' There is no proportionality proviso (as exists with Article 8, for example). In a strongly worded judgment in *Limbuela*, discussed below, Baroness Hale observed about s. 55(1) that it has taken the New Poor Law principle of less eligibility 'to an extreme which the Poor Law itself did not contemplate, in denying not only all forms of state relief but all forms of self sufficiency, save family and philanthropic aid, to a particular class of people lawfully here' (at [77]).

As Morris (2009: 71) notes, s. 55

> was introduced by means of a late amendment in the [House of Lords]. It was allowed only 15 minutes' debate in the House of Commons, was not included in the White Paper which preceded the Bill, and was the subject of severe reservations by the Joint Committee on Human Rights [references omitted]. The political process being redundant, the courts became the dialogic community in which these issues were debated (there being no right of appeal to the First-tier Tribunal (Asylum Support)).

Morris (2009: ch. 4) demonstrates the way in which the use of the courts became an overt strategy, co-ordinated by the Housing and Immigration Group, an informal group of lawyers who effectively hijacked the process. Rather than seeking out individual test cases, the strategy was a 'blitz' campaign, flooding the courts with emergency judicial review applications (being, of course, lucrative for those involved as well) which, in itself, caused what Palmer (2007: 257–62) describes as 'a crisis in the administrative courts' – the Court of Appeal in *Limbuela* referring to the fact that there were 666 other similar cases awaiting determination. Charities and voluntary agencies were involved in supporting cases through witness statements demonstrating the lack of alternative sources of support for claimants affected by the s. 55 prohibition. Harlow and Rawlings (2009: 740) refer to this episode of administrative justice as involving 'guerrilla warfare' ('the courts repeatedly attacking harsh measures and central government responding with various heavy armaments ranging from primary legislation to propaganda (use of the media)') or as 'a protracted "litigation game" played for high stakes'.

In *R* v. *Secretary of State for the Home Department ex p Limbuela* [2006] 1 AC 396, the House of Lords had to decide whether, and at what point, an individual asylum seeker is subject to 'inhuman and degrading treatment' so as to fall within the prohibition in Article 3 and, thus, require the Secretary of State to take positive action. It was found that s. 55 constituted 'treatment' when combined with the refusal to allow asylum seekers the opportunity to seek and gain alternative employment. It became 'inhuman and degrading' when 'a late applicant with no means and no alternative sources of support, unable to support himself, is, by the deliberate action of the state, denied shelter, food or the most basic necessities of life' (Lord Bingham, at [7]). The high threshold would be crossed 'if there were persuasive evidence that a late applicant was obliged to sleep in the street, save perhaps for a short and foreseeably finite period, or was seriously hungry, or unable to satisfy the most basic requirements of hygiene' (at [9]). 'Mere' destitution in itself is unlikely to be sufficient to cross the threshold because the s. 55 cases operate under a stricter regime than section 95 cases but rough sleeping on its own may be sufficient to give rise to the required degradation and humiliation (Lord Hope, at [58]–[60]; Lord Scott, at [72]; Lord Brown, at [101]). It is also clear that the requirement in s. 55 is to act before the breach takes place (at [61]) because the section requires the Secretary of State to 'avoid' a breach occurring (at [62]).

The 1948 Act

From the outset of the statutory controls on asylum seekers' access to housing, a strategy was developed to draw on little-used provisions in the 1948 Act by way of substitution to the other housing provisions. The most relevant provision remaining extant in that Act was that concerned with the provision of 'residential accommodation for persons aged eighteen or over who by reason of age, illness, disability or any other circumstances are in need of care and attention which is not otherwise available to them' (s. 21(1)(a)). This provision was, at one time, combined with the predecessor provision to the homelessness legislation (s. 21(1)(b)) which was subsequently repealed. However, that provision was, by something of a mysterious quirk, re-introduced in an enforceable departmental circular (LAC 93(10); see Cowan 1995; also the historical description given by Baroness Hale in the *Slough* case, discussed below, at [7]–[13]). The provision applies wherever a person is subject to immigration control or their presence in the UK is, for some reason, illegal because it offers 'the final hope of keeping the needy off the streets': *R (O)* v. *Wandsworth LBC* [2000] 1 WLR 2539, 2552, *per* Brown LJ.

In *R (M)* v. *Slough BC* [2008] 1 WLR 1808, the question arose as to whether a person subject to immigration control whose needs were for medication prescribed by her doctor and a fridge to put the medication in, fell within s. 21(1)(a) or s. 95. The House of Lords unanimously found that those needs were insufficient to fall within s. 21(1)(a) because, although the need for care and attention is one of the conditions precedent for the operation of s. 21(1)(a), 'care and attention' meant 'looking after' (*R (Wahid)* v. *Tower Hamlets LBC* [2003] HLR 2, at [32], *per* Hale LJ; the *Slough* case, at [33], *per* Baroness Hale). M did not require 'looking after', she required a fridge (her medical needs being catered for by the NHS):

> Looking after means doing something for the person being cared for which he cannot or should not be expected to do for himself: it might be household tasks which an old person can no longer perform or can only perform with great difficulty; it might be protection from risks which a mentally disabled person cannot perceive; it might be personal care, such as feeding, washing or toileting. This is not an exhaustive list. The provision of medical care is expressly excluded. (at [33], *per* Baroness Hale)

On the other hand, a person who was totally blind, requiring assistance with finding his way around his accommodation and surrounding area, dressing, shopping, laundry and housework, some of which are accommodation-specific needs, does fall within s. 21(1)(a) (*R (Zarzour)* v. *Hillingdon LBC* [2009] EWCA Civ 1529).

In *R* v. *Hammersmith and Fulham LBC ex p M* (1998) 30 HLR 10 (p. 20), the Court of Appeal held that s. 21(1)(a) was engaged in the case of certain asylum seekers because 'any other circumstances' included the circumstances under which those asylum seekers found themselves (despite the fact that these provisions of the 1948 Act 'were probably not intended to cover the situation which has now arisen': *R* v. *Newham LBC ex p Gorenkin* (1998) 30 HLR 278, *per* Carnwath LJ). A complicated body of case law quickly arose in which, for example, a claimant was excluded from support if they brought the problem on their own head (*R* v. *Kensington and Chelsea RLBC ex p Kujtim* (2000) 32 HLR 579); it was proper for the authority to provide support using vouchers or free supermarket food (*R* v. *Secretary of State for Health ex p Hammersmith & Fulham LBC* (1998) 30 HLR 525). The 1948 Act was subsequently amended because, as the Home Office put it, in its White Paper, it was not just an expensive form of provision, but also:

> The Court of Appeal judgments relating to the 1948 Act meant that, without warning or preparation, local authority social services departments were presented with a burden which is quite inappropriate, which has become increasingly intolerable and which is unsustainable in the long term, especially in London, where the pressure on accommodation and disruption to other services has been particularly acute. (Home Office 1998: para. 8.14)

The 1948 Act was amended in the 1999 Act (s. 116), so that the s. 21(1)(a) duty only applies in the following circumstances:

> (1A) A person to whom section 115 of the Immigration and Asylum Act 1999 (exclusion from benefits) applies may not be provided with residential accommodation under subsection (1)(a) if his need for care and attention has arisen solely –
> (a) because he is destitute; or
> (b) because of the physical effects, or anticipated physical effects, of his being destitute.

In subsequent cases, the question has arisen as to the extent of this provision as well as the interaction between s. 21(1)(a) and s. 95, the 1999 Act. In *R (Westminster CC)* v. *NASS* [2002] 1 WLR 2956, Lord Hoffmann, giving the leading judgment, drew a distinction between the able-bodied destitute, on the one hand, and the infirm destitute, on the other. The former were excluded from the 1948 Act as a result of the amendment (i.e. s 21(1A)), thus placing the obligations on NASS/UKBA, the latter were not – that was the effect of the word 'solely' in s. 21(1A) (*per* Lord Hoffmann at [32]). Thus, to fall within s. 21(1)(a), a person subject to immigration control must show what has come to be termed 'destitution plus'. That is, where 'an applicant's need for care and attention is to any material extent made more acute by some circumstance other than the mere lack of accommodation and funds, then, despite being subject to immigration control, he qualifies for assistance' (*R (O)* v. *Wandsworth LBC* [2000] 1 WLR 2539, 2548, *per* Brown LJ).

Failed asylum seekers

Where an application for asylum has been unsuccessful, any support provided under s. 95, the 1999 Act, terminates on the occupier being given notice, which is usually 28 days if granted asylum. Such occupiers have no security of tenure (Housing Act 1985, Sch. 1, para. 4 (as amended); Housing Act 1988, Sch. 1, para. 12A) and are excluded tenancies for the purposes of the Protection from Eviction Act 1977 (s. 3A(7A)). Support provided under the 1948 Act can continue in certain circumstances provided that the household complies with removal directions (Sch. 3, para. 6, the 2002 Act). Where the 1948 Act is inapplicable, s. 4, the 1999 Act (as amended), provides that:

> (2) The Secretary of State may provide, or arrange for the provision of, facilities for the accommodation of a person if –
> (a) he was (but is no longer) an asylum-seeker, and
> (b) his claim for asylum was rejected.
> (3) The Secretary of State may provide, or arrange for the provision of, facilities for the accommodation of a dependant of a person for whom facilities may be provided under subsection (2).

The scheme is, like s. 95, residual. It operates where the 'failed asylum seeker' appears to be destitute and any one or more of the following apply (Asylum (Provision of Accommodation for Failed Asylum Seekers) Regulations 2005, SI 2005/930, reg. 3):

> (a) he is taking all reasonable steps to leave the United Kingdom or place himself in a position in which he is able to leave the United Kingdom, which may include complying with attempts to obtain a travel document to facilitate his departure;
> (b) he is unable to leave the United Kingdom by reason of a physical impediment to travel or for some other medical reason;
> (c) he is unable to leave the United Kingdom because in the opinion of the Secretary of State there is currently no viable route of return available;
> (d) he has made an application for judicial review of a decision in relation to his asylum claim –
> (i) in England and Wales, and has been granted permission to proceed pursuant to Part 54 of the Civil Procedure Rules … or
> (e) the provision of accommodation is necessary for the purpose of avoiding a breach of a person's Convention rights, within the meaning of the HRA.

Section 4 support is routinely referred to as 'hard cases' support in that the applicant must appear not just destitute but also fulfil one of the other conditions – vouchers and housing are provided. In 2009, there were 10,150 successful applications for support (Home Office 2010), although this is the limit of the published statistics to date. It may be that one can read from *Limbuela* some positive duty in relation to reg. 3(2)(e) and, certainly, the threshold is likely to be reached regularly (Sweeney 2008). Failure to comply with removal directions also disentitles an application both to individuals (Sch. 3, the 2002 Act) and, potentially, to households with dependent children (ibid., as amended by s. 9, Asylum and Immigration (Treatment of Claimants etc.) Act 2004). The power in relation to dependent children, however, was not used from February 2008–2009 (JCHR 2009: para. 1.61).

The justification for this residual, basic provision in s. 4 is, in essence, to reduce any potential 'pull' factors to potential asylum seekers, particularly those found to be 'bogus' or 'undeserving' in some way. As Fox and Sweeney (2010: 302) point out, framing the debate in this way means that 'the impact of human experience of the asylum seeker is marginalized, even rendered irrelevant'. Furthermore, in terms of the s. 4 process, they point out (at p. 307) that 'in reality, [the failed asylum seeker is] likely to face administrative delays, complex application processes, and, ultimately, barriers in accessing housing which is capable of functioning as home'. Expanding on those bureaucratic problems, Lewis (2009: para. 2.3.2), whose research was conducted with agencies in Leeds, identified long and variable waiting times, up to several months, so that such a failure is 'a worsening cause of destitution in Leeds'. The JCHR (2007: para. 105) also found delays and 'evidence of an unacceptably high error rate in the processing of applications for support'. The significance of this problem was reinforced by Lewis' finding that only 9 per cent of failed asylum seekers were removed from Leeds (para. 3.1).

Applicants whose application for s. 4 support is unsuccessful have a right of appeal to the First-tier Tribunal (Asylum Support), although this does not extend to the location, nature and quality of any accommodation offered. Decisions of that tribunal are appealable to the Upper Tribunal. An application must be made within three working days of receipt of the decision (Tribunal Procedure Rules 2008, rule 22, with a discretion to extend the time limit). Public funding is not available for representation at such hearings. The current generic evidence suggests, not unreasonably, that representation at tribunals is correlated with increased success rates (Genn and Genn 1989) and the evidence suggests, unsurprisingly perhaps, that the same is true of Tribunal hearings on s. 4 appeals (ASAP 2007: 13–14).

Other persons from abroad

A person who is in the UK in breach of immigration laws (as well as certain failed asylum seekers whom the Secretary of State certifies have failed without reasonable excuse to take reasonable steps to leave the UK voluntarily or place themselves to leave voluntarily: Sch. 3, para. 7A, 2002 Act; and EEA nationals: para. 5) is not entitled to support under the 1999 Act, the 1948 Act, or the welfare and support provisions of the Children Act 1989, unless that person is a minor (Sch. 3, para. 1). However, those exclusions do not apply if, otherwise, the Secretary of State would be in breach of Treaty rights or the ECHR.

In *Birmingham CC* v. *Clue* [2010] 4 All ER 423, that dilemma faced Ms Clue who was also offered funds to return to Jamaica (her home country) by Birmingham City Council, with the possibility of a further resettlement grant. She had lived in the UK since 2000, having arrived with her daughter. She had three further children with a British citizen (so that those three children were British citizens). She applied to the Home Office on her and her eldest daughter's behalf for indefinite leave to remain, on the ground that her eldest daughter had been living in the UK for more than 7 years (an established ground for the exercise of discretion in her favour). Before that application was determined, she applied to Birmingham for assistance. Birmingham refused assistance for the family as a result of the application of Sch. 3, the 2002 Act.

The Court of Appeal gave a wide-ranging judgment, drawing on Article 8, ECHR, which provides for the right to respect for 'private and family life', subject to proportionality provisos, and which has 'reined in' the impact of Sch. 3 (Burton and Gask 2010: 1000). Dyson LJ began by making the important observation that 'private' life was a broader concept than 'family' life (by reference to *Boultif* v. *Switzerland* (2001) 33 EHRR 50) because the former concept embraced 'the totality of social ties between settled migrants and the community in which they are living' (*Boultif*, at [59]). In essence that enabled Dyson LJ to distinguish other authorities which would have determined the matter against Ms Clue (*R (Kimani)* v. *Lambeth LBC* [2004] 1 WLR 272; *R (Grant)* v. *Lambeth LBC* [2005] 1 WLR 1781). Where an applicant has no other forms of assistance available, and 'the only potential impediment [to returning to the country of origin] is practical in nature', it is open to a local authority to arrange transport back to the country of origin to avoid a breach of that person's Convention rights.

However, where the 'potential impediment is legal in nature' so that returning to the country of origin would in itself breach that person's Convention rights, then different considerations apply. Where Article 8 is engaged, and there has been no application for leave to remain in the UK, the question for the local authority concerns whether a return to the country of origin would breach Article 8 (although, in family cases, where the children have spent their formative years in the UK, a return would be likely to breach Article 8: at [59]). In such cases, though, the local authority is 'entitled to have regard to the calls of others on its budget in deciding whether an interference with a person's article 8 rights would be justified and proportionate within the meaning of article 8(2)' (at [73]).

On the other hand, if the applicant for assistance has also applied for leave to remain,

> save in hopeless or abusive cases, the duty imposed on local authorities to act so as to avoid a breach of an applicant's Convention rights does not require or entitle them to decide how the Secretary of State will determine an application for leave to remain or, in effect, determine such an application themselves by making it impossible for the applicant to pursue it. (at [63])

The point is that, if the applicant is forced to leave the UK, they would not be able to pursue their application or appeal for leave to remain. In such a situation, the financial resources of the local authority are irrelevant (at [72] providing that the applicant would otherwise be entitled to those services and is destitute).

European Economic Area nationals

The UK's accession into the European Union brought with it obligations to facilitate workers' free movement within the EU. They are, however, ineligible for housing as homeless persons, ineligible for an allocation of housing, and ineligible for HB unless they fall within certain categories of households who are entitled (respectively: Housing Act 1996 ss. 185 and 193(6)(a), 160A(5), including regs. 3–5, the Allocation of Housing and Homelessness (Eligibility) (England) Regulations 2006, SI 2006/1294; and reg. 10, Housing Benefit Regulations 2006, SI 2006/213). Broadly, only those applicants and members of their family who are 'qualified persons' are eligible but they must also be habitually resident in the Common Travel Area (unless exempt from that test). A person who is not exercising their Treaty rights, but who is in the UK lawfully in the sense that they have not been removed from the UK by the Secretary of State, does not have a 'right to reside' and is, therefore, ineligible for assistance (*Abdirahman* v. *Secretary of State for Work and Pensions* [2008] 1 WLR 254). It is necessary, thus, to consider the rights of residence of EU applicants for assistance.

EEA nationals who are exercising Treaty rights, which includes full or part-time work (as well as jobseekers) or study, do not require leave to enter or remain in the UK, and are, therefore, entitled to a right to reside in the UK (Directive 2004/38/EC (the 2004 Directive); Immigration (European Economic Area) Regulations 2006 (the IEEA Regulations), SI 2006/1003, regs. 5 and 6; cf. *Barnet* v. *Ismail* [2006] EWCA Civ 383). They are qualified persons under the IEEA Regulations as indeed are their other family members. That qualification extends, in the case of workers, to 'former workers', such as temporary unemployment after an illness or accident; in certain circumstances related to length of previous employment, or unemployment, or are looking for employment (and have a genuine chance of engagement), to those who have lost work involuntarily and are jobseekers or have entered vocational training; or have given up work to enter vocational training related to their previous employment (IEEA Regulations, reg. 6(2); cf. Article 7, 2004 Directive, which appears to be less restrictive). Students must be enrolled on a recognised course, have comprehensive sickness insurance, and have sufficient resources not to become a burden on the social assistance scheme of the UK during their residence (IEEA Regulations, reg. 4(1)(d)). Jobseekers are explicitly denied an allocation of housing and entitlement to homelessness assistance (Allocation of Housing and Homelessness (Eligibility) (England) Regulations 2006, SI 2006/1294, regs. 4(1)(b) and 6(1)(b)).

To exercise rights as a worker, the work must be more than 'marginal or ancillary' and must perform services of economic value that are genuine and effective, under the direction of another person, and for remuneration (see, for example, *DM Levin* v. *Staatssecretaris van Justitie* Case 53/81; *Vatsouras* v. *Arbeitsgemeinschaft (ARGE) Nürnberg 900* Case 22/08). The standard is relatively low. Thus, a person who undertook work as a steward at the Wimbledon tennis championships for a fixed 2-week period was a 'worker' because this was genuine and effective and, without his services, the Wimbledon organisers would have had to employ somebody else (*Barry* v. *Southwark LBC* [2009] HLR 30). That decision was relevant to Southwark's obligations to Mr Barry as a homeless person because the status of worker continues in certain circumstances for 6 months after involuntary unemployment (reg. 6(2)(b)(ii), IEEA Regulations); before the end of that period, Mr Barry had an accident which left him unable to work. He, therefore, retained his worker status.

All EEA nationals (including those from the A8 and A2 states, as to which see below) enjoy a right to reside if they have 'resided legally for a continuous period of 5 years in the host Member State' (Article 16, 2004 Directive, brought into force, albeit in narrower terms, by reg. 15 (1), IEEA Regulations). The meaning of 'reside legally' is highly contested (including, at the time of writing, two references to the Court of Justice of the European Union from UK courts: *SSWP* v. *Lassal* [2009] EWCA Civ 157, and see now, the judgment of the C-162/09 *SSWP* v. *Lassal*; by the Supreme Court in *McCarthy* v. *SSHD*), and it is currently unclear whether it is permissible to 'count' periods before the IEEA Regulations came into force (*Lassal*, although the Advocate-General's opinion in that case is that such periods should be counted: http://eur-lex.europa.eu/ LexUriServ/LexUriServ.do?uri=CELEX:62009C0162:EN:HTML). However, in *Lekpo-Bozua* v. *Hackney LBC* [2010] EWCA Civ 909, the Court of Appeal held that 'reside legally' meant in accordance with the terms of the 2004 Directive, in particular Recital 17 to the 2004 Directive. That recital requires 'compliance with the conditions laid down in this Directive' for the right to permanent residence. One of the conditions is that the person must not be an unreasonable burden on the social assistance system of the host state.

Rights given under the 2004 Directive are equally available to certain family members of the worker on the basis that to do otherwise would place obstacles in the way of the right of free movement (see, among other sources, Article 12, Regulations EC 1612/68 (the 1968 Regulations)). Those rights of the children or of the parent who has actual custody of the children, irrespective of nationality, are not lost by the death or departure from the Member State of the citizen, 'if the children reside in the host Member State and are enrolled at an educational establishment, for the purpose of studying there, until the completion of their studies' (Article 12, 2004 Directive). The 2004 Directive replaced certain of the 1968 Regulations but, significantly, not Article 12 of the 1968 Regulations.

In *Teixeira* v. *Lambeth LBC* (Case C-480/08) and *Ibrahim* v. *Harrow LBC* (Case C-310/08), the European Court of Justice held that the 2004 Directive had not affected the interpretation of Article 12 of the 1968 Regulations (see *Baumbast and R* Case C-413/99) so that children of migrant workers (who have in the past worked but whether or not they are working at the time), who are residing in the host Member State, are entitled to equal treatment in access to education, which gives them an independent right of residence in the host Member State, on which the primary carer's right depends. This meant that the primary carer has an independent right of residence in the host Member State, irrespective of whether they are workers or have sufficient resources and comprehensive sickness cover for themselves, or their relationship with the worker (see Article 7, 2004 Directive), indeed a right of residence in their own right. This is because, were the result different, that would effectively deprive the child of its right to education (see also Article 8, ECHR – *Ibrahim*, at [31]; *Teixeira*, at [39]). The guidance provided by the DWP on these judgments (DWP 2010a – for the purposes of income support, among other benefits, which can also determine the income entitlement for HB) suggests that the right is dependent on the child still being in general education and under eighteen, but that may be questionable (see *Teixeira*, at [81]); additionally, it suggests that the primary carer must also be a parent, but that is not apparent on the face of either the relevant provisions or the two cases (see http://nearlylegal.co.uk/blog/2010/05/ibrahimteixeira-guidance/).

A8 and A2 nationals

In May 2004, ten new states joined the EU (A8 states, as two of the new accession states, Cyprus and Malta, were not included in the restrictions discussed below) and in January 2007, two further states joined (A2 states). Although nationals of those states had the same rights as other EEA nationals in principle, EU states were given transitional powers to derogate from those rights for a limited period. The UK has done so (for A8 and A2 nationals respectively, these regulations are the Accession (Immigration and Worker Authorisation) Regulations 2004, SI 2004/1219 (the 2004 Accession Regulations) and the Accession (Immigration and Worker Authorisation) Regulations 2006, SI 2006/3317 (the 2006 Accession Regulations)). The 2004 Accession Regulations, which were due to run out in 2009, have been extended to 30 April 2011; the 2006 Accession Regulations end on 31 December 2011 (although they can be extended for a further two years). The basis for these derogations rests on two 'themes' – the consequences of immigration of A8 and A2 nationals for service provision and the implications for community cohesion – although these themes were 'rooted in assumptions regarding the economic benefits of new immigration, toward a more sceptical position' (Robinson 2007: 101–2). In fact, as Robinson (2007: 105 and 108) points out, less than 1 per cent of all social rented lettings in England were to A8 nationals and these were in the less popular property types (see further, Pemberton 2009).

Under both these sets of regulations, the UK has derogated from nationals of these states Treaty rights by developing a worker registration scheme applicable only to those nationals. These schemes broadly require: in the case of A8 nationals, registration of their employment with the Secretary of State for 12 months on commencing employment; and, in the case of A2 nationals, the more restrictive requirement of registration only for certain types of employment. There are exclusions from the registration requirement in certain circumstances, but the basic principle is that the person cannot be a jobseeker for the purposes of the IEEA Regulations if they are not registered (reg. 4(2), the 2004 Accession Regulations; reg. 6(2), 2006 Accession Regulations). Thus, their eligibility is similarly restricted.

Habitual residence

A person who is not habitually resident in the Common Travel Area (the UK, Isle of Man, Republic of Ireland, or the Channel Islands) is generally not eligible for the assistance considered in this part of this book (Allocation of Housing and Homelessness (Eligibility) (England) Regulations 2006, SI 2006/1294, regs. 3(c) (Class C), 4(1), 5(1)(c) (Class C), 6(1); Housing Benefit Regulations 2006, SI 2006/213, reg. 10(2); for a scathing critique of the development of this concept, see Adler 1995). In general, 'an appreciable period of time and a settled intention' are required to demonstrate a habitual residence (*Re J* [1990] 2 AC 562, 578; see also *Nessa* v. *Chief Adjudication Officer* [1999] 1 WLR 1937; *Shah* v. *Barnet* [1983] 1 All ER 226; *Swaddling* v. *Adjudication Officer* Case C90/97, at [29]–[31]). The Homelessness Code of Guidance (CLG 2006e: para. 9.16) draws a distinction between those who have resided in the Common Travel Area for more than 2 years, in which case it 'is likely' that they pass the habitual residence test; and, in cases of residence for less than 2 years, further enquiries are required. Annex 10 to the code contains a list of non-exclusive factors to be considered: why the applicant has come to the UK; whether the applicant is joining or rejoining family or friends; the applicant's plans; length of residence in another country; their 'centre of interest' (e.g. a home, job, friends, clubs, finance accounts – at paras. 17–18).

Homelessness and allocations – family members

As originally conceived, where a family member of an eligible applicant was ineligible, no account was to be taken of the ineligible family member for the purposes of the local authority's decision as to whether the (eligible) applicant was homeless or threatened with homelessness and had a priority need (Housing Act 1996, s 185(4)). In *Morris* v. *Westminster CC* [2006] 1 WLR 505, the Court of Appeal, by a majority, found this provision to be in breach of Articles 8 and 14, Sch. 1, HRA, because it clearly affected family life and was disproportionate to the policy objective (as a 'response to the problems of benefit tourism and unlawful migration': at [48], *per* Sedley LJ). It could only be justified if there were 'very weighty' or 'solid' grounds for it, or it was a reasonable and proportionate response, but those justifications provided by the Secretary of State were neither weighty nor solid (at [83](iii), *per* Auld LJ).

The government's response was tardy (JCHR 2010: para. 156); indeed, it was not until the introduction of s. 314 and Sch. 15, Housing and Regeneration Act 2008 that the 1996 Act was amended. The first amendment to s. 185(4) was to make the exclusion only apply where the main applicant is eligible but subject to immigration control (other than being an EEA or Swiss national) – Arden et al. (2010: para. 3.72) suggest that it will apply in relation to applicants who have been granted refugee status, indefinite leave to remain or humanitarian protection.

Second, the 2008 Act amendments insert a new category of 'restricted cases' into the 1996 Act. These restricted cases occur where an eligible applicant relies on an otherwise ineligible family member (a 'restricted person') to qualify as homeless or in priority need. The full housing duty owed in restricted cases is, so far as reasonably practicable, to make an offer of a private AST for a term of at least 12 months (ss. 193(7AA)–(7AD)). The duty ends when the household accepts that offer having been given certain information about the consequences of refusal of the offer and its right to a review of the suitability of the accommodation offered (ss. 193(7AA)–(7AB)). The justification for this difference of treatment was on the basis that 'the provision of long-term social housing – it is a scarce resource which brings valuable benefits with it, including the right to buy – is another matter' (HL Debs, col. 819 (9 July 2008), Baroness Andrews; see also JCHR 2008: para. 91). Despite this attempt to deal with *Morris*, the JCHR has remained unconvinced that these new provisions are themselves compatible with Articles 8 and 14 (JCHR 2008, paras. 92–5; 2010: para. 157).

As regards an allocation of social housing, Part VI of the Housing Act 1996 does not have an exclusion for these types of cases other than if they fall within the categories of homeless person who would otherwise be accorded 'reasonable preference' (s. 167(2) and (2ZA), 1996 Act – see Chapter 7). However, that having been said, in other cases, it is open to a local authority to take account of the immigration status of the members of an applicant's household – indeed, depending on the individual local authority's policy, that is likely to be a relevant consideration albeit one which may differ depending on the ineligible family member's age and dependency on the applicant (*R (Ariemuguvbe)* v. *Islington LBC* [2010] HLR 14).

Conclusions

The complexity of the law on eligibility belies a fairly simple policy of alignment of immigration and housing assistance. That policy has taken its inspiration from ill-informed and unfortunate anecdote and myth, as well as seeking to respond to concerns raised by the marginal far-right parties. This chapter demonstrates that access to housing assistance has been significantly constrained by the concept of eligibility. That concept does not halt the media and politician-inspired headlines and it is certainly true that more could be done by politicians, academics and practitioners to demonstrate the inadequacy of the apparently pervading 'legal consciousness', for want of a better expression. Morris' concept of civic stratification offers a useful way of thinking about eligibility because it enables the various levels to be visualised as well as offering a differentiated version of citizenship.

9

Access to the private rented sector

Contents

Previous chapters in this part have considered the rules about access to social housing through homelessness legislation and the general law on allocating social housing. They noted that accessing PRS accommodation may be one outcome of any such application. In this chapter, consideration is given to three broader issues about access to the PRS: the terms of the agreement; tenancy deposits; and state support for rent payments (HB). These issues do not necessarily arise when a landlord and tenant actually enter into an agreement – most often, other than possibly HB, neither party gives much thought to them at that point. Issues about HB can arise at the outset or during the currency of the agreement (if, for example, the tenant loses their employment). However, the point of entry into the agreement is the crucial moment to which the law looks when problems in the relationship subsequently arise. Access to HB may determine whether a tenant can afford the rent 'negotiated' at the outset. Payment of a tenancy deposit upfront, before the tenancy commences, can cause problems for either party at the point at which the tenancy is determined. The final issue considered in this chapter relates to tenure shifts – where an owner sells their property and then rents it straight back. These arrangements cause particular problems, which are discussed in this section (and to which we return in Chapter 16 below).

Contractual terms

It is usual today for tenants to be given a written contractual agreement by their landlord. Although short-term tenancies of less than 3 years can be granted orally as a matter of strict property law (s. 54(2), Law of Property Act 1925; s 2(5), Law of Property (Miscellaneous Provisions) Act 1989), it is usually the case that they are granted in writing because, amongst other reasons, that facilitates any subsequent claim of the landlord to possession. The common law assumes that the terms of the agreement are freely negotiated, like any other contract. However, certain terms are implied into residential tenancies, or superimposed on the contract, as a matter of common law and statute – amongst others, these give the tenant certain rights, for example to quiet enjoyment and security of tenure as well as placing obligations on the landlord, subject to certain criteria, to conduct certain repairs to the property. These extra-contractual rights are considered in more depth in Chapters 11 and 13 below.

That assumption of the common law may not be unreasonable in certain parts of the sector, but most often one is dealing with terms which are not the subject of negotiation and nor are they intended to be. In Part I, we noted that many landlords are 'amateurs' in the sense that they have limited, if any, legal expertise; tenants are in a similar position. Even in areas where there is a plentiful supply of privately rented property, which might give more scope for negotiation, one might question whether landlords and tenants actually appreciate the nature of the bargain into which they are entering or anticipate future problems in the relationship (which is, after all, the essence of good drafting of any document) (see, generally, Ellickson 2008). They can hardly be blamed for this lack of knowledge – the law is complex and advice rarely sought. As the Law Commission (2001: 11) noted, landlords fall foul of the law through inadvertence; tenants are equally confused about their rights and responsibilities; non-specialist lawyers find this area of law difficult to understand.

In a series of papers drawing on interviews with landlords and younger tenants, Lister (2002; 2005; 2007) demonstrates how the formal contract between landlord and tenant gave way to informal sets of understandings developed at the outset through the interactions between landlord and tenant. Neither party expected to negotiate about terms and rents. If the tenant sought to negotiate, 'it was perceived [by the landlord] as denoting financial insecurity and a potential risk' (2002: 99). Lister's point was that by focusing on legal requirements, 'social factors of relationships are overlooked which are significant and have a greater impact on behaviour than at first credited' (2007: 72). Thus, social expectations of the relationship, combined with the emotional or sentimental attachments (including with the property) should be regarded as significant. Lister emphasises the role of trust, which might be regarded as a central aspect of all ongoing relations (see Macneil 1981: 1034). When trust breaks down between the parties, attachments can become more evident through unlawful action. So, one of the consistent findings in research about unlawful evictions is that landlords regard the property as 'theirs', which underpins their belief that they are entitled to possess it without recourse to due process of law (see Nelken 1983; Marsh et al. 2000).

There has been a more general shift, partly reflecting these understandings of the landlord–tenant relationship, towards a 'consumer approach'. The shift is currently at the stage of what might be referred to as an emerging governing mentality, one which has not quite been accepted formally within law and is, in itself, contested. There are a number of strands to the development of this mentality. First, the Law Commission proposed that reforms to the landlord–tenant relation should be guided by the consumer approach. One consequence of that approach was the need to develop model tenancy agreements, which contained all necessary terms in plain and intelligible language (Law Commission 2006). The government's subsequent review argued that it was not clear whether the Law Commission reform suggestions 'offer a substantial improvement' to the existing framework (Rugg and Rhodes 2008: 82). Nevertheless, that review did suggest that there was a need for written tenancy agreements, a proposal which was subsequently accepted by the government (CLG 2010a: paras. 24–6). Given the Coalition government's deregulatory desire, that proposal (along with other reforms to the PRS) has been ruled out (CLG 2010g).

A further way in which the consumer perspective has infiltrated the letting sector (both private and public) has been through European regulations concerned with unfair terms in consumer contracts between a 'seller or supplier' and a 'consumer' (Council Directive 93/13/EEC). These have been incorporated into English law in the Unfair Terms in Consumer Contracts Regulations 1999 (SI 1999/2083). These provisions have been held to apply to both private and public landlords (*R (Khatun)* v. *Newham LBC* [2002] HLR 29) as well as between a letting agent and non-business landlord (*Office of Fair Trading* v. *Foxtons Ltd* [2009] EWHC 1681).

Where a term is not 'core' to the agreement, and has not been individually negotiated, it 'shall be regarded as unfair if, contrary to the requirement of good faith, it causes a significant imbalance in the parties' rights and obligations arising under the contract, to the detriment of the consumer' (reg. 5). Core terms are those which are the essence of the price, the main subject-matter of the contract, which were regarded as more likely to have been negotiated between the parties (*Abbey National plc* v. *Office of Fair Trading* [2009] EWCA Civ 116, at [52]). The requirement of good faith is 'one of fair and open dealing', which might be expressed as transparency and not taking advantage of the consumer (*Director General of Fair Trading* v. *First National Bank plc* [2002] 1 AC 481, at [17], Lord Bingham). All terms, core or not, must be drafted in plain, intelligible language and, where there is doubt about their meaning, 'the interpretation most favourable to the consumer shall prevail' (reg.7).

The OFT produces written guidance setting out certain terms which it regards as potentially unfair as well as how the regulations are interpreted by the OFT (OFT, 2005). This notes that fairness depends not only on how a contractual term is intended to be used, but also how it could be used (which depends on its breadth) (para. 2.6). Unfair terms are likely to be those which seek to exclude or restrict the landlord's express or implied obligations (ch. 3). In relation to rights of the landlord to re-enter the property on the tenant's default (forfeiture clauses), the OFT states that it does not object to the inclusion of such clauses provided that the landlord makes clear the circumstances under which the landlord is entitled to re-enter. In other words, a right of re-entry on its own is unlikely to be sufficient; the right must be in plain language and cannot give the landlord greater powers to end the tenancy than they would have under the law (paras. 4.16–8).

Tenancy deposits

The one specific area in which policy on landlord–tenant relations seemed to be at odds with the broader deregulatory agenda was tenancy deposits. Here policy had belatedly accepted that reliance on contract and more informal mechanisms had proved inadequate: the need for a greater emphasis on consumer protection was acknowledged. Tenancy deposits were regularly cited by welfare organisations as being the most problematic area of landlord–tenancy relations: landlords made unjustified or unexplained deductions, or withheld deposits completely, all of which had consequences for households in terms of securing alternative accommodation and their risk of homelessness (NACAB 1998).

In tune with its broader concerns about regulation-as-burden on landlords (see Blandy 2001), the government initially opted for the promotion of a self-regulation scheme. However, few landlords joined these schemes (Rugg and Bevan 2002); the government then 'suggest[ed] that legislation may be likely, *although the costs and benefits of such intervention must be fully assessed*' (ODPM 2002: 6). Rugg and Bevan (2002: 6.3.18) also cautioned that even bodies representing tenants 'were agreed that the issue of deposit mismanagement is not so pressing as to require the introduction of a full-sector regulatory framework. The widespread lack of a perceived problem with deposits by landlords and agents is likely to bring such a framework into disrepute and may lead to extensive – and expensive – non-compliance.' While the government's position suggested a less than committed approach to enforcing the self-regulation of deposits, political pressure during the legislative process meant that provisions for such a scheme were introduced into the 2004 Housing Bill at a late stage (on 20 October 2004, on the third and final day of the report stage in the House of Lords, responding to concerns raised by Lord Best). Perhaps as a result of that lateness and the government's commitment issues, the provisions were not well-drafted.

The provisions are contained in ss. 212–5 and Schedule 10, Housing Act 2004, and only concern deposits held under an AST. In summary, the purposes of the provisions were to ensure that deposits were properly protected and to provide an alternative dispute resolution scheme which takes such issues away from the court. Lord Bassam, a government whip (and formerly a leader of the squatters' movement), introduced the amendments (see HL Debs, vol. 665, col. 884), saying they will

> streamline the proceedings for tenancy deposits to make it easier for tenants to enforce sanctions against non-compliant landlords … A landlord or a letting agent on his behalf now has 14 days *from receiving the deposit* to ensure that it is safeguarded by a scheme, that he has complied with the initial requirements of the scheme and to provide a tenant with information about that scheme and its operation. *Until this is done*, the landlord is unable to regain possession of the property using the usual 'notice only' grounds for possession.

> Additionally, we have cut down the number of court hearings required to enforce the provisions. *If the landlord or his agent has not complied within 14 days*, the tenant can now apply for a court order requiring the landlord to either return the deposit or pay it into a custodial scheme and an order requiring the landlord to pay the tenant an amount equivalent to three times the deposit. *We believe that this provides a greater certainty for landlords that they will face a financial penalty if they do not comply with the provisions …*

> We have put something in place in legislation which will not only stand the test of time but, more importantly, will match the very understandable concerns over tenancy deposits expressed by tenants – and to a degree by landlords – over a considerable period of time …

> We have introduced these amendments with the aim of dealing with the worst abuses in the private rented sector. Obviously those abuses have a disproportionate effect on the poorest members of our communities.

This lengthy quotation provides the essence of the case both for intervention and the intensive scheme developed. Since the 2004 Act came into force, all tenancy deposits paid by tenants to landlords must be protected with an authorised scheme from the time that they are received (s. 213(1); the reference throughout to the word 'paid' means that the money must have been handed over by the tenant to the 'landlord', and does not refer to money retained by the landlord: *UK Housing Alliance* v. *Francis* [2010] HLR 28, at [9], Longmore LJ). The definition of a landlord includes 'a person or persons acting on [the landlord's] behalf in relation to the tenancy or tenancies' – which is wide enough to include a managing agent. A deposit is defined as any money intended to be held by the landlord or otherwise as security for the performance of the tenant's obligations or the discharge of any of the tenant's liability arising under or in connection with the tenancy (s. 212(8)); a deposit cannot consist of property other than money (s. 213(7)).

The 'initial requirements of an authorised scheme' must have been complied with by the landlord within 14 days of receipt of the deposit (s. 213(3)). The initial requirements are 'such requirements imposed by the scheme as fall to be complied with by a landlord on receiving such a tenancy deposit' (s. 213(4)). The landlord must provide certain information to the tenant about the scheme, initial requirements and the operation of these statutory provisions (s. 213(5)) in a prescribed form or to the same effect as such a form (s. 213(6)(a)) within 14 days of receipt of the deposit (s. 213(6)(b)). These provisions override any other agreement between the parties, i.e. they cannot contract out of these provisions.

Failure to comply with the initial requirements of an authorised scheme, failure to provide the information in the correct format, or, in effect, being misinformed by the landlord that a scheme applies to the deposit, entitles the tenant or any person who pays the deposit on behalf of the tenant to apply to the county court (s. 214(1)–(2)). In those cases and where the court is not satisfied that the deposit is being held in accordance with a scheme, the court must, as it thinks fit, either order the person holding the deposit to return that deposit or require the deposit to be held in accordance with such a scheme, within 14 days (s. 214(3)). Then, the following appears:

> The court must also order the landlord to pay to the applicant a sum of money equal to three times the amount of the deposit within the period of 14 days beginning with the date of the making of the order. (s. 214(4))

This penalty is potentially severe. There is also a further penalty in the nature of a restriction on a defaulting landlord's ability to obtain possession of the property:

(1) If a tenancy deposit has been paid in connection with a shorthold tenancy, no section 21 notice may be given in relation to the tenancy at a time when –
   (a) the deposit is not being held in accordance with an authorised scheme, or
   (b) the initial requirements of such a scheme (see section 213(4)) have not been complied with in relation to the deposit.
(2) If section 213(6) is not complied with in relation to a deposit given in connection with a shorthold tenancy, no section 21 notice may be given in relation to the tenancy until such time as section 213(6)(a) is complied with. (s. 215)

The right of the landlord to terminate an AST by using the section 21 notice procedure is discussed in Chapter 11 below, but, in summary, it entitles a landlord to a mandatory possession order 2 months after it has been served (but not before the tenancy has lasted 6 months). This is the prime right of the landlord and the restriction in s. 215 is highly significant.

The amateur nature of landlordism meant that it was not long before a stream of cases arrived in the county courts. They demonstrated just how poorly the legislation had been drafted; county court judges were unable to agree on the proper construction of the provisions (and their judgments do not bind other county court judges). The full story of these judgments can be traced back (www.nearlylegal.co.uk/blog; or www.nicmadge.co.uk/Tenancy_Deposits. php). This left considerable uncertainty in how the provisions work.

In particular, different decisions at county court level emerged regarding the situation where the landlord put the deposit into a scheme after they or the tenant had brought proceedings for possession or the mandatory award. Some courts accepted the argument that the remedies under s. 214(3) and (4) only arose if the landlord had not provided the tenant with the prescribed information at all; some accepted that they arose if the landlord had not done so within 14 days. In the joined cases of *Tiensia* v. *Universal Estates, Honeysuckle Properties Ltd* v. *Fletcher* [2010] EWCA Civ 1224, the Court of Appeal resolved this issue, by a majority, in favour of the apparently defaulting landlord. In both cases, the landlords had protected the deposit late – well after the 14-day period was over. Were they liable for the s. 214(4) penalty? The court held that they were not (Rimer LJ, with whom Thorpe LJ agreed, giving the reasoned judgment for the majority); indeed, if the landlord protected the deposit at any time up to the court hearing, the landlord would not be liable. The court did so on the basis of a construction of the penalty provision which meant that it only referred to a failure to comply with the initial requirements of the scheme (which do not include any scheme specific requirements: [35]) and *not* the requirement that compliance must take place within 14 days of receipt of the deposit (at [37]). Second, the (present) tense in ss. 214(1) and (2) referred to whether these obligations had been performed at all, and not whether they had been performed within the 14-day period (at [38]). Third, if it were to be read the other way, the s. 215 bar on obtaining possession would be permanent. Fourth,

> Such interpretation appears to me to be not only firmly supported by what I would regard as the carefully chosen statutory language, it is also a properly precise, or strict, one to apply to legislation such as section 214 that is manifestly penal in intent. Moreover, it is an interpretation that is consistent with the purpose of the legislation. That purpose is to achieve the due protection of deposits paid by tenants, ideally within the 14-day period but, if not, then later. It cannot be its purpose to punish landlords who may for example, for innocent reasons, be just a day late in securing such protection. (at [39])

Rimer LJ was making the point that the purpose of the provisions was simply that landlords protect the deposit; his narrow, perhaps pragmatic, reading both of the provisions and their purpose meant that all sides would be satisfied.

Sedley LJ disagreed, arguing that the majority needed to face up to the fact that their construction had drained the provisions of their effect; indeed, it had eviscerated the legislative scheme (at [49]–[50] and [52]). He accepted that the outcome of his construction – that failure to comply with the initial requirements within 14 days meant that the landlord would permanently be unable to terminate the tenancy – was 'morally questionable but perfectly explicable: Parliament has decided that recovery is to be in the tenant's hands, that it is to depend on the simple question of compliance or non-compliance, and that strict liability for non-compliance will catch the devious and encourage the others. That is a matter for legislators, not for us.' (at [50])

The effect of *Tiensia* is that the intentions as expressed by Lord Basham have been avoided as a result of poor draftsmanship. Nevertheless, the s. 215 bar remains significant – a landlord cannot serve a section 21 notice until the deposit has been protected. It was common practice in relation to some tenancies for landlords to serve a section 21 notice at the outset of the tenancy to ensure that they would be able to take possession of the property at the end of the term. If, as would be likely, the landlord had not complied with the initial requirements of the scheme, and/or had not given the tenant notice of the terms, that section 21 notice could not subsequently be relied upon (*Delicata* v. *Sandberg*, Central London CC, 2 June 2009).

Housing Benefit

Housing benefit (HB) is a means tested form of assistance to cover all or part of the contractual rent between a landlord and occupier when a property is the tenant's home (s. 130(1)(a), Social Security Contributions and Benefits Act 1992). Around 20 per cent of occupiers in the PRS are in receipt of HB. The HB market forms a distinctive sub-sector of the PRS (Rugg and Rhodes 2008: 18), but, at a more micro-level, it has been said that there are distinctions within this sub-sector between 'dominant', 'concentrated' or 'dispersed' HB markets (CURS et al. 2009a: 41–5). Such differentiation is an important local characteristic because it affects landlord and tenant behaviour generally as well as, for example, willingness to negotiate over rents.

As befits most welfare schemes of assistance, HB is incredibly complex. It has recently been the subject of reform which has been designed to increase the choice and responsibility of occupiers and reduce the scheme's complexity. In the first section on this subject, entitlement is discussed; the critiques of HB as was are then considered; the new scheme is then analysed. Only the barebones of the law are examined here (and the discussion does not include pensioners' entitlements, which effectively operate under an almost separate scheme – Kemp 2007: 114). In the final section, the Coalition government's highly controversial reforms to HB are discussed.

Entitlement

In essence, HB is parasitic on other benefits. A person entitled to Income Support or Jobseeker's Allowance is generally entitled to HB as well. Where a person is in work or has certain other income, they are entitled to HB but their entitlement is reduced by 65 pence for every pound of income over the threshold (s. 130(3)(b), Social Security Contributions and Benefits Act 1992; reg.71, Housing Benefit Regulations 2006, SI 2006/213 (references in this section are to these regulations unless stated otherwise)). Certain capital of less than £6,000 generally does not affect the level of HB payment, but capital between £6,000–16,000 reduces entitlement (capital does not include one's home, which raises difficult issues in certain situations: Hopkins and Laurie 2009). Entitlement is reduced where a 'non-dependent' – broadly somebody who could and should contribute to the rent (reg. 3) – also occupies the property (reg. 74).

There are a number of anti-fraud provisions in the regulations – indeed, as discussed below, the possibility of widescale fraud has been a major policy driver in the regulations. Certain non-transparent relationships are excluded from HB claims altogether (reg. 9; *R v. Stratford-upon-Avon Housing Review Board ex p White* [1999] 31 HLR 126). No HB is payable where, for example, the tenancy has not been granted on a commercial basis (reg. 9(1)(a)).

Particular issues arise when an owner in difficulties with their mortgage sells the property to a company on condition that the company lets the property back to the owner, the so-called sale-and-rentback arrangement (discussed below). This transaction is potentially caught by these anti-fraud provisions which treat the former owner as not liable to pay rent in respect of a property which the claimant has owned in the previous 5 years, 'save that this sub-paragraph shall not apply where [the claimant] satisfies the appropriate authority that he or his partner could not have continued to occupy that dwelling without relinquishing ownership' (reg. 9(1)(h)). In two cases before the Upper Tribunal, it has been said that the claimant has to address the steps taken to explore the alternatives before entering into such arrangements; the question is not one of the claimant's perception but what alternatives were available to the claimant; further, 'could not' in the proviso to reg. 9(1)(h) was about practical compulsion – a claimant could not be expected to get themselves further into debt by borrowing against a credit card to meet mortgage payments, which would be the height of financial irresponsibility (*CH/2340/2008* [2008] UKUT 11; *CH/3571/2008* [2009] UKUT 20; see generally Marston and Wilding 2009).

HB is payable against the contractual rent, but there are certain charges disregarded from the contractual rent, such as water rates and some unrelated service charges. That is not meant to say that HB covers the entire contractual rent. There are certain policy priorities which have dictated that maximum HB payable is set below the eligible contractual rent. One particular policy priority has, perhaps not surprisingly, been to restrict the overall HB budget, discussed further below.

In 1996, the Conservative government introduced particular regulations for 'young persons' between the ages of 16 and 25 years old. The reason given for this restriction was that HB should not make a person under 25 better off than they would otherwise have been had they remained in the parental home or take on better quality accommodation than they would be able to afford if they were in work (for discussion, see Rugg 1999). These regulations restrict the young person claimant's maximum HB to what is known as a 'single room rent', that is a single room in a shared house, as assessed by a rent officer (see below for discussion of the rent officer). This was subsequently expanded by the New Labour government to include not just a single room but also a shared room as well (see Rent Officers (Housing Benefit Functions) Order 1997, SI 1997/1984, as amended). The effect of this restriction has been quite dramatic, leading to 'a steady and substantial decline' in claims made by such claimants for HB (which the New Labour expansion did nothing to alter), despite demand amongst this group for PRS accommodation (Harvey and Houston 2005: 35). Landlords have also been more wary of renting to this age group (ibid. p. 37; Kemp and Rugg 1998).

Entitlement could be reduced in certain areas as a sanction for failure to co-operate with rehabilitation efforts where a household had been evicted on an ASB ground (s. 130B–G, Social Security Contributions and Benefits Act 1992; see Chapter 15 below). This rule derived from the 2000 Green Paper, which drew a parallel with the use of financial mechanisms to discipline landlords when it floated the possibility of using the HB system as a means of enforcing conformity to desirable norms. The rights/responsibilities dichotomy was explicitly proffered as the rationale for making the payment of HB conditional on the tenant's behaviour (DWP 2003: para. 1). The essential question posed by this document was why should the state offer financial support to people 'who behave without regard to their neighbours' (para. 9). The consultation paper was keen to point out that there should be little impact on landlords (para. 14; Annex B).

In one sense, this entitlement restriction has turned out to be a symbolic policy intervention – by 23 February 2009, no local authority had begun the process of reducing HB entitlement as a result of ASB. The symbolic element, though, is significant, because it further demonstrated a shift in the nature of the welfare state away from entitlements to one in which a contractual approach dominates and which aligns welfare payments with the rather different motivations of the criminal justice system. As Rodger (2006: 131) has put it, 'the implicit model of behaviour informing the Labour government's policy strategy against incivility is one of punitive operant conditioning' – a combination of behaviour modification through negative sanctions and re-socialisation.

The role of the rent officer

The HB scheme falls within the purview of the DWP, whereas housing policy falls within the currently constituted CLG. As Kemp (1994) acknowledged, there are considerable tensions between these two departments. On the one hand, the DWP's reasonable concern is to constrain and reduce the growth of HB; on the other hand, CLG's policy prescription has been to revive the PRS and one major policy tool it has used was to enable landlords 'to secure a reasonable rate of return on their investment' (DoE 1987a: 3.16). It was recognised from the outset of the deregulated PRS that there would need to be some control over rents where HB was payable, but it was said that HB 'would take the strain' of the inevitable increases in rents. What has transpired over time, then, is that the HB sub-sector effectively operates within centrally controlled rental parameters.

Kemp (1993: 67) noted that the policy conflict was resolved by mediating controls over allowable HB through an expanded role for rent officers. Rent officers became responsible for a variety of different determinations over the years following the introduction of the Housing Act 1988 reforms to the PRS. Overall responsibility for the rent service has been contracted out and falls within the Valuation Office Agency (VOA) (a revenue and customs executive agency).

HB was restricted, for example, in cases where the rent was unreasonably high, in relation to rents for equivalent properties in the locality (the local reference rent), and rent officers were made responsible for the single-room rent determination. Rent officers made these determinations drawing on a startling breadth of discretion, leading to allegations of arbitrary decision-making (Bramley 1995: 14) and inconsistency (Kemp and McLaverty 1994: 113), as well as unreality (the regulations presuppose the existence of a market for the type of accommodation and that market is not dependent on HB). Determinations involve what Valverde (2003b: 48–53) has described as the deployment of knowledge and administrative, on-the-job expertise, a non-scientific empirical knowledge (see Kemp and McLaverty 1993: 98). Harvey and Houston (2005: 50) note the following practices in relation to single room rent determinations:

> It was clear that rent officers in most areas were having difficulty in finding sufficient evidence. Measures were used, such as casting the net over a very wide area and/or using 'similar' accommodation and/or in practice looking at the student market for supporting information (although this is not taken into account in the formal decision-making). Reflecting the lack of variation in the low income 'single room' part of the market, the resulting figure was usually uniform across the case study area concerned.

Determinations by rent officers are made now in relation to the 'broad rental market area' (BRMA), a term which has been substituted for the word 'locality'. The background to this substitution is the confusion over the breadth of 'locality' (R (Saadat) v. The Rent Service [2002] HLR 613, at [15], Sedley LJ), despite an attempt to give broad discretion to rent officers in making that determination (Sch. 1, para. 4(6), Rent Officers (Housing Benefit Functions) (Amendments) Order 2001, SI 2001/3561). In R (Heffernan) v. The Rent Service [2008] 1 WLR 1702, the House of Lords struck down a rent officer decision that the locality of a flat in Sheffield Central was the whole of the Sheffield area, including certain outlying rural areas. It is, for these purposes, unnecessary to delve too deeply into their Lordships reasoning because, shortly after the decision, the DWP laid a further Statutory Instrument before Parliament substituting the phrase 'broad rental market area' for 'locality'. The definition of BRMA for the local housing allowance (LHA) is as follows:

> (4) [The BRMA] means an area within which a person could reasonably be expected to live having regard to facilities and services for the purposes of health, education, recreation, personal banking and shopping, taking account of the distance of travel, by public and private transport, to and from those facilities and services.
>
> (5) [A BRMA] must contain –
> > (a) residential premises of a variety of types, including such premises held on a variety of tenures; and
> > (b) sufficient privately rented residential premises to ensure that, in the rent officer's opinion, the [LHA] for the categories of dwelling in the area for which the rent officer is required to determine a [LHA] is representative of the rents that a landlord might reasonably be expected to obtain in that area. (Rent Officers (Housing Benefit Functions) Amendment (No. 2) Order 2008, SI 2008/3156, inserting these provisions into Sch. 3B(4), Rent Officers (Housing Benefit Functions) Order 1997).

This provision effectively returns the position to what it was considered to be prior to the decision in Heffernan. Thus, provided that it meets the criteria, the whole of Sheffield including rural areas could indeed be a BRMA. This is significant because one might imagine that there will be considerable differentiation between inner and outer area rents, which will impact on (i.e. potentially lessen) the allowable amounts for the LHA. However, *Heffernan* remains relevant to the extent that it explains the subtle alterations in the scope of the regulations. For example, it is to be noted that there is no quality threshold for the facilities and services mentioned in sub-para. (4) as there was in the previous regulations. That is because, otherwise, there could be considerable room for argument in whether an area of 100 sq. km or more has sufficient access to the facilities and services of the appropriate quality: 'the possible difficulties involved in resolving such an argument speak for themselves' (at [62]). Equally, there is no restriction to any particular neighbourhood or neighbourhoods – the BRMA clearly can be extensive provided that the relevant facilities and services are available within reasonable distance by public or private transport. It is that latter proviso which effectively provides one limit to the BRMA but the notion of reasonableness is flexible – the guidance issued by the VOA suggests that people living in rural areas expect to travel greater distances, for example (VOA 2009: 3). The other limits are contained in sub-para. 5: the BRMA must have mixed tenures and, perhaps more importantly, sufficient PRS properties to determine that the LHA represents what a landlord might reasonably be expected to obtain. As regards the latter criterion, the VOA Guidance (2009: 4) makes the following observation:

Lettings information representing 10–15% or more of the private rented sector should provide a reliable representation of a broad rental market. (It should be noted that the size of the Private Rented Sector (PRS) cannot be determined by the amount of lettings information that the VOA holds – the extent of the PRS must be independently assessed by using other data such as census data.)

Of considerable interest (perhaps as a future research question) concerns the interaction between the local authority, which pays out and controls access to HB, and the rent officers. There is an undertaking from the VOA that, although the final decision is that of the rent officer, it will consult with local authorities as to the extent of the BRMA (VOA 2009: 5).

The BRMA was not a concept which was alien to rent officers prior to the 2008 order. Indeed, it underpins the LHA. However, the LHA evaluation reveals certain problems in setting the LHA. Under the previous regime, rent officers 'had regular contact with a range of landlords and tenants that both referrals and the related inspections had previously provided'; the LHA, as effectively a more administrative procedure, removes those 'regulatory conversations' from decision-making because the LHA is set without reference to any particular property. The process had, therefore 'reduced [rent officers'] ready access to quantitative and qualitative market information'. The relevant market information was compiled through 'regular "formal" surveys of landlords and agents and strengthening existing informal contacts with them, subscribing to electronic lettings information where available and expanding the use of advertisements for lettings in newspapers, Post Offices and shops' (CURS et al. 2009b: 30).

Critiques

Other than what has already been discussed above, the HB scheme was the subject of fairly extensive critiques, not all of which were based on anything more than economic assumptions. In summary, the critiques of the pre-LHA scheme were that it was too complex, and that it encouraged: passivity, upmarketing, fraud and created a perverse disincentive against seeking employment. Each is now taken in turn.

Complexity is, in many respects, part-and-parcel of any long-running scheme which has been the subject of detailed regulations, and which have altered over time (what Kemp (2007: 122) refers to as 'complexity creep'). At times, the DWP (and its predecessors) have engaged in a game of cat and mouse with the courts. Indeed, *Heffernan* and its predecessors demonstrate that adverse (in the sense that they do not accord with current practice) judicial findings of higher courts have simply been overturned subsequently through amending regulations re-installing current practice. More generally, though, there has been a problem of over-specificity in regulations which, while meant to be of general application, cannot account for some individual circumstances. The tendency to over-specify detail in regulations means that they are altered, sometimes quite subtly, in response to other individual claims. Thus, the area has become overly regulated and has developed a complexity which belies the fact that its purpose is to assist people on no or low incomes. In particular, the non-dependent deduction provisions have been the subject of concern because of their complexity.

There are sub-issues about complexity relating to the administration of HB. There have been historic concerns about administrative problems leading to delays in the payment of HB. Claims are required to be processed within 14 days but, with rising anxiety about the cost of HB fraud leading to increasing checks on claims, this deadline can be a moveable feast in a proportion of local authorities (Audit Commission 2002). Having said that, recent evidence is of improved performance in the processing of HB claims, with pockets of poor performance in certain areas (Pawson et al. 2010). The average time taken to process new claims across local authorities was 42 days in 2003/2004 which was reduced to 25 days in 2007/2008 (see www.dwp.gov.uk/asd/asd1/hb_ctb/performance.asp). However, as Stephens (2005: 124) notes, HB is relatively cheap to administer, with costs similar to the early 1990s. Even so, error rates in determinations have also been quite high, leading to over- and under-payments. Complicated rules exist regarding the repayment of over-payments, drawing a distinction between official error (which does not require repayment) and overpayments where the claimant has contributed to the mistake or omission (see Housing Benefit and Council Tax Benefit Circular A15/2009: 54–9). Irvine et al. (2008) found that error rates had risen and were higher than rates of fraud on the system by 2006 (although there has also been an overall reduction in error rates since 2002/2003: DWP 2009: 2.5).

Second, the argument has been that the HB scheme has created passive recipients because HB was set against the eligible rent. In around half of all cases, HB covers the entire rent. As a result, there were no incentives on either landlord or tenants to negotiate over the contractual rent, particularly where it was unclear at the outset what the rent officer determination would be regarding the maximum rent payable. There is limited evidence available on this issue. A further related issue was that, as HB could be (and as a matter of course, usually was) paid direct to landlords by the local authority, at the instigation of the occupier (reg. 96(1)(a), 2006 Regulations), this meant that the occupier effectively had no 'connection' with the payment of their rent.

Third, given that HB covered the entire eligible rent, there were concerns that recipients might occupy accommodation that was too large for their needs or too costly. The regulations were rewritten during the 1990s to deal with this problem. However, as Stephens (2005: 123) observes, evidence of this effect was hard to establish but, drawing on Kemp (1992b), there was no evidence to suggest that upmarketing was, or had been, a significant problem.

Fourth, recent policy debates have focused on fraud by claimants and landlords on the HB system. Error and fraud rates were high and of concern to the government, which consequently placed various obligations on claimants to provide relevant documentation as well as inform the local authority of any change in circumstances. How one defines fraud is, of course, a central issue here. Does it apply in cases where the claimant is simply unaware of the reporting requirement, avoids reporting a change in circumstances, or deliberately does not inform the local authority? The regulations are riddled with exceptions, designed to combat fraud, and discretion on the local authority to stop payments in certain cases (which, of course, adds to the complexity of entitlement).

Finally, it was said that HB creates a perverse disincentive to seeking employment because it covers the eligible rent at 100 per cent and because the effect of the taper for earnings has a potentially significant effect. Quite simply, receipt of HB created an 'unemployment trap' and a 'poverty trap', effects which were exacerbated by the time taken to make redetermination after a change in circumstance. As Stephens (2005: 122) put it, although these traps could be demonstrated on paper, 'there is relatively little evidence to indicate its impact on actual behaviour'. Cannizzaro (2009: 10) suggested,

> The links between eligible rents, HB and work incentives depend on a number of factors that include, but are not dominated by rent levels. The characteristics of the claimant and the job choice they make also interact and determine whether or not the financial gain to work is high enough to induce a move into employment.

The government sought to ease the effect of transition into work through an extended payments scheme: where a claimant has been in receipt of a qualifying benefit for 26 weeks and obtains employment (or increases their earnings from employment), they are entitled to HB at the full rate for a further 4 weeks (reg. 72, 2006 Regulations). The government was consulting on altering this rule with a new 'transition into work payment' with a longer qualification period for eligibility but substituting 3 months for 4 weeks (DWP 2009: 4.8–9). All of this was, no doubt, for the best but the key issue lay in its translation into the everyday experiences and understandings of claimants themselves. Turley and Thomas (2006: ch 2) found a lack of knowledge amongst claimants about in-work benefits, whether they were out of work or in work and not claiming. Indeed, the knowledge of those out of work was 'essentially limited and invariably confused' (at para. 2.2.1).

The local housing allowance

The LHA was designed to meet at least some of these critiques. At its heart lay notions of responsibility and choice (albeit inadequately articulated: King 2006). The idea behind the LHA is that it provides claimants with a flat rate, a kind of monetary housing voucher, depending on their household size, composition and location.

It dealt with complexity in part only. Rent officers fix the LHA in the BRMA based on the number of bedrooms required by households. They take the median from the basket of rents in that BRMA. That rate is then applied throughout that BRMA and published as such. To this extent, the LHA is designed to be transparent. Thus, the range of previous determinations which rent officers used to make in respect of a specific household and a specific property are no longer required (hence the lack of contact noted above). Delays should, as a result, fall out of that element of the process. However, the complexity of the entitlement rules, fraud and error devices, remains.

It dealt with passivity by entitling claimants to receive the full LHA amount whatever their actual rent. This creates incentives on tenants to negotiate with landlords and shop around. If their actual rent is below the LHA, they are entitled to retain the difference up to a maximum of £15 per week; if the rent is above the LHA, the occupier must fund the difference (hence, dealing with the upmarketing critique).

Claimants themselves are paid the LHA. There are two purposes for that change: first, it is designed to enable claimants to open bank accounts, which is regarded as part of a work-entry requirement and financial inclusion; second, it is designed also to 'empower' claimants to manage their incomes and pay their rents (DWP 2002: 18). There is a tension here with the purpose of HB, that is to ensure occupiers are able to meet their rental payments; and, indeed, there are provisos for those tenants who are likely to have difficulty in managing their affairs, it is improbable that they will pay their rent, and the claimant has more than 8 weeks of rent arrears (regs. 95–6, 2006 Regulations) – in these cases, HB is to be paid direct to landlords (which, on one interpretation of 'responsibility', rather undermines the LHA: King 2006). HB officers are required to make these decisions, a new role which was not entirely welcomed by them (CURS et al. 2009b: 54; Stares 2010). It is up to the claimant themselves, in conjunction with their landlord and support services, to make a case for vulnerability (which rather shifts the burden of proof and may, in itself, prove to be an irrational policy). The evaluation of the LHA pathfinders found inconsistency between and within the pathfinder local authorities as to their implementation of these rules (CURS et al. 2009b: 55). In relation to the 8-week arrears rule, authorities approached this issue in different ways during the pathfinders, some making large cheques out to landlords, but sending them to the claimant's address (thus not offending the LHA principle in the sense that the claimant had to pass the cheque on to the landlord), and some intervening before the 8-week period (ibid. p. 57–8).

New Labour concerns

However, certain policy problems emerged with the implementation of the LHA. One might say that these problems might not have existed had the DWP waited for the outcome of the evaluation of the LHA pathfinders before deciding to roll out the LHA across all local authorities (the evaluations were finally published in 2010: Rhodes and Bevan 2010; Hartfree et al. 2010; Walker and

Niner 2010). Be that as it may, the problems have emerged partly as a result of the changed policy environment after the credit crisis in 2007–2008. The key concern was, of course, to limit public spending in this new environment.

The LHA was a target for a number of reasons. First, the average amount of LHA exceeding rents was estimated at £11. On one view, this suggests that the scheme was working well and tenants were negotiating effectively with their landlords. On another view, this excess drove up costs compared to the previous system (which limited HB to the eligible rent). The government recognised that there is an elasticity between the eligible rent and the LHA, which landlords might exploit by raising rent levels to the LHA maximum. In the 2009 Budget, the government announced that it would limit the LHA to the eligible rent, but subsequently recognised that such a change undermined the essence of the LHA (i.e. choice and responsibility). Therefore, it engaged in a further round of consultations on reform (DWP 2009: 3.9–11). A final point here concerned the government's responses to 'press coverage … about a family who have been receiving very high rates of Housing Benefit to live in a property in London' (DWP 2008) – the LHA was subsequently capped at a five-bedroom rate, leaving some large households with a potential rent shortfall.

The evaluation from the national roll-out of the LHA, however, demonstrated that most claimants had only a limited understanding of the LHA (and some claimants were unaware of the change to the LHA); where claimants did demonstrate an awareness of the LHA, it was of the direct payments' rules. Claimants 'claimed to have had no awareness of their entitlement when embarking on their property search. However, where claimants lacked awareness of their actual entitlement, they often had a "rough idea" based on the amount of HB they had previously received.' (Hartfree et al. 2010: 16) As many claimants were unaware of their entitlement, they made an educated (albeit often inaccurate) guess. Where claimants did negotiate with the landlord,

> the negotiation was borne out of necessity as tenants had agreed to take the property and then discovered that their LHA entitlement would not cover their rent. In most cases these negotiations were successful and the rent was reduced. Whilst there was evidence of some negotiation taking place in relation to rent levels, there was little to suggest that tenants felt empowered to negotiate as a result of LHA. (ibid p. 49)

Research with landlords, by contrast, found greater knowledge of LHA rates – indeed, whatever method was used to set rents, most appear to have checked the rent against the LHA, at least, if not set the rent by reference to the LHA rate (Rhodes and Bevan 2010: ch 2).

Second, the calculation of the LHA by rent officers takes account of all rents in the BRMA, whether high or not, and set the LHA at the median level. This meant that, in some areas, the LHA is 'distorted by the presence of large numbers of expensive properties; properties most working households could never consider renting' (DWP 2009: 5.6). The DWP, therefore, proposed to exclude the most expensive rents from the LHA calculation (para. 5.13).

Third, there were concerns about the safeguard procedures in relation to when payments might be made to landlords directly rather than to the occupier themselves. It will be remembered that a key element of the LHA scheme was payment to the occupier to encourage choice and responsibility as part of their empowerment. The DWP, in a wonderful turn of phrase, was considering 'returning an element of choice to customers which would enable them to decide to have their benefit paid directly to the landlord' (para. 6.10). If the purpose of the scheme was to encourage choice and responsibility on the part of the customer through the payment mechanism, then this comment bore more than a hint of irony. That having been said, the evaluation of the national roll-out did find considerable differences in the degree of flexibility of HB authorities in the payment of rent direct to landlords and that independent advisers were concerned that the safeguard was not operating efficiently for all claimants (Hartfree et al. 2010: ch 5). Further, research with landlords found less knowledge on this issue, despite it being a significant complaint of the landlords surveyed (Rhodes and Bevan 2010: ch 7).

Indeed, when considered in the round, the proposed reforms involved a kind of recalibration of HB which almost returned it to its pre-LHA days. The government had always been sensitive to media concerns about exploitation of the system by landlords and tenants, and to the need to reduce its expense on HB. Both of those were, no doubt, reasonable concerns, but it should also be remembered that, when the sector was subject to rent deregulation (from fair to market rents) in the late 1980s, reliance was placed upon HB to meet the increased rents.

Discretionary housing payments

Under the Discretionary Financial Assistance Regulations 2001 (SI 2001/1167), local authorities have the power to make payments by way of financial assistance to persons who are entitled to HB and 'appear [to the local authority] to require some further financial assistance (in addition to the benefit or benefits to which they are entitled) in order to meet housing costs' (reg. 2(1)). As the title of the regulations suggests, such payments are discretionary and they are also subject to certain limits (reg. 3). Walker and Niner (2005) found certain gatekeeping practices in place – such as insufficient or no publicity for the scheme, and 'red tape' – but, even where claimants provided sufficient information and completed the application form, claims were decided in some areas on the basis of a 'feeling'. By way of contrast to the complex formal rules on HB, these payments are made on the basis of limited criteria. Although only one of their case studies had a formal policy on such payments, decisions tended to be made by senior officers and are capable of being reviewed (reg. 8).

Coalition reform

In the emergency Budget in 2010, the incoming Coalition government made a number of proposals for changes to the LHA that were planned to take effect either immediately or within the next few years. Some of these changes had been suggested by the outgoing New Labour government, but the immediate changes were: to remove the LHA for five-bedroom properties so that the maximum payable would be for a four-bedroom property; to set absolute caps centrally on the amount of LHA; and to shift away from using the median rent to set the BRMA to using the 30th percentile of rents, thus reducing the LHA; the excess between the eligible rent and the LHA, which had been kept by the tenant (up to a maximum of £15), will be removed; occupiers in need of a carer will be entitled to an extra-bedroom rate. Discretionary housing payments were to be increased, but to only 4 per cent of the potential gain to the Treasury of the total reform package, thus leaving tenants effectively unable to use such payments in the case of a shortfall (Social Security Advisory Committee 2010: para. 4.12). Part of the Coalition government's case for change was that HB should be geared to what people in that accommodation would expect to pay; however, that case was undermined by the DWP's own research, which argued that this was, in essence, a false binary (between in work and out of work) because many low-income working households were in receipt of HB and

> although this cannot be fully evidenced – that low income households in the PRS could be more appropriately viewed as a continuum with those in slightly higher paid and more secure jobs at one end [low-income working households] to people unlikely to be able to access and keep secure, reasonably paid jobs at the other (HB claimants). In the middle are those who may move in and out of benefit as circumstances change. (Walker and Niner 2010: 44)

However, there were other major concerns. Setting the LHA cap centrally and removing the five-bedroom rate effectively means that many households are likely to be priced out of certain areas and will have to move, sometimes great distances. The cap appeared to have been set 'quite arbitrarily' and the potential risks were not justified by reference to the proposed savings (Social Security Advisory Committee 2010: 4.21). Furthermore, the impact of removing the five-bedroom rate was not supported by an equalities impact assessment, and 'the [DWP] cannot properly assess the impact of the proposed measure on the group most likely to be affected – ethnic minority families' (Social Security Advisory Committee 2010: 4.17).

The Social Security Advisory Committee made a damning assessment of the proposed reforms, arguing that:

> In our view these proposed measures are neither a coherent expression of the Government's objectives for improving incentives and making work pay, nor a certain formula for achieving savings to the public purse as a whole. At the same time, the rationale for the measures suggests that the underlying problem that

needs to be addressed is one of under supply of affordable housing, particularly in economically vibrant parts of the country …

Apart from the potential financial hardship, the human costs, the child poverty and other wider negative impacts of these proposed changes, we also see them as being out of step with the broader thrust of policies to incentivise work and to make work pay. (ibid. paras. 6.1 and 6.5)

The government went ahead with its plans, despite these critiques which were shared by a number of other interest groups and media (see Helm and Asthana 2010), but delayed their start until April 2011 with transitional provisions to assist those with ongoing tenancies and rental obligations at that date (Social Security Advisory Committee 2010). The transitional provisions also enable HB to be paid direct to the landlord in a further circumstance, 'the relevant authority considers that it will assist the claimant in securing or retaining a tenancy' (reg. 2(8)). The apparent intention of this provision is that it offers a quid pro quo: in return for landlords lowering the rent to HB levels, they will be entitled to rent direct ('However, Ministers are clear this is likely to be a temporary agreement to provide an incentive to landlords to lower their rents and is by no means a return to direct payments being made to landlords as a matter of course.': DWP 2010b). There are further reforms to come, including a proposal to reduce, to 90 per cent, the allowable HB of a person who has been entitled to Jobseeker's Allowance for more than 12 months; and a mooted proposal to increase the age range for the single room rent from 25 to 35 years' old.

Tenure shifting: sale-and-rentback

Access to the PRS may also arise through a tenure-shifting route – where the owner of a property sells it to a buyer, usually a company, who/which then rents it back to the buyer, usually on an AST. Various commitments may be given to the former owner by the buyer about the length of the term of the tenancy and the buyer may offer the former owner the opportunity to buy the property back after (say) 10 years. These sales usually take place at an undervalue, and sometimes involve staged payments, with a certain proportion at the outset with the rest to be paid after (say) 10 years on a specific event (see the 'deal' in *UK Housing Alliance* v. *Francis*, at [1]). As we discuss in Chapter 16 below, sale-and-rentback agreements have caused, and continue to cause, considerable problems for law. This is partly because many of the commitments entered into by the buyers are not put into writing, but are oral assurances (for example, 'you can stay in the property for as long as you like, provided you pay the rent') which are dependent on the individual negotiation between the buyer and the seller-renter (see, for example, *In the Matter of the North East Property Buyers Litigation* [2010] EWHC 2991 (Ch), Appendix 1); and, in general, there are particular issues for property law when such assurances are made. Partly also, questions arise as to the priority of interest between the mortgage lender and the seller-renter. These issues are 'parked' for now.

Considerable concern was expressed about these arrangements because of the risk that seller-renters were entering into these transactions without understanding their effect, and the transactions were not always regarded as in the seller-renters' best interests. In the 2008 Budget, HM Treasury requested that the OFT conduct a market study. This estimated that the number of such transactions that had taken place was around 53,000, most firms were small, the sector had grown very fast, and the industry was still evolving (OFT 2008: ch. 3.2–21). Further, there were considerable risks for the seller-renter, in that often they did not see the buyer's valuation, which might also be revised downwards at a crucial stage (such as when the seller-renter was due in court to deal with mortgage arrears); buyers were unaware of the limited security they were receiving under the terms of the AST, which might also result in significant increases in rent; buyer default on the mortgage resulted in risks to the occupier; there were concerns about the advice offered by the buyer; and that most seller-renters will rely on HB, but their eligibility for HB is not straightforward (see above) so that initial assumptions proved unfounded after sale; further, many seller-renters did not shop around (3.30–60; 4.9–21). They also found that there had been exploitation of people who were in difficult circumstances – 'Most consumers interviewed by our researchers were left with the firm impression that their tenancy would be unlimited.' (at 5.10) There were concerns that intermediaries, including solicitors, were not providing full and proper advice (see, for example, the 'vague' advice given to the buyer in *Scrowther* v. *Waltermill Properties* [2009] EW Misc 6 (EWCC) Newcastle-upon-Tyne County Court, at [40]–47]).

The case for regulation was clear, particularly as self-regulation was not a viable option given the wide range of buyers in the market (see also Treasury Select Committee 2009: 27–31). This recommendation was accepted by the government (Department for Business, Enterprise and Regulatory Reform 2008; Treasury 2009b), which placed regulatory responsibility with the FSA (FSMA 2000 (Regulated Activities) (Amendment) Order 2009, SI 2009/1342). Given the extreme concern about the need for immediate regulation, the FSA made interim regulation (FSA 2009b) followed by full regulation (2010b). These regulations require all sale-and-rentback firms to be registered with the FSA and to comply with its regulatory principles. In particular, these regulations require full disclosure of certain information and provide that the tenancy cannot be brought to an end on certain of the mandatory grounds (including Ground 8 for non-payment of rent) and the buyer can only rely on a ground for possession if it is 'fair' to do so (amended rule 2.6A.5B). Further, the buyer must ensure that any mortgage lender has seen the terms of the tenancy agreement with the seller-renter and agrees in writing to it. The buyer must give the seller-renter clear warnings about the transaction, including that they should **'Consider these schemes only as a last resort**. Make sure you have looked at all other options first.' (original emphasis)

Many of the issues which have arisen should not arise in the future if the buyers conform to these principles. At present, though, there are many examples of difficult issues of property and housing law which do arise in this context. For example, it is perfectly possible for a transaction at an under-value to be overturned if the seller-renter subsequently becomes bankrupt or insolvent, although the burden of showing it is at an undervalue is on the seller-renter's creditors (*Delaney* v. *Chan* [2010] EWHC 6 (Ch)). A collateral contract under which the buyer promises to pay a withheld proportion of the sale price to the seller-renter after (say) 10 years may well have to comply with certain formalities in a contract for the sale of an interest in property; failure to comply with those formalities will render the agreement void, requiring the buyer to return the money immediately (*Scrowther* v. *Waltermill Properties* [2009] EW Misc 6 (EWCC) Newcastle–upon-Tyne County Court, at [67]–[75], HHJ Behrens, who nevertheless expressed some doubt on the point and gave leave to appeal). Certain of the terms must pass the 'fairness' test in the Unfair Terms in Consumer Contracts Regulations 1999 (discussed above), which raise trans-action-specific issues (compare *UK Housing Alliance* v. *Francis* [2010] HLR 28, especially at [27], and *Scrowther*, at [76]–[87]).

However, perhaps the best example of the problems created arose in *Redstone Mortgages plc* v. *Welch*, Birmingham County Court, 22 June 2009 (HHJ Worster). Welch was the buyer and Redstone her lender. The report is short but demonstrates the complex problems which arise when a person who is essen-tially an amateur engages in such a transaction. Welch made a number of oral representations to the seller-renters (the Jacksons): they would be entitled to remain in the property while they were paying rent (a representation which was fraudulent because the contract of sale gave Welch vacant possession when the sale was completed); and the tenancy was entitled 'short assured tenancy'. Welch failed to pay four instalments of the mortgage and Redstone sought possession of the property. HHJ Worster held that the agreement, in fact, created an AT which bound Redstone (although cf. the *North East Property Buyers Litigation*, which found that such matters did not bind the mortgage lenders; this latter case is currently on appeal).

Conclusion

Access to the PRS is an issue which is commonly ignored and regarded as the proper domain of the individual relationship between landlord and ten-ant. Such motivations tie in with the current policy vision of the PRS as well as of regulation. That vision, as discussed in Chapter 3 above, sees the PRS as an important tenure within the housing system which needs to grow in size to meet demand. Regulation is regarded as the pitfall, leading to a decline in the size of the sector. The evidence for the latter observation lies in the twentieth century until the deregulation in the Housing Act 1988. The landlord lobby is influential and anti-regulationist (Cowan and Carr 2008). As a result, much is left to the individuals to negotiate terms. It is only at the margins or in isolated cases (such as tenancy deposits) that regulation has entered the domain in a way which suggests a lack of coherence.

HB, which at one time regulated that segment of the market that relied on it, was also liberated giving room for negotiation between landlord and occupier on the question of price, although much of the ideology underpinning the original idea of the LHA has been reworked. If a key purpose of the LHA was to offer an incentive to tenants to negotiate their rents down (so that they could retain a portion of the LHA paid to them), the Coalition government's reforms have effectively returned to the old HB idea but with fairly savage cutbacks and with more to come.

The final matter considered in this chapter has been the tenure-changing effects of sale-and-rentback agreements. These create considerable complexity because, like the PRS more generally, they have been entered into by amateurs, on the basis of representations of (at best) dubious validity, with dramatic consequences (to which we return in Chapter 16).

10

Access to owner-occupation

Contents

In this chapter, we look at access to owner-occupation, first focusing on generic issues around access to mortgage finance, and subsequently, more specifically, on access to low-cost ownership (focusing on shared ownership and the RTB). The preface to the discussion in this chapter is contained in Chapter 2, in which the promotion of 'home ownership' and the regulation of the mortgage market was discussed. We are at a point in the housing market cycle in which there has been much wringing of hands, consideration given to greater regulation of access to mortgage finance, together with the active promotion of alternatives, sometimes labelled 'intermediate home ownership' (IHO). Separately to that cycle, access of sitting tenants to ownership through the RTB, discussed in outline in Chapter 4, has also contracted as a result of various recent statutory limitations. Nevertheless, the apparent virtues of home ownership have remained dominant in policy statements, which continue to promote its benefits. The RTB is also discussed in this chapter in greater detail.

Mortgage finance

For most households, access to ownership is impractical without the aid of some form of financial assistance. This section begins with a general consideration of the regulation of access to mortgage finance, and then drills down to the more specific and limited legislative and judicial controls over that process. There are important links between this section and Chapter 14 below concerning repossession, as inadequate or unchecked assessments by lenders and/or their intermediaries at the outset may be reflected in the types of households against which possession is subsequently sought (see Chapter 2).

Regulatory problems and solutions

The regulatory problems have arisen for the FSA by a combination of 'irrational exuberance' on the part of some borrowers, a failure by some lenders to undertake a proper assessment of borrowers' ability to repay the money lent, together with 'an explosion in the number of mortgage products available to meet the demand', so that high-risk loans accounted for a significant market share (FSA 2009: 2.6; Scanlon et al. 2008; Williams 1997; Dudleston 2001, noting the increased riskiness of certain 'flexible mortgage' products). Certainly, the ready availability of credit caused by the import of securitisation underlay these regulatory problems, but it also caused a shift in the way in which mortgage lending occurred.

Rather than approach a customer-facing bank or building society for a loan, borrowers often obtain loans through financial intermediaries, including mortgage brokers, themselves regulated by the FSA. This settlement was particularly the case in the sub-prime market (Stephens and Quilgars 2008: 204–5). The temptation, therefore, was for borrowers to overstate their income and understate their expenditure (if, indeed, they were aware of it), and for intermediaries (who stand to gain from the deal) to do the same (FSA 2006; Stephens and Quilgars 2008: 210–11; FSA 2009). The problem was exacerbated by the growth in 'non-income verified mortgages', such as those where the borrower 'self-certified' their income. These types of product, initially designed for the self-employed, 'grew way beyond the consumer groups for which they were originally intended' (FSA 2009: 4.46), and arrears rates for borrowers who took these mortgages (at increased interest rates) 'can be up to three or four times higher than that of an income verified borrower' (ibid. para. 4.53).

A narrow legal jurisdiction

A series of judicial decisions at the turn of the century sought to balance the desire to retain the sanctity of the contractual bargain inherent in the mortgage transaction against the possibility of exploitation of the borrower by the lender. The result is an extremely narrow jurisdiction: the courts will only become involved in mortgage transactions where the agreement is '(1) unfair and unconscionable, or (2) in the nature of a penalty clogging the equity of redemption, or (3) inconsistent with or repugnant to the contractual and equitable right to redeem' (*Kreglinger* v. *New Patagonia Meat Company Ltd* [1914] AC 25, 61, Lord Parker). Unfairness and unconscionability, in this triumvirate, do not bear their ordinary meaning. Rather they have a specific, narrow construction, as Browne-Wilkinson J suggested:

> it is not enough to show that, in the eyes of the court, [the mortgage bargain] was unreasonable. In my judgment a bargain cannot be unfair and unconscionable unless one of the parties to it has *imposed the objectionable terms in a morally reprehensible manner*, that is to say, in a way which affects his conscience.' *Multiservice Bookbinding Ltd* v. *Marden* [1979] Ch 84, 109 (emphasis added)

Thus, judicial intervention in a mortgage bargain on these principles is rare (for such an example, see *Jones* v. *Morgan* [2001] EWCA Civ 995). This is particularly so, as few standard mortgages these days affect the right of borrowers' to redeem the mortgage (that is, the right to pay back the mortgage lender in full).

Other jurisdictions

More recent statutory interventions provide some level of redress for a borrower where the relationship between themselves and their creditor is 'unfair' to the borrower because of any term of the agreement or related agreement; the way in which the creditor has exercised or enforced any of their rights under the agreement or related agreement; or any act or omission by, or on behalf of, the creditor (s. 140A, Consumer Credit Act 1974, as amended by the Consumer Credit Act 2006; although this provision does not apply to most first mortgages as they are regulated mortgage agreements protected by the FSMA 2000 – see s 16(6C), Consumer Credit Act 1974). What is unfair is something of a moot point (see Brown 2007), although the courts 'shall have regard to all matters it thinks relevant' (s. 140A(2)).

Low-cost home ownership

A suite of low-cost home ownership initiatives were rolled out by the incoming Conservative government in 1979. Most of these initiatives had foundations in different legislative and local interventions. The RTB, the most trumpeted policy, had previously existed, but as a power in the hands of local authorities. Other, perhaps less well-known initiatives, had grown up through local intervention. In this section, we begin with a discussion of one such less well-known initiative that has since become a major plank in housing policy since the early 1990s (at the latest): IHO. We then move on to discuss the RTB, with a focus on its mechanics. Finally, there is discussion of certain alternative low-cost ownership schemes.

Intermediate home ownership

Just like the RTB, IHO has a long history, going back to the formation of the new model housing associations in the 1960s and was pioneered by Birmingham City Council in the mid-1970s (with different models in the different states of the UK) (see generally Forrest et al. 1984). The significance of IHO cannot now be overstated, both in historical terms and current housing policy. McDermont (2010: 118–9) has identified IHO as a push factor into the mixed funding arrangements which became a feature of the PRP sector from the mid-1980s, because of their reliance on private finance. Since the late 1980s, it has been recognised that we may be reaching the natural end point of sustainable home ownership, but that there remained pent-up demand for it among households for whom otherwise it would be unaffordable (see, for example, DoE 1987b: para. 1.7; DoE 1995a: ch. 2). As house prices increased, particularly in London and the South-East, ownership became unaffordable to a larger proportion of households. IHO is designed to reach out to these groups in the context of the clear policy desire to enable households to enter into home ownership for the first time (DETR/DSS 2000 : paras. 4.38–4.40).

In essence, IHO widens the net of home ownership to lower income groups, because buyers purchase a share of a property, usually paying some sort of periodic fee to the provider on the remainder. It is intermediate both because it offers something between buying and renting, but also because it assumes that buyers will move on to 'full' ownership at some stage in the future. The major providers of IHO are PRPs, but private sector housebuilders have also developed schemes (particularly during economic downturns) and variants on them have been promoted, or at least considered, by private sector providers (see Treasury/CLG 2006; CLG 2008e); indeed, there are issues over competition between PRPs and private housebuilders, particularly during economic downturns (Burgess et al. 2009). IHO is a policy intervention and, as discussed in the next section, one at the heart of housing policy, but the process of mapping IHO onto legal frameworks is rather old-fashioned. That use of old-fashioned legal concepts has caused considerable difficulty for buyers if they are unable to pay their periodic fee to the provider (see Chapter 16 below).

Policy context

Although there have been funding troughs, in general terms IHO has been well-served by housing grants from the Housing Corporation and its successor, the HCA. Between 1990–1991 and 1993–1994, IHO captured between 11%

and 17.5% of the overall development programme for housing associations in England, rising to 28.5% in 1996–1997 (Bramley and Dunmore 1996: 109–10). That proportion rose to 30% in 2004–2005, and the Housing Corporation's 2006–2008 investment programme devoted £970 million to IHO out of £3.9 billion (Hills and Lomax 2007: 15). Other developments have been funded without grant by associations (around 12% in 2007: Spenceley 2008: 12).

The number of shared ownership and other IHO units in which PRPs had a share was just over 114,000 in 2007, of which 85% were shared ownership units (Spenceley 2008: 11); by March 2009, this had increased to 135,200 (HCA 2010: para. 75); in 2008–2009, there were 22,970 IHO completions and 22,730 in 2007–2008 (HCA 2010). This represents a relatively small proportion of stock available in the social housing sector (approximately 10%: Hills and Lomax 2007: 13) and of PRPs involved in the sector (22%: Spenceley 2008: 11), but it was dwarfed by the intentions of central government as regards its development (ODPM 2005b; CLG 2007b). In its 2007 Green Paper, CLG aimed to deliver at least 25,000 new shared ownership and shared equity properties a year until 2010–2011, with additional properties provided through local authority-backed local housing companies (CLG 2007b: 70). The Coalition government's programme for government is equally forthright: 'We will promote shared ownership schemes and help social tenants and others to own or part-own their home.' (CLG, 2010b: para. 12)

The central reasons for the promotion of IHO are that it essentially fulfils a number of aims of housing policy. It is targeted on those on low incomes, those currently occupying social housing, key workers, regional priorities, as well as homeless households and/or those on social housing waiting lists for accommodation, thus plausibly contributing to meeting housing need. As Clarke (2010) has put it: 'This has been termed the "double whammy" effect whereby both acute housing need by the poorest households seeking social rented housing, and the aspirations of better-off existing tenants for home ownership can be met simultaneously.' The empirical basis for this objective is less clear, partly because of the need for buyers to have financial security and partly because some social housing occupiers may well have left the sector at some point in the future in any event (see, for example, NAO 2006a: paras. 44–7; Clarke 2010). The data suggests that only 26 per cent of buyers had been renting a property through a PRP or local authority (HCA 2010: figure 15). It also requires the PRP and local authority to work together, passing potential buyers on to providers, which has not always been a facilitative relationship (Rowlands and Murie 2008: para. 2.27).

Eligibility criteria are developed centrally in policy documents and rolled out by 'agents', who 'have effectively targeted first time buyers but this group is not necessarily the most important local priority group' (see ECOTEC 2008: para. 3.5.1.3). These criteria include certain key workers who have an income of less than £60,000 per annum. Buyers have tended to be slightly younger than RTB purchasers, and more usually without children (Bramley et al. 2002). There are considerable regional variations – 45 per cent of shared ownership properties in 2007 were in London and the South East (Spenceley 2008: 11; HCA 2010: figure 6), where there is better value for money (Bramley et al. 2002: 82–4).

It fulfils the aspiration of both policy-makers and households to facilitate growth in home ownership; contributes to the development of mixed-tenure estates, regeneration, and sustainability; as well as enabling more people to share in asset wealth (ODPM 2005b: paras. 1.4 and 2.1). It offers a stepping stone to full ownership although there is only weak evidence of this, particularly in terms of mobility (Wallace 2008). As a result of fulfilling these aims, it offers value for money against a number of indicators in regions where house price markets are strong, but a weak case in other regions (Bramley et al. 2002: 82–4). Furthermore, receipts from IHO purchases can be recycled into further development and/or cross-subsidise other activities, thus making the investment go further.

Perhaps as a result of its development 'beyond the state' by PRPs, it has evolved through a number of different schemes, none of which have had legislative form (indeed, this remains the case, beyond their inclusion within the definition of 'social housing' in the Housing and Regeneration Act 2008, s. 70). This becomes relevant by way of comparison with the RTB – whereas the RTB is replete with statutory provisions, affecting each step of the transaction, amendments to those provisions, and supplementing case law, IHO has barely any case law concerning access to it. It has only recently become a 'hot topic' in terms of legal intervention and then only as regards the method of eviction (as to which see Chapter 16 below).

The variety of different schemes were slimmed down after 2005 and marketed under the label 'HomeBuy' (ODPM 2005b; see also Low Cost Home Ownership Task Force 2003). The intention was to simplify the complex arrangements and different processes underpinning the array of IHO schemes. HomeBuy incorporates four different generic schemes – social HomeBuy; new build HomeBuy; HomeBuy direct; and rent to HomeBuy (which also incorporate the first time buyers' initiative) – and two specialist schemes – for older people and people with long-term disabilities (see ODPM 2005b). The scheme under which buyers found a suitable property on the open market and purchased it with a provider – known as 'open market HomeBuy' or 'do-it-yourself shared ownership' – no longer exists. Not surprisingly, given its complexity, various research evaluations have found a misunderstanding of the IHO product among potential and actual buyers, as well as front-line staff (see, for example, Rowlands and Murie 2008: para. 2.25). Nevertheless, there appear to be high levels of satisfaction with the tenure among existing shared owners (TSA 2009b).

The different IHO schemes currently available are now briefly outlined:

- Social HomeBuy enables certain PRP and local authority occupiers to part-buy the properties they are currently occupying at the right-to-acquire discount (see below). The discount applies on all subsequent purchases of extra shares. This discount has been described as 'unattractive' and the main target group of buyers are those who would not otherwise have the right to buy or acquire their property (Rowlands and Murie 2008: ch 2). Providers must bid to run this scheme and so it is not necessarily available in all areas. PRPs are the predominant providers. Any discount is repayable if the property is resold within 5 years of the purchase.

- New build HomeBuy is what was once described as 'conventional shared ownership', where a PRP builds and markets new properties for IHO. Access to the scheme is through HomeBuy agents, who assess the buyer's eligibility and ability to sustain their interest in the property. Buyers purchase a minimum share of 25% of the property up to a maximum of 75%, the landlord retaining the freehold in the property. Buyers must buy the maximum share they can afford; they pay rent to the provider on the outstanding share at no more than 3% of its value. The type of arrangement this scheme entails is discussed below.

- HomeBuy direct is a scheme under which a buyer purchases a minimum equity share of 70 per cent of a property (which must be valued at no more than £300,000), with the developer and the state retaining the remaining share. HomeBuy agents market the scheme and assess buyer's eligibility. Eligibility is as follows: 'HomeBuy Direct homes are available to people who cannot afford to buy a home on the open market and earn less than £60,000 per annum. Priority will be given to social tenants and key workers whose household income is less than £60,000' (HCA 2009). The buyer pays nothing for the first 5 years on the developer/HCA's share, after which 'a low equity charge is levied of 1.75% rising at RPI+1% p.a.' (Housing Corporation 2008: 5). The developer/HCA shares the capital appreciation in the property as well as any loss.

- Rent to HomeBuy is a scheme under which a potential buyer pays a reduced rent on their property for up to 5 years, enabling them to save the remaining amount to have enough capital to pay a deposit and obtain a mortgage. The buyer buys between 25–75 per cent of the property, but may buy the whole. The scheme appears to have developed as a result of recognition of the current difficulties first-time buyers have in obtaining a mortgage where they have insufficient capital to pay a deposit. HomeBuy agents again assess eligibility. The scheme is restricted to first-time buyers with a combined income of less than £60,000 (www.homesandcommunities.co.uk/rent_to_homebuy, accessed 11 May 2010).

Shared ownership types

There is some weak evidence that IHO buyers perceive themselves to be 'owners' (Clarke 2010), but, as Bright and Hopkins (2010) analogise, IHO in law bears a similarity to the 'Emperor's New Clothes' tale. Although there are variations on the theme, generally IHO boils down to two particular types of legal arrangement. The buyer buys either (a) the freehold but a share in the equity of the property (HomeBuy direct), or (b) a long lease of the purchased share (most of the other scheme types) (Bright and Hopkins, 2009: 338). Although, in principle, complex legal issues can arise in relation to the former type, the main problems have arisen with type (b) on which this section focuses. It should, however, be stressed that these are the types which predominate within the social housing sector (including some profit-making organisations).

Under the long-lease type, the provider retains the freehold title to the property. The buyer obtains a long lease representing their share, usually of 99 years; they pay a sub-market rent on the remainder, which should be set at no more than 3 per cent of the open market valuation of the valuation of the provider's share. Although the lease is long, it will usually attract the protection of the Housing Act 1988 and is usually an AT (the exclusions to security of tenure in Sch. 1, Housing Act 1988, discussed in Chapter 11 below, are unlikely to apply because of the high rental element).

The Housing Corporation/TSA promulgates model leases, which funded providers can either adopt or use their own provided they have the core terms of the model leases (see CML et al. 2010: para. 14). Buyers usually purchase a minimum stake of 25 per cent, although different schemes have different minimum amounts, and they can subsequently purchase further shares either en bloc or incrementally in a minimum 10 per cent until they own the property outright.[1] Subsequent purchases are referred to as 'staircasing' (and there are different rules about staircasing in certain protected rural areas). There is no provision for downward staircasing in the model leases (only upwards), although some individual providers do have such provisions in their agreements (see CML et al. 2010: paras. 6 and 62–74). That limitation is effectively to protect the PRP's business planning and mortgagees. Most schemes have minimum periods of ownership and there may be other restrictions depending on, for example, if the development was built through a section 106 agreement or in certain protected areas (Housing (Right to Enfranchise) (Designated Protected Areas) (England) Order 2009, SI 2009/2098).

There are a number of key provisions in the model leases. The buyer takes entire responsibility for repairs to and maintenance of the property, *irrespective of the share purchased*; they may have to pay a service charge in relation to common parts; there are restrictions on alienation of the whole or part of the property to protect public funds, and rights of pre-emption. However, a further key provision, often overlooked in the policy and evaluation literature, is a mortgagee protection clause, designed to give further comfort to lenders by entitling them to recover part of their loss where they take enforcement action on default by the buyer, provided that the loan had been approved in advance by the provider (cll. 6.1–6.6). This clause effectively removes at least part of any commercial disadvantage to the mortgagee because the provider underwrites part of

---

[1] Enfranchisement, if it were available, is not permitted: Leasehold reform Act 1967, Sch. 4A, para. 3A (inserted by s. 301, Housing and Regeneration Act 2008); Housing (Shared Ownership Leases) (Exclusion from Leasehold Reform Act 1967) (England) Regulations 2009, SI 2009/2097.

the lender's loss (giving an incentive to the provider to ensure that its financial checks are sufficiently robust at the outset) (see CML et al. 2010: para. 15 and 18–23). Nevertheless, there is some evidence that the range of lending products which is available for a standard purchase is not available to those buying a share through IHO, so that loans are more expensive for IHO (CCHPR 2008; McKee 2010: 44–5).

The right to buy

The policy impact of the RTB has already been discussed (see Chapter 4 above). In this section, the mechanics of the RTB are examined. The scheme of the RTB is essentially simple, although it has become more complex over the years. In essence, a secure tenant is entitled to require their landlord to convey the property occupied by the tenant to the tenant. Certain criteria must be satisfied before the right arises and is exercisable. The price is determined by a valuation less a discount to the tenant, the discount depending generally on how long the tenant has occupied the property. The scheme has become more complex, in part, because of the need to develop the bare bones provided by the Housing Act 1980, to penalise recalcitrant landlords, and to pull back from what are now considered to be the excesses of the regime which operated in the 1980s and 1990s and which were regarded as having undesirable consequences. The general default position appears now to be that the RTB is a 'sacred cow' which, nevertheless, and to mix metaphors, requires recalibration (Goodlad and Atkinson 2004).

Coercion

The RTB has always been premised upon the belief that a significant proportion of tenants would want to exercise it and a suspicion that local authorities would do their utmost to wriggle out of the legislative straitjacket. Central government adopted the approach that would provide maximum control over recalcitrant local authorities under the guise of protecting the choice of tenants:

> Tenants wishing to become owners will expect the House to ensure that they have a right to buy which cannot be circumvented or ignored. If Parliament enacts this legislation it is right to expect all councils and landlords falling within the provisions of the Bill to carry out their duties responsibly and speedily. (HC Debs, vol. 976, col 1447, Michael Heseltine; cited in Forrest and Murie 1991: 205)

In taking this policy option, central government clearly opted for individual rights (the tenant-purchaser) against collective provision (local authority and its other tenants).

At every stage, either the tenant or the landlord can force the other's hand. As such, it was a brilliant scheme, designed to reduce local discretion and power, and in the process dismantle the notion of welfare state housing (if it existed).

In particular, by s. 164(1), the Secretary of State has a general power of intervention where 'tenants generally, a tenant or tenants of a particular landlord, or tenants of a description of landlords, have or may have difficulty in exercising effectively and expeditiously the right to buy'. Few other statutory provisions better represented the changed relationship between central and local government than this one. It matched 'implicit coercion on tenants to buy their property [with] coercion on local authorities to engage in the process of selling them' (Cowan 1999: 345). Even Lord Denning regarded that power as 'a most coercive power' (see *Norwich CC* v. *Secretary of State for the Environment* [1982] 1 All ER 737, and Forrest and Murie 1991: ch 9). Unlike practically all other statutory duties on local authorities at that time, the DoE put authorities' response to the new duties under rigorous surveillance: 'Impressions of progress or delay were also obtained from letters of complaint from or on behalf of tenants, from press reports and from informal discussion between the Department and local authorities' (Forrest and Murie 1991: 208). Any sign of delays would be met with formal approaches. The Norwich saga is instructive for the council's refusal to sell was neither absolute nor based on inefficiency. Rather, the council was concerned at being able to balance its obligations to those in housing need against those who wished to purchase their accommodation (ibid. p. 212).

Scheme mechanics

The current scheme can be found in the Housing Act 1985, Part V, as amended. The secure tenant (or, where there is more than one, secure tenants) have a right to buy the property they occupy provided they have lived there for more than 5 years (if their occupation began after the implementation of s. 180, Housing Act 2004, or 2 years before this time). Certain landlords are excluded, though, from the RTB (Sch. 5). In particular, charitable PRPs have managed to maintain their exclusion, despite occasionally fierce pressure on and from government to include them (McDermont 2010: 61–2).

The RTB is not exercisable 'if the tenant is subject to an order of the court for possession of the dwelling-house' (s. 121(1)). Thus, if a possession order is granted at any stage before completion of the purchase, the RTB ceases to be operable. Equally, if (for some reason) the tenant loses their secure status, they also lose their right to buy (*Muir Group HA* v. *Thornley* (1992) 25 HLR 89). The wording was altered by the Housing and Regeneration Act 2008, s. 325, in line with the two-stage possession process (after *Harlow DC* v. *Hall* [2006] HLR 27, discussed in Chapter 14 below) but the intention remained the same: 'to prevent undeserving tenants (ie those whose conduct is seriously in breach of the terms of their tenancy to warrant a court order) from being able to buy their homes. This is not just a question of withholding a reward from the tenant concerned, but also of retaining the local authority's control over somebody whose behaviour adversely affects others.' (CLG 2007c para. 18)

That policy has not always been entirely clear, particularly because of the default policy prescription in favour of sale. In *Taylor* v. *Newham LBC* [1993]

25 HLR 290, the applicant had reached the stage where she was entitled to apply for an injunction to enforce the RTB. Before she had done so, however, Newham issued proceedings to recover possession of the property on the basis of 'acts of an aggressive, violent, insulting and offensive nature, and being, as it was alleged, the product of hostility born of racial enmity [against the local Asian community].' It was on this basis that the council sought to defend Ms Taylor's subsequent application for an injunction. This defence was unsuccessful for, as it was held, the injunction can only be set aside on narrow grounds. Sir Thomas Bingham MR made it clear that the intention of Parliament overrode all other considerations:

> [The history of the RTB is that] it was introduced for the first time in 1980 at a time when a number of local authorities strongly resisted parting with the ownership of publicly owned accommodation to those who then lived in it, and it seems to me that we should be doing great violence to the obvious intention of Parliament if we did not recognise that it was Parliament's intention to block to the maximum the opportunities open to reluctant landlords to obstruct the acquisition of title by their tenants. (p. 298)

It followed that Ms Taylor's rights overrode the obvious social problems caused by enabling an alleged racist to buy their own property in the area where the alleged acts had taken place.

In *Bristol CC* v. *Lovell* [1998] 1 WLR 446, a similar issue arose for the House of Lords concerning an alleged drug dealer. This person had 'suitably adapted [his property] to the trade, with steel grilles over doors and windows, kennels for Rottweiler dogs, surveillance cameras to check visitors, a radio scanner tuned to police frequency and equipment for locating covert listening devices' (Lord Hoffmann). He had accepted the terms of the council's proposed conveyance. He sought to defend the council's possession proceedings by counterclaiming for an injunction to complete the transaction under s. 138(3). Before the possession proceedings had been heard, an interlocutory application for the injunction was brought and decided in Mr Lovell's favour. The House of Lords disagreed. The majority held in favour of the council on two grounds, one essentially practical, the other substantive. The practical ground was that the court is entitled, in the exercise of its discretion as to case management, to hear cases in whatever order it wishes on the basis of what appears 'just and convenient'. This is difficult to accept in the light of the other accepted assertion that this discretion could not be used to overrule the policy of the statute nor the rights which it gave to tenants (Lord Hoffmann). The policy of the Act, as we have seen, was to give rights to the tenant at the expense of the landlord. It was only in defeating the purpose of the enforcement provisions of the Act – to force recalcitrant landlords to convey the property – that this discretion might be exercised. Thus, in order to do what was undoubtedly (on the alleged facts) just and convenient, the House of Lords had to remould the policy of the legislation. *Taylor* could be distinguished because, in that case, there was no question as to the judge's discretion on this point, only as to whether the injunction was discretionary or not.

The substantive ground related to a concession made by counsel for Lovell that the council would have been able to continue with its possession action after the grant of the injunction on the basis that Lovell remained a tenant until the actual conveyance. Lord Lloyd found that concession surprising ('To my mind Parliament cannot have intended that the Council should be able, in effect, to reverse a mandatory injunction by obtaining a subsequent order for possession') but nevertheless accepted it. Other members of the House of Lords believed the concession proper. Indeed, Lord Clyde based the majority of his reasoning upon this point. The difficulty with it, though, is precisely that raised by Lord Lloyd. The effect of a grant of possession after the grant of the injunction does violence to the nature and rationale of the injunction: to force the council to make the grant. Of course, as Lord Clyde pointed out, other matters require checking (in the ordinary way of the conveyancing process) but this does not answer the point that the council can avoid the effect of the injunction by subsequently seeking possession of the property.

Other powers are now available to a landlord in such cases, including making an application to a court to suspend the tenant's right to buy for a period in cases of certain ASB (s. 121A), although the period of suspension can still count towards the qualifying period. The tenant's application is also suspended where the landlord has applied for a demotion order or an order for possession on the nuisance ground (Ground 2) (s. 138(2A); see Chapter 15 below).

The qualifying period had been 3 years, originally, but this oscillation perhaps demonstrates the different policy motivations of governments – from encouraging sale to encouraging the tenant to commit to the community before purchasing (essentially through a retrenchment mechanism). Certain periods of occupation as a public sector tenant of a different property count towards the qualifying period of the new property (Sch. 4; and may count even after the landlord has obtained a possession order on the former property: *Manchester CC* v. *Benjamin* [2009] 1 WLR 2202, cf. s. 121(1)). Equally, a secure tenant retains their right to buy even after a transfer of their property to a different landlord – this is known as the preserved right to buy (ss. 171A–C) – a particularly important right when a secure tenant is considering whether or not to vote for (or against) an LSVT because, after transfer, they will no longer be secure tenants but will take an AT. However, this preserved right to buy can also create anomalies because of the exclusion of certain organisations like charitable PRPs, which are excluded from the RTB, and former co-ownership tenancies (see Alder and Handy 1997: 189).

Subject to certain exceptions, the secure tenant begins the process by serving on their landlord written notice claiming the RTB (s. 122). The landlord must then serve written notice generally within 4 weeks admitting or denying the secure tenant's RTB (s. 124).

Valuation

The date on which that application is received by the local authority is the relevant date for valuation. The property is valued by the landlord on the basis of its open market value and as if it is being sold by a willing seller with vacant possession (s. 127). Certain matters are disregarded from the valuation, including any improvements to the property made by the tenant (or neglect), and it is assumed that the service charge or improvements levied by the landlord will not exceed its estimates. Valuation is an inexact science, at best, and is generally done by using comparator properties. The degree to which the valuer instructed by the landlord will inspect the property was found to be variable and dependent on a number of factors – for example, if the valuer was external to the local authority and paid per property, the research suggested that the price paid affected the way the property was valued (from a 'drive-by' valuation to a more intensive approach); some landlords failed to pass the relevant information to the valuer; and, as important, at the time of the valuation, the valuer was unlikely to have access to all the available market transactions (because of delays in the conveyancing process) (Plimmer et al. 2007).

The tenant can apply to the District Valuer to appeal the valuation – indeed, the process was remarkably simple, just involving a cross in a box. The incidence of appeals varied between areas and for no apparent reason – Dixon et al. (2006) suggested that friendship networks, communication with the landlord, and the length of time the original valuer spent at the property were among the potential indicators of likelihood to appeal. They recorded that the District Valuer adopted a quasi-adjudicative stance, as there is no appeal from the District Valuer's decision (the only challenge could be by way of judicial review which, in itself, would present many obstacles, not the least the high threshold required for such an application). The information available to the District Valuer was more complete, because of their access to better systems and because, by that stage, conveyancing delays on comparable properties were likely to have been dealt with. The District Valuer is also required to conduct an internal inspection of the property. Where the District Valuer's determination of the value was flawed in some way – where there was a significant error or a failure to take account of representations made by tenant or landlord – there may be a further determination of value (ss. 128A–B; this is designed to deal with the situation where internal checks reveal that a valuation is flawed as a result of errors of fact – CLG 2007c: para. 49).

Once the landlord has the initial valuation, it serves a written notice on the tenant stating the price of the property less the discount, together with other information including whether there are known structural defects as well as estimates and information about service charges and improvements (ss. 125 and 125A–C). Within 12 weeks, the tenant must serve written notice on the landlord informing the landlord whether or not the tenant intends to proceed with the RTB transaction (s. 125D). The landlord may, in the absence of such a notice, serve a written notice on the tenant requiring the tenant to serve that notice within 28 days; failure to serve such a notice terminates the RTB transaction (s. 125E). The landlord has the power to correct clerical errors after service of that notice, although the nature and extent of that power has yet to be determined (*Nessa* v. *Tower Hamlets LBC* [2010] HLR 37) as well as such errors or omissions made by the secure tenant (s. 177).

'As soon as all matters relating to the grant have been agreed or determined', the landlord must make the grant of the relevant interest, provided there are no more than 4 weeks of rent arrears and the landlord is not seeking a demotion order or a possession order on the basis of Ground 2 (s. 138). Failure to disclose a structural defect as required in the section 125 notice is not a matter 'relating to the grant', reflecting a narrow construction of the word 'grant', limited to matters relevant to the conveyance (*Ryan* v. *Islington LBC* [2009] EWCA Civ 578, cf. *Scinto* v. *Newham LBC* [2009] EWCA Civ 837, where the council bound itself not to grant the interest until it had rectified serious structural problems which, thus, became a matter relating to the grant).

Discount

The critical underpinning of the RTB is the right of the secure tenant to a discount from the valuation, based on length of qualifying period and subject to a maximum amount (unless the discount reduces the price below a cost-floor relating broadly to purchase and refurbishment costs within 10 years: ss. 129–31). The current level of discount depends on when the qualifying period began – if it began before January 2005 (when the amending provisions of the Housing Act 2004 came into force), the starting point is a discount of 32% for a house and 44% for a flat, increasing by 1% (for a house) or 2% (for a flat) for each additional year, and up to a maximum of 60% (for a house) or 70% for a flat (s. 129). Past studies suggest that it is this discount which enables buyers to 'upmarket' subsequently in a relatively short period (Jones and Murie 2006: 182). The New Labour government reduced the cash level of the maximum amount of discount based on regional sale prices to account for 'the pressure on social housing resources' (DETR 1998: para. 23), leading to maximum amounts ranging from £22,000–38,000 (Housing (Right to Buy) (Limits on Discounts) Order 1998, SI 1998/2997), which were later further reduced for certain London and South-Eastern local authority areas to £16,000 (Housing (Right to Buy) (Limits on Discount) (Amendment) Order 2003, SI 2003/498). These changes in discount levels were a significant cause of a 'sharp peak' in RTB applications in the first quarter of 1999 as a result of information and misinformation about the changes, some of which suggested that these changes were the first step towards the abolition of the RTB (Marsh et al. 2003: 29–30).

The landlord may require the discount (less the cost of certain improvements) to be repaid if the buyer subsequently disposes of their interest within 5 years (s. 155(2)). The time period had been 3 years but was amended by the

Housing Act 2004 (which also allows for a reduction of 20 per cent for each full year without such a disposal: s 155A(3)). The 2004 Act also made a rather more subtle alteration, concerning the calculation of the amount to be repaid – it relates the repayment to the percentage of the value of the property sold, as opposed to the actual discount (which, perhaps might be referred to as 'discount+'). In effect, this stops the buyer from enjoying any 'windfall gains as a result of house price inflation' (Carr et al. 2004: 7.30).

Delay

Where there are delays in the transaction and all relevant matters have been agreed, the landlord has the power to serve on the tenant a notice requiring them to complete the transaction (ss. 140–1). Not surprisingly, given the policy genus of the RTB, more extensive rights are given to secure tenants to compel their landlords to perform their side of the equation – if the landlord delays in serving notices under ss. 124 or 125, or 'where the tenant considers that delays on the part of the landlord are preventing him from exercising expeditiously his right to buy …', the secure tenant may serve an initial notice of delay (s. 153A). The landlord may then serve a counter-notice if it believes in good faith that it has a right to insist on the terms it is offering (although good or bad faith is neither here nor there when dealing with 'a hard edged question of fact': *Guinan* v. *Enfield LBC* (1997) 29 HLR 456, cf. *Southwark LBC* v. *Dennett* [2008] HLR 23, at [9] and [26], although Carnwath LJ, at [41], left open whether a counter-notice would only be invalid if the authority had no reasonable basis in public law terms for serving it). The significance of the secure tenant's notice is that, from the date in the notice to the date on which a counter-notice (if any) is served, the secure tenant may then serve an operative notice of delay, which entitles the secure tenant to various remedies including that any payments of rent count towards the purchase price (and, if the delay lasts more than 12 months, a further 50 per cent): s. 153B. Those payments of rent include payments made by way of HB entitlement (*Hanoman* v. *Southwark LBC* [2009] 1 WLR 1367). That operative notice may even be served where a counter-notice wrongly identifies that the landlord has taken the relevant action (*Dennett*).

Exploitation

During the first New Labour government, policy issues began to be considered around a roughly hewn concern about the exploitation of the RTB. Exploitation broadly referred to conduct which, while lawful, was tinged with some sort of conduct which was morally problematic (see, for example, Nelken 1983). Research into this exploitation (Jones 2003) broadly found three particular types – assistance by unrelated companies; assistance by friends or relatives; and exercising the RTB when properties have been scheduled for demolition (so as to obtain compensation payments and the open market value).

Perhaps due to the nebulous nature of the concept of exploitation, the actual numbers of properties bought as a result of it was hard to gauge. It was

suggested that there were about twenty companies, mostly operating region-
ally, although market economics (such as declining rents) may have altered
their number. Companies either offer assistance in the RTB procedure, including valuation appeals, or (more shadily) provide a cash payment to the buyer
in return for a 20-year lease on the property at a peppercorn rent *and* a formal commitment to sell the property to the company at the end of the discount
period then in operation (3 years). Effectively, the buyer obtains an upfront
cash payment (which, the research suggested, was mostly used by the buyer
as a down payment on another property or to move abroad: Jones 2003: 4.29).
There was no misrepresentation by the companies but the regular leafleting and
advertisements offered 'a potential hard sell of their activities and the encouragement of tenants to take on financial commitments they cannot afford or to
make decisions they will subsequently regret' (ibid. para. 4.43).

In *McGuane* v. *Welch* [2008] 2 P&CR 24, such a transaction was set aside
on technical grounds where the buyer was assisted by an individual (who was
employed by one of these companies). The individual clearly was not well-
versed in transactional formalities, failing to have relevant documents stamped
(for taxation purposes) which were then inadmissible before a court. Although
there had been a bargain between the buyer and the individual, the court
refused to intervene because of the 'unsettling features of the transaction ...
The lack of independent advice [to the buyer], the incorrect information given
by [the individual] to the solicitors acting for [the buyer], the vendor and mortgagor, and the substantial undervalue all take this case out of the ordinary run
of contracts for the sale of land'. (Mummery LJ, at [46])

Other mechanisms of sale

The power of sale

Local authorities have had a power of sale for some time which exists in addition to the RTB, enabling non-occupiers the opportunity to purchase a council property (now contained in ss. 32–3, Housing Act 1985). In *Porter* v. *Magill*
[2002] 2 AC 357, the House of Lords held that such a power can only be exercised for the purposes for which it was given and the promotion of the political advantage of one party was not such a purpose. Westminster City Council,
then controlled by the Conservative party under Dame Shirley Porter, had
engaged in such a programme in key marginal wards (under the label 'Building
Stable Communities') in order to retain power in what was then (the 1980s)
a Conservative 'flagship' council (see, generally, Cowan 2003; Hosken 2006;
Dimoldenberg 2006).

The right to acquire

The right to acquire enables certain PRP tenants to buy certain properties at a
discount. Those properties must have been built or acquired through the use
of public money (s. 16) and certain properties are exempt. The discount is not

as generous as under the RTB, ranging from £9,000–16,000 depending on area (and the amount of discount has not been increased since the scheme began), but in most other respects the scheme operates along similar lines to the RTB scheme. Given the low discount, the few properties that are eligible, and the range of alternatives, it is, perhaps, not surprising that this scheme has only accounted for 2,520 sales to August 2009. It is included here for two reasons – first, because it offers a point of comparison to the RTB scheme (which can only really be explained by the favourable position allocated to PRPs in housing policy, albeit, in this context, rather against the grain); and, second, because, the applicable scheme for an occupier is almost entirely dependent on the roulette wheel of the allocations process.

Incentive schemes

Various incentive schemes are (and have been) available to PRP and local authority tenants, which, in essence, give a current tenant cash as an incentive to buy a home in the private sector (s. 129, Housing Act 1985, as amended – see ODPM 2002). In the local authority sector, the scheme is known as the 'cash incentive scheme'; in the PRP sector, there have been 'tenant's incentive schemes'.

Conclusion

Access to home ownership has played a pivotal role in post-war housing policy. The pre-eminence of ownership has been enhanced by successive governments from 1979 onwards. At the level of politics, it has been argued that home ownership is the most natural tenure, which the population generally desires, although this is at best debatable. Rather, it reflects the fact that alternative tenures have declined leaving little else other than properties for sale into home ownership in some areas. The movement into home ownership has also been facilitated (and engineered) by the ease with which money became available sporadically throughout the twentieth and twenty-first centuries. The power of the mortgage contract has been such that it has not required to be altered to any degree since the foundation of the modern system of property law in 1925.

The ideological supremacy ascribed to home ownership by all major parties has found expression in the various aspects of government policy which have promoted it to low-income groups as part of a financial inclusion agenda. It provides the context for the discussion of the expansion in low-cost home ownership as well as the sweeteners used by government to influence people into the tenure. Certainly, as regards the RTB, there are considerable pressures on landlords to complete these transactions. The major development in the last twenty years has been in relation to 'intermediate home ownership schemes', the predominance of which has been emphasised by its pride of place in the policies of the present and past governments. Yet, as is discussed in Chapter 16 below, serious legal issues arise with such transactions to the extent that there must be real concerns as to their appropriateness.

Part III
Rights and responsibilities

Introduction to Part III

This part of the book is concerned with the social and legal construction of individual rights in housing. As in earlier chapters, we are concerned to flesh out and explain the disparities, actual and theoretical, between law, policy and practice. The framework which guides this discussion explicitly recognises that the current focus no longer reflects the grants of rights to occupants. But the animating question in this part concerns the balance between rights and responsibilities – these should not be seen as being in opposition to each other (and certainly not in the current political settlement) but as the same side of the coin; or, perhaps, as poles on a continuum.

Garland (1996) has argued that the criminal justice system has, out of necessity, extended its reach into other domains. This is because the failure of the state to control the upward spiral of crime has represented a challenge to the state's capacity to protect the public. The concentration now is upon the *criminologies of everyday life* (p. 450; original emphasis) – the acceptance that crime affects us all and there is little that the state can do to stop it. However, at the same time as strategies have been developed to cope with that acceptance, 'the political arm of the state has frequently engaged in a form of denial which appears increasingly hysterical in the clinical sense of that term' (p. 459). This has led to a 'show of punitive force' which attempts to re-establish the sovereign authority of the state: 'punishment is an act of sovereign might, a performative action which exemplifies what absolute power is all about' (p. 461).

This bifocal understanding of criminology could equally have been written about recent developments and thinking in housing rights. It becomes particularly apparent, for sure, when anti-social and nuisance behaviour is discussed. Even our language crosses over into modern understandings of policing – 'zero tolerance', 'risk management', etc. – let alone our purpose – to divide off the inherently anti-social using the 'eliminative ideal'. As Rutherford (1997) argued, again in the context of criminal justice: 'Put bluntly, the eliminative ideal strives to solve present and emerging problems by getting rid of troublesome and disagreeable people with methods which are lawful and widely supported.' (1997, 117) Housing has always been a key tool in the criminal justice process – in the monitoring and control of the occupation of, and exclusion from, property – but the past twenty years have provided a legislative shroud for these processes.

One also sees this eliminative ideal in operation in thinking about arrears. Whatever tenure, with the exception of the PRS, possession is said to be a last resort and the goal is sustainability. Arrears are a natural product of everyday life and every bit a part of the capitalist process. Households are required now to be active managers of their rent account, rather than passive recipients of HB. It is the housing equivalent of the current ideological underpinning of citizenship. Just as we are all enjoined, or responsibilised, into protecting our possessions from situational theft, households are responsibilised into actively managing their mortgage/rent. There is nothing inherently 'wrong' with this – indeed, it seems sensible, although it does give rise to concerns about the vulnerable – but we need to recognise that it has a different vision of the social citizen and a different mentality of government. There has been a shift from social security to what O'Malley (1992: 257) refers to as 'privatised actuarialism (prudentialism)'.

At a more mundane level, the point about the arrears process is that it saves some and eliminates others from the tenure; and, as we see, understandings of the 'last resort' are flexible. There is an unpalatable remaining question about this elimination, for households cannot be literally eliminated: what happens to the excluded? Once excluded from social housing, it is unlikely that they will be able to access it again because access laws enable them to be excluded. Home ownership and mortgages are often out of the question. Consequently, there is a developing realisation that the excluded commonly end up in the poorest end of the PRS.

All of this reflects a marked shift from the 1960s and 1970s when the central concern of housing lawyers lay in the protection of individual rights ('due process'). Although today's concern is about individual responsibility, and the conditionality of rights, those pockets of rights which remain are being re-evaluated and made fit for today's purposes. However, those purposes reflect an ideological shift that has been profound. We see this most clearly in Chapter 11 where the Coalition government is actively seeking to roll back the boundaries of housing rights in the name of localism, but perhaps a shift towards particular understandings of the market may be a better way of thinking about that ideological shift. It reflects an economic and efficiency-based understanding of housing need; and one which has the market for social and private housing at its heart. Parts of the terrain remain untouched, partly because the ideological project is also a pragmatic one. Governments cannot be seen to 'go soft' on harassment and unlawful eviction, or remove landlord repairing obligations. These rights remain in place; however, it is noticeable that, as regards the former, few prosecutions are ever made, fines are low and prison sentences rare; and, as regards the latter, a combination of the funding regime and insecurity of tenure are likely to have diminished its significance in the private sector. This, perhaps, is one of the paradoxes of rights – even though they may continue to exist, broader contexts render them impotent.

There is a further theme undercutting the general discussion in this part: tenure *is* important. In fact, the only way one can think about housing rights is through tenure because it is tenure that *defines* the rights which households obtain. Significantly, this is the starting point for this part of the book when we analyse security of tenure. That discussion underpins the subsequent chapters. Private sector tenants get private sector tenancies; public sector tenants get public sector tenancies; PRP tenants get an awkward mixture between the two (reflecting the awkward public–private distinction inherent in the PRP operation). Thus, one can only regard housing rights by tenure and this makes tenure seem extremely odd – in Part II we noted how tenure was often an irrelevance when households access a particular sector; 'social' mechanisms treat tenure indifferently, although there will be a clear PRS preference in the future if the Localism Bill remains unchanged. Yet, we find tenure the essential starting point for an examination of rights and, indeed, of responsibility. The reason seems to depend on the different regulatory mechanisms applicable in each tenure. Tenure explains the repairing strategies employed by occupiers and landlords (although this is shown to be dependent upon the methods used to regulate each tenure). It explains the history of approaches to ASB – which predominantly focused on social housing estates – and although modern policy understandings appear tenure neutral, this is often more a politically correct discourse. It is clear what households are going to be targeted and why. It is like a discussion of mothering using gender neutral language.

11

Security of tenure

Contents

Tenure is the oddest thing. We use it differently between disciplines, and the various statutory overlays on it seem, at times, incomprehensible. The purpose of this chapter is to set out the different regimes in relation to each tenure as identified in housing policy, and used throughout this book: owner-occupation; private renting; PRP renting; local authority renting.

The focus in this chapter is on the nature and degree of *security* in each such tenure. Security, in this sense, refers to the rights that the occupier has in their property; or, to put it another way, the ease or difficulty with which the provider (including a mortgage lender) is entitled to take possession from the occupier. What is often regarded as the most secure form of tenure – ownership – turns out to be less secure.

Setting the tenures side by side in this chapter also fulfils a further purpose, emphasising the oddity of tenure by comparison with each other. This is important because, as we saw in Part II of this book, the type of tenure accessed by a household is not necessarily related to the point of entry – a homeless household may be offered a private sector tenancy, a licence of a property (in whatever sector), a shared ownership lease, a PRP tenancy, and one could go on; and, in Part I, we noted how the regulation of social housing was converging.

The point is that the choices which are made at the point of entry determine the nature and degree of security to which the household becomes entitled. Further, choices made subsequently – such as whether to vote for or against an LSVT, or to take advantage of a sale-and-rentback offer – may alter the security of tenure framework for the household. Security of tenure, on the other hand, has its roots in housing regulation (Part I of this book). This is, perhaps, the absurdity of security of tenure, responding to superimposed structures without reference to the mode of access. As Ellickson (2008: 93) observes, households are highly unlikely to structure their affairs 'in the shadow' of 'endgame laws'. However, those endgame laws, a phrase which might sum up the notion of security of tenure, are key to understanding the household's rights during its occupation as well as defending any claim to possession.

This chapter proceeds through layers of analysis. It begins with a summary of the position at property law, developing into 'traditional' landlord and tenant law. There is a certain amount of repetition with earlier chapters here (especially Chapter 1 and Chapter 3) which is unavoidable as what follows is dependent on that analysis. Rather than repeating the analysis of earlier chapters, however, the approach taken in this chapter is to set out a series of principles to determine the distinction between a lease and a licence. The chapter then goes on to the domain of housing law, considering the security of tenure of households in each (housing policy) tenure, as well as the position where no security exists. Apparently distinct arrangements – sale-and-rentback and shared ownership (discussed in particular in Chapter 16 below) – in fact take place within these regimes. Those arrangements have caused, and continue to cause, considerable anxiety within housing law and policy. Although they seem 'shiny brand new', they are anything but new, operating according to traditional precepts of law. This chapter excludes consideration of initiatives which manipulate security of tenure in the specific context of anti-social and nuisance behaviour (introductory tenancies, demoted tenancies, family intervention tenancies), as these initiatives are considered separately in Chapter 15 below.

Property law

The proper starting point for a consideration of security of tenure is property law because the notion of security of tenure feeds off, or was overlain on, property law. The techniques of property law, therefore, were not just the foundation for subsequent interventions but also, as a result, the crucial starting point for analysis of a household's rights and responsibilities. This is not the place for a detailed excursus on property law, but it is important that certain rules and identifications of property law are considered at the outset. A housing lawyer must have a basic understanding of these principles. There are three parts to this section. The first considers the role of tenure in property law, noting that it is a largely irrelevant concept as it has given way to the 'doctrine of estates'. The second provides a brief outline of the significance of formalities in property law – the formal way of creating an estate in land and the consequences of avoiding those formalities. The third focuses specifically on the relationship of landlord and tenant.

Tenure and estates

Gray and Gray (2009: 1.3.1), perhaps shockingly, observe that 'perhaps the most striking feature of English land law has been the absence, within its conceptual scheme, of any overarching notion of ownership'. In short, ownership of land is an unknown concept in property law; it has become a convenient shorthand to describe what may appear to be the practical reality. The doctrine of tenure described the relationship between the overlords and their subjects within the feudal context after the Norman Conquest – a parcel of land in return for services – but this doctrine has since become something of an irrelevance (the statute *Quia Emptores* 1290 prohibited the creation of further sub-tenures, which, in turn, effectively caused its demise over time).

The doctrine of tenure's irrelevance was, in a sense, neither here nor there. It had been superseded by the doctrine of estates and it is this doctrine that denotes what is 'owned'. The doctrine simply denotes the length of time that the 'owner' is entitled to exercise rights and responsibilities over the land. The types of modern estate most commonly used today are the fee simple absolute in possession and the term of years absolute; or, more colloquially, the freehold and leasehold (the latter also equating with tenancy). They are the most commonly used because they are the only estates now capable of existing 'at law' (s. 1(1), Law of Property Act 1925); other interests in those estates, most notably (for the purposes of this book) certain mortgages, are recognised 'at law' (s. 1(2), Law of Property Act 1925). That is not to say that other estates and interests are not capable of existing at all; they are not recognised by the common law but by a different system of rules, known as equity. Whereas equity follows the law, unless there is contrary intention, there cannot be a vacuum in the ownership of an estate at law; hence, the currency of the freehold and leasehold estate. These estates are what is sold on the open market.

The freehold estate lasts effectively for ever, or until there is no person entitled to it (at which point it reverts back to the Crown). The leasehold interest, on the other hand, has a certain commencement, continuation and termination point – in an early case, it was said that all other words in a lease 'are but babble' (*Say* v. *Smith* (1530) 1 Plowd 269) – although the position may now be slightly more complex because of the interplay between law and equity (*Berrisford* v. *Mexfield Housing Co-Operative Ltd* [2010] HLR 44, currently on appeal to the Supreme Court; see the discussion in Loveland 2010). The time period of a leasehold interest can be of any particular duration, so long as (in theory) it is certain. Sometimes, one does come across a purported tenancy granted for the life of the occupier – such a tenancy, although uncertain on its face, is saved by the operation of s. 149(6), Law of Property Act 1925, which creates out of such a grant a tenancy for 90 years with provision for earlier determination on the death of the relevant occupier.

The other particular significance of the rules of equity occurs where two or more persons claim an interest over the same property. Somewhat confusingly, where two or more people own an interest in the same property concurrently, the interests of these people are described in property law as either 'joint tenants' or 'tenants in common', although they have little to do with the rules about leasehold interests and should be conceptually separated. They are also held by means of a trust, which separates out the interests of the parties at law and in equity, the latter determining the extent of the shares. At law, the only joint ownership recognised is the joint tenancy (s. 36(2), Law of Property Act 1925), whereas both are recognised in equity. The other key difference between joint tenancy and tenancy in common is that, in the former, the right of survivorship operates. The right of survivorship means that, on the death of one of the joint tenants, the other joint tenant (or joint tenants) takes the whole property irrespective of provisions in the deceased's will. In principle, in the case of a tenancy, such a tenancy can be determined by one of those joint tenants giving a notice in the correct form to the landlord (*Hammersmith & Fulham LBC* v. *Monk* [1992] 1 AC 478 – but see Chapter 16 for a qualification to this principle).

As between cohabitants, the question often arises as to the shares of each in the property. The primary rule is that, where they have set out their shares in an appropriate form, it is that document which governs the extent of their interest (*Goodman* v. *Gallant* [1986] Fam 106). Unfortunately, despite the simplicity of that basic rule, much cost has been expended because of the failure of households and their advisors to heed it. Failure to do so means that, at the endgame, if the parties are not married or civil partners, the laws of equity determine the nature and extent of the parties' interests through the principles of constructive trust and proprietary estoppels. The basic rule of the former is that equity follows the law, unless there is contrary intention, so that where the parties are both legal owners, their shares will be 50:50 (*Stack* v. *Dowden* [2007] 2 AC 432);

the basic rule of the latter is that equity may grant a remedy if a person embarks on a detrimental course of conduct in reliance on a representation made by the legal owner (*Thorner* v. *Major* [2009] 1 WLR 776; *Yeoman's Row Management Ltd* v. *Cobbe* [2008] 1 WLR 1752).

Formalities

Certain formalities are prescribed before an estate or interest in property can be granted or sold off. Failure to comply with these formalities is hugely problematic as it may leave the purported disposition void and of no effect. They are, therefore, important but sometimes ignored particularly where lay persons seek to engage in property law relationships with each other. Thus, for example, the creation of a legal estate in land requires a deed (s. 52, Law of Property Act 1925; s. 1, Law of Property (Miscellaneous Provisions) Act 1989); it also usually requires registration at the Land Registry before it can take effect at law if the estate is either a freehold or a leasehold with a term of more than 7 years (ss. 7(1), 4(2), Land Registration Act 2002).

Rights can be created which, while not recognised by law, are recognised in equity. This is most often achieved by means of a contract. The validity of such contracts depends on compliance with strict formalities – they must be in writing, incorporating all the terms of the agreement (or by reference to another document), and signed by, or on behalf of, all parties (s. 2, Law of Property (Miscellaneous Provisions) Act 1989). Failure to comply with those formalities renders the contract void (subject to possible resuscitation through the constructive trust and proprietary estoppel – see, though, the issues in respect of the latter in *Yaxley* v. *Gotts* [2000] Ch 162). The significance of these formalities can be demonstrated through their effect on a previously established practice of granting a charge over a property by handing title deeds to a bank in return for a loan. By virtue of s. 2, such a practice is now of no effect because it does not comply with the relevant formalities (*United Bank of Kuwait* v. *Sahib* [1997] Ch 107).

There is an important exception to the formalities requirements in respect of leases for less than or exactly 3 years. These may be made orally (s. 54(2), Law of Property Act 1925; s. 2(5)(a), Law of Property (Miscellaneous Provisions) Act 1989), although not assigned orally (*Crago* v. *Julian* [1992] 1 WLR 372). They must, however, take effect in possession immediately and be at the best rent reasonably obtainable (*Long* v. *Tower Hamlets LBC* [1998] Ch 197).

Landlord and tenant

The relationship of landlord and tenant (or lessor and lessee – the terms are interchangeable) is perhaps the most important concept within housing law because, as we develop in the next section and subsequent chapters in this part, it underpins the identification of the rights and responsibilities of the provider and occupier, as well as the occupier's security. Therefore, it is essential to be able to identify the type of occupation agreement. The usual distinction which needs to be drawn is between a lease and a licence. This was discussed in Chapter 3 above. For the sake of convenience, this distinction is presented here in terms of a series of principles:

Principle 1: the essence of a lease is that the occupier has the right of exclusive possession. This right means that the occupier can exclude all, including the landlord, from the property. The landlord may reserve to themselves limited rights of entry to the property (for example, to conduct repairs, and usually on giving reasonable notice to the occupier).

Principle 2: whether an occupier is entitled to exclusive possession is a question of law and fact – the subjective intentions of the parties are not relevant to that determination. Thus, the labels that the parties apply to an agreement are irrelevant.

Principle 3: an occupier who has the right of exclusive possession is 'exceptionally' not necessarily a tenant. Their occupation may be referable to some other type of arrangement or there was no intention to create legal relations (for example, granted out of friendship or charity). The intention and nature of the grantor is key to the determination of whether the arrangement fits into these categories.

Principle 4: a lease must take effect for a certain term. This has been discussed above but is repeated here because it is central to the identification of the relationship. If the term is uncertain, no lease can take effect. However, it is possible to imply a term from the periodic payment of rent.

Principle 5: a lease may require a rent to be paid. Rent is not an absolute requirement (s. 205(1)(xxvii), Law of Property Act 1925; *Ashburn Anstalt* v. *Arnold* [1989] Ch 1) but provides an indication of intention as to the type of right created; if there is no rent payable, this may indicate that the situation falls within principle 3 above.

Principle 6: it appears that a grant to two or more persons can only take effect as a lease if those persons take as joint tenants (for discussion, see Sparkes 1987). If the parties take under separate agreements, the question is whether those agreements are 'interdependent' (joint tenants) or 'independent' of each other (licensees); to put this another way, the question is whether those agreements can be read together (joint tenants) or not (licensees). The existence of separate rental obligations here is, or may be, significant.

Principle 7: Although the existence of the security of tenure legislation should not affect the construction of the agreement between the parties, the court will strike out terms which are 'pretences', which are designed to avoid the creation of a tenancy and its consequences in terms of security of tenure.

Principle 8: if the grantor does not have title to grant a tenancy, it is possible for a tenancy to arise nevertheless, as a result of an 'estoppel' on the basis that the grantor represents that they have power to make the grant and the occupier relies on that representation to their detriment. One outcome of this type of situation is that the grantor is then subject to the repairing obligations considered in Chapter 13 below.

Questions of termination of leases without security of tenure are dealt with below and in Chapters 14–16.

Security of tenure

In the introduction to this chapter, the point was made that the security of tenure provisions appear absurd because tenure (in housing policy terms) may be largely accidental and its consequences largely unforeseen. Policy-makers do not recognise security of tenure in those terms. Rather, the identification of security of tenure with a particular tenure is the product of the different forms of *regulation* of each tenure and the different purposes security has served historically. So, for example, in the long history of council housing, council tenants only gained rights against their landlords in 1980 as the era of 'patronage' came to an end and the era of consumerism was beginning (see Loveland 1992). Security given to PRP tenants has varied according to the directions from which the PRP has gleaned development funds. The current position of mixing public and private funds means that PRP tenants' security commonly falls between the public and private regimes. The policy desire to encourage the private rental market has affected the level of security given to tenants in the PRS. No matter how and by whom the accommodation is accessed, the regulation of each sector has predetermined the level of security given to occupiers in each sector.

This focus on regulation, as opposed to access, being the determining factor is perhaps not unnatural, although it does create absurdities. However, it also marks (and masks) a deep-rooted set of ideological underpinnings, which have produced legal complexity. The Law Commission, in its review of the development of security of tenure, made this important point:

> Legal complexity is in large part the result of political decisions taken at different stages in the development of housing law about which categories of agreement should or should not fall within the scope of any regulatory scheme. Legislators have in the past thought it right to make a large number of special provisions for particular situations … They have resulted in the complexity that now confronts us. (2002a: para. 3.4)

Past Conservative governments have been keen to deregulate and decontrol the PRS as far as possible because they believed that excessive regulation and control of the private sector was constraining that sector's development. Regulation of private sector landlord or lender interests are sometimes regarded almost as expropriation, a removal of that person's rights over their property or security (see also Honore 1980). Such views were often replicated within the judiciary, where a focus on strict contractual rights conflicts with statutory security. This conflict is an underlying feature of much of the case law, which means that the legislation was often narrowly construed (i.e. construed against the interests of the occupier). Hand (1980: 358; see also Robson and Watchman 1981) made this point when she argued that:

> [T]he courts made no secret of their dislike for the whole idea of a statutory ten-ant since he did not fit easily into the accepted categories of proprietary interests. They therefore moved towards the position that he had a purely personal right. Parliament had not made its intentions sufficiently clear. To give the statutory tenant property rights was to remove them from the landlord and this the courts were unwilling to do.

Partington (1980: 30), however, observed that, as no study had been conducted on judicial views of security of tenure, any 'casual empiricism' should be treated with some caution, an approach which sits more easily with current judicial attitudes.

In this section, each tenure is considered separately in the following order: owner-occupation; private renting; PRPs; local authority. The section begins with a brief discussion of ownership – it is brief because this issue is particu-larly considered in Chapter 14 below. Subsequently, private renting and local authority security are analysed through the following structure: (i) qualifying conditions, (ii) excluded agreements, (iii) any rights granted to the occupier by statute, (iv) the nature of the security (i.e. the ways in which, and reasons why, an occupier might be evicted). The section on PRPs is more discursive because the regime builds on that existing in the PRS. The final section, however, looks at the position where the occupier has no security.

Ownership

Few households are able to afford to buy a property without the assistance of a mortgage. The rights of the mortgage lender are significant. Indeed, uncon-strained, the occupier may find that they have no security at all in law, except through convention and regulation, for it has traditionally been said that the mortgage lender is entitled to go into possession of the property 'as soon as the ink is dry' on the mortgage deed (or, now, the land register), unless they have expressly or impliedly agreed to limit or exclude this right (*Four-Maids Ltd* v. *Dudley Marshall (Properties) Ltd* [1957] Ch 317 at 320, Harman J). Further, it is also said that the rights of an owner-borrower with a mortgage come down to the right to pay the lender back, known as the equity of redemption (*City of London BS* v. *Flegg* [1988] AC 54).

There is no requirement on the mortgage lender to obtain a court order for possession of the property (*Ropaigealach* v. *Barclays Bank plc* [2000] 1 QB 263), although a wise lender will not usually exercise its self-help remedy because of the potential for the commission of a criminal offence (s. 6, Criminal Law Act 1977). It is usual now for lenders to limit their right to possession to circumstances where there has been a breach of a term of the mortgage document – so, for example, in *Horsham Properties* v. *Clark* [2009] 1 WLR 1255, at [18], the lender restricted its rights to certain defaults of the borrower, including the failure to make one or more monthly payments when they are due or a failure to pay any other part of the mortgage debt within 1 month of it becoming due.

Legal mortgagees have other remedies (the powers of sale and to appoint a receiver), although these may be dependent on the borrower's default (see ss. 103 and 109, Law of Property Act 1925, in relation to the power of sale and receivership respectively). It is usual for the mortgage lender to obtain possession before sale of the property (because sale with vacant possession is likely to net a higher value and be less problematic). However, the mortgage lender or their appointed receiver may sell the property with the 'owners' still living in it; the effect of such a sale is usually to deprive the owners of their entire interest in the property if the sale discharges the mortgage; it also does not engage any of the human rights of the 'owners', particularly if the sale is by the receiver under contractual powers in the mortgage agreement (*Horsham Properties* v. *Clark* [2009] 1 WLR 1255).

What in some circumstances a mortgage lender cannot do, however, is to take risks at the potential expense of the owner. Thus, in *Palk* v. *Mortgage Services Funding Ltd* [1993] Ch 330, the Court of Appeal was faced with a disagreement between lender and borrower over whether the property should be rented out or sold, in a circumstance where there was negative equity (the value of the outstanding loan was greater than the value of the property at that time). The borrower wanted to sell the property as soon as was possible, even though there would be a considerable debt outstanding. The lender wished to rent the property out until the property market increased again, although it was uncertain when this would be. However, if the property were rented out, there would still be an annual shortfall of £15,000 owed to the lender. The jurisdiction of the court was wide – under s. 91(2), Law of Property Act 1925, the court is entitled to make an order 'on such terms as it thinks fit' in relation to the sale. In *Palk*, the court ordered that the mortgagor should be entitled to sell the property. What seemed to influence the court was that the lender was effectively gambling on the state of the housing market and using the Palk's property as stake money. As Nicholls V-C suggested, if it wished to do this, the lender could purchase the property itself.

Palk was heard during a recession when there was considerable public anxiety over the increasing number of property repossessions. This context particularly seemed to affect the court which, it may be argued, was swayed by its views of the lender's approach. In *Polonski* v. *Lloyds Bank* [1998] 1 FLR 896, the court ordered a sale in similar circumstances to *Palk*. Jacobs J was influenced by two factors: first, he argued that the bank would only be disadvantaged by the sale because the 'mortgage payments are currently being met by the state'.

Second, the borrower was regarded as wanting to do the right thing (move from a relatively poor neighbourhood where she feared for her child's future to a more affluent neighbourhood).

In 1997, the Court of Appeal attempted to circumscribe this jurisdiction in *Cheltenham & Gloucester BS* v. *Krausz* (1997) 29 HLR 597. The issue in *Krausz* was whether a mortgage rescue scheme, under which a PRP was to buy the property, could take effect after the lender had obtained a warrant for possession under the section 91(2) jurisdiction. The court was influenced by the judges' 'past experience of hopeless applications for leave to appeal against possession orders … There will be a danger, if the mortgagee does not obtain possession, that the mortgagor will delay the realisation of the property by seeking too high a price or deliberately procrastinating on completion [of the sale].' (p. 603) Two other reasons provided were that the court would enter into an 'area of difficult factual enquiry' as to the common benefit of the lender and borrower; and there would be difficulties in lenders 'monitoring the negotiations of [borrowers] who are permitted time to market their properties' (ibid.). Consequently, it was held that the jurisdiction opened up by the decision in *Palk* only applied where the lender was not actively seeking possession.

What we find, therefore, is that an 'owner' owns nothing but an estate in land and, if there is a legal mortgage, their security is limited, and potentially more limited than a tenant with security of tenure. This aspect of the 'endgame' is the natural counterbalance to the claim that ownership provides 'ontological security' to the owners (see, for example, Saunders 1990); as Fox (2007) notes, it is framed in the interests of the lenders which are always paramount and protected, because of the concerns that, if it were otherwise, mortgage lending for ownership would be constricted.

Private renting

Under the Housing Act 1988, two distinct but interrelated types of security of tenure regimes have been in operation: the AT and the AST. Prior to this Act, security of tenure in the PRS was generally governed by the Rent Act 1977, itself a consolidation of earlier legislation (Rent Act 1965 and Rent Act 1974). The underlying basis for protection under both the 1977 and 1988 Acts is that the occupier has a tenancy. Prior to the 1988 Act, landlords sought to avoid giving the protection offered by the Acts to tenants either through licence agreements or other mechanisms. To a certain extent, the decision of the House of Lords in *Street* v. *Mountford* stymied such attempts, although its effect was 'rapidly neutralized' by the effect of the Housing Act 1988 to be discussed below (see Vincent-Jones 1987). Under the protection of the 1977 Act, the tenant's security was described as 'status of irremoveability' during the currency of protection. This term was used to denote the limits on the landlord's rights to evict the tenant, as well as the right (until 1989) of *two* successions given to the tenant. On the death of the tenant, their successor would be entitled to take the tenant's interest;

and, on the death of the successor, a further succession was permitted. The 1988 Act, however, removed the right of second succession. The focus in this section, however, is on the AT and AST. The latter, which is the most common current form of security of tenure, may be described as a 'status of moveability'.

The Conservative government, working under the prevailing economic theory that rent control or rent regulation together with security of tenure was responsible for the decline in the PRS (see IEA 1972; Turner and Malpezzi 2003; cf. Radin 1986), used the 1988 Act as part of a series of incentives designed to revive the PRS. No more Rent Act tenancies could be created (and restrictions were placed on the right of succession under the 1977 Act). In fact, the AT closely resembles the 1977 Act regime as regards the level of security of tenure (albeit more simplified). There were, however, significant alterations to the grounds on which courts can grant possession orders. The principal innovation of the 1988 Act was the creation of the AST. Initially, all tenancies granted after the 1988 Act came into force were ATs *unless* the landlord served a notice on the tenant that the tenancy was to be an AST. In the Housing Act 1996, however, the notice requirement was swapped around so that the landlord must serve a notice on the tenant if the tenancy is to be an AT. Where no notice is served the tenancy is an assured shorthold. The case for change was that many landlords were being caught out by the notice requirement, thus granting ATs rather than ASTs (see DoE 1995). The central difference between an AT and an AST lies in their termination.

Qualifying conditions

By virtue of s. 1, 1988 Act:

(1) A tenancy under which a dwelling-house is let as a separate dwelling is for the purposes of this Act an assured tenancy if and so long as –
  (a) the tenant or, as the case may be, each of the joint tenants is an individual; and
  (b) the tenant or, as the case may be, at least one of the joint tenants occupies the dwelling-house as his only or principal home; and
  (c) the tenancy is not one which, by virtue of subsection (2) or subsection (6) below, cannot be an assured tenancy.

This definition built on, and altered, previous approaches so that much of the case law under the previous security of tenure regimes is relevant to the interpretation of s. 1. The first point is that the 1988 Act regime, as with previous regimes, only applies to tenancies. It excludes licences. There is no logical reason beyond the history of the Rent Acts why this should be so – the Law Commission's view (2002a: paras. 6.8 and 9.39–40) was that security should apply to all contracts for rent which confer the right to occupy premises as a *home*, as the fine distinctions in law between leases and licences did not necessarily correspond with the use of property. That more modern 'take' on the arrangement makes sense, but has not yet been favoured.

The expression 'if and so long as' is to be noted – this means that if, at any time, the conditions are not fulfilled, then the tenant loses the security of the 1988 Act. Further, security only attaches if the tenant is an individual, a carefully chosen word which excludes a company (which, while being a legal 'person', is not an individual).

The premises concerned must be a 'dwelling-house', which can also be part of a house (s. 45). Perhaps counter-intuitively, this old-fashioned expression extends well beyond a house or part of a house to a single room. The question for the House of Lords in *Uratemp Ventures Ltd* v. *Collins* [2002] 1 AC 301 was whether a single room in a hotel, without cooking facilities, could be a dwelling-house. The House of Lords adopted an expansive definition, so that Lord Millett, in the leading speech, asked 'whether, at the date when the proceedings were brought, it was the tenant's home. If so, it was his dwelling.' (at [58]) The absence of cooking facilities was neither here nor there; indeed, Lord Irvine went so far as to suggest that a room without a bed might be a 'dwelling' ('every case is for the judge of trial but I would have no difficulty with a conclusion that one could live in a room, which is regarded and treated as home, although taking one's sleep, without the luxury of a bed, in an armchair, or in blankets on the floor': at [4]; cf. Lord Bingham at [12]: 'If a room were so small and cramped as to be unable to accommodate a bed, I should be inclined to doubt whether it would qualify to be called a dwelling-house because, although sleeping in premises may not be enough to make them a dwelling-house, premises will not ordinarily be a dwelling-house unless the tenant sleeps there.'). As their Lordships explained, the interpretation of the expression 'dwelling-house' must take account of the statutory context – the purpose of the legislation being to provide security to tenants in their own home – and modern conditions. Lord Steyn pointed out:

> there has been an explosion in the growth of self-service cafeteria, sandwich shops, takeaway shops, home delivery services and other fast food outlets. One only has to look under the entry 'Food and Drink Delivered' in the most recent edition of the Yellow Pages for Central London (2000/2001) to realise the scale of this development in the eating habits of large numbers of people of all ages.

Thus, the meaning of dwelling-house concerns whether, in light of the purpose of the statute and modern life, premises can be regarded as the tenant's 'home' (a concept which, in itself, is contested – see, for example, Fox 2007); however, the structure itself must be a fixture (*Chelsea Yacht & Boat Co. Ltd* v. *Pope* [2000] 1 WLR 1941).

The dwelling-house must also be let as *a* separate dwelling. It is perfectly possible for there to be individual ATs/ASTs of rooms in a house, but a property let as several dwellings will not fall within this expression (*St Catherine's College* v. *Dorling* [1980] 1 WLR 66). Where the tenants share some part of the premises with others, except the landlord, but have exclusive occupation of part of the premises, that is sufficient for the 'separate dwelling' criterion (s. 3). However, where the tenant shares some part of the premises with the landlord, then that exception does not apply (s. 3(1)(a); Sch. 1, para. 10 and Part III, designed to encourage potential landlords to rent out a room in their property for which there are also taxation advantages).

Finally, the premises must be the individual's 'only or principal home'. This is a relatively narrow expression (compared with the 1977 Act) which implies that continued residence is not necessary. In *Brown* v. *Brash* [1948] 2 KB 247, it was held that the tenant must have both an 'inward intention to return' as well as some 'formal, outward, and visible sign of [possession]' (p. 254). That case actually concerned the meaning of the word 'residence' but is equally applicable to the 1988 Act (see, for example, *Crawley BC* v. *Sawyer* (1988) 20 HLR 98, a case under the 1985 Act, which also uses the only or principal home test). In *Amoah* v. *Barking & Dagenham LBC* [2001] 82 P&CR DG6, the question was whether a tenant who had been imprisoned for 12 years nevertheless occupied his premises as his only or principal home. Etherton J summarised the case law on this test as follows:

> A. Absence by the tenant may be sufficiently prolonged or unintermittent to compel the inference, prima facie, of a cesser of possession or occupation. The question is one of fact and degree.

> Assuming an absence sufficiently prolonged to have this effect:

> 1. The onus is on the tenant to repel the presumption that his possession has ceased.
> 2. In order to repel it he must at all events establish a de facto intention on his part to return after his absence.
> 3. While there is no set limit to the length of absence, the tenant must be able to demonstrate a 'practical possibility' or 'a real possibility' of the fulfilment of his intention to return within a reasonable time.
> 4. The tenant must also show that his inward intention is accompanied by some formal, outward and visible sign of this intention to return, which sign must be sufficiently substantial and permanent that in all the circumstances it is adequate to rebut the presumption that the tenant, by being physically absent from the premises for a prolonged period, has ceased to be in possession of it. (Transcript, pp. 15–16; cited in *Sheffield CC* v. *Wall* [2010] HLR 47, at [52].)

It was found that Mr Amoah had no other place to which he could return on release; he had left his furniture in the premises; his step-daughter retained the keys to the premises, having been given them by the council, to act as the caretaker and she paid the rent. Therefore, the presumption that the premises were not his only or principal home was, on the facts, rebutted.

Excluded agreements

Section 1(1)(c) excludes certain tenancies from the operation of the security of tenure provisions. The excluded tenancies are set out in Sch. 1, 1988 Act. The Act only bites on tenancies granted after the Act comes into force. Also excluded are the following: tenancies at a low or no rent (less than £1,000 per annum in London and £250 per annum elsewhere); holiday, student, agricultural, local authority, fully mutual housing association lettings as well as lettings of licensed (i.e. for selling intoxicating liquor) premises.

Similarly, tenancies at a high rent are excluded because it is assumed that the 'luxury' end of the market does not require protection (Rugg and Rhodes 2008: 83). The high rent was originally set at £25,000 but was increased at the suggestion of Rugg and Rhodes ('a failure to institute a change might lead to the creation of a growing tenancy class "outside" the AST regulations, where tenants would have very limited rights': ibid.), to £100,000 per annum (Assured Tenancies (Amendment) (England) Order 2010, SI 2010/908). This upper limit applies irrespective of when the tenancy was created (and may lead to issues regarding protection of the tenant's deposit: http://nearlylegal.co.uk/blog/2010/03/housing-act-changes/). (For an attempt to use the upper limit to contract out of the security of tenure provisions, see *Bankway Properties Ltd v. Pensfold-Dunsford* [2002] 1 WLR 1369, discussed in Chapter 3 above; also, Bright 2002.)

Statutory rights

The rights of an assured tenant are limited. They are not entitled to assign, part with or sub-let any part of the dwelling-house without the consent of the landlord (s. 15). In the past, rent was either controlled or regulated. However, under the 1988 Act, there is no provision relating to rent – landlords can charge whatever the market will bear. Indeed, once in occupation under a periodic tenancy, the landlord is entitled to increase the rent, although the tenant has the right to refer that proposed increase to the Rent Assessment Committee (ss. 13–14, 1988 Act). In the case of an AST, the tenant also has the right to apply to the committee during the first 6 months of the agreement 'for a determination of the rent which, in the committee's opinion, the landlord might reasonably be expected to obtain under the [AST]' (s. 22(1)). Realistically, though, few applications are made because of the limited security of tenure in an AST and the prospect of retaliatory eviction if such an application were made.

The significant benefit of this and other security of tenure regimes is that they allow for rights of succession; that is, on the death of a tenant, a further person from a limited class of persons is entitled to take the tenancy of the same property on the same terms as the deceased tenant. This principle mimics and alters the position at common law regarding tenancies, which pass with the estate of the deceased through their will or in accordance with the rules of intestacy (where there is no will) (see Law Commission 2002b: ch. 7). Under the 1988 Act, the rules of succession are altered in relation to periodic tenancies only (s. 17). They allow for *one* succession (which includes the operation of the right of survivorship on the death of the joint tenant(s): s. 17(2)(b)) and only to a person who is the tenant's spouse or civil partner – or who has lived as such (i.e. the status was not the subject of formality; see also *Ghaidan* v. *Mendoza* [2004]

HLR 46, in which the House of Lords read a similar provision under the Rent Act 1977 to include those living together as if they were husband and wife, so as to include same-sex couples) – and 'immediately before the death, the tenant's spouse or civil partner was occupying the dwelling-house as his or her only or principal home' (s. 17(1)(b)).

Security of tenure

The principal benefit of the security regime is that a tenancy cannot be terminated by the landlord without a court order (s. 5); such an order can only be made on limited grounds (s. 7, and the grounds for possession in Sch. 2). A fixed-term tenancy which comes to an end by effluxion of time (i.e. at the end of the term), nevertheless remains in operation as a periodic tenancy on the same terms as the previous tenancy, the period being that for which rent was *last* payable under the previous tenancy (s. 5(3)). In *Church Commissioners for England v. Meya* [2007] HLR 4, the question for the Court of Appeal was this: 'On the expiry of an assured shorthold tenancy for a term of 1 year less a day at a rent of £x per annum payable by equal quarterly payments in advance on the usual quarter days, is the statutory periodic tenancy which arises under s. 5 of the Housing Act 1988 (the Act) a periodic tenancy under which the period of the tenancy is yearly or quarterly?' (at [1]). Ward LJ stressed the word 'last', which qualifies the word 'payable', and because the last rent payable was for a quarterly period, that was the period of the new tenancy (at [20]–[1]).

Prior to seeking possession, the landlord must serve a notice of proceedings (s. 8(1)(a); although the court may dispense with it where it is 'just and equitable' to do so (s. 8(1)(b)), except where the landlord is proceeding on the basis of the mandatory ground for rent arrears, Ground 8 (s. 8(5)). The notice sets out the ground(s) relied on, although the court has discretion to alter or add other grounds (s. 8(2)); the earliest date on which the landlord will commence proceedings (s. 8(3)(b)); as well as the particulars of breach (which can be brief as long as they are sufficient to convey to the recipient the nature of the breach or to enable them to work out how much is owed: *Torridge DC v. Jones* (1986) 18 HLR 107, *Marath v. McGillivray* (1996) 28 HLR 484).

There are eight mandatory and ten discretionary grounds for possession. In theory at least, the court must make an order for possession if one of the mandatory grounds are proven – this is covered in greater detail in Chapter 16 below where the impact of the HRA is discussed. In summary, the current position is that the court must also consider the proportionality of the claim to possession but it is unclear whether this limitation applies to private landlords. Under the discretionary grounds, the landlord must show not just that the ground is established but also that it is reasonable to grant possession (s. 7(4)). The discretionary grounds for rent arrears and nuisance are considered in Chapters 14 and 15 below, where there are discussions of the construction of 'reasonableness' in those contexts. In summary, the position is that the court should take account of all relevant facts and circumstances in weighing whether it is reasonable to make an order for possession. The judge must take into account all relevant circumstances and 'he must do so in what I venture to call a broad, common-sense way as a man of the world, and come to his conclusion giving such weight as he thinks right to the various factors in the situation' (*Cumming* v. *Danson* [1942] 2 All ER 652, 655, Lord Greene MR). Under the discretionary grounds for possession, the court has an extended jurisdiction to adjourn or postpone possession or suspend the execution of an order for possession on terms (s. 9, 1988 Act). The effect of this extended jurisdiction, which at one stage was thought to cause considerable problems, is discussed in Chapter 14 below ('tolerated trespassers').

There are *three* grounds for possession based upon arrears of rent, one of which is *mandatory*. For monthly tenancies, the mandatory ground was shown where more than 3 months' rent was in arrears (Ground 8). This period was reduced to 2 months (and 8 weeks for weekly tenancies) (s. 101, Housing Act 1996). The government's reason for this change was that for a private landlord 'having a tenant who does not pay the rent can be financially very difficult' (DoE 1995: para. 2.14). Yet, where the tenant is reliant on HB (which is paid 4 weeks in arrears, whereas rent is practically always claimed in advance), concerns were expressed that this reduction could prove problematic. The Conservative government's answer was that, after service of the notice, it still takes a few months to obtain a court order and, provided the rent is paid off by that time, the ground can no longer be shown.

The principal difference between the AT and the AST lies in the level of security of tenure (otherwise the regimes are broadly similar). Essentially, the AST can be brought to an end at any time after the tenancy has been in existence for 6 months. The procedure for retaking possession is simplicity itself: the landlord serves a notice on the tenant in writing, giving the tenant not less than 2 months to leave (s. 21(1)(b)). More precisely, the notice must state that 'after a date specified in the notice, being the last day of a period of the tenancy and not earlier than two months after the date the notice was given, possession of the dwelling-house is required by virtue of this section' (s. 21(4)(a)). Subsequently, the landlord must obtain a court order (which is again mandatory) unless the tenant leaves earlier; there is an accelerated possession procedure available to landlords making such an application, which, in essence, is paper-based unless the tenant has a defence to the claim (CPR 55, Part II).

There has been a difficult question, however, about the interpretation of s. 21(4)(a) (at which *Meya* was partly directed), concerned with the meaning of the phrase 'the last day of the period of the tenancy'. The most authoritative discussion of the issue is contained in *McDonald* v. *Fernandez* [2004] HLR 13. Here the notice stated that the possession was required on a certain day (4 January 2003), which was the day after the last day of the period of the tenancy (3 January 2003). Hale LJ said that 'the subsection is clear and precise. Nor is it difficult for landlords to comply. They know when the period ends ... [one purpose of the provision] is to give the courts a clear and simple set of criteria which trigger their mandatory duty to order possession' (at [23]). The notice was, therefore, invalid. Bright (2007: 63) suggests that this 'ruling ... reintroduces technicality and creates unnecessary traps', but equally the landlord could have rescued their notice by using a form of words to save the notice from invalidity, but did not do so (see *Lower Street Properties* v. *Jones* (1996) 28 HLR 877, at 882, Kennedy LJ).

It should be noted, however, that no notice under s. 21 may be served where the landlord has not complied with the tenancy deposit protection rules (s. 215(1), Housing Act 2004; *Tiensia*, discussed in Chapter 9 above, does not affect this rule).

Thus, the central advantage of the assured shorthold is that the landlord can retake possession with minimal requirements and the tenant's security is consequently minimal. The other grounds for possession available in respect of ATs equally apply to ASTs. It is hardly surprising, then, that the AST has become the tenancy form most commonly granted by landlords because they are able to obtain possession so quickly and neatly. However, the ease with which the landlord can gain possession also has its pitfalls for housing policy. If one aim of housing policy is to improve the quality of the housing stock and, more specifically, to ensure that the vulnerable are not taken advantage of, the ease with which a landlord can take possession may not assist either aim. An AST occupier who complains about the state and condition of the premises or about the level of rent which the landlord is asking under the agreement may well be met with what is known as 'retaliatory eviction' (see Law Commission 2002a: 6.159–6.174; the Citizens Advice Bureau campaign, www.retaliatoryeviction.com/; cf. Rugg and Rhodes 2008: 79–81, where it is said that the problem is complex to quantify and, further, 'It cannot be denied that there will be landlords who evict tenants who complain about property condition; at the same time, it has to be admitted that there are tenants who will claim unfair eviction in the hope that this will improve their chance of getting a social housing tenancy.').

The final point about security of tenure in the PRS is that a prior mortgage is not bound by a subsequently created tenancy (of whatever type). This is an example of the general principles of priority of interests in property law – first in time prevails (s. 28, Land Registration Act 2002) – and the priority rules on registration of a security interest in land (s. 30, Land Registration 2002) (see *Britannia BS* v. *Earl* [1990] 1 WLR 422). If the lender consents to the tenancy, then the tenancy will take priority. However, by the Mortgage Repossessions (Protection of Tenants etc.) Act 2010, a tenant is given limited protection where the lender seeks possession against the landlord, or obtains a warrant for eviction against the landlord in the case of an unauthorised tenancy. The Act gives the court a discretion either to postpone the date of possession for 2 months on the application of the tenant; or to stay or suspend execution of an order for possession, where the tenant has requested an undertaking from the lender not to enforce the order for two months and the lender has refused (s. 1). As the tenant may not be aware that the lender has obtained a possession order, the

Act also extends the notification requirement to include the tenant or occupier of the property using a prescribed form (s. 2; Dwelling Houses (Execution of Possession Orders by Mortgagees) Order 2010, SI 2010/1809). Mortgage lenders must now give a notice addressed to 'the tenant or occupier' not less than 14 days before they execute a warrant, which is in the prescribed form and contains information about the exercise of the tenant's rights under the 2010 Act (CPR 55.10(4A)). Although the rights are limited, these provisions have already been used to some effect in county courts (*Bank of Scotland* v. *Ashraf*, Romford CC, 5 October 2010 (2010) December *Legal Action* 36; *GMAC RFC Ltd* v. *Jones*, Lambeth CC, 15 November 2010 (2011) January *Legal Action* 36) and the CLG has issued guidance on their use (CLG 2010f).

Private registered providers

We have noted in earlier chapters how PRPs have, at different times, been regarded as being private sector, public sector, or quasi-public sector. That difference is naturally reflected in the types of security of tenure regime within which the tenancies they provide fall. So, in the period 1977–1980, PRP tenants had no security of tenure ('presumably because the … landlords were non-profit making bodies and considered socially responsible' – Stewart 1996: 199). Between 1980 and 1988, PRP tenants were put within the secure tenancy regime, principally (it seems) because the Conservative government was keen to widen the definition of the public sector in order to widen the scope of the RTB. However, the RTB, by amendment in the House of Lords accepted by the Conservative government, did not apply to charitable PRPs. The 1980 Act regime applied to all tenancies granted by PRPs prior to its introduction.

The position changed from the introduction of the 1988 Act for two reasons. The mixed funding regime provided a significant impetus because it was assumed that private lenders would only be willing to make loans to PRPs if the security of tenure available to tenants was the same as private sector tenants and (importantly) rents were subject to market principles: 'This [use of AT and AST regimes] should give [PRPs] the essential freedom and flexibility in setting their rents to enable them to meet the requirements of private sector finance instead of relying on funding from public sources.' (DoE 1987b: para. 4.6) A further reason for the shift to private sector security of tenure regimes was so that PRPs themselves would fall out of the public sector regime and, thus, not be 'counted' as part of public expenditure.

Thus, in short, PRP tenants now fall within the 1988 Act regime, as described above. This includes those tenants who have been the subject of an LSVT, as their landlord no longer fulfils the 'landlord condition' for the security of tenure regimes under the Housing Act 1985 (see below); and it also includes 'conventional' shared ownership (where the shared owner buys a long lease – it is that lease which will fall within the 1988 Act regime). Be that as it may, the regulatory desire of the Housing Corporation was to equalise PRP tenants as closely as possible with the status and security of council tenants. Thus, from an early stage, the Housing Corporation's Tenant's Guarantee made it clear that PRPs were to grant 'the most secure form of tenure possible', which meant that other than in 'exceptional circumstances' PRPs were to grant ATs (Housing Corporation 1997: para. C3), which the subsequent shift to tenants' charters (reflecting the different sectors in which PRPs operate) did not diminish. PRP tenants were also to be given additional rights to consultation on certain issues, to information, to participate in housing management, plus additional rights to repair, take in lodgers, assign tenancies, exchange properties, as well as alternative complaints mechanisms (using the housing ombudsman scheme).

These rights were not incorporated into the tenancy agreement and questions arose as to their enforceability in law (see, for example, Stewart 1996: 223), which *Weaver v. London & Quadrant HT* [2009] 1 All ER 17, at first instance effectively disposed of in the context of rent arrears (and which was not the subject of appeal). The terms of the contract in that case said that '[i]n providing a housing service we will comply with the regulatory framework and guidance issued by the Housing Corporation'. It was argued that this created a legitimate expectation in Ms Weaver that L&Q would indeed comply with that framework and guidance. However, Richards LJ said (at [87]):

> I do not think that it can be read as a clear, unambiguous and unqualified promise or commitment to do everything set out in the guidance issued by the Housing Corporation. The guidance is by its nature guidance, not prescription. The regulatory provisions … place the Housing Corporation in a strong position to ensure that it is substantially followed, but there is nothing that turns it into the equivalent of a statutory rule-book, and the Housing Corporation looks not just at whether the guidance has been followed but at whether alternative action has been taken to achieve the same objectives .… The statement in LQHT's standard terms and conditions cannot have been intended to give the guidance a status it does not have under the statute or in the Housing Corporation's own practice … Moreover, if the statement has the character of a promise, there is no reason why it should not be treated as a contractual promise, since it features in the contractual terms and conditions; but it is no part of the claimant's case that the statement is contractually binding. If it lacks the qualities to give it contractual force notwithstanding that it is located in a contract, I am not satisfied that it can properly be treated as having the qualities that justify its enforcement in public law as a legitimate expectation.

In any event, the regulatory guidance (concerned with use of the mandatory ground for possession for rent arrears as a last resort) was itself not sufficiently precise (at [88]).

The Housing Corporation's *Performance Standards* (1997) also contained similar comments to the Tenant's Guarantee about the level of security of tenure ('the most secure form of tenancy possible compatible with the purpose of the housing means issuing all new tenants with assured periodic tenancies': para. G1.1). However, there were two particular exceptions enabling PRPs to grant ASTs under a 'local lettings' scheme or under a 'starter tenancy' scheme (see Standard H2.2; and para. 14; following on from Page 1993). The subsequent *Regulatory Code* (Housing Corporation 2005) did not contain similar provisions but provided a general assertion regarding proper management that PRPs should provide good quality housing, inter alia 'by offering the most secure form of tenure compatible with the purpose of the housing and the sustainability of the community' (para. 3.5.2). The TSA, in its regulatory framework (2010a: 25), followed that approach: 'Registered providers shall offer and issue the most secure form of tenure compatible with the purpose of the housing and the sustainability of the community', and, by way of guidance on that standard, that PRPs 'shall publish clear and accessible policies which outline their approach to tenancy management' (at para. 3.1). This regulatory history is relevant because it demonstrates the development of the understanding of security of tenure by both the regulators as well as PRPs themselves. Starter tenancies are common for PRP tenants, which raises concerns about the use of the section 21 notice procedure in such cases.

It is also the case that many PRPs extend the security of tenure to their tenants in different ways by the mechanisms of policy, practice and/or contract. For example, their policy may expressly disavow the use of the section 21 notice procedure, or the use of Ground 8 (mandatory eviction for rent arrears). Such policies and practices are particularly prevalent among LSVT PRPs where the offer made to existing tenants prior to the vote on transfer includes such a commitment in relation to the use of Ground 8, usually for a set period of (say) 5 years, to neutralise concerns about transfer (Pawson and Mullins 2010: 213). Thus, in one recent survey, just 11.5% of LSVT respondents used Ground 8; indeed, just 40.4% of non-LSVT respondents used it (Pawson et al. 2010: 76). The same study also suggested geographical disparity in its use (higher incidence in London; virtual absence in the South West).

Where ASTs are used, there are usually procedures for seeking possession which extend the requirements of the section 21 notice, including (for example) a process enabling the tenant to appeal to the PRP against its decision to end the starter tenancy/AST. *Eastlands Homes Partnership Ltd* v. *Whyte* [2010] EWHC 695 (QB) is a most instructive case as to the operation of public law principles in this precise context and demonstrates the practical issues which may arise in the operation of such a policy. In essence, the PRP failed to follow its own policy (indeed, was unable to produce part of it), breached principles of natural justice by failing to provide relevant documents to Ms Whyte in advance of an internal appeal hearing, and failed to inform her of her right to a further appeal (as the PRP was unaware of this right in their own policy). Further, the conduct of the internal appeal hearing itself was flawed:

> There is no indication in the minutes that the attention of the appeal panel was drawn to the [PRP's] normal policy in relation to rent arrears. There is also no evidence that the appeal panel was asked to consider whether the failure by the Defendant to pay was deliberate [as required by the PRP's policy]. It had evidence

before it to the contrary in that the appeal letter adverted to difficulties regarding housing benefit. These were important matters, because it was crucial for the appeal panel to be satisfied that there was good reason to depart from the normal policy. The modest size of the arrears at the time emphasised the need for careful scrutiny. (at [57])

In the post-*Weaver* (Court of Appeal) environment (discussed in Chapter 5 above), such a decision trailblazes the potential future issues for PRPs in the management of tenancies.

Local authority

Until the Housing Act 1980, local authority tenants had few enforceable rights against their landlords in the way of security of tenure, as local authority provision was expressly excluded from the protection afforded to other tenants (see, in particular, *Shelley* v. *London CC* [1949] AC 56). The reason for this lack of protection was related to the relationship between central and local government; as Loughlin (1986: 114, original emphasis) puts it, 'Central government's role traditionally has been *advisory* rather than *supervisory*.' Loveland (1992: 344) argued that a further important context was the relationship between central and local government: 'Tightly drafted statutes or interventionist case law would have overridden the traditional expectation that councils should govern their local areas, rather than simply administer centrally defined services on an agency basis.' This might be regarded as the period of trust in local authorities. Stewart's discussion (1996: 126) of the *Shelley* case is instructive as, she argues, 'the public position of the local authority ensures that it can be trusted to act in a public-spirited and fair way in the general public interest as a landlord'.

The shift to more tightly drafted statutes and interventionist case law occurred when the central–local government relationship began to break down in the mid-1970s. Even so, as Hoath (1982: 4) pointed out, it was 'increasingly illogical' to have an elaborate system of protection for tenants in a dwindling PRS, but excluding an expanding public sector. The relationship of trust and fairness was regarded as a 'nowadays unconvincing' basis (Finer 1974: 388). The economic context of recession and public spending constraint was also an influential factor (Kay et al. undated: 1–2). Although it has been argued that tenants were granted rights *in order to* grant them the RTB (Smith and George 1997), it was also the case that security of tenure emerged after a lengthy campaign focusing on the council tenant as consumer (see Loveland 1992; National Consumer Council 1976; Housing Services Advisory Group 1977), and was one of the foundations for the growth of the law centre movement (Public Health Advisory Service 1976: 26, cited in Stewart 1996: 135).

There was, then, a cross-party consensus on the need for a security of tenure regime for council tenants – the Labour government's 1979 Housing Bill contained a set of individual rights, based on the acceptance of their need in the Green Paper (DoE 1977: 51–6), which mostly found themselves in the

Conservatives' 1980 Act. That having been said, implementation of the rights by councils after the 1980 Act came into force was patchy: 'The majority of councils have not implemented the rights effectively. Many have not even met the minimum legal requirements' (Kay et al. undated: ix). This mirrored the apparent lack of interest by central government (ibid. p. 40); so, 'While the right to buy was advertised several times on television and in national newspapers, the DoE confined promotion of the rest of the Tenants' Charter to a slim official pamphlet.' (Loveland 1992: 352) Thus, the national structures meant that little information was given to individual tenants, who were then unable to exercise their rights for which, in any event, councils themselves were not ready.

The rights are now contained in the Housing Act 1985, Part IV.

Qualifying conditions

The security of tenure provisions bite *at any time* when the premises have been let as a separate dwelling, the occupier meets the 'tenant condition' and the landlord meets the 'landlord condition' (ss. 79–81). The phrase 'at any time' has been highlighted because it is different from the 1988 Act and means that it is possible to go into, out of, and back into the regime (what has been described as an 'ambulatory effect'). The notion of 'letting' has a more expansive definition, however, as the provisions also apply to a licence to occupy a dwelling-house whether or not for payment 'as they apply to a tenancy' (s. 79(3)), other than one granted 'as a temporary expedient' (s. 79(4)). In *Westminster CC* v. *Clarke* [1992] 2 AC 288, the House of Lords held that only licences which *also* convey the right to exclusive possession to the licensee fell within the scope of s. 79(3) (see Cowan 1992b). Other than these distinctions, the discussion of the 1988 Act principles similarly applies here. Thus, the tenant (or tenants) must be an individual who occupies the premises as their only or principal home. The key difference, however, concerns the landlord condition, which is (inter alia) a local authority or a HAT. These organisations can only grant secure tenancies.

Excluded agreements

Schedule 1, 1985 Act, specifies a number of occupation agreements which are excluded from protection including: long leases (defined in s. 115 and include leases for more than 21 years or granted under the RTB); certain short-term agreements (commonly referred to as the North Wiltshire scheme, whereby a landlord leases or licences accommodation to an authority with vacant possession for a specified period: Cowan 1992a); introductory, demoted and family intervention tenancies (unless, in the case of family intervention tenancies, the landlord informs the tenant that it is to be secure); asylum seekers and certain displaced persons; and certain employment-related exclusions. Accommodation granted to homeless persons under Part VII, Housing Act 1996 cannot be secure tenancies, unless the landlord informs the tenant that it is to be secure.

Statutory rights

Prior to the 1980 Act, tenancy agreements commonly placed many obligations on the tenant without giving tenants any rights (see the critique of Saunders 1990; and Chapter 4 above). The 1980 Act included what was termed the Tenants' Charter. It has since been amended but it contains a series of rights which appear superficially potent but their potency is reduced by limitations on their exercise. The following are a selection: secure tenants have the right to take in lodgers, make improvements to the property and be compensated for them, and have a right to repair and recover the costs of the repairs.

Particularly important have been the rights to information about tenancy rights and conditions (s. 104) and consultation (s. 106; including over a decision to transfer stock to a private landlord: s. 106A) that were discussed in Chapter 4 above. Each of these rights is delimited in some way or other so as to reduce its potency. For example, the right to be consulted does not go so far as to cover the level of rents, 'one of the most important collective concerns for tenants' (Gilroy 1998: 26); and 'the economic disadvantage of most tenants limits their right to undertake improvements' (Stewart 1996: 153). *R (Beale)* v. *Camden LBC* [2004] HLR 48 provides further salient evidence of the limits of the right to consultation. The case concerned the consultation process leading to the transfer of the management of Camden's stock to an ALMO. Beale and colleagues were involved in opposition to the process under the Defend Council Housing banner. Their argument was that it was incumbent on Camden to present arguments against their proposal to the tenants; in short, that the publicity should be balanced to enable the tenants to make their own decision. The court found, however, that the main requirements were that the council had to make arrangements which permitted tenants to inform themselves of the proposal; and a court will only interfere if it is satisfied that no reasonable council would deem the arrangements appropriate (relying on *R* v. *Brent LBC ex p Morris* (1997) 30 HLR 324). There was no obligation on the council to canvass the '*dis*advantages' of its proposal (*Beale*, at [33], original emphasis).

The further statutory right is the right of succession. As under the 1988 Act, there can only be one succession but, at present, the succession can be to a broader category of person who:

> occupies the dwelling-house as his only or principal home at the time of the tenant's death and either –
> (a) he is the tenant's spouse or civil partner, or
> (b) he is another member of the tenant's family and has resided with the tenant throughout the period of twelve months ending with the tenant's death (s. 87(1))

The definition of spouse or civil partner is expanded by the mechanism of including those living as spouse or civil partner within the definition of member of the tenant's family (s. 113; see also *Ghaidan* v. *Mendoza* [2004] HLR 46, in which the House of Lords read a similar provision under the Rent Act

1977 to include those living together as if they were husband and wife, so as to include same-sex couples). The tenant's family is limited to include certain close relatives (parent, grandparent, child, grandchild, brother, sister, uncle, aunt, nephew or niece: s. 113(1)(b)). Where more than one person is entitled to succeed, then the spouse or civil partner is to be preferred, after which it is within the discretion of the landlord if there is no agreement between the individuals entitled (s. 89(2)). The Act does not affect the common law rule regarding the right of survivorship after a joint tenancy; where one of the joint tenants dies, the other joint tenant is the successor and there can be no further succession even if the other joint tenant no longer occupies the premises (*Solihull MBC v. Hickin* [2010] 1 WLR 2254). This case provides cause for an observation that the joint tenancy should be severed (or the tenancy re-granted in the sole name of the remaining occupier) as soon as possible after one joint tenant has left.

Tenants are generally precluded from assigning their tenancy, subject to certain exceptions (s. 91(1)), or sub-letting their properties without the prior consent of their landlord (s. 93(1)(b)). There have been regular campaigns against housing tenancy fraud in the social sector (including PRPs), focusing in part on unlawful sub-letting, which is estimated to affect 2.5% of tenancies in London and 1% elsewhere (Audit Commission 2010: 19; CLG, 2009f).

What if the tenant sub-lets the property while acting under a relevant disability? Does it unlawfully discriminate against that tenant to seek possession against them? The answer to these questions now depends on the construction of the Equality Act 2010, ss. 15 and 19. Under the previous DDA provisions, it was unlawful discrimination to evict or subject the disabled person to other detriment (s. 22(3)(c)), except where the premises were small and the accommodation was shared with the landlord (s. 23). Detriment included serving a notice to quit (*Manchester CC v. Romano* [2005] 1 WLR 2775) but was better thought of as one composite process from service of the notice to possession (*Malcolm v. Lewisham LBC* [2008] 1 AC 1399). Discrimination was defined as:

a person ('A') discriminates against a disabled person if –
(a) for a reason which relates to the disabled person's disability, he treats him less favourably than he treats or would treat others to whom that reason does not or would not apply; and
(b) he cannot show that the treatment in question is justified.

In *Malcolm v. Lewisham LBC* [2008] 1 AC 1399, Mr Malcolm sublet his premises which meant that he lost his security of tenure. Lewisham Council was, therefore, entitled to serve a notice to quit terminating his tenancy (in accordance with the rules outlined below 'no security') and did so. Mr Malcolm had a disability (schizophrenia) which, it was found, existed at the time of the sub-let and was not controlled by medication. His eviction was a pure housing management decision and, thus, held not to be 'related to' his disability; the disability had to cause the decision to evict in some way; thus, the landlord had to have knowledge of the tenant's disability. Further, and perhaps more damaging, was the House of Lords' decision about the identity of the others with which to compare the treatment (i.e. 'less favourably than … others to whom that reason does not or would not apply'). Those others were said to be persons without a relevant disability who have sublet a Lewisham premises and gone to live elsewhere (cf. Baroness Hale, dissenting, at [70]–[81]). As Lewisham Council would have taken the same action in those cases, it was not discrimination.

The Equality Act 2010, s. 15, has overtaken the interpretation in *Malcolm*. Indeed, it was specifically designed to reverse the effect of *Malcolm*. Section 15 now defines discrimination in such cases in rather more simple terms:

(1) A person (A) discriminates against a disabled person (B) if –
   (a) A treats B unfavourably because of something arising in consequence of B's disability, and
   (b) A cannot show that the treatment is a proportionate means of achieving a legitimate aim.
(2) Subsection (1) does not apply if A shows that A did not know, and could not reasonably have been expected to know, that B had the disability.

Realistically, by the time of trial (assuming the tenant has pleaded discrimination), a landlord will know of the disability; thus, if the possession process is composite, this defence is unlikely to be available to the landlord. This is not to say that a disability will always trump the landlord's right to possession (on whatever ground), but the landlord will have to show that the treatment is a proportionate means of achieving a legitimate aim, which Lewisham may well have been able to show in *Malcolm* in any event (as it was accepted that they were a hard-pressed social landlord, with demand exceeding supply of their housing stock). (Readers are also referred to the discussion of general duties in relation to disability equality in s. 49A(1), DDA, replaced by s. 149, Equality Act 2010, in Chapter 6 above, which are equally applicable here.)

Security of tenure

In order to terminate a secure tenancy, the landlord must obtain a court order (s. 82) on certain grounds (s. 84(1), Sch 2, 1985 Act). The process is similar to the 1988 Act in that the landlord must serve a 'notice of seeking possession' on the tenant(s), containing specified information including the ground(s) for possession on which the landlord is relying, although the court has discretion to dispense with notice where it considers it 'just and equitable' to do so (s. 83(1)(b)); the date after which proceedings may be brought; and summary particulars of the breach(es). There are 16 grounds for possession: Grounds 1–9 require not only that the ground be made out but also that it is reasonable to grant possession; Grounds 9–11 require that the ground is made out and suitable alternative accommodation is to be provided; and Grounds 12–16 require that the ground is made out, it is reasonable to grant possession and suitable alternative accommodation is to be provided. The criterion of reasonableness remains as it does for the 1988 Act.

The differences between the 1988 Act and 1985 Act grounds are significant, beyond a different form of words with a similar meaning, and include the following: there are no mandatory grounds under the 1985 Act (currently) and, in particular, there is no mandatory ground for rent arrears under the 1985 Act; there is no equivalent ground in the 1985 Act to Ground 11 (persistent delay in paying rent); the 1985 Act has a discretionary ground for possession based on the tenant or a person acting at their instigation knowingly or recklessly making a false statement inducing the landlord to grant the tenancy (Ground 5); whereas certain of the 1985 Act grounds require that suitable alternative accommodation be provided to the tenant, under the 1988 Act there is a sole (discretionary) ground where 'Suitable alternative accommodation is available for the tenant or will be available for him when the order for possession takes effect' (Ground 9).

As with the 1988 Act, the court has extended discretion in possession cases (except under Grounds 9–11) (s. 85). The wording is slightly, but materially, different from that under the 1988 Act, which was sufficient to enable the House of Lords to draw a distinction between the 1985 and 1988 Acts in relation to the 'tolerated trespasser' doctrine (*Knowsley HT* v. *White* [2009] 1 AC 636; see Chapter 14 below).

No security

An array of arrangements confer no statutory security of tenure on the occupier, because they do not fall within the scheme of the 1985 and 1988 Acts; for example, lettings by resident landlords fulfilling the criteria for exclusion from the 1988 Act. Recently, difficult questions have arisen in respect of fully mutual co-operative housing associations which, while registered with the TSA, nevertheless do not offer security of tenure under the 1988 Act (Sch. 1, para. 12(h)) and nor do they fulfil the landlord condition under the 1985 Act. Thus, tenants of such co-operative bodies are excluded from the protective embrace of these Acts (see *Joseph* v. *Nettleton Road Housing Co-operative Ltd* [2010] EWCA Civ 228; *Berrisford* v. *Mexfield Housing Co-operative Ltd* [2010] EWCA Civ 811).

In such circumstances, the only protection beyond the terms of the contract between the parties and the common law, lies in the requirement under the Protection from Eviction Act 1977 that a notice to quit a tenancy or a periodic licence must be in writing, containing certain information, and give at least 4 weeks (or the contractual period, if longer) before it is to take effect (s. 5(1) and 5(1A)). After such a notice has been served, if the occupier continues lawfully residing in the premises, then they may only be evicted by due process of law, that is to say, a court order (s. 3(1) and (2)), a provision which amends the landlord's common law self-help remedy of ejectment. These provisions do not, however, apply to 'excluded' tenancies and licences (s. 5(1B)) –where the occupier shares accommodation in certain circumstances with the landlord/licensor or a member of their family (s. 3A, 1977 Act), a provision designed to encourage occupiers to 'rent a room'.

The contract may, however, limit the grounds on which the landlord can claim possession of the property. If it does so in a way which fetters the landlord's right to terminate the contract at the end of a period, it is void (*Prudential Assurance* v. *London Residuary Body* [1992] 2 AC 386; the question whether the tenancy still has a status in equity is currently before the Supreme Court on appeal in *Berrisford*). In the case of fully mutual co-operatives, the question has arisen as to whether their exclusion from the statutory regimes raises an incompatibility with Articles 8 and 14, Sch. 1, HRA (*Joseph*) but was neatly sidestepped on the facts by the Court of Appeal (as, even if the occupier was right, he would have failed on the facts). As a result, this area remains live; even if the Supreme Court finds that *Berrisford* enjoyed a tenancy in equity, it is likely that the proportionality principle discussed in Chapter 16 below may be found to apply to fully mutual co-operative tenants.

The future

The Localism Bill is designed in part to implement certain controversial, heavily trailed changes to what has become known as the 'tenancy for life' in the social sector (that is, either an assured or secure tenancy). The expression 'tenancy for life' is (hopefully by now, clearly) not a legal term of art but a controversial description of the secure and AT regimes which local authorities and PRPs respectively use. Rather than take the opportunity offered by the Law Commission to simplify the current security of tenure arrangements, unfortunately the Localism Bill creates a yet further type of tenancy, which can form part of what has become known as the 'social offer': a 'flexible tenancy'.

The discursive narrative underlying these reforms is of a more marketised sector, one which is closer to the private than the social sector. It represents a sea-change in the identity of the social, but one which is consistent with the current direction of the welfare state. The link that has been drawn in social housing policy is between employment, including a mobile welfare force, and security of tenure (which parallels the link between receipt of benefits and actively looking for work) (see generally, CLG 2009b regarding social housing allocation). Thus, the consultation paper on which the housing parts of the Localism Bill are based, made clear:

> Stable and secure social housing should provide a firm basis on which people can build a successful future. But far too often, the security and subsidised rent that social housing provides do not appear to help tenants to independence and self-sufficiency. (CLG 2010e: 1.5)

The link between, and concern about, security and job-seeking can be traced back some distance in policy pronouncements by housing ministers, but the evidence on which that link and concern is based is not clear. Indeed, as regards labour mobility, the evidence is mixed – the evidence from qualitative work with households suggests that local social and family networks are more important than labour market considerations (Fletcher 2009).

The second narrative is a concern that households which access social housing, rightly allocated on the basis of need, may not subsequently have the same level of need – in short, needs change over time. Yet, they have 'lifetime' security.

> [S]ocial landlords are required – by inflexible, centrally-determined, rules – to grant in the vast majority of cases lifetime tenancies that can take no account of how individuals' and households' circumstances might change in the future. In some instances those tenancies can be inherited by family members, who may be in no need of housing. (CLG, 2010e: para. 1.9)

> In addition, the current system is inflexible in relation to rents, providing social tenants with heavily-subsidised rents for the duration of their time in the sector, regardless of their changing need and ability to pay. (ibid. para. 1.10)

This narrative returns to the themes which were dominant during the financial crisis in the 1920s and 1930s, at which point similar concerns were expressed about making the best value use of social housing (see Committee of Local Expenditure 1932; Ministry of Health, 1933); of course, the current financial 'crisis' gives rise to the same concerns. The central point here, though, is that this reasoning exposes a fundamental policy contradiction between, on the one hand, sustainability, which has become a key underpinning of housing management, and, on the other hand, the need for better use of the social housing stock at a time of crisis. Sustainability is as much about commitment to a neighbourhood as it is to preserving a valuable tenancy. For example, one of the key motivations for CBL, it will be remembered, was that it would assist with local sustainability because households living there had actually, actively chosen the area (although the claims for its qualitative benefits might have been exaggerated: Cowan and Marsh 2001a). It can properly be suggested that social housing management has been re-imagined around the concept of sustainability (a point developed in relation to rent arrears in Chapter 14 below) because of concerns over the effects on communities of *un*sustainable housing. The possible provision of short-term 'affordable' tenancies appears to run counter to that set of understandings because short-term housing is hardly likely to engender commitments to local areas.

The government's answer to this point appears to be that it is not a requirement that providers offer that type of tenancy for that length of time, but the social offer gives providers the opportunity to select tenancy length and type from a flexible menu of potential tenancy terms – a fixed-term tenancy of at least 2 years (the precise length of the term is subject to local variation) – some of which at least should have the rent set at an 'affordable' level, said to be 80 per cent of the market rent, which will retain such tenancies within the ambit of the regulator as they will still be considered 'social housing' (Housing and Regeneration Act 2008, ss. 68–9; although there will be revisions to the tenancy standard set by the TSA – TSA 2010d). Such properties will be allocated in the same way as they are currently (see Chapter 7 above). Approximately four-ninths of the total budget for new social housing will be set aside to deliver these new tenancies (£2 billion out of the £4.5 billion: see the Ministerial Statement, Localism Bill and Social Housing, 9 December 2010). There is a suggestion at least that annual rent rises will be pegged to an RPI+½% formula during the currency of the fixed term

For PRPs, different considerations may apply depending on the type and locale of their operation – for example, national players with relationships with local authorities may have to be more flexible than (say) an LSVT association which has the entire social housing stock in an area (and, therefore, a better bargaining position) – as well as whether they are allowed to offer such tenancies by the regulator. What appears clear already is that larger PRPs will be in a better position to offer value for money in their bid to develop affordable rent schemes, so their development may signal further amalgamation in the sector, although the outcomes will also depend on whether 'localism' is more than a symbolic rallying cry (if so, then this may favour local PRPs) – the history of the development of the PRP sector does not inspire confidence that it will be, particularly as value for money has been emphasised. Further, PRPs with good relationships with a local authority (or authorities) will be in a better position to bid for funding from the HCA (there is a 'premium on co-operation and trust: 3-way on-going dialogue and discussions – providers, local authorities, HCA': Mcgregor 2010). What also appears clear is that the development of flexible tenancies will impact on the allocation of social housing as so much of the newly developed property will have to be offered on that 'flexible' basis.

This new regime, however, will not affect those tenancies already in existence (presumably because of the human rights and public law issues which would otherwise arise). The menu is to be set locally reflecting local priorities (hence its pre-statutory setting in the Localism Bill) (CLG 2010e: para. 1.20) and 'landlords will be free to make decisions on tenancies that take account of the needs of individual tenants and the needs of the local community, and that enable the efficient management of their stock' (para. 1.26). To facilitate this approach, there is to be a new strategic tenancy policy (paras. 2.17–21), together with a requirement on individual landlords to publish it (2.45–6), and it is to be complemented by a new tenancy standard for PRPs indicating the available flexibility (paras. 2.41–4). The purpose of the rent level, in essence, is to enable PRPs at least to recycle that revenue into the provision of further affordable homes (although there is a 'robbing Peter to pay Paul' element, as it is recognised that the rent is likely to be met by HB). The flexible tenancy process has already been set in train in relation to PRPs (from April 2011).

Six months prior to termination of the fixed term, the landlord is to serve a notice indicating that it is 'minded not to' reissue the tenancy, and providing certain information, including the tenant's right to seek a review of the decision (para. 2.32). If, after a review, the tenant still wishes to challenge the landlord's decision, they will be able to do so by making an application to the county court on a point of law including material error of fact (ibid.). Sure to be included in any such challenge is the proportionality of the decision to evict (see Chapter 16 for discussion). Housing media reports have already suggested that the development of the principles of proportionality are currently causing uncertainty about the viability of the flexible tenure regime; whatever, it is clear that, as currently conceived, this new scheme will give rise to difficult questions both of public law as well as human rights law.

Finally, rights of succession are to be confined in the case of tenancies granted subsequent to the implementation of the Localism Bill to a more limited class of possible successors, only including the spouse or partner of the deceased tenant (although landlords will be free to offer greater rights in their agreements) (para. 2.36).

Conclusion

Although there is relative stability in the nature of security of tenure in the private sector (including ownership), the social sector is at a crossroads with the future hard to predict. It appears that the PRS is offering a partial model for the development of security of tenure in the social sector, and that the new affordable rent regimes will level the playing field between the social and PRS sectors (the latter having complained for some time about unevenness: Cowan and Carr 2008). Greater complexity will be caused by the development of a yet further tenancy type and policy-makers have managed to avoid the fundamental question addressed in this chapter: the absurdity of security of tenure (or so it might be regarded). It is not immediately obvious why there should be a schism between the types of tenure offered by the two different social housing providers; nor that PRPs should be offering what is, on any view, a hybrid (part private sector, part regulation) and a lesser form than council tenants; nor that security should be linked to concepts of property law. When one looks at tenure from the perspective of the household, tenure type is often an accident (and more so in the future) depending on ability to pay, location and other factors. Furthermore, the tenure which may be regarded publicly as offering the most security, we find, offers potentially the least, largely for historical reasons about the development of property law.

The only explanations for these absurdities are, first, history and, second, regulation. The significance of history for understanding the present almost goes without saying (hence the link between security and letting), but history does not provide a justification for the current settlement in and of itself. Different regulation between tenures follows the different funding regimes, which provides the principal logic; but there has been a shift in the regulation of the social sector towards equalisation, with a focus on the tenant – as Cave suggested (2007: 2.15), 'all social housing providers fulfil similar housing needs' and, further, that regulation should focus on the domain rather than individual tenures (see, especially, 2007: 4.9). Therefore, this justification has become less relevant. It becomes apparent, then, that the sole remaining justification lies in the different funding arrangements and the concern that, if security of tenure was equalised across the social sector, this would affect the willingness of private lenders to finance further developments at the levels (and price) they have done. The development of the single social tenancy is, therefore, on hold (although, it might be observed, this has already been achieved in Scotland).

12

Harassment and unlawful eviction

Contents

Harassment and unlawful eviction of tenants is both a crime and civil cause of action. It is not possible to tell the extent of the issue with any accuracy, as there are no published statistics of such management problems. We do know that in 2008, there were twenty-seven prosecutions brought under the relevant Act (the Protection from Eviction Act 1977), of which fourteen defendants were found guilty (Home Office 2010: table S5.1). We know that 11 per cent of tenants in the PRS were either slightly or very 'dissatisfied' with their landlords (a slightly higher proportion of tenants on HB), but, as Rugg and Rhodes (2008: 60) correctly identify, satisfaction surveys tell us little if anything. It is likely that, given the limited security of tenure in much of the PRS, most of the management problems between landlord and tenant that are, or approach being, harassment and/or unlawful eviction go unreported (Kemp 2004: 168; see Rauta and Pickering 1992; Jew 1994, who estimated that there may have been 144,180 households who had been, or were being, harassed by their landlords). Tenants may not appreciate the proper processes which landlords are required to go through before obtaining possession of the property – indeed, qualitative research with tenants suggests that 'many believed that they remained in their properties as a result of the good faith of their landlords and not as a result of legal frameworks of security of tenure' (Cowan 2001: 254).

What we have to go on, then, is largely anecdotal and individual case history-based (see, for example, Carlton et al. 2003; Rugg 2008: 15). A particularly fine anecdotal example of alleged harassment can be found described at http://nearlylegal.co.uk/blog/2010/08/on-the-naughty-step-drop-the-dead-donkey-redux/, concerning the actions of a landlord who, having served what appears to have been an invalid notice seeking possession, then arrived at the property with the GMTV cameras, describing the occupier as a 'squatter', with the GMTV 'anchor', Sally Smedley, asking: 'why can't the landlord turn up with the police, or turn the electricity off, as so many viewers have emailed to say they should do this?'

In this chapter, I seek to answer that question both through an analysis of the relevant law, but also, and at a deeper level, also seeking an answer to the question as to how such misperceptions have become rooted in what might be termed 'landlord culture'. The first section addresses the policy background and the development of the law. Given the above, it seems almost inconceivable today to remember that, just around forty-seven years ago, harassment and unlawful eviction were such major issues that they contributed to the downfall of a government and emergency remedial legislation. However, that was the case and that is where this chapter begins.

Background

Although there have been laws penalising unlawful eviction and harassment since 1924, the profile of this area of landlord and tenant law was forever raised by the circumstances surrounding the property management career of Perec Rachman (Milner Holland 1965). Whatever is known about this career (and much is shrouded with secrecy), it is certainly true that it contributed to the downfall of the Conservative government, emergency legislation to deal with the supposed problems was brought forward by the new Labour administration in 1964, and a new word – Rachmanism – entered the English language. Rachman was implicated in the Profumo affair (the war minister, Profumo, slept with prostitutes, who were living in Rachman's properties and involved with Russian agents) which led to the downfall of the MacMillan government.

Rachman's methods were said to be threefold (at least): he would offer secure tenants a sum of money to give up their occupation (a practice known as 'winkling'); he would introduce tenants into the properties whom, he or his agents believed, would make life difficult for the secure tenants living in the property making the latter gradually leave the property; third, he charged exorbitant rents for slum property. Yet, such actions would not breach the criminal law, nor would they constitute a civil wrong. Winkling was, and still is, regarded as a legitimate commercial practice and not harassing action; there would be considerable difficulty in finding a landlord responsible for the acts of others; and the third was not an offence *per se* – rather the law simply required the landlord to repay any overcharging to the tenant.

It was the abuses of the 'creeping decontrol' Rent Act 1957 – under which protected tenancies would become decontrolled once the protected tenant left the property – which were most publicised. Rachman was regarded as primarily responsible for these abuses, and became something of a media bête noire, but he was also regarded as the worst example of a broader brand of exploitation. Publicity given to his practices led to an emergency debate in the House of Commons, as well as the setting up of the Milner Holland Committee. One of the first acts of the incoming Labour government in 1964 was to pass 'emergency' legislation protecting people from eviction. The Conservative party was keen also to have 'stiff deterrent penalties', and large commercial landlords supported the action so that the Rachman stigma could be diverted (Nelken 1983: 30 and 38).

The incoming Labour government's election manifesto had promised such emergency legislation. It offered a compromise position and, in doing so, was much assisted by the Milner Holland Committee report. That report approached the issue of unlawful eviction and harassment by first discarding the term 'Rachmanism' because 'it has no precise meaning and is used by different persons to mean different things' (Milner Holland 1965: p. 162). It classified 'abuses' into the following twelve heads (pp. 163–4):

(1)   Tenants unlawfully turned out of or excluded from their homes.

With the object of securing vacant possession, tenants subjected to:

(2)   Assault
(3)   Interference with their accommodation or its services
(4)   Interference with personal possessions.
(5)   Deliberate introduction of unwelcome or undesirable tenants into other accommodation in the building.
(6)   Any other deliberate or persistent annoyance.
(7)   Threat of any items (1)–(6)
(8)   Tenants tricked or misled into leaving controlled accommodation
(9)   Rents in excess of controlled rents obtained for controlled property by threats of other improper means.
(10) Exorbitant rents demanded as the alternative to eviction.
(11) Deliberate withholding of rent books or the information which should be shown in them.
(12) Any other form of abuse, persecution, ill-treatment or unfair practices to which tenants have been subject.

They characterised heads 1–8 as landlords trying to get rid of tenants 'by unlawful or reprehensible means'; 9–10 were 'unlawful and oppressive' means of gaining higher rents; 11 was already covered by earlier legislation; and 12 was a catch-all category. Noticeably absent from these headings was winkling or other 'commercial' practices. The committee was directly responsible for the shape of

the subsequent legislation as part of the 'kitchen cabinet' of the housing minister, Richard Crossman. Thus, only 1–8 fell to be dealt with under unlawful
eviction and harassment legislation. Practices 9–10 were dealt with by allowing
the tenant the means to have reimbursement of any excess. David Nelken's classic study of this period and its implementation suggests that the legislation had
been successful because 'the response to Rachmanism reflected and reinforced
established boundaries of propriety and impropriety in the use and abuse of
property rights' (1983: 27).

Thus, the law tends not to treat commercial practices by commercial landlords as unlawful. Instead, the law tends to 'catch' amateur or resident landlords who are unfamiliar with the law or simply did not want the occupier to
remain living with them. A particular finding of Nelken's study, for example,
was that resident landlords were more likely to be prosecuted because they were
less likely to cooperate with the enforcement agency, due to the nature of the
disputes between occupiers living cheek by jowl (although such a finding has
less salience today, as the Housing Act 1988 almost entirely deregulated this
sub-sector: s. 3A, Protection from Eviction Act 1977). Amateurism remains an
issue, particularly with a new generation of private landlords, introduced as a
result of the buy-to-let schemes (Scanlon and Whitehead 2005), who have come
into the market in search of profit (discussed in Chapter 3 above).

From the outset, enforcement of the new law was placed in the hands of local
authorities and not the police, a position which was subsequently endorsed by a
further committee on the Rent Acts (Francis 1971). That committee drew attention to the following difficulties faced by the police in such cases: a constable
on the spot is in no position to work out whether the occupier is a 'residential
occupier' (as to which, see below); in the case of allegations of harassment, these
take some time to investigate, and constables are in no position to take immediate action; and the police have no power of arrest in these circumstances
(Francis 1971: 106). Nelken (1983: 104) adds that the police probably saw their
role as limited because 'in all cases of domestic types of dispute the normal
police response is to try and sort out the matter and maintain order rather than
strive to bring any prosecution'. Even today, we find the police being the subject of civil actions for assisting in unlawful evictions and, despite considerable
attempts by local authorities to educate and train local police in the relevant
principles, the police appear to work sometimes in ignorance of those principles (Cowan and Marsh 2001b: 839–40; also see, for example, *Cowan* v. *Chief
Constable for Avon and Somerset Constabulary* [2002] HLR 44, where it was
held that there was no duty of care arising out of the tort of negligence where
the police assisted in an unlawful eviction by a landlord without knowledge of
the relevant offences).

Such has been the power of the images conjured up by Rachmanism that
leading commentators on the PRS have suggested that this represents a significant reason why few financial institutions have been willing to enter the sector as landlords (Crook and Kemp 1996; 1998). Indeed, the ongoing impact

of 'the ghost of Rachman' has been that, when the Conservative government deregulated the sector in the Housing Act 1988, they were so concerned about potential landlord abuse that they strengthened both civil and criminal law concerning unlawful eviction and harassment.

The law

In this section, we look at both the criminal and civil law. As the latter is partly derived from the former, our investigation begins with the crimes of unlawful eviction and harassment.

Criminal law

The relevant offences are now contained in the Protection from Eviction Act 1977. They can be committed either by 'any person' or a more restricted group – including, but not limited to, the landlord – against a 'residential occupier'. The phrase 'residential occupier' means 'a person occupying the premises as a residence, whether under a contract or by virtue of any enactment or rule of law giving him the right to remain in occupation or restricting the right of any other person to recover possession of the premises' (s. 1(1)).

This requires, first, that there be occupation of the property as a residence (which suggests that the test in *Brown* v. *Brash*, considered in Chapter 11, applies); and, second, that the occupation is based on a contractual agreement or some other statutory provision or rule which enables the occupier to remain in the property. The latter criterion seems to include all persons who are entitled to occupy the premises until the expiry of a court order for possession, or otherwise up to the termination of their right of occupation (where there is no statutory requirement for possession proceedings). For example, occupiers under ATs and ASTs are residential occupiers. They remain so until the landlord has successfully brought possession proceedings and the court order has expired. After the possession order has expired, the person is no longer a residential occupier. Other than cases where there is a resident owner (either landlord or licensor), the Act makes it unlawful to recover possession without a court order (s. 3(1)). In these cases, the person remains a residential occupier until the court order has run its course. Even where the occupier does not fall within the definition, it is an unwise person who uses the ancient common law self-help right of ejectment (Criminal Law Act 1977, s. 6 – criminal offence to recover possession by intentionally or recklessly using violence to secure entry to premises when a person occupying the premises objects to such entry).

Unlawful eviction

The offence of unlawful eviction is committed in one of two circumstances. First, it occurs where 'any person unlawfully deprives the residential occupier of

any premises of [that person's] occupation of the premises or any part thereof';
second, it occurs where any person 'attempts' to do the same (s. 1(2)). While the
word 'eviction' is not explicitly used, it is said that the act must have the character of an eviction. Locking up part of the premises, or obstructing the occupier's
use of part of the premises would count for this purpose because the offence
can occur in relation to part of the premises. An eviction is unlawful when the
owner does not use the correct procedure for terminating a person's occupation. The Act does not prescribe a particular mental state (*mens rea*) which is
required before the offence is proved. This either means that no particular mental state is required, or (and more likely) the general principle of criminal law
that guilt is shown only if the defendant intended the act, or was reckless (see
below), applies.

In *R* v. *Yuthiwattana* (1984) 16 HLR 49, the Court of Appeal found that
the offence of unlawful eviction would not be committed in cases which they
described as '"locking out" or not admitting the occupier on one or even more
isolated occasions, so that in effect he continues to be allowed to occupy the
premises but is then unable to enter'– such matters were better regarded as falling within the criminal harassment provision (see below). While the deprivation did not have to be permanent, the offence was committed when the
occupier 'effectively has to leave the premises and find other accommodation'
(p. 63). However, in *Costelloe* v. *Camden LBC* (1986) Crim LR 250, the Court of
Appeal made the apparently contradictory point that the temporal quantity of
the exclusion was immaterial. The critical question was said to be 'what was the
nature of the exclusion; was it designed to evict the occupier? If so the conduct
fell within s 1(2).'

Harassment 1

There are two offences of harassment of a residential occupier. The first (original) offence must be split between the required *mens rea* and the acts which
the defendant must do (*actus reus*) in order to fit within the offence.

The mental element is as follows: when any person *intends* to cause the residential occupier to give up occupation of the premises or any part thereof, *or*
to refrain from exercising any right or pursuing any remedy in respect of the
premises or any part thereof. While it is not necessary to prove that the defendant has breached the civil law (*R* v. *Burke* [1991] 1 AC 135, 146–7), the requisite
level of intention is nevertheless difficult to prove. The defendant must specifically intend either that the occupier give up the premises or that the occupier will
not exercise any rights in relation to the premises: 'The court is not entitled to
automatically draw the conclusion that the defendant had the necessary intent
just because the harassing conduct caused the victim to give up occupation (or
refrain from the exercise or pursuit)' (Arden et al. 2002: 150). If the defendant is
reckless as to the result, this may also found a criminal prosecution (Ashworth
1978: 78). In this context, recklessness would probably be decided according to
a subjective test (liability would exist if the person knows or suspects or is aware

of the risk that the occupier would give up the premises or that the occupier would not exercise any rights in relation to the premises).

In *Schon* v. *Camden LBC* (1986) 18 HLR 341, the landlord wanted to build a bathroom in a room directly above the tenant's flat. The landlord requested the tenant leave for 2 weeks, offering a hotel room (a request which was rejected by the tenant). The works went ahead and the tenant's ceiling caved in. The Court of Appeal held that these actions did not show an intention to cause the tenant to give up the occupation of the premises. Rather, they disclosed an intention only to require the tenant to leave the accommodation for a limited period of time.

The *actus reus* is that the act(s) complained of must be likely to interfere with the peace or comfort of the residential occupier or members of the household, or persistently withdraws or withholds services reasonably required for the occupation of the premises as a residence. The first limb (acts likely to interfere with the peace and comfort) must relate to a positive act, and not an omission to act (although one act is sufficient: *R* v. *Polycarpou* (1978) 9 HLR 129). The second limb (persistently withdrawing or withholding services) does not apply to those services which are provided voluntarily by the landlords (*McCall* v. *Abelesz* [1976] 1 QB 585). Arden et al. (2002: 147) regard this proposition, however, as no longer being good law as it conflicts with the express wording of the Act as well as being based on the proposition, subsequently held to be unnecessary (*R* v. *Burke* [1991] AC 135), that the defendant had breached the residential occupier's legal rights; equally, the requirement of persistence means that there need be only one act but there must be deliberate continuity (for example, leaving gas or electricity cut off for a period of time).

Harassment 2

The second offence was introduced by way of amendment to the 1977 Act (s. 1(3A)) in the Housing Act 1988, in response to claims that the requirement to prove a specific intent under harassment 1 made convictions rather difficult. The new offence differs from the old one in the following ways: the offence can only be committed by the landlord or the landlord's agent (such as a letting agent) and not by 'any person'; the *mens rea* required is that the landlord or agent must *know, or have reasonable cause to believe*, that the acts are likely to cause the residential occupier to give up occupation of the premises or any part thereof, *or* to refrain from exercising any right or pursuing any remedy in respect of the premises or any part thereof. Otherwise the offence is the same as harassment 1.

Defence

Where the landlord believes, or has reasonable cause to believe, that the residential occupier had ceased to reside in the premises, the defendant has a good defence. In *R* v. *Phekoo*, a landlord honestly believed that the occupiers were squatters (they were sub-tenants). It was suggested that such a belief was sufficient, provided it was honestly and reasonably held; on the other hand a defence which lacks credibility both as a matter of belief and grounds for such a belief was rejected in *Kalas* v. *Farmer* [2010] HLR 25. In *West Wiltshire DC* v. *Snelgrove*, an *obiter* distinction was drawn between mistake of fact and mistake of law, the former being a defence and the latter going to mitigation: 'No doubt a mistaken belief as to whether or not they were contravening the statute would have been highly relevant by way of mitigation and thus on the issue of penalty. In my judgment, however, it could not have provided them with a defence.' (1998) 30 HLR 57, 63, *per* Simon Brown LJ. That distinction did not avail the council in *Wandsworth LBC* v. *Osei-Bonsu* (1999) 31 HLR 515, in which Simon Brown LJ doubted his earlier comment. He said:

> Certainly it now seems to me necessary to qualify the absolute proposition that a mistaken belief as to the law cannot be relevant or available as a defence. As appears from paragraph 17–22 of Archbold (1998 edition) and the cases cited thereunder, the rule of law that ignorance of the law does not excuse is a rule only with regard to the criminal law: a mistake as to the civil law may have the effect of negativing *mens rea*. Classically that is so, for example, in a 'claim of right' defence to a charge of theft or criminal damage in respect of property which the accused mistakenly believes is his own.

That did not assist Wandsworth council either, however, as its belief that the tenancy had been determined could not have been reasonably held as the notice to quit given by Mr Osei-Bonsu's wife was too short.

Protection from Harassment Act 1997

Somewhat dislocated from the argument hitherto because it has its roots in issues arising outside the subject matter, the Protection from Harassment Act 1997 nevertheless has the potential to be equally relevant in some cases. The complexity of the 1977 Act potentially makes successful prosecutions rather difficult. The 1997 Act, by way of contrast, seems to enable prosecutions to be brought on much simpler grounds. The 1997 Act was a product of a different set of events and political pressures. Before the 1997 general election, a debate arose about the proper protection of people from 'stalkers' as well as more general concerns regarding the limits to a person's privacy. The Conservative government was able to resuscitate its proposed protection for people in these circumstances amidst what might be described as an atmosphere akin to a law and order auction. Thus, the Protection from Harassment Act 1997 was rushed through Parliament at this time without proper debate or questioning as to its ambit.

The Act creates three offences which may be relevant:

- A person is guilty of an offence if they pursue a 'course of conduct' which amounts to harassment of another *and* which that person knows or ought to know amounts to harassment of the other (s. 1; there are certain exceptions in sub-s. (3)). The phrase 'ought to know' is judged against what a 'reasonable person in possession of the same information would think'. An offence is committed in these circumstances (s. 2).

- In the same circumstances, the person against whom the harassment has occurred may claim damages and an injunction. Breach of that injunction entitles that person to apply for a warrant of arrest (s. 3).
- A person whose course of conduct causes another to fear, on at least two occasions, that violence will be used against him is guilty of an offence if he knows or ought to know that his course of conduct will cause the other to fear on each of those occasions (s. 4; there are certain exceptions in sub-s. (3)). Once again, the phrase 'ought to know' is judged against what a 'reasonable person in possession of the same information would think'.

These offences are broad enough to cover a significant proportion of unlawful eviction and harassment cases.

Civil law

Until the introduction of the Housing Act 1988, s. 27 (the statutory torts), tenants had to rely on rather arcane principles such as the breach of the implied (or express) contractual term, known as a covenant, of 'quiet enjoyment' – the ancient common law right that 'the tenant's lawful possession of the land will not be substantially interfered with by the acts of the lessor or those lawfully claiming under him' (*Southwark LBC* v. *Mills* [2001] AC 1, Lord Hoffmann) – or a species of trespass and conversion (two tortious wrongs). It would be wrong to suggest that those other principles are no longer of any relevance but their significance has been reduced by the statutory torts. As we have seen, the statutory torts were introduced to penalise landlords in damages, but, as we go on to consider, their development may also have had a hand in the decline in prosecutions.

The torts can be committed by the landlord or any person acting on the landlord's behalf – although damages are only payable by the landlord (causing problems in cases where the landlord is not in the country: *Sampson* v. *Wilson* (1997) 29 HLR 18). They are in similar terms to the offences described above of attempted unlawful eviction (actual and constructive) and harassment 2, which are not to be mechanistically applied but rather in relation to the acts or omissions as a whole (*Abbott* v. *Bayley* (2000) 32 HLR 72); and contain the similar defence where the defendant believed and had reasonable cause to believe that the residential occupier had ceased to reside in the property at the time when they were deprived of occupation (s. 27(8)(a)).

Other complete defences are where the defendant believed, and had reasonable cause to believe, that 'he had reasonable grounds for doing the acts or withdrawing or withholding the services in question' (s. 27(8)(b); if 'before the date on which proceedings to enforce the liability are finally disposed of', the residential occupier is reinstated in the property so that 'he becomes again the residential occupier', or a court makes an order reinstating the residential occupier (s. 27(6)(a) and (b)). In *Tagro* v. *Cafane* [1991] 1 WLR 378, at [16]-[17] *per* Lord Donaldson, it was held that reinstatement 'does not consist in merely handing the tenant a key to a lock which does not work and inviting her to resume occupation of a room which has been totally wrecked'; moreover, the residential occupier has a choice that they can make between accepting reinstatement (and, thus, provide a defence to a claim) or making a claim.

A partial defence, at least as far as it mitigates the damages, occurs where the conduct of the former residential occupier or any person living with them 'was such that it is reasonable to mitigate the damages for which the landlord in default would otherwise be liable'; or, before the proceedings were begun (i.e. the claim for damages: *Tagro*, at [21], *obiter*), the landlord offered to reinstate the former residential occupier but that offer was unreasonably refused (or, if alternative accommodation had been obtained, it would have been unreasonable to refuse that offer) (s. 27(7)(a) and (b)). As regards the former, in parliamentary debates it was suggested that: 'The conduct of a tenant will have to be very bad indeed for a court to decide that it is reasonable to mitigate damages that are clearly designed as a penalty for committing an unlawful act.' (HC Debs, col. 392 (9 November 1988)).

In *Regalgrand Ltd* v. *Dickerson* (1997) 29 HLR 620, the landlords changed the locks on the door while the tenants were moving out. They claimed £707 arrears of rent and the tenants counterclaimed for unlawful eviction. Statutory damages assessed at £12,000 were reduced by £10,500 by the judge, and upheld on appeal, because the tenants were in arrears of rent. The Court of Appeal said (at p. 625) that the conduct must be considered in the light of the surrounding facts and that each case will be fact-dependent. In *Osei-Bonsu*, the conduct in question was Mr Osei-Bonsu's violence towards his wife, which caused her to leave, obtain an ouster order against him, and serve an albeit invalid notice to quit. In the circumstances, the Court of Appeal reduced the damages by two-thirds:

> True, Wandsworth mistook their rights in law and are thus liable to a statutory damages award for wrongful eviction. But that eviction was clearly the culmination of an unbroken chain of events starting with the respondent's conduct … [A]ny ouster order postulates grave misconduct and if, as I conclude, the respondent's conduct was not merely deserving of condemnation but also precipitated the course of events leading logically to his dispossession, that in my judgment amply satisfies the requirements of this provision and makes it appropriate to mitigate the damages substantially.

The assessment of damages has been a contested arena. Early cases seemed to adopt an approach which reflected the purpose of the provision – to penalise the landlord in damages for the wrong caused; later cases have, however, pulled back from that and made a significant dent to that purpose. Section 28 determines the assessment of damages, which are assessed as the difference between:

(a) the value of the interest of the landlord … determined on the assumption that the residential occupier continues to have the same right to occupy the premises as before that time; and

(b) the value of the interest determined on the assumption that the residential occupier has ceased to have that right. (s. 28(1))

Considerable problems have arisen over the valuation for the purpose of assessing the level of damages. For example, in *Jones* v. *Miah* (1993) 26 HLR 60, four different sets of valuers were instructed and each interpreted the formula incorrectly (according to the Court of Appeal). In the beginning, this meant that the level of damages awarded was often rather high. However, the deterrent effect of this statutory remedy has been reduced in most situations in which unlawful eviction and harassment occur (according to the Milner Holland report 1965 – i.e. multiple occupation and where the level of security is low).

In *Melville* v. *Bruton* (1997) 29 HLR 319, M was a tenant of premises which also contained two other tenants. M was unlawfully evicted and, at first instance, was awarded £15,000 (the difference between the rival valuations being £2,000). The valuation took no account of the presence of other occupiers. The issue about valuation was raised for the first time by the Court of Appeal, where it was held that the proper basis for valuation was a 'factual' as opposed to a 'notional' basis ('otherwise that which the landlord is ordered to pay to the tenant is not the value of the profit occasioned by his wrong but a fine which may be far greater'). This meant that the damages reflected the market value of the property with *all the occupiers* less the market value without the complainant. In multiply occupied property, the difference in value will be minimal because the value of the property lies in vacant possession which would not be capable of being granted if other occupiers are present.

The Court of Appeal expanded on this approach in *King* v. *Jackson* (1998) 30 HLR 539. K was let a flat on an AST and was unlawfully evicted 6 days before her interest came to an end. At first instance, K was granted £11,000 damages. The Court of Appeal found that such an amount for being deprived of 6 days' occupation was 'manifestly wrong' and the amount was in fact 'extremely small'. K was granted £1,500 damages for breach of the covenant of quiet enjoyment. It also seems that, as an assured shorthold can be terminated after 2 months' notice, the level of damages would be minimal in all cases outside the original term of the tenancy; the same must also be true where the property, although occupied (say) as a secure tenancy, is jointly occupied in circumstances where the other joint tenant could serve a valid notice to quit (*Osei-Bonsu*, although note the Court of Appeal did not re-open the valuation because it had been agreed by counsel before the county court).

The reasoning in *Melville* (which can, on this point, all be found at p. 325) provides an important counterbalance to the original legislative purpose of providing an important deterrent against such actions. It was argued by counsel for the claimant that, where a property has ten tenants, it would make nonsense of the law if each of the first nine tenants were to receive nominal damages but the tenth 'would scoop the pool'. All that could be offered against that argument was the belief that it would be as 'incongruous' if each of the ten tenants was to claim full damages. However, one can surely posit that this was precisely the intention of Parliament, for how else could the section provide an effective deterrent?

It was then argued that the background to the sections was that it was enacted at the 'height of the property boom' to counteract the incentive that landlords had to 'winkle out inconvenient tenants whose presence was preventing their making large profits'. While this was found 'persuasive' by the court, the next step in the argument did not find favour. That step required the court to 'ensure that the legislation continues to provide real protection to tenants, real deterrence to landlords'.

The court found that three opposing arguments counterbalanced the position. First, courts should not make assumptions about meanings because of some such 'extraneous and supervening reason'. Parliamentary intention, then, is irrelevant here. Second, the court made a sweeping empirical proposition: 'in the much changed conditions that now obtain, the incentive to landlords to evict tenants is much reduced indeed, it is difficult to see why in the ordinary case a landlord should wish to evict a tenant at a rack rent who is paying his rent'. Third, there was no reason to think that the Act was meant to provide all tenants with substantial damages – 'had that been the intention some means of calculation not dependent on changing values would have been adopted'. Finally,

> It is legitimate to reflect that, whereas during the property boom [the other civil law] rights were perceived to provide an inadequate deterrent to wrongful eviction, the position may well be different in the current climate. It should also be remembered that harassment and wrongful eviction are criminal offences.

As a result Melville was awarded £500 in substitution for the £15,000 awarded in the county court. The CPR amend the standard position as to allocation of cases when a claim is made for unlawful eviction and/or harassment so that such claims are allocated to the fast track (or multi-track) and not to the small claims track which would otherwise inappropriately be the case (CPR 26.7(4)).

Enforcement

In this section, we consider why, despite the very real and unpleasant nature of much of the practices of unlawful eviction and harassment, so few persons responsible are prosecuted. It will be remembered that, although the police do have powers of prosecution in such cases, the main enforcement agency is the local authority. Why do local authorities prosecute so few cases? One answer may be that fewer occupiers complain, perhaps out of lack of knowledge of the law, a recognition that their security in the property was marginal in any event, a belief that the property is the landlord's home to do with as they will, a legitimation of the landlord's conduct where the occupier has been at fault in some way (perhaps by not paying the rent), and a failure by the police to intervene (Cowan 2001: 254–7). However, that tells only part of the story.

Of equal interest to what might be termed the legal consciousness of the occupiers is the role and understandings of the regulatory enforcers. There is now a considerable body of socio-legal research which considers the exercise of prosecutorial discretion amongst non-police agencies (see generally, Sanders et al. 2010: 410–23 for a summary). One aspect of that literature discusses the process of regulatory capture (under which the regulator takes on the perspective of the regulated – see, for example, Mullins 1997). In these studies, two regulatory strategies are commonly found to operate. First, 'compliance' strategies seek to remedy existing problems and prevent others arising through the regulator using co-operative and conciliatory approaches. Second, 'deterrence' strategies involve the regulator giving prosecution a pivotal role for any number of reasons (from retribution to utilitarian) (Hawkins 1984). Compliance-type strategies predominate amongst non-police agencies responsible for enforcement, the role of the regulator is one of bargaining, negotiation and 'constant vigilance' – the aim is to secure the remedy of current regulatory breaches and prevent future breaches. Prosecution is regarded as the antithesis of such a strategy – although its threat may well be used to enforce compliance – because it effectively ends the relationship. Hutter (1989) has found evidence of 'persuasive' and 'insistent' strategies within the 'compliance' category and has drawn attention to the probability that different areas may have different policies and practices *and* these may also vary within one area. The type of strategy adopted tends to reflect the agency's background philosophy (Carson 1970).

These diagnoses have now to be set in the context of the particularly influential attitude within government towards regulation more generally – that it stifles the market and will lead to market exit. From this perspective, the starting assumption is that it is desirable to limit or eliminate regulation. The argument taps into more fundamental contemporary discourses to neutralise calls for greater regulation, as Tombs (2002: 124) suggests:

> The range and nature of the neutralization techniques currently offered in a society such as Britain can only be understood in the context of the facts that the spirit of entrepreneurialism, ideologies of free enterprise and the illegitimacy of external regulation have become elevated to the status of almost unquestionable moral truths.

Starting policy discussion from the presumption that regulation is undesirable, coupled with techniques such as regulatory impact assessments, automatically places those arguing for regulation on the defensive (e.g. Morgan 2003) and, more profoundly, effectively limits the available range of solutions.

Studies of regulatory crime almost without exception note the limited use of prosecution and discuss a number of similar factors which lead to the adoption of compliance strategies. Chief amongst these factors are the often paltry penalties handed out to those organisations which are successfully prosecuted;

the often inadequate funding of the regulatory agency; the belief that regulatory crime is often technically complex; the lack of unequivocal support for the regulatory agencies' activities; and the regulatory agencies' understanding of the morality of the regulatees' actions. Further, as some have suggested (see, especially, Pearce and Tombs 1990), 'regulatory crimes' are often distinguishable from 'real crimes'. As Sanders (1996: xvii) asserts, 'perhaps it is the lack of enforcement which creates the non-criminogenic image'. Although there is much of similarity between, on the one hand, a study of local authority approaches to dealing with deviance amongst landlords and others towards residential occupiers, and, on the other, those more generic understandings of regulatory agencies, Cowan and Marsh (2001b) draw on data gained from a government-funded study of local authority enforcement officers (tenancy relations officers (TROs)) to argue that there are also distinguishing features of the situation in the PRS. In what follows, I draw on Hawkins' use of the concepts 'surround', 'field' and 'frame' to reconsider that data (2002). Although Cowan and Marsh's data is over 11 years old, it nevertheless is likely to remain of explanatory value, not least because many of the tendencies in housing policy and practice referred to there have been extended. Moreover, subsequent developments in the area of non-police prosecutions are likely to have exacerbated the non-prosecutions strategy further, because these reviews of regulatory enforcement were against the use of the criminal sanction (Hampton 2005; Macrory 2006). What we can see below also is the point that Hawkins makes strongly – surround, field and frame overlap and interact at almost every turn.

Cowan and Marsh sub-titled their paper 'From "Rachmanites" to "partners"' to denote the shift in housing policy understandings of the PRS which were also crucial in appreciating what Hawkins (2002: 48–50) refers to as the 'surround' of the regulatory role. The policy image of the landlord has turned almost 180 degrees so that the policy discourse about the landlord no longer refers to the social pariah status exemplified by Rachman(ism); rather, as we have seen, housing policy is fixated by the 'many good landlords' in the sector (DETR/DSS 2000: 45), whom we want to protect, and the concern that they might fall victim to the unscrupulous tenant. The landlord is now regarded as serving a useful social purpose, particularly in facilitating job-related migration. Rather than benign (or malign) neglect, the sector is now favoured by government intervention to stimulate the market and protect landlords. It is the small minority of landlords which are regarded as causing the problem. Further, the de- (or in-)security in the PRS was a significant factor as TROs emphasised its 'easy access' (and, by implication, easy exit) nature so that tenants can simply move on rather than support a prosecution against their landlord. One should also add that the last thirty years have involved not just deregulation of the sector but an ethos that regulation is, quite simply, bad and unhelpful to business.

The 'field' is related to the surround, in that it 'is something defined by, and acted on by the organisation' (Hawkins 2002: 50). Relevant considerations from the Cowan and Marsh data here are the role, for example, of civil penalties. Complainants would be told that they might be better off securing compensation rather than seeking prosecution. As they put it: 'Thus, the paradoxical effect of the increasing rights of occupiers in this area was that they have in some instances been used to deter and deny prosecution; or put another way, the individual capital gain of the occupier is set against the public interest of prosecuting the deviant landlord and, in such a contest, capital gain is the winner.' (p. 846) Most significantly, though, the field, perhaps overlapping with the surround here, was limited by a number of different factors: the shaping and operation of public sector organisations, through the various 'new public management' initiatives (e.g. CCT and Best Value); and the emphasis on joint working. The new mantras of preventing homelessness and using the PRS to accommodate homeless households work against the instrumental use of prosecution. It was notable that TROs' performance indicators concerned prevention of homelessness, for example. Although local authorities are regulating landlords, they are also providing information, knowledge, accreditation, fast-tracking through HB, and other services. Landlords were 'partners in meeting housing need', even in those areas where there was competition for consumers between social and private landlords.

The final part of the Hawkins approach is the better understood sociological concept of 'frame' – how do TROs make sense of individual decisions by framing them? Here what was crucial as a dividing practice was the cult of amateurism in the sector because it raised a key question (also paralleled by discussion in the cases) as to whether a prosecution should be used to sanction ignorance of the law. The emphasis in most cases of tenancy relations was on mediation and conciliation. As Nelken neatly showed, the types of landlords who are responsible for much of the crime (or, more accurately, that which is reported to the local authority) are far from the Rachman stereotype. Cowan and Marsh's study also suggested that most landlords responsible for unlawful eviction and harassment were individuals operating in the sector as a sideline to their main or other business. The essential point about this counter-stereotype was that TROs by-and-large understood what led this type of landlord into breaking the law. TRO approaches were, therefore, premised upon *working with* this type of landlord, to provide them with the understanding to evict the occupier in accordance with the law. The most commonly cited reason for unlawful eviction or harassment was that landlords believed that the property that was the subject of the lease remained their own. Landlord crime was therefore something which could be rectified by a little legal advice – which in the majority of cases was true – occasionally backed up by a threat of prosecution.

A final aspect of the framing of individual disputes was that tenancy relations is clearly a subjective value-laden enterprise. So, for example, the principal cause of harassment and unlawful eviction in our study areas was non-payment of rent, and this was principally due to the failure of HB to be paid within the correct timescale or to HB not covering the full amount of the rent. Landlord crime might then be characterised as an inevitable frustration with local authority procedures, or tenants not filling out benefit forms correctly. When the occupier had been involved in the stigmatised range of actions which fell within the umbrella term 'anti-social behaviour', landlord crime might be regarded by local authority officers as 'six of one and half a dozen of the other'.

What might be said then is that, at the individual level, reductions in security of tenure have disempowered households in the sector. At the organisational level, the interweaving of tenancy-relations work with broader private sector strategies and homelessness duties means that prosecution is almost inevitably constructed as a less desirable course of action. In areas of housing stress, the absence of alternative accommodation makes it imperative for local authorities to work with the PRS, irrespective of whether this is seen as desirable. It is perhaps no surprise that there are bureaucratic impediments in the way of prosecution, but the Best Value regime also further reduced the attractiveness of pursuing prosecutions, which carry large costs but only indistinct benefits. Similarly, it may be of little surprise that TROs take a view about the morality of both landlord and tenant behaviour in determining the action they will take. Yet, it seems clear that morality is constructed by reference to the surround and frame, as suggested by Hawkins, and displaced onto judicial attitudes.

Conclusions

Harassment and unlawful eviction provide an interesting and powerful study of 'law in action'. It must be emphasised that 'law' is not a static thing and nor can it be seen in isolation. Diverse influences impact on its formation, implementation and operation at different points in time. The current focal point of housing policy is not just economic but also focused on occupiers' responsibility, so that we forget (perhaps conveniently) our collective housing history. That, of course, serves housing policy as it seeks to rely more and more strongly on the private sector.

The discursive nature of housing policy has fundamentally shifted and, as a result, private landlords are constructed as being mostly good (as if such a binary good–bad is fixed in time). Perhaps they are, and this explains the low level of prosecutions for unlawful eviction and harassment. One should not discount that obvious explanation. The alternative explanations are, however, more compelling, quite simply because they reflect empirical observation of the practices of TROs. Readers may consider placing this chapter against Chapter 15 concerning ASB. What we have here is rather complex law protecting residential occupiers against certain interference with their home that is rarely prosecuted (it is unclear how many civil claims are made each year); what we have in Chapter 15 is clear, relatively simple law that is regularly used against defaulting occupiers.

13

Property state and condition

Contents

This chapter concerns the state and condition of property, including the private and public law obligations of landlords and local authorities. It is helpful when reading the material in this chapter to bear in mind three points:

1. The state and condition of housing was the concern which gave rise to an incipient housing and public health policy in the nineteenth century, and the then understandings about the cause of disease remain relevant. The Labour government in the 2000s did address the consequences of this history through two devices, the creation of a statutory risk-based HHSRS in the Housing Act 2004, Part I, and the non-statutory 'decent homes' test. Their development was founded on increasingly better understandings of the relationship between poor quality housing and health (on which there is now a considerable literature, see, for example, Prevalin et al. 2008). These have not affected the private law obligations, however, although in some cases there are overlaps.

2. Building on those new definitions, data from the 2008 English Housing Survey found that 7.4 million homes (33 per cent) were 'non-decent' with the highest proportion of non-decent homes in the PRS (44 per cent)(CLG

2010c: para. 2.21). Further, a potentially serious hazard under the HHSRS was present in around 4.8 million homes in 2008 (22 per cent) (para. 2.18).

3.   When specifically considering the PRS, one has to bear in mind the findings in Chapters 3 and 11 above about the limited security of tenure. As Burridge and Ormandy (2007: 558) have put it, in a withering critique: 'Private tenants may enjoy limited rights bestowed by legal text-books and upheld by judicial proclamation in theory, but such rhetoric is exposed by the realities of insecurity, procedural technicality, and legal complexity that demands expert but unreachable legal services'. One of the particular points made in that comment is that, despite relatively strong protection for disrepair in law, it is rendered practically useless by the temporary nature and easy accessibility of private renting. One can put this point rather differently to explain the policy inertia – the policy dilemma has been framed as a concern that further policy intervention will reduce the supply of housing in the much-needed PRS.

The chapter begins with a brief appreciation of the historical development of the law, a discussion of the response to unfitness, followed by an examination of tenants' individual private law rights to force their landlord to repair the property. The chapter then moves on to the assessment and enforcement of local authorities' public duties under the HHSRS and the decent homes strategy (see also Chapter 3 above).

Historical development

In the opening chapter, we looked at the history of housing law and policy. Much of the material there is equally relevant for an understanding of the historical development of law and policy regarding the state and condition of property. That is because those antecedents are intimately related to the law considered in this chapter. In this section, those antecedents are summarised in the form of key points to bear in mind in reading the subsequent material. Those key points are as follows:

1.   The Victorian concern was essentially one of public health which then metamorphosed into a concern with the state and condition of non-working and working-class (privately rented) properties.

2.   That concern was animated by the moral effects of poor quality and overcrowded housing. The question, as framed by the Royal Commission on the Housing of the Working Classes (1885a: 14), was: 'Is it the pig that makes the stye or the stye that makes the pig?'

3.   One of the key turning points was the Royal Commission on the Housing of the Working Classes in 1885, but the developments to which that gave rise subsequently had been foreshadowed by earlier interventions of a public health nature, including an attempt at what we might refer to now as an area clearance strategy.

4. The developments occurred against an apparent dominant influence of *laissez faire* (Wohl 1977: 19), but it must be remembered that, as the Royal Commission on the Housing of the Working Classes (1885a: 3) put it in the opening sentence of their report: 'The subject of the housing of the Working Classes in Your Majesty's Kingdom is one which has been continually before the public for more than 30 years.'

5. Intervention in the field of public health seems to have been accepted as legitimate as it was divorced from free trade or freedom of contact; however, the judicial approach was to take a narrow construction of such provisions and a refusal to develop the common law further into the realms of establishing property standards and conditions.

Let us take that last point about the judicial approach as a point from where further analysis might begin. As Atiyah has demonstrated in his classic text, *The Rise and Fall of Freedom of Contract* (1979: 469), although much lip service was paid by the courts to Ricardian free market economics, judges of the time were not entirely consistent: 'at no time did this austere and amoral market law ever wholly represent the practice of the Courts'. A key moment concerned whether the principle of *caveat emptor* – let the buyer beware – was applicable within the landlord and tenant domain. *Caveat emptor* is almost the embodiment of free-market economics, and one to which land law itself clearly subscribed.

It was, however, perfectly plausible for the developing principles of consumer protection to be applied to contracts made between landlord and tenant. These new rules implied terms into contracts that property would be fit for purpose. They were limited to certain types of contract. But, in the case of *Smith* v. *Marrable* [1843] 11 M&W 6, such a term was implied into a contract for the letting of a furnished house to Lady Marrable in Brighton. Lady Marrable took occupation of the property but left 'as soon as she can take another, paying a week's rent, as all the bedrooms occupied but one are so infested with bugs that it is impossible to remain'. Although the judges appear to have scouted around to find precedents ('I am glad that authorities have been found to support the view which I took of this case at the trial': Lord Abinger CB, at p. 694), the principle of law was said to be that 'A man who lets a ready-furnished house surely does so under the implied condition or obligation – call it which you will – that the house is in a fit state to be inhabited' (Lord Abinger, ibid.). Further, it was said:

> [I]f the demised premises are incumbered with a nuisance of so serious a nature that no person can reasonably be expected to live in them, the tenant is at liberty to throw them up. This is not the case of a contract on the part of the landlord that the premises were free from this nuisance; it rather rests in an implied condition of the law, that he undertakes to let them in a habitable state.

The case was subsequently reduced in effect (and by the same judges) so that the rule, *caveat emptor*, became predominant once again. In *Sutton* v. *Temple*, heard a mere 10 months later in 1843, the court held that the *Smith* v. *Marrable* rule was applicable only in cases where the property was let furnished. In *Sutton*, grazing land had been let but 'old paint' was found on the grass which killed off some of the cattle grazing there. Smith was distinguished (Lord Abinger, p. 1112). The authorities on which *Smith* v. *Marrable* was founded were doubted by Parke B, and Rolfe B would have been prepared to overrule that case.

In *Hart* v. *Windsor* [1845] 12 M&W 68, a case regarded as so important that it was reported early and straight after *Sutton* in the law reports, the precedents for the decision in *Smith* were discussed at length. Parke B held that those authorities were not good law and, further, that *Smith* 'cannot be supported on the ground on which I rested my judgment' (p. 1122). Indeed, he went further and equated the rules with broader principles of land law: 'though in the case of a dwelling-house taken for habitation, there is no apparent injustice in inferring a contract of this nature, the same rule must apply to land taken for other purposes – for building upon, or for cultivation and there would be no limit to the inconvenience which would ensue' (p. 1122). The *Smith* principle was thereafter found to apply only in the exceptional case of the short-term let of *furnished* property. Most property at this time was unfurnished leasehold and so the common law did not touch upon the ordinary living conditions of the majority. The reason for moving away from the implied condition partly reflected a fixation upon the agricultural leases but, as Reynolds (1974: 368; cf. Robinson, 1976) points out,

> the social reality was that the Industrial Revolution of the previous decades had seen the very structure of English society change from one dependent upon an agrarian economy to one based upon industry … It was at this crucial time of urbanisation and slum formation that the judges looked to the agrarian lease as providing a justification for their decisions.

The failures of the common law to provide appropriate remedies for unfitness and disrepair gave way to statutory reform which attempted to ameliorate health issues in insanitary housing.

So, for example, the early legislation concerning lodging houses in 1851 was the terrain of the newly formed police, who were given powers of registration, inspection and enforcement through the courts. Slum clearance powers and improvement schemes had been created in the Cross and Torrens Acts (1868 and 1875 respectively) about which Gauldie (1974: 267) makes the following observation:

> The acknowledged purpose of the new Act, the 'improvement' of our cities, the creation of better public health by the removal of the focus of disease, was almost unanimously approved. It was, in fact, for most people, if not for the immediate instigators of reform, not the real reason why they were prepared to suffer bureaucratic interference with private property. The first and most sweeping improvement schemes were deliberately driven through the most criminal areas, with the dispersal of criminals from their haunts, and the suppression of crime as the first motive. The fact that these haunts were in most cases also

the most insanitary parts of the cities was a secondary consideration. The frequency with which the emotive phrase 'dens of vice' crops up is some indication of attitude.

This suspicion was, perhaps, confirmed by the lack of replacement housing built.

As the focus of the legislation was on public health, the individual relationship between landlord and tenant was largely left unaffected. Enforcement was generally by third parties and this was a period in which different enforcement mechanisms were being tried and tested (Atiyah 1979). It was not until the Housing of the Working Classes Act 1885 that Parliament introduced an implied condition of fitness for human habitation into the contract between landlord and tenant (against the furious protests of the judiciary – see Reynolds 1974: 381). The provision was, perhaps unsurprisingly, narrowly interpreted, but it remains an important provision (at the symbolic level – see below) in that it interfered for practically the first time in the landlord–tenant relationship. It brought into effect, in slightly different form, a recommendation of the 1885 Royal Commission that 'there should be a simple power by civil procedure for the recovery of damages against owners or holders of property by those who have suffered injury or loss by their neglect or default in sanitary matters' (1885a: 56). It is unclear where this recommendation came from. Certainly, its subsequent use, particularly the introduction of a power in the landlord to enter the property to check it, was regarded with concern because of its use as a tool of surveillance (Reynolds 1974).

The legacy of this period is of intervention in housing, but in the field of public health. The interventions themselves appear both extensive as well as faltering. Enforcement seems to have focused on area clearance of the dangerous classes, a broad concoction of pauperised persons and criminalised classes (Cowan and McDermont 2006: ch 2). The carving out of the public health niche had legitimated intervention in housing and, gradually, it also appears it made intervention between landlord and tenant acceptable, if controversial.

Unfitness

Section 15 of the Housing of the Working Classes Act 1885 included an implied condition that the letting of property for habitation should, at its commencement, be 'in all respects reasonably fit for human habitation'. The Marquess of Salisbury said that: 'I look to this clause more than to any other to diminish the death-rate that is caused by insanitary dwellings' (cited in Law Commission, 1996, para. 4.8). Subsequently, legislation made it clear that landlords and tenants were not able to contract out of its protection. In the common law world, the fitness provision was startlingly bold for the period and at least eighty years ahead of its time. It was not until 1970 that the US Court of Appeal in the District of Columbia held that similar provisions should apply to rented accommodation (*Javins* v. *First National Realty Corporation* (1970) 428 F.2d 1071).

Yet, by this time, the English provision, which has never been repealed, had fallen into disuse (it is now s. 8, Landlord and Tenant Act 1985). Attached to the provision were rent limits which, while they were low, covered 'with the exception of London, nearly all of the working classes of the Kingdom' (John Burns MP, cited in Law Commission 1996: para. 4.9). The rent limits were increased in the early part of the twentieth century, and the provision upgraded after certain judicial assaults upon its impact (see Reynolds 1974). Rent limits were finally increased in the Housing Act 1957. The rent limits then put in place, which remain today, are £52 generally and £80 for inner London – these are *per annum* figures, not weekly. The Law Commission suggested a number of reasons why the rent limits were not updated, while accepting that it is not 'easy to account': 'the extension of local authority housing, the decline in private sector lettings engendered by the Rent Acts, and the rise in owner occupation' (1996: para. 4.13). Additionally, they suggested that the development of the implied covenants to repair (see below) had made this provision anachronistic (paras. 4.14–7). In *Quick* v. *Taff-Ely BC* [1986] QB 809, the Court of Appeal deprecated the failure to increase the rent levels which, by that time, had made the provision largely obsolete. Lawton LJ said (p. 821):

> When I read the papers in this case I was surprised to find that the plaintiff had not based his claim on an allegation that at all material times the house let to him by the defendant council had not been fit for human habitation. The uncontradicted evidence, accepted by the trial judge, showed that furniture, furnishings and clothes had rotted because of damp and the sitting-room could not be used because of the smell of damp. I was even more surprised to be told by counsel that the provisions of the Housing Act 1957, as amended by the London Government Act 1963, did not apply to the plaintiff's house. By section 6 of the 1957 Act, on the letting of a house at a specified low rent, a covenant is implied that the landlord will keep it in a condition fit for human habitation. For most of the time the plaintiff was in occupation of the house let to him by the defendant council it is arguable that it was not fit for human habitation. Unfortunately, the figures which were fixed as being low rents have not been changed for over 20 years. In 1965 a low rent outside central Greater London was one not exceeding £52 per annum. The present-day equivalent of that figure, when inflation is taken into account, is over £312. The plaintiff's rent of £6.75 per week in 1976 was well above the statutory figure. This case would seem to indicate that a new definition of a low rent is needed.

The Law Commission argued that the duty should be revived, and applied to all landlords in whichever sector letting property for less than 7 years (cf. Smith, 1994). Three objections were considered (paras. 8.17 *et seq.*): the proposals would lead to increased costs which would have to be borne by landlords or tenants; the applicability to local authority lettings; and, third, the effect on renovation grants. The (perhaps surprising) stridency of the Law Commission's rejection of these criticisms ('we consider that the cost is justified by the injustice we seek to remedy': para. 8.18; 'we can see no case for a blanket exclusion of local authority lettings': para. 8.25) have a slightly unreal air. Central government's concern was to entice more property into the PRS through deregulation and diminishing obligations upon landlords, attempting to make renting more profitable. Furthermore, if government was and is worried about rising rents (because of HB), then broadening the implied condition was unlikely to be a political possibility. There is an uncomfortable reality that, while meant to benefit a class of people who occupy the worst sort of property in the sector, such laws may work to their detriment because cheap accommodation becomes scarce(r), and upgraded accommodation becomes more expensive (see Hirsch 1981; Meyers 1975).

Repairing obligations

The law

Since 1961, in all leases for less than 7 years, landlords (whether public or private) have an obligation to repair the structure and exterior of the dwelling-house framed in the following terms:

(1) In a lease to which this section applies ... there is implied a covenant by the lessor –
   (a) to keep in repair the structure and exterior of the dwelling-house (including drains, gutters and external pipes),
   (b) to keep in repair and proper working order the installations in the dwelling-house for the supply of water, gas and electricity and for sanitation (including basins, sinks, baths and sanitary conveniences, but not other fixtures, fittings and appliances for making use of the supply of water, gas or electricity), and
   (c) to keep in repair and proper working order the installations in the dwelling-house for space heating and heating water.

(1A) If a lease to which this section applies is a lease of a dwelling-house which forms part only of a building, then, subject to subsection (1B), the covenant implied by subsection (1) shall have effect as if –
   (a) the reference in paragraph (a) of that subsection to the dwelling-house included a reference to any part of the building in which the lessor has an estate or interest; and
   (b) any reference in paragraphs (b) and (c) of that subsection to an installation in the dwelling-house included a reference to an installation which, directly or indirectly, serves the dwelling-house and which either
      (i) forms part of any part of a building in which the lessor has an estate or interest; or
      (ii) is owned by the lessor or under his control.

(1B) Nothing in subsection (1A) shall be construed as requiring the lessor to carry out any works or repairs unless the disrepair (or failure to maintain in working order) is such as to affect the lessee's enjoyment of the dwelling-house or of any common parts, as defined in section 60(1) of the Landlord and Tenant Act 1987, which the lessee, as such, is entitled to use.

Subsection (1A) extends the scope of the covenant to certain common parts, where the dwelling forms part of a larger building (overturning the restrictive interpretation applied to the section in *Campden Hill Towers* v. *Gardner* [1977] QB 823), although such a term may also be implied as a matter of common law in relation to access points (*Liverpool CC* v. *Irwin* [1977] AC 239). Although the landlord may not contract out of these provisions, the terms of the agreement between landlord and tenant may extend the landlord's obligations. It is to be noted that the obligation is to 'keep' the relevant parts of the property in repair, which means the same as a covenant to repair and implies that the 'obligation of the [person with the burden of the covenant], if the premises are not in tenantable repair when the tenancy begins, is to put them into, keep them in, and deliver them up in tenantable repair' (*Proudfoot* v. *Hart* [1890] 25 QBD 42, p. 50, Lord Esher MR). As Lord Hoffmann put it, 'Keeping in repair means remedying disrepair. The landlord is obliged only to restore the house to its previous good condition' (*Southwark LBC* v. *Mills* [2001] 1 AC 1, 8).

The court's construction of these statutory obligations has been to narrow them at almost every opportunity (see Reynolds 1974). There are three particular limitations: first, the landlord must have notice of the disrepair; second, the construction of the word 'repair'; third the scope of the landlord's defence.

As regards the first, despite the landlord's right of access to the property, liability generally only arises where a landlord is put on inquiry as to whether repairs are needed and does not respond within a reasonable time from the receipt of the notice (*Calabar Properties* v. *Stitcher* [1984] 1 WLR 287; although not as regards the common parts: *Melles & Co* v. *Holme* [1918] 2 KB 100). In order to engage the landlord's liability for breach of the section 11 covenant, the landlord must have sufficient notice of the relevant defects, whether they be latent or patent, that would put a reasonable person on inquiry as to the need for repair (*McCarrick* v. *Liverpool Corporation* [1947] AC 219; *O'Brien* v. *Robinson* [1973] AC 912; *British Telecom plc* v. *Sun Life Society plc* [1995] 4 All ER 44, 51–2; see also the contrary views of the notice requirement by Reynolds 1974, and Robinson 1976). Such notice may be actual, in which case it may be given informally (*McGreal* v. *Wake* (1984) 13 HLR 107), or imputed. Imputed notice may come from a contractor who has express or implied authority to accept complaints on the landlord's behalf (*Sheldon* v. *West Bromwich Corporation* (1973) 13 HLR 23). The notice need not be precise but such as to put a reasonable landlord on enquiry as to the need for repairs. The notice need not be in writing and may be given by a third party (*McGreal*). Where the landlord has notice of the need for repairs, and unsuccessfully seeks to enter the property to conduct works due to the claimant's action, there is a breach of covenant by the claimant and a break in the chain of causation of the landlord's liability for disrepair.

As regards the second issue, the obligation under s. 11 is to keep the property in repair. It does not extend to 'improvement', 'renewal', or 'replacement' which existed prior to the commencement of the tenancy (*Quick* v. *Taff-Ely BC*

[1986] QB 809; *Stent* v. *Monmouth DC* (1987) 19 HLR 19). However, where an inherent defect causes disrepair to items which fall within the scope of the section 11 covenant, then the landlord will be required to remedy the disrepair to those items (*Stent* v. *Monmouth DC* (1987) 19 HLR 19). Further, in certain circumstances where the inherent defect in the property will cause the same disrepair again and again, the landlord can be compelled to remedy the inherent defect. As Forbes J put it in *Ravenseft Properties Ltd* v. *Davstone (Holdings) Ltd* [1980] QB 12, p. 21, in a case involving a tenant's repairing covenant, 'The true test is …, that it is always a question of degree whether that which the tenant is being asked to do can properly be described as repair, or whether on the contrary it would involve giving back to the landlord a wholly different thing from that which he demised.'

An excellent example of the parameters of this limitation can be found in *Quick* v. *Taff-Ely BC* [1986] QB 809. The Court of Appeal found that the covenant did not protect the tenant against loss of amenity, although the covenant might require the remedying of an inherent defect. The property itself had an inherent defect which caused condensation at such a rate that all the tenants' fittings became mouldy and ruined. The court held that this property was not in disrepair as the covenant only applied to the physical exterior of the property and not to its 'lack of amenity or inefficiency'. Earlier cases had found that repairs could include the remedying of inherent defects in the property but Dillon LJ was concerned that this should be restricted to circumstances when it was 'the only practicable way of making good the damage'. Dillon LJ argued:

> [T]he liability of the local authority was to keep the structure and exterior of the house in repair, not the decorations. Though there is ample evidence of damage to the decorations and to bedding, clothing and other fabrics, evidence of damage to the subject-matter of the covenant, the structure and exterior of the house, is far to seek …[T]here is no evidence at all of physical damage to the walls, as opposed to the decorations, or the windows.

Third, it has been held by the courts, and transposed into the section 11 covenant, that the standard of repair of the relevant parts of the property must be related to 'the age, character and prospective life of the dwelling-house and the locality in which it is situated' (s. 11(3); *Proudfoot* v. *Hart*). A run-down property in a run-down area must, therefore, be considered in that context. As Parke B put it in *Payne* v. *Haine* (1847) 16 M&W 541:

> The cases all shew that the age and class of the premises let, with their general condition as to repair, may be estimated in order to measure the extent of the repairs to be done. Thus a house in Spitalfields may be repaired with materials inferior to those requisite for repairing a mansion in Grosvenor Square; but this lessee cannot say he will do no repairs, or leave the premises in bad repair, because they were old and out of repair when he took them.

In *Newham LBC* v. *Patel* (1978) 13 HLR 77, p. 83, it was conceded by the council that the property was in such a state of disrepair that any repairs would be 'wholly useless' (Templeman LJ). Mr Patel had been offered the property at a low rent to reflect its state of disrepair. Further, as Ormerod LJ put it (p. 85): 'If the prospective life of the dwelling-house, as in this case, is short, then it is perfectly proper, sensible and reasonable to adjust the landlord's obligations accordingly and not to seek to impose a construction on the statute, which can only be described as pedantic.'

Procedure

Even despite the above limitations, the Law Commission noted that 'actions to enforce [the implied covenant] are a commonplace and appear routinely in the daily lists of some county courts' (1996, para. 5.12). At one stage, it was suggested that one large city council spent more in defending claims to disrepair than it did in actually repairing properties, which, on any view, might be regarded as a perverse effect of the law. In his review of civil justice, Lord Woolf (1998: ch. 16, paras. 59–72) encouraged the various interest groups to develop a pre-action protocol (PAP), the purpose of which, in part, was to reduce the number of civil claims made by developing a procedure to govern the conduct of matters before the need for making a claim arose. The protocol came into effect only in 2003 'because the social landlords and the tenant lawyers had great difficulties in reaching a consensus'. It enables joint experts to be appointed and for issues to be resolved at an early stage. Community Legal Service funding is generally available in such claims, subject to eligibility, provided that the prospects of success are sufficiently clear and above borderline, and, in practice that the matter be allocated to the fast-track trial process (although this funding may be withdrawn in some cases after the legal aid review). That allocation requires that the tenant be seeking an order requiring the landlord to carry out repairs or other work, the cost of which is above £1,000; and the financial value of the claim is above £1,000 (CPR 26.6(1)(b)). A key issue, then, often turns on the financial value of the claim, which is now considered.

Damages

The measure of damages for breach of a repairing covenant is governed by the general principle that an award of damages is designed to restore the tenant to the position they would have been in but for the breach (*Calabar Properties Limited* v. *Stitcher* [1984] 1 WLR 287; *Wallace* v. *Manchester CC* (1998) 30 HLR 1111; *Shine* v. *English Churches Housing Group* [2004] HLR 42). This reflects the loss of value of the tenancy to the tenant. There is no single general principle beyond that. Three methods of quantifying the damages have been suggested: a notional reduction in rent; a global award for discomfort and inconvenience; or some combination of the two provided they do not overlap (as they are alternative expressions of each other) (*Wallace* v. *Manchester CC* (1998) 30 HLR 1111; *Shine* v. *English Churches Housing Group* [2004] HLR 42). Whichever method is used, general damages should only exceed the rent payable by the tenant during the relevant period if the facts warrant it (generally relating to the conduct of the landlord) (*Shine* at [104]; *Earle* v. *Charalambous* [2007] HLR 8, at [32], Carnwath LJ). Assessment of quantum is really an art rather than a science, particularly in disrepair cases and, while the obligation to conduct repairs arises when the disrepair occurs, damages depend on when the landlords had notice (except as regards common property).

Other remedies

A range of other remedies beyond the express terms of the agreement and s. 11 may apply. Reference is made here to the covenant for quiet enjoyment; s. 4(1), Defective Premises Act 1972; and statutory nuisance. Others, such as the ordinary law of nuisance (particularly as regards such things as cockroach and vermin infestations) may well apply in addition (see, generally, Luba et al. 2010).

As regards the covenant for quiet enjoyment, *Southwark LBC* v. *Mills* [2001] 1 AC 1 concerned a property which had no sound insulation and 'The tenants can hear not only the neighbours' televisions and their babies crying but their coming and going, their cooking and cleaning, their quarrels and their lovemaking' (p. 7, Lord Hoffmann). Lord Hoffmann observed that, read literally, a covenant for quiet enjoyment would cover precisely these facts. However, that literal reading could not stand in the way of centuries of case law which had limited the operation of the covenant to the following: 'a covenant that the tenant's lawful possession of the land will not be substantially interfered with by the acts of the lessor or those lawfully claiming under him' (p. 10). 'Substantial interference' meant that the tenant must not be able to use the property in an 'ordinary lawful way' (p. 10), which may well include noise. However, the covenant only covers *prospective* interference, emphasised by the use of his word 'will' in the definition. As the defect had been there at the time of the grant of the tenancy, the covenant did not, therefore, cover the problems faced by the tenants of this block.

As regards the Defective Premises Act 1972, s. 4(1) provides that, where it is a term of the tenancy that the landlord is obliged to repair or maintain the premises, the landlord:

> owes to all persons who might reasonably be expected to be affected by defects in the state of the premises a duty to take such care as is reasonable in all the circumstances to see that they are reasonably safe from personal injury or from damage to their property caused by a relevant defect.

This section creates a tortious duty owed by the landlord to persons 'expected to be affected by defects' in the property. It imposes no obligations beyond the repair and maintenance obligations discussed above. However, s. 4(2) of the 1972 Act extends the notice requirement in the following way:

The said duty is owed if the landlord knows (whether as the result of being noti-fied by the tenant or otherwise) or if he ought in all the circumstances to have known of the relevant defect.

Actual or constructive knowledge of the defect is therefore sufficient. Such notice can be provided by the tenant, or come to the landlord by other means (for example, through a third party's intervention) (*Clarke* v. *Taff Ely BC* (1984) 10 HLR 44).

Finally, there are the provisions concerning statutory nuisance in the Environmental Protection Act 1990, as amended, and the still extant Public Health Act 1936, as amended. These provisions return to the historical develop-ment of the law in this area considered in the previous section, as they substan-tially replicate the provisions from the nineteenth-century statutes, but have been considerably limited by judicial intervention over the years (see Malcolm and Pointing 2006). Section 79(1)(a) lists statutory nuisances as including 'any premises in such a state as to be a nuisance or injurious to health' (derived from s. 8, Nuisances Removal Act 1855). In *Birmingham CC* v. *Oakley* [2005] 1 AC 617, the House of Lords by a majority decided that this provision did not cover an unhygienic arrangement of a property in which the occupants had to pass through a kitchen, after having gone to the toilet, before they could wash their hands. As Malcolm and Pointing (2006: 41) pithily put it, 'it was the practice itself that was unhygienic and not the state of the premises'.

The tolerated trespasser: specific issues

The concept of the tolerated trespasser is discussed further in Chapter 14 below. The specific issue, in relation to property state and condition, relates to the cir-cumstances in which a tolerated trespasser can have their tenancy regarded as continuing uninterrupted through the period of 'toleration', so as to bring a claim for disrepair to include the period during which their tenancy was in abeyance. Prior to the Housing and Regeneration Act 2008, one of the con-sequences of the finding that an occupier was a 'tolerated trespasser' was that the occupier could not bring a disrepair claim because, in effect, there was no tenancy on which the repairing obligations might 'bite' (*Burrows* v. *Brent LBC* [1996] 1 WLR 1448; *Lambeth LBC* v. *Rogers* (2000) 32 HLR 361, 367).

An occupier in this position now has two options. They could make an appli-cation under s. 85, Housing Act 1985, effectively to change the possession order into a PPO. Alternatively, they might make a 'satellite' application as part of a disrepair claim. Schedule 11, Housing and Regeneration Act 2008, enables such an application to be made in the following circumstances:

(3) In proceedings on a relevant claim the court concerned may order that the new tenancy and the original tenancy are to be treated for the purposes of the claim as –
  (a) the same tenancy, and

(b) a tenancy which continued uninterrupted throughout the termination period.

(4) The following are relevant claims –

(a) a claim by the ex-tenant or the ex-landlord against the other for breach of a term or condition of the original tenancy –

(i) in respect of which proceedings are brought on or after the commencement date,

or

(ii) in respect of which proceedings were brought, but were not finally determined, before that date,

(b) a claim by the ex-tenant against the ex-landlord for breach of statutory duty in respect of which proceedings are or were brought as mentioned in paragraph (a)(i) or (ii), and

(c) any other claim of a description specified by the appropriate national authority by order.

The court, then, has discretion as to whether to regard the tenancy as continuing. The remaining question concerns the circumstances under which the court will exercise that discretion in favour of the occupier. In *Austin* v. *Southwark LBC* [2010] 3 WLR 144, Baroness Hale observed: 'Even if some local authority landlords might have welcomed not being under a contractual obligation to repair properties for which the occupier was not paying the full rent, they would also have acknowledged that it could not be right for them to be able to charge the equivalent of the full rent which was calculated on the basis that they did have an obligation to repair' ([54]). That suggests at least that the discretion might be exercised with a 'light touch'. In *Chase* v. *Islington LBC* (reported in (2010) *Legal Action* October; also at http://nearlylegal.co.uk/blog/2010/10/fair-limit-on-damages/), albeit at county court level (and, therefore, a non-binding authority), the court made clear that the discretion was to be exercised in light of all the circumstances of the case, including the extent to which the breach of the order was technical and the importance of granting relief on those circumstances. The court could also, it was said, impose conditions on the grant of relief, for example by limiting the amount of damages recoverable.

Housing Health and Safety Rating System: science and pseudo-science

This section turns from individual remedies for disrepair to the public law obligations of local authorities in respect of unsafe housing. The HHSRS consigns much of the previous law concerned with fitness for human habitation, based as it was on the nineteenth-century conceptions, to the historical dustbin. The HHSRS itself, by contrast, is based on multidisciplinary and interdisciplinary assessments of the health and safety risks of a particular property. The bare bones of the law are contained in the Housing Act 2004, Part I, but this is supplemented by statutory instrument and guidance, to which local authorities must have regard (s. 9, 2004 Act).

The background to the Act is set out by Burridge and Ormandy (2007), who were the primary movers in the formulation of the standard and developed the processes and practices contained in the guidance. There was some considerable time between the first suggestions for reforms they made and the 2004 Act, but this enabled a review to be conducted of the evidence-base for 'housing-related health risks, developments in the epidemiology of diseases, the causation of structure-related illness, and the incidence and causes of accidents in the home' (p. 561). At heart, the HHSRS is a scientifically based assessment, dependent on professional judgment and up-to-date technical knowledge (p. 562). The focus is on threats to health and safety and is not generally concerned with matters of quality, comfort and convenience (CLG 2006f: para. 1.06).

The purpose of the HHSRS is to enable local authorities to assess the condition of 'residential premises' and to provide for certain enforcement action (s. 1(1)). 'Residential premises' includes a 'dwelling' (s. 1(4)), which 'means a building or part of a building occupied or intended to be occupied as a separate dwelling' (s. 1(5), and thus includes an HMO). The obligation to make an HHSRS assessment of a property arises both generally and specifically. Generally, a local housing authority must keep the housing conditions in its area under review with a view to identifying any action that may need to be taken by it (s. 3(1)). Specifically, for example, if a local housing authority considers as a result of any matters of which it has become aware under s. 3 or for any other reason, that it would be appropriate for any residential premises in its district to be inspected with a view to determining whether any Category 1 or 2 hazard exists on those premises, the authority must arrange for such an inspection to be carried out (s. 4(1)).

The purpose of an HHSRS assessment is to assess the category of hazard. 'Hazard' is defined by s. 2(1) as

> any risk of harm to the health or safety of an actual or potential occupier of a dwelling or HMO which arises from a deficiency in the dwelling or HMO or in any building or land in the vicinity (whether the deficiency arises as a result of the construction of any building, an absence of maintenance or repair, or otherwise).

The Housing Health and Safety Rating System (England) Regulations 2005 (SI 2005/3208) expand on the meaning of hazard. Regulation 3(1) states that a hazard is of a prescribed description for the purposes of the Act where the risk of harm is associated with the occurrence of twenty-nine matters or circumstances listed in Sch. 1. Those matters or circumstances range from damp and mould growth, excess cold/heat, asbestos, crowding, light and noise, and others. Regulation 6 provides the method of calculation for the seriousness of the hazard, which is the likelihood, during the period of 12 months beginning with the date of the assessment, of a relevant occupier suffering any harm as a result of that hazard as falling within one of the range of ratios of likelihood contained in table 1 (reg. 6(2)). Regulation 7 divides hazards into bands (Band A–J) based on a numerical score, which represents the seriousness of the hazard (reg. 6(5)). There are two categories of hazard, Category 1 and Category 2 (s. 2). Regulation 8 provides that hazards in Bands A, B or C are Category 1 hazards.

Despite the science behind the assessment idea, the appeal to 'risk', and the training of environmental health officers, an HHSRS assessment, which usually appears as a series of calculations based on the classes of harm on one page producing a final numerical score, is as much an art as a science, if not more so. That assertion is, to an extent, based on personal experience, as opposed to a valid social scientific method, but the guidance provided by the Lands Tribunal (which is the appeal court in such matters, beyond the Residential Property Tribunal) is as follows:

> It seems to me important that RPTs when determining cases under Part 1 of the Act should bear in mind the nature of such assessments as these and their limitations. The complicated set of provisions is designed to produce a numerical score for each hazard that is under consideration so that it can be seen to fall within a particular band and in either category 1 or category 2. The great danger of a numerical score produced in this way is that it creates the impression of methodological accuracy, whereas the truth may be that it is the product of no more than a series of value judgments based on little understood statistics of questionable validity. (*Bolton MBC* v. *Patel* [2010] UKUT 334 (LC), at [38])

The category of hazard determines the obligations on the local authority, which are under a duty to take the appropriate enforcement action in relation to Category 1 hazards (s. 5(1)) and powers in relation to Category 2 hazards (s. 7(1)). The enforcement action can take the following forms: an improvement notice (s. 11); a prohibition order (s. 20); emergency remedial action (s. 40); a demolition order (s. 265(1) or (2), Housing Act 1985); and declaring the area to be a clearance area (s. 289(2), Housing Act 1985). Where only one of those actions is possible, the local authority must take that action: s. 5(3). The HHSRS enforcement guidance suggests a compliance-based approach that the decision to take enforcement action must be used flexibly: 'The decision to take enforcement action will require a judgement as to the necessity for intervention, given the authority's priorities and wider renewal policies and, where appropriate, their knowledge of a landlord and his or her compliance history' (CLG 2006g: para. 2.2). Formal enforcement policies should take account of the views of tenants, landlords and owners, as well as other factors such as the types of properties in which the worst conditions can be found (para. 2.16; see also paras. 2.18–19).

Although the 2004 Act applies to 'residential premises', it appears that, despite local authorities having a duty to assess residential premises owned by them, public housing is excluded from the enforcement duties (despite the mandatory wording of s 5). This is because, before enforcement action is taken, the local authority must serve a notice on certain person(s). For example, an improvement notice, hazard awareness notice, and emergency remedial action must be served, in the case of a dwelling, on the person having control of the dwelling (respectively Sch. 1, para. 2(2); s. 28(7); s. 40(7)); a prohibition order must be served, inter alia, in relation to a flat on every person who is 'authorised to permit persons to occupy the whole or part of the building' (Sch. 2, para. 2(2)(b)). However, in general, local authorities cannot serve such notices on themselves. This was the decision under earlier legislation in *R* v. *Cardiff CC ex p Cross* (1983) 6 HLR 1. Even so, Lord Lane LCJ stressed that this conclusion was limited:

> It is confined strictly, because Sections 9 and 16 of the [1957] Act may in certain circumstances apply even though the house is owned by a local authority. For example it may apply where it is owned by a local authority outside that local authority's own area. It may apply where the local authority, even in their own area have an interest in the house but someone else is in control of the house: for example, it may be owned by the local authority, and yet it may be that a property company have taken a long lease from the local authority and the property company in turn may have let it to a tenant on weekly terms. The conclusion is limited to a case where the local authority in charge of the area is the body having control of the house.

Can such a distinction between council and other tenants survive the implementation of Articles 8 and 14, Sch. 1, HRA (right to respect for family/home and non-discrimination respectively), which together would seem to imply that such differential treatment in respect of a person's home would be problematic? The approach of the courts has been to limit the application of Article 14 so that it is not self-standing (*Petrovic* v. *Austria* [2001] 33 EHRR 14 at [28]); and, when in conjunction with Article 8, it has been said that the ECtHR 'has taken a more nuanced approach, reflecting the unique feature of article 8 …: that it is concerned with the failure to accord *respect*' (*M* v. *Secretary of State for Work and Pensions* [2006] 2 AC 91, at [83], Lord Walker, original emphasis). Further, 'the cases in which article 14 has been considered in conjunction with the family life limb of article 8 [are] all (whichever way they were ultimately decided) concerned with measures very closely connected with family life' (at [84]). The expression 'very closely connected' has been described as a 'high threshold' (*R (Harrison)* v. *Secretary of State for Health* [2009] EWHC 574 (Admin), Silber J at [89A]). In *R (Erskine)* v. *Lambeth LBC* [2003] EWHC 2479 (Admin) at [43]–[4], Mitting J found that the different treatment of council tenants as opposed to other tenants, inherent in the legislation concerning the then provisions about fitness for human habitation (s. 189[1] and Part VI, Housing Act 1985), was not such as to breach Articles 8 and 14, Sch. 1, HRA:

> It is plain that the principal purpose of the legislation, as originally enacted, and as re-enacted over the years, was to protect and promote public health, and to

---

[1] The relevant part of section 189 was as follows: 'where the local housing authority are satisfied that a dwelling house … is unfit for human habitation, they shall serve a repair notice on the person having control of the dwelling house'.

improve the condition of low cost housing stock. It was not the protection or pro-motion of the rights, such as those to be found in Article 8, of individuals. As such, therefore, section 189 and Part VI are not 'within the ambit' of Article 8 as explained in *Petrovic*. [43]

The 2004 Act, on first blush, also appears to be written to reflect the deci-sion in *Cross*. So, for example, where a prohibition order is operative, security of tenure under the Rent Act 1977 or the Housing Act 1988, but significantly not the Housing Act 1985, acts to stop possession being obtained. All that having been said, difficult questions are likely to arise in the post-welfare settlement of social housing, when a local authority has contracted out the management, as opposed to the ownership of its stock, to an ALMO or TMO. Here, the answer may lie in the management agreement between the organisation and the authority. The issue, of course, does not arise where the local authority has parted with ownership of its stock under an LSVT, for example.

Decent homes

The New Labour government established in 2000 a non-statutory 'soft' target that all social tenants should have a decent home by 2010 (ODPM 2003b: 14). The HHSRS also underpins the decent homes strategy:

> To be decent, a dwelling should be free of category 1 hazards, and the existence of such hazards should be a trigger for remedial action unless practical steps can-not be taken without disproportionate expense or disruption. Landlords should consider the circumstances very carefully in the interests of the occupiers of the dwelling before concluding that a hazard cannot be dealt with effectively, and in such cases should ensure that the occupiers are fully aware of the position. (CLG 2006b: para. 2.20)

Somerville (2004; cited in Pawson and Mullins 2010: 202) has criticised the def-inition as being too narrow and setting a relatively low benchmark, but it has nevertheless been an unachievable target.

The plan included £22 billion to improve housing and communities, £5 bil-lion for affordable homes, at least £1 billion for key-worker housing, as well as support for home ownership and new growth areas. The action plan has been presented as a common-sense strategy – who could argue that all tenants should not have a decent home, or argue against the ideal of sustainable com-munities? – but it underpinned the New Labour strategy to reduce local author-ity housing provision (see Chapter 4 above; Cowan and McDermont 2006: 98). However, it is also the case that, whatever the ideological implications of the policy, it has achieved a considerable amount after decades of neglect in the sec-tor: between 2001–2008, the investment 'had ... reduced the sector-wide non-compliance rate from 38 per cent to 18 per cent' (Pawson and Mullins 2010: 202–3).

Conclusion

Although this chapter has stretched itself over a considerable period of the history of housing, including the foundation stones both of housing policy and the statutory interference in the relationship between landlord and tenant, it might be felt that we have yet to develop a proper strategy in civil and public law for dealing with unhealthy housing. Individual rights have been restricted by court decisions; statutory provisions regarding fitness for human habitation are moribund; public law decisions regarding the HHSRS are not enforceable in respect of a significant proportion of the housing stock, and, in any event, compliance policies are likely to dominate the sector and are encouraged by guidance; it is significant in this light that perhaps the most important developments have arisen not from formal law but from the soft targets set by New Labour with financial and consequential organisational strings attached.

14

Arrears

Contents

This chapter concerns *discretionary* grounds for a claim to possession of property brought by either a mortgage lender or landlord (mandatory possession proceedings are considered in Chapter 16 below). Although the principles and procedures are different, the reasons for arrears arising in the first place are often not dissimilar between tenures (relationship breakdown, loss of employment by one or both partners, and, at a general level, inability to meet financial commitments), although certain prominent reasons are tenure specific (HB issues for rented accommodation, risky lending practices with ownership). While much high-profile government policy energy is given over to 'saving' owners in arrears during times of crisis, one hears much less about policy initiatives to assist tenants in arrears, which tend to be left to good practice-type initiatives at the level of individual landlord. When it comes to possession, however, the regulatory rhetoric is exactly the same across tenures: possession should be the last resort. It is the interpretation of that phrase 'last resort', however, which is variable. That is the socio-legal question, viz. at what point does the lender/landlord reach the 'last resort'?

The first section focuses on mortgage arrears and the second on tenant arrears. In that latter section, however, the predominant focus is on social housing, for two reasons. First, quite simply, there is more that is known about social-rented evictions – indeed, very little is known about private-rented evictions on discretionary grounds for arrears; and second, there is an important social scientific question about the changing construction of the 'social' in relation to social housing here (again).

Mortgage arrears and possessions

This section is split into four parts, but is clearly related to the regulation of the mortgage industry (Chapter 2 above) and access to ownership (Chapter 10 above) because it might be said that arrears arise, in part, because of the previously (and perhaps current) poor regulation of lending practices, and the resultant over-extension of households not just when they purchase but also subsequently (second mortgages and equity-release arrangements). The first part discusses borrowers' responses to arrears; the second deals with the government's response to the mortgage crisis from 2008; third, and related to that, the Civil Justice Council's (CJC) PAP on mortgage possessions is discussed; finally, there is discussion of the content of mortgage possession hearings.

Let us, first, discuss the nature and scale of the issue. Between 2005–2009, the numbers of possession claims in the county court were 107,993 (2005), 123,033 (2006), 128,520 (2007), 133,001 (2008), and 87,248 (2009); about two-thirds of those, on average, resulted in a court order (including a suspended possession order (SPO)). There are a number of matters to note about these statistics. First, the number of possession claims was actually rising before the 'credit crunch' occurred, so, as Ford and Wallace (2010: 134) suggest, that episode '*magnified* rather than *created*' the crisis (original empahsis). Second, the geographical distribution of court orders for possession is skewed, with the highest proportion occurring in the North West, whereas the southern regions are below the expected regional share of the owner-occupied dwellings in England (Ford et al. 2010: para. 3.39). Third, there was, in fact, a quite dramatic reduction in 2009, which was, in itself, counter-intuitive as one would have expected rather more possession claims during this period. One of the issues to be discussed below are the reasons for that decline and whether it is 'real' in the sense that it was not caused by external factors which, were they to cease, would lead to an increase – certainly, the number of borrowers in arrears did not decline in 2009 (and there were concerns that it was going to be a bumper year). It may be that the years 2009–2010 have been temporary blips, dependent on the poor performance in the property market in addition to the other factors discussed below.

Responding to arrears

According to the Council for Mortgage Lenders (CML), '176,100 mortgages (1.55% of the total) had arrears of 2.5% or more of the outstanding balance at the end of September, down from 178,200 at the end of June, and from 203,800 a year earlier' (CML 2010). While the legal focal point is clearly on possession proceedings, such proceedings in fact account for only a small proportion of households in arrears losing their properties. The mortgage lenders, themselves, may not bring possession proceedings; and borrowers in arrears have other means of exiting, for example selling or renting the property or simply handing the keys in to the mortgage lender.

As regards the latter, Ford et al. (2010: para. 3.8) conducted an analysis of the Survey of English Housing for 2005–2008 and found that, of 381,000 households which contained someone who had experienced voluntary or compulsory possession or sold because of financial pressure, some 246,000 such households had sold and a further 80,000 had given voluntary possession (handed the keys to the mortgage lender). One key difference noted in this research, regarding borrowers, between the current climate and the last housing crash in the late 1980s/early 1990s was the much greater use today of insolvency-related strategies, such as voluntary arrangements, because of the multiple debts and over-indebtedness of some borrowers, which made giving up ownership the inevitable outcome (paras. 5.35–41). Equally, the threat by the mortgage lender of going to court might stimulate the decision to give up voluntarily (paras. 5.31–4).

As regards lender strategies, the main differences between the current situation and that of the late 1980s/early 1990s are twofold: first, the different types of lender in the marketplace and the risks they have taken, leading to differentiation and segmentation of strategies between different types of lender; second, perhaps more prosaically, the nature and content of regulation.

As regards the first, we have already discussed (in Chapter 2 above) the significance of securitisation and the sub-prime mortgage market. Unsurprisingly, arrears in the sub-prime sector were at higher levels than in the prime sector (up to eight times as high as the 'prime' sector – Stephens and Quilgars 2008: 207) and it has been reported that lenders in the sub-prime sector were less likely to be willing to negotiate or tolerate arrears than the prime sector and more likely to resort to use of courts as part of their arrears strategies (ibid.: 208; Munro et al. 2005). However, as regards the latter point, there are a range of factors involved in mortgage lenders' individual decisions, principally related to the market place itself. As Ford and Wallace (2009: 16) put it: 'Falling house prices, falling transactions, the costs of possession and the extent of exposure to risk, are central factors influencing how lenders respond to arrears.' Thus, even in the sub-prime sector, while the market is weak, it may be more beneficial to the lender to be more willing to negotiate with borrowers so as to avoid 'crystallising' the loss (ibid. p. 17).

It is important to note that this increased willingness to negotiate represented a major cultural change within lenders, which had previously adopted a fairly blunt 'pay or possess' strategy (Ford and Wallace 2010), although these processes were in train in the 1990s (Ford et al. 1995: 44). Thus, there has been a significant shift towards earlier intervention and negotiation. Lenders have a 'forbearance toolkit' but this cultural shift is ongoing: 'variation in forbearance practice exists within any one lender as well as between lenders' (Ford and Wallace 2010: 143).

The second difference highlighted above is the regulatory dimension to arrears management. Arrears management is a new and developing practice, which became the subject of a voluntary code of conduct sponsored by the CML in 1999, but was overtaken by the regulatory oversight of the FSA in 2004. The MCOB rules 12 and 13 are concerned with arrears and possessions, and are at the time of writing the subject of consultation to tighten the principles and rules (FSA 2010a). The rules require that court action for possession should be a last resort, 'where all else has failed' (MCOB 13.3.2E(f)).

Where customers fall into arrears, the rules require that certain information is to be given to them and there should be a degree of transparency. However, the MCOB regulatory standards regarding charging for arrears letters and administration of arrears, in some cases, have not been effected on a thought-out basis with significant puzzling variations across lenders, which are poorly explained to borrowers (FSA 2010a : ch. 4); with two sub-prime lenders being fined for excessive arrears charges (ibid. para. 4.4). Transparency of operations remains a concern over the key issue of customer knowledge of possession policies. As McMurtry (2007) puts it:

> More questionable [than the provision of statements of policy required by the rules] is whether the rules will produce an equivalence of treatment for different borrowers in regulated contracts with different lenders following different enforcement policies. It is to be regretted that there remains scope for the adoption of highly divergent approaches and the standard expected cannot, in any sense, be regarded as exacting. (See also Whitehouse 1998; 2010.)

While the MCOB rules may appear significant, Ford and Wallace (2010: 141–2) suggest that these had limited impact on lenders (or, at least, lenders were reluctant to attribute changes in strategies to the regulation and intervention). In 2009, the FSA noted that: 'It is clear that many firms have not exercised forebearance but moved quickly to repossess properties.' (FSA 2009: para. 7.5) and are consulting on whether to convert 'guidance' into binding rules (FSA 2010).

For debts and other security interests not covered by the MCOB, such as second charges, the OFT has responsibility for regulation in respect of 'irresponsible lending practices' (s. 25(2B), Consumer Credit Act 1974, as amended). The OFT guidance makes clear, once again, that possession (or application for a charging order – a method of turning an unsecured debt effectively into a debt secured over property) should be a last resort in the context of a proportionate response to debt (OFT 2010: para. 7.14).

Responding to 'crisis'

Although the FSA's consultation and approach to its code, together with the OFT's explanation of its approach to irresponsible lending, may constitute the regulatory state's approach to the potential possessions crisis which emerged as a real probability in the late 2000s, the government itself was also taking action to deal with what appeared (in October 2008) to be an 'enormous' problem (Stephens 2008: 6). That action encompassed a range of activities: reversing trends in state support for mortgage interest; schemes to support borrowers to remain in their properties; and access to debt advice services for borrowers.

In the 1990s, private insurance schemes were developed to insure borrowers against missed mortgage payments. It was clear that this mortgage payment protection insurance (MPPI) was not the panacea that some had considered it to be in the 1990s. Early schemes did not insure against certain risks and had wide exclusions from cover. Those households most at risk of falling into arrears often had most difficulty in obtaining insurance as well as being most unlikely to take up the insurance (Burchardt and Hills 1997: 25; Ford and Kempson 1997; Pryce and Keoghan 2002). Even so, MPPI had been the reason for the reduction in the payment of income support for mortgage interest from the mid-1990s: for the first 9 months of any claim for income support, borrowers received no help with their mortgage payments (Social Security (Income Support and Claims and Payments) Amendment Regulations 1995, SI 1995/1613, reg. 8(1)) as MPPI would/should cover those in need of assistance during those first 9 months.

One of the New Labour government's earliest announced interventions in 2008 was to reverse that trend, entitling benefits to be paid towards borrowers' mortgage interest payments from 13 weeks of arrears being accrued; doubling the capital limit on which eligibility for assistance was calculated to £200,000; and paying the interest at a generous fixed rate (above the interest on most mortgages), although this was reduced to the average mortgage interest rate from October 2010 (see Ford et al. 2010: para. 3.30–1). That was not just in recognition of the lack of success of MPPI, but also that income support for mortgage interest had been successfully used in the 1990s in conjunction with lenders exercising forebearance, thus contributing to a reduction in repossessions at that time. What central government did not do in 2008, unlike in the early 1990s, was to make a compact with lenders linking direct receipt of that benefit by lenders with their forebearance (Williams and Wilcox 2009: 2). Nevertheless, as part of the package of reforms announced in November 2008, the government did agree with major lenders that those lenders would wait at least 3 months before commencing possession proceedings, in order to explore all other alternatives including forebearance.

Two 'new' schemes were also announced at that time: the 'mortgage rescue scheme' and the 'homeowners mortgage support' (see Wilcox et al. 2010).
Under the rescue scheme, a borrower facing repossession either engaged in a
sale-and-rentback arrangement with a PRP (the borrower sells the property to
the PRP and the PRP grants them an AST for a minimum period of 3 years at
80 per cent of the market rent) or the PRP lent money to the borrower in return
for a shared-equity arrangement (similar to the shared-ownership model). The
PRP then also brought the property into line with the decent homes standard. The HCA provided generous funding for these schemes to PRPs, over and
above the usual grant rate, to secure their involvement (Wilcox et al. 2010: para.
4.18). One of the overriding rationales for this scheme was the prevention of
homelessness and to limit the demand for social housing – thus, the borrower
must fulfil the criteria for a 'successful' homelessness applicant (see Chapter 6
above). There were also price caps and the extent of negative equity must not
exceed 20 per cent. The borrower, however, must be able to contribute 3 per
cent of the purchase price; the mortgage lender was requested to write off their
losses, which some were willing to do because of the benefits to them of not taking possession of a property in a declining market and selling it.

The administration of the rescue scheme was both complex, involving a
number of referrals from different agencies (with a 'fast-track team' taking
over for a limited period to deal with referrals from lenders), housing options
appraisals, homelessness assessments, as well as the usual conveyancing process; and cumbersome, on average taking between 10 and12 months from original approach to completed sale (Wilcox et al. 2010: 5.37; see *Cheltenham &
Gloucester Building Society* v. *Krausz* (1997) 29 HLR 597, where a mortgage
rescue scheme came unstuck because the market picked up between the time
of the offer and completion, making the mortgage lender's claim to possession
compelling). Not surprisingly, there were early teething problems (e.g. Wilcox
et al. 2010: 5.44) but, by March 2010, 629 applicants had been 'rescued', mostly
into the sale-and-rentback scheme, but there were concerns about ongoing debt
and ability to meet the rent levels (ibid. paras. 6.23–32).

Under the homeowners mortgage support scheme, the borrower entered into
an arrangement with their lender, under which the mortgage became an interest only mortgage (i.e. the monthly payments were not of capital) and the borrower paid a minimum of 30 per cent interest for up to 2 years. This scheme was
not a success in its own right – indeed, it presented a classic implementation
problem as, from its inception, it 'appeared classically "top-down"' (Wilcox et al.
2010: 7.7); the criteria for eligibility were set at a threshold which was restrictive
(ibid. para. 7.5); the 'prevailing view amongst lenders and advisors [is] that the
scheme is cumbersome to administer, too narrow in its applicability and with a
lack of clarity about its remit' (ibid. para. 7.21). The direct effect was that support for the scheme from lenders was 'subdued' and, in fact, was only used in
thirty-two cases between April 2009 to March 2010 (ibid. para. 7.37). However,
the scheme did influence the lenders' development of forbearance strategies

through the publicity it generated. As a result, the scheme might be said to have been indirectly successful.

The pre-action protocol

In November 2008, the CJC issued a *Pre-Action Protocol for Possession Claims based on Mortgage or Home Purchase Plan Arrears in respect of Residential Property* (CJC 2008; 'the mortgage PAP') to govern mortgage possession claims. Protocols were devised as a procedural method for prescribing certain steps to be taken before a relevant claim is made together with demonstrable consideration of alternatives for resolving potential claims, usually with sanctions for non-performance (for example, in terms of non-recovery of costs by the non-performing party). Their purpose is to avoid claims either entirely or by diverting them to alternative dispute resolution fora. They do *not* change (indeed, are not capable of changing) the substantive law.

The purpose of the mortgage PAP is that: 'It is in the interests of the parties that mortgage payments or payments under home purchase plans are made promptly and that difficulties are resolved wherever possible without court proceedings. However in some cases an order for possession may be in the interest of both the lender and the borrower.' (para. 1.3) It applies to practically all residential mortgages (whether first, second or subsequent charges: para. 3.1). It prescribes the steps that mortgage lenders must take, which generally follow the good practice in the sector set out by the CML as well as the regulatory requirements of the MCOB. It reinforces the 'last resort' nature of a possession claim. For example, it says (para. 7.1) that:

> The court takes the view that starting a possession claim is usually a last resort and that such a claim should not normally be started when a settlement is still actively being explored. Discussion between the parties may include options such as:
> (1) extending the term of the mortgage;
> (2) changing the type of a mortgage;
> (3) deferring payment of interest due under the mortgage; or
> (4) capitalising the arrears.

What it does not do, however, is to prescribe sanctions for non-performance beyond requiring the parties to explain the actions that have been taken to comply with it (para. 9.1); and the mortgage PAP has been much criticised for this omission (see, for example, Marshall 2009, noting geographical variations in court practice as a result; Whitehouse 2009: 813, where the mortgage PAP is regarded as 'little more than a conduit, conveying a polite request to all lenders that they consider whether court proceedings are essential'). In all likelihood, the lack of sanctions represented a compromise between the interests of the lender community (which was virulently against the draft mortgage PAP during consultation) and the interests of the government in having the mortgage PAP engaged before a prospective tide of possession claims.

All that having been said, though, it is clear that the mortgage PAP had a disciplining effect on mortgage lenders, perhaps because they were concerned about the impact of non-compliance in individual claims or delays in obtaining possession as a result of non-compliance. Ford and Wallace (2010: 141–2) noted that its introduction caused lenders to review their strategies and practices, amending their ICT systems to ensure they could demonstrate compliance with its terms, and revisiting neglected forbearance tools (see also Williams and Wilcox 2009: 3). Ford et al. (2010) noted that its introduction had the immediate effect of reducing possession claims while lenders adapted their administrative processes, but that its influence has perhaps transcended the lack of sanction (at paras. 3.34 and 7.46–7 respectively). Whitehouse (2010) calls for further research into the impact of the mortgage PAP on the judicial process of dealing with possession claims to which we now turn.

Mortgage possession proceedings

Whitehouse (2010) makes the valuable point that the mortgage agreement in law has changed its form subtly over time but the substance of the agreement has never changed, despite its changing social use. In theory, as discussed in Chapter 11 above, the mortgage lender has no need to bring a claim for possession of property – the lender has an absolute right which may be the subject of express or implied limits or conditions – and the statutory powers of the court can be sidelined should a mortgage lender take that path (*Ropaigealach* v. *Barclays Bank plc* [2000] QB 263). Given that there is no requirement on a mortgage lender to bring possession proceedings, it may appear somewhat bizarre that the borrower has a statutory right to resist such a claim; however, that is the position in English law. It works on the basis that lenders will generally bring a court-based claim to possession before obtaining it. In such circumstances, the borrower can resist the claim by using the tortuously worded Administration of Justice Act 1970, s. 36 and Administration of Justice Act 1973, s. 8. Under s. 36, the court may adjourn a claim, suspend or stay the execution of a possession order, or postpone a possession order, if the property is a dwelling-house and 'it appears to the court that in the event of its exercising the power the mortgagor is likely to be able within a reasonable period to pay any sums due under the mortgage or to remedy a default consisting of a breach of any other obligation arising under or by virtue of the mortgage'.

The section was devised to deal with the limits placed on the previous equitable jurisdiction taken by the courts of chancery from 1936, but effectively limited in *Birmingham Citizens Permanent Building Society* v. *Caunt* [1962] Ch 883. The Payne Committee, set up to consider the balance between the mortgage lender's rights and the borrower's home decided on this limitation, in part because it placed trust and confidence in the building society community and the courts' exercise of discretion. However, the section was restrictively interpreted at the outset so that the phrase 'sums due' was said to include not just the missed payments but the whole amount owed under the mortgage because, in the usual course of events, the terms of the agreement make all such sums due on default by the borrower (*Halifax Building Society* v. *Clark* [1973] 2 All ER 33; *Habib Bank Ltd* v. *Tailor* [1982] 3 All ER 561). Thus, s. 8, Administration of Justice Act 1973, in part, clarified that 'sums due' relates to only those 'amounts as the [borrower] would have expected to be required to pay if there had been no such provision for earlier payment'. It also provided that the borrower was required to be able to pay not only that amount (plus interest) within the 'reasonable period' but also 'that [the borrower] is likely to be able by the end of that period to pay any further amounts that [the borrower] would have expected to be required to pay by then on account of that sum'. This means, in effect, that the borrower must be able to continue to pay towards the mortgage and the arrears during that reasonable period.

The sections effectively accept but limit the lender's right to possession. In other words, the court has discretion to broker a forbearance agreement provided the borrower is likely to be able to repay the sums owing within a reasonable period and likely to be able to continue to make the mortgage payments. On this basis, the lender will be successful if a possession order is made, but it will also be successful if the judge exercises the discretion to delay the grant of possession in order to make an order as to payment (because the lender will potentially recoup its losses) (see Whitehouse 1998: 172). Furthermore, the lenders' costs of bringing the actions in the first place are added to the amount owed by the borrower because the mortgage agreement will usually provide for the borrower to be responsible for the lender's costs of obtaining possession (see *First National Bank* v. *Syed* [1991] 2 All ER 250; cf. Bates 2005, where it is suggested that the Unfair Terms in Consumer Contracts Regulations may assist borrowers).

It was that latter fact about the costs of claims being paid for by the borrower which was influential in the current leading case on the interpretation of the 'reasonable period', *Cheltenham and Gloucester BS* v. *Norgan* [1996] 1 WLR 343. Prior to that case, courts had adopted the definition of the reasonable period to be 2 years as a rule of thumb (although there were geographical variations). The court held that the starting point in this case was that the rest of the mortgage term should be regarded as the reasonable period. One of the consequences of this rule of thumb was that there were repeated applications for possession, the costs of each being added to the mortgage. The parties in this case had been to court 'with depressing frequency', including a 3-day trial which was the subject of the appeal:

> One advantage of taking the period most favourable to the mortgagor at the outset is that, if his or her hopes of repayment prove to be ill-founded and the new instalments initially ordered as a condition of suspension are not maintained but themselves fall into arrear, the mortgagee can be heard with justice to say that the mortgagor has had his chance, and that the section 36 powers (although of course capable in theory of being exercised again and again) should not be employed

repeatedly to compel a lending institution which has already suffered interruption of the regular flow of interest to which it was entitled under the express terms of the mortgage to accept assurances of future payment from a borrower in whom it has lost confidence. (at p. 354, Waite LJ)

There were a number of additional key factors in favour of the 'reasonable period' being the term of the mortgage in this case. There was about 12 years left for the mortgage to run; the borrowers retained some equity in the property; and the CML voluntary code, to which the claimant subscribed, required its members to consider a range of alternatives to possession, including capitalisation of the missed payments (see, in particular, p. 357, Evans LJ). Evans LJ offered a 'practical summary' of the judgments in the form of questions for the judge:

> (a) How much can the borrower reasonably afford to pay, both now and in the future? (b) If the borrower has a temporary difficulty in meeting his obligations, how long is the difficulty likely to last? (c) What was the reason for the arrears which have accumulated? (d) How much remains of the original term? (e) What are relevant contractual terms, and what type of mortgage is it, i.e. when is the principal due to be repaid? (f) Is it a case where the court should exercise its power to disregard accelerated payment provisions (section 8 of the Act of 1973)? (g) Is it reasonable to expect the lender, in the circumstances of the particular case, to recoup the arrears of interest (1) over the whole of the original term, or (2) within a shorter period, or even (3) within a longer period, i.e. by extending the repayment period? Is it reasonable to expect the lender to capitalise the interest or not? (h) Are there any reasons affecting the security which should influence the length of the period for payment? In the light of the answers to the above, the court can proceed to exercise its overall discretion, taking account also of any further factors which may arise in the particular case. (at pp. 357–8)

The key point is that it will not be every case in which the 'reasonable period' should be the rest of the mortgage agreement's term, although that should be the starting point; *Norgan* was, perhaps, a strong example of the merits of that starting point. However, the court noted the need for a more intrusive statement of the borrower's income and expenditure than had previously been the case as a result (at p. 353, Waite LJ).

A different approach is taken by the courts in cases of voluntary sale by the borrower where the mortgage lender is seeking possession. In such cases, the courts have tended to say that, provided there is clear evidence that a sale will occur within 6 to 12 months, that should be regarded as a 'reasonable period' (*National and Provincial Bank* v. *Lloyd* (1995) 28 HLR 459). However, in *Bristol & West BS* v. *Ellis* (1997) 29 HLR 282, the Court of Appeal said that the extent of the period depended on the circumstances of the case:

> It all depends on the individual circumstances of each case, though the important factors in most are likely to be the extent to which the mortgage debt and arrears are secured by the value of the property and the effect of time on that security. Where the property is already on the market and there is some indication of delay on the part of the mortgagor, it may be that a short period of suspension of only a

few months would be reasonable (see *e.g.* [*Target Home Loans* v. *Clothier* (1992) 25 HLR 48]). Where there is likely to be considerable delay in selling the property and/or its value is close to the total of the mortgage debt and arrears so that the mortgagee is at risk as to the adequacy of the security, immediate possession or only a short period of suspension may be reasonable. Where there has already been considerable delay in realising a sale of the property and/or the likely sale proceeds are unlikely to cover the mortgage debt and arrears or there is simply no sufficient evidence as to sale value, the normal order would be for immediate possession. (pp. 287–8)

One final amendment protects tenants of the borrower against possession being claimed 'over their heads' by the mortgage lender. A tenancy agreement granted after a mortgage will not bind the mortgage lender, unless the lender has consented to the tenancy taking priority over the mortgage – in principle, therefore, the lender is therefore entitled to possession irrespective of the existence of the tenancy agreement (*Britannia BS* v. *Earl* [1990] 1 WLR 422) but possibly such an order would not be granted if the mortgage lender is not seeking possession in good faith (*Quennell* v. *Maltby* [1979] 1 WLR 318, *quaere* whether *Quennell* is good law, or restricted to its own facts, because the right to possession does not depend on the mortgage lender's motivations in theory). The Mortgage Repossessions (Protection of Tenants) Act 2010 and the Dwelling Houses (Execution of Possession Orders by Mortgagees) Regulations 2010 (SI 2010/1809) alter the rules regarding possession claims to provide limited protection to certain private-sector tenants (see Chapter 11 above).

Rent arrears

This section is split into five parts. In the first part, consideration is given to the significant changes affecting social-housing management regarding arrears of rent. What we find is that there has been a shift from generic housing management to subject-specific expertise. The second part concerns the significant PAP affecting claims for rent arrears. The third and fourth parts discuss the issues arising around rent arrears possession claims, first, in law, and second, from the position of the judges hearing such claims. The final part discusses the problematic, baleful concept of the 'tolerated trespasser' and the attempts at resolving the problems it created both in the courts and legislation.

The focus in this section is on social housing rent arrears possession cases as few private landlords will use the discretionary grounds for rent arrears, preferring the mandatory grounds, especially the mandatory notice procedure for terminating an AST. On the other hand, secure tenancies can only be terminated for rent arrears on discretionary grounds; and many PRPs, which grant either ATs or ASTs, rely only on discretionary grounds for rent arrears (just 25 per cent of PRPs surveyed in one study relied on mandatory grounds – Pawson et al. 2010: table 5.10).

Just as with mortgage lenders, there was clear regulatory guidance in the PRP sector that possession claims should be a last resort (Housing Corporation 2005: 3.2c). The Housing Corporation issued a circular in 2007 which stated that rent arrears possession claims

> should not be started against a tenant who can demonstrate that they have:
> - a reasonable expectation of eligibility for housing benefit;
> - provided the local authority with all the evidence required to process a housing benefit claim; and
> - paid required personal contributions towards the charges.

The TSA's regulatory framework (2010: 3.1) does not repeat that level of pre-scription, but makes clear that '[PRPs] shall develop and provide services that will support tenants to maintain their tenancy and prevent unnecessary evictions'. Good practice guidance for local authorities on rent arrears has consistently made clear the position that possession claims should be a last resort (see ODPM 2005c). As we shall see, the rent arrears PAP for social landlords reinforces the position that possession should be a last resort.

Managing rent arrears

It is helpful to keep in mind the significance of rent arrears possession claims in social housing management. Revenue from rent is a significant element in the business operation of social landlords – in the case of PRPs, it is used to service the debt and loans are made, as well as their terms, on the basis that a certain proportion of the rent will be collected. Decisions to seek possession, therefore, should be seen as part of the wider matrix of the funding and regulation of social housing. Non-payment of rent puts the business operation in jeopardy; however, tenancy turnover also 'generates significant costs for landlords, as each additional property falling vacant incurs revenue costs in relation to repair, cleaning and reservicing the property as well as the costs in lost rent while it remains empty and the costs of reletting the property to another tenant' (Pawson and Munro 2010: 146). Thus, social landlords must balance their business operations, which may account for their selection processes at the point of letting (Cowan et al. 2009).

Most social housing possession claims are brought at least on a rent arrears ground either solely or in combination with another ground for possession (such as nuisance). The statistics range from 90% in one study (Neuberger 2003) to 98% of notices served on the grounds of rent arrears and 93% of evictions related to rent arrears, representing 0.64% as a proportion of stock (Pawson et al. 2005). However, as with mortgage possessions, there are a number of voluntary possessions in the sector as well (Pawson and Munro 2010).

The causes of rent arrears are similar to the causes of mortgage arrears – loss of employment or changes in employment status, relationship breakdown, low-income status, multiple debts. However, there is one compounding factor in relation to the social sector – the administration of HB. Approximately 59 per cent of social renting households are in receipt of HB (about 2.27 million households) (CLG 2010c: tables 3.2 and 3.4), which is either received as a rebate, if the landlord is a local authority (that is, a reduced rent payable to the local authority landlord), or by way of payment if the landlord is a PRP (usually made directly to the PRP – although this may change in the future).

A number of studies have demonstrated how problematic administration of HB (including delays in processing claims, recovery of overpayments, the verification framework, and communication difficulties between housing department and HB administration) produced rent arrears and court-based action for their recovery (Pawson et al. 2005; Blandy 2007). In some cases, landlords served notices before commencing possession claims to *force* HB departments to process claims (Pawson et al. 2005; 2010). That having been said, there is more recent evidence that HB administration has improved nationally, although pockets of poor performance remain, so that the average time taken to process new claims has reduced from 42 days in 2003/2004 to 25 days in 2007/2008 (Pawson et al. 2010). Although it is difficult to draw a clear correlation, this improvement may be one reason also why the number of possession claims have reduced since 2004/2005.

This development ties in with subtle shifts in social housing management regarding rent arrears. Social housing management tends to undulate and conform to the expression 'what goes around comes around'. There has been a tendency to move from generic housing management, under which officers have general management (including rent arrears) of a 'patch', to specific roles, such as dealing with rent arrears alone, and back again. At present, there has been a shift towards the specific roles for a number of reasons. Rent arrears management is not perhaps the most glamorous element of social housing management, and generic housing officers may not prioritise this part of their job. A focus on revenue, however, within the organisation is likely to target rent arrears management as a specific task. Equally importantly, though, one of the key policy priorities in recent years has been the prevention of homelessness and stopping the 'revolving door' of eviction from social housing was regarded as contributing to that endeavour. Finally, it was recognised that strategies designed to prevent rent arrears were more cost-effective than the cure (see, especially, ODPM 2005c).

Thus, a number of changes have accompanied the shift towards specific rent arrears officers. At the symbolic level, they may be labelled 'income maximisation officers' or 'local account managers', both to demonstrate to tenants that the organisation is taking rent arrears management seriously as well as give an element of prestige to the role itself; and they may be part of a central team of officers, as opposed to being patch-based (Pawson et al. 2010). These titles also symbolise the shift in culture within organisations as they seek to assist their occupiers literally to maximise their income through receipt of benefits (and some PRPs and local authorities employ in-house welfare benefits advisors for this purpose). Occupiers are assisted with their HB claims at the outset of their occupation. Equally, officers generally seek to 'responsibilise' their occupiers into, in the housing management vernacular, 'taking responsibility for their rent account'; occupiers are no longer regarded as passive recipients of state bounty through HB but are required to be actively ensuring that their rent account is up-to-date. The model for all of this is private sector debt collection, but there is one 'stand-out motif' and that is that sustaining a tenancy is *the* primary concern and eviction is regarded as a failure (Pawson et al. 2010: 95).

The rent arrears pre-action protocol

In October 2006, the CJC issued the *Pre-action Protocol for Possession Claims based on Rent Arrears* (CJC 2006; the 'rent arrears PAP'). Unlike the mortgage arrears PAP, the rent arrears PAP contains significant penalties for non-compliance with its terms:

> If the landlord unreasonably fails to comply with the terms of the protocol, the court may impose one or more of the following sanctions –
> (a) an order for costs;
> (b) in cases other than those brought solely on mandatory grounds, adjourn, strike out or dismiss claims. (para. 14)

Although there has been no research into the operation of the rent arrears PAP across courts, anecdotal experience suggests that failure to follow it will, in some courts, result in the adjournment of a claim, at best. Indeed, as stated in the preamble to the rent arrears PAP, its terms do no more than has been suggested as good practice, including contact with the tenant to assess their financial circumstances and ability to pay, providing the rent statements regularly, assist with benefits claims, and make adjustments where the occupier has a relevant impairment. In particular, the rent arrears PAP says that a claim should not be made where the occupier has provided the authority with all documents required for an HB claim with an expectation that they will receive an amount towards the rent from HB, and the occupier has paid other sums not covered by HB (such as certain utilities) (para. 7). Further, the landlord should 'make direct contact with the relevant HB department before taking enforcement action' (ibid.).

It is clear that the PAP has been particularly influential in shaping the changes in housing management. For example, it is usual for the same officers responsible for rent arrears management, or another housing officer, to present the social landlord's claim to possession in court (unlike mortgage lenders) or appear in person as a witness. Failure to comply with the rent arrears PAP may then leave a direct imprint on that person and the organisation if the judge takes a view on the landlord's approach to the protocol and court practice suggests that they require such compliance (in one court, apparently, requiring a checklist to be completed by the landlord: Pawson et al. 2010: 46). Pawson et al. (2010: 84–6) found that PRP practice had been altered significantly in consequence of the rent arrears PAP, and the three most common areas of change were a more-structured, thorough and consistent practice (including better documentation of pre-action casework); a more pro-active, preventative approach; increased awareness of vulnerability issues.

Equally, though, Pawson et al. (2010: ch. 6) were able to demonstrate how the operationalisation of the expression 'last resort' by PRPs and individual offic-ers differs depending on the context of their operation, the significance to the organisation of rent arrears management, and the relationship of the officer with the tenant. There are key questions here, such as whether the tenant has engaged with the officer, and the officer's perception of the willingness of the tenant to take responsibility for the rent account, down to the officer's use of the organisation's ICT rent arrears management system (that is, to what extent does the system, which prompts certain actions at certain stages, manage the officer or the officer manage the system?). While the key motif may be sustainability, that motif must be manipulated in the everyday work of the officer.

Discretionary rent arrears possession claims: the law

The landlord must show, in relation to a secure tenancy, that 'rent lawfully due from the tenant has not been paid' (Ground 1, Sch. 2, Housing Act 1985); in relation to an AT, the landlord must show that:

> Some rent lawfully due from the tenant
> (a) is unpaid on the date on which the proceedings for possession are begun; and
> (b) … was in arrears at the date of the service of the notice under that section relating to those proceedings. (Ground 10, Sch. 2, Housing Act 1988)

And/or:

> Whether or not any rent is in arrears on the date on which proceedings for pos-session are begun, the tenant has persistently delayed paying rent which has become lawfully due. (Ground 11, Sch. 2, Housing Act 1988)

There is no equivalent to Ground 11 in the Housing Act 1985 for secure tenan-cies. In addition to proving that the relevant ground is available to the landlord, the landlord must also demonstrate that it is 'reasonable' for the court to make a possession order (s. 84(2), Housing Act 1985; s. 7(4), Housing Act 1988). The court has a wide discretion regarding reasonableness and most factors are rele-vant (including compliance with the rent arrears PAP) (*Cresswell* v. *Hodgson* [1951] 2 KB 92; *Cumming* v. *Danson* [1942] 2 All ER 653). In *Cresswell*, the Court of Appeal said (p. 95):

> the county court judge must look at the effect of the order on each party to it. I do not see how it is possible to consider whether it is reasonable to make an order unless you consider its effect on landlord and tenant, firstly if you make

it and secondly if you do not. I do not think we should say anything which restricts the circumstances which the county court judge should take into consideration.

So, for example, the following may be relevant factors: issues with HB, the length of the tenancy, the behaviour of the tenant, the ability of the tenant to meet the rental obligation; and the arrears of rent involved.

Both the 1985 and 1988 Acts extend the discretion of the court regarding the orders it may make – the court may stay or suspend execution of the order or postpone the date for possession (s. 85(2); s. 9(1)) and, in such circumstances, the court can impose terms on the payment of the rent and arrears (s. 85(3); s. 9(2)). Once a decision on 'reasonableness' has been made by the judge, it is extremely difficult to persuade a higher court to overturn that judgment – indeed, usually, this can only be done if the judgment is outside the margins of acceptability because there has been an error of principle, mistake of law or the decision was plainly wrong (see, for example, *Whitehouse* v. *Lee* [2010] HLR 11; *Bracknell Forest BC* v. *Green* [2009] HLR 38).

There are certain procedural requirements for beginning a claim and the evidence which the landlord must demonstrate (CPR 55 and the Practice Direction). In general terms, a court is entitled to decide the claim at the first hearing, or it may make case management directions (CPR 55.8). That hearing is not a 'trial', a technical but important point because the order can be set aside on the broader grounds in CPR 3.1(2) than the stricter considerations for setting aside trial judgments elsewhere in the CPR (*Forcelux Ltd* v. *Binnie* [2010] HLR 20). However, those stricter requirements may be relevant in local authority possession cases (at least) (*Hackney LBC* v. *Findlay* [2011] EWCA Civ 8; express reference to s. 85(2), Housing Act 1985, at [24] suggests that this may be limited to local authorities, but the judgment appears to be framed wider as well, because of the significance placed by the Court of Appeal on the general principle of finality to proceedings, the relevance of the rent arrears PAP, and 'best practice of social landlords' to inform the tenant of the proceedings – at [24] – together with its description of *Forcelux* as an unusual case).

Rent arrears possession claims: judicial perspectives

The social reality of possession claims provides an important context for the consideration of the law. Claims are usually heard on 'possession days' in courts and busy days can lead to lists of around sixty claims. Each claim is allocated five minutes. Claims which appear to raise tricky issues of principle or fact are adjourned off to other days. District judges hearing such claims in county courts have four or five possible decisions on a claim – they may dismiss it, adjourn it, make an order but suspend its execution (SPO), make a possession order but postpone its effect until a future date which may or may not be specified (PPO), or grant an outright possession order.

In order to get through the list, district judges, like other 'street-level bureaucrats' (Lipsky 1980), need coping strategies or mechanisms to simplify the job, otherwise it may become unmanageable. They also need ways to cope with the 'emotional labour' of doing the job (see, in particular, Roach Anleu and Mack 2005). Cowan, Blandy and Hunter et al. (2006) develop typologies of district judge approaches to possession proceedings from their interviews with 26 such judges. They describe three particular types – the patrician, the formalist and the liberal – suggesting that these types respond differently in terms of their role, the understanding of the cause and nature of the problem, and their depiction of the occupier's behaviour. The researchers also encountered what they called the 'idiosyncrat', who did it their own way, actively going against the grain (p. 566). The point of this approach was not to suggest that district judges adopt one such type or, indeed, do not develop their style of judging over time, but rather to explain the differences between their approaches. The regular critique is that different courts will decide the same cases differently and, further, different judges in the same court will decide the same cases differently. In some respects, of course, that is the point of the discretion vested in the district judge.

The types of coping strategies employed by district judges include the client-processing mentality, which engaged Michael Lipsky in his studies of street-level bureaucracy (1980; Hunter et al. 2005; Cowan and Hitchings 2007). Although all cases are, by their nature, different, they are also repetitive and the limits of the enquiry mean that they can also be categorised by the district judge, so that informal rules and routines develop. For example, they may have a rule not to make any form of possession order when the arrears are less than (say) £500, but above which they will make an SPO or PPO (their choice of the type of order perhaps being determined by current practice and thinking in relation to the tolerated trespasser concept, see below). They may develop strategies to discriminate between the worthy and unworthy (or deserving and undeserving), to develop trust in the landlord through its representative (which may result in less attention being given to the paperwork, for example). Further, as Cowan and Hitchings (2007: 373) note:

> [District judges] acted out their version of the social in possession proceedings, which could be a powerful driver in their work. Social landlord cases were treated differently from private renting and mortgage possession cases. In some courts, there were social landlord possession 'days', partly because of the sheer numbers and partly because the principles were different from the private sector. Our [district judge] interviewees clearly marked out social landlord cases as *different*. For example, it was said that social landlords should lean in favour of the tenant, should not bring proceedings where housing benefit was at issue, or should not apply for a mandatory possession order. For some of our interviewees there was a clear link made between the trust they placed in the landlord and the social nature of that landlord.

The 'worthy tenant' demonstrated their adherence to the rule of law through attendance at the hearing – more often than not, a non-attending occupier was the one against whom a possession order was made because they were not regarded as demonstrating sufficient willingness to pay nor respect for the court. Finally, Cowan and Hitchings noted how rent arrears possession procedures (from court practice to the arrangement of waiting areas) were designed to obtain agreements between landlord and tenant, at the door of the court, which could then be rubber-stamped by the district judge. This was a rational strategy on the part of the district judges simply to enable them to get through the list.

Thus, what appears to be a legalistic process, unconstrained by rights of appeal (effectively) and by case law, turned out to be a narrowly confined 'series of taken-for-granted assumptions …. In order to cope with their caseload, DJs produced principles and rules from their discretion.' (Cowan and Hitchings 2007: 379) Further,

> Lipsky assists us with empathizing with the DJs in our study, if not sympathizing with the predicament in which they find themselves. We are able to explain away some of the more tendentious approaches and strategies by naturalizing them through an examination of context. We could not say that we found some approaches tasteful (to say the least), nor that we approved of them. Indeed, sitting in a courtroom observing an occupier being told off by somebody who clearly revels in the role is an experience to make even the hardiest empiricist squirm.

In other words, the approach taken by district judges in rent arrears possession cases is both complex, depending on a range of actors often related to their understanding of the 'social', and simplified, through processes of rule-making, routine and trust. Parts of the process, including the district judge's explanation of the outcome to the tenant can, in their own way, be as telling about the district judge as about the tenant.

The tolerated trespasser

There is little doubt that the 'tolerated trespasser' debacle has been one of the worst blots on the legal landscape; created by judicial interpretation (probably incorrectly in the first place: *Knowsley HT* v. *White* [2009] AC 636; *Austin* v. *Southwark LBC* [2010] UKSC 10) in 1986 (*Thompson* v. *Elmbridge BC* [1987] 1 WLR 1425, with little by way of reasoning) and subsequently nodded into effect by the House of Lords with little discussion (because it was not directly in issue: *Burrows* v. *Brent LBC* [1996] 1 WLR 1448; see the discussion in *Austin* at [21], Lord Hope).

It has been judicially described as a 'conceptually peculiar, even oxymoronic, status' (Lord Neuberger, in *White*, at [79]); 'this unfortunate zombie-like creature achieved a sort of half-life only through a series of judicial decisions in which courts failed, or did not need, to face up to the theoretical and practical contradictions inherent in the notion' (Lord Walker, in *Austin*, at [43]); the early judicial decisions 'set the law on a course which was wrong in principle and

wrong in practice. They produced a position with which no-one was happy –
neither the landlords nor the tenants' (Baroness Hale, in *Austin*, at [56]).

Just what is this unliked, oxymoronic creature, the tolerated trespasser? Put
simply, it is a secure tenant's status after the conditions attached to an SPO have
been breached. Practically all SPOs (or, indeed, PPOs) granted on the basis
of rent arrears are breached, usually fairly immediately if HB is in payment in
arrears; and usually for no fault of either landlord or tenant, the lack of fault
being irrelevant for these purposes. That having been said, though, most social
landlords would not seek a warrant to evict an occupier who has made some
payments to the rent account for the reasons given above. However, in law, they
are so entitled (or entitled to apply). There were further undesirable consequences: the statutory RTB was, in theory, ended; the landlord had no repairing
obligations because there was no tenancy (but these rights revived with the tenancy: *Lambeth LBC* v. *Rogers* (1999) 32 HLR 361); it was unclear whether the
landlord had obligations under the Defective Premises Act 1972; it was unclear
whether the tolerated trespasser had any 'rights' which survived a stock transfer (see *Bristol CC* v. *Hassan* [2006] 1 WLR 2582, at [34]). However, the tenancy might be revived by order of the court, setting out new conditions, which
would also revive some of those obligations and, in the case of the repairing
covenant, it could be backdated; or, perhaps exceptionally, a new tenancy could
be inferred from the actions of the landlord such as treating the tolerated trespasser as a tenant (cf. *Burrows*).

The reason for this unfortunate outcome depended on the interpretation
of the statutory provisions and the relevant court order. The focus here is on
secure tenancies because the House of Lords subsequently held that the tolerated trespasser outcome did not afflict the AT regime (*White*); it could not do
so in relation to secure tenancies because of the line of unchallenged authority
from *Thompson*, which had been assumed to be correct and acted on in 'tens of
thousands of cases', particularly after Parliament had sought to solve the problem (*White*, [92]–[3], Lord Neuberger).

The problem arose by the combination of ss. 82 and 85, Housing Act 1985.
Section 82(2) states: 'Where the landlord obtains an order for the possession of
the dwelling-house, the tenancy ends on the date on which the tenant is to give
up possession in pursuance of the order.' Section 85, headed 'extended discretion of court in possession claims', says at (2)–(4):

(2) On the making of an order for possession of such a dwelling-house on any
      of those grounds [for possession], or at any time before the execution of the
      order, the court may –
      (a) stay or suspend the execution of the order, or
      (b) postpone the date of possession,
   for such period or periods as the court thinks fit.
(3) On such an adjournment, stay, suspension or postponement the court –
      (a) shall impose conditions with respect to the payment by the tenant of
            arrears of rent (if any) and rent or payments in respect of occupation

after the termination of the tenancy (mesne profits), unless it considers that to do so would cause exceptional hardship to the tenant or would otherwise be unreasonable, and

(b) may impose such other conditions as it thinks fit.

(4) If the conditions are complied with, the court may, if it thinks fit, discharge or rescind the order for possession.

In *Thompson*, the standard form of order (Form N28) then in use gave possession to the landlord but it was not to be 'enforced for 28 days in any event, and for so long thereafter as the defendant punctually pays … [the arrears and] costs by instalments of £10 per week in addition to the current rent'. The two-judge Court of Appeal, in an *ex tempore* judgment, said that this order suspended the tenancy but that, on breach, the tenancy immediately comes to an end. In 1993, the standard form order was amended so that the opening paragraph said: 'The court has decided unless you make the payments as set out in paragraph 2 you must give the plaintiff possession of [property] on …[insert date].' This did not ameliorate the problem; there was a further amendment in 2001: '1. The defendant give the claimant possession of … on or before … 20 … 5. This order is not to be enforced so long as the defendant pays the claimant the rent arrears and the amount for use and occupation [and costs, totalling] by the payments set out below in addition to the current rent.' The 2001 amendment made matters worse. In *Harlow DC* v. *Hall* [2006] 1 WLR 2116, the Court of Appeal (in quite dramatic circumstances) held that this order, in fact, terminated the secure tenancy on the date set out in the opening paragraph even if the occupier did not breach the order (in accordance with s. 82(2)), and it was only the execution of that order which para. 5 suspended (in accordance with s. 85(2)). Subsequently, in *Bristol CC* v. *Hassan* [2006] 1 WLR 2582, the Court of Appeal formulated a suggested standard form order which postponed possession to an unspecified date to be fixed by the court on the application of the landlord if the terms of the order were breached. This was the standard form of order (Form N28A) which courts tended to use thereafter, instead of an SPO when making an order short of outright possession.

As Baroness Hale put it in *Austin* (at [46]): 'It is a fair assumption that there are many old possession orders around which had an effect which the court making them would have avoided if it had known how to do so. The acquisition of trespasser "status" was accidental not intentional. It was also very common.' A tolerated trespasser could, however, apply to the court for an order which retrospectively revived the tenancy prior to execution of the original possession order (s. 85(2)), and which also retrospectively revived the repairing obligation as well as the RTB. In *Austin*, it was held that the tolerated trespasser's next of kin could also make such an application which would then enable a succession to the tenancy to occur.

A practice also emerged for 'proleptic' discharge of the order – in other words, a paragraph was inserted into the order to the effect that the order would be of no effect if the arrears and other payments (such as costs) were made in full (for example: 'Upon payment of the arrears in full, claim do stand dismissed', para. 6 of the order in *Honeygan-Green* v. *Islington LBC* [2009] AC 636, at [64]; or 'When you have paid the total amounts mentioned, the plaintiff will not be able to take any steps to evict you as a result of this order', para. 4 of the order in *Porter* v. *Shepherds Bush HA* [2009] AC 636, at [59]). It had previously been held that such a clause was of no effect; and further, perhaps even more illogically, if the order itself had been breached but the tolerated trespasser paid off the amount owed in full, then they could not apply to the court under s. 85(2), because the order had no effect and could not be amended, nor under s. 85(4), because the order had not been complied with (*Marshall* v. *Bradford MDC* [2002] HLR 428; *Swindon Borough Council* v. *Aston* [2003] HLR 610). The House of Lords in *White* held that those cases had been wrongly decided on this point, that a proleptic discharge could be included in the original order, and did not need to be related to the other terms of the order (cf. Lord Mance, in dissent on this point at [7]–[26]).

The Housing and Regeneration Act 2008, Sch. 11, has resolved most of the issues which might now arise in relation to previous tolerated trespassers by the expedient of creating 'replacement tenancies' which arose at the date of commencement of the schedule, provided that the occupier fulfils the 'home condition' (that the property has been their only or principal home throughout: para. 16(2)) and the ex-landlord is entitled to let the property (para. 16(1)(a)(ii), causing issues to arise if the property has been the subject of an LSVT but again ameliorated by the Housing (Replacement of Terminated Tenancies) (Successor Landlords) (England) Order 2009, SI 2009/1262, see CLG 2009e: 23–30). The replacement tenancy is a secure tenancy on the same terms as the previous secure tenancy (paras. 17–19) and for certain specified purposes ('relevant purposes'), determining whether the occupier is a successor and for the qualifying period for the RTB, treated as being the same and continuous and uninterrupted (para. 21(1)–(2)). However, where the former tolerated trespasser brings a claim of a specified type ('relevant claims'), including disrepair, the court has a discretion whether to treat the two tenancies as the same or continuing uninterrupted (para. 21(3)–(4)). The schedule has also cured the drafting 'defect' in the 1985 Act by making clear that a secure tenancy only ends on the date of execution of the possession order (Part I, although, after *Porter* v. *Shepherds Bush HA*, the government decided not to alter s. 85(4) – CLG 2009e: paras. 18–20).

Conclusions

There is a certain amount of overlap between owner-occupiers and social renters both in the causes of arrears and their consequences. Relationship breakdown, loss of employment, multiple debts, the uncertainty of welfare benefits are all causes of housing debt. Social renters are more likely to have arrears as a result of HB issues, to be sure, but at a general level the causes are the same.

Equally, the consequences are the same at least in terms of regulation – possession is, or should be, the last resort. However, as this chapter has demonstrated, the procedure for dealing with housing debt is rather different, let alone the law. There are differences between the terms of the PAPs, although their effect may not be entirely dissimilar (with attempts being made at compliance), and the approach of the courts to their different jurisdictions, albeit both heavily dependent on interpretation of the word 'reasonable', tends to be different.

The nature of the obligation entered into by the owner with the mortgage lender is, of course, different in law from the nature of the obligation entered into by the occupier with the social landlord. The government has sought to protect owners from the consequences of losing their home as a result of mortgage arrears, but it has done little to protect the social tenant from the same consequence. Fox (2007) argues that the value of 'home' – a concept beyond tenure, in the sense that it is not tenure-dependent – is one which the law can and should recognise. It does, of course, do so formally by recognition of the compatibility of the different sets of procedures and legal values with the European Convention of Human Rights (it being assumed, rightly, that the processes described in this chapter are compliant with the Article 8 right to respect for home and family life – see *Manchester CC* v. *Pinnock* [2010] UKSC 45, at [55]–[6]). However, it is equally important to recognise that possession proceedings based on arrears are context dependent, the context being the separate histories of each sector and, in particular, the private nature of mortgage lending as opposed to the public nature of social housing.

15

Anti-social behaviour

To say that ASB has been a policy and legislative, as well as academic, focus for the past fifteen or so years would be an understatement. There have been a range of interventions – legislative and non-legislative – aimed at preventing further bad conduct and encouraging good conduct. Crawford (2009: 817–18) identified eighteen noteworthy 'regulatory tools' with ASB at their heart since 1996, not all of which were new, but which had been significantly expanded in scope and use in recent years. The relationship between ASB and housing, in particular, tenure, has been one of the cornerstones of this regulatory intervention, although it is also right to say that the policy rhetoric is now oriented in a more tenure-neutral way. Nevertheless, the discovery of, and interventions to deal with, ASB have lead to a seismic shift in the way housing tenure, specifically social housing, is managed and its residents controlled. These processes were already in place but have been magnified and intensified, and the evidence is that most of the interventions are used by social landlords and against their residents at the residents' request.

This chapter begins by locating the definition of ASB at a broad level, narrowing down to its focus on tenure. One of the key questions here is why was it that social housing was initially targeted? Equally, the consequences of that focus at the level of housing management are discussed in this section, drawing attention to the recalibration of the housing management role. The next section begins with some of the 'softer', non-statutory regulatory tools in operation, moving on to the forms of injunction currently in operation, to the new form of social housing tenure (introductory and starter tenancies, the demoted tenancy and family intervention tenancy), and then to claims for possession based on nuisance, the close relative of ASB. The presentation of the material here is designed to reflect the rational, pyramid structure of interventions (Ayres and Braithwaite 1992); but it should always be borne in mind that such a neat structure is not always operationalised in practice, so that interventions can begin at the top of the pyramid. The final section, by way of conclusion, offers further observations.

Locating anti-social behaviour

Before digging down into the formal legal definitions of ASB, this section begins with some broad commentary on the nature and notion of ASB, but its primary focus is to demonstrate the tenure basis of the definition and, as importantly, the consequences of that tenure focus.

Defining anti-social behaviour

As we go on to see in the next section, the definition of ASB is not necessarily fixed by the acts of the perpetrator but by their effects on the community, locality or neighbourhood.

For example, Prior (2009: 9) noted the Home Office website definition of ASB as 'any activity that impacts on other people in a negative way'. It is an 'affective' concept, driven by local perceptions of metaphor and interpretation (Atkinson and Flint 2003; Mackenzie et al. 2010). Those local perceptions are themselves driven by feelings of insecurity and a demand for greater security through reclaiming the neighbourhood (Home Office 2003a: paras. 1.5–7; Millie 2007; Johnsen and Fitzpatrick 2010). Different official lists of the type of behaviour constituting ASB have been produced at different times and for different purposes (Carr and Cowan 2006: 58–64).

It has been notable that there is an absence of any comprehensive national dataset (Prior 2009: 7) and social landlords have not maintained recording systems capable of mapping trends in the number and location of complaints (Pawson, Davidson and Lederle 2007). A one-day count of ASB was conducted in 2003, using questionable statistical techniques. This discovered 66,107 reports made to participating agencies, equating 'to more than one report every 2 seconds or around 16.5 million reports every year. ASB recorded on the day of the count cost agencies in England and Wales at least £13.5m; this equates to around £3.4b a year.' (Home Office 2003b) In effect, the answer to the question of definition has been: 'you know it when you see it' (Millie 2007: 613); or to regard its existence as common sense; or to make rhetorical assertions about its existence and linking it with a societal breakdown in respect and responsibility (Home Office 2003a). Critics are decried (a personal favourite, drawn from *The Guardian*, is the following comment, 'After all, they [i.e. perpetrators of ASB] cannot *all* be sent to live next door to nice Professor Ashworth', the Vinerian professor of English law, who dared to criticise the Crime and Disorder Bill in 1998: Bennett 1998).

The disappointing lack of centrally collected data has not been mirrored by a lack of academic endeavour. Scott and Parkey (1998: 329), in an early attempt at definition, identified a 'spectrum … comprising three distinct (yet potentially interrelated) phenomena, these being: neighbour disputes, neighbourhood problems and crime problems'. Hunter et al. (1998: 2) suggested that the choice of label used – nuisance, disputes, behaviour – 'may well reflect a conclusion about the appropriate response: punitive responses to "anti-social behaviour", and attempts to mediate agreement in "neighbour disputes"'. Cowan and McDermont (2006) identified the lack of definition as a classic example of obscurity as a tool of governance, in the sense that the definitional obscurity enabled greater regulatory intervention (see also Prior 2009: 18).

That having been said, the statistical evidence does not suggest that the majority of the population suffer ill-effects from ASB (Millie 2007). Drilling down into the available statistical data, however, enables certain patterns to emerge. Millie et al. (2005) and Upson (2006) found a link between ASB concerns and relative deprivation, reflecting data on broader concerns linking fear of crime with poverty (Pantazis 1999); the National Audit Office (2006b: para. 1.6) noted its higher effects (in terms of perception) in 'hard-pressed' areas, those living in social rented housing, or from an ethnic minority; Flatley et al. (2008) similarly found that the following factors were most strongly associated with high levels of ASB: levels of deprivation, low levels of community cohesion, being a victim of crime in the previous 12 months, not living in northern regions of England, age, and living in an area for 3 or more years.

The emergence of anti-social behaviour

The emergence of ASB as a phenomenon was due to a number of contextual factors which were not necessarily interrelated but coalesced around its identification as a policy problem demanding intervention. One not inconsequential factor was the pioneering 'neighbours from hell' type of television programme, which began in the early 1990s (Jacobs et al. 2003: 441). A second factor was a shift in understandings of the causes of crime, so that they became regarded in certain criminological strands as situational and choice-based, requiring preventative solutions (Crawford 2003 : 484–5). Third, there was a rapidly emerging discourse about crime and policing that placed risk at its heart (classically, see Feeley and Simon 1992; O'Malley 1992; Ericson and Haggerty 1997), largely because of a recognition that crime control was a failing enterprise (as the 'political arm of the state has frequently engaged in a form of denial [of its limits] which appears increasingly hysterical in the clinical sense of that term' – Garland 1996: 459). Fourth, and linked to that shift to risk, was the untroubled policy transference of the 'broken windows' thesis (Wilson and Kelling 1982; Crawford 1999: 816) from the US to the UK, which diagnosed the problem of crime as starting with low levels of ' "untended" behaviour' leading to the breakdown of community (see, in particular, Home Office 2003b: paras. 1.8–10, 'The spiral of anti-social behaviour'); as well as the different ways in which the 'new' concepts of the 'underclass' and social exclusion began to be operationalised in social policy (Murray 1990; Levitas 2005). Fifth, there was a shift at the heart of British politics to a contractualist ideology through which reciprocal rights and responsibilities were both recognised as of equal weight (Squires 2008: 307). Sixth, there was a recognition within politics of a breakdown in criminal justice, arising from an over-zealous adherence to due process at the risk of victims and respectful, civilising conduct (Crawford 1999: 815; Squires 2006; Powell and Flint 2009).

One consequence of the 'broken windows' thesis was an intensification of policing on low-level behaviours, which could take the form and style of 'zero tolerance' and micro-management (Crawford 1999: 814). An alternative format for intervention was through the 'community', a largely imagined form of different spatial characteristics, which became 'responsibilised' into crime control strategies and techniques. The foundations of David Cameron's current predilection for the 'Big Society' can be found in much of these engagements for the crime prevention approach pursued by previous governments emphasised 'active citizenship', 'partnerships' and 'multi-agency working' (Cowan 1997; Crawford 1997). Furthermore, 'within state agencies themselves, organizational change has been introduced to further these ends, with promotion of strategic planning, inter-agency co-operation, and shared decision making between departments which were previously separate' (Garland 1996: 453). These developments themselves had already been in place for some time (see, for example, Sampson et al. 1988), but were reinforced by New Labour's adoption of 'joined-up' working. The manifestations include the introduction of multi-agency crime and disorder strategies, numerous regeneration schemes (particularly coming from the Social Exclusion Unit (SEU) and the New Deal policies), together with the introduction of multi-agency risk assessments of certain persons (see, for example, SEU 1998).

A slightly tangential point about the 'location' of ASB is that there is con-siderable local variation in the use of the regulatory interventions identified in the next section of this chapter (NAO 2006b). Most areas use the lower-level types of contractual interventions, such as acceptable behaviour con-tracts (ABCs), but other types of intervention, such as demoted tenancies, were used by less than half of the then existing Crime and Disorder Reduction Partnerships; the explanation for this variation was differences in demog-raphy and deprivation levels (Cooper et al. 2009: 19). There are also variations in the types of interventions used between agencies (and possibly also within agencies, although there is no data on this point) (Pawson et al. 2005 – see below).

Locating housing

In its earliest incarnations, the policy focus on ASB was also located as a focus on ASB in council housing. The DoE consultation paper (DoE 1995c: para. 1.1) began with the following assertion: 'Anti-social behaviour by a small minority of tenants and others is a growing problem on council estates.' Social housing – for the field soon expanded to include PRPs – was a soft target for this focus on ASB, partly because the early interventions were directed at it. The 'neighbours from hell' programmes in the early 1990s depicted social housing with a clear message: 'social housing estates were an inferior form of tenure occupied in the main by dysfunctional families who were unable to coexist peacefully with other residents' (Jacobs et al. 2003: 441).

Social housing organisations had been expressing concern about crime and low-level nuisance for some time, partly because of the appearance of new estates which had proved difficult to let (SEU 1998; Watt and Jacobs 2000) and partly because criminological literature had already identified certain types of social housing as inherently problematic (focusing, for example, on allocations policies which concentrated stigmatised households in unpopular housing – see, for example, Bottoms et al. 1992; Page 1993). They had taken on board the 'environmental determinism' literature (e.g. Newman 1972) that suggested that the architecture of new building could 'design out' crime.

It is also right to note, as does Donoghue (2010), that the available research does suggest that social housing tenure is correlated with higher perceptions of ASB than other tenures, and residents were complaining about ASB. In this vein, Pawson et al. (2005: para. 2.4) noted that there were about 135,000 ASB incidents in social housing (grossing up this figure from the results of a pos-tal questionnaire) and that 'the consensus among social landlords seems to be that there is a genuine underlying upward trend in the problem itself'. The twin processes of residualisation and marginalisation discussed in Chapter 4 above were also very much in evidence in this discussion (see also Murie 1997). A central point is that ASB is largely found in social housing 'because the physical presence of "investigatory" people and technology ensure that it will be found.

Anti-social behaviour is thus partly a *product* of social housing management.'
(Brown 2004: 210–11, original emphasis)

However, the focus on social housing must also be seen in context. The history of social housing can be written as a history of the control and correction of morals, its provision being regarded (certainly by the Victorian philanthropists) as a means of reforming the souls of the poor (see Clapham et al. 1990; Cowan and McDermont 2006; McDermont 2010; Damer 1974; 2000). It has various techniques at its disposal for doing so today, including the allocations/lettings scheme (which might be seen as a process of risk management: Cowan et al. 1999), the tenancy agreement, but, most importantly, a cadre of professional housing officers with management responsibilities. There is an explicitly moral dimension to housing management today, which increasingly encourages self-regulation and responsibility amongst its occupants 'as governing bodies presume to know what constitutes good, appropriate and responsible conduct' (Flint 2002: 622; Haworth and Manzi 1999; Flint 2004) and are increasingly focusing on their propagation (ibid. p. 625). Brown (2004: 206) notes how ASB case reports 'note the level of cleanliness of the perpetrator's home, unusual appearance and personal hygiene, and not only the volume of music but also, if the perpetrator had particularly poor taste, the name of the singer and song'.

Increasingly, social housing management has been reconfigured with specific teams designed to deliver an ASB strategy (Pawson et al. 2005), in conjunction with other organisations through multi-agency partnerships, and employing ex-police officers, communities, as well as software packages in their governance of the populations:

> One motivation here is to expand and refine the surveillance and regulation of particular spaces and specific populations within them. This has its corollary in social landlords' increasingly sophisticated use of bespoke anti-social behaviour software packages such as *REACT* and *Caseworks* and Geographical Information Systems enabling patterns of incidents or complaints to be mapped and analysed and for hotspots to be identified. (Flint and Pawson 2009: 427)

Housing management, a process which has not been fixed definitionally (see Chapter 4 and Chapter 5 above), was able to accommodate these developments – indeed, it largely welcomed them – although they did cause tensions in their operation. For example, Flint (2002: 634) notes how multi-agency working 'risked blurring the discrete governing identity of housing agencies'; and McCarthy (2010) suggests that those multi-agency meetings are led, for the most part, by the police who 'construct and directly steer the discussions towards pre-set agendas'. As Brown (2004: 207) notes, a new profession has formed around ASB, 'but the discourse is one of "common sense" morality rather than pathology'. As the government recognised:

> The focus of housing management is increasingly shifting to become more closely linked with wider neighbourhood management objectives, such as tackling crime and anti-social behaviour, in addition to the more traditional tenancy

and property management that housing managers undertake. (CLG 2007a: para. 7)

In 1995, an influential lobbying organisation, the Social Landlords Crime and Nuisance Group, was set up and appears to have had the ear of policy-makers. It now represents a large body of social landlords and related organisations, with lobbying, training and 'best practice' roles. There was, then, a 'confluence of interests between policing and social housing', through which resources have been levered into the sector but raised concerns about the 'social' response to the issue (Cowan et al. 2001).

The early location of ASB in social housing has been a defining feature of the legislative landscape as discussed in the next section. However, other regulatory forms do appear in the PRS and there has been a recognition that anti-social tenants, who may have been evicted from social housing, exist in the PRS. Thus, selective licensing and HMO licensing have ASB as one of their targets (DTLR 2001; see Chapter 4 above). The issue, though, is the lack of fixity in the identity of private landlords and tenants: 'It is the very amorphousness of this shifting body of individuals, their lack of homogeneity, their lack of need for community relations, and indeed, their amateurishness which creates the central problem of governance – governing the ungovernable' (Carr et al. 2007: 108; Nixon et al. 2003). There are no corresponding regulatory interventions to work with owner-occupiers, although in principle some of the injunctions discussed below can be granted against owner-occupiers, landlords and tenants.

Regulatory and other interventions

In this section, we consider the 'law' concerning the array of regulatory and other interventions through which social housing management seeks to regulate the behaviour of its occupiers and extending the web to other perpetrators of ASB. For the reasons identified in the previous section, it is social housing managers (and the police) who largely have these powers, many of which have been developed entrepreneurially by such landlords or requested by them from central government leading to primary legislation. Before beginning, though, it is important to note that there is no general liability on social landlords in relation to the nuisance acts of their tenants (*Hussain* v. *Lancaster CC* [2000] 1 QB 1). There is no need to take any form of action in relation to ASB against those tenants (beyond the preparation of a strategy). However, a failure to take action may in limited circumstances lead to the landlord adopting the nuisance (and, thus, becoming liable: *Brumby* v. *Octavia Hill HT* [2010] EWHC 1793 (QB), applying the principle from *Sedleigh-Denfield* v. *O'Callaghan* [1940] AC 880).

Non-statutory interventions

A range of non-statutory methods of regulating the conduct of occupiers has been developed by social landlords, sometimes in conjunction with other agencies such as the police. These initiatives include a more precise drafting of the tenancy agreement to restrict the types of behaviours in which occupiers can engage both in the dwelling but also outside it, in the neighbourhood or locality, as well as widening the responsibilities to include visitors and other occupiers of the property. Spelling out such responsibilities clearly and precisely is designed to inform the occupier but also facilitate a claim for possession or an injunction against the occupier. Commentators note that, as a result, tenancy agreements have become lengthier and attention has been drawn to the practices of certain landlords which have tenancy-signing ceremonies (mirroring the ceremonies of newly naturalised persons) (see Flint 2004; Flint and Nixon 2006: 949–50), perhaps to counteract the apparent ignorance of occupiers of their responsibilities (Lister 2006). Further, some landlords have developed complimentary 'good neighbour agreements' to reinforce the interlocking nature of the responsibilities of occupiers (Flint 2004).

Other interventions, while the occupation agreement is running, include an increased use of mediation between neighbours and forms of 'contractual governance', such as ABCs (Crawford 2003: Flint and Nixon 2006: 947–8). ABCs are widely used in the sector (Pawson et al. 2005). Their 'main aim is to lead perpetrators towards recognition both of the impact of their behaviour, and of the need to take responsibility for their actions' (Home Office 2007: 2). They 'cede considerable discretion and quasi-judicial decision-making authority to non-judicial officers' as part of a broader shift to summary justice (Crawford 2009: 820). ABCs are not 'contracts' as recognised by law (there is no consideration either way) and there is no formal sanction for their breach; they are voluntary (in the sense that a household is not required to enter into such an agreement), but they use the contractual language as a form of 'reciprocal contracting' which 'is more likely to affect the behaviour of the parties than the imposition of compulsion by coercive fiat from the state' (Crawford 2003: 489). Agencies, by way of reciprocal obligation, should offer support to address the underlying causes of the behaviour (Home Office 2007). When minors are involved, parents make the contracts on behalf of the minor. However, as Vincent-Jones (2006: 269) suggests: 'The casting of individual responsibilities in contractual terms may be used to focus attention on the state's own reciprocal obligations, and on whether it is delivering its side of the bargain. This opens up new possibilities for increased accountability.'

Refusing an ABC or breaching one can constitute evidence to assist with, or support, a possession claim. Such criminal and pre-criminal sanctioning processes are combined by some social landlords with more positive schemes designed as rewards for good behaviour. Some landlords have developed incentive schemes to reward a 'good customer' through which those customers apply for benefits including shopping vouchers, enhanced repairs services, and other benefits (such as free flower seeds) (Lupton et al. 2003). These schemes have the tripartite purpose of rewarding active tenants, particularly those who do voluntary community work, encourage housing management to 'go the extra mile', and tackle the stigmatisation of the sector through rebranding the image and reputation of social housing (Flint 2004: 162–4).

Forms of injunction

In this section, three forms of injunction are considered, in which social housing organisations are, or may be, involved: anti-social behaviour injunctions (ASBIs); anti-social behaviour orders (ASBOs); and dispersal orders. Social landlords have the power to make an application for either an ASBI or ASBO, and work with police to fashion and oversee areas designated for dispersal orders. The focus in this section is on the ambit of the law, which has, since 1996, developed into a set of coercive powers of considerable breadth. Other forms of injunction are available to local authorities, in particular such as by virtue of s. 222, Local Government Act 1972, but that power should only be exercised in exceptional cases if the local authority could also obtain an ASBO (*Birmingham CC* v. *Shafi* [2009] 1 WLR 1961). There are signs, however, that the range of injunctions and orders available will be much reduced in the future (Wintour and Stratton 2011).

Anti-social behaviour injunctions

ASBIs were and are primarily injunctions designed for use by social housing managers. They were originally introduced in the Housing Act 1996, Part V, but subsequently amended by the Anti-Social Behaviour Act 2003 and the Police and Justice Act 2006. The relevant powers and criteria are contained in ss. 153A–E. Any social landlord, including a charitable housing trust, can apply for an ASBI (s. 153E(7)–(8)). The social landlord must satisfy the court of the following condition:

> that the person against whom the injunction is sought is engaging, has engaged or threatens to engage in housing-related conduct capable of causing a nuisance or annoyance to –
>
> (a) a person with a right (of whatever description) to reside in or occupy housing accommodation owned or managed by a relevant landlord,
> (b) a person with a right (of whatever description) to reside in or occupy other housing accommodation in the neighbourhood of housing accommodation mentioned in paragraph (a),
> (c) a person engaged in lawful activity in, or in the neighbourhood of, housing accommodation mentioned in paragraph (a), or
> (d) a person employed (whether or not by a relevant landlord) in connection with the exercise of a relevant landlord's housing management functions. (s. 153A(3))

The expression 'housing-related' means 'directly or indirectly relating to or affecting the housing management functions of a relevant landlord' (s. 153A(1)); and the word 'conduct' means 'conduct anywhere'. An ASBI can also be obtained against the unlawful use of premises (s. 153B) or against breach of

Court, 78/82 Victoria Road, Aldershot GU11 1SS on Thursday 04th
November 2004 at 14.00 pm.

If you do not attend at the time shown the court may make an injunction
order in your absence. You are entitled to apply to the court to reconsider
the order before that day.

And it is ordered that

Susan Collette [sic] Hartless shall

(4) Leave Midhurst Road, Liphook by 6.00 pm on 29 October 2004.

(5) Exercise proper and reasonable parental control over [AH, BH, CH and
DH] in order to prevent them from behaving in any of the ways referred to
in this order.

It is further ordered that

(6) A Power of Arrest pursuant to Section 153C of the Housing Act 1996 be
attached to paragraphs (1) (2) (3) (4) of this order.

(7) The costs of this application reserved

THIS ORDER SHALL REMAIN IN FORCE UNTIL THE 29 April 2005
unless before then it is revoked by further order of the court.'

The plan attached to the order embraced a large part of Liphook. (at [2]–[3])

The form of order effectively excluded Ms Hartless from her home and the
locality.

First, the court reaffirmed that a without notice injunction is a most extreme
form of order and there should be a 'very good reason' for departing from the
general rule that notice must be given: 'needless to say, the more intrusive the
order, the stronger must be the reasons for the departure' (at [63]). Second, it
would be 'inconceivable' that a court would grant a without notice injunction
unless both conditions in s. 153C(1) were satisfied and the risk of significant
harm to one of the relevant persons during the short period between the time
of service and the return date (at [81]). Third, the court confirmed the practice
that the without notice order should normally last for 6 months with a full hearing shortly to take place at which the order might be varied or discharged (at
[85]). Fourth, care should be taken in drafting witness statements in support of
the injunction so that they do not advocate for the order ('Mr Macdonald's own
statement resembled more closely the opening speech for the prosecution in a
criminal trial': at [101]) and are specific enough to enable the perpetrator(s) to
respond to the allegations (ibid.). Fifth, as regards the use of hearsay evidence:

> The willingness of a civil court to admit hearsay evidence carries with it inherent
> dangers in a case like this. As Mr Macdonald said, rumours abound in a small
> housing estate, and it is much more difficult for a judge to assess the truth of what
> he is being told if the original maker of the statement does not attend court to be
> cross-examined on his/her evidence. The emphasis placed by section 4(2)(b) of
> the [Civil Evidence Act 1995] on contemporaneity merely goes to highlight the
> importance of a landlord giving a tenant contemporary notice of any complaints
> that are made against his/her behaviour, so that the tenant is not faced in court
> with serious complaints made by anonymous or absent witnesses about matters
> that took place, if at all, many months previously. ([135])

The relative ease with which an ASBI may be obtained, by way of contrast to the slightly more stringent approaches taken by the courts in relation to ASBOs may well explain why the ASBI appears to have become the injunction of choice for most social landlords (Pawson, Davidson and Lederle 2007; Flint and Pawson 2009: 421). In 2009/2010, local authorities alone obtained 1,123 ASBIs (CLG 2010d: 14). However, Flint and Pawson (2009: 422) offer the explanation that ASBIs are 'of value mainly in terms of their capacity for rapid deployment, and in countering certain forms of "hard to prove" criminal activity ... [PRPs] have preferred injunctions over ASBOs because there is no routine necessity for consultation with other parties, as would be required for the latter.'

Anti-social behaviour orders

As suggested above, despite their higher profile than ASBIs, ASBOs are now used more infrequently than ASBIs. There is some similarity in the defining criteria for both, although their statutory derivation is different. ASBOs derive from the powers open to social landlords contained in the Crime and Disorder Act 1998 (as amended, in particular by the Anti-Social Behaviour Act 2003, s. 85, which enabled all social landlords, including HATs, to apply: s. 1(1A), Crime and Disorder Act 1998). The notion of a 'social landlord' has been expanded so as to enable a local authority to contract out its functions under ss. 1–1F, Crime and Disorder Act 1998 to 'one or more housing managers whereby the housing manager, or an employee of the manager, may exercise any relevant function' (Local Authorities (Contracting out of Anti-Social Behaviour Functions) (England) Order 2007, SI 2007/1441, Article 2, under powers granted to the Secretary of State in s. 1A(2), 1998 Act; see, generally, CLG 2007a). The functions can, therefore, be contracted out to ALMOs, TMOs and Private Finance Initiative consortia (CLG 2007a: para. 5), subject to certain conditions including the requirement that the relevant manager consults with the local authority before exercising any function (Article 3(2)(a)).

Section 1(1), 1998 Act, enables a social landlord to apply to the magistrates' court for an ASBO

> if it appears to the authority that the following conditions are fulfilled with respect to any person aged 10 or over, namely –
> (a) that the person has acted, since the commencement date, in an anti-social manner, that is to say, in a manner that caused or was likely to cause harassment, alarm or distress to one or more persons not of the same household as himself; and
> (b) that such an order is necessary to protect persons from further anti-social acts by him.

An organisation which decides to make an application for an ASBO must consult with their police and/or local authority counterparts (s. 1E, 1998 Act). A magistrates' court may make such an order, which prohibits certain conduct provided that the prohibitions 'are those necessary for the purpose of protecting persons … from further anti-social acts by the defendant' (s. 1(6)). The order may last for not less than 2 years (although certain parts of the order may last for a shorter period: *Lonergan* v. *Lewes Crown Court* [2005] 1 WLR 2570, at [13]). Breach of an ASBO is a criminal offence (s. 1(10)). ASBOs may also be made by a county court in the course of other proceedings, or by a criminal court on conviction (ss. 1B and 1C, the latter sometimes being described as a CrASBO). An ASBO may be made against a child whom the local authority is looking after, but only subject to certain requirements reflecting the conflict of interest that will exist between the different constituent parts of the authority (see *R (M)* v. *Sheffield Magistrates' Court* [2005] FLR 81).

An application for an ASBO involves a civil, not a criminal, process, because the purpose of the procedure is to impose a prohibition and not a penalty – which has the important consequence that hearsay evidence can be used by the applicant (*R (McCann)* v. *Crown Court at Manchester* [2003] 1 AC 787, e.g. at [68] Lord Hope; [94] Lord Hutton), subject to the statutory safeguards regarding that evidence (see Civil Evidence Act 1995, especially s. 4). However, that having been said, because there is a potential interference with the alleged perpetrator's rights under Article 6, Sch. 1, HRA (right to a fair trial of the determination of civil rights and obligations), the heightened civil standard of proof applies.

Magistrates are required, when considering s. 1(1)(a) 'to be sure' that the defendant has acted in an anti-social manner; the inquiry under s. 1(1)(b) 'does not involve a standard of proof: it is an exercise of judgment and evaluation' (*McCann*: [37], Lord Steyn; [82], Lord Hope). As the Court of Appeal put it, the test is 'one of necessity. Each separate order prohibiting a person from doing a specified thing must be necessary to protect persons from further anti-social acts by him' (*R* v. *Boness* [2005] EWCA Crim 2395, at [29], Hooper LJ). In *McCann*, the House of Lords made their underlying rationales for these points clear, by reference to a balance of the rights of the alleged perpetrator against the interests of the community (especially [113], Lord Hutton) and the purpose of the 1998 Act in protecting the 'weak and vulnerable' from criminal and sub-criminal activities 'which the existing law failed to deal with satisfactorily' (especially [1] and [16], under the rubric 'the social problem', Lord Steyn; on which, see Carr and Cowan 2006; cf. Donoghue 2010).

In terms of the drafting of an ASBO, the cases demonstrate a consistent line of reasoning that the prohibitions must be 'clear, comprehensible and enforceable; otherwise they amount to no more than beating the wind' (*Heron* v. *Plymouth CC* [2009] EWHC 3562 (Admin), at [3], Moses LJ). There must be a practical way of policing the order (*Boness*, at [47]). The prohibitions must be targeted at the individual (*Heron*, [8]), and be proportionate; they may include effective curfews or football-banning prohibitions (e.g. *Lonergan*); and, if the evidence suggests, can prohibit the wearing of a hooded top (*R (B)* v. *Greenwich Magistrates' Court* [2009] HLR 24). Crucially, also, they must be based on clear findings of fact and magistrates must give reasons for the orders, which need only be short and simple (*Heron* at [12] and [14]).

The final point concerns publicity for ASBOs. In *R (Stanley)* v. *Metropolitan Police Commissioner* [2005] HLR 8, it was held that one of the concomitants of an ASBO is publicity. As that might infringe the perpetrator's rights under Article 8, Sch. 1, HRA (right to respect for family and home), the authority should also consider whether such publicity was necessary and proportionate to its legitimate aims. Although the authority in that case had not done so, that did not matter on the merits. As Kennedy LJ said (at [40]):

> The resident of Brent who was informed, in an attempt to restore confidence, that several ASBOs had been obtained might turn out to be invaluable in enforcing one of those orders, particularly having regard to the relatively wide terms of the orders under consideration in this case. It is clear to me that whether publicity is intended to inform, to reassure, to assist in enforcing the existing orders by policing, to inhibit the behaviour of those against whom the orders have been made, or to deter others, it is unlikely to be effective unless it includes photographs, names and at least partial addresses. Not only do the readers need to know against whom orders have been made, but those responsible for publicity must leave no room for misidentification.

Subsequently, Home Office guidance (2005: 2) suggested that '**publicity should be expected in most cases**' (original emphasis) while maintaining that there should be a 'correlation between the purposes of publicity and the necessity test'. Cobb (2007) draws attention to what he describes as the governance of ASB through publicity and the 'ethopolitics of shame' – that is to say, the self-regulatory impetus provided from the shaming through publicity.

Dispersal orders

Under the Anti-Social Behaviour Act 2003, a police officer (superintendent or above: s. 36) may, after obtaining the consent of the relevant local authority (or authorities) (s. 31(2)), make a 'dispersal order', where the officer

has reasonable grounds for believing –
(a) that any members of the public have been intimidated, harassed, alarmed or distressed as a result of the presence or behaviour of groups of two or more persons in public places in any locality in his police area (the 'relevant locality'), and
(b) that anti-social behaviour is a significant and persistent problem in the relevant locality. (s. 30(1))

The authorisation by the superintendent (or above) must specify the reasonable grounds for so believing, not in great detail, but sufficient to provide 'a proper thought-out basis for making the authorisation and expressing that basis in written form, which can later be examined and challenged' (*Sierny* v. *DPP* [2007] Crim LR 60, at [28], Nielson J; s. 31(1)). The authorisation can be for no more than 6 months (s. 30(2)). The area covered by the dispersal order must be publicised in the local press and conspicuously in the zone (s. 31(3)), and should be written in a readily understandable way to those likely to be affected by it (*Carter* v. *CPS* [2010] 4 All ER 990, [6], Thomas LJ). Further, as it is an 'interference with the liberty of the subject' and 'by a novel route', proper procedures need to be in place for the authorisation, direction and infringement (ibid. [4]).

Once an order has been made and publicised, police constables and police community support officers have various powers to move people on. Where a minor under the age of sixteen is in the dispersal zone without adult control between 9pm and 6am, a constable in uniform can 'remove the person to the person's place of residence unless he has reasonable grounds for believing that the person would, if removed to that place, be likely to suffer significant harm' (s. 30(6)). Social landlords have been centrally involved in the use of these orders (Flint and Pawson 2009: 426), but Crawford's analysis (2008: 774; see also Crawford and Lister 2007) is that such orders 'can be read as a pre-eminent form of "control signal". They operate as much through the symbolic properties they impart, as through their instrumental capacity to regulate behaviour.' Thus, they can raise false expectations about police resources for the zone (ibid. p. 775).

Alternative forms of tenure

One of the most striking aspects of the focus on ASB has been the numbers of alternative forms of tenure it has spawned. Typically, these enable social landlords either to offer lower security of tenure or to reduce long-term security; if a decision to evict is made, this is subject to an internal review; if the decision remains to evict, the tenancy can be terminated simply and cheaply, with mandatory eviction (so that the court has no discretion (in theory) as to whether or not to make the possession order – see Chapter 16 below). The actual eviction process is discussed in the next chapter which is concerned with mandatory eviction claims and their compatibility with the HRA. However, attention here is drawn to the following types of alternative tenures available to social landlords: introductory or 'starter' tenancies; demoted tenancies; family intervention tenancies.

Introductory and starter tenancies

Local authorities were empowered to grant introductory tenancies by the Housing Act 1996, Part V, as part of the 'fight against nuisance neighbours'. This regime was specifically requested by a number of authorities which were concerned about the rise of ASB on their estates. It only applies to local authorities and HATs and only if those landlords decide, after consultation, to exercise their discretion to introduce the regime. After deciding to enter the scheme, every subsequent grant of a tenancy and exclusive possession licence (ss. 124 (2) and 126(1)) is an introductory tenancy and not secure. Where the new occupier has been a secure tenant before, or an AT of a PRP, they are excluded from the regime. Introductory tenants have broadly similar rights to secure tenants (ss. 131–137).

The central difference between a secure and introductory tenant lies in the ability of the landlord to seek possession of the property. The introductory tenancy lasts for 1 year (after which it automatically becomes secure) (s. 125(2), 'the trial period'); however, the trial period can be extended by 6 months – subject to a notice setting out the reasons for the extension as well as informing the tenant of their right to request a review of that decision within 14 days – being served on the tenant at least 8 weeks before the end of the trial period (s. 125A and B).

It was rightly termed a 'probationary' tenancy because, during that period, the introductory tenant can be evicted much more speedily on a mandatory basis provided the local authority has followed the correct procedure (s. 127). The procedure is simple: the landlord serves a notice of proceedings on the tenant and that must contain certain information, including the reasons for the decision to seek possession and the tenant's right to seek a review of that decision within 14 days (s. 128). Once the review, if any, has been conducted and the landlord decides to continue to seek possession, application is made to the county court. Thus, the landlord can proceed from notice to eviction in a short period of time.

On review, it is perfectly proper for a local authority to decide to suspend further action – for example, where there are rent arrears, by giving the tenant the opportunity to pay the current rent and an amount towards the arrears – and a failure to keep to the terms of such a decision does not require a further notice (and review) unless there is a 'substantial' or 'significant' difference in the reasons for pursuing a claim for possession. So, in *Cardiff CC* v. *Stone* [2003] HLR 47, the tenant failed to keep to such an arrangement regarding rent arrears made in the review decision, and the local authority commenced a claim for possession. The Court of Appeal held that there was no 'substantial difference' between the original notice and the ground for the claim: the failure to pay rent promptly in full. On the other hand, in *Forbes* v. *Lambeth LBC* [2003] HLR 49, there was a significant difference between the original notice and the ground, although based on ASB, but the reasons for pursuing the claim for possession were based on different facts which required a further review to question the facts and the reasonableness of the local authority's decision. The cases do not sit easily with each other, but in the latter, Crane J held (at [34]) that the review decision had, in fact, decided not to confirm the decision in the notice to seek possession. Thus, a further notice and review would have been required in any event.

PRPs have rather different non-statutory powers to grant starter tenancies (originally granted in 1999 by the Housing Corporation), although they do not have to do so with all their new tenancies. They were entitled to do so

as part of a managed strategy for dealing with ASB either:
- across their whole stock;
- across their stock in a local authority area; or
- in defined street areas or estates. (Housing Corporation 2007b: 8)

There has always been sufficient 'wriggle room' in the regulatory guidance which, while it requires PRPs to grant the 'most secure form of tenure', which is usually an AT, there is a proviso that such tenure should be 'compatible with the purpose of the housing and the sustainability of the community' (TSA 2010a). A starter tenancy is essentially an AST for a period of 12 months, and it is usually a term of the tenancy agreement that the tenant can seek a review of a decision to terminate the tenancy within a certain period (see Chapter 11 above).

Despite concerns that introductory and starter tenancies might lead to greater evictions, and detrimentally affect particularly vulnerable persons and others who do not 'fit', Pawson et al. (2005: 40) found that, though the evidence base was limited and not entirely conclusive, those with introductory tenancies were no more likely to be evicted than longer-established tenants. Indeed, they report that there were perceived benefits of the regimes (strengthening the landlord's hand during the first year of the tenancy) with one landlord, in particular, reporting (p. 65) that

> in practice, the procedures involved in the (internal) review of a Notice Seeking Possession issued to a household with an Introductory Tenancy (where invoked by the tenant) were 'more onerous' than going to court. It was also asserted that, recognising the relative finality of serving a Notice in respect of an Introductory Tenancy, landlords were reluctant to use this power except as an absolute last resort.

However, that having been said, it is known that many evictions from introductory tenancies are for rent arrears and not ASB (Hunter et al. 2000; Pawson et al. 2005).

Additionally, as developed in Chapter 16, what appears to be a 'mandatory' requirement on the court to make a possession order on its face does not always turn out to be so simple.

Demoted tenancies

The demoted tenancy regime was introduced by the Anti-Social Behaviour Act 2003 by way of amendments made to the Housing Acts 1985 (s. 82A), 1988 (s. 6A) and 1996 (ss. 143A–P). It is clearly modelled on the introductory tenancy regime, so the discussion above applies here and is not repeated, save that the demoted tenancy lasts for 12 months. The essential difference is that the household is already an occupier with a secure or an AT – it is that tenancy which is demoted. As secure tenancies have been granted by local authorities, HATs and PRPs, they have the power to apply for a demoted secure tenancy (s. 82A(1)); PRPs can apply for a demoted AT (s. 6A(1)). The landlord applies to the county court for an order demoting the tenancy made on the following criteria:

> The court must not make a demotion order unless it is satisfied –
> (a) that the tenant or a person residing in or visiting the dwelling-house has engaged or has threatened to engage in
>   (i) housing-related anti-social conduct, or

(ii) conduct to which section 153B of the Housing Act 1996 (use of premises for unlawful purposes) applies, and

(b) that it is reasonable to make the order. (s. 6A(4), 1988 Act; s 82A(4), 1985 Act).

The phrase 'housing-related anti-social conduct' is defined by reference to the same phrase in s. 153A(1) (s. 6A(7A), 1988 Act; s. 82A(7A), 1985 Act), concerning ASBIs. As regards reasonableness, the discussion below concerning possession claims and reasonableness applies likewise here. However, it should be borne in mind that a demotion is 'a far more drastic step than the making of a suspended possession order' (*Manchester CC* v. *Pinnock* [2010] HLR 7, at [27], CA) and that it 'is obviously a Draconian sanction' albeit not as draconian as an immediate order for possession (*Washington Housing Company Ltd* v. *Morson* [2005] EWHC 3407 (Ch), [67], cited in Luba et al. 2010: 183). Such comments were made before the Supreme Court decision in *Pinnock*, discussed in the next chapter, which ameliorates the process, but the sentiment remains the same – the court has potentially less far-reaching jurisdiction on demoted tenancies than a suspension or postponement.

Family intervention tenancies

Family intervention tenancies (FITs) were created by the Housing and Regeneration Act 2008, ss. 297–8, and by way of additions to the categories of tenancy excluded from the security of tenure protections in the Housing Acts 1985 and 1988. These provisions formalise the practices of social landlords, initially through certain pioneer projects (such as the Dundee Family Project) and which were subsequently endorsed in central government's Respect policy through support and provision of resources for family intervention projects. They have a twin aspect: punitive sanctions combined with rehabilitation through therapeutic strategies (Nixon et al. 2010; Parr 2010). In some respects, the statutory provisions create something of a meal out of those informal processes and practices, despite good intentions (see CLG 2009d: paras. 12–13). They are non-secure occupation agreements (Sch. 1, para. 4ZA, 1985 Act; Sch. 1, para. 12ZA, 1988 Act), which are terminable on a notice to quit of the appropriate length (s. 298, 2008 Act; s. 3, Protection from Eviction Act 1977). The notice must, however, be preceded by a 'minded to' notice which, inter alia, gives the household the reasons why the landlord will be seeking the order and entitles the household to seek a review of the decision within 14 days (s. 298(2)). However, a statutory review is not formally open to PRP occupiers – the CLG guidance makes the following observation, though:

> There is no statutory review process of the decision to terminate the Family Intervention Tenancy for [PRP] Family Intervention Tenancies, but there is a clear regulatory expectation of fairness. Eviction should be the last resort and only after due process. The Tenant Services Authority expects [PRPs] to offer a review process which closely parallels that offered by local authorities. (CLG 2009d: para. 49)

In essence, a statutory FIT can arise when a possession order has been made against a household (which does not have to be a family) on a nuisance or domestic violence ground; such an order could, in the opinion of the social landlord, have been made in relation to such a tenancy; or could have been made if the household had had such a tenancy. The FIT is for the purposes of the provision of 'behaviour support services' – the FIT is clearly related to Behaviour Support Agreements in the guidance (CLG 2009d: paras. 34–44). Furthermore, before the FIT commences, the landlord must serve a notice with the following information:

(5) A notice under this sub-paragraph is a notice stating –
   (a) the reasons for offering the tenancy to the new tenant;
   (b) the dwelling-house in respect of which the tenancy is to be granted;
   (c) the other main terms of the tenancy (including any requirements on the new tenant in respect of behaviour support services);
   (d) the security of tenure available under the tenancy and any loss of security of tenure which is likely to result from the new tenant agreeing to enter into the tenancy;
   (e) that the new tenant is not obliged to enter into the tenancy or (unless otherwise required to do so) to surrender any existing tenancy or possession of a dwelling-house;
   (f) any likely action by the landlord if the new tenant does not enter into the tenancy or surrender any existing tenancy or possession of a dwelling-house.

Thus, although a FIT is voluntarily entered into, para. (f) above will offer the household a clear steer.

It would be fair to say that the FIT and associated programmes have given rise to clear divisions within the academic community. On the one hand, the actual outcomes for households have appeared to be positive in terms of behaviour-change (Nixon et al. 2007; White et al. 2008). Nevertheless, there is some disquiet about their intrusive effects, their authoritarian nature, the coercive techniques and their enforcement of terms and conditions (see, for example, Garrett 2007; cf. the more nuanced response from Nixon 2007), and the gendered nature of such interventions (Nixon and Hunter 2009). In an excellent, sophisticated account of qualitative research with five households subject to a FIT, Parr (forthcoming) demonstrates how households are subject to the surveillance and scrutiny of agencies: 'project workers spell out to families the consequences that may befall them should they fail to meet their side of the support plan agreement as a key part of what was described as a "challenging" and "assertive" approach' (p. 9). That became a constant worry and imposition for the households, emphasised by their lack of alternative housing options. Nevertheless, those effects were balanced by the degree and depth of support offered by individuals and agencies to the households, which led to relationships of trust and 'family' being created. Parr concludes with the observation that 'a fundamental contradiction was identified between the role of the project workers as "help-givers" and housing officers responsible for enforcing compliance with tenancy agreements and other legal tools such as ASBOs'.

Possession

The current law

All landlords have the option of claiming possession against their occupiers on the basis of the occupiers' nuisance. The relevant grounds, which are discretionary, are Ground 2 (secure tenancies, Sch. 2, Housing Act 1985) or Ground 13 (ATs, Sch. 2, Housing Act 1988). These are in similar terms, as amended:

> The tenant or a person residing in or visiting the dwelling-house –
> (a) has been guilty of conduct causing or likely to cause a nuisance or annoyance to a person residing, visiting or otherwise engaging in a lawful activity in the locality, or
> (b) has been convicted of –
>   (i) using the dwelling-house or allowing it to be used for immoral or illegal purposes, or
>   (ii) an indictable offence committed in, or in the locality of, the dwelling-house.

They are usually also supplemented in practice by Grounds 1 and 12 (1985 and 1988 Acts respectively) because there has been an alleged breach of the tenancy obligations in such cases.

Leaving aside para. (b), it will be immediately noticed that the nuisance grounds are cast widely. The ground is proved not just when the tenant has been engaging in such acts, but also other occupiers and visitors, so that the absence of the tenant's personal blame is not a relevant consideration at this stage (although it may affect a decision on whether it is reasonable to make a possession order: *Kensington and Chelsea RLBC* v. *Simmonds* (1997) 29 HLR 507, 512; *Portsmouth CC* v. *Bryant* (2000) 31 HLR 906, 915 and 921; see also Nixon and Hunter 2001); the conduct, which can be sub-criminal, need only be '*likely* to cause a nuisance or annoyance' (emphasis added), nuisance being widely drawn (beyond its technical definition in the tort of nuisance) and annoyance is yet wider; and the conduct should affect not just other tenants, but others 'engaging in a lawful activity in the locality', the word 'locality' having been framed deliberately to encompass a wide area. Further, the usual provisions as to service of a notice preceding the possession claim are altered in cases brought under Grounds 2 or 14, so that a claim can be brought immediately after service (s. 83A(1), 1985 Act; s. 8(4), 1988 Act).

As these are discretionary grounds, the landlord must also show reasonableness, and there is a connection between the type and level of conduct and reasonableness here, so that the broad principles of reasonableness outlined in the previous chapter are interpreted slightly differently. The 1985 and 1988 Acts were amended (by the Anti-Social Behaviour Act 2003) so that, in considering reasonableness under the nuisance grounds, the court must consider, in particular

(a) the effect that the nuisance or annoyance has had on persons other than the person against whom the order is sought;

(b) any continuing effect the nuisance or annoyance is likely to have on such persons;

(c) the effect that the nuisance or annoyance would be likely to have on such persons if the conduct is repeated. (s. 85A(2); s. 9A, 1988 Act)

These provisions give statutory form to the position at which the courts had already arrived (see, for example, *Kensington and Chelsea RLBC* v. *Simmonds* (1997) 29 HLR 507, 511); the provision's 'effect is to codify and mandate the already existing jurisprudence' (*Knowsley HT* v. *McMullen*, [2006] HLR 43, at [4]).

If it is reasonable to make a possession order, a third issue arises, whether the order should be suspended or postponed. Those two issues commonly elide, in that it may only be reasonable to make the order if it can be suspended on satisfactory terms (*McMullen*, at [53]). However, as regards whether to suspend the order, the focus should be not so much on the past, but on the future so as to devise the best method of protecting others against the recurrence of the behaviour (*Manchester CC* v. *Higgins* [2006] HLR 14, at [55]). There is no point in suspending an order if the inevitable outcome will be a breach (*Canterbury CC* v. *Lowe* (2001) 33 HLR 53; *Higgins*, at [37]). Such an assessment can only be made on a risk-based prediction and, as Ward LJ put it in *Higgins*, 'If history were predictive of the future then the future would seem bleak.' (at [41]); or, to use another well-worn phrase, 'the shadow of the past is too heavy upon the present' (*Lambeth LBC* v. *Howard* (2003) 33 HLR 636, at [33], Sedley LJ).

There has been some discussion in the cases, particularly by Sedley LJ, of the significance of Article 8, Sch. 1, HRA, and specifically the requirement of proportionality (*Howard*, at [29]–[32]; cf. *Solon South West Housing Association Ltd* v. *James* [2005] HLR 24, [69]). In *Webb* v. *Wandsworth LBC* [2008] EWCA Civ 1643, at [24], Sedley LJ referred to the failure of the trial judge to take account of the fact that the property provided a home for the tenant's three children and a grandchild. The significance of such comments is likely to have been diluted by the approach taken by the Supreme Court in *Manchester CC* v. *Pinnock* [2010] 3 WLR 1441, at [55]–[6], where the court said that, where reasonableness must be shown: 'It therefore seems highly unlikely, as a practical matter, that it could be reasonable for a court to make an order for possession in circumstances in which it would be disproportionate to do so under article 8.' (at [56])

A number of points have arisen about those second and third issues which can be summarised as follows: the effect of the inability of the tenant to control a third party; the existence of an ASBO and/or other interventions against the perpetrator; where the nuisance stops prior to the trial of the claim and the seriousness of the nuisance; and the effect of a perpetrator's failure to show remorse. These points are often interconnected but are taken separately for analytical convenience. There is a final point concerned with the interaction between this law and the DDA.

In *McMullen*, the tenant was a vulnerable female, who had an IQ of 63, and needed her son, the perpetrator, living with her. Neuberger LJ commented on an *obiter* view expressed by Sedley LJ which suggested that, in such circumstances it may be unreasonable to make an order against such a tenant 'and it will almost certainly be unreasonable to make an outright order against such a person' (*Bryant*, p. 917). Neuberger LJ disagreed with that assertion in strong terms, in part because the exercise of judgment on reasonableness turns on the particular facts of the case (at [28]). Further,

> It can also be said, at least in many cases, that there is a stronger, not a weaker, case for not suspending an order for possession based on nuisance where the tenant's point is that she cannot control the nuisance-maker. If reasonableness indicates an order for possession, what, it may be asked, is the point of suspending it, if the tenant is incapable of ensuring compliance? However, there can be some point in suspending in such a case especially if, as here, the nuisance-causer is no longer a child and is related to the tenant. If he is aware that, by continuing the nuisance, he will lose his home, and that the tenant will lose her home, there may be some hope that he will see sense, and behave. (at [31])

Indeed, if the tenant is unable to control a nuisance-maker, who remains in the property, that would assist the landlord in obtaining an immediate possession order (at [33]). However, perhaps in contradiction to that comment, it has been said that it is not permissible to use a suspended or postponed order 'as a means of bringing pressure to bear on a third party to modify behaviour over which the tenant himself or herself has not influence or control' (*Webb*, at [23], Sedley LJ).

The existence of an ASBO and/or other interventions has been regarded as a 'double-edged sword' – it raises the prospect that the behaviour will be controlled but it also illuminates the significance of past breaches (*Webb*, [14], Wilson LJ). A possession order and an ASBO are 'conceptually quite different' and there is certainly no intrinsic rule that the existence of an ASBO should prevent a possession order being made (*McMullen*, at [37]). On the one hand, an ASBO 'will be strong but not conclusive evidence that the tenant will have forfeited his entitlement to remain in possession' (*Higgins*, at [36]). On the other hand, it may also assist a tenant where the perpetrator is a third party whom the tenant cannot control (*McMullen*, at [44]). In one case, the trial judge's reliance on alleged, but unproven breaches of an ASBO fatally infected the decision to postpone a possession order (*Webb*).

Where the nuisance stops or is in abeyance at the date of the trial, the issue is said to turn on the seriousness of the past acts, although efforts to improve behaviour are to be taken into account (*Howard*; *Sandwell MBC* v. *Hensley* [2008] HLR 22). Thus, these two issues often elide, albeit analytically distinct.

In cases of serious criminal activity, such as the cultivation of cannabis on a large scale or drug dealing, the courts

> stress the serious nature of a breach of a condition which involves the committing of a criminal offence. The more serious the offence, the more serious the breach. Convictions of several offences will obviously be even more serious. In such circumstances, it seems to me that the court should only suspect the order if there is cogent evidence which demonstrates … a sound basis for the hope that the previous conduct will cease. (*Hensley*, at [17]; also *Bristol CC* v. *Mousah* (1998) 30 HLR 32)

A criminal punishment is irrelevant (ibid. [23]). The seriousness of the offence should also be considered in light of the role of a provider of social housing to ensure that its properties are properly managed and are kept free of such criminal activity ([25]). As Gage LJ put it, in the absence of 'cogent evidence providing a real hope that the [tenant] had mended his ways, the council was in all the circumstances entitled to an outright order' (at [26]). Arden LJ suggested that, in such a case of serious and serial drug-related offences, the tenant would have to show a 'strong case to resist and immediate possession order' (at [27]).

Frankly, it never serves a tenant (or, indeed, anyone) well to show little or no remorse for their actions. It is an issue of significance in terms of the risk-based jurisdiction as to the consideration of a suspension or postponement of the order for, if the tenant or perpetrator shows little or no remorse or acceptance of their conduct, then the shadow of the past is likely to bear heavily on the future, so that an immediate possession order may be more likely (*James*, especially, [78], Carnwath LJ; *Hensley*; *Higgins*).

Finally, there has been an issue of the proper course of action for a landlord in cases where the occupier has a disability (as defined by the DDA 1995 or Equality Act 2010). In *Manchester CC* v. *Romano* [2005] 1 WLR 2775, the Court of Appeal came down firmly on the enforcement side of the line. As the court put it:

> the council must prove that if it did not take this action someone's health or safety would be endangered. It does not have to prove that that person's health or safety has actually been damaged. The World Health Organisation has since 1948 adopted the following definition of the word 'health':
>> 'Health is a state of complete physical, mental and social well-being and not merely the absence of disease and infirmity'.
>
> If health is endangered, that state is put at risk. The statute does not use the words 'seriously endangered', and when interpreting the 1995 Act compatibly with the European Convention on Human Rights, it is necessary to bear in mind not only the Convention rights of the disabled person but also the Convention rights of his neighbours. (at [69]–[70])

Under the Equality Act, ss. 15 and 19, one might suspect that there would be a similar process in order to establish the legitimacy and proportionality of the landlord's actions, within the context of reasonableness. However, in *Romano*, it is to be noted that the Court of Appeal pointed out the significance of inter-agency working in such cases at an early stage (at [117]–[20]).

The future

On 11 January 2011, the housing minister, Grant Shapps announced that there would be a consultation paper published which would give details of a mandatory ground for possession in cases of ASB:

> Ministers believe this will lead to a faster and fairer courts process – being found guilty of housing related anti-social behaviour in one court will provide automatic grounds for eviction in the county court, removing the need to prove the incidents of anti-social behaviour for a second time.

To speed up the courts process further, Mr Shapps announced that he would be exploring jointly with the justice department whether there were any unnecessary obstacles to the swift resolution of ASB possession cases where serious harm is being caused to individuals and communities.

In a brilliant rebuke to the minister, Nearly Legal wrote an open letter to him (http://nearlylegal.co.uk/blog/2011/01/dear-mr-shapps/), pointing out the potential impact of *Pinnock* (discussed in Chapter 16) and describing the outline proposals as a 'chocolate teapot'.

Conclusions

The conclusions to this chapter are more in the way of observations on the state of both the academic and judicial positions. There is no doubt that ASB has spawned some important developments in our thinking, at a social-theoretical level as well as by way of legal remedies. As regards academic approaches, the predominant focal points fall within the penumbra of what has been termed the 'responsibilisation thesis' – in summary, that we all have responsibility for controlling crime; and the associated notion that there is a renewed ethic, sometimes regarded as specifically neo-liberal or even advanced liberal, of self-control and self-responsibility in the interests of the community. Squires (2006), I think rightly, regards responses to ASB as part of a web of the criminalisation of social policy; but I think, perhaps differently from Squires, that the relationship between social policy and crime control is historically connected, which has made the current inter-penetration thinkable and possible. What is clear is that the emergence of contractual and quasi-contractual forms of governance, which draw on regulatory ideals (in a different, more punitive way than is asserted in the better regulation literature: Crawford 2009), represent relatively novel, innovative forms of social control.

What is also clear is that these forms of governance particularly affect marginal, socially excluded, and vulnerable populations, often with mental health issues – who are often also the primary targets of ASB (Manders 2009; Parr 2009; Donoghue 2010). They are also highly gendered, having a disproportionate impact on female-headed households, despite being framed in a gender-neutral way, 'which facilitates a return to Victorian notions of womanhood, where the failure of women to control the behaviour of members of their families is presented as a failure of parenting and citizenship' (Nixon and Hunter 2009).

16

Mandatory possession proceedings

In a range of possession proceedings, provided the landlord has complied with relevant formalities, the judge must make an order for possession. These are mandatory cases, so that the judge's role is, in essence, procedural rather than substantive. At least, that used to be the case and it is likely still to be true in many cases. However, a substantive issue has emerged, partly as a result of the incorporation of the European Convention on Human Rights into English law in the HRA. That the UK has been a signatory to the Convention since its foundation, but this issue has only really emerged relatively recently, may have been a question of jurisdiction and, simply, proximity (bringing rights back home, the government's strapline for the HRA, focused minds on their ambit). The nearer the jurisdiction is to national law, the more influential it is likely to be; and, indeed, in mandatory possession proceedings, it has been influential. The central question concerns the extent to which such proceedings must have reference to proportionality. This derives from Article 8 of the European Convention and Sch. 1, HRA. It is in these terms:

Right to respect for private and family life
1. Everyone has the right to respect for his private and family life, his home and his correspondence.
2. There shall be no interference by a public authority with the exercise of this right except such as is in accordance with the law and is necessary in a democratic society in the interests of national security, public safety or the economic well-being of the country, for the prevention of disorder or crime, for the protection of health or morals, or for the protection of the rights and freedoms of others.

Proportionality derives from the question of whether such proceedings are 'necessary in a democratic society' (para. 2). Generally, such proceedings are 'in accordance with the law', because they are in accordance with statutory provisions or the common law, and so that point is conceded.

This chapter begins by setting out the range of possible types of mandatory possession proceedings non-inclusively. Certain of those types have been discussed in previous chapters. However, some have been held over to this chapter and they are discussed here. There then follows a discussion of the development of proportionality in mandatory possession cases until what is described as the 'watershed' moment – the decision in *Manchester CC* v. *Pinnock* [2010] 3 WLR 1441 – and the ambit of proportionality in mandatory possession cases. As has been suggested on the Nearly Legal blog, *Pinnock* is 'the new giant on the scene, one judgment to rule them all and in its 9 strong constitution bind them' (www.nearlylegal.co.uk/blog/2010/11/brave-new-world-or-same-old-story/; the reference to the nine-strong constitution is to the highly unusual nine justice bench of the Supreme Court) – in short, it is potentially the most significant housing law case of all time. It requires full consideration and thought. The final section considers specific issues in relation to mandatory possession proceedings concerned with shared ownership and sale-and-rentback, where the Article 8 issue may arise but in conjunction with other issues.

Mandatory possession proceedings: the range

A landowner or their derivative in title should be entitled to bring mandatory possession proceedings in the following range of circumstances:

1. where the occupier began their occupation of the land as a trespasser and has no legal right to remain on the land;
2. where the occupier has no security of tenure because they are excluded from those regimes;
3. where the occupier is precluded from succeeding to the tenancy by the relevant rules;
4. where the occupier had security of tenure, but lost it
    a. because they no longer fulfil the qualifying conditions; or
    b. because they occupied with others as joint tenants and one of the joint tenants has served a notice to quit the property, thus ending the entire tenancy;
5. where the occupier has security of tenure under the Housing Act 1988, and the landlord is proceeding on one of the mandatory grounds for possession;
6. where the occupier has a demoted, introductory, or FIT and the landlord is seeking possession.

Point 1 appears self-evident, although there are specific issues when one is dealing with occupation by travellers and squatters, for example. Before *Pinnock*, the major interventions were caused in these claims. Points 2, 3, 4a, and 5 have been discussed in Chapter 11 and require no further elaboration here. The types of tenancy discussed in Point 6 have been discussed in previous chapters, but the method of termination requires further examination here, as does point 4b, which has not been discussed previously.

Joint tenants and termination

Where one or more joint tenants under a tenancy serves a notice to quit on their landlord, in theory this notice ends the tenancy. Any security of tenure which the occupation attracted is effectively ended when the notice period runs out, provided that the notice is properly constituted and served. The notice should be clear and unequivocal, and allow for the correct period (at least 28 days). This is sometimes known as the rule in *Hammersmith and Fulham LBC* v. *Monk* [1992] 1 AC 478, in which this point was established. A properly constituted notice destroys the tenancy in its entirety even if the other joint tenant(s) does not know of the notice to quit and has no wish to bring the tenancy to an end. The rule in *Monk* proceeded on a contractual analysis of the lease, noting that one of two or more joint landlords could serve such a notice, and so it must follow that one of the joint tenants could do likewise. Some disquiet was expressed by Lord Browne-Wilkinson about the outcome:

The revulsion against Mrs. Powell being able unilaterally to terminate the appellant's rights in his home is property based: the appellant's property rights in the home cannot be destroyed without his consent. (p. 491H)

However, it was the contractual analysis which 'triumphed' in the House of Lords. This was a significant victory for social housing managers who had pioneered its use in cases of domestic violence, rehousing the person against whom the violence occurred (who also served the notice) and evicting the perpetrator relatively simply. This approach was encouraged in a series of policy pronouncements from the 1980s, particularly because it demonstrated a holistic (and tough) approach to the aftermath of domestic violence (see e.g. Home Office 1990). Successive attempts to dismantle its effects after the introduction of the HRA were unsuccessful (see Cowan and Gallivan 2010).

Introductory, demoted and family intervention tenancies

Although introductory, demoted and FITs have different statutory foundations, the latter two were drafted substantially to mirror the introductory tenancy regime and follow its pattern. In essence, in order to terminate such a tenancy, the landlord must serve a notice informing the tenant that the landlord has decided to seek possession; the reasons for that decision; the date after which proceedings will be issued (not being earlier than would otherwise have been possible if the landlord had served a notice to quit); the tenant's right to request a review of that decision within 14 days of the date of service of the notice; and that if the tenant needs help or advice about the notice, or what to do about it, the tenant should consult a Citizens Advice Bureau, a housing aid centre, a law centre or a solicitor (respectively ss. 128–9, 143E–F, Housing Act 1996, and s. 298, Housing and Regeneration Act 2008; in relation to the latter, as the FIT is terminated by a notice to quit, the landlord's notice indicates the date after which that notice will be served, rather than the date after which proceedings will be issued: s. 298(2)(d)). There are slight differences in the way in which these provisions are worded (for example, the wording of s. 298(4)(a), which requires the landlord to review the decision appears to be independent of the tenant's request for the same), but, in general, the effect appears to be the same. Even if the notice contains a 'bad' reason, that will not invalidate the notice 'unless, for instance, the bad reason somehow infects the good faith of the landlord' (*Manchester CC* v. *Pinnock* [2010] 3 WLR 1441, at [117]).

Regulations make provision for the conduct of the review (respectively: Introductory Tenants (Review) Regulations 1997, SI 1997/72; Demoted Tenancies (Review of Decisions) (England) Regulations 2004, SI 2004/1679; Family Intervention Tenancies (Review of Local Authority Decisions) (England) Regulations 2008, SI 2008/3111). These regulations generally provide that the review is to be conducted by a different, more senior officer, who was not involved in the original decision; tenants may request an oral hearing within 14 days of the notice but, in any event, the tenant is entitled to make written representations; the tenant is entitled to be accompanied by their representative, if any (which may or may not be someone who is professionally qualified), and they are entitled to call their own evidence, put questions to any person who gives evidence, and request that the hearing be postponed (which the landlord may grant or refuse); and the hearing may be adjourned.

What comes across, then, is that the review procedure must be conducted broadly in accordance with the usual principles of natural justice – it is at the crossover between an administrative–adjudicative process, and the principles of adjudication properly apply. For example, evidence of acts occurring after the notice are relevant, provided that the tenant or the landlord has an appropriate opportunity to deal with that evidence (*Manchester CC* v. *Pinnock* [2010] 3 WLR 1441, at [116]; the same must also be true of introductory tenancies and FITs). Furthermore, it is also clear that the landlord is entitled to rely on *any* act or omission of the tenant, whether or not that constitutes a breach of the tenancy agreement, subject only to rationality and proportionality (at [115], presumably provided that the breaches are part of a previous pattern, as to which see below; the same must also be true of introductory tenancies and FITs). The landlord may decide, following a review, effectively to postpone a decision to evict, for example, on terms about the tenant or their household's behaviour; breach of such terms will not require the landlord to serve a second notice (*Cardiff CC* v. *Stone* [2003] HLR 47).

The key point for the purposes of this chapter is that, provided that this procedure has been properly followed, the court *must* make an order for possession (s. 127(2); 143D(2); termination of the FIT is by a notice to quit, on which the court must make an order for possession).

Proportionality

The position at which the UK courts have now arrived is that mandatory possession proceedings are subject to a requirement of proportionality; the question for the court is whether it would be disproportionate to evict the tenant. However, there are a number of provisos. This point took some time to reach, but demonstrates the absolute influence of ECtHR jurisprudence as it developed over the course of the first decade of the twenty-first century. In this section, I sketch out that development, before moving on to the watershed moment – which I take to be the Supreme Court judgment in *Manchester CC* v. *Pinnock*. In the absence of further guidance on the meaning of proportionality in this context, I sketch out certain principles of general application in cases of mandatory possession. I then move on to consider the reach of the proportionality principle – a key question following *Pinnock*.

Development

Prefatory comments

To get to this position, there have been four decisions of the highest UK court (House of Lords/Supreme Court): *Harrow LBC* v. *Qazi* [2004] 1 AC 983; *Kay* v. *Lambeth LBC* [2006] 2 AC 465; *Doherty* v. *Birmingham CC* [2009] 1 AC 367; ending with *Pinnock*. Each of these decisions pushed the boundary a little further. Each of these decisions was interspersed with a number of ECtHR decisions: *Blecic* v. *Croatia* (2004) 41 EHRR 185; *Connors* v. *UK* (2004) 40 EHRR 189; *McCann* v. *United Kingdom* [2008] 47 EHRR 40; *Cosic* v. *Croatia*, ECHR Application 28261/06, 15 January 2009; *Zehentner* v. *Austria*, Application No 20082/02, 16 July 2009; *Paulic* v. *Croatia*, Application No 3572/06, 22 October 2009; *Kay* v. *UK*, Application No 37341/06, 21 September 2010.

By way of further preface, it is necessary to fill in two gaps concerning the implementation of the HRA, and that concerns precedent, and the options open to the court when it considers that a provision is incompatible with Convention rights.

As regards the former, by virtue of s. 2, HRA, a UK court 'must take into account' a judgment of the ECtHR, but it does not need to give effect to it (the rationale is based on certainty: *Kay*, at [43], Lord Bingham). The question about the extent to which UK law must, or should, follow the ECtHR has, accordingly, been a continuing question, answered in this context, emphatically, by the Supreme Court in favour of following the ECtHR. There were good reasons for doing so, to which we will come shortly.

As regards the incompatibility point, a higher court has two options when confronted with a potential incompatibility. These options are governed by s. 3, HRA. The first option is to make a declaration of incompatibility, and leave it to Parliament to remedy that deficiency (that was what the Court of Appeal did in relation to the eligibility issue in *Morris* v. *Westminster CC* [2006] 1 WLR 505, discussed in Chapter 8 above). A county court is not entitled to make a declaration of incompatibility and the proper approach is for that court to adjourn the hearing to enable the compatibility point to be argued in the High Court. The alternative option is what has become known as 'reading down' the relevant provision so that it becomes compatible (that was the option taken by the House of Lords in *Ghaidan* v. *Mendoza* [2004] HLR 46, in relation to same-sex couples and succession to tenancy). It is the latter option which is the one favoured by the HRA: '*So far as it is possible to do so*, primary legislation and subordinate legislation must be read and given effect in a way which is compatible with Convention rights' (s. 3(1), emphasis added).

The unfolding story

The UK story begins not with *Qazi*, in fact, but much earlier, when the parameters of the new, special judicial review procedure governing certain claims against public authorities were set. A question arose as to whether, if a tenant is seeking to deploy public law arguments by way of defence to a possession claim, that defence needed to be pursued through formal judicial review proceedings or could be done by way of defending the possession claim in the county court. That was the issue in *Wandsworth LBC* v. *Winder* [1985] AC 461, where the House of Lords held that the tenant could take the latter option; and that the full range of defences were open to the defendant in such cases. In essence, the question that arose subsequently was the extent to which such public law defences enabled mandatory possession proceedings to be compatible with Article 8. It was that line which held sway in the cases prior to *Pinnock*. Thus, in *Qazi*, the House divided and came to a property law-focused position regarding the interpretation of Article 8 in the context of mandatory possession proceedings (the case concerned the rule in *Monk*). Although the reasoning of the majority was not entirely consistent, it might be said by way of synthesis that it was there held that, where the landlord is relying on an unqualified contractual and proprietary right to possession, and entitled to mandatory possession as a result, Article 8 could not defeat that right (see, generally, Loveland 2004).

In *Kay* and *Doherty*, the line held by the House of Lords was that there were two possible routes of challenge, known as 'gateway (a)' and 'gateway (b)'. This was in direct response to the ECtHR decision in *Connors* (which concerned Travellers being evicted from a site on the basis of certain allegations which they did not have the opportunity to question, as the local authority terminated their licence), but recognising that a public law defence would have been open in that case (see in particular Lord Brown, at [210]). These gateways were explained by Lord Hope, in *Kay* at [110], in a much-quoted formulation as follows:

> (a) if a seriously arguable point is raised that the law which enables the court to make the possession order is incompatible with art 8, the county court in the exercise of its jurisdiction under the Human Rights Act 1998 should deal with the argument in one or other of two ways: (i) by giving effect to the law, so far as it is possible for it do so under s 3, in a way that is compatible with art 8, or (ii) by adjourning the proceedings to enable the compatibility issue to be dealt with in the High Court. (b) if the Defendant wishes to challenge the decision of a public authority to recover possession as an improper exercise of its powers at common law on the ground that it was a decision that no reasonable person would consider justifiable, he should be permitted to do this provided again that the point is seriously arguable: *Wandsworth London Borough Council* v. *Winder* [1985] AC 461. The common law as explained in that case is, of course, compatible with art 8. It provides an additional safeguard.

Gateway (a), however, could generally not be opened by tenants in mandatory possession proceedings – that was the *Qazi* principle, as expressed by Lord Brown in *Kay*:

> Where no statutory protection is afforded to occupiers that should be assumed to be Parliament's will: sometimes that will be clearly evident from the terms of the

governing legislation ... even, however, where the owner's rights arise at common law, the absence of statutory protection must surely be ... the result of a deliberate decision by Parliament to leave the owner's right to recover possession in these cases unqualified. ... it is not unrealistic to regard the general law as striking the required balance. (at [203])

Furthermore, and here there was a minor but important difference between the majority and minority in *Kay*, the minority took the view that the occupier's personal circumstances were relevant to a gateway (b) challenge in the context of an Article 8 defence to mandatory possession proceedings, so that, 'in highly exceptional circumstances' (at [36], Lord Bingham), Article 8 might assist an occupier; the majority disagreed with that view.

By *Doherty*, however, it was clear that the ECtHR had moved much further than the UK courts had believed. In *McCann*, in which the ECtHR held that the rule in *Monk* was incompatible with Article 8, the court said, at [53]:

> As in *Connors*, the 'procedural safeguards' required by Art 8 for the assessment of the proportionality of the interference were not met by the possibility for the applicant to apply for judicial review and to obtain a scrutiny by the courts of the lawfulness and reasonableness of the local authority's decisions. Judicial review procedure is not well adapted for the resolution of sensitive factual questions which are better left to the County Court responsible for ordering possession. In the present case, the judicial review proceedings, like the possession proceedings, did not provide any opportunity for an independent tribunal to examine whether the applicant's loss of his home was proportionate under Art 8(2) to the legitimate aims pursued.

In *Doherty*, the House of Lords moved a little further towards the position of the ECtHR, a position again encapsulated in the judgment of Lord Hope, who argued (at [55]) that:

> I think that in this situation it would be unduly formalistic to confine the review strictly to traditional *Wednesbury* grounds. The considerations that can be brought into account in this case are wider. An examination of the question whether the respondent's decision was reasonable, having regard to the aim which it was pursuing and to the length of time that the appellant and his family have resided on the site, would be appropriate. But the requisite scrutiny would not involve the judge substituting his own opinion for that of the local authority. In my opinion the test of reasonableness should be, as I said in para 110 of *Kay*, whether the decision to recover possession was one which no reasonable person would consider justifiable.

In truth, though, it became difficult to discern quite what difference there was between the modification of *Kay* in *Doherty*, and the position taken by the minority in *Kay* (*Doherty* is discussed deftly by Loveland 2009).

What also emerged from *Doherty* was a strong critique of the ECtHR's understanding of mandatory possession proceedings as they occurred in England. Perhaps the strongest of these critiques was in Lord Scott's judgment (at [82]–[7]), who argued that *McCann* was based on a 'mistaken understanding of the procedure in this country', and a misunderstanding of the various factors which would have been taken into account by the judge, who would have considered the proportionality of the public authority's decision.

In retrospect, that level of critique was misplaced. Not only did the ECtHR pursue the *Connors* line of authority in subsequent cases not involving the UK (*Cosic*, *Zehentner*, *Paulic*), but also, when Mr Kay's (and others') case(s) appeared before the ECtHR, it reinforced its view in those judgments, simply applying that line of authority to *Kay*, and holding that the UK had not gone far enough. The question then arose whether the UK had gone far enough in *Doherty*; on this point, the ECtHR offered a rather cryptic response (see [73]), but this was sufficient to demonstrate that the ECtHR was not going to back down; in the end, it was the Supreme Court, in *Pinnock*, which decided to follow the ECtHR line of authority in preference to the UK line.

Jurisdiction and scale: contestation or conversation?

It is easy to portray the above discussion as one of contestation between the UK highest courts and the ECtHR. The high point of that contestation can be seen, perhaps, in the judgment of Lord Scott in *Doherty*. Certainly, that was the way I saw it while living through the debate from the margins. It was exciting, and it did feel like a battle. It is rare for a single House of Lords' decision to be overturned within a few years, but what was happening were constant modifications until *Pinnock* effectively reversed the previous three House of Lords' decisions. It probably had to do so, because an unsuccessful defence to a mandatory possession claim by a tenant would be likely to lead to an application to the ECtHR, which was equally likely to be successful (there are applications pending before the ECtHR in at least two pre-*Pinnock* cases: *Wandsworth LBC* v. *Dixon* [2009] EWHC 27; *Poplar HARCA* v. *Howe* [2010] EWHC 1745).

With the considerable assistance of my colleagues,[1] I now see this rather differently; rather than a 'battle', I see it as raising questions of jurisdiction and scale which are neatly and harmoniously resolved (as to which see, generally, Valverde 2009). De Sousa Santos (1987: 283) writes that different scales of legality are 'constituted by different legal spaces operating simultaneously on different scales and from different interpretive standpoints. So much is this so that in phenomenological terms and as a result of interaction and intersection among legal spaces one cannot properly speak of law and legality but rather of interlaw and interlegality'. And, as Valverde (2009: 142–3) comments, part of the salience of this notion is that the plurality implied by interlegality also means that 'one and the same authority can use different gazes at different times – or even at the same time'.

---

[1] This section is based on some of the ideas in a paper prepared by Caroline Hunter, Hal Pawson and myself, and delivered at the Society of Legal Scholars annual conference, University of Southampton, 2010.

Interlaw and interlegality underpin the development towards, and understandings of, proportionality. On one level, they demonstrate the harmonious
interaction between the highest UK court (House of Lords or Supreme Court)
and the ECtHR. These courts have engaged in constructive dialogue with each
other (to use the House of Lords' expression in *R* v. *Horncastle* [2010] 2 AC 373;
R (Purdy) v. *DPP* [2010] 1 AC 345, at [34], Lord Hope), and the ECtHR has
led the UK courts to a position which approximates with their requirements.
In essence, those notions of interlaw and interlegality are what this discussion
is about: the overlapping jurisdictions and agents, their different scales of operation, and their different social realities. The search should be for the internal
logics of the different scales to demonstrate not just their difference and incom-
mensurability (which would come as little surprise to any socio-legal scholar);
but also the purpose of reference to jurisdiction and scale is not to denounce
one scale by reference to the principles of another scale but rather to offer a version which puts abstract principles of law and the everyday work of housing
officers in separate blackboxes which are rarely connected (Valverde 2009).
That is what the House of Lords and Supreme Court were seeking to achieve –
co-existence and harmonious separation. For the ordinary, everyday work of
housing officers and county courts are as relevant to this discussion as abstract
legal principles and values. What the UK courts were trying to protect were the
internal logics of mandatory possession proceedings. As Cowan et al. (2010)
put it, these internal logics were twofold:

> First, and most significantly, there is protection of the integrity of the process.
> Time and again in the cases, we are told that most gateway (b) claims [could],
> and should, be disposed of summarily, presumably as part of the list. Even Lord
> Bingham, who was in the minority in *Kay*, was clear that this was '… an import-
> ant aspect of these appeals, and one that has caused the House much concern' but
> was a concern which could be assuaged by the high standard (which all Counsel
> who appeared accepted) to be applied.
>
> Second, it follows from that first point certainly as an outcome but, we sug-
> gest, also as part of the internal logic of public law itself, that considerable lati-
> tude is to be given to social housing providers in their possession claims. Part
> of the rationality behind that principle is deference to the nature of mandatory
> possession proceedings, as developed by the courts and appears in statutory pro-
> visions. … This suggests an empirical conclusion, which may not be warranted,
> that social housing providers make rational, lawful decisions which comply with
> their policies and procedures. Curtailing the defences of occupiers only makes
> sense when this internal logic of the process is applied.

The ECtHR certainly accepted the first point that these authors made, as indeed
did Lord Bingham in *Kay*. The point at issue, though, was whether, and to what
extent, it was appropriate to give that measure of deference to the decision-
making of authorities exercising functions of a public nature.

Successive refinements of the gateway (b) defence were made by the Court
of Appeal and High Court before *Pinnock*. In particular, in *Stokes* v. *Brent LBC*

[2010] EWCA Civ 626, the Court of Appeal held that the tenant could not call for full disclosure at the initial possession hearing unless it was decided that the tenant's defence was substantial (in accordance with CPR 55.8(2); at which point case management directions may be given which are likely to include disclosure). This meant that the tenant would be unlikely to be able to uncover procedural and substantive defects in the landlord's decision-making prior to the hearing in order to demonstrate that the defence was 'seriously arguable'. Indeed, amid the welter of higher court decisions on the ambit of gateway (b), there were only four successful defences (*Doherty*; *McGlynn v Welwyn Hatfield DC* [2010] HLR 10 (legitimate expectation); *Eastlands Homes Partnership Ltd v. Whyte* [2010] EWHC 695 (QB) (procedural impropriety); *Barber* v. *Croydon LBC* [2010] HLR 26 (irrationality)).

By way of additional summary of that welter of authority on gateway (b), the following general principles can be deduced:

a. The proper location for hearing a gateway (b) defence is the county court and the 3-month time limit used in relation to applications for judicial review does not apply (*Winder*).

b. The full range of public law defences, as influenced by the jurisprudence derived from the European Convention on Human Rights, are available to the defendant (*Kay/Doherty*). This includes a defence that is based on the occupier's legitimate expectation and procedural impropriety on the part of the claimant (*McGlynn*).

c. Such defences should only be raised when they have real and obvious substance – overly technical defences will not be permitted (*Brent LBC* v. *Corcoran* [2010] HLR 43, at [26], Jacob LJ).

d. The defendant's personal circumstances which are known to the claimant may be relevant to a gateway (b) defence, in particular the length of time which the defendant has lawfully occupied the property; and the provision of alternative accommodation (respectively, *Kay* at [210], *per* Lord Brown; *Defence Estates* v. *JL* [2009] EWHC 1049 (Admin); *Central Bedfordshire Council* v. *Taylor* [2010] 1 WLR 446). However, on their own, personal circumstances are insufficient to mount a gateway (b) defence successfully (although they are relevant to the exercise of discretion as to whether, and for what period, to suspend a possession order).

e. It is a 'rare' or 'exceptional' case which surmounts the higher threshold requirement that a case be 'seriously arguable' (*Kay*; on 'seriously arguable', see, especially, the first instance judgment of King J in *Stokes* v. *LB Brent* [2009] EWHC 1426 (QB)).

f. Although the landlord would be better served in a claim for possession by giving consideration to the relevant facts prior to their decisions, there is no requirement for it so to do when it is relying on a claim for possession as of right. Nor is there a requirement for the claimant to give reasons for their decisions unless the situation is 'exceptional'.

g. The court's consideration should be directed at all decisions taken by a claimant throughout their claim for possession (as far as the execution of a warrant of possession) (*Taylor*, at [39]–[41]; *Mullen*, at [68]–[75]; *Barber*; cf. *Doran* v. *Liverpool CC* [2009] 1 WLR 2365).

h. A county court cannot substitute its decision for that of the claimant – the usual range of public law remedies are available, although it appears that a county court is unable to make such orders and so, if successful, the matter must be remitted to the High Court.

The watershed moment: *Pinnock*

Pinnock has expanded the grounds of challenge so that an occupier can now also plead a proportionality defence, although it is clear that a challenge to a decision on public law principles (gateway (b)) also remains. A successful gateway (b) challenge may fall within a proportionality defence, but this is not necessarily the case (see the discussion of proportionality below).

In *Pinnock*, the narrow issue for the Supreme Court concerned whether the requirement on the judge to grant possession to a landlord of a demoted tenancy was compatible with Article 8; and, if so, whether it was open to the demoted tenant to bring a gateway (b) defence in those same proceedings; and whether the ambit of a gateway (b) challenge enabled Mr Pinnock to dispute the factual basis on which Manchester had decided the review. The Court of Appeal had held that it was so compatible, in part because one had to look at the whole process from application for a demoted tenancy (with the reasonableness requirement) together with the process for termination. Further, it was held that the statutory provisions, in requiring the court to make an order if there had been compliance with the process, required any gateway (b) challenge to be made by separate application for judicial review, but any challenge to the procedure could be dealt with by the county court judge. The Court of Appeal was necessarily constrained by authority in so reading the provisions.

The Supreme Court, however, rewrote the rule book (Lord Neuberger providing the sole judgment of the nine-judge court). It focused on the jurisprudence of the ECtHR, and drew the following conclusions:

(a) Any person at risk of being dispossessed of his home at the suit of a local authority should in principle have the right to raise the question of the proportionality of the measure, and to have it determined by an independent tribunal in the light of article 8, even if his right of occupation under domestic law has come to an end ....

(b) A judicial procedure which is limited to addressing the proportionality of the measure through the medium of traditional judicial review (i e, one which does not permit the court to make its own assessment of the facts in an appropriate case) is inadequate as it is not appropriate for resolving sensitive factual issues ....

(c) Where the measure includes proceedings involving more than one stage, it is the proceedings as a whole which must be considered in order to see if article 8 has been complied with ....

(d) If the court concludes that it would be disproportionate to evict a person from his home notwithstanding the fact that he has no domestic right to remain there, it would be unlawful to evict him so long as the conclusion obtains – for example, for a specified period, or until a specified event occurs, or a particular condition is satisfied. (at [45]; references to ECtHR authority for each proposition have been removed)

This was an 'unambiguous and consistent' line of authority (at [46]). As regards the extent to which account should be taken of that line of authority, the court said that, although the general principle is that the court is not bound to follow every decision of the ECtHR:

> Where, however, there is a clear and constant line of decisions whose effect is not inconsistent with some fundamental substantive or procedural aspect of our law, and whose reasoning does not appear to overlook or misunderstand some argument or point of principle, we consider that it would be wrong for this Court not to follow that line. (at [48])

Therefore, the court hearing the possession claim must have the power to assess the proportionality of the order for possession and resolve any dispute of fact (at [49]). As a result, the Supreme Court 'read down' the mandatory nature of the demoted tenancy possession proceedings to enable the county court judge also to consider the proportionality of the eviction as well as decide disputed questions of fact (at [73]–[88]).

> After all, the tenant's [proportionality] argument in such circumstances would be within the scope of the ambit of section 143D(2), namely that 'the procedure under sections 143E and 143F has not been [lawfully] followed', since lawfulness must be an inherent requirement of the procedure. It must equally be open to the court to consider whether the procedure has been lawfully followed, having regard to the defendant's article 8 Convention rights and section 6 of the HRA. (at [77])

As it happened, none of this helped the Pinnock household themselves. This was partly because the process should be seen as a whole – a judge would have found that it was reasonable to make a demoted tenancy less than 2 years previously – and it would be a most unusual case in which the household was able to deploy proportionality successfully (at [107]). There had been three serious offences since the demoted tenancy order was made, which were not breaches of the tenancy agreement (resisting arrest at the property, causing death by dangerous driving, burglary). The Pinnock's defence was that they had lived in the property for 30 years; they were not responsible for the offences (it was their children who no longer lived at the property); Mr Pinnock could not therefore be treated as responsible for their behaviour; and there were other ways of dealing with the behaviour, such as by an ASBO or ASBI, rather than obtaining possession. The Supreme Court did not accept these arguments. These were serious offences which, while unrelated to the tenancy agreement (which did not matter, as there was no requirement in the statute that they should be), were committed when the children visited their parents:

> For the Council to evict Mr Pinnock on such grounds may well seem to him harsh. However, in the light of the history, the demotion order, the interests of their neighbours, and the Council's right and duty to manage and allocate its housing stock, the decision cannot be characterised as unreasonable or dispro-portionate. (at [128])

There are grounds for suggestion that the Supreme Court might have been less convinced were the acts relied on by the local authority not repetitions of the former events. As the court put it:

> there appears to be no express fetter on the nature of the grounds which a local authority can invoke for seeking possession against a demoted tenant. It would seem that, as in this case, local authorities seeking possession against demoted tenants in practice normally rely on repetitions of the type of incidents which gave rise to the demotion order. It may well be that the nature of the grounds upon which possession can be sought against demoted tenants is limited in that way, as a matter of law. However, that would involve implying some sort of limita-tion into the statute, as there is no express provision which would prevent a local authority relying on, say, the fact that it has a more deserving potential occupier of the premises in question. We say no more on the matter since the point does not arise in this appeal, and it was not the subject of any argument. (at [106])

Proportionality: meaning and effect

The approach in *Pinnock*

The Supreme Court also considered the meaning and effect of the incorp-oration of this concept into English law in this context; it is not an unknown concept in English law, to which we return below. However, in the context of mandatory possession proceedings, the Supreme Court, perhaps unfortunately, felt that 'the wide implications of this obligation will have to be worked out. As in many situations, that is best left to the good sense and experience of judges sitting in the County Court' (at [57]). Certain guidance was provided by the Supreme Court, however, more at what might be termed a meta-level, partly because the court was due to hear the appeals in *Salford CC* v. *Mullen* [2010] HLR 35 (concerned with introductory tenancies and Part VII accommodation), in which it envisaged that it would give further guidance.

The first point of significance here concerns the previous position that it would only be exceptional cases that would be able to maintain the defence (a position which had been accepted by the ECtHR). The Supreme Court regarded it as 'unsafe and unhelpful' to use exceptionality as the criterion. The starting point is that, unless the landlord believes that there are particularly strong or unusual reasons for seeking possession, it is not necessary for it to plead the same. The public authority landlord's rights and obligations – to possession coupled with the duties regarding the distribution and management of its housing stock, including allocation, redevelopment, refurbishment, transfer of occupants who are over-occupying or to sheltered/warden-assisted housing – are clearly established. However, 'The question is always whether the eviction is a proportionate means of achieving a legitimate aim' (at [52]).

The further guidance given by the Supreme Court on the ambit of proportionality was, first, that it did not envisage that the acceptance of the doctrine of proportionality would impact on the discretionary grounds for possession where reasonableness must also be shown. Six further general points were made (at [59]–[64]). First, the conditions for establishing the proportionality defence rely on the occupier showing that the property is their 'home'. Second, the Article 8 defence must be raised by the occupier. Third, the court will usually consider the issue summarily so that if, 'as will no doubt often be the case', the facts do not suggest the defence will succeed, it should be dismissed. Fourth, the effect of Article 8 may, 'albeit in exceptional cases', require the grant of an extended period of possession, suspending the order, or refusing it altogether. Fifth, certain procedural and statutory provisions may require revisiting (including the postponement of possession in cases of exceptional hardship to 42 days: s. 89, Housing Act 1980). Sixth, proportionality is more likely to be a relevant issue if the occupier is vulnerable as a result of mental illness, physical or learning disability, poor health or frailty, which may require the body exercising functions of a public nature to explain why it is not securing alternative accommodation.

Proportionality: general approach

The starting point here is the decision of the Privy Council in *de Freitas* v. *Permanent Secretary of Ministry of Agriculture, Fisheries, Lands and Housing* [1999] 1 AC 69, p. 80 (Lord Clyde), which suggested a three-stage test. The court should ask itself

> whether: (i) the legislative objective is sufficiently important to justify limiting a fundamental right; (ii) the measures designed to meet the legislative objective are rationally connected to it; and (iii) the means used to impair the right or freedom are no more than is necessary to accomplish the objective.

This test was subsequently accepted and adopted as determining the 'contours' of proportionality (e.g. *R(Daly)* v. *Home Secretary* [2001] 2 AC 532, [27], Lord Steyn; *A* v. *Secretary of State for the Home Department* [2005] 2 AC 69, at [30], Lord Bingham). In *Huang* v. *Secretary of State for the Home Department* [2007] 2 AC 167, at [19], the House of Lords unanimously recognised that an aspect of proportionality 'which should never be overlooked or discounted' is 'the need to balance the interests of society with those of individuals and groups'. The 'fair balance' of those interests lies at the heart of the Convention rights (citing *R (Razgar)* v. *Secretary of State for the Home Department* [2004] 2 AC 368).

In *Daly*, Lord Steyn further observed (at [27]–[8]): (a) there is an overlap between proportionality and traditional grounds for review, but the intensity of a proportionality review is somewhat different; (b) proportionality review may require the reviewing court to assess the balance struck by the decision-maker (not merely whether the decision is perverse); (c) proportionality may go further than traditional judicial review in requiring attention to be directed 'to the relative weight accorded to interests and considerations'; (d) proportionality goes beyond a 'heightened scrutiny test' in judicial review proceedings.

Although proportionality in essence requires a balance to be drawn, the ECtHR applies a test of 'margin of appreciation' in favour of participating states. Such a test is inapt in a national context. Thus, the test has been framed differently by the UK courts, essentially as one of appropriate deference to the context, or, as Lord Hope put it, a 'margin of discretion' which is context-dependent (*A* v. *Secretary of State for the Home Department* [2005] 2 AC 69, at [107]; on this notion, see, in particular: Rivers 2006; Young 2009). A decision-maker is not necessarily required to make their decision in the same way as a court might assess the question of proportionality (*R (SB)* v. *Governors of Denbigh High School* [2007] 1 AC 100, at [68], Lord Hoffmann). However, as Baroness Hale has observed, 'the views of the local authority are bound to carry less weight where the local authority has made no attempt to address that question' (*Belfast CC* v. *Miss Behavin' Ltd* [2007] 1 WLR 1420, at [37]).

The 'intensity' of the proportionality review and, indeed, the deference accorded to the decision-making body depends on the type of right under consideration. It is variable in other words (*R (SB)* v. *Governors of Denbigh High School* [2007] 1 AC 100, at [30], Lord Bingham). In this context, Article 8 is, of course, a qualified right but it is significant that the ECtHR, in its consistent line of decisions on this issue, has made clear that: 'The loss of one's home is a most extreme form of interference with the right to respect for the home.' (*McCann* v. *UK* [2008] 47 EHRR 40, at [50]) It is, therefore, arguable that the intensity of review should be high in this context.

A proportionality test requires the judge to make their own reasoned decision as to whether, in all the circumstances, a decision is proportionate. As Lord Bingham put it in the *Denbigh* case, 'The domestic court must now make a value judgment, an evaluation, by reference to the circumstances prevailing at the relevant time' and be judged *objectively* by the court (at [30]). In parenthesis, it might be added that the 'relevant time' is the time at which the relevant measure is being applied (*Wilson* v. *First County Trust Ltd (No. 2)* [2004] 1 AC 816). However, it is clear that proportionality involves a different evaluative judgment from a *Wednesbury*-type review and entitles the presiding judge to substitute their decision for that of the council.

In principle, each decision made by the landlord exercising functions of a public nature in the course of a possession claim is open to scrutiny on the basis of proportionality. This follows from the decisions prior to *Pinnock*, which were concerned with the authority's decisions on which a gateway (b) defence will 'bite', and are *a fortiori* equally applicable post-*Pinnock* (indeed, that appears implicitly accepted in Pinnock – see [81]).

Proportionality: summary of relevant principles

It may assist readers to have a summary of relevant principles which can be derived from the authorities:

a. Where a proportionality defence is available to mandatory possession proceedings, it must follow that the 'gateway (a)' defence is unarguable.

b. The relevant question is whether the eviction is a proportionate means of achieving a legitimate aim.

c. The intensity of the proportionality review, which should apply in cases where the right to respect for the home is in issue, is high because of the significance of the right and its breach.

d. The court should, in such cases, assess the balance struck by the decision-maker and direct attention to the relative weight accorded to interests and considerations. This review requires an objective value judgment.

e. A margin of discretion is appropriately accorded to decision-makers.

f. There is no requirement for the decision-maker to conduct a full-blown 'proportionality review', but the decision-maker's views will carry little weight if they do not consider the balance of interests.

g. The following are relevant considerations as part of the fair balance of interests: the landlord's housing management rights and responsibilities; the landlord's unencumbered property right; the occupier's personal circumstances, particularly relating to vulnerability; the consequences of an order for possession (see also *Kryvitska* v. *Ukraine* (ECtHR, 2 December 2010), at [50]).

h. Each 'micro-decision' taken by the landlord in initiating and continuing a possession claim in the exercise of its functions of a public nature is, in principle, separately and properly the subject of the proportionality assessment.

i. The court is entitled to decide disputed questions of fact where those facts are relevant to the case.

j. The court is entitled to substitute its own decision (on the facts and proportionality) for that of the decision-maker.

k. If a proportionality defence is successfully made out, the court has a range of options by way of remedy (refuse, adjourn, suspend, postpone, extended period for possession).[2]

---

[2] Excellent textbook accounts of the doctrine of proportionality can be found in Craig 2008: 621–45; Harlow and Rawlings 2009: 120–6; for a particularly stimulating, general discussion of the issues, see Hickman 2010, especially ch. 5.

It is difficult to over-estimate the change of mindset which this set of principles requires both of English law as well as landlord practice, to which we now turn.

Landlord practice: private registered providers and the use of Ground 8

It will be remembered from Chapter 11 that Ground 8 is the mandatory possession ground for rent arrears under the Housing Act 1988 (for ATs and ASTs). It requires that there are at least two months' (or eight weeks', depending on the rent period) rent arrears at the date of service of the notice seeking possession and at the date of the hearing. If those simple facts are shown, the court must then make an order for possession; there is no discretion. The rent arrears PAP does not apply to a claim brought under this ground. Other than in the proper management of the court list or where the tenant has a possible defence, the judge hearing the claim can only adjourn it on exceptional grounds:

> there may occasionally be circumstances where the refusal of an adjournment would be considered to be outrageously unjust by any fair-minded person. We hold that the power to adjourn a hearing date for the purpose of enabling a tenant to reduce the arrears to below the Ground 8 threshold may only be exercised in exceptional circumstances ... But the fact that the arrears are attributable to maladministration on the part of the housing benefit authority is not an exceptional circumstance. It is a sad feature of contemporary life that housing benefit problems are widespread. To a substantial extent, these are no doubt the product of lack of resources. But we do not consider that the nonreceipt of housing benefit can, of itself, amount to exceptional circumstances which would justify the exercise of the power to adjourn so as to enable the tenant to defeat the claim. (*North British HA* v. *Matthews* [2005] 1 WLR 3133, at [32])

PRPs which use this ground should do so as a 'last resort' (as with their general powers of tenancy termination). They do not need to use it, and many do not (as discussed in Chapter 11). In the period before *Pinnock*, when the scope of the two gateways was being widely discussed within the housing law profession as well as being much (perhaps over) litigated, Pawson et al. (2010) conducted their research into the use of Ground 8 by PRPs (although the research was broader). Lawyers might have anticipated that the issue would have been much discussed and considered by PRPs. There was, of course, no reason why that should have been the case, other than perhaps a colonisation of one jurisdiction/scale by another. What the Pawson et al. research found, by way of contrast, was the limited penetration of the gateways discourse into PRP practice. In their online questionnaire sample of PRPs, which used Ground 8, only 7.7 per cent (n=4) indicated that human rights issues influenced the decision whether or not to use Ground 8.

The factor most commonly cited as one of the reasons for the use of Ground 8 was rent arrears (73 per cent). While this may not be a particularly surprising finding (perhaps the surprising element is that *only* 73 per cent cited this reason), statistics on 2007/2008 evictions showed that tenants evicted under Ground 8 had higher arrears than those whose homes were repossessed on other grounds. However, the difference in the average figures across all responding associations – £2,600 compared with £2,300 – was fairly modest suggesting that this reason (i.e. level of arrears) might not have been the only factor involved in decision-making. Other factors cited as reasons for using Ground 8 were: where the tenant failed to respond to attempts at contact; where the tenant was believed to be no longer living at the property; and the tenant's 'other behaviour' (most likely some form of nuisance or ASB – 51.9 per cent of respondents (n=27)). The picture which emerged from this data suggests that a proportionality argument might be possible in certain of these cases, particularly where the tenant has not had an opportunity to respond to allegations made about their 'other behaviour'. Jurisdiction, then, becomes relevant here too, for that choice of jurisdiction underscores the greater ease with which (in theory) the PRP might obtain possession. As Ground 8 was chosen for its greater efficiency than the nuisance-based grounds, it enabled PRPs and the law to operate in an orderly way, pigeon-holing the relevant information in the relevant boxes. Jurisdiction also emerged as a factor in another, perhaps more subtle, way in the online survey. A quarter of respondents (n=13) which used Ground 8 did so to by-pass the procedural requirements of the PAP on rent arrears.

In their case studies, the researchers found that jurisdiction and scale were significant but approached differently. Statistics and benchmarking form a critical part of rent officer practice, suggesting the significance of the power of audit as a scale of law. Public law considerations were largely irrelevant, although there was recognition of the controversy about the use of Ground 8 by social landlords.

Most internal written policies were framed differently, but one common theme was that use of Ground 8 was termed a 'last resort' or for use in 'exceptional circumstances' or 'where appropriate', but there were different ways of conceptualising when this arose depending on the broader environment in which the association found itself. It was clear that Ground 8 was used, in particular, by many officers as 'a threat' or, less pejoratively, 'a lever' to make tenants pay off their arrears. Some officers also stressed that, while orders may be sought and made under Ground 8, they would not seek to enforce them if the occupier made an offer to repay the arrears. For these reasons, conversely, Ground 8 was not regarded as an eviction tool, but a tenancy sustainment tool – as one PRP officer put it, 'a tool to focus people's minds'.

The data also suggested that Ground 8 would be used in practice to by-pass other mandatory procedures which were regarded as problematic for one reason or another. In theory, for example, a tenant who abandons their tenancy so that the property is not the tenant's 'only or principal home' loses their security of tenure. Possession should follow. However, proving abandonment is not necessarily a simple matter. Equally, within an organisation, responsibility for such proceedings may fall on a different part of the organisation (such as legal services). It may take some time to put such a case together, during which rent

arrears would rise and which would have an impact on a rent officer's performance rating. Possession in such abandonment cases might be sought on the
basis of Ground 8. For the same reasons, the same approach might be used in
cases where it was believed that the tenant had sub-let the property.

What this research suggests, then, is that there may be some scope in our
post-*Pinnock* world for the operation of proportionality in such cases, taking
account of the individual PRP policy, the reasons for seeking to use Ground 8 in
that individual case, and the process adopted by the PRP for making that decision; the evidence may also suggest that the 'exceptional' may be rather more
common than the Supreme Court believed.

Future issues

One of the key questions is the extent of the reach of the proportionality doctrine. There are two possible answers to this question, although there is doubt in
relation to both. The first answer is that proportionality only applies in the case
of those core public authorities, as well as hybrid public authorities, which are
exercising functions of a public nature. If this were the case, then there would
be a certain number of tricky issues. The status of PRPs would be very much in
issue, partly because of the wide effect it would potentially have on their practices. If *Weaver* is right – and, as will be remembered from Chapter 5 above,
there must be some doubt about the extent of the Court of Appeal's interpretation, let alone the outcome – then PRPs would be covered. The real questions,
then, are the extent to which it reaches further (the potential 'Heineken effect').
For example, there are questions over the extent to which the PRS might find
itself subject to the proportionality doctrine – and thus, we might find a potential remedy to the retaliatory eviction problem discussed in Chapter 11; or, perhaps, this might be limited to where there is a greater element of 'publicness',
such as where a PRS landlord provides housing through nomination arrangements with the local authority or in satisfaction of the local authority's Part VII
duties. There are arguments both ways here (Lord Mance reserved this question
in *YL* v. *Birmingham CC* [2008] 1 AC 95, at [85], for example; Baroness Hale
hinted at an answer at [55]; cf. Lord Neuberger, at [135] and [164]); perhaps the
question was easier when one was applying public law principles only under
gateway (b) because it has not been suggested that a private landlord would be
amenable to judicial review.

There is an alternative way of answering this question: it is a non-question.
The HRA is applied by the court, and the court is a core public authority. A
court must exercise all its functions in accordance with the HRA; therefore,
the court cannot order possession without considering the proportionality of
the outcome. The identity of the actual parties is an irrelevance. This is what is
sometimes termed 'the horizontal application' of the HRA because it may apply
between two private parties (see, for example, Hunt 2001; Hickman 2010).
There are odd cases where it appears (or it can be argued) that the courts have
proceeded on this assumption without directly addressing the point (*Ghaidan*

v. *Mendoza* [2004] 2 AC 557 is such a case). There is much to be said for such an approach – there are no divisions (all tenures are part of the social), and no costly litigation; probably also, the state would have to answer for (say) the notice and writing-based procedure for terminating an AST in the ECtHR, were a challenge brought by a tenant. That having been said, though, there is much to be said for tightening up the qualifying criterion – the breadth of proportionality might suggest that the qualifying criteria should be narrowed; there would be concerns stemming from the (legal) regulation-as-burden line of argument, and that extra regulation may push potential or current landlords away from the market.

The other central question here concerns the parameters of proportionality in the context of mandatory possession proceedings and the extent of deference to the public authority's decision-making practice. Much hinges on the Supreme Court's approach in *Salford CC* v. *Mullen*, judgment in which is currently anticipated.

The problems of tenure-shifting

In this section, two aspects of tenure-shifting are considered: sale-and-rent-back arrangements; and IHO (intermediate home ownership, aka shared ownership). I proceed on the basis that Article 8 is probably not applicable in the former; but is applicable in the latter, at least where the landlord is a PRP or local authority. The former contains issues which draw largely on property law principles; the latter raises difficult questions of property and housing law, with an additional smattering of the HRA. The analysis in this section hinges on the discussion about these types of arrangement in Chapters 9 and 10 above. These two examples demonstrate that, although tenure-shifting may be a significant policy device and of some potential benefit, the legal implications of each of these types of transactions are capable of causing a major headache for policy-makers, law, and the consumer (and, one might add, there has been little thought given to the latter's position).

Sale-and-rentback

In a sale-and-rentback arrangement, the seller-renter will usually take under an AST. There may also have been representations made to the seller-renter by the buyer at the time of sale as to the length of such an agreement (over and above the actual term of the tenancy). It is perfectly possible that, if the seller-renter relied on such a representation, the buyer would be bound by it (and it may also bind any further person interested in the property). However, the key issue which has emerged is whether the seller-renter's interest will bind the buyer's mortgage lender. The issue usually arises where the buyer becomes bankrupt or insolvent, or otherwise unable to meet the mortgage payments. In such a case, the lender may seek possession. The lender will be bound by the AST if it consented to the AST taking priority over its own interest. If the AST was created before the mortgage, then it may bind the mortgage lender if it was made by a deed or the buyer is in 'actual occupation' at the date of the transfer to the lender (s. 30, Sch. 3, paras. 1 and 2, Land Registration Act 2002). But, equally, in theory, if the AST is made after the mortgage, then the mortgage should take priority (s. 28).

Timing is everything. It is also extremely messy, partly because it was held in *Abbey National BS* v. *Cann* [1991] AC 56 that where a purchase is made with a mortgage, and the buyer needed the mortgage to complete the purchase, the two transactions (sale and mortgage) take place simultaneously; there is no moment in time (or, as it was put in *Cann*, no *scintilla temporis*) between those two transactions. If there is no such moment in time, then the buyer cannot grant rights, including the AST to the seller-renter, *prior* to the creation of the mortgage. Further, where the contract, completion and registration occur on the same day, these are all assumed to be one and the same transaction without a moment in time between them (*Nationwide* v. *Ahmed* (1995) 70 P&CR 381). Assuming that *Cann* was correctly decided (and there may be some doubt), there may be another interpretation of its outcome, and that is that the House of Lords were simply taking account of the realities of the transaction (which was undoubtedly the basis for the decision in *Cann*).

In *Redstone Mortgages plc* v. *Welch*, Birmingham County Court, 22 June 2009 (HHJ Worster), the judge took the latter approach. It was therefore open to him to find that the reality of the transaction was that the buyer never obtained the property free from the seller-renter's interest. That meant that the seller-renter's interest had to precede the lender's interest. That approach was approved by the High Court in *Delaney* v. *Chan* [2010] EWHC 6 (Ch), albeit that it was not in issue in that case. However, in *In the Matter of the North East Property Buyers Litigation* [2010] EWHC 2991 (Ch), HHJ Behrens took the former, narrower interpretation of the decision in *Cann*. From a property lawyer's perspective, that reading of *Cann* is the orthodox approach. It was also argued in the *North East Property Buyer's Litigation* that the seller-renter's rights could affix to the contract (before the transfer of the property to the buyer), but the extension of *Cann* in *Ahmed* stood in the way of that argument particularly as, in each of the cases before HHJ Behrens, contract and completion took place on the same day; further, in order for the seller-renter's rights to bind the mortgage lender, they had to be property rights, and not personal rights (Sch. 3, para. 2, Land Registration Act 2002):

> prior to completion the occupiers' equitable rights were at best personal and not proprietary. At that stage (prior to completion) the vendors were in possession and entitled to remain in possession by virtue of their ownership of their properties. NEPB had no right to possession prior to completion and could not therefore grant a proprietary right to possession. As the rights were personal rights they could not give rise to overriding interests. They became proprietary rights as against NEPB on completion. (at [54])

The problem was that all the seller-renters had, on this interpretation, was a mere hope that they would be offered an AST after the sale, and that mere hope was a personal right against the buyer. Here, it may be that HHJ Behrens can be criticised for not considering the possibility of an estoppel binding on the buyer and lender prior to sale, although it is recognised that there are problems in the way of such an argument (there would then follow the difficult question of whether the estoppel was sufficiently mature to bind the mortgage lender – s. 116, Land Registration Act 2002 – a question which, by itself, is by no means easy, see *Henry and Mitchell* v. *Henry* [2010] 1 All ER 988, at [46]–[7], for example).

Intermediate home ownership

In an IHO lease, where the shared owner defaults on their rent or mortgage, or breaches a term of their lease, the question arises as to the proper routes for possession. The owner's mortgage lender may use the procedure for recovery of possession outlined in Chapter 14 above if the default is on mortgage payments. Where the mortgage lender seeks possession, the IHO buyer has the usual protections afforded to owners under the Administration of Justice Acts 1970 and 1973, together with the PAP; and the lender also has the benefit of the mortgagee protection clause discussed in Chapter 10 above. The owner's landlord may use the processes in the Housing Act 1988 (where the landlord is a PRP) in order to obtain possession. They may use one of the discretionary grounds, or they may use the mandatory grounds (including Ground 8 discussed above). Now, and here is the significant point, if the PRP is successful in obtaining possession, the shared owner walks away with *nothing*; they have no proprietary entitlement because they have no tenancy; and, if they have no tenancy, their 'share' (together with any capital appreciation) is lost unless the PRP offers *ex gratia* to repay it. The average equity share purchased initially has ranged from 37–47 per cent (HCA 2010: figure 9). If one accepts that such a result just seems wrong and unfair, one still needs to clothe such a gut feeling in legal garb, but the available range of clothes are ill-fitting. A range of arguments were deployed in the one case on this subject, *Richardson* v. *Midland Heart Limited*, Birmingham Civil Justice Centre (ChD), 12 November 2007, and a further set were to be deployed in *Catalyst HA* v. *Hart*, although that case was settled.

Possession

The available data on possession is incomplete – a surprising omission given that so much data about PRP performance is collected centrally. It is known that, in 2008/2009, 432 shared-ownership properties were repossessed by the lender (0.38%) (HCA 2010: para. 61). However, it has been said that the proportion of shared owners in arrears is higher than for other first-time buyers or RTB owners (Bramley et al. 2002: 130; at p. 133, the proportion of repossessions was estimated at 0.77% as opposed to 0.21% for other owners in 2000). Such a finding is understandable because of the higher costs of IHO and the low (as well as potentially unstable) income of occupiers. It is also known that at least three PRPs seek possession using Ground 8 (Pawson et al. 2010: 59). Where the buyer defaults on their mortgage or lease, they may be entitled to staircase down (although the conditions for such action are often strict so that many buyers will find themselves unable to do so), but there is no obligation on the PRP to allow this.

Guidance

Given the significance of the problem, and the high policy/political stakes, it might have been hoped that there would be clear guidance about when possession should be sought or, indeed, on what ground(s). Unfortunately, the guidance does not do so. Rather, it focuses on the proper interaction between PRP and mortgage lender (CML/NHF 2009; CML et al. 2010: paras. 67–70). So, a PRP which intends to claim possession of the property is usually required under the terms of an undertaking with the lender to give reasonable notice to that lender. The purpose of the notice is to provide 'sufficient time [to the lender] to resolve the problem, so avoiding the need for the [PRP] to take legal action that could result in the loss of the mortgage security' (para. 86). A mortgagee may have, and take, the option of 'final staircasing' (buying the remaining share) or simply enforce its security in the usual ways. The PRP must also give a separate notice to the lender of at least 28 days about the possible possession proceedings and the grounds on which the action will be based (paras. 87–8).

Further guidance is provided by the CML and NHF (2009). This is not particularly aimed at protecting the buyer, but, again, at the interactions between the PRP and lender, setting out the actions which they should take (in terms of communication between them) before commencing a claim to possession. The guidance *notes* do, however, make a number of observations about PRPs and possession, and it is worth quoting these in full:

> [PRP]s can offer a range of support to leaseholders who are in financial difficulty, from showing where to get financial advice through to using the Recycled Capital Grant Fund to allow households to 'downward staircase' when someone is in danger of losing their home.

> The key rule when considering taking action over arrears is not to seek possession where there is a reasonable alternative. If this is not possible, [PRP]s are legally entitled to use Ground 8, which is one of the mandatory grounds for possession of an assured tenancy listed in Housing Act 1988 Schedule 2.

> However, the use of Ground 8 is an extreme step in the context of shared ownership housing, the effect of which is similar to forfeiture. It should not be necessary where the [PRP] and lender work jointly to resolve the problem, if possible with the shared owner.

When the use of Ground 8 is unavoidable, the decision should be taken at an appropriately senior level in an organisation, and the lender should be told that this course of action is intended at least 28 days before notice is served.

It is most important that both parties understand the requirements placed on the other in respect of the borrower/tenant, and take these fully into account when dealing with arrears/possession.

Midland Heart v. *Richardson*

In *Richardson*, Ms Richardson bought a 50 per cent stake in the property on a conventional IHO basis – long lease – without a mortgage. She paid £29,500. In 2003, her ex-partner was imprisoned and Ms Richardson was forced to leave the property having received threats. She moved to a women's refuge. Rent arrears built up because, after 12 months, HB ceased to be paid in respect of both properties. By the time of the possession claim, there were about 16 months' rent arrears (approximately £1,941), which had increased to around £3,000 at the date of the hearing. Ms Richardson tried unsuccessfully to sell the property (which had been vandalised in her absence). By that time, it was worth approximately £151,000. In 2005, Midland Heart sought possession on the basis of Ground 8.

The arguments deployed for Ms Richardson relied particularly on property law devices – it was argued that there were two tenancies crafted out of the single formal long lease, an AT and a long lease; and that there was a trust of the freehold – but these devices were properly rejected by HHJ Gaunt QC in the Birmingham County Court. Bright and Hopkins (2009), in their discussion of this case, found alternative property law arguments, based on resulting and constructive trusts or proprietary estoppel, to be similarly wanting on the facts of this case at least.

The outcome was that Ms Richardson lost not just her £29,500 but also her share of the increase in value of the property – she lost everything (although it is reported that Midland Heart offered an *ex gratia* payment of £29,500, less the rent arrears and costs of repair – judgment at [24]). As HHJ Gaunt QC put it:

> That all said, I have found this case troubling. Miss Richardson has had a rough ride in life and has now lost what is probably her only capital asset. Moreover, she lost it in proceedings brought at a time when, to the knowledge of the [PRP], she was actively seeking to sell the house to pay off her debts and the housing association was itself involved in that process. I must say that I find the stance taken by the housing association strange in the circumstances and I have not received any adequate explanation. There may, of course, be many facts and matters in the background that I know not of and so I do not intend to be unduly critical. I simply comment on the timing. (at [23])

The court was not addressed on the possible effect of the Human Rights Act 1998 and, more specifically, Articles 8 and 1, First Protocol (and, indeed, given the state of the law at that time, that may not have been an unreasonable omission). Such issues may have been raised on appeal but the appeal was discontinued   (http://nearlylegal.co.uk/blog/2010/03/richardson-v-midland-heart-appeal-is-no-more/). An Article 8 proportionality argument may stand some prospects of success at least in a Ground 8 claim, after *Pinnock*, although much will rest on the individual circumstances of the shared owner and the factual matrix (including the way in which the property was marketed and any representations made by the HomeBuy agent or equivalent). However, even if such a defence is successful, there are a range of outcomes, not just dismissing the claim, but also 'albeit in exceptional cases' granting an extended period for possession or suspending the order for possession on the happening of any event (*Pinnock* at [62]). Such orders do not necessarily protect the buyer's premium (or share in the increase in value of the property).

The same is true of 'successful' defences to a discretionary ground for possession, under which the court has the power to stay, suspend or postpone possession. Indeed, the making of the possession order, under whatever ground, will deprive the leaseholder of their interest in the property. As the tenant's interest can only be assigned to a new purchaser, who would have to take possession under the possession order made, it follows that the market value of the property will be significantly reduced, if not wiped out, by the lack of security any incoming occupier would take possession under. The shared owner's interest is blighted by the possession order. It makes no real difference that outright possession has not been ordered.[3]

Article 1, First Protocol

Perhaps the best (and, possibly, only) way to protect the buyer's interest is through the deployment of an argument based on Article 1 of the First Protocol. That Article, which is contained in Sch. 1, Part II, HRA, is concerned with the 'protection of property', and so, in theory, it seems apt to do precisely that in the IHO context, albeit that it is a qualified right:

> **Article 1**
>
> Every natural or legal person is entitled to the peaceful enjoyment of his possessions. No one shall be deprived of his possessions except in the public interest and subject to the conditions provided for by law and by the general principles of international law.
>
> The preceding provisions shall not, however, in any way impair the right of a State to enforce such laws as it deems necessary to control the use of property in accordance with the general interest or to secure the payment of taxes or other contributions or penalties.

A number of points can be made about this Article, both generally and specifically in this context:

a.   The definition of 'possessions' is broad and includes rights flowing from the identification of an item as property (such as the right of alienation), assets

---

[3] I am grateful to Iain Colville, barrister, Arden Chambers, for this point.

and other claims, such as those based on a legitimate expectation (*Marckx v. Belgium* (1979) Series A No. 31, at [63]; *Pye* v. *UK* (2008) 46 EHRR 1083, at [61]).

b. Article 1 contains three rights: the first sentence of the first paragraph being general; the second sentence of the first paragraph and the second paragraph being particular instances of interference with the right to peaceful enjoyment of property; and the latter are therefore construed in light of the general principle in the first sentence of the first paragraph (*Pye*, at [52]; *Sporrong & Lonnroth* v. *Sweden* (1982) Series A No. 52, at [61]). The ECtHR usually proceeds by examining whether there has been a breach of the second or third rights before considering the general right (ibid.).

c. As regards 'deprivation', the ECtHR appears to look at the substance of the matter – so, for example, a successful claim of adverse possession was not a 'deprivation' of ownership rights but regulated questions of title; rather, that system involved a 'control of use' and fell within the second paragraph (*Pye*, at [66]).

d. An interference with the peaceful enjoyment of possessions
must strike a 'fair balance' between the demands of the general interest of the community and the requirements of the protection of the individual's fundamental rights … in particular, there must be a reasonable relationship of proportionality between the means employed and the aim sought to be realised by any measure depriving a person of his possessions.

In determining whether this requirement is met, the Court recognises that the State enjoys a wide margin of appreciation with regard both to choosing the means of enforcement and to ascertaining whether the consequences of enforcement are justified in the general interest for the purpose of achieving the object of the law in question …

94. Compensation terms under the relevant legislation are material to the assessment whether the contested measure respects the requisite fair balance and, notably, whether it imposes a disproportionate burden on the applicants. In this connection, the Court has already found that the taking of property without payment of an amount reasonably related to its value will normally constitute a disproportionate interference and a total lack of compensation can be considered justifiable under Article 1 of Protocol No. 1 only in exceptional circumstances (*Jahn* v. *Germany* [2004] ECHR 36 at [93]–[4], 'Recapitulation of the relevant principles'; see also *James* v. *UK* (1986) Series A No. 98, especially at [54], noting that compensation does not, however, guarantee a right to 'full' compensation).

e. A failure to offer compensation is not necessarily determinative that the rights have been breached (*Jahn* itself (context of reunification of Germany)).

f. The 'margin of appreciation' is particularly wide in the context of the 'public interest' and in housing, when aimed at 'securing greater social justice in the sphere of people's homes, even where such legislation interferes with existing contractual relations between private parties and confers no direct benefit on the State or community at large'; indeed, the width of the margin is such that the ECtHR will respect the state's position on the public interest 'unless that judgment be manifestly without reasonable foundation' (*James*, at [46]–[7]).

g.   Finally, it is significant to note that the ECtHR arrogates jurisdiction to itself even if the primary dispute is between two private parties, but where the proper application of the law engages the rights (see, in particular, the discussion in *Pye*, at [75]).

The limits of an Article 1, First Protocol 'defence' must also be stressed. The interference in possession through a successful claim on a Housing Act 1988 ground is not in issue; what is in issue is whether that interference is disproportionate to the buyer's financial stake in the property. It is the equivalent of forfeiture *without* relief (and the court has shown itself willing to interfere where a state's act stops short of expropriation: *Sporrong*), but the framing of the issue is only about the expropriation of the buyer's financial stake and not about their interest in the property.

That having been said, though, it is the combination of the failure of the state to regulate this point beyond the Housing Act 1988, combined with the lack of compensation to the buyer, which frames this issue within the terms of Article 1, First Protocol. In my view, it represents the best opportunity for some restitution of the buyer's share (although there are some contraindications from the ECtHR – see, for example, *Marckx* v. *Belgium* Application No. 6833/74, 13 June 1979). Ms Richardson's case is instructive in this regard – she lost £29,500 (or £75,500, if you account for the uplift in the property market) because of rent arrears of around £3,000. The rent arrears, on the facts of the case, arose because of the refusal of HB authority to pay both for her place in the refuge as well as the IHO rent for more than 52 weeks. It was clear, on any reading of the case, that she could not and would not return to the IHO property because of her fears for her personal safety (and no doubt was cast on their genuineness).

If this is not resolved, however, major issues will continue to exist with this significant element of housing policy. Despite consistent government statements in support of IHO in the past few years, when considerable publicity and anxiety has been caused by this issue, it is notable that no government has intervened to deal with it. As a result, there must be some concern about its viability (despite the Coalition government's continued support for it).

Conclusions

This chapter seems a fitting way to end a book on housing law and policy. It deals with three areas, which might be regarded as constituting the immediate future of housing law, while also raising major questions for housing policy. These are not narrow, technical debates about law – although they may be read as such; they are state of the art, and they tell us much about a potentially radical reconceptualisation of the subject (in both senses of the word). By way of conclusion to this chapter, the discussion is broadened so as to relate the above more directly to housing policy.

It is perhaps easiest to discuss IHO first, because the policy implications of the debate about possession against the shared owner are just so significant. If *Richardson* is right, and there is no way around it, then this major aspect of housing policy is likely to be dead in the water – surely, few if any households would take the risk of losing their capital because they are unable to make two rental payments; and it would be perfectly proper to advise households of the risks they face (it must be wondered how potential IHO buyers are advised now?); equally, the buyer's lenders are likely to be concerned about whether they will get their loan back. But *Richardson*'s consequences may be ameliorated by reference to the HRA, although there remains some doubt about the extent to which it will be possible. It might also be anticipated that future IHO cases will raise the *Weaver* issue about whether PRPs are exercising functions of a public nature at all, but, if so, which of those functions count as private. Although IHO is termed 'social housing' under the Housing and Regeneration Act 2008, and there has been considerable public funding put into these schemes, they are, by their nature, of a different type from general needs rented housing.

If there is no such thing as mandatory possession proceedings any more – which would seem a reasonable extrapolation from *Pinnock*, on the basis that such proceedings would be inherently incompatible with the HRA – this raises a major issue across the board. Mandatory possession proceedings in county courts are likely to be very different enterprises. It cannot be possible to engage in the sort of analysis of Mr Pinnock's defence which the Supreme Court did in *Pinnock* (nine pages' worth) in every possession claim. However, the repercussions of *Pinnock* are likely to be felt beyond the current and into the future. If the Localism Bill passes its parliamentary passage unscathed, it will create fixed-term tenancies which can be ended by a notice/review procedure followed by supposedly 'mandatory' possession proceedings; if the housing minister decides to press ahead with his plan, there will be 'mandatory' possession proceedings in certain (at least) cases of ASB. The outcome of *Pinnock* will be just as applicable in these cases as it was found to be in the demoted tenancy regime. Proportionality will apply across the board. There are likely to be few 'straightforward' mandatory possessions. The Coalition government's view on the impact of *Pinnock* is unclear, but it would seem to create potential barriers in certain cases where the property is the occupier's home and they raise an Article 8 defence.

The odd one out, though, appears to be sale-and-rentback. This does not appear to be a government priority beyond ensuring that the marketplace for such transactions is properly regulated. Although such transactions form part of the government's mortgage rescue scheme, they are of an entirely different type and are not affected by the discussions above (except, perhaps, in some cases). However, these types of tenure-swapping transaction (like IHO) raise serious questions for the ways in which the law can 'handle' them. The evident failure of the law is because it seems able to operate only in monochrome – a fitting way to end this book?

Postscript

After this book had been completed, the Supreme Court gave judgment in *Hounslow LBC* v. *Powell* [2011] 2 WLR 287. This postscript only addresses the effect of that judgment on the analysis contained in Chapter 16 above, concerned with proportionality defences to mandatory possession proceedings (I have resisted the temptation to deal with other after-events, such as the Court of Appeal decision in *Gladehurst Properties Ltd* v. *Hashemi* [2011] EWCA Civ 604 and the High Court decision in *Potts* v. *Densley* [2011] EWHC 1144 which further the destruction of the tenancy deposits regime, discussed at pp. 224–8 above, and amendments to that regime in the Localism Bill; as well as the ongoing saga about the impact of the HB changes and the flexible tenancy regime).

It will be remembered that, in *Manchester CC* v. *Pinnock* [2010] 3 WLR 1441, the Supreme Court accepted that it was now time for the defence of proportionality based on Article 8, Schedule 1, Human Rights Act 1998, to be accepted as a challenge to mandatory possession proceedings in domestic courts. Although the Supreme Court did provide certain limited guidance in *Pinnock*, as discussed at p. 391 above, it was recognised that the appeals in *Powell* were likely to provide the opportunity for more guidance to be given (at [59]).

In *Powell*, the linked cases concerned introductory tenancies and non-secure occupation agreements in satisfaction of temporary accommodation duties under the homelessness provisions in Part 7, Housing Act 1996. The Supreme Court accepted that proportionality defences were, in principle, available in those cases (at [50]–[6], Lord Hope; [78]–[9], Lord Phillips). In contrast to the approach taken in *Pinnock*, where the Supreme Court spent considerable time dealing with the proportionality of Mr Pinnock's eviction, the Supreme Court in *Powell* devoted less time to rejecting the defences. Only in Ms Powell's case (non-secure tenancy, rent arrears as a result of the termination of an HB claim) would the court have remitted the matter to the county court for an assessment of proportionality. It did not do so because the council had made an offer of suitable alternative accommodation. In the other linked cases concerned with introductory tenancies, the defence of proportionality was not seriously arguable. It is notable that Lord Phillips (at [93]) approved the comment of Waller LJ in *R (McLellan)* v. *Bracknell Forest DC* [2002] QB 1129, at [97], where it was said that it is not a requirement for the council to be satisfied that breaches of an introductory tenancy scheme had taken place – the right question is always whether it is reasonable for the council to proceed to terminate the tenancy.

Those were the outcomes, but the way in which the Supreme Court reached those conclusions has left some room for doubt and provided only limited clarification beyond the issues raised directly in these appeals. It will be remembered that, in *Pinnock*, it was said that whether a case was 'exceptional' was an outcome and not a criterion ('exceptionality is an outcome and not a guide': at [51]). This was a reference back to the judgment of Lord Bingham in *Kay* v. *Lambeth LBC* [2006] 2 AC 465, who said that it would only be in exceptional cases that such a defence based on personal circumstances would be seriously arguable. In *Pinnock*, the Supreme Court had effectively said that exceptionality was an empirical question which could only be answered after the data had been generated. Yet both in *Pinnock* and *Powell*, it is also fair to say that the judgments contain references to 'exceptional' cases only being sufficient to cross the proportionality threshold – Lord Phillips, for example, in *Powell* summarised what he regarded as 'an accurate statement of fact' in relation to introductory tenancies from *Pinnock* that 'it will only be "in very highly exceptional cases" that it will be appropriate for the court to consider a proportionality argument' (at [92]). *Powell* is perhaps more strident on this issue.

This issue – exceptionality – may well have to be revisited. It may be that the statutory (or common law) basis for the possession claim is significant. Both *Pinnock* and *Powell* are clear that the rights given to the occupier by the particular regime under which they occupy are more than background noise, and provide the essential context – so, Lord Phillips justified the assertion of accuracy on the basis that, under the introductory tenancy regime, the threshold to cross for justifying the termination of such a tenancy is low, and there are procedural safeguards in place (including the right to review the decision). Those safeguards are unavailable in some other claims, such as, for example, in a *Hammersmith & Fulham LBC* v. *Monk* [1992] 1 AC 478 type claim (discussed at pp. 380–1 above). However, at present, there is a lack of clarity leading to possible inconsistency in county courts.

Next, it will also be remembered that the Supreme Court in *Pinnock* advocated the possible use of a wider range of potential orders beyond an outright possession order, to include adjourning the claim, suspending or postponing the order, or, indeed, refusing the order altogether (at [62]). One possible reason for this extension of the range of possible orders was a concern over the compatibility of s. 89, Housing Act 1980, with Article 8, an issue that was not fully argued in *Pinnock* (at [63]). Section 89(1) gives courts the power to postpone the giving-up of possession by an occupier, in cases of exceptional hardship, to a date not later than 6 weeks after the making of the order (subject to certain exceptions in sub-s. (2)).

The issue over the compatibility of s. 89 with Article 8 was fully argued in *Powell*. The Supreme Court held that the terms of s. 89 were sufficiently strong so that a 'reading down' of that provision was impermissible ([62], Lord Hope); and the section was not per se incompatible with Article 8 as there was no evidence to show that the maximum period of 6 weeks is insufficient to meet the needs of cases of exceptional hardship ([64], Lord Hope). In agreement, Lord Phillips, however, sounded a note of caution:

> In any situation where the judge dealing with an application for a possession order has power to refuse to make the order on the ground that it would infringe article 8, no question of incompatibility can arise in relation to section 89. That section merely increases the options open to the judge. He can (i) make an immediate order for possession; (ii) make an order the operation of which is postponed up to the limit permitted by section 89; (iii) refuse to make the order on the ground that it would infringe article 8. The clear limit on the judge's discretion to postpone the operation of the order may thus, in rare cases, have the consequence that the order is refused, whereas it would otherwise have been granted, subject to postponement of its operation for a greater period than section 89 permits. This is not a consequence that Parliament can have envisaged. (at [103])

So, if the order would, in the view taken by the judge, have to be postponed for longer than 6 weeks, it would be proper for the judge to refuse to make the order. Lord Phillips' comment may turn out to be of limited assistance. After all, if a proportionality defence is found to be 'exceptional', then the county court can simply adjourn or refuse the order on the basis of the proportionality defence; if not 'exceptional', then it may be unlikely that s. 89 will come into play as the circumstances may not be sufficiently 'exceptional' to fall within that section.

Third, in my discussion of the principles of proportionality at pp. 392–4 above, I have suggested that the questions addressed by the House of Lords in *Huang* v. *Secretary of State for the Home Department* [2007] 2 AC 167 are relevant to the basis of the proportionality review. That approach is no longer tenable. In *Powell*, the Supreme Court rejected the need for such a 'structured approach' ([41], Lord Hope). The reasoning for this rejection comes back to what the landlord for these purposes needs to plead in its claim. It is taken as read that the 'public' landlord has ownership rights in these cases, which it is seeking to vindicate in the claim, combined with public obligations in terms of the allocation and management of their housing stock. The type of structured approach advocated in *Huang*, while important in certain cases, 'would give rise to the risk of prolonged and expensive litigation, which would divert funds from the uses to which they should be put to promote social housing in the area' ([41], Lord Hope). Further, it would collapse the distinction created by Parliament between secure and non-secure tenancies (ibid.).

Fourth, there is a developing issue over the nature of, and need for, reasons to be given before seeking possession in such cases. This issue raises the question discussed above about the limiting effects of the Court of Appeal decision in *Stokes* v. *Brent LBC* [2010] EWCA Civ 626 (see pp. 387–8 above). The facts of *Powell* and the linked cases did not call for this discussion, but Lord Hope noted that there is no statutory requirement for reasons to be given and the council does not need to justify its motives for seeking possession (at [47]). Lord Phillips was slightly more forthcoming in his discussion (at [114]–[17]). In his view, without being given reasons, the occupier 'will be denied the opportunity of displacing the presumption that the authority's action will serve a legitimate aim' (at [114]). He did not suggest that there is a requirement on the council to give reasons 'in the first instance' to justify to the court its application or to plead the reasons for seeking the order; but the tenant must be informed of the reason(s), so that they can decide whether to mount the proportionality defence (at [116]). This is significant because, at the first hearing of a possession claim, the court may decide the claim and make an order unless the occupier can show that 'the claim is genuinely disputed on grounds which appear to be substantial' (CPR 55.8(2)). Unless the occupier has reasons before that hearing, it will be difficult to get over that threshold (let alone the 'seriously arguable' threshold). County court practice is developing on this point but it may be that, in some courts, where an Article 8 issue is raised in a possession list, such defences will be taken out of the list.

Fifth, it is now clear from both *Pinnock* and *Powell* that significant deference is to be accorded to the decision-making body. As Caroline Hunter and I have noted (paper on file with the author):

> The assumption is that the decision-maker has made correct decisions in accordance with its duties – hence it is unnecessary for them to plead directly to their reasons for wanting possession – but this is, of course, an empirical observation (and there is plenty of evidence which suggests the contrary in the context of housing management).

Lord Hope in *Powell* (at 35]) demonstrates the twin concerns of both deference to the decision-making body intertwined with the efficient administration of court possession lists:

> Practical considerations indicate that it would be demanding far too much of the judge in the county court, faced with a heavy list of individual cases, to require him to weigh up the personal circumstances of each individual occupier against the landlord's public responsibilities. Local authorities hold their housing stock, as do other social landlords, for the benefit of the whole community. It is in the interests of the community as a whole that decisions are taken as to how it should best be administered. The court is not equipped to make those decisions, which are concerned essentially with housing management. This is a factor to which great weight must always be given, and in the great majority of cases the court can and should proceed on the basis that the landlord has sound management reasons for seeking a possession order.

Deference is required because, were it otherwise, the court possession list might become unmanageable (see the discussion at pp. 386–8 above).

Finally, neither *Pinnock* nor *Powell* address the question as to the amenability of a private landlord or other private body to a challenge based on Article 8 (or indeed, Article 1, First Protocol). This remains a live issue and one which, even if successful, will give rise to competing policy considerations on proportionality.

David Cowan
Bristol/London
June 2011

Bibliography

Adler, M. (1995), 'The habitual residence test: A critical analysis', *Journal of Social Security Law* 2(2): 179–95.

Albon, R. and Stafford, D. (1987), *Rent Control*, London: Croom Helm.

Alder, J. and Handy, C. (1997), *Housing Associations: The Law of Social Landlords*, London: Sweet & Maxwell.

Allen, C. (2003), 'Desperately seeking fusion: On "joined-up thinking", "holistic practice" and the *new* economy of welfare professional power', *British Journal of Sociology* 54(2): 287–306.

Anderson, I. and Morgan, J. (1997), *Social Housing for Single People? A Study of Local Policy and Practice*, Housing Policy and Practice Unit, University of Stirling.

Andrews, R., Boyne, G., Law, J. and Walker, R. (2005), 'External constraints on local service standards: The case of the Comprehensive Performance Assessment in English local government', *Public Administration* 83(3): 639–56.

Anie, A. Daniel, N., Tah, C. and Petruckevitch, A. (2005), *An Exploration of Factors Affecting the Successful Dispersal of Asylum Seekers*, Home Office Online Report 50/05, London: Home Office.

Arden, A., Orme, E. and Vanhegan, T. (2010), *Homelessness and Allocations*, London: LAG.

Arden, A. and Partington, M. (1983), *Housing Law*, London: Sweet & Maxwell.

Arden, A., Partington, M., Carter, D. and Dymond, A. (2002), *Quiet Enjoyment*, London: LAG.

Ashworth, A. (1978), 'Protecting the home through criminal law', *Journal of Social Welfare and Family Law* 1(2): 76–85.

Asylum Support Appeal Project (ASAP) (2007), *Failing the Failed? How NASS Decision Making is Letting Down Destitute Rejected Asylum Seekers*, London: ASAP.

Atiyah, P. (1979), *The Rise and Fall of Freedom of Contract*, Oxford University Press.

Atkinson, R. and Blandy, S. (2005), 'Introduction: International perspectives on the new enclavism and the rise of gated communities', *Housing Studies*, 20(2): 177–86.

(2007), 'Panic rooms: The rise of defensive homeownership', *Housing Studies*, 22(4): 443–58.

Atkinson, R. and Flint, J. (2003), 'Order born out of chaos? The capacity for information social control in disempowered and "disorganised" neighbourhoods', *Policy and Politics* 32(3): 333–50.

Audit Commission (2002), *Housing Benefit: The National Perspective*, London: Audit Commission.

(2007), *Housing Key Lines of Enquiry (KLOE) Guidance Notes*, London: Audit Commission.

(2008), *Short Notice Inspection of Housing Associations – Statement of Methodology*, London: Audit Commission.

(2010), *Protecting the Public Purse 2010: Fighting Fraud against Local Government and Local Taxpayers*, London: Audit Commission.

Ayres, I. and Braithwaite, J. (1992), *Responsive Regulation: Transcending the Deregulation Debate*, Oxford University Press.

Back, G. and Hamnett, C. (1985), 'State housing policy formation and the changing role of housing associations in Britain', *Policy and Politics* 13(4): 397–412.

Bailey, R. (1973), *The Squatters*, London: Penguin.

(1976), *Blunt Powers, Sharp Practices*, London: Shelter.

Bailey, R. and Ruddock, J. (1972), *The Grief Report*, London: Shelter.

Baker, C. (2009), 'Ahmad and allocations: Telescopes, law and policy', *Journal of Housing Law* 12(4): 69–72.

Baker, T. (2000), 'Insuring morality', *Economy and Society* 29(4): 559–77.

Ball, M. (1983), *Housing Policy and Economic Power: The Political Economy of Owner-Occupation*, London: Methuen.

(1986), *Home Ownership: A Suitable Case for Reform*, London: Shelter.

Barker, K. (2004), *Delivering Stability: Securing our Future Housing Needs*, London: CLG.

Barlow, J. and Duncan, S. (1989), 'The use and abuse of housing tenure', *Housing Studies* 3(4): 219–31.

Barnes, P. (1984), *Building Societies: The Myth of Mutuality*, London: Pluto.

Bates, J. (2005), 'Costs in mortgage possession proceedings: An unfair contract term?', *Journal of Housing Law* 13(1): 31–2.

Bauman, Z. (2005), *Liquid Life*, Cambridge: Polity.

Bellman, H. (1927), *The Building Society Movement*, London: Methuen.

Bennett, C. (1998), 'Hell on the range', *The Guardian*, 7 March.

Berry, F. (1974), *Housing: The Great British Failure*, London: Croom Helm.

Best, R. (1991), 'Housing associations 1890–1990', in S. Lowe and D. Hughes (eds.), *A New Century of Social Housing*, Leicester University Press.

(1997), 'Housing associations: A sustainable solution?', in P. Williams (ed.), *Directions in Housing Policy*, London: Paul Chapman.

Bines, W., Kemp, P., Pleace, N. and Radley, C. (1993), *Managing Social Housing*, London: HMSO.

Birkinshaw, P. (1982), 'Homelessness and the law: The effects and response to legislation', *Urban Law and Policy* 5(3): 225–95.

Black, J. [2005], 'The emergence of risk-based regulation and the new public risk management in the United Kingdom', *Public Law*: 512–48.

(2008), *Forms and Paradoxes of Principles Based Regulation*, Law, Society and Economy Working Papers 13/2008, London School of Economics.

(2010), *Managing the Financial Crisis – The Constitutional Dimension*, Law, Society and Economy Working Papers 12/2010, London School of Economics.

Black, J., Hopper, M. and Band, C. (2007), 'Making a success of principles-based regulation', *Law and Financial Markets Review*, May: 191–206.

Blandy, S. (2001), 'Housing standards in the private rented sector and the three Rs: Regulation, responsibility and rights', in D. Cowan and A. Marsh (eds.), *Two Steps Forward: Housing Policy into the New Millennium*, Bristol: Policy Press.

(2007), 'The impact of housing benefit on social landlords' possession actions in the county courts', *Journal of Social Security Law* 14(1): 29–46.

Blandy, S. and Goodchild, B. (1999), 'From tenure to rights: Conceptualising the changing focus of housing law in England', *Housing Theory and Society* 16(1): 31–42.

Blandy, S. and Lister, D. (2005), 'Gated communities: (Ne)gating community development?', *Housing Studies,* 20(2): 287–302.

Blandy, S. and Robinson, D. (2001), 'Reforming leasehold: Discursive events and outcomes, 1984–2000', *Journal of Law and Society* 23(3): 384–408.

Blomley, N. (2005), 'The borrowed view: Privacy, propriety, and the entanglements of property', *Law and Social Inquiry* 30(4): 617–61.

Boddy, M. (1980), *The Building Societies*, Basingstoke: MacMillan.

  (1989), 'Financial deregulation and UK housing finance: Government–building society relations and the Building Societies Act, 1986', *Housing Studies* 4(1): 92–104.

Boddy, M. and Lambert, C. (1988), *The Government–Building Society Connection: From Mortgage Regulation to the Big Bang*, Working Paper 75, School for Advanced Urban Studies, University of Bristol.

Bond, L., Sautkina, E. and Kearns, A. (2011), 'Mixed messages about mixed tenure: Do reviews tell the real story?', *Housing Studies* 26(1): 69–94.

Bone, J. and O'Reilly, K. (2010), 'No place called home: The causes and consequences of the UK housing "bubble"', *British Journal of Sociology* 61(2): 231–55.

Bottomley, A. (2007), 'A trip to the mall: Revisiting the public/private divide', in H. Lim and A. Bottomley (eds.), *Feminist Perspectives on Land Law*, London: Routledge-Glasshouse.

Bottoms, A., Clayton, A. and Wiles, P. (1992), 'Housing markets and residential community crime careers: A case study from Sheffield', in D. Evans, N. Fyfe and D. Herbert (eds.), *Crime, Policing and Place: Essays in Environmental Criminology*, London: Routledge.

Bottoms, A. and Wiles, P. (1986), 'Housing tenure and residential community crime careers in Britain', in A. Reiss, and M. Tonry (eds.), *Crime and Justice: A Review of Research – Communities and Crime*, University of Chicago Press.

Bowes, A. and Sim, D. (2002), 'Patterns of residential settlement among black and minority ethnic groups', in P. Somerville and A. Steele (eds), *'Race', Housing and Social Exclusion*, London: Jessica Kingsley.

Bowley, M. (1945), *Housing and the State*, London: Allen & Unwin.

Boyne, G., Day, P. and Walker R. (2002), 'The evaluation of public service inspection: A theoretical framework', *Urban Studies* 39(7): 1197–212.

Bramley, G. (1993), 'Quasi-markets and social housing', in J. Le Grand and W. Bartlett (eds), *Quasi-Markets and Social Policy*, Basingstoke: MacMillan.

  (1995), *Too High a Price: Homeless Households, Housing Benefit and the Private Rented Sector*, London: Shelter.

Bramley, G. and Dunmore, K. (1996), 'Shared ownership: Short-term expedient or long-term major tenure?', *Housing Studies* 11(1): 105–31.

Bramley, G., Morgan, J., Cousins, L., Dunmore, K., Three Dragons Consultancy and MORI Social Research (2002), *Evaluation of the Low Cost Home Ownership Programme*, London: ODPM.

Bramley, G. Munro, M. and Pawson, H. (2004), *Key Issues in Housing: Policies and Markets in 21st-Century Britain*, Basingstoke: Palgrave.

Bridges, L., Sunkin, M. and Meszaros, G. (1995), *Judicial Review in Perspective*, London: Cavendish.

Bright, S. (2002), 'Avoiding tenancy legislation: Sham and contracting out revisited', *Cambridge Law Journal* 61(1): 146–68.

(2007), *Landlord and Tenant Law in Context*, Oxford: Hart.

Bright, S. and Hopkins, N. [2009], '*Richardson v Midland Heart Ltd*: Low cost home ownership – Legal issues of the shared ownership lease', *Conveyancer and Property Lawyer* 337–49.

(2010), 'Shared ownership: Home, meaning and identity', paper presented at the Association for Law, Property and Society annual meeting, Washington DC, 2010.

Brown, A. (2004), 'Anti-social behaviour, crime control and social control', *Howard Journal of Criminal Justice* 43(2): 203–11.

Brown, S. [2007], 'The Consumer Credit Act 2006: Real additional mortgagor protection?', *Conveyancer and Property Lawyer* 316–41.

Buck, T. (1991), 'Rents and income: A legal overview', in D. Hughes and S. Lowe (eds.), *A New Century of Social Housing*, Leicester University Press.

Building Research Establishment (BRE) (2007), *Evaluating the Impact of HMO and Selective Licensing: The Baseline before Licensing in April 2006*, London: CLG.

(2010), *Evaluation of the Impact of HMO Licensing and Selective Licensing*, London: CLG.

Burchardt, T. and Hills, J. (1997), 'From public to private: The case of mortgage payment insurance in Great Britain', *Housing Studies* 13(3): 311–24.

Burgess, G., Grant, F. and Whitehead, C. (2009), *Low Cost Home Ownership and the Credit Crunch: A Report on Regional Markets and Competition with Private Developers*, London: TSA.

Burnett, J. (1986), *A Social History of Housing 1915–1985*, London: Methuen.

Burridge, R. and Ormandy, D. (2007), 'Health and safety at home: Private and public responsibility for unsatisfactory housing conditions', *Journal of Law and Society* 34(4): 544–66.

Burton, J. and Gask, A. (2010), 'Humanity, 1: 0 Policy', *New Law Journal*, 16 July, 160(7426): 1000–1.

Butler, S. (1998), *Access Denied: The Exclusion of People in Need for Social Housing*, London: Shelter.

Cabinet Office (1991), *The Citizen's Charter*, Cm 1599, London: HMSO.

(2000), *Review of the Public Sector Ombudsmen in England: A Report by the Cabinet Office*, London: HMSO.

Cain, M. and Kulcsar, K. (1981–1982), 'Thinking disputes: An essay on the origins of the dispute industry', *Law and Society Review* 16(3): 375–402.

Cairncross, L., Clapham, D. and Goodlad, R. (1997), *Housing Management, Consumers and Citizens*, London: Routledge.

Cairncross, L., Morrell, C., Darke, J. and Brownhill, S. (2002), *Tenants Managing: An Evaluation of Tenant Management Organisations in England*, London: ODPM.

Cambridge Centre for Housing and Planning Research (CCHPR) (2008), *Low Cost Home Ownership: Affordability, Risks and Issues*, Cambridge: CCHPR.

Cannizzaro, A. (2009), *Impacts of Rents on Housing Benefit and Work Incentives*, Working Paper no. 38, London: DWP.

Carlen, P. (1994), 'The governance of homelessness: Legality, lore and lexicon in the agency-maintenance of youth homelessness', *Critical Social Policy* 41:18–29.

Carlton, N., Heywood, F., Izuhara, M., Pannell, J., Fear, C. and Means, R. (2003), *The Harassment and Abuse of Older People in the Private Rented Sector*, Bristol: Policy Press.

Carnwath, R. (1978), *A Guide to the Housing (Homeless Persons) Act 1977*, London: Charles Knight & Co.

Carr, H. (2005a), "'Someone to watch over me": Making supported housing work', *Social and Legal Studies* 14(3): 387–408.

(2005b) "'People will say we're in love": Talking dirty about tenancy deposits', paper presented at the Socio-Legal Studies Association Conference, University of Liverpool, 29–31 March.

Carr, H., Cottle, S., Baldwin, T. and King, M. (2004), *The Housing Act 2004: A Practical Guide*, Bristol: Jordans.

Carr, H. and Cowan, D. (2006), 'Labelling: Constructing definitions of anti-social behaviour', in J. Flint (ed.), *Housing and Anti-Social Behaviour: Perspectives, Policy and Practice*, Bristol: Policy Press.

Carr, H., Cowan, D. and Hunter, C. (2007), 'Policing the housing crisis', *Critical Social Policy* 27(1): 100–18.

Carr, H., Cowan, D., Hunter, C. and Wallace, A. (2010), *Tenure Rights and Responsibilities*, York: Joseph Rowntree Foundation.

Carson, W. (1970), 'White-collar crime and the enforcement of factory legislation', *British Journal of Criminology* 10(4): 383–98.

Carter, D. and Cowan, D. (2010), 'Contracting-out decision-making: Unanswered questions', *Journal of Housing Law* 13(2): 24–5.

Carter, M. and Ginsburg, N. (1994), 'New government housing policies', *Critical Social Policy* 41: 100–10.

Cave, M. (2007), *Every Tenant Matters: A Review of Social Housing Regulation*, London: CLG.

Centre for Housing Research (1989), *The Nature and Effectiveness of Housing Management*, London: HMSO.

Centre for Urban and Regional Studies (CURS), Centre for Housing Policy and Centre for Research in Social Policy (2009a), *Local Housing Allowance Final Evaluation: The Survey Evidence of Claimants' Experience in the Nine Pathfinder Areas*, London: DWP.

(2009b), *Local Housing Allowance Final Evaluation: Implementation and Delivery in the Nine Pathfinder Areas*, London: DWP.

Central Housing Advisory Committee (CHAC) (1938), *The Management of Municipal Housing Estates, Report of the House Management and Housing Associations Sub-Committee of the Central Housing Advisory Committee*, London: HMSO.

(1949), *Selection of Tenants and Transfers and Exchanges*, Third Report of the Housing Management Sub-Committee of the CHAC, London: HMSO.

(1959), *Councils and their Houses: Management of Estates*, London: HMSO.

(1969), *Council Housing Purposes, Procedures and Priorities*, London: HMSO.

Chaplin, R., Jones, M., Martin, S., Pryke, M., Royce, C., Saw, P., Whitehead, C. and Yang, J. (1995), *Rents and Risks – Investing in Housing Associations*, York: Joseph Rowntree Foundation.

Chartered Institute of Housing (CIH) (2006), *Ways and Means: Local Authorities' Work with the Private Rented Sector*, Coventry: CIH.

Checkland, S. and Checkland, E. (1974), *The Poor Law Report of 1834*, Harmondsworth: Penguin.

Civil Justice Council (CJC) (2006), *Pre-action Protocol for Possession Claims based on Rent Arrears*, London: Civil Justice Council.

(2008), *Pre-Action Protocol for Possession Claims based on Mortgage or Home Purchase Plan Arrears in Respect of Residential Property*, London: Civil Justice Council.

Clapham, D. and Franklin, B. (1994), *The Housing Management Contribution to Community Care*, York: Joseph Rowntree Foundation.

Clapham, D., Kemp, P. and Smith, S. (1990), *Housing and Social Policy*, Basingstoke: MacMillan.

Clapham, D. and Kintrea, K. (1986), 'Rationing, choice and constraint: The allocation of public housing in Glasgow', *Journal of Social Policy* 15(1): 51–66.

Clarke, A. (2010), 'Shared ownership: Does it satisfy government and household objectives?', in S. Monk and C. Whitehead (eds.), *Making Housing More Affordable: The Role of Intermediate Tenures*, Oxford: Wiley Blackwell.

Clarke, A. and Kohler, P. (2005), *Property Law*, Cambridge University Press.

Clarke, J. and Newman, J. (1997), *The Managerial State*, London: Sage.

Cleary, E. (1965), *The Building Society Movement*, London: Elek.

Cloatre, E. (2008), 'TRIPS and pharmaceutical patents in Djibouti: An ANT analysis of socio-legal objects', Social and Legal Studies 17(2): 263–81.

Cobb, N. (2007), 'Governance through publicity: Anti-social behaviour orders, young people, and the problematization of the right to anonymity', *Journal of Law and Society* 34(3): 342–73.

Cochrane, A. (2004), 'Modernisation, managerialism and the culture wars: The reshaping of the local welfare state in England', *Local Government Studies* 30(4): 481–96.

Cole, I. (2008), *The Cole Report: Delivering Cross-Domain Regulation for Social Housing*, London: CLG.

Cole, I. and Furbey, R. (1994), *The Eclipse of Council Housing*, London: Routledge.

Cole, I., Gidley, G., Ritchie, C., Simpson, D. and Wishart, B. (1996), *Creating Communities or Welfare Housing? A Study of New Housing Association Developments in Yorkshire and Humberside*, Coventry: CIH.

Cole, I. and Goodchild, B. (1995), 'Local housing strategies in England: An assessment of their changing role and content', *Policy and Politics* 23(1): 49–60.

Cole, I. and Powell, R. (2010), 'The future of Arms Length Management Organisations: The uncertain fate of a social housing hybrid', *People, Place and Policy Online* 4(2): 50–61.

Cole, I. and Robinson, D. (2000), 'Owners, yet tenants: The position of leaseholders in flats in England and Wales', *Housing Studies* 15(6): 595–612.

Coleman, A. (1986), *Utopia on Trial*, London: Hilary Shipman.

Commission on Integration and Community Cohesion (CICC) (2007), *Our Shared Future*, London: CICC.

Committee on Local Expenditure (1932), *Report of the Committee on Local Expenditure (England and Wales)*, Cmd 4200, London: HMSO.

Communities and Local Government (CLG) (2006a), *Dealing with 'Problem' Private Rented Housing*, Housing Research Summary 228, London: CLG.

(2006b), *A Decent Home: Definition and Guidance for Implementation*, June 2006 – Update, London: CLG.

(2006c), *Strong and Prosperous Communities: The Local Government White Paper*, Cm 6939-I, London: CLG.

(2006d), *Strong and Prosperous Communities: The Local Government White Paper*, Cm 6939-II, London: CLG.

(2006e), *Homelessness Code of Guidance for Local Authorities*, London: ODPM.

(2006f), *Housing Health and Safety Rating System Guidance, Guidance about Inspections and Assessment of Hazards given under Section 9*, London: CLG.

(2006g), *Housing Health and Safety Rating System Enforcement Guidance*, London: CLG.

(2007a), *Delivering Housing and Regeneration: Communities England and the Future of Social Housing Regulation*, London: CLG.

(2007b), *Homes for the Future: More Affordable, More Sustainable*, Cm 7191, London: CLG.

(2007c), *Clarifying the Right to Buy Rules*, London: CLG.

(2008a), *Residents' Choice: Guidance on Tenant Management and Other Options Supported through the Tenant Empowerment Programme*, London: CLG.

(2008b), *Local Choice, Local Control: Statutory Guidance on Tenant Management for Local Authorities and Local Authority Tenants*, London: CLG.

(2008c), *Self-Financing of Council Housing Services: Summary of Findings of a Modelling Exercise*, London: CLG.

(2008d), *Allocation of Accommodation: Choice Based Lettings*, Code of Guidance for Local Housing Authorities, London: CLG.

(2008e), *The Pomeroy Review of Prospects for Private Sector Shared Equity*, London: CLG.

(2009a), *Exclusion of New Council Housing from the Housing Revenue Account Subsidy System and Pooling: Guidance for Local Authorities*, London: CLG.

(2009b), *Fair and Flexible, Statutory Guidance on Social Housing Allocations for Local Authorities in England*, London: CLG.

(2009c), *Homelessness Code of Guidance for Local Authorities: Supplementary Guidance on Intentional Homelessness*, London: CLG.

(2009d), *Guidance on the Use of Family Intervention Tenancies*, London: CLG.

(2009e), *Tolerated Trespassers: Guidance for Social Landlords*, London: CLG.

(2009f), *Tackling Unlawful Subletting and Occupancy: Good Practice Guidance for Social Landlords*, London: CLG.

(2009g), *The Private Rented Sector: Professionalism and Quality*, Government Response to the Rugg Review, Consultation, London: CLG.

(2009h), *Reform of Council Housing Finance*, Consultation, London: CLG.

(2010a), *The Private Rented Sector: Professionalism and Quality*, Summary of Responses and Next Steps, London: CLG.

(2010b), *The Coalition: Our Programme for Government on Communities and Local Government*, London: CLG.

(2010c), *English Housing Survey: Headline Report 2008–09*, London: CLG.

(2010d), *Local Authority Housing Statistics, England, 2009/10*, London: CLG.

(2010e), *Local Decisions: A Fairer Future for Housing*, London: CLG.

(2010f), *Guidance to the Mortgage Repossessions (Protection of Tenants etc) Act 2010*, London: CLG.

(2010g), 'Shapps promises "no more red tape" for private landlords', London: CLG, www.communities.gov.uk/newsstories/housing/16026231.

(2010h), *Homelessness Prevention and Relief: England 2009/10 Experimental Statistics*, London: CLG.

(2010i), *Council Housing: A Real Future*, Prospectus, London: CLG.

(2010j), 'Eric Pickles to disband Audit Commission in new era of town hall transparency', news release, 13 August 2010, London; CLG.

(2010k), *A Review of Social Housing Regulation*, London: CLG.

Communities and Local Government (CLG) and Department for Children, Schools and Families (DCSF) (2010), *Provision of Accommodation for 16 and 17 year old Young People who may be Homeless and/or Require Accommodation*, Guidance to Children's Services Authorities and Local Housing Authorities about their duties under Part 3 of the Children Act 1989 and Part 7 of the Housing Act 1996 to Secure of Provide Accommodation for Homeless 16 and 17 year old Young People, London: CLG/DCSF.

Communities and Local Government (CLG) Select Committee (2008), *The Supply of Rented Housing*, Eighth Report of Session 2007–08, HC 457–1, London: TSO.

Cooper, C., Brown, G., Powell, H. and Sapsed, E. (2009), *Exploration of Local Variations in the Use of Anti-Social Behaviour Tools and Powers*, Research Report 21, London: Home Office.

Council for Mortgage Lenders (CML) (2010), 'Mortgage arrears and possessions fall in third quarter', www.cml.org.uk/cml/media/press/2769 (accessed 03 January 2011).

Council for Mortgage Lenders (CML)/National Housing Federation (NHF) (2009), *Guidance for Handling Arrears and Possession Sales of Shared Ownership Properties*, London: CML/NHF, www.cml.org.uk/cml/policy/guidance.

Council for Mortgage Lenders (CML), National Housing Federation (NHF), Homes and Communities Agency (HCA) (2010), *Shared Ownership: Joint Guidance for England*, London: CML/HCA/NHF.

Cowan, D. (1992a), 'Policy and the "North Wiltshire scheme"', *Local Government Review* 587–8.

[1992b], 'A public dimension to a private problem', *Conveyancer and Property Lawyer* 285–292.

(1995), 'Accommodating community care', *Journal of Law and Society* 22(2): 212–30.

(1997), *Homelessness: The (In-)appropriate Applicant*, Aldershot: Dartmouth.

(1999), *Housing Law and Policy*, Basingstoke: MacMillan.

[2001], 'Harassment and unlawful eviction in the private rented sector – A study of law in(-)action', *Conveyancer and Property Lawyer* 249–64.

(2003), '"Rage at West*s*inster": Socio-legal reflections on the power of sale', *Social and Legal Studies* 12(2): 177–98.

(2008a), 'A review of the reviews', *Journal of Housing Law* 11(3): 47–50.

(2008b), 'Nominations: A practical issue', *Journal of Housing Law* 11(2): 26–7.

Cowan, D., Blandy, S., Hunter, C., Nixon, J., Hitchings, E., Pantazis, C. and Parr, S. (2006), 'District judges and possession proceedings', *Journal of Law and Society* 33(4): 547–71.

Cowan, D. and Carr, H. (2008), 'Actor-network theory, implementation, and the private landlord', in M. Partington, *Law's Reality: Case Studies in Empirical Research on Law*, *Journal of Law and Society* 35 (Special Research Issue): 149–166.

Cowan, D. and Dearden, N. (2001), 'The minor as (a) subject: The case of housing law', in J. Fionda (ed.), *Legal Concepts of Childhood*, Oxford: Hart.

Cowan, D. and Gallivan, T. (2010), 'The rule in *Hammersmith and Fulham LBC v Monk* reconsidered', *Journal of Housing Law* 13(6): 107–11.

Cowan, D., Gilroy, R. and Pantazis, C. (1999), 'Risking housing need', *Journal of Law and Society* 26(4): 403–26.

Cowan, D., Halliday, S. and Hunter, C. (2006), 'Adjudicating the implementation of homelessness law: The promise of socio-legal studies', *Housing Studies* 21(3): 381–400.

Cowan, D. and Halliday, S. with Hunter, C., Maginn, P. and Naylor, L. (2003), *The Appeal of Internal Review: Law, Administrative Justice and the (Non-)emergence of Disputes*, Oxford: Hart.

Cowan, D. and Hitchings, E. (2007), '"Pretty boring stuff": District judges and housing possession proceedings', *Social and Legal Studies* 16(3): 363–83.

Cowan, D., Hunter, C. and Pawson, H. (2010), 'Jurisdiction and scale: Mandatory possession proceedings', paper presented to the Society of Legal Scholars annual conference, September 2001, University of Southampton.

Cowan, D. and Marsh, A. (2001a), 'New Labour, same old tory housing policy?', *Modern Law Review* 64(2): 260–79.

(2001b), 'There's regulatory crime and then there's landlord crime: from "Rachmanites" to "partners"', *Modern Law Review* 64(6): 831–54.

(2005), 'From need to choice, welfarism to advanced liberalism? Problematics of social housing allocation', *Legal Studies* 25(2): 22–48.

(2009), 'Ahmad: Some reflections', *Journal of Housing Law* 12(4): 73–6.

Cowan, D. and McDermont, M. (2006), *Regulating Social Housing: Governing Decline*, London: Routledge-Glasshouse.

(2009), 'Obscuring the public function: A case study of social housing', *Current Legal Problems* 159–89.

Cowan, D., McDermont, M. and Morgan, K. (2008), *Risk, Trust and Betrayal: A Social Housing Case Study*, Final Report to the ESRC, Grant Ref. RES-000–22–1930, School of Law, University of Bristol, www.bristol.ac.uk/law/research/centres/themes/nominations/nominationsreport.pdf.

Cowan, D., McDermont, M. and Prendergrast, J. (2006), *Governing and Governance: A Social Housing Case Study*, CMPO Working Paper 06/149, Bristol: Centre for Market and Public Organisation.

Cowan, D. and Morgan, K. (2009), 'Trust, distrust and betrayal: A social housing case study', *Modern Law Review* 72(2): 157–81.

Cowan, D., Morgan, K. and McDermont, M. (2009), 'Nominations: An actor-network approach', *Housing Studies* 24(3): 281–300.

Cowan, D., Pantazis, C. and Gilroy, R. (2001), 'Social housing as crime control: An examination of the role of housing management in policing sex offenders', *Social and Legal Studies* 10(4): 435–57.

Craig, Paul (2008), *Administrative Law*, London: Sweet & Maxwell.

Craig, Peter (1986), 'The house that jerry built? Building societies, the state and the politics of owner-occupation', *Housing Studies* 1(2): 87–108.

Cranston, R. (1985), *Legal Foundations of the Welfare State*, London: Weidenfeld & Nicolson.

Crawford, A. (1997), *The Local Governance of Crime: Appeals to Community and Partnerships*, Oxford: Clarendon.

(1999) *The Local Governance of Crime: Appeals to Community and Partnerships*, Oxford University Press.

(2003), 'Contractual governance of deviant behaviour', 30(4), *Journal of Law and Society*: 479–505.

(2008), 'Dispersal powers and the symbolic role of anti-social behaviour legislation', *Modern Law Review* 71(5): 734–52.

(2009), 'Governing through anti-social behaviour: Regulatory challenges to criminal justice', *British Journal of Criminology* 49(4): 810–31.

Crawford, A. and Lister, S. (2007), *The Use and Impact of Dispersal Orders: Sticking Plasters and Wake-Up Calls*, Bristol: Policy Press.

Crook, A. (1992), 'Private rented housing and the impact of deregulation', in J. Birchall (ed.), *Housing Policy in the 1990s*, London: Routledge.

Crook, A., Hughes, J. and Kemp, P. (1995), *The Supply of Privately Rented Homes: Today and Tomorrow*, York: Joseph Rowntree Foundation.

Crook, A. and Kemp, P. (1996), 'The revival of private rented housing in Britain', *Housing Studies* 11(1): 51–68.

(2002), 'Housing investment trusts: A new structure of rental housing provision?', *Housing Studies* 17(5): 741–54.

Cullingworth, J. (1973), *Problems of an Urban Society*, vol. 2: *The Content of Planning*, London: Allen and Unwin.

Daintith, T. (1994), 'The techniques of government', in J. Jowell and D. Oliver (eds.), *The Changing Constitution*, Oxford: Clarendon.

Daly, G., Mooney, G., Poole, L. and Davis, H. (2005), 'Housing stock transfer in Birmingham and Glasgow: The contrasting experiences of two UK cities', *European Journal of Housing Policy* 5(3): 327–41.

Damer, S. (1974), 'Wine Alley: The sociology of a dreadful enclosure', *Sociological Review* 22(2): 221–48.

(1976) 'A note on housing allocation', in M. Edwards, F. Gray, S. Merrett, and J. Swann (eds.), *Housing and Class in Britain*, London: Russell Press.

(1980), 'State, class and housing: Glasgow 1885–1919', in J. Melling (ed.), *Housing Social Policy and the State*, London: Croom Helm.

(2000), "Engineers of the human machine': The social practice of council housing management in Glasgow, 1895–1939', *Urban Studies* 37(11): 2007–26.

Damer, S. and Madigan, R. (1974), 'The housing investigator', *New Society,* 25 July: 226.

Darling, J. (2009), 'A city of sanctuary: The relational re-imagining of Sheffield's asylum politics', *Transactions of the Institute of British Geographers* 35: 125–40.

Daunton, M. (1983), *House and Home in the Victorian City*, London; Edward Arnold.

Davidson, M. and Piddington, J. (2007), *Implementing Decent Homes in the Social Sector*, London: CLG.

Day, P., Henderson, D. and Klein, R. (1993), *Home Rules: Regulation and Accountability in Social Housing*, York: Joseph Rowntree Foundation.

Day, P. and Klein, R. (1995), *The Regulation of Social Housing*, London: NHF.

Dean, M. (1991), *The Constitution of Poverty: Toward a Genealogy of Ethical Liberal Governance*, London: Routledge.

(1992), 'A genealogy of the government of poverty', *Economy and Society* 21(3): 215–51.

Department for Business, Enterprise and Regulatory Reform (BERR) (2008), *Government Response to Office of Fair Trading (OFT) Sale and Rent Back Market Study*, London: BERR.

Department for Work and Pensions (DWP) (2002), *Building Choice and Responsibility: A Radical Agenda for Housing Benefit*, London: DWP.

(2003), *Housing Benefit Sanctions and Anti-social Behaviour*, London: DWP.

(2008), *Consultation on the Housing Benefit Amendment Regulations 2009*, London: DWP.

(2009), *Supporting People into Work: The Next Stage of Housing Benefit Reform*, Consultation Paper, London: DWP.

(2010a), *Right to Reside – Parent and Primary Carer of a Child in Education*, Memo DMG 30/10, London: DWP.

(2010b), 'Housing benefit reforms will restore fairness to broken system', press release, 30 November.

(2010c), *Universal Credit: Welfare that Works*, London: DWP.

Department of the Environment (DoE) (1971), *Fair Deal for Housing*, Cmnd 4728, London: HMSO.

(1977), *Housing Policy – A Consultative Document*, London: HMSO.

(1987a), *Finance for Housing Associations: The Government's Proposals*, London: DoE.

(1987b), *Housing: The Government's Proposals*, London: HMSO.

(1994), *Access to Local Authority and Housing Association Tenancies*, London: HMSO.

(1995a), *Our Future Homes: Opportunity, Choice and Responsibility*, Cm 2901, London: DoE.

(1995b), *More Choice in the Social Rented Sector*, Consultation Paper, London: DoE.

(1995c), *Anti-social Behaviour on Council Estates: A Consultation Paper on Probationary Tenancies*, London: DoE.

(1996), *Allocation of Housing Accommodation and Homelessness*, London: DoE.

Department of the Environment, Transport and the Regions (DETR) (1997), *Modernising Local Government: Improving Local Services through Best Value*, Consultation Paper, London: DETR.

(1999a), *Licensing of Housing in Multiple Occupation – England*, Consultation Paper, London: DETR.

(1999b), *Tenant Participation Compacts,* Consultation Paper, London: DETR.

(1999c), *Best Value in Housing Framework,* Consultation Paper, London: DETR.

(2001), *Health and Safety in Housing*, Consultation Paper, London: DETR.

Department of the Environment, Transport and the Regions (DETR)/Department of Social Security (DSS) (2000), *Quality and Choice: A Decent Home for All – The Housing Green Paper*, London: DETR/DSS.

Department of Health (DoH) (2000), *Framework for the Assessment of Children in Need and their Families*, London: DoH.

Department of Transport, Local Government and the Regions (DTLR) (2001), *Selective Licensing of Private Landlords*, Consultation Paper, London: DTLR.

de Sousa Santos, B. (1987) 'Law: A map of misreading. Toward a postmodern conception of law', *Journal of Law and Society* 14(3): 279–302.

Dimoldenberg, P. (2006), *The Westminster Whistleblowers: Shirley Porter, Homes for Votes and Scandal in Britain's Rottenest Borough*, London: Politico.

Disability Rights Commission (DRC) (2005), *The Duty to Promote Disability Equality: Statutory Code of Practice*, England and Wales, London: DRC.

Dixon, T., Pottinger, G., Marston, A., Plimmer, F. and Daly, J. (2006), *Valuing for Right to Buy: A Review of the Valuation Process in Sales of Local Authority Housing to Sitting Tenants*, London: ODPM.

Doling, J. and Ford, J. (1991), 'The changing face of home ownership: Building societies and household investment strategies', *Policy and Politics* 19(1): 109–18.

Donnison, D. (1967), *The Government of Housing*, London: Pelican.

Donoghue, J. (2010), *Anti-Social Behaviour Orders? A Culture of Control*, Basingstoke: Palgrave.

Downe, J. and Martin, S. (2006), 'Joined up policy in practice? The coherence and impacts of the local government modernisation agenda', *Local Government Studies* 32(4): 465–88.

Dudleston, A. (2001), 'The flexible mortgage: A risk-reducing product?', *Housing Studies* 16(2): 163–77.

Dunn, R., Forrest, R. and Murie, A. (1987), 'The geography of council house sales in England: 1979–85', 24(1), *Urban Studies*: 47–59.

Dwelly, T. and Cowans, J. (2006), *Rethinking Social Housing*, London: Smith Foundation.

Dwyer, P. and Brown, D. (2008), 'Accommodating "others"?: Housing dispersed, forced migrants in the UK', *Journal of Social Welfare and Family Law* 30(3): 203–18.

ECOTEC (2008), *Evaluation of the HomeBuy Agents in the Delivery of the National Affordable Housing Programme 2006/08*, London: ECOTEC.

Ellickson, R. (2008), *The Household: Informal Order around the Hearth*, New Jersey: Princeton.

Elton, L. (2006), *Review of Regulatory and Compliance Requirements for RSLs*, London: Housing Corporation.

Englander, D. (1983), *Landlord and Tenant in Urban Britain, 1838–1918*, Oxford University Press.

Equality and Human Rights Commission (EHRC) (2011), *The Essential Guide to the Public Sector Equality Duty: England (and Non-Devolved Bodies in Scotland and Wales)*, London: EHRC.

Ericson, R. and Haggerty, K. (1997), *Policing the Risk Society*, Oxford University Press.

Evans, R. and Long, D. (2000), 'Estate-based regeneration in England: Lessons from Housing Action Trusts', *Housing Studies* 15(2): 301–18.

Ewick, P. and Silbey, S. (1999), *The Common Place of Law: Stories from Everyday Life*, University of Chicago Press.

Feeley, M. and Simon, J. (1992), 'The new penology: Notes on the emerging strategy of corrections and its implication', 30(2), *Criminology*: 452–74.

Felstiner, W., Abel, R . and Sarat, A. (1980–81), 'The emergence and transformation of disputes: Naming, blaming, claiming ...', *Law and Society Review* 15(3): 631–48.

Financial Ombudsman Service (FOS) (2009), *Aggregate Complaints Statistics 2006–2009 (H1)*, London: FOS.

(2010), *Annual Report 2009/10*, London: FOS.

Financial Services Authority (FSA) (2006), *The FSA's Risk-Assessment Framework*, London: FSA.

(2008a), *Mortgage Code of Business*, London: FSA.

(2008b), *The Supervision of Northern Rock: A Lessons Learned Review*, London: FSA.

(2009), *Mortgage Market Review*, Discussion Paper 09/3, London: FSA.

(2009b), *Regulating Sale and Rent Back: An Interim Regime*, 09/06, London: FSA.

(2010a), *Mortgage Market Review: Responsible Lending*, London: FSA.

(2010b), *Sale and Rent Back (Full Regime)*, London: FSA.

Finer, M. (1974), *Report of the Committee on One Parent Families*, vol. I, Cmnd 5629, London: HMSO.

Fitzpatrick, S. (2005), 'Explaining homelessness: A critical realist perspective', *Housing, Theory and Society* 22(1): 1–17.

Fitzpatrick, S. and Pawson, H. (2007), 'Welfare safety net or tenure of choice? The dilemma facing social housing policy in England?', *Housing Studies* 22(2): 163–82.

Flatley, J., Moley, S. and Hoare, J. (2008), *Perceptions of Anti-social Behaviour: Findings from the 2007/08 British Crime Survey*, London: Home Office.

Fletcher, D (2009), 'Social tenants, attachment to place and work in the post-industrial labour market: Underlining the limits of housing-based explanations of labour immobility?' *Housing Studies* 24(6): 775–92.

Flinn, M. (1965), *Report on the Sanitary Condition of the Labouring Population of Gt. Britain /by Edwin Chadwick, 1842*, Edinburgh University Press.

Flint, J. (2002), 'Social housing agencies and the governance of anti-social behaviour', *Housing Studies* 17(4): 619–37.

— (2004) 'Reconfiguring agency and responsibility in the governance of social housing in Scotland', 41(1), *Urban Studies*: 151–72.

Flint, J. and Nixon, J. (2006), 'Governing neighbours: Anti-social behaviour orders and new forms of regulating conduct in the UK', *Urban Studies* 43(5/6): 939–55.

Flint, J. and Pawson, H. (2009), 'Social landlords and the regulation of conduct in urban spaces in the United Kingdom', *Criminology and Criminal Justice* 9(4): 415–35.

Ford, J., Bretherton, J., Jones, A. and Rhodes, D. (2010), *Giving up Home Ownership: A Qualitative Study of Voluntary Possession and Selling because of Financial Difficulties*, London: CLG.

Ford, J., Burrows, R. and Nettleton, S. (2001) *Home Ownership in a Risk Society*, Bristol: Policy Press.

Ford, J. and Kempson, E. (1997), *Bridging the Gap? Safety-nets for Mortgage Borrowers*, Centre for Housing Policy, University of York.

Ford, J., Kempson, E. and Wilson, M. (1995), *Mortgage Arrears and Possessions: Perspectives from Borrowers, Lenders and the Courts*, London: HMSO.

Ford, J. and Wallace, A. (2009), *Uncharted Territory? Managing Mortgage Arrears and Possessions*, London: Shelter.

Forrest, R., Lansley, S. and Murie, A. (1984), *A Foot on the Ladder? An Evaluation of Low Cost Home Ownership Initiatives*, Working Paper no. 41, School for Advanced Urban Studies, University of Bristol.

Forrest, R. and Murie, A. (1984), *Right to Buy? Issues of Need, Equity and Polarisation in the Sale of Council Houses*, Working Paper no. 39, School for Advanced Urban Studies, University of Bristol.

— (1991), *Selling the Welfare State: The Privatization of Public Housing*, London: Routledge.

Forrest, R. Murie, A. and Williams, P. (1990), *Home Ownership: Differentiation and Fragmentation*, London: Unwin Hyman.

Foucault, M. (1991), 'Governmentality', in G. Burchell, C. Gordon and P. Miller, (eds.), *The Foucault Effect: Studies in Governmentality*, University of Chicago Press.

Fox, L. (2007), *Conceptualising Home: Theories, Law and Policies*, Oxford: Hart.

Fox O'Mahoney, L. and Sweeney, J. (2010), 'The exclusion of (failed) asylum seekers from housing and home: Towards an oppositional discourse', *Journal of Law and Society* 37(2): 285–314.

Francis, H. (1971), *Report of the Committee on the Rent Acts*, Cmnd 4609, London: HMSO.

Franklin, B. (2000), 'Demands, expectations and responses: The shaping of housing management', *Housing Studies* 15(6): 907–28.

Franklin, B. and Clapham, D. (1997), 'The social construction of housing management', *Housing Studies* 12(1): 7–28.

Furbey, R., Wishart, B. and Grayson, J. (1996), 'Training for tenants: "Citizens" and the enterprise culture', *Housing Studies* 11(2): 251–69.

Galanter, M. (1974), 'Why the "haves" come out ahead: Speculations on the limits of legal change', *Law and Society Review* 9(1): 95–160.

(2004), 'The vanishing trial: An examination of trials and related matters in federal and state courts', *Journal of Empirical legal Studies* 1(3): 459–570.

Garland, D. (1996), 'The limits of the sovereign state: Strategies of crime control in contemporary society', *British Journal of Criminology* 36(3): 445–71.

(2001), *The Culture of Control: Crime and Social Order in Contemporary Society*, Oxford University Press.

Garrett, P. (2007) '"Sinbin" solutions: The "pioneer" projects for "problem families" and the forgetfulness of social policy research', *Critical Social Policy* 27(2): 203–30.

Gauldie, E. (1974), *Cruel Habitations: A History of Working-Class Housing 1780–1918*, London: Unwin.

Genn, H. (1999), *Paths to Justice: What People Do and Think about Going to Law*, Oxford: Hart.

Genn, H. and Genn, Y. (1989), *The Effectiveness of Representation at Tribunals*, London: LCD.

Gibb, K. and Munro, M. (1993), *Housing Finance in the UK: An Introduction*, Basingstoke: MacMillan.

Gilad, S. (2008a), 'Exchange without capture: The UK Financial Ombudsman Service's struggle for accepted domain', *Public Administration* 86(4): 907–24.

(2008b), 'Accountability or expectations management? The role of the ombudsman in financial regulation', *Law and Policy* 30(2): 227–53.

(2009), 'Judging conflicting demands: The case of the UK Financial Ombudsman Service', *Journal of Public Administration Research and Theory* 19(2): 661–80.

(2010), 'Why the "haves" do not necessarily come out ahead in informal dispute resolution', *Law and Policy* 32(3): 283–312.

Gilroy, R. (1998), 'Bringing tenants into decision making', in D. Cowan (ed.), *Housing: Participation and Exclusion*, Aldershot: Dartmouth.

Ginsburg, N. (1988), 'Institutional racism and local authority housing', *Critical Social Policy* 4–19.

(1989), 'The Housing Act 1988 and its policy context: A critical commentary', *Critical Social Policy* 25: 56–73.

Glastonbury, B. (1971), *Homeless Near a Thousand Homes*, London: Allen & Unwin.

Goodchild, B. and Karn, V. (1997), 'Standards, quality control and house building in the UK', in P. Williams (ed.), *Directions in Housing Policy*, London: Paul Chapman.

Goodlad, R. (1993), *The Housing Authority as Enabler*, Coventry: CIH.

Goodlad, R. and Atkinson, R. (2004), 'Sacred cows, rational debates and the politics of the right to buy after devolution', *Housing Studies* 19(3): 447–63.

Gray, F. (1979), 'Consumption: Council house management', in S. Merrett (ed.), *State Housing in Britain*, London: Routledge & Kegan Paul.

Gray, K. and Gray, S. (2009), *Elements of Land Law*, London: Butterworths.

Gregory, P. and Hainsworth, M. (1993), 'Chameleons or Trojan horses? The strange case of housing action trusts', *Housing Studies* 8(1): 109–19.

Greve, J., Page, D. and Greve, S. (1971), *Homelessness in London*, Edinburgh: Scottish Academic Press.

Griffith, A. (2008), 'CLACs: Are they worth it?', *Legal Action*, June: 10–11.

Griffiths, D., Zetter, R. and Sigona, N. (2006), 'Integrative paradigms, marginal reality: Refugee community organisations and dispersal in Britain', *Journal of Ethnic and Migration Studies* 32(5): 881–98.

Griffiths, M., Parker, J., Smith, R., Stirling, T. and Trott, T. (1996), *Community Lettings: Local Allocations Policies in Practice*, York: Joseph Rowntree Foundation.

Gurney, C. (1999a), 'Pride and prejudice: discourses of normalisation in public and private accounts of home ownership', *Housing Studies* 14(2): 163–85.

(1999b), 'Lowering the drawbridge: A case study of analogy and metaphor in the social construction of home-ownership', *Urban Studies* 36(7): 1705–22.

Hacking, I. (1991), 'How should we do the history of statistics?', in G. Burchell, C. Gordon, and P. Miller (eds.), *The Foucault Effect: Studies in Governmentality*, University of Chicago Press.

Halliday, S. (1998), 'Researching the "impact" of judicial review on routine administrative decision-making', in D. Cowan (ed.), *Housing: Participation and Exclusion*, Aldershot: Dartmouth.

[2000a], 'The influence of judicial review on bureaucratic decision-making', *Public Law* 110–22.

(2000b), 'Institutional racism in bureaucratic decision-making: A case study in the administration of homelessness law', *Journal of Law and Society* 27(3): 449–71.

(2004), *Judicial Review and Compliance with Administrative Law*, Oxford: Hart.

Hamlin, C. (1998), *Public Health and Social Justice in the Age of Chadwick – Britain, 1800–1854*, Cambridge University Press.

Hampton, P. (2005), *Reducing Administrative Burdens: Effective Inspection and Enforcement,* London: HM Treasury.

Hancher, L. and Moran, M. (1989), 'Organising regulatory space', in L. Hancher and M. Moran (eds.), *Capitalism, Culture and Economic Regulation*, (reproduced in R. Baldwin, C. Scott and R. Hood (eds.), *A Reader on Regulation*, Oxford University Press).

Hand, C. [1980], 'The statutory tenancy: An unrecognised proprietary interest?', *Conveyancer and Property Lawyer* 351–70.

Harlow, C. and Rawlings, R. (2009), *Law and Administration*, Cambridge University Press.

Harris, N. (1999), *Social Security Law in Context*, Oxford University Press.

Harrison, J. (1992), *Housing Associations after the 1988 Housing Act*, Working Paper no. 108, School for Advanced Urban Studies, University of Bristol.

Hartfree, Y., Whitfield, G., Waring, A., Sandu, A. and Hill, K. (2010), *Tenants' and Advisers' Early Experiences of the Local Housing Allowance National Rollout*, Research report no. 688, London: DWP.

Harvey, J. and Houston, D. (2005), *Research into the Single Room Rent Restrictions*, Research Report no. 243, London: DWP

Hawes, D. (1986), *Building Societies – The Way Forward*, Occasional Paper no. 26, School for Advanced Urban Studies, University of Bristol.

Hawkins, K. (1984), *Environment and Enforcement*, Oxford University Press.

(2002), *Law as Last Resort: Prosecution Decision-Making in a Regulatory Agency*, Oxford University Press.

Haworth, A. and Manzi, T. (1999), 'Managing the "underclass": Interpreting the moral discourse of housing management', *Urban Studies* 36(1): 153–65.

Helm, T. and Asthana, A. (2010), 'Councils plan for exodus of poor families from London', *The Observer*, 24 October.

Henderson, J. and Karn, V. (1987), *Race, Class and State Housing: Inequality and the Allocation of Public Housing in Britain*, Aldershot: Gower.

Hickman, T. (2010), *Public Law after the Human Rights Act*, Oxford: Hart.

Hills, J. (2008), *Ends and Means: The Future Roles of Social Housing in England*, CASE Report 34, London School of Economics.

Hills, J. and Mullings, B. (1990), 'Housing: A decent home for all at a price within their means?', in J. Hills (ed.), *The State of Welfare: The Welfare State in Britain since 1974*, Oxford University Press.

Hills, S. and Lomax, A. (2007), *Whose House is it Anyway? Housing Associations and Home Ownership*, London: Housing Corporation/Coventry: CIH.

Hirsch, W. (1981), 'Landlord–tenant relations law', in P. Burrows and C. Veljanovski (eds.), *Economic Approach to Law*, London: Butterworths.

Hoath, D. (1982), *Council Housing*, London: Sweet & Maxwell.

  (1983), *Homelessness*, London: Sweet & Maxwell.

Holmans, A. (1987) *Housing Policy in Britain*, London: Croom Helm.

Home Office (1990), *Domestic Violence*, Circular 60/1990, London: Home Office.

  (1998), *Fairer, Faster and Firmer: A Modern Approach to Immigration and Asylum*, Cm 4018, London: TSO.

  (2003a), *Respect and Responsibility – Taking a Stand against Anti-social Behaviour*, Cm 5778, London: Home Office.

  (2003b), *The One Day Count of Anti-social Behaviour*, London: Home Office.

  (2005), *Publicising Anti-Social Behaviour Orders*, Home Office Guidance, London: Home Office.

  (2007), *Acceptable Behaviour Contracts and Agreements*, London: Home Office.

  (2010), *Control of Immigration: Quarterly Statistical Summary, United Kingdom*, London: Home Office.

Home Office Border and Immigration Agency (2008), *The Path to Citizenship: Next Steps in Reforming the Immigration System*, London: UKBIA.

Homes and Communities Agency (HCA) (2009), *HomeBuy Direct: Buyers' Guide*, London: HCA.

  (2010), *Data Compendium: A Collation of Published Data about the Intermediate Market*, London: HCA.

Honore, A. (1980), *The Quest for Security: Employees, Tenants, Wives*, London: Stevens.

  (1987) 'Ownership', in A. Honore (ed.), *Making Laws Bind*, Oxford: Clarendon.

Hopkins, N. and Laurie, E. (2009), 'The "value" of property rights in social security law', *Journal of Social Security Law* 16(2): 180–206.

Hosken, A. (2006), *Nothing like a Dame: The Scandals of Shirley Porter*, London: Granta.

Housing Corporation (1997), *Performance Standards*, London; Housing Corporation.

  (2003), *The Social Housing Grant (Capital) General Determination 2003*, London: Housing Corporation/HCA, http://cfg.housingcorp.gov.uk/gserver.php?show=conWebDoc.10606&outputArea=2.

  (2005), *The Regulatory Code and Guidance*, London: Housing Corporation.

  (2007), *Tenancy Management: Eligibility and Evictions*, Circular 02/07, London: Housing Corporation.

(2008a), *Report of the Ujima Inquiry*, London: Housing Corporation.

(2008b), *HomeBuy Direct: Prospectus*, London: Housing Corporation.

(2008c), *National Affordable Housing Programme 2008–11: Prospectus*, London: Housing Corporation.

Housing Ombudsman Service (HOS) (2010), *Annual Report and Accounts 2009*, London: HOS.

Housing Services Advisory Group (1977), *Tenancy Agreements*, London: DoE.

Hunt, M. (2001), 'The "horizontal effect" of the Human Rights Act: Moving beyond the public–private distinction', in J. Jowell and J. Cooper (eds.), *Understanding Human Rights Principles*, Oxford: Hart.

Hunter, C., Blandy, S., Cowan, D., Nixon, J., Hitchings, E. and Pantazis, C. (2005), *The Exercise of Judicial Discretion in Rent Arrears Cases*, London: DCA.

Hunter, C., Mullen, T. and Scott, S. (1998), *Legal Remedies for Neighbour Nuisance: Comparing Scottish and English Approaches*, York: Joseph Rowntree Foundation.

Hunter, C., Nixon, J. and Shayer, S. (2000), *Neighbour Nuisance, Social Landlords and the Law*, Coventry: CIH.

Hutter, B. (1989), 'Variations in regulatory enforcement styles', *Law and Policy* 11(2): 153–74.

Hynes, P. (2009), 'Contemporary compulsory dispersal and the absence of space for the restoration of trust', *Journal of Refugee Studies* 22(1): 97–121.

Institute of Economic Affairs (IEA) (1972), *Verdict on Rent Control*, IEA Readings no. 7, London: IEA.

Ipsos MORI (2009) *Attitudes to Housing: Findings from Ipsos MORI Public Affairs Monitor Omnibus Survey (England)*, London: CLG.

Irvine, A., Davidson, J. and Sainsbury, R. (2008), *Reporting Changes in Circumstances: Tackling Error in the Benefit System*, Research Report no. 497, London; DWP.

Jacobs, K., Kemeny, J. and Manzi, T. (1999), 'The struggle to define homelessness: A constructivist approach', in S. Hutson and D. Clapham (eds.), *Homelessness: Public Policies and Private Troubles*, London: Cassell.

(2003), 'Power, discursive space and institutional practices in the construction of housing problems', *Housing Studies* 18(4): 429–46.

Jacobs, K. and Manzi, T. (2000), 'Performance indicators and social constructivism: Conflict and control in housing management', *Critical Social Policy* 20(1): 85–103.

James, R. (1997), *Private Ombudsmen and Public Law*, Aldershot: Dartmouth.

Jeffers, S. and Hoggett, P. (1995), 'Like counting deckchairs on the *Titanic*: A study of institutional racism and housing allocations in Haringey and Lambeth', *Housing Studies* 10(3): 325–44.

Jew, P. (1994), *Law and Order in Private Rented Housing: Tackling Harassment and Illegal Eviction*, London: Campaign for Bedsit Rights.

Johnsen, S. and Fitzpatrick, S. (2010), 'Revanchist sanitization or coercive care? The use of enforcement to combat begging, street drinking and rough sleeping in England', *Studies* 47(8): 1703–23.

Joint Committee on Human Rights (JCHR) (2007), *The Treatment of Asylum Seekers*, Tenth Report of Session 2006–07, vol. 1, HL Paper 81-1, HC 60-1, London: TSO.

(2008), *Monitoring the Government's Response to Human Rights Judgments: Annual Report 2008*, Thirty-First Report of Session 2007–08, HL Paper 173, HC 1078, London: TSO.

(2009), *Legislative Scrutiny: Borders, Citizenship and Immigration Bill*, Ninth Report of Session 2008–09, HL Paper 62, HC 375, London: TSO.

(2010), *Enhancing Parliament's Role in Relation to Human Rights Judgments*, Fifteenth Report of Session 2009–10, HL Paper 85, HC 455, London: TSO.

Jones, C. (2003), *Exploitation of the Right to Buy Scheme by Companies*, London: ODPM.

(2007), 'Private investment in rented housing and the role of REITS', *European Journal of Housing Policy* 7(4): 383–400.

(2009), *Government Review of Regulation and Redress in the UK Housing Market*, Final Report to the Department for Communities and Local Government (CLG) and the Department for Business, Enterprise and Regulatory Reform (BERR), London: BERR.

Jones, C. and Murie, A. (2006), *The Right to Buy: Analysis and Evaluation of a Housing Policy*, Oxford: Blackwell.

Jones, M. (1988), 'Utopia and reality: The utopia of public housing and its reality at Broadwater Farm', in N. Teymur, T. Markus and T. Woolley (eds.), *Rehumanizing Housing*, London: Butterworths.

Karn, V. (1993), 'Remodelling a HAT: The implementation of the Housing Action Trust legislation 1987–92', in P. Malpass and R. Means (eds.), *Implementing Housing Policy*, Buckingham: Open University Press.

(ed.) (1997), *Ethnicity in the 1991 Census*, vol. 4, London: HMSO.

Karn, V., Lickiss, R. and Hughes, D. (1997), *Tenants' Complaints and the Reform of Housing Management*, Aldershot: Dartmouth.

Karn, V., Kemeny, J. and Williams, P. (1985), *Home Ownership in the Inner City: Salvation or Despair?*, Aldershot: Gower.

Karn, V. and Sheridan, L. (1994), *New Homes in the 1990s*, Manchester/York: University of Manchester and Joseph Rowntree Foundation.

Kay, A., Legg, C. and Foot, J. (Undated), *The 1980 Tenants' Rights in Practice: A Study of the Implementation of the 1980 Housing Act Rights by Local Authorities 1980–1983*, London: Housing Research Group, City University.

Kearns, A. (1990), *Voluntarism, Management and Accountability: Report of a Postal Survey of Housing Association Management Committee Members in Great Britain*, Centre for Housing Research, University of Glasgow.

Kearns, A. and Stephens, M. (1997), 'Building societies: Changing markets, changing governance', in P. Malpass (ed.), *Ownership, Control and Accountability: The New Governance of Housing*, Coventry: CIH.

Kemeny, J. (1992), *Housing and Social Theory*, London: Routledge.

Kemp, P. (1992a), 'Rebuilding the private rented sector?', in P. Malpass and R. Means (eds.), *Implementing Housing Policy*, Buckingham: Open University Press.

(1992b), *Housing Benefit: An Appraisal*, London: Social Security Advisory Committee.

(1994), 'Housing allowances and the fiscal crisis of the welfare state', *Housing Studies* 9(4): 531–42.

(1997a), 'Ideology, public policy and private rental housing since the war', in P. Williams (ed.), *Directions in Housing Policy*, London: Paul Chapman.

(1997b), 'Burying Rachman', in J. Goodwin and C. Grant (eds.), *Built to Last*, London: Roof.

(2000), *Shopping Incentives and Housing Benefit Reform*, Coventry: Joseph Rowntree Foundation and CIH.

(2004), *Private Renting in Transition*, Coventry: CIH.

(2007), 'Housing benefit in Britain: A troubled history and uncertain future', in P. Kemp (ed.), *Housing Allowances in Comparative Perspective*, Bristol: Policy Press.

Kemp. P. and Keoghan, M. (2001), 'Movement into and out of the private rented sector in England', *Housing Studies* 16(1): 21–38.

Kemp, P. and McLaverty, P. (1993), 'Determining eligible rent for rent allowances: A case study of public policy implementation', in P. Malpass and A. Baines (eds.), *Housing and Welfare: Housing Studies Association Conference Proceedings Spring 1993*, School for Advanced Urban Studies, University of Bristol.

(1994), 'The determination of eligible rents for housing benefit: The implementation by local authorities of central government policy', *Environment and Planning C* 12(1): 109–21.

Kemp, P. and Rugg, J. (1998), *The Single Room Rent: Its Impact on Young People*, Centre for Housing Policy, University of York.

Kemp, P. and Williams, P. (1991), 'Housing management: An historical perspective', in D. Hughes, and S. Lowe, (eds.), *A New Century for Municipal Housing*, University of Leicester Press.

King, P. (2006), 'What do we mean by responsibility? The case of UK housing benefit reform', *Journal of Housing and the Built Environment* 21(1): 111–25.

(2010), *Housing Policy Transformed: The Right to Buy and the Desire to Own*, Bristol: Policy Press.

Kleinman, M. (1993), 'Large-scale transfers of council housing to new landlords: Is British social housing becoming more European?', *Housing Studies* 8(3): 163–78.

Laffin, M. (1986), *Professionalism and Policy: The Role of the Professions in the Central–Local Government Relationship*, Aldershot: Gower.

Langley, P. (2008), 'Sub-prime mortgage lending: A cultural economy', *Economy and Society*: 37(4): 469–94.

Langstaff, M. (1992), 'Housing associations: A move to centre stage', in J. Birchall (ed.), *Housing Policy in the 1990s*, London: Routledge.

Law Commission (1996), *Landlord and Tenant: Responsibility for State and Condition of Property*, Law Com. no. 238, London: HMSO.

(2001), *Reform of Housing Law: A Scoping Paper*, London: Law Commission.

(2002a), *Renting Homes 1: Status and Security*, Consultation Paper, LC CP 162, London: Law Commission.

(2002b), *Renting Homes 2: Co-Occupation, Transfer and Succession*, Consultation Paper, LC CP 168, London: Law Commission.

(2003), *Renting Homes*, Law Com. no. 284, London: Law Commission.

(2006a), *Housing: Proportionate Dispute Resolution*, Issues Paper, London: Law Commission.

(2006b), *Housing: Proportionate Dispute Resolution*, Further Analysis, London: Law Commission.

(2006c), *Renting Homes: The Final Report*, vol. 1: Report, Law Com. no. 297, London: Law Commission.

(2007), *Encouraging Responsible Renting*, Consultation Paper, Law Com. no. 181, London: Law Commission.

(2008), *Housing: Encouraging Responsible Letting*, Law Com. no. 312, London: Law Commission.

Leather, P., Revell, K. and Appleton, N. (2001), *Developing a Voluntary Accreditation Scheme for Private Landlords: A Guide to Good Practice*, London: DETR.

Le Grand, J. (1997), 'Knights, knaves or pawns? Human behaviour and social policy', *Journal of Social Policy* 26(2): 149–69.

(2003), *Motivation, Agency, and Public Policy: Of Knights, Knaves, Pawns and Queens*, Oxford University Press.

Levison, D. and Robertson, I. (1989), *Partners in Meeting Housing Need: Local Authority Nominations to Housing Associations in London: Good Practice Guide*, London: NFHA.

Levitas, R. (2005), *The Inclusive Society? Social Exclusion and New Labour*, Basingstoke: Palgrave.

Lewis, H. (2009), *Still Destitute: A Worsening Problem for Refused Asylum Seekers*, York: Joseph Rowntree Charitable Trust.

Lewis, N. and Harden, I. (1982), 'The Housing Corporation and "voluntary housing"', in A. Barker (ed.), *Quangos in Britain*, Basingstoke: MacMillan.

Lidstone, P. (1994), 'Rationing housing to the homeless applicant', *Housing Studies* 9(4): 459–72.

Lipsky, M. (1980), *Street-Level Bureaucracy: Dilemmas of the Individual in Public Service*, New York: Russell Sage Foundation.

Lister, D. (2002), 'The nature of tenancy relationships – Landlords and young people in the private rented sector', in S. Lowe and D. Hughes (eds.), *The Privately Rented Sector in a New Century*, Bristol: Policy Press.

(2005), 'Controlling letting arrangements? Landlords and surveillance in the private rented sector', *Surveillance and Society* 2(4): 513–28.

(2006), 'Tenancy agreements: A mechanism for governing anti-social behaviour?', in J. Flint (ed.), *Housing, Urban Governance and Anti-Social Behaviour: Perspectives, Police and Practice*, Bristol: Policy Press.

(2007), 'Controlling letting arrangements in the private rented sector?', in D. Hughes and S. Lowe (eds.), *The Private Rented Housing Market: Regulation or Deregulation?*, Aldershot: Ashgate.

Lloyd-Bostock, S. and Mulcahy, L. (1994), 'The social psychology of making and responding to hospital complaints: An account model of complaint processes', *Law and Policy* 16(2): 123–47.

Longmate, N. (2003), *The Workhouse*, London: Pimlico.

Loughlin, M. (1986), *Local Government in the Modern State*, London: Sweet & Maxwell.

Loveland, I. (1991a), 'Administrative law, administrative processes, and the housing of homeless persons', *Journal of Social Welfare and Family Law* 13(1): 4–26.

(1991b), 'Legal rights and political realities: Governmental responses to homelessness in Britain', *Law and Social Inquiry* 18(2): 249–311.

(1992), 'Square pegs, round holes: The "right" to council housing in the post-war era', *Journal of Law and Society* 19(2): 339–61.

(1993), 'The politics, law and practice of "intentional homelessness": 1 – Housing debt', *Journal of Social Welfare and Family Law* 15(2): 113–99.

(1995), *Housing Homeless Persons*, Oxford University Press.

[2004], 'The impact of the Human Rights Act on security of tenure in public housing', *Public Law* 594–611.

[2009], 'A tale of two trespassers: Reconsidering the impact of the Human Rights Act on rights of residence in rented housing', *European Human Rights Law Review* (2): 148–69 (Part 1); (4): 495–511 (Part 2).

[2010], 'Security of tenure for tenants of fully mutual housing co-operatives', *Conveyancer and Property Lawyer* 461–83.

Low Cost Home Ownership Task Force (2003), *A Home of My Own*, Report of the Government's Low Cost Home Ownership Task Force, London: Housing Corporation.

Luba, J. and Davies, L. (2010), *Housing Allocation and Homelessness*, Bristol: Jordans.

Luba, J., Gallagher, J., McConnell, D. and Madge, N. (2010), *Defending Possession Proceedings*, London: LAG.

Lupton, M., Hale, J., Sprigings, N., and Chartered Institute of Housing (CIH) (2003), *Incentives and Beyond? The Transferability of the Irwell Valley Gold Service to other Social Landlords*, London: ODPM.

Lyons, M. (2007), *Place-Shaping: A Shared Ambition for the Future of Local Government*, London: TSO.

Mabey, S. and Tillet, P. (1980), *Building Societies: The Need for Reform*, London: Bow Group.

Mackenzie, S., Bannister, J., Flint, J., Parr, S., Millie, A. and Fleetwood, J. (2010), *The Drivers of Perceptions of Anti-Social Behaviour*, Research Report 34, London: Home Office.

Macneil, I. (1981), 'Economic analysis of contractual relations: Its shortfalls and the need for a "rich classificatory apparatus"', *Northwestern Law Review* 75(3): 1018–63.

Macrory, R. (2006), *Regulatory Justice: Making Sanctions Effective*, London: Cabinet Office.

Malcolm, R. and Pointing, J. (2006), 'Statutory nuisance: The sanitary paradigm and judicial conservatism', *Journal of Environmental Law* 18(1): 37–54.

Malos, E. and Hague, G. (1993), *Domestic Violence and Housing*, School for Applied Social Sciences, University of Bristol.

Malpass, P. (1990), *Reshaping Housing Policy: Subsidies, Rents and Residualisation*, London: Rutledge.

(1991), 'The financing of public housing', in D. Hughes and S. Lowe (eds.), *A New Century of Social Housing*, Leicester University Press.

(1994), 'Policy making and local governance: How Bristol failed to secure City Challenge funding (twice)', *Policy and Politics* 22(3): 301–12.

(1997), 'Introduction', in P. Malpass (ed.), *Ownership, Control and Accountability: The New Governance of Housing*, Coventry: CIH.

(1999), 'Housing policy: does it have a future?', *Policy and Politics* 27(2): 217–32.

(2000a), *Housing Associations and Housing Policy: A Historical Perspective*, Basingstoke: MacMillan.

(2000b), 'The discontinuous history of housing associations in England', *Housing Studies* 15(2): 195–212.

(2003), 'The wobbly pillar? Housing and the British postwar welfare state', *Journal of Social Policy* 32(4): 589–606.

(2005), *Housing and the Welfare State: The Development of Housing Policy in Britain*, Basingstoke: Palgrave.

(2008), 'Housing the new welfare state: Wobbly pillar or cornerstone?', *Housing Studies* 23(1): 1–20.

Malpass, P. and Mullins, D. (2002), 'Local authority housing stock transfer in the UK: From local initiative to national policy', *Housing Studies* 17(4): 673–86.

Malpass, P. and Murie, A. (1999), *Housing Policy and Practice*, Basingstoke: MacMillan.

Malpass, P. and Warburton, M. (1993), 'The new financial regime for local authority housing', in P. Malpass and R. Means (eds.), *Implementing Housing Policy*, Buckingham: Open University Press.

Malpass, P., Warburton, M., Bramley, G. and Smart, G. (1993), *Housing Policy in Action: The New Financial Regime for Council Housing*, School for Advanced Urban Studies, University of Bristol.

Manders, G. (2009), 'The use of anti-social behaviour powers with vulnerable groups: Some recent research', *Social Policy and Society* 9(1): 145–53.

Manzi, T. (2007), 'Cultural theory and the dynamics of organizational change: The response of housing associations in London to the Housing Act 1988', *Housing, Theory and Society* 24(4): 251–71.

Marsh. A. (2004), 'The inexorable rise of the rational consumer? The Blair government and the reshaping of social housing', *European Journal of Housing Policy* 4(2): 185–207.

Marsh, A., Cowan, D., Cameron, A., Jones, M., Kiddle, C. and Whitehead, C. (2004), *Piloting Choice Based Lettings: An Evaluation*, London: ODPM.

Marsh, A., Forrest, R., Kennett, P., Niner, P. and Cowan, D. (2000), *Harassment and Unlawful Eviction of Private Rented Sector Tenants and Park Home Residents*, London: DETR.

Marsh, A., Kennett, P., Forrest, R. and Murie, A. (2003), *The Impact of the 1999 Changes to the Right to Buy Discount*, London: ODPM.

Marshall, T. (2009), 'Anger in court', *Roof* May/June: 28–30.

Marston, J. and Wilding, K. [2009], 'Credit crunch, housing benefit and sale and rent back agreements', *Conveyancer and Property Lawyer* 413–27.

McAuslan, P. [1989], 'Administrative Justice – A necessary report?', *Public Law*, 402–13.

McCarthy, D. (2010), 'Self-governance or professionalized paternalism? The police, contractual injunctions and the differential management of deviant populations', *British Journal of Criminology* 50(5): 1–18.

McCormack, J. (2009), '"Better the devil you know": Submerged consciousness and tenant participation in housing stock transfers', *Urban Studies* 46(2): 391–411.

McDermont, M. (2007a), 'Territorializing regulation: A case study of "social housing" in England', *Law and Social Inquiry* 32(2): 373–98.

(2007b), 'Mixed messages: Housing associations and corporate governance', *Social and Legal Studies* 16(1): 71–94.

(2010), *Governing, Independence, and Expertise: The Business of Housing Associations*, Oxford: Hart Publishing.

McDermont, M., Cowan, D. and Prendergrast, J. (2009), 'Structuring governance: A case study of the new organisational provision of public service delivery', *Critical Social Policy* 29(4): 677–702.

Mcgregor, F (2010), 'Proposals and programme management', presentation at the TSA Affordable Rent Seminar, London: TSA, www.tenantservicesauthority.org/server/show/ConWebDoc.20992/changeNav/14567 (accessed 10 January 2011).

McKee, K. (2009), 'Regulating Scotland's social landlords: Localised resistance to technologies of performance management', *Housing Studies* 24(2): 155–72.

(2010), 'Promoting homeownership at the margins: The experience of low-cost homeownership purchasers in regeneration areas', *People, Place and Policy Online* 4(2): 38–49.

McMurtry, L. (2007), 'Mortgage default and repossession: Procedure and policy in the post-*Norgan* era', *Northern Ireland Legal Quarterly* 58(2): 194–210.

Mearns, A. (1883), *The Bitter Cry of Outcast London: An Inquiry into the Condition of the Abject Poor*, London: Review of Reviews.

Merrett, S. (1979), *State Housing in Britain*, London: Routledge & Kegan Paul.

(1982), *Owner Occupation in Britain*, London: Routledge.

Meyers, C. (1975), 'The covenant of habitability and the American Law Institute', *Stanford Law Review* 27(3): 879–903.

Millie, A. (2007), 'Looking for anti-social behaviour', *Policy and Politics*: 35(4): 611–27.

Millie, A., Jacobson, J., McDonald, E. and Hough, M. (2005), *Anti-Social Behaviour Strategies: Finding a Balance*, Bristol; Policy Press.

Millward, R. (2005), '"We are announcing your target": Reflections on performative language in the making of English housing policy', *Local Government Studies* 31(5): 597–614.

Milner Holland, Sir (1965), *Report of the Committee on Housing in Greater London*, Cmd 2605, London: HMSO.

Ministry of Health (1930), *Eleventh Annual Report 1929–30*, Cmd 3667, London: HMSO.

(1931), *Twelfth Annual Report 1930–31*, Cmd 3937, London: HMSO.

(1933), *Fourteenth Annual Report 1932–1933*, Cmd 4372, London: HMSO.

Ministry of Justice (MoJ) (2010), *Proposals for the Reform of Legal Aid in England and Wales*, London: MoJ.

Mnookin, R. and Kornhauser, L. (1979), 'Bargaining in the shadow of the law: The case of divorce', *Yale Law Journal* 88(3): 950–78.

Morgan, B. (2003), 'The economization of politics: Meta-regulation as a form of nonjudicial legality', *Social & Legal Studies* 12(4): 489–523.

Morgan, B. and Yeung, K. (2007), *An Introduction to Law and Regulation: Text and Materials*, Cambridge University Press.

Morris, J. and Winn, M. (1990), *Housing and Social Inequality*, London: Hilary Shipman.

Morris, L. (2009), *Asylum, Welfare and the Cosmopolitan Ideal: A Sociology of Rights*, London: Routledge-Glasshouse.

Mulcahy, L. and Tritter, J. (1998), 'Pathways, pyramids and icebergs? Mapping the links between dissatisfaction and complaints', *Sociology of Health and Illness* 20(6): 825–47.

Mullins, D. (1997), 'From regulatory capture to regulated competition: An interest group analysis of the regulation of housing associations in England', *Housing Studies* 12(3): 301–19.

(2006), 'Exploring change in the housing association sector in England using the Delphi method', *Housing Studies* 21(2): 227–51.

Mullins, D. and Craig, L. (2005), *Testing the Climate: Mergers and Alliances in the Housing Association Sector*, CURS, University of Birmingham

Mullins. D., Murie, A., Leather, P. and Lee, P. (2006), *Housing Policy in the UK*, Basingstoke: Palgrave.

Munro, M., Ford, J., Leishman, C. and Kofi Karley, N. (2005), *Lending to Higher Risk Borrowers: Sub-Prime Credit and Sustainable Home Ownership*, York: Joseph Rowntree Foundation.

Murie, A. (1997), 'The social rented sector, housing and the welfare state in the UK', *Housing Studies* 12(4): 437–61.

(1998), 'Secure and contented citizens? Home ownership in Britain', in A. Marsh and D. Mullins (eds.), *Housing and Public Policy: Citizenship, Choice and Control*, Buckingham: Open University Press.

Murie, A. and Nevin, B. (2001), 'New Labour transfers', in D. Cowan and A. Marsh (eds.), *Two Steps Forward: Housing Policy into the New Millennium*, Bristol: Policy Press.

Murie, A., Niner, P. and Watson, C. (1976), *Housing Policy and the Housing System*, London: Allen & Unwin.

Murray, C. (1990), *The Underclass*, London: IEA.

National Association of Citizens Advice Bureaux (NACAB) (1998), *Unsafe Deposit*, London: NACAB.

National Audit Office (2006a), *A Foot on the Ladder: Low Cost Home Ownership Assistance*, HC 1048 Session 2005–2006, London: NAO.

(2006b), *Tackling Anti-Social Behaviour*, HC 99 Session 2006–2007, London: NAO.

National Centre for Social research (NCSR) (2008), *Housing in England 2006/07*, London: CLG.

National Consumer Council (1976), *Tenancy Agreements*, London: National Consumer Council.

National Federation of Arms Length Management Organisations (NFALMO) (2009a), *A Future for ALMOs – Within Local Communities*, London: NFALMO.

(2009b), *What Next for ALMOs?*, London: NFALMO.

National Federation of Arms Length Management Organisations (NFALMO), National Federation of Tenant Management Organisations, Councils with ALMOs Group (2009), *Local Authority, ALMO and TMO Relationships – A Good Practice Guide*, London: NFALMO.

Neale, J. (1997), 'Homelessness and theory reconsidered', *Housing Studies* 12(1): 47–61.

Nelken, D. (1983), *The Limits of the Legal Process: A Study of Landlords, Law and Crime*, London: Academic Press.

Neuberger, J. (2003), *House Keeping: Preventing Homelessness through Tackling Rent Arrears in Social Housing*, London: Shelter.

Newman, O. (1972), *Defensible Space*, London: Architectural Press.

Nield, S. (2010), 'Responsible lending and borrowing: where to low-cost home ownership?', 30(4) *Legal Studies*: 610–32.

Nixon, J. (2007), 'Deconstructing "problem" researchers and "problem" families: A rejoinder to Garrett', *Critical Social Policy* 27(4): 546–64.

Nixon, J., Blandy, S., Hunter, C. and Reeves, K. (2003), *Tackling Anti-social Behaviour in Mixed Tenure Areas*, London: ODPM.

Nixon, J. and Hunter, C. (2001), 'Taking the blame and losing the home: Women and anti-social behaviour', *Journal of Social Welfare and Family Law* 23(4): 395–410.

(2009), 'Disciplining women and the governance of conduct', in A. Millie (ed.), *Securing Respect: Behavioural Expectations and Anti-social Behaviour in the UK*, Bristol: Policy Press.

Nixon, J., Parr, S., Hunter, C., Sanderson, D. and Whittle, S. (2007), *The Longer-Term Outcomes Associated with Families who have Worked with Intensive Family Support*, London: ODPM.

Nixon, J., Pawson, H. and Sosenko, F. (2010), 'Rolling out anti-social behaviour families projects in England and Scotland: Analysing the rhetoric and practice of policy transfer', *Social Policy and Administration* 44(3): 305–25.

Noble, D. (1981), 'From rules to discretion: The Housing Corporation', in M. Adler and S. Asquith (eds.), *Discretion and Welfare*, London: Heinemann.

Office of Fair Trading (OFT) (2005), *Guidance on Unfair Terms in Tenancy Agreements*, London: OFT.

(2008), *Sale and Rent Back – An OFT Market Study*, OFT 1018, London: OFT.

(2009), *Second Charge Lending – OFT Guidance for Lenders and Brokers*, OFT 1105, London: OFT.

(2010), *Irresponsible Lending – OFT Guidance for Creditors*, OFT 1107, London: OFT.

Office of the Deputy Prime Minister (ODPM) (2002), *Revision of the Code of Guidance on the Allocation of Accommodation*, London: ODPM.

(2003a), *Major Repairs Allowance*, London: ODPM.

(2003b), *Sustainable Communities: Building for the Future*, London: ODPM.

(2004a), *Housing Health and Safety Rating System Guidance*, London: ODPM.

(2004b), *An End to End Review of the Housing Corporation*, London: ODPM.

(2004c), *Guidance on Arms Length Management of Local Authority Housing*, London: ODPM.

(2004d), *Pooling of Housing Capital Receipts*, London: ODPM.

(2004e), *A Decent Home: Definition and Guidance for Implementation*, London CLG.

(2005a), *Sustainable Communities: Settled Homes; Changing Lives*, London: ODPM.

(2005b), *HomeBuy – Expanding the Opportunity to Own*, Consultation Paper, London: ODPM.

(2005c), *Improving the Effectiveness of Rent Arrears Management – Good Practice Guidance*, London: CLG.

Office of the Deputy Prime Minister (ODPM) Select Committee (2004a), *The Role and Effectiveness of the Housing Corporation*, Eighth Report of Session 2003–2004, HC 401–1, London: TSO.

(2004b) *Housing, Planning, Local Government and the Regions: Decent Homes*, Fifth Report of Session 2003–2004, vol. 1, Report, together with formal minutes: House of Commons papers 2003–2004, 46-I, London: TSO.

O'Malley, P. (1992), 'Risk, power and crime prevention', *Economy and Society* 21(3): 252–75.

(2004), *Risk, Uncertainty and Government*, London: Glasshouse.

PA Consulting (2008), *The Private Finance Initiative for Housing Revenue Account Housing: The Pathfinder Schemes Baseline Report*, London: CLG.

Page, D. (1993), *Building for Communities*, York: Joseph Rowntree Foundation.

Palmer, E. (2007), *Judicial Review, Socio-Economic Rights and the Human Rights Act*, Oxford: Hart.

Pantazis, C. (1999), 'Fear of crime: Vulnerability and poverty', *British Journal of Criminology* 40(3): 414–36.

Paris, C. (2002), *Housing in Northern Ireland*, Coventry: CIH.

Parker, J., Smith, R. and Williams, P. (1994), *Access, Allocations and Nominations: The Role of Housing Associations*, London: HMSO.

Parr, S. (2009), 'The role of social housing in the "care" and "control" of tenants with mental health problems', *Social Policy and Society* 9(1): 111–22.

(2010), 'Family policy and the governance of anti-social behaviour in the UK: Women's experiences of intensive family support', *Journal of Social Policy* http://journals.cambridge.org/action/displayAbstract?fromPage=online&aid=7923990&fulltextType=RA&fileId=S0047279410000735.

Partington, M. (1980), *Landlord and Tenant*, London: Weidenfeld & Nicolson.

(1990), 'Rethinking British housing law: The failure of the Housing Act 1988', in M. Freeman (ed.), *Critical Issues in Welfare Law*, London: Stevens & Sons.

(1993), 'Citizenship and housing', in R. Blackburn (ed.), *Rights of Citizenship*, London: Mansell.

Pawson, H. (2007), 'Local authority homelessness prevention in England: Empowering consumers or denying rights?', *Housing Studies* 22(6): 867–84.

(2009), *Analysis of English Local Authority Housing Management Performance 2007/08*, York: Housing Quality Network.

Pawson, H., Davidson, E. and Lederle, N. (2007), *Housing Associations' Use of Anti-social Behaviour Powers*, London: Housing Corporation.

Pawson, H., Davidson, E. Morgan, J., Smith, R. and Edwards, R. (2009), *The Impacts of Housing Stock Transfers in Urban Britain*, York: Joseph Rowntree Foundation.

Pawson, H., Flint, J., Scott, S., Atkinson, R., Bannister, J., McKenzie, C. and Mills, C. (2005), *The Use of Possession Actions and Evictions by Social Landlords*, London: CLG.

Pawson, H. and Jacobs, K. (2010), 'Policy intervention and its impact: Analysing New Labour's public service reform model as applied to local authority housing in England', *Housing, Theory and Society* 27(1): 76–94.

Pawson, H., Jones, C., Donohoe, T. Netto, G., Fancy, C., and Clegg, S. and Thomas, A. (2006), *Monitoring the Longer Term Impact of Choice Based Lettings*, London: CLG.

Pawson, H. and Kintrea, K. (2002), 'Part of the problem or part of the solution? Social housing allocation policies and social exclusion in Britain', *Journal of Social Policy* 31(4): 643–67.

Pawson, H. and Mullins, D. (2003), *Changing Places: Housing Association Policy and Practice on Nominations and Lettings*, Bristol: Policy Press.

(2010), *After Council Housing: Britain's New Social Landlords*, Basingstoke: Palgrave MacMillan.

Pawson, H. and Munro, M. (2010), 'Explaining tenancy sustainment rates in British social rented housing: The roles of management, vulnerability and choice', *Urban Studies* 47(1): 145–68.

Pawson, H., Netto, G., Jones, C., Wager, F., Fancy, C. and Lomax, D. (2007), *Evaluating Homelessness Prevention*, London: CLG.

Pawson, H. and Sosenko, F. (2007), *Sector Restructuring*, Sector Study 61, London: Housing Corporation.

Pawson, H., Sosenko, F., Cowan, D., Croft, J., Cole, M. and Hunter, C. (2010), *Investigation of Rent Arrears Management Practices in the Housing Association Sector*, London: TSA.

Peach, C. and Byron, M. (1994), 'Council house sales, residualisation and Afro-Caribbean tenants', *Journal of Social Policy* 23(3): 363–83.

Pearce, F. and Tombs, S. (1990), 'Ideology, hegemony and empiricism', *British Journal of Criminology* 30(4): 423–43.

Pemberton, S. (2009), 'Economic migration from the EU "A8" accession countries and the impact on low-demand housing areas: Opportunity or threat for housing market renewal pathfinder programmes in England?', *Urban Studies* 46(7): 1363–84.

Phillips, D. (2006), 'Moving towards integration: The housing of asylum seekers and refugees in Britain', *Housing Studies* 21(4): 539–53.

Piratin, P. (1978), *Our Flag Stays Red*, London: Lawrence & Wishart.

Pleace, N., Quilgars, D., Jones, A. and Rugg, J. (2007), *Tackling Homelessness: Housing Associations and Local Authorities Working in Partnership*, London: Housing Corporation.

Plimmer, F., Pottinger, G. and Dixon, T. (2007), 'Valuation "accuracy" within the right to buy process', *Journal of Building Appraisal* 2(2): 102–25.

Poovey, M. (1995), *Making a Social Body: British Cultural Formation 1830–1864*, University of Chicago Press.

Powell, R. and Flint, J. (2009), '(In)formalisation and the civilizing process: Applying the work of Norbert Elias to housing-based anti-social behaviour interventions in the UK', *Housing, Theory and Society* 26(3): 159–78.

Power, A. (1987), *Property before People*, London: Allen & Unwin.

Power, M. (1997), *The Audit Society: Rituals of Verification*, Oxford University Press.

Pressman, J. and Wildavsky, A. (1973), *Implementation: How Great Expectations in Washington are Dashed in Oakland; or, Why it's Amazing that Federal Programs Work at All, This Being a Saga of the Economic Development Administration as Told by Two Sympathetic Observers who Seek to Build Morals on a Foundation of Ruined Hopes*, Berkeley, University of California Press.

Prevalin, D., Taylor, M. and Todd, J. (2008), 'The dynamics of unhealthy housing in the UK: A panel data analysis', *Housing Studies* 23(5): 679–96.

Price, S. (1958) *Building Societies: Their Origin and History*, London: Franey.

Prior, D. (2009), 'The "problem" of anti-social behaviour and the policy knowledge base: Analysing the power/knowledge relationship', *Critical Social Policy* 29(1): 5–23.

Procacci, G. (1991), 'Social economy and the government of poverty', in G. Burchell, C. Gordon and P. Miller (eds,), *The Foucault Effect: Studies in Governmentality*, University of Chicago Press.

Prosser, T. (forthcoming), '"An opportunity to take a more fundamental look at the role of government in society": The spending review as regulation', *Public Law*.

Pryce, G. and Keoghan, M. (2002), 'Unemployment insurance for mortgage borrowers: Is it viable and does it cover those most in need?', *European Journal of Housing Policy* 2(1): 87–114.

Pryke, M. (1994), 'Coping with some of the new risks of social housing in England', in W. Bartlett and G. Bramley (eds.), *European Housing Finance – Single Market or Mosaic*, School for Advanced Urban Studies, University of Bristol.

Public Health Advisory Service (1976), *Interim Report*, London: Public Health Advisory Service.

Radin, M. (1986), 'Residential rent control', 15(2), *Philosophy & Public Affairs*: 350–80.

Randolph, B. (1993), 'The re-privatization of housing associations', in P. Malpass and R. Means (eds), *Implementing Housing Policy*, Buckingham: Open University Press.

Rashman, L., Downe, J. and Hartley, J. (2005), 'Knowing creation and transfer in the Beacon Scheme: Improving services through sharing good practice', *Local Government Studies* 31(5): 683–700.

Rauta, S. and Pickering, R. (1992), *Private Renting in England 1990*, London: HMSO.

Ravetz, A. (2001), *Council Housing and Culture: The History of a Social Experiment*, London: Routledge.

Reid, B., Vickery, L., Bradburn, A. and Verster, B. (2007), *Learning from Arms Length Management Organisations – The Experience of the First Three Rounds*, London: CLG.

Rex, J. and Moore, R. (1967), *Race, Community and Conflict: A Study of Sparkbrook*, Oxford University Press

Reynolds, J. (1974) 'Statutory covenants of fitness and repair: Social legislation and the judges', *Modern Law Review* 37(3): 377–98.

Rhodes, D. (2007), 'Buy to let landlords', in D. Hughes and S. Lowe (eds.), *The Private Rented Housing Market*, Aldershot: Ashgate.

Rhodes, D. and Bevan, M. (2010), *Private Landlords and the Local Housing Allowances System of Housing Benefit*, Research Report no. 689, London: DWP.

Rivers, J. (2006), 'Proportionality and variable intensity of review', *Cambridge Law Journal* 65(1): 185–207.

Roach Anleu, S. and Mack, K. (2005), 'Magistrates' everyday work and emotional labour', *Journal of Law and Society* 32(4): 590–614.

Robertson, D. (2006), 'Cultural expectations of homeownership: Explaining changing legal definitions of flat "ownership" within Britain', *Housing Studies* 21(1): 35–52.

Robinson, D. (2007), 'European Union accession state migrants in social housing in England', *People, Place and Policy Online*: 98–111 1(3).

(2010), 'New immigrants and migrants in social housing in Britain: Discursive themes and lived realities', *Policy and Politics* 38(1): 57–77.

Robinson, D., Reeve, K. and Casey, R. (2007), *The Housing Pathways of New Immigrants*, York: Joseph Rowntree Foundation.

Robinson, M. (1976), '"Social legislation" and the judges: A note by way of rejoinder', *Modern Law Review* 39(1): 43–54.

Robson, P. and Halliday, S. (1998), *Residential Tenancies*, Edinburgh: Green & Sons.

Robson, P. and Poustie, M. (1996), *Homeless Persons and the Law*, London: Butterworths.

Robson, P. and Watchman, P. (1981), 'Sabotaging the Rent Acts', in P. Robson and P. Watchman (eds.), *Justice and Lord Denning*, London: Butterworths.

Rodger, J. (2006), 'Antisocial families and withholding welfare support', *Critical Social Policy* 26(1): 121–43.

Rose, N. (1999), *Powers of Freedom – Reframing Political Thought*, Cambridge University Press.

Rose, N. and Miller, P. (1992), 'Political power beyond the state: Problematics of government', *British Journal of Sociology* 43(2): 173–205.

Rose, N. and Valverde, M. (1998), 'Governed by law?', *Social and Legal Studies* 7(4): 541–51.

Rowlands, R. and Murie, A. (2008), *Evaluation of Social HomeBuy Pilot Scheme for Affordable Housing*, London: CLG

Royal Commission (1885a), *Royal Commission on the Housing of the Working Classes*, vol. 1, London: HMSO.

(1885b), *Royal Commission on the Housing of the Working Classes*, vol. 2: *Minutes of Evidence*, London: HMSO.

Rugg, J. (1999), 'The use and "abuse" of private renting and help with rental costs', in J. Rugg (ed.), *Young People, Housing and Social Policy*, London; Routledge.

(2008), *A Route to Homelessness? A Study of Why Private Sector Tenants become Homeless*, London: Shelter.

Rugg, J. and Bevan, M. (2002), *An Evaluation of the Pilot Tenancy Deposit Scheme*, London: ODPM.

Rugg, J. and Rhodes, D. (2003), '"Between a rock and a hard place": The failure to agree on regulation for the private rented sector in England', *Housing Studies* 18(6): 937–46.

(2008), *The Private Rented Sector: Its Contribution and Potential*, York: Centre for Housing Policy.

Rugg, J. and Wilcox, S. (1997), *Taking the Strain?: The Impact of Changes to the Housing Benefit Regulations on Housing Associations*, York: Centre for Housing Policy.

Rutherford, A. (1997), 'Criminal policy and the eliminative ideal', *Social Policy and Administration* 31(1): 116–28.

Rutter, J. and Latorre, M. (2009), *Social Housing Allocation and Immigrant Communities*, Research Report 4, London: EHRC.

Sainsbury, R. (1992), 'Administrative justice: Discretion and procedure in social security decision-making', in K. Hawkins (ed.), *The Uses of Discretion*, Oxford University Press.

Sales, R. (2002), 'The deserving and the undeserving? Refugees, asylum seekers and welfare in Britain', *Critical Social Policy* 22(3): 456–78.

Sampson, A., Stubbs, P., Smith, D., Pearson, G. and Blagg, H. (1988), 'Crime, localities and the multi-agency approach', *British Journal of Criminology* 28(3): 478–93.

Sanders, A. (1996), 'Prosecution in common law jurisdictions', in A. Sanders (ed.), *Prosecution in Common Law Jurisdictions*, Aldershot: Dartmouth.

Sanders, A., Young, R. and Burton, M. (2010), *Criminal Justice*, Oxford University Press.

Saunders, P. (1990), *A Nation of Home Owners*, London: Allen & Unwin.

Scanlon, K., Lunde, J. and Whitehead, C. (2008), 'Mortgage product innovation in advanced economies: More choice, more risk', *European Journal of Housing Policy* 8(2): 109–31.

Scanlon, K. and Whitehead, C. (2005), *The Profile and Intentions of Buy-to-Let Investors*, London: CML.

Schifferes, S. (1976), 'Council tenants and housing policy in the 1930s: The contradictions of state intervention', in M. Edwards, F. Gray, S. Merrett and J. Swann (eds.), *Housing and Class in Britain*, London: Russell Press.

Schofield, J. and Sausman, C. (2002), 'Symposium on implementing public policy: Learning from theory and practice', *Public Administration* 82(2): 235–48.

Scott, S. and Parkey, H. (1998), 'Myths and reality: Anti-social behaviour in Scotland', *Housing Studies* 13(3): 325–45.

Seebohm, F. (1968), *Report of the Committee on Local Authority and Allied Personal Social Services*, Cmnd 3703, London: HMSO.

Short, J. (1982), *Housing in Britain: The Post-War Experience*, London; Methuen.

Smiles, S. (1859/2002), *Self-Help*, Oxford University Press.

Smith, N. and George, G. (1997), 'Introductory tenancies: A nuisance too far?', *Journal of Social Welfare and Family Law* 19(2): 307–19.

Smith, P. [1994], 'Repairing obligations: A case against radical reform', *Conveyancer and Property Lawyer* 186–99.

Smith, S. and Mallinson, S. (1996), 'The problem with social housing: Discretion, accountability and the welfare ideal', *Policy and Politics* 24(3): 339–57.

Social Exclusion Unit (SEU) (1998), *Bringing Britain Together: A National Strategy for Neighbourhood Renewal*, Cm 4045, London: HMSO.

Social Security Advisory Committee (2010), *Housing Benefit (Amendment) Regulations 2010 (SI 2010/2835), The Rent Officers (Housing Benefit Functions) Amendment Order 2010* (SI 2010/2836), London: TSO.

Somerville, P. (2004), 'Transforming council housing', paper presented to the Housing Studies Association Conference, Sheffield.

Sparkes, P. (1987), 'Co-tenants, joint tenants, and tenants in common', *Anglo-American Law Review* 18(1): 151–64.

Spenceley, J. (2008), *Trends in Housing Association Stock in 2007*, Dataspring Briefing Paper on behalf of the Housing Corporation, Cambridge: Dataspring.

Spicer, N. (2008), 'Places of exclusion and inclusion: Asylum-seeker and refugee experiences of neighbourhoods in the UK', *Journal of Ethnic and Migration Studies* 34(3): 491–510.

Spicker, P. (1987), 'Concepts of need in housing allocation', *Policy and Politics* 15(1): 17–27.

Squires, P. (2006), 'New Labour and the politics of anti-social behaviour', *Critical Social Policy* 26(1): 144–68.

(2008), 'The politics of anti-social behaviour', *British Politics* 3(2): 300–23.

Stares, R. (2010), 'Direct pressure', *Roof* (January/February): 32–3.

Stephens, M. (1997), 'Windfall wars', in J. Goodwin and C. Grant (eds.), *Built to Last?*, London: Roof.

(2005), 'An assessment of the British housing benefit system', *European Journal of Housing Policy* 5(2): 111–29.

(2007), 'Mortgage market deregulation and its consequences', *Housing Studies* 22(2): 201–20.

(2008), *The Government Response to Mortgage Arrears and Repossessions*, Housing Analysis and Surveys Expert Panel Papers 6, University of York.

Stephens, M. and Quilgars, D. (2008), 'Sub-prime mortgage lending in the UK', *European Journal of Housing Policy* 8(2): 197–215.

Stewart, A. (1996), *Rethinking Housing Law*, London: Sweet & Maxwell.

Stewart, A. and Burridge, R. (1989), 'Housing tales of law and space', *Journal of Law and Society* 16(1): 65–82.

Sunkin, M. (1987), 'What is happening to applications for judicial review?', *Modern Law Review* 60(3): 432–57.

Sweeney, J. [2008], 'The human rights of failed asylum seekers in the United Kingdom', *Public Law* 277–301.

Talbot, L (2008), *Critical Company Law*, London: Routledge-Cavendish.

Tang, C. (2008), 'Between "market" and "welfare": Rent restructuring policy in the housing association sector, England', *Housing Studies* 23(5): 737–59.

Tenant Services Authority (TSA) (2009a), *Building a New Regulatory Framework: A Discussion Paper*, London: TSA.

(2009b), *Existing Tenants Survey 2008: Shared Owners*, London: TSA.

(2010a), *The Regulatory Framework for Social Housing in England from April 2010*, London: TSA.

(2010b), *Regulatory and Statistical Return 2010*, London: TSA.

(2010c), *Rents, Rent Differentials and Service Charges for Private Registered Providers: 2011–12*, London: TSA.

(2010d), *Affordable Rent – Revisions to the Tenancy Standard*, London: TSA.

Tenant Services Authority (TSA)/Audit Commission (2010a), *Transitional Arrangements for the Inspection of Registered Social Housing Providers*, Joint statement by the TSA and Audit Commission, November 2010, London: TSA/Audit Commission.

(2010b), *Tenant Involvement: Assessing Landlords' Progress*, London: TSA/Audit Commission.

Tenant Services Authority (TSA)/Housing Ombudsman Service (HOS) (2010), *Tenant Services Authority and Housing Ombudsman Service: Interim Protocol*, London: TSA/HOS.

Thatcher, M. (1993), *The Downing Street Years*, London: Harper Collins.

Thomas, A. and Snape, D. (1995), *In from the Cold*, London: DoE.

Tiesdell, S. (2001), 'A forgotten policy? A perspective on the evolution and transformation of Housing Action Trust policy, 1987–99', *European Journal of Housing Policy* 1(3): 357–83.

Titmuss, R. (1974), *Social Policy*, B. Abel-Smith and K. Titmuss (eds.), London: Unwin Hyman.

Tombs, S. (2002), 'Understanding regulation?', *Social and Legal Studies* 11(1): 113–33.

Torgerson, U. (1987), 'Housing: The wobbly pillar under the welfare state', in B. Turner, J. Kemeny and L. Lundquist (eds.), *Between State and Market: Housing in the Post-Industrial Era*, Stockholm: Almquist & Wiksell.

Treasury (2008), *The Building Societies (Funding) and Mutual Societies (Transfers) Act 2007: A Consultation*, London: HM Treasury.

(2009a), *Mortgage Regulation: A Consultation*, London: HM Treasury.

(2009b), *Regulating the Sale and Rent Back Market: A Consultation*, London: HM Treasury.

Treasury/Department for Business, Innovation and Skills (2010a), *A New Approach to Financial Regulation: Judgment, Focus and Stability*, Cm 7874, London: HM Treasury.

(2010b), *A New Approach to Financial Regulation: Consultation on Reforming the Consumer Credit Regime*, London: HM Treasury.

HM Treasury/Department for Communities and Local Government (2006), *Report of the Shared Equity Task Force*, London: HM Treasury/CLG.

Treasury Select Committee (2008), *The Run on the Rock*, Fifth report of Session 2007–2008, vol. 1, HC 56-I, London: TSO.

(2009), *Mortgage Arrears and Access to Mortgage Finance*, Fifteenth report of Session 2008–2009, HC 767, London: TSO.

Turley, C. and Thomas, A. (2006), *Housing Benefit and Council Tax Benefit as In-Work Benefits: Claimants' and Advisors' Knowledge, Attitudes and Experiences*, Research Report 383, London: DWP.

Turner, B. and Malpezzi, S. (2003), 'A review of empirical evidence on the costs and benefits of rent control', *Swedish Economic Policy Review* 10(1): 11–56.

Turner, D. and Whiteman, P. (2005), 'Learning from the experience of recovery: The turnaround of poorly performing authorities', *Local Government Studies* 31(5): 627–54.

Upson, A. (2006), *Perceptions and Experience of Anti-social Behaviour: Findings from the 2004/05 British Crime Survey*, London: Home Office.

Valuation Office Agency (VOA) (2009), *Guidance: Broad Rental Market Area*, London: VOA.

Valverde, M. (2003a) 'Police science, British style: pub licensing and knowledges of urban disorder', *Economy and Society* 32(2): 234–52.

(2003b), *Law's Dream of a Common Knowledge*, New Jersey: Princeton.

(2009), 'Jurisdiction and scale: "Legal technicalities" as resources for theory', *Social and Legal Studies* 18(2): 139–57.

Van Ham, M. and Manley, D. (2009), 'Social housing allocation, choice and neighbourhood ethnic mix in England', *Journal of Housing and the Built Environment* 24(2): 407–22.

Vincent-Jones, P. (1987), 'Exclusive possession and exclusive control of private rented housing: A socio-legal critique of the lease–licence distinction', *Journal of Law and Society* 14(4): 445–58.

(2001), 'From housing management to the management of housing: The challenge of Best Value', in D. Cowan and A. Marsh (eds.), *Two Steps Forward: Housing Policy into the New Millennium*, Bristol: Policy Press.

(2006), *The New Public Contracting*, Oxford University Press.

Wainwright, T. (2009), 'Laying the foundations for a crisis: Mapping the historic-geographical construction of residential mortgage backed securitization in the UK', *International Journal of Urban and Regional Research* 33(2): 372–88.

(1997), 'Rent setting in local government', *Local Government Policy Making* 23(4): 39–46.

(1998), 'Pricing public housing services: mirroring the market?', *Housing Studies* 13(4): 549–66.

(2003), 'Setting the rents of social housing: The impact and implications of rent restructuring in England', *Urban Studies* 40(10): 2023–47.

(2006), 'Getting a policy to "stick": Centralising control of social rent setting in England', *Policy and Politics* 34(2): 195–217.

Walker, B. and Niner, P. (2005), 'The use of discretion in a rule-bound service: Housing benefit administration and the introduction of discretionary housing payments in Great Britain', *Public Administration* 83(1): 47–66.

(2010), *Low Income Working Households in the Private Rented Sector*, Research Report no. 698, London: DWP.

Walker, R. (1997), 'New public management and housing associations: From comfort to competition', *Policy and Politics* 26(1): 71–86.

(2000), 'The changing management of social housing: The impact of externalisation and managerialisation', *Housing Studies* 15(2): 281–99.

Walker, R. and Smith, R. (1999), 'Regulatory and organisational responses to restructured housing association finance in England and Wales', *Urban Studies* 36(4): 737–54.

Wallace, A. (2008), *Achieving Mobility in the Intermediate Housing Market: Moving Up and Moving On?*, York: Joseph Rowntree Foundation.

Wallace, A. and Ford, J. (2010), 'Limiting possessions? Managing mortgage arrears in a new era', *International Journal of Housing Policy* 10(2): 133–54.

Walters, W. (2000), *Unemployment and Government: Genealogies of the Social*, Cambridge University Press.

Warburton, M. (1996), 'The changing role of local authorities in housing', in S. Leach, Howard David & Associates (eds.), *Enabling or Disabling Local Government*, Buckingham: Open University Press.

Watchman, P. (1980), 'The origin of the 1915 Rent Act', *Law and State* 5(1): 20–50.

Watchman, P. and Robson, P. (1981), 'The homeless persons obstacle race', *Journal of Social Welfare and Family Law* 3(1): 1–15 (Part 1); 65–82 (Part 2).

Watson, S. (1999) 'A home is where the heart is: Engendering notions of homelessness', in P. Kennett and A. Marsh (eds.), *Homelessness: Exploring the New Terrain*, Bristol: Policy Press.

Watt, P. and Jacobs, K. (2000), 'Discourses of social exclusion: An Analysis of *Bringing Britain Together: A National Strategy for Neighbourhood Renewal*', *Housing, Theory and Society* 17(1): 14–26.

White, C., Warrener, M., Reeves, A. and LaValle, I. (2008), *Family Intervention Projects: An Evaluation of their Design, Set-Up and Early Outcomes*, London: DCSF.

Whitehouse, L. (1998), 'The impact of consumerism on the home owner', in D. Cowan (ed.), *Housing: Participation and Exclusion*, Aldershot: Dartmouth.

(2009), 'The mortgage arrears pre-action protocol: An opportunity lost', *Modern Law Review* 72(5): 783–814.

(2010), 'Making the case for socio-legal research in land law: Renner and the law of mortgage', *Journal of Law and Society* 37(4): 545–68.

Widdowson, B. (1981), *Intentional Homelessness*, London: Shelter.

Wilcox, S. (1997), *Housing Finance Review 1997/98*, York: Joseph Rowntree Foundation.

Wilcox, S., Wallace, A., Bramley, G., Morgan, J., Sosenko, F. and Ford, J. (2010), *Evaluation of the Mortgage Rescue Scheme and Homeowners Mortgage Support*, London: CLG.

Williams, N., Sewel, J. and Twine, F. (1987), 'Council house sales and the electorate: voting behaviour and ideological implications', *Housing Studies* 4(3): 274–82.

Williams, P. (1997), 'A more flexible system of finance for home ownership', in T. Dwelly (ed.), *Sustainable Home Ownership: The Debate*, York: Joseph Rowntree Foundation.

Williams, P. and Wilcox, S. (2009), *Minimising Repossessions*, Housing Analysis and Surveys Expert Panel Papers, University of York.

Wilson, J. and Kelling, G. (1982), 'Broken windows: The police and neighborhood safety', *Atlantic Monthly* (March): 29–37.

Wintour, P. (2008), 'Labour: If you want a council house, find a job', *The Guardian*, 5 February.

Wintour, P. and Stratton, A. (2011), 'Theresa May unfolds new "toolkit" to tackle anti-social behaviour', *The Guardian*, 31 January.

Wohl, A. (1977), *The Eternal Slum: Housing and Social Policy in Victorian Britain*, London: Edward Arnold.

Woodward, R. (1991), 'Mobilising opposition: The campaign against housing action trusts in Tower Hamlets, *Housing Studies* 6(1): 44–58.

Woolf, Lord H. (1998), *Access to Justice*, Final Report, London: DCA.

Woolf, M. (2010), 'British to jump housing queue', *The Sunday Times*, 29 August.

Young, A. (2009), 'In defence of due deference', *Modern Law Review* 72(4): 554–80.

Zebedee, J. (2009), *Guide to Housing Benefit and Council Tax Benefit 2010–11*, London: Shelter.

Index